Processes

Virtual Memory

Threads

Modules

Message Queues

WND

Memory

Windows® 95

Heaps

System Programming
SECRETS™

Structures

Window Classes

Thread Synchronization

PI Spying

Portable Executable Files

Paging

Win16Mutex

Contexts

Ring 0

Win32 API Incompatibilities

ree System Resources

Tasks

Shared Memory

MATT PIETREK

Windows® 95 System Programming SECRETS™

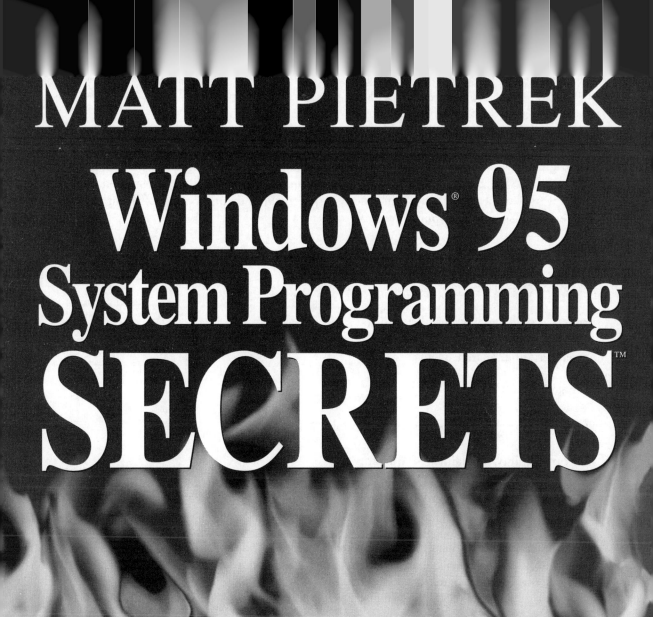

MATT PIETREK

Windows® 95
System Programming
SECRETS™

Windows 95 System Programming SECRETS
Published by
IDG Books Worldwide, Inc.
An International Data Group Company
919 East Hillsdale Boulevard, Suite 400
Foster City, CA 94404

Library of Congress Catalog Card No.: 95-75057

ISBN 1-56884-318-6

Printed in the United States of America

Second Printing, March, 1996

10 9 8 7 6 5 4 3 2

Distributed in the United States by IDG Books Worldwide, Inc.

  Published in the United States

FOR MORE INFORMATION...

For general information on IDG Books in the U.S., including information on discounts and premiums, contact IDG Books at 800-434-3422.

For information on where to purchase IDG's books outside the U.S., contact Christina Turner at 415-655-3022.

For information on translations, contact Marc Jeffrey Mikulich, Foreign Rights Manager, at IDG Books Worldwide; fax number: 415-655-3295.

For sales inquiries and special prices for bulk quantities, contact Tony Real at 800-434-3422 or 415-655-3048.

For information on using IDG's books in the classroom and ordering examination copies, contact Jim Kelly at 800-434-2086.

Windows 95 System Programming SECRETS is distributed in Canada by Macmillan of Canada, a Division of Canada Publishing Corporation; by Computer and Technical Books in Miami, Florida, for South America and the Caribbean; by Longman Singapore in Singapore, Malaysia, Thailand, and Korea; by Toppan Co. Ltd. in Japan; by Asia Computerworld in Hong Kong; by Woodslane Pty. Ltd. in Australia and New Zealand; and by Transword Publishers Ltd. in the U.K. and Europe.

Welcome to the world of IDG Books Worldwide.

IDG Books Worldwide, Inc. is a subsidiary of International Data Group, the world's largest publisher of computer-related information and the leading global provider of information services on information technology. IDG was founded more than 25 years ago and now employs more than 7,500 people worldwide. IDG publishes more than 235 computer publications in 67 countries (see listing below). More than fifty million people read one or more IDG publications each month.

Launched in 1990, IDG Books Worldwide is today the #1 publisher of best-selling computer books in the United States. We are proud to have received 3 awards from the Computer Press Association in recognition of editorial excellence, and our best-selling *...For Dummies™* series has more than 18 million copies in print with translations in 24 languages. IDG Books, through a recent joint venture with IDG's Hi-Tech Beijing, became the first U.S. publisher to publish a computer book in the People's Republic of China. In record time, IDG Books has become the first choice for millions of readers around the world who want to learn how to better manage their businesses.

Our mission is simple: Every IDG book is designed to bring extra value and skill-building instructions to the reader. Our books are written by experts who understand and care about our readers. The knowledge base of our editorial staff comes from years of experience in publishing, education, and journalism — experience which we use to produce books for the '90s. In short, we care about books, so we attract the best people. We devote special attention to details such as audience, interior design, use of icons, and illustrations. And because we use an efficient process of authoring, editing, and desktop publishing our books electronically, we can spend more time ensuring superior content and spend less time on the technicalities of making books.

You can count on our commitment to deliver high-quality books at competitive prices on topics consumers want to read about. At IDG, we value quality, and we have been delivering quality for more than 25 years. You'll find no better book on a subject than an IDG book.

John J. Kilcullen

John Kilcullen
President and CEO
IDG Books Worldwide, Inc.

IDG Books Worldwide, Inc. is a subsidiary of International Data Group, the world's largest publisher of computer-related information and the leading global provider of information services on information technology. International Data Group publishes over 235 computer publications in 67 countries. More than fifty million people read one or more International Data Group publications each month. The officers are Patrick J. McGovern, Founder and Board Chairman; Kelly Conlin, President; Jim Casella, Chief Operating Officer. International Data Group's publications include: **ARGENTINA'S** Computerworld Argentina, Infoworld Argentina; **AUSTRALIA'S** Computerworld Australia, Computer Living, Australian PC World, Australian Macworld, Network World, Mobile Business Australia, Publish!, Reseller, IDG Sources; **AUSTRIA'S** Computerwelt Oesterreich, PC Test; **BELGIUM'S** Data News (CW); **BOLIVIA'S** Computerworld; **BRAZIL'S** Computerworld, Connections, Game Power, Mundo Unix, PC World, Publish, Super Game; **BULGARIA'S** Computerworld Bulgaria, PC & Mac World Bulgaria, Network World Bulgaria; **CANADA'S** CIO Canada, Computerworld Canada, InfoCanada, Network World Canada, Reseller; **CHILE'S** Computerworld Chile, Informatica; **COLOMBIA'S** Computerworld Colombia, PC World; **COSTA RICA'S** PC World; **CZECH REPUBLIC'S** Computerworld, Elektronika, PC World; **DENMARK'S** Communications World, Computerworld Danmark, Computerworld Focus, Macintosh Produktkatalog, Macworld Danmark, PC World Danmark, PC Produktguide, Tech World, Windows World; **ECUADOR'S** PC World Ecuador; **EGYPT'S** Computerworld (CW) Middle East, PC World Middle East; **FINLAND'S** MikroPC, Tietoviikko, Tietoverkko; **FRANCE'S** Distributique, GOLDEN MAC, InfoPC, Le Guide du Monde Informatique, Le Monde Informatique, Telecoms & Reseaux; **GERMANY'S** Computerwoche, Computerwoche Focus, Computerwoche Extra, Electronic Entertainment, Gamepro, Information Management, Macwelt, Netzwelt, PC Welt, Publish, Publish; **GREECE'S** Publish & Macworld; **HONG KONG'S** Computerworld Hong Kong, PC World Hong Kong; **HUNGARY'S** Computerworld SZT, PC World; **INDIA'S** Computers & Communications; **INDONESIA'S** Info Komputer; **IRELAND'S** ComputerScope; **ISRAEL'S** Beyond Windows, Computerworld Israel, Multimedia, PC World Israel; **ITALY'S** Computerworld Italia, Lotus Magazine, Macworld Italia, Networking Italia, PC Shopping Italy, PC World Italia; **JAPAN'S** Computerworld Today, Information Systems World, Macworld Japan, Nikkei Personal Computing, SunWorld Japan, Windows World; **KENYA'S** East African Computer News; **KOREA'S** Computerworld Korea, Macworld Korea, PC World Korea; **LATIN AMERICA'S** GamePro; **MALAYSIA'S** Computerworld Malaysia, PC World Malaysia; **MEXICO'S** Compu Edicion, Compu Manufactura, Computacion/Punto de Venta, Computerworld Mexico, Macworld, Mundo Unix, PC World, Windows; **THE NETHERLANDS'** Computer! Totaal, Computable (CW), LAN Magazine, Lotus Magazine, MacWorld; **NEW ZEALAND'S** Computer Buyer, Computerworld New Zealand, Network World, New Zealand PC World; **NIGERIA'S** PC World Africa; **NORWAY'S** Computerworld Norge, Lotusworld Norge, Macworld Norge, Maxi Data, Networld, PC World Ekspress, PC World Nettverk, PC World Norge, PC World's Produktguide, Publish& Multimedia World, Student Data, Unix World, Windowsworld; **PAKISTAN'S** PC World Pakistan; **PANAMA'S** PC World Panama; **PERU'S** Computerworld Peru, PC World; **PEOPLE'S REPUBLIC OF CHINA'S** China Computerworld, China Infoworld, China PC Info Magazine, Computer Fan, PC World China, Electronics International, Electronics Today/Multimedia World, Electronic Product World, China Network World, Software World Magazine, Telecom Product World; **PHILIPPINES'** Computerworld Philippines, PC Digest (PCW); **POLAND'S** Computerworld Poland, Computerworld Special Report, Networld, PC World/Komputer, Sunworld; **PORTUGAL'S** Cerebro/PC World, Correio Informatico/Computerworld, MacIn; **ROMANIA'S** Computerworld, PC World, Telecom Romania; **RUSSIA'S** Computerworld-Moscow, Mir - PK (PCW), Sety (Networks); **SINGAPORE'S** Computerworld Southeast Asia, PC World Singapore; **SLOVENIA'S** Monitor Magazine; **SOUTH AFRICA'S** Computer Mail (CIO),Computing S.A.,Network World S.A., Software World; **SPAIN'S** Advanced Systems, Amiga World, Computerworld Espana, Communicaciones World, Macworld Espana, NeXTWORLD, Super Juegos Magazine (GamePro), PC World Espana, Publish; **SWEDEN'S** Attack, ComputerSweden, Corporate Computing, Macworld, Mikrodatorn, Natverk & Kommunikation, PC World, CAP & Design, DataIngenjoren, Maxi Data,Windows World; **SWITZERLAND'S** Computerworld Schweiz, Macworld Schweiz, PC Tip; **TAIWAN'S** Computerworld Taiwan, PC World Taiwan; **THAILAND'S** Thai Computerworld; **TURKEY'S** Computerworld Monitor, Macworld Turkiye, PC World Turkiye; **UKRAINE'S** Computerworld, Computers+Software Magazine; **UNITED KINGDOM'S** Computing /Computerworld, Connexion/Network World, Lotus Magazine, Macworld, Open Computing/Sunworld; **UNITED STATES'** Advanced Systems, AmigaWorld, Cable in the Classroom, CD Review, CIO, Computerworld, Computerworld Client/Server Journal, Digital Video, DOS World, Electronic Entertainment Magazine (E2), Federal Computer Week, Game Hits, GamePro, IDG Books, Infoworld, Laser Event, Macworld, Maximize, Multimedia World, Network World, PC Letter, PC World, Publish, SWATPro, Video Event; **URUGUAY'S** PC World Uruguay; **VENEZUELA'S** Computerworld Venezuela, PC World; **VIETNAM'S** PC World Vietnam.

DEDICATION

To Elma Swails
Who was my biggest fan
She always read my books cover to cover

CREDITS

Publishing Director
John Osborn

Senior Acquisitions Manager
Amorette Pedersen

Managing Editor
Kim Field

Editorial Director
Anne Marie Walker

Production Director
Beth A. Roberts

Project Editor
Clare A. Mansfield

Manuscript Editors
Teresa Frazier
Susan Pink

Technical Editor
James Finnegan

Composition and Layout
Dusty D. Parsons
Ronnie K. Bucci

Proofreader
Mildred Rosenzweig

Indexer
Elizabeth Cunningham

Cover Design
Draper and Liew Inc.

ACKNOWLEDGMENTS

Numerous people helped me out and provided moral support during the writing of *Windows 95 System Programming SECRETS*. For starters, my thanks to Trudy Neuhaus, Amy Pedersen, Clare Mansfield, and everybody else associated with IDG Books. They're all pros at what they do, and they all did their part to smooth out the occasional bumps that came up during the course of producing this book.

My manuscript editors, Teresa Frazier and Susan Pink, were the unsung heroes of this book. Believe it or not, the original text that computer authors send to the publisher is often badly organized, contradictory, and filled with little goof-ups that would be mortally embarrassing if they appeared in print. The job of the manuscript editor is to go through *everything* the author submits and clean it up. Teresa and Susan did a fabulous job of slogging through my highly technical material, and constantly amazed me by finding problems that I never would have spotted. They didn't just stop there, though. They made many suggestions that I incorporated into the book and feel the book is better for. Not to mention that they did all this under intense deadline pressure. My hat's off to them.

James Finnegan was my technical editor for this book. Although he'll deny it, his contributions to this book were invaluable. Jim is a fellow contributing editor for *Microsoft Systems Journal*. Simply put, he knows his stuff. More than just being my tech editor, Jim is also a great friend. Jim's most important contribution to this book was to hang out on the phone with me for hours at a time while we discussed things like the price of Star Wars figurines, old video games, writer gossip, obscure bits of 80386 trivia, or the latest Microsoft lunacy of the week. My wife says that Jim is my virtual coffee klatch buddy. As Jim puts it: "I'm trying to throw tacks in the road to slow you down so that I can catch up."

Teri Schiele (the Windows 95 SDK program manager) was my beta buddy. She was great about letting me rant and rave about what I felt were major deficiencies in Windows 95. She took this "input" and actually got something done about some of it. I pestered her quite a bit, and made her life difficult from time to time. Nonetheless, she didn't give up on me, and stuck with me through the entire beta. I certainly wouldn't want to try and fill her shoes, given everything that she's responsible for.

Also from Microsoft are Gretchen Bilson, Eric Maffei, Joanne Steinhart, and the rest of the *Microsoft Systems Journal* gang. Gretchen in particular was instrumental in getting me on the Windows 95 beta. She stuck up for me on more than one occasion when certain people within Microsoft weren't thrilled over things I said about Windows 95 in *Microsoft Systems Journal* articles and columns. *Microsoft Systems Journal* and the people who work there have been great to me over the past couple of years, and I hope to continue our excellent working relationship.

Several people helped fill gaps in my Windows 95 knowledge. Andrew Schulman explained some of the finer points of VxDs to me. (And no, I still haven't written a VxD!) Eli Boling from Borland (Mr. TLINK32) reviewed Chapter 8, and added many valuable insights. And let's not forget the guys at Nu-Mega, either: Dom Basile (Mr. SoftIce/W), Peter Hurley, and Tom Gunither. They're all Windows 95 Wizards, and we've all had many long conversations about the implementation of Windows 95. This book is significantly richer in information content because of their help.

Speaking of Nu-Mega, everybody there was very supportive of my book efforts. Special thanks to the owners Jim Moskun and Frank Grossman. Also, Kenny Kutney pitched in and wrote the professional-looking install program for this book's programs and source code. (His install program is much better looking than what I'd have come up with on my own.)

Reminding me that there are more important things than computers were my two boys, Gunther and Theodore. They're actually twin dachshunds who are total clowns, and who think they're humans with just a bit too much fur. Throughout my work on this book, they were at my knee, silently asking me to stop and play with them. I'm glad I took the opportunity to do so on numerous occasions.

Finally, and most importantly, my wife April has my eternal gratitude for putting up with me during the seemingly interminable time it took to write this book. Since I work full time at Nu-Mega, this book was written during nights and weekends. April spent most of those nights and weekends without me, and I can't thank her enough for doing without me and running the house on her own.

The publisher would like to give special thanks to Patrick McGovern, without whom this book would not have been possible.

ABOUT THE AUTHOR

Matt Pietrek is the "Under the Hood" columnist for *Microsoft Systems Journal*. He also writes for *PC Magazine* and other publications, and is the author of *Windows Internals* (Addison-Wesley, 1993) and co-author of *Undocumented Windows* (Addison-Wesley, 1992). In addition to his writing, Matt is the senior software architect for the BoundsChecker series of products from Nu-Mega Technologies. He lives in Nashua, New Hampshire, and his e-mail address is 71774.362@compuserve.com.

Contents Summary

Foreword XXVII

Introduction XXIX

Chapter 1: Putting Windows 95 in Perspective 1

Brush up on the historical background of the Win32 operating systems, Windows NT, Win32s, and Windows 95. You can read about the relative strengths and weaknesses of each system, as well as alternative Win32 environments such as OS/2 Warp and the Phar Lap TNT DOS extender.

Chapter 2: What's New in Windows 95 15

In this chapter, you'll receive a broad architectural overview of Windows 95, and learn why Windows 95 evolved from Windows 3.1, rather than having been written from scratch. High-level issues such as memory management, thread synchronization, and improvements to the windowing system are also described.

Chapter 3: Modules, Processes, and Threads 69

By examining Windows 95's modules, processes, and threads, you can unravel the data structures that KERNEL32 uses to implement them. Augmenting this chapter the pseudocode for the Win32 functions that rely on these data structures. In addition, you can read about thread local storage and structured exception handling.

Chapter 4: USER and GDI Subsystems 185

Microsoft reworked the windowing, messaging, and graphics subsystems of Windows 3.1 for Windows 95. To better understand what this means, learn all about the 32-bit USER and GDI heaps, and the effect that the new data structures in the 16-bit USER heap have on the free system resources.

Chapter 5: Memory Management 273

Thirty-two-bit memory management in Windows 95 is a complicated area. In this hefty chapter, you can explore the topic in detail by delving into paged-based virtual memory, separate address spaces, and shared memory. Each Win32 memory management API is also described using pseudocode.

CHAPTER 6: VWINKERNEL32386 .... **423**

In Windows 95, there are three essential kernel components: the 16-bit KRNL386, the 32-bit KERNEL32, and the ring 0 VWIN32.VXD. (If you put them all together, you get VWINKERNEL32386.) As you examine the relationship between these kernels, you'll discover many useful — albeit undocumented — functions along the way.

CHAPTER 7: WIN16 MODULES AND TASKS **477**

Not to be overlooked, the 16-bit KERNEL data structures of Windows 95 deserve a good bit of explanation. Although Windows 95 is a 32-bit operating system, much of the system's state is reflected in data structures also present in Windows 3.1. These data structures include the task database and the 16-bit module database, and go a long way toward explaining the intricacies of the Windows 95 architecture.

CHAPTER 8: THE PORTABLE EXECUTABLE AND COFF OBJ FORMATS **555**

To fully understand Windows 95, you need to understand the Portable Executable file format, which is the native executable format for both Windows 95 and Windows NT. In this chapter, you can also learn more about the COFF format OBJ and LIB files that linkers use to create PE files.

CHAPTER 9: SPELUNKING ON YOUR OWN **621**

If you want to really get into the nuts and bolts of Windows 95, Chapter 9 gives you the means to do so. You'll learn to use file-dumping tools and API spying programs, as well as how to examine assembler listings to find things such as local variables, parameters, if statements, and so forth. The chapter concludes with a collection of helpful hints.

CHAPTER 10: WRITING A WIN32 API SPY **685**

Building on the information presented in earlier chapters, this chapter shows you how to create a user-extendable API function spying tool. This spy program can log API function calls as well as their parameter values.

Contents

FOREWORD XXVII

INTRODUCTION XXIX

Assumptions About You, the Reader xxx
The Pseudocode xxxi
The Sample Programs xxxi

CHAPTER 1: PUTTING WINDOWS 95 IN PERSPECTIVE 1

Positioning the Win32 Operating Systems 5
The Windows NT implementation 7
The Win32s implementation 8
The Windows 95 implementation 10
Win32 implementations outside Microsoft 12
Development Considerations 13
The Future of Win32 14
Summary 14

CHAPTER 2: WHAT'S NEW IN WINDOWS 95? 15

Similarities to Windows 3.1 17
Improvements over Windows 3.1 23
DOS is dead (almost) 24
The windowing system 24
Changes to the messaging system 27
The interaction between 16- and 32-bit processes 29
The Win16Mutex 31
The Windows 95 GDI 33
System resource cleanup 34
Decreased memory consumption below 1MB 35
Brand-New Features 36
The Windows 95 Win32 implementation 36
The Windows 95 Win32 system DLLs 37
The ring 0 components of Windows 95 38

Process management 40

Thread management 43

Process and thread synchronization 45

Module management 49

The Windows 95 address space 50

Windows 95 memory management 52

Memory mapped files 55

Structured exception handling 56

The registry 57

Additions to USER 59

System information and debugging 60

"Dirty Little Secrets" About Windows 95 63

Anti-hacking code 64

The Win32 API farce 66

Free system resource fudging 67

Win16 isn't dead 67

Summary 68

CHAPTER 3: MODULES, PROCESSES, AND THREADS 69

Win32 Modules 71

IMTEs (Internal Module Table Entries [?]) 73

The IMTE structure 74

The MODREF structure 78

Module-Related API Functions 80

GetProcAddress and IGetProcAddress 80

x_FindAddressFromExportOrdinal 86

x_FindAddressFromExportName 89

GetModuleFileName and IGetModuleFileName 92

GetModuleHandle and IGetModuleHandle 95

x_GetMODREFFromFilename 98

x_GetHModuleFromMODREF 99

KERNEL32 Objects 100

Windows 95 Processes 102

What's a Process Handle? What's a Process ID? 103

The Windows 95 Process Database (PDB) 106

GetExitCodeProcess and IGetExitCodeProcess 114

SetUnhandledExceptionFilter 115

OpenProcess 116

SetFileApisToOEM 117

The Environment Database 117
    GetCommandLineA 119
    GetEnvironmentStrings 120
    FreeEnvironmentStringsA 120
    GetStdHandle 121
    SetStdHandle 121
Process Handle Tables 122
Threads 124
What's a Thread Handle? What's a Thread ID? 126
The Thread Database 128
The Thread Information Block (TIB) 136
Thread Priorities 138
    GetThreadPriority 139
    SetThreadPriority 140
    CalculateNewPriority 141
    SetPriorityClass 143
    GetPriorityClass 145
Thread Execution Control 146
    GetThreadContext and IGetThreadContext 146
    x_ThreadContext_CopyRegs 150
    SetThreadContext and ISetThreadContext 151
    SuspendThread and VWIN32_SuspendThread 154
    ResumeThread 156
Structured Exception Handling 157
    Structured exception handling and parameter validation 163
    GetCurrentDirectoryA 164
    x_invalid_param_handler 166
Thread Local Storage 169
    TlsAlloc 170
    TlsSetValue 172
    TlsGetValue 173
    TlsFree 174
Miscellaneous Thread Functions 176
    GetLastError 176
    SetLastError 177
    GetExitCodeThread and IGetExitCodeThread 177
The Win32Wlk Program 178
    Under the hood of Win32Wlk 181
Summary 184

CHAPTER 4: USER AND GDI SUBSYSTEMS **185**

The Windows 95 USER Module 186
   USER32 thunking example 189
   32-bit heaps 195
   The mysterious GetFreeSystemResources issue 202
   The mixed 16-/32-bit nature of the windowing system 211
   Messaging system changes 214
   Per-thread message queues 218
   Per-queue system windows 224
   Changes to (H)WND structures in Windows 95 226
   Changes to Windows 95 window classes 233
   The SHOWWND program 237
   Pseudocode for select 16-bit USER.EXE functions 239
   USER32 isn't just thunks to USER.EXE 248
   Unicode support in Windows 95 (Huh?) 257
The Windows 95 GDI Module 260
   GDI objects 263
   New Win32 GDI functions available to Win16 applications 270
Summary 271

CHAPTER 5: MEMORY MANAGEMENT **273**

Windows 95 Page-Based Memory Management 274
   Memory paging 274
   Memory paging versus selectors 277
The Address Space of a Windows 95 Win32 Process 279
Sharing Memory 286
"Copy on Write" in Windows 95 (or the Lack Thereof) 290
The PHYS Program 292
   Examining shared memory with PHYS 298
   Examining copy on write with PHYS 298
   Cool stuff in the PHYS program (for advanced readers) 299
Memory Contexts (Advanced Stuff) 303
The Windows 95 Memory APIs 309
The VMM Functions 310
The Win32 Virtual Functions 312
   VirtualAlloc 313
   mmPAGEToPC 318
   VirtualFree 319
   VirtualQueryEx 321

VirtualQuery and IVirtualQuery 323
VirtualProtectEx 325
VirtualProtect and IVirtualProtect 327
VirtualLock and VirtualUnlock 328
The Win32 Heap Functions 329
The Win32 heap header and heap arenas 332
The Windows 95 heap header 335
The WALKHEAP program 339
GetProcessHeap 342
HeapAlloc and IHeapAlloc 343
HPAlloc 344
hpCarve 348
ChecksumHeapBlock 351
HeapSize and IHeapSize 352
HeapFree and IHeapFree 354
hpFreeSub 357
HeapReAlloc and IHeapReAlloc 360
HPReAlloc 362
HeapCreate 366
HPInit 369
HeapDestroy and IHeapDestroy 373
HeapValidate 377
HeapCompact 377
GetProcessHeaps 377
HeapLock 378
HeapUnlock 378
HeapWalk 379
The Win32 Local and Global Heap Functions 379
Win32 local heaps 380
LocalAlloc and ILocalAlloc 383
LocalLock and ILocalLock 387
LocalUnlock 390
LocalFree and ILocalFree 392
LocalReAlloc and ILocalRealloc 396
LocalHandle and ILocalHandle 400
LocalSize and ILocalSize 402
LocalFlags 405
LocalShrink 407
LocalCompact 408

The Win32 Global Heap Functions 408
    GlobalAlloc 408
    GlobalLock 408
    GlobalUnlock 409
    GlobalFree 409
    GlobalReAlloc 409
    GlobalSize 409
    GlobalHandle 409
    GlobalFlags and IGlobalFlags 410
    GlobalWire 410
    GlobalUnWire 410
    GlobalFix 410
    GlobalUnfix 411
    GlobalCompact 411
Miscellaneous Functions 411
    WriteProcessMemory and ReadProcessMemory 411
    GlobalMemoryStatus and IGlobalMemoryStatus 414
    GetThreadSelectorEntry and IGetThreadSelectorEntry 417
    The C/C++ compiler's malloc and new functions 420
Summary 422

CHAPTER 6: VWINKERNEL32386 423

A Crash Course in VxDs 425
    Calling VxD functions from other VxDs 426
    Calling VxD functions from Win16
        (protected mode) code 427
Calling VxD Functions from Win32 Code 431
Where Can I Find Win32 VxD Services? 438
Win32 VxD Services Provided by VMM 439
Calling Win32 VxD Services on Your Own 441
Examining VWIN32.VXD 444
    The VWIN32.VXD ring 0 VxD service API 445
    The VWIN32.VXD 16-bit protected mode API 446
    The VWIN32.VXD Win32 VxD service API 447
The VWIN32 TDBX 454
How the Three Windows 95 Kernels Communicate 457
    VWIN32 knowledge of KRNL386 458

VWIN32 knowledge of KERNEL32.DLL 460
KERNEL32.DLL knowledge of VWIN32 460
KERNEL32.DLL knowledge of KRNL386.EXE
    (or, What Microsoft isn't telling you) 461
KRNL386 knowledge of KERNEL32.DLL 465
KRNL386 knowledge of VWIN32 466
The Win32 VxD Service Spy (W32SVSPY) 466
    A sample W32SVSPY session 469
    Technical challenges in writing W32SVSPY 472
Summary 476

CHAPTER 7: WIN16 MODULES AND TASKS 477

Why Have 16-bit Representations of 32-bit Modules and
    Processes? 478
16-bit Modules 479
The NE Header 482
    New module database fields in Windows 95 492
The Segment Table 492
The Resource Table 495
The Entry Table 499
The Resident and Nonresident Names Tables 501
HMODULEs versus HINSTANCEs 503
Module-Related Functions 505
    The GetModuleHandle function 505
    The GetExePtr function 510
    The GetProcAddress function 515
16-bit Tasks 521
Some Common Misconceptions about Tasks 525
The Task Database (TDB) 526
Task-Related Functions 536
    The GetCurrentTask() function 537
    The IsTask() function 537
    The GetTaskQueue() function 538
    The MakeProcInstance() function 540
    The TaskFindHandle() function 544
The SHOW16 Program 547
Summary 554

CHAPTER 8: THE PORTABLE EXECUTABLE AND
COFF OBJ FORMATS **555**

The PEDUMP Program 559
Basic Win32 and PE Concepts 559
The Section Table 570
Commonly Encountered Sections 576
  The .text section 577
  The Borland CODE and .icode sections 579
  The .data section 579
  The DATA section 580
  The .bss section 580
  The .CRT section 580
  The .rsrc section 580
  The .idata section 581
  The .edata section 581
  The .reloc section 581
  The .tls section 582
  The .rdata section 583
  The .debug$S and .debug$T sections 585
  The .drective section 585
  Sections containing $ (OBJs/LIBs only) 585
  Miscellaneous sections 586
PE File Imports 586
  The IMAGE_THUNK_DATA DWORD 590
  Putting IMAGE_IMPORT_DESCRIPTORs and
    IMAGE_THUNK_DATAs together 591
PE File Exports 593
  Export forwarding 598
PE File Resources 599
PE File Base Relocations 602
The COFF Symbol Table 605
The COFF Debug Information 611
The COFF Line-Number Table 613
Differences Between PE Files and COFF OBJ Files 614
COFF LIB Files 615
  Linker members 618
  The Longnames member 620
Summary 620

CHAPTER 9: SPELUNKING ON YOUR OWN **621**

Spelunking Overview 623
Spelunking with File-Dumping Tools 624
Spelunking with Spying Tools 634
Spelunking Using Disassembly 642
   Zen and the art of disassembly 643
   Recognizing common code sequences and
     conventions 646
   A disassembly example 667
Advanced Hacking Tips 672
   Using SoftIce/Windows 673
   Using hardware breakpoints 675
   The VxD . (dot) commands 676
   The VAR2MAP utility 676
   Identifying VxD services 678
   Identifying Win32 VxD services 679
   Identifying parameter validation and Ixxx functions 680
   Using the debug version 681
   Pentium-optimized code 682
Summary 683

CHAPTER 10: WRITING A WIN32 API SPY **685**

Intercepting the Functions 687
Injecting a DLL into Another Process 692
Using the Debug API to Control the Target Process 695
Building Stubs to Log API Functions 697
Parameter Information Encoding 699
Function Return Values 701
The APISPY32 Code 705
Win32s-Specific Code 729
The APISPYLD Code 730
Notes on Using APISPY32 744
Intercepting Functions in Your Own Programs 746
Summary 753

APPENDIX A: THE UNDOCUMENTED KERNEL32.DLL IMPORT LIBRARY 760

INDEX 761

FOREWORD

Windows 95 System Programming SECRETS is Matt
Pietrek's third major work on how to truly understand
Microsoft Windows. Matt has been mucking about with this
Windows stuff for quite some time. His life as techno-guru
began when he graduated in 1988 from the University of
Santa Cruz with a degree in physics but only two computer
courses under his belt. After joining the tech support depart-
ment at Borland, he quickly distinguished himself by tying for
the lowest score in an evaluation that gauged "employee sym-
pathy for the customer."

Life was rosier in Borland's R&D division. There Matt wrote
TDUMP and WinSpector, and even admits to having worked on
the OS/2 Turbo Debugger. He was richly rewarded for his efforts
by being laid off during one of Borland's many staff pogroms.
Matt finally came into his own at Nu-Mega, where today he is
chief architect for the Bounds-Checker family of products.

I first met Matt at the spring Software Development conference in 1991, an event where we Windows advocates were
still a minority. Charles Petzold and I were panelists for a
Windows versus OS/2 debate. We were soundly trounced by
the other panelists, and heckled by the audience for predicting
that the dominant PC OS of the very near future was going to
be Windows.

It seems as if Matt, Charles and I were proven right — in fact, Windows has now transcended the realm of technology and become a part of pop culture. During its opening weekend, Windows 95 grossed more than *Jurassic Park*. Thankfully, when you look beyond all the hype, there is plenty of steak to go with the sizzle. An end-user migration from Windows 3.*x* to Windows 95 finally rids us of the memory model agitation we've experienced for years, and enables us to live out our lives entirely in 32 bits.

If Windows is a big labyrinthian cave, then this book is for those of us who want to venture farther into the cave than the Win32 API will take us. Matt is the foremost guide to the innermost caverns of Windows 95. (In fact, the working title to this book was *Spelunking Windows*.) Many of the other "current" Windows 95 developer books (including the first edition of the "unauthorized" one) promise to show you all the dark chambers, but were in fact written a year or more ago. In an effort to be first, the authors of some of those books jumped the gun, exploring Chicago no further than its May 1994 beta 1 release. Some of those works are now riddled with obsolete information and misleading supposition.

Matt, on the other hand, scrutinized all the iterations of Chicago — including the retail release of Windows 95 — to bring you the up-to-date information contained here. So strap on your safety helmet, light that lamp, and start spelunking.

Eric J. Maffei
Editor-in-Chief
Microsoft Systems Journal
New York, September 1995
ericm@microsoft.com

INTRODUCTION

*O*f late, Microsoft has been asking, "Where do you want to go today?" The company hasn't been shy about promoting Windows 95 as the means by which we'll reach our destination. What we as programmers need to know is whether Windows 95 is the appropriate vehicle for getting there. Almost everybody will agree that Windows NT is a Cadillac (or Mercedes Benz, if you prefer)—it's well built and loaded with options. The question is: Is Windows 95 a Chevrolet or a go-cart? The only way to find out is to pop the hood and look for yourself. That's the purpose of the book you're now holding. Only by examining the fundamentals of an operating system such as Windows 95 is it possible to tell whether it's composed of tail fins and chrome, or serious safety and comfort features.

You might be wondering why programmers like me keep taking apart the fundamental pieces of operating systems such as Windows 95. Wouldn't it be better to focus our efforts on new technologies like OLE, MFC, or the latest graphics or multimedia APIs? Although some programmers prefer to learn just enough to get by, other programmers have an insatiable need to understand all the layers of code down to the bare metal. Maybe we just don't want to trust our code to run atop the unexamined code of others. Whatever the reason, *Windows 95 System Programming SECRETS* is a book for these programmers. Knowledge is power, and the more knowledge you have about a system like Windows 95, the more control you have over it.

Windows 95 System Programming SECRETS is by no means an authoritative look at all aspects of the Windows 95 architecture and implementation. Rather, I self-indulgently chose to concentrate on the areas that I'm particularly interested in. I hope that somewhere within the contents of this tome, you'll find something of particular interest or use to you in your own Windows 95 programming.

ASSUMPTIONS ABOUT YOU, THE READER

To cover any significant ground in this book, I needed to make certain assumptions about my reading audience. In a nutshell, my main assumption is that the reader of this book is a competent Windows programmer who's done at least some Windows 3.*x* programming. This book isn't a "How do I write a program for Windows 95?" book. There are already plenty of books available for programmers who want to learn the basics of Windows 95 programming.

Rather, *Windows 95 System Programming SECRETS* assumes that you know *how* to program in Windows 3.1 or Windows 95, and that you now want to go on to the next step: understanding *why* Windows 95 works as it does.

By knowing what goes on inside the theoretical black box of Windows 95, you'll be able to make sense of the rituals you perform to accomplish tasks in Windows 95—rituals that you might otherwise perform blindly. Likewise, when (heaven forbid) you find a bug in your program, the debugging process goes much faster if you understand how Windows 95 works. How's this? If you grasp what Windows is doing (or should be doing), you can usually identify where your program goes off-track much earlier in the debugging process.

The examples in this book are written in C, with a bit of assembler mixed in. The pseudocode I present for various Windows 95 functions is also based on the C language. Therefore, to get the maximum benefit from this book, you should know C/C++. You can probably squeak by if you program in some other compiled language such as Borland Pascal/Delphi.

The Pseudocode

Since the goal of this book is first and foremost to show how Windows 95 works, I provide pseudocode for various functions in the system DLLs. This pseudocode usually resembles compilable C code. However, when it makes sense to break the rules of strict C syntax for the sake of clarity, I do. The pseudocode is based on the debug version of Windows 95, which provides many helpful diagnostics strings and other tidbits that make it easier to see exactly what Windows is doing. If you're not running the debug version of Windows 95, you really should be. The debugging DLLs for Windows 95 give very useful information when something goes wrong. If you resist the debug version and try stepping through the retail build, be prepared for discrepancies between what you see in your debugger and the pseudocode from this book.

The Sample Programs

Windows 95 System Programming SECRETS includes quite a few programs for exploring Windows 95 on your own. All these programs (both the .EXEs and the source files) are included on the disk that accompanies this book. I absolutely despise books that take up (pad) 30 pages at a time with source code listings. For this reason, almost none of the source code for these programs appears here. The one exception is the APISPY32 program in Chapter 10. The focus of Chapter 10 is building a Win32 API spy, and a close examination of the source code is necessary to demonstrate the concepts involved.

If you read *Microsoft Systems Journal* or *PC Magazine*, you may have seen some of the programs from this book in their earlier incarnations. In fact, several of the chapters in this book were excerpted in the aforementioned magazines. However, if you've read these articles, don't skip over the corresponding sections in this bookThe programs have evolved since they originally appeared in magazine form. And, there are reams of material that didn't make it into the magazine articles for space reasons.

For example, the PEDUMP program from Chapter 8 has almost doubled its amount of functionality since it first appeared in *Microsoft Systems Journal*. Likewise, the APISPY32 program that appeared in *Microsoft Systems Journal* worked with beta 2 of Windows 95, but broke in later builds. The APISPY32 program from this book works with the shipping Windows 95, as well as with .EXEs that use the extensions introduced in NT 3.51.

PUTTING WINDOWS 95 IN PERSPECTIVE

A WIN32 OVERVIEW

*A*s I write this, Microsoft is madly churning out copies of Windows 95, in the wake of its August debut.

Windows NT, on the other hand, has been available for two years — and in many people's minds has flopped. The perception is that NT is slow and a resource hog. (Windows NT 3.5 was a substantial improvement over the first NT release, however, and many of the initial complaints were dealt with. I quite enjoy developing in Windows NT now.) The Win32s libraries, which run atop Windows 3.1 and which were released at the same time as Windows NT 3.1, are widely regarded as being incredibly buggy and ultimately not worth the effort of working with.

Things just haven't looked too bright for the future of 32-bit Windows programming until the release of Windows 95. Now, like it or not, you'll have to come face to face with Win32 programming if you want to stay in the Microsoft camp and keep up with the latest technologies. Microsoft is putting all its eggs in the Win32 basket. Even though 16-bit Windows 3.x applications will continue to be supported in future Microsoft operating systems, 16-bit programs won't be able to take advantage of many new features. Given that Win32 is the future (according to Microsoft, anyway), the big question is "Where should you be focusing your programming efforts?"

While the primary focus of this book is on the architecture and implementation of Windows 95, this operating system is the newcomer to the Win32 playing field. Even though Windows NT and Win32s have been shipping for quite some time, many of you probably didn't pay much attention to Win32 programming until Windows 95 came along. Microsoft's master strategy for the Win32 application programming interface (API) and the scaleability of its operating systems have been with us for three years now. It would be foolish to pretend that Windows 95 is brand new, and without a history. In addition, although Windows 95 is currently getting all the press, in the halls of Microsoft, it's the NT team that's building Microsoft's operating system of the future. Microsoft intends Windows NT and Windows 95 to merge in the future, and the result will be based more on Windows NT technology than on Windows 95. Therefore, before digging into the nitty-gritty technical details of Windows 95, I'll use this chapter to provide a sense of Microsoft's Win32 strategy over the past several years and to show how Windows 95 fits into the picture. Believe me, the remainder of the book will be chock-full of information about Windows 95 and how it's implemented. But this first chapter is important to put Windows 95 into the larger context of Win32 programming and the Win32 (API).

No doubt Microsoft won't like some of what I'll say here, since its mantra has long been "There's just one Win32 API. Write one program and have it run on all our systems." Although this sounds like a nice idea, it breaks down in practice.

Probably the best way to start this discussion is to define the term *Win32*. Used properly, Win32 defines a set of operating-system functions (an API) that application programs can use to carry out their work. This set of functions is called the *Win32 API*. When Microsoft first introduced Windows NT, many programmers were confused about the difference between the terms "Win32" and "Windows NT." Windows NT is just one implementation of the Win32 API. However, since it was the first announced Win32 implementation, some programmers had a hard time differentiating between the operating system (Windows NT) and its API (Win32).

Since one of Microsoft's major goals with respect to Win32 is to provide easy porting to the Win32 API, the Win32 API functions are very similar to the Windows 3.*x* API in those areas covered by Windows 3.*x* (for instance, in window management and display output).

If Microsoft had limited the use of the Win32 API to just Windows NT, Windows 95 would have turned out very different than it did. However, Microsoft committed to implementing the Win32 API on several operating systems. Each operating system is optimized for a specific situation and hardware environment. For powerful high-end machines where robustness and security are of primary importance, Windows NT is the implementation of choice. For low-end 386 machines that are still running Windows 3.1 with limited memory, the Win32s libraries were the optimal Win32 solution until Windows 95 arrived on the scene. The important point from Microsoft's perspective is that by writing your programs using the Win32 API, the same executable can presumably run on any Win32 implementation.

In theory, the Win32 API implementation in each operating system should gloss over any underlying differences in hardware or low-level operating system design. This relates to Microsoft's "Scaleable Architecture" campaign, promoted around the time of the first Win32 developer's conference in July of 1992. As the name Win32 implies, one of the key advantages of switching to the Win32 API from the Windows 3.*x* API is 32-bit code. In defining the Win32 API, Microsoft also outlined a new 32-bit executable file format. This format is known as the PE (Portable Executable) format and is derived from the UNIX System common object file format V (COFF). The Win32 API and the PE format are a matched set. All Win32 operating system implementations (even on non-Intel platforms) use the PE format as their primary executable format. By using the same executable format for all Win32 operating systems, Microsoft hopes to guarantee that a properly written Win32 program will run on all Win32 implementations. Of course, portability only goes so far. While the executable format is portable, you still can't run a program compiled for the DEC Alpha on a computer with an Intel CPU (at least, not without very complex emulation software).

Shortly after Windows NT was put into the public arena, Microsoft announced another implementation of the Win32 API called Win32s. The idea behind Win32s is that a collection of DLLs and virtual device drivers (VxDs) provided by Microsoft could be added to an existing Windows 3.1 machine to enable it to run Win32 programs. Unfortunately, some of the desirable features that Windows NT brings to the party weren't achievable under the architecture imposed by running atop Windows 3.1. Thus was born the concept of the Win32s subset. The Win32s libraries provide some, but not all, of the API functions that Windows NT and Windows 95 have. In fact, the *s* in Win32s stands for *subset* (or, depending on your experience with Win32s, a variety of other less flattering words). The major downfall of Win32s is that it doesn't support many features of modern operating systems, such as threads and separate address spaces. *Threads* are a feature of advanced operating systems that allow more than one portion of a program to execute at once (or at least appear to operate this way). A classic use of threads is to use one thread to handle printing, while another thread continues to respond to user input. Win32s is also hamstrung by some of the limitations of Windows 3.*x*. (More on this in "The Win32s implementation" section later in the chapter.)

Like Win32s, Windows 95 provides only a subset of the full Win32 API as defined by Windows NT. Microsoft originally dubbed this subset *Win32c* (the *c* stands for *Chicago*, which was the original code name for Windows 95). The Win32c API subset includes all the functions in Win32s, and adds a significant number from the full NT API set. Hopes are high for the success of Windows 95, because even though its API is a subset of Windows NT's, Windows 95 contains most of the features programmers find desirable in an advanced operating system — for example, threads and separate address spaces (both features that Win32s lacks). Programmers generally love separate address spaces because this feature prevents buggy programs from overwriting another program's data or, more importantly, from overwriting the operating system itself. Windows 95 also requires less memory than Windows NT, making it a more suitable choice for the average desktop PC.

Unlike the Windows NT team, the Windows 95 team didn't consider portability to other processors to be a major goal. That's because the Intel market is large enough to enable Microsoft to have two mostly separate Win32 development efforts. The Windows NT group produces a portable Win32 implementation, but one that isn't optimal for any given platform. The Windows 95 group produces a Win32 implementation that is optimized for the Intel 80386 class of CPUs. If Microsoft didn't have a version optimized for the Intel platform, it would likely lose ground to operating systems that do, such as OS/2 Warp. In fact, many people think OS/2 and Windows 95 are very similar and that Windows 95 is an "OS/2 killer."

A while ago, Microsoft ditched the term "Win32c" because it seemed to highlight the differences between Windows NT and Windows 95 and was confusing programmers. In place of the term "Win32c," Microsoft started claiming that there is just one Win32 API, and that a program written for the Win32 API will run on all the Win32 implementations. The reality, however, is that programmers still have to consider the functions that Windows 95 implements as a proper subset of the Windows NT (Win32) API. Microsoft's concern seemed to be that programmers might be holding off on writing to the Win32 API since they didn't know which subset to target. Later on, Microsoft tried to further enforce this "Just one Win32 API" mindset by making support for both Windows NT and Windows 95 a requirement to use the Microsoft Win32 Logo on a product.

Of course, trying to feather over the differences among API subsets is complete nonsense. There are differences between the subsets, and they do matter. For example, developers discovered that it was difficult for them to obtain Microsoft's Win32 Logo program because the differences between the Windows NT and Windows 95 Win32 implementations made it next to impossible to meet Microsoft's requirement that its products support both implementations. (Eventually, enough whining by developers caused Microsoft to revise its logo requirements.) And, as a second example, it's clear that a program that relies on multiple threads to do its job can't run on Win32s since Win32s doesn't support multithreading. The result of these differences is that, in order to program effectively, programmers will have to pay attention to the Win32 subsets and understand the underlying operating system.

POSITIONING THE WIN32 OPERATING SYSTEMS

To clarify the underlying architecture of the current Win32 platforms, I've come up with an audio-system analogy (see Figure 1-1) that nicely illustrates the relationships between the platforms. For the sake of this discussion, pretend that audio compact disks don't exist and that cassette tapes are the best available form of recorded music.

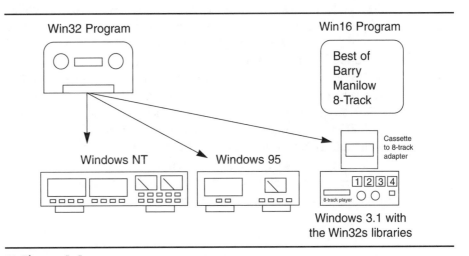

Figure 1-1

This audio-system analogy clarifies the underlying architecture of the current Win32 platforms and shows how they are related to each other.

In my analogy, Win32 programs are like cassette tapes, and 16-bit Windows 3.*x* programs are like the older, clunkier 8-track tapes. Similarly, a Win32 operating system is like a cassette tape player that can play and record cassette tapes, and Windows 3.*x* is like an 8-track player and is limited to 8-track tapes.

Given this scenario, if you were an audiophile and wanted top-of-the-line stereo components, you'd purchase a high-quality cassette deck with all the bells and whistles — that is, you'd purchase Windows NT. On the other hand, if you're strapped for cash and wanted to play cassette tapes, but had only an 8-track player, what would you do? You might decide to get an adapter for your 8-track player that will permit you to listen to cassettes. In Windows programming, Win32s is the equivalent of this cassette-to-8-track adapter. You plug Win32 programs into the Win32s adapter, which in turn plugs into Windows 3.1 (the 8-track tape player). When using these tape adapters, you're limited in what you can do. For instance, you can't use an 8-track adapter to record onto a cassette tape. Also, the sound quality isn't anywhere near as good as playing the cassette on a cassette deck would be (since there's an extra layer of electronics and tape heads between the 8-track tape and the cassette deck tape head). Likewise, Win32s has limits on what it can do: The full Win32 API isn't supported, nor are features such as threads available.

Where does Windows 95 fit in? Windows 95 would be the equivalent of a basic-model cassette deck, with some of its components scrounged from an 8-track player (and a pretty new face plate). Windows 95 has a lot of new 32-bit code, but also borrows heavily from the Windows 3.1 code base for features such as window management. For the most part, the Windows 95 cassette deck does everything that the Windows NT premium-quality cassette deck does, but it lacks some high-end features — for example, it doesn't support security or double-byte character sets (a.k.a. *Unicode*) like NT does. On the positive side, however, the Windows 95 basic-model cassette deck doesn't require anywhere near the amount of fancy, sophisticated electronics inside, so it's cheaper to produce. In other words, Windows 95 won't have nearly as much code as NT, so it will take up less room in memory and run faster.

With this rather corny analogy safely tucked away in the attic of your mind, let's zoom in and examine each of Microsoft's Win32 implementations to see how they relate to one another.

The Windows NT implementation

The primary goals of Windows NT are robustness and portability to other platforms. Much of the code is written in portable C or C++ rather than in hand-optimized assembler for the target platform. The emphasis on stability makes NT an ideal development platform, even if you're targeting Windows 95, Win32s, Windows 3.*x*, or DOS. On the other hand, portability and stability come at a cost. All the C/C++ code in NT adds up to a large footprint in memory just to get the system booted. A minimum usable Windows NT development machine is a 486 with 16MB of memory. Even with that hardware, NT won't be as fast as a system running OS/2 or Windows 95. (In defense of Windows NT, however, the 3.5 version was significantly better than NT 3.1, which is the version many programmers based their first impressions on.)

One of the primary reasons for NT's robustness is its protected subsystem architecture. In the protected subsystem, the operating-system code that implements the API functions runs in a different address space and process than that of the calling program. The most important subsystem in Windows NT is the Win32 subsystem. The Win32 subsystem is its own process, with most of the USER and GDI code placed in a DLL called WINSERV.DLL. When your program makes a call to an API function such as TextOut, you're not making a direct call to the real TextOut code. Instead, a stub in NT's GDI32.DLL copies your parameters into a region of memory accessible by both your process and the Win32 subsystem process. Your thread then signals the Win32 subsystem process that there's a function request waiting for it and then goes to sleep. When the Win32 subsystem process sees the signal that there's work to do, it processes the request (doing things such as putting a text string to the screen) and then informs the calling process's thread that the function has completed. This subsystem client/server model also applies to other operating system "flavors" that NT supports, such as OS/2 1.*x* and POSIX.

The advantage of protected subsystems is that their address space is better protected against memory overwrites and other bugs in application program code. In operating systems without this subsystem model (such as Windows 3.*x* and Windows 95), the operating-system code and data is mapped into the address spaces of all processes, making it possible for a buggy program to overwrite and crash the operating system. The disadvantage to the subsystem model is increased execution time. Every call to an operating-system function theoretically causes a process switch and memory context change. This is expensive, clock-cycle–wise, with estimates of 2000–3000 clock cycles for the average call. For this reason, the NT developers optimized some heavily used routines so that they wouldn't require a process switch. In addition, certain GDI calls can be batched so there doesn't have to be a process switch for each call.

All this improved robustness for Win32 applications is great, but what about existing 16-bit applications that are run under NT? Sixteen-bit Windows programs run under a cooperatively multitasking model, and expect to be able to access memory belonging to other tasks. NT keeps 16-bit tasks at arm's length by running them in a separate process known as WOW (Windows On Windows). By default, 16-bit Windows applications run in a single "WOW box," which is essentially a multithreaded DOS box.

The WOW box is a Windows 3.1-like "sandbox" inside of which 16-bit applications can do anything they want; their actions don't corrupt anything outside the box.

The WOW subsystem communicates with the Win32 subsystem code to perform display output, allowing 16- and 32-bit windows programs to interact on the same screen. Windows NT 3.5 introduced the ability to run each Win16 application in its own WOW box, increasing stability among several applications running Win16 at the expense of additional memory.

I'm introducing the WOW subsystem in this section because it's an important architectural difference between Windows NT and Windows 95. (Windows 95 runs Win16 applications in the same address space as the current Win32 application.) The only real downside to the WOW subsystem in NT is that 16-bit Windows applications run slower than they would under Windows 3.1 running on the same machine.

The Win32s implementation

In contrast to Windows NT, Win32s is yet another layer on the already shaky DOS and Windows house of cards. Win32s isn't an operating system in and of itself; rather, it's a set of extension libraries for Windows 3.1. Likewise, Windows 3.x isn't a true operating system by itself, either. Instead, it rests rather dicily on the unprotected real mode operations of DOS. The code for implementing the Win32 API with Win32s adds another precariously balanced layer because it relies on the VxDs and system DLLs from Windows 3.1.

With few exceptions (such as memory mapped files), if a particular piece of functionality isn't in Windows 3.1, the equivalent Win32 function isn't in the Win32s subset. A good chunk of the Win32s code is nothing more than thunks to go from your 32-bit program down to the 16-bit Windows 3.1 code that does the actual work. *Thunks* are the programming equivalent of patching things together with chewing gum, string, and bailing wire. Thunks in Win32s and Windows 95 are small chunks of code that handle the transitions between 16- and 32-bit code.

The limitations of Win32s are numerous. First and foremost, it doesn't support multithreading. 'Nuff said on that point. A second Win32s flaw is its single address space for all Win16 and Win32 programs. Since Windows 95 and NT have separate address spaces for Win32 programs, this relegates Win32s to the "abandon as soon as you can" category. Win32 programs running under Win32s can see the memory of other Win32 programs, as well as the memory of 16-bit programs, making memory corruption a very real possibility.

A third mark against Win32s is the lack of per-process DLL data. In NT and Windows 95, the data area of a DLL is instanced on a per-process basis (by default). In simpler terms, this means that you can safely use global variables in DLLs without worrying that another process will call the DLL and overwrite the variable with another value. Since DLLs under Win32s share the same data area between all users of the DLL (just like under Windows 3.1), you can run into nasty bugs. Typically, your program and its DLLs will work fine under NT or Windows 95, but crash in Win32s/Windows 3.1. This is yet another reason to forget that Win32s ever existed, now that Windows 95 is here.

Another group of Win32 problems that don't exist in Windows NT and Windows 95 relates to process scheduling and the messaging system. In Windows NT and Windows 95, threads are switched pre-emptively. In addition, Windows NT and Windows 95 give each thread its own message queue, and a separate input system thread assigns mouse and keyboard events to the appropriate queue. These two design factors allow one thread to be as unresponsive and take as much time as it wants without affecting other programs. In contrast, Win32s is stuck with the hopelessly problem-prone Windows 3.1 cooperative multitasking model. In order for one task to run, another task has to yield the CPU by calling a function such as GetMessage or PeekMessage. If a task doesn't retrieve its messages and yield the CPU in a timely manner, the user can't switch to or use other programs.

The bottom line? Win32s has a reputation of being cranky and prone to crashes or other strange behavior. If you're getting the feeling that I don't think Win32s isn't worth the trouble, you're right. Thank goodness Windows 95 is finally here to take its place.

The Windows 95 implementation

The best way to describe the Windows 95 Win32 implementation is to say that it's Win32s done properly. Another way to think of Windows 95 is to conceive of it as incorporating the best features of Windows NT implemented in the Win32s style. Windows 95 contains just the right amount of advanced operating-system features without going overboard in terms of code size and speed. In fact, the Window 95 memory footprint is roughly the same as Windows 3.1 with Win32s installed, making Windows 95 an ideal replacement for Win32s.

Under the hood, Windows 95 has a stronger resemblance to Windows 3.1 and Win32s than it does to Windows NT. Like Windows 3.1, the lowest layer of Windows 95 is ring 0 system code consisting of the Virtual Machine Manager (VMM) and assorted VxDs. The code running at CPU ring level 0 is theoretically the most stable and trusted code, so it has more access to the hardware and operating-system data than the application-level code running at ring level 3 of the CPU. Also, as in Windows 3.1, there is one virtual machine set up for running Windows programs and a separate virtual machine for each DOS session you start. In the system virtual machine that's used by Windows programs, you'll find the familiar ring 3 system DLLs: USER, KERNEL, and GDI, along with their 32-bit equivalents: KERNEL32, USER32, and GDI32.

Like Win32s, Windows 95 implements a big chunk of its code in the 16-bit system DLLs and uses thunks to transfer from 32-bit programs down to the 16-bit code. Almost all of the windowing and messaging system code resides in the 16-bit USER.EXE, just as in Windows 3.1. Trying to convert the massively complex windowing system code in USER.EXE to 32 bits would have led to a large size increase and incompatibilities with existing 16-bit programs. Neither of these problems was acceptable to Microsoft, since backward compatibility with existing hardware and software was not up for debate. Therefore, the windowing and messaging system in Windows 95 is essentially an updated version of the Windows 3.1 code. The updates are primarily to allow the 16-bit components to interface with the 32-bit components, as well as to add whatever functionality was needed to implement the Win32 functions that Windows 95 supports.

The implementation of the 32-bit GDI API in Windows 95 is split between existing code in the 16-bit GDI.EXE and new code in GDI32.DLL. Wherever possible and reasonable, the Windows 95 GDI32 functions thunk down to the existing 16-bit GDI code. With regard to the KERNEL APIs, Microsoft's statements have indicated that the 32-bit KERNEL32.DLL doesn't thunk down to the 16-bit KRNL386.EXE. However, Andrew Schulman proved conclusively in *Unauthorized Windows 95* that KERNEL32 does in fact call down to KRNL386.EXE. We'll also be scrutinizing Microsoft's statements on this topic later on in the book, especially in Chapter 3.

In the previous section I described some of the problems with Win32s: no threading support, a single address space, the lack of per-process DLL data, and cooperative multitasking. For the most part, Windows 95 corrects these issues; that is, it works like NT. Windows 95 32-bit programs can have threads (although 16-bit tasks cannot), and data in DLLs is per-process. However, some corners have been cut. For example, each process in Windows 95 gets its own address space, but all loaded system DLLs are visible to a Windows 95 process, not just the DLLs that the process has loaded itself. In addition, the memory of all Win16 tasks and some of the DOS memory below 1MB is visible to the currently running Win32 process. In other words, parts of DOS, Win16 programs, and the current Win32 process all intermingle in the same address space, unlike in Windows NT. As Chapter 5 shows, memory corruption is still a possibility in Windows 95, but the likelihood of a 32-bit programming bashing memory that it doesn't own is much less than under Win32s.

One of the hot topics about Windows 95 is its not-very-smooth multi-tasking behavior in the presence of 16-bit programs. Windows 95 really does have preemptive multitasking, but a badly behaved 16-bit program can cause other threads to jam up at the entrance to 16-bit DLLs such as USER.EXE and GDI.EXE. The problem is that the 16-bit system DLLs are nonreentrant. That is, they don't expect to be switched away from while they're in the middle of doing something. Since many of the Win32 API functions thunk down to the system DLLs, some method to prevent a thread switch at an inopportune moment is necessary. Many solutions were discussed and hotly debated during the early design period of Windows 95.

The solution that was finally decided on as the most palatable of numerous bad options is known as the Win16Mutex. The Win16Mutex is essentially a mutual exclusion semaphore that needs to be acquired upon entry to the 16-bit system DLLs such as USER.EXE and GDI.EXE. The Win16Mutex means that only one thread can be executing at a time through the 16-bit system code. This in itself wouldn't be so bad, but to prevent other problems, the Win16Mutex is "owned" whenever a 16-bit application is executing. The unfortunate ramification is that a 16-bit program that doesn't yield properly by calling GetMessage or PeekMessage can prevent the user interface threads of 32-bit applications from executing.

The implications of the Win16Mutex are twofold. First, the sooner you move your application to 32 bits, the better. If a system isn't running any badly behaved 16-bit programs, the Win16Mutex will almost never be a source of trouble. (As pointed out in *Unauthorized Windows 95*, no

Windows 95 system is completely free of Win16 tasks, since the system itself uses one or two 16-bit tasks. However, these system tasks are good about yielding control to other tasks, and thereby are good about releasing the Win16Mutex.)

The second implication of the Win16Mutex involves threading. If you're doing time-critical work, you'll probably want to split your application into multiple threads (for instance, a user interface thread and one or more worker threads). The Win16Mutex doesn't affect threads that aren't thunking down to 16-bit code like USER or GDI. These threads will continue to be pre-emptively scheduled and executed, even if the entire user interface is tied up with an ill-behaved 16-bit program that's not yielding. The most likely way to get hung up in your Win32 application while waiting for the Win16Mutex is by calling USER and GDI functions. With advance planning, you can avoid calls that might block in your time-sensitive threads.

Win32 implementations outside Microsoft

The previous three sections have focused on the Win32 platforms provided by Microsoft. However, the Win32 API is sufficiently well defined and full featured enough to enable other companies to implement it. The example most people are aware of is OS/2 Warp. With the advent of all these Win32 operating systems from Microsoft, IBM saw the writing on the wall. Even though the Win32 API competes directly with the native OS/2 API, IBM's more recent versions of OS/2 have support for a subset of the Win32 API. At the time of this writing, the Win32 subset supported by OS/2 is Win32s, although no doubt IBM is looking at supporting the Windows 95 subset in the future.

Nearer and dearer to my heart is Win32 for DOS. Even though I primarily run either Windows 95 or Windows NT, I still boot DOS and Windows 3.1 frequently. When I do this, I hate not having all my programming utilities available that I wrote using the Win32 API. Luckily, I don't have to forego my tools when operating in a nonnative Win32 supporting environment. Both Phar Lap and Borland make DOS extenders that support enough of the Win32 API to allow console mode programs to run under DOS or Windows 3.1. If you use any graphics or windowing system functions, these DOS extenders won't fill the bill, but often a console mode program (like my PEDUMP from Chapter 8) is all you need.

Phar Lap's DOS extender is called TNT; Borland's DOS extender comes with the Borland DOS Power Pack. Using these extenders, you can write generic C/C++ programs that use functions such as printf and fread without concern for whether your program will be running under Windows NT, Windows 95, or DOS.

Using the Phar Lap or Borland DOS extenders can be as simple as changing a line or two in your linker options. You can continue to use your existing Win32 compiler without any changes. The idea behind these DOS extenders is that you use the special program supplied with the DOS extender as the DOS stub program in your Win32 executable. If you run the EXE under Windows 95 or NT, the operating system ignores the stub program. If you run the program from DOS, the stub program loads the DOS extender and brings in the code that provides the Win32 API subset under DOS.

Interestingly, Microsoft itself used the TNT DOS extender in its first release of Visual C++ 32-bit edition. Since there were programmers who wanted to develop for Win32s but didn't have an NT machine, Microsoft couldn't make Windows NT a requirement for running the compiler (CL.EXE) and linker (LINK.EXE). By using the TNT extender, the Microsoft tools run as native Win32 console mode applications for programmers developing on NT and as DOS extended applications for Win32s developers. The majority of Borland's command-line tools are also Win32 applications and continue to use the Borland Power Pack DOS extender to this day.

DEVELOPMENT CONSIDERATIONS

If you decide that your next great project is going to run on both Windows 95 and Windows NT (and heaven help us, maybe even Win32s), the selection of your primary development platform is critical. If you get your program to work correctly on Windows 95, and don't use features specific to Windows 95, there's a pretty good chance that the code will run unmodified on Windows NT. On the other hand, Windows 95 isn't as robust as Windows NT. You may spend quite a bit more time rebooting in Windows 95 than you do under Windows NT (at least I do). This point lends credence to the argument that NT is the ideal Win32 development platform.

The choice of whether to develop on Windows NT or Windows 95 seems to be intensely personal. Some developers abhor the Windows 3.1-style shell of NT 3.5 and would much rather work in Windows 95. It's likely that those same people aren't doing the kind of development work that tends to put the system in an unstable state. Others, like me, routinely put the system at risk by doing things such as writing debuggers and poking around at the operating system and therefore enjoy the incredible robustness of Windows NT. In all my work, I've crashed Windows NT only once or twice over a period of two years, whereas I routinely crash Windows 95. (This isn't because Windows 95 is inherently unstable, it's just that the design of NT makes it more resistant to hard system crashes.) But despite the robustness of Windows NT, I still find myself developing quite a bit on Windows 95 because there are tools such as SoftIce/W available for it that aren't yet available for Windows NT. In short, there is no good answer to this question. Both Windows NT and Windows 95 have merits as your Win32 development platform or choice.

The Future of Win32

About the time this book was published, Microsoft was working on the next major revision of NT, code-named Cairo. Cairo will use the Win32 API, and is supposed to be extremely object oriented, even down to its file system. Cairo should also sport Microsoft's post-Windows 95 thoughts on user interface design. Since Cairo will be a revision of the NT code base, its platform independence may be achieved at the cost of increased code size and slower performance. Perhaps Microsoft is betting that the average machine's performance and available memory will have increased significantly by the time Cairo arrives.

Although Windows 95 is not the end of Microsoft's 32-bit Intel-specific operating-system line, the Windows 95 architecture may only live on for a few more years. If hardware prices and capabilities are conducive to running Cairo and its successors on average desktop systems, Microsoft may discontinue developing two Win32 operating systems in parallel. On the other hand, if the majority of user's hardware won't support running the portable Cairo code base, Microsoft will certainly continue to develop an Intel-specific Win32 platform that allows them to keep their market share.

Summary

This concludes my whirlwind rendition of how Windows 95 relates to other Win32 implementations and the Win32 story to date. In Chapter 2, the focus will be entirely on Windows 95. Specifically, it will provide an overview of what's new in Windows 95 relative to Windows 3.1. The remainder of the book will then dig down into the dirty details of what is sure to be the most widely studied and supported Win32 platform ever.

What's New in Windows 95?

2

F or nearly two years, people have been speculating about what Windows 95 is. Some have described Windows 95 as NT Lite — but Windows 95 isn't just a "light" version of NT. Others have described Windows 95 as Win32s on steroids— and although there are some striking similarities between the two operating systems, that description isn't really right either. Windows 95 is much more than a bulked up Win32s.

This chapter provides an overview of Windows 95 from a programming and architectural point of view. Since most users will be converting to Windows 95 from Windows 3.1, I used Windows 3.1 as the baseline for the various comparisons I make.

The portions of the architecture I describe are those that almost every Windows application deals with. The majority of the topics I discuss fall into the traditional KERNEL, USER, and GDI troika. The view of Windows 95 given here is by no means complete. There are many topics — such as OLE 2.0, Plug and Play, MAPI (Mail API), and TAPI (Telelphony API) — that are beyond the scope of what I can hope to describe in this book.

Throughout this chapter, I describe some Windows 95 features and architectural concepts that are technically Win32 features and concepts rather than Windows 95-specific. These features have existed in NT for quite some time. However,

Windows 95 will be the first real exposure to Win32 programming for many programmers. Since this book is first and foremost about Windows 95, I say Windows 95 in many places where it would be more technically correct to say "Win32" or "NT and Windows 95."

As I see it, Windows 95 has two fundamental, if sometimes conflicting, requirements:

- Provide an implementation of the Win32 API with all the goodies of Windows NT (threads, separate address spaces, virtual memory, and so on), without the space-eating features such as security and support for the Unicode standard.

- Run existing MS-DOS and 16-bit Windows applications on a 4MB machine as well or better than Windows 3.1 would on the same machine.

The first requirement represents Microsoft's admission that not every computer has the processing power or memory needed to run Windows NT. Although NT is a great "No Compromises" operating system, its resource requirements exceed that of the average 4MB desktop PC. Windows 95 brings a respectable subset of NT's capabilities to users who don't have NT-capable hardware but also don't need all the overhead of a bulletproof operating system like NT or UNIX. Since there are tens of millions of non-NT-capable machines, Microsoft gave up NT's portability to get a powerful Win32 implementation that runs on the average desktop PC. While the Win32 API layers are very similar between NT and Windows 95, Windows 95's implementation ties it to the 80386 class of Intel CPUs. The capability to bring Win32 to a vast number of machines made it worth the expense of maintaining two operating systems.

The second requirement for Windows 95 needs to be specified very clearly. Note that Microsoft doesn't claim you can run a couple of large applications smoothly on a 4MB Windows 95 machine. Instead, Windows 95's target is this: On machines with 4MB or more, Windows 95 will run no worse than Windows 3.1, given equivalent program loads. I think applications that run better on a 4MB machine than on Windows 3.1 will be the rarity. However, it's reasonable to expect that applications will run as well on Windows 95 as they did on Windows 3.1. (Bear in mind that almost everyone considers 8MB to be a usable minimum for Windows 3.1, so running "as well as" isn't the same thing as "running well.") Since Windows 95 can't give up Windows 3.1 features, it's clear that the Win32 support needs to be shoehorned into space freed by tightening and tuning the Windows 3.1 code. This is where most of the Windows 95 design compromises come into play.

I've divided this chapter into four main sections:

- How Windows 95 is the same as Windows 3.1
- How Windows 95 has improved on already-existing Windows 3.1 features
- New features introduced in Windows 95
- "Dirty little secrets" about Windows 95

This chapter provides a high-level view of the changes and additions to Windows 95 and defers the in-depth discussion to subsequent chapters. Where appropriate, I'll give pointers to other chapters in the book where you can find more information.

SIMILARITIES TO WINDOWS 3.1

Microsoft has gone to great lengths to convince people that Windows 95 is a brand new operating system, built from the ground up. However, you shouldn't believe everything you're told. If you make a few small changes (which I'll describe next), you can make a persuasive argument that a Windows 95 system is actually running Windows 3.1. That's because under the hood, Windows 95 is primarily an evolution of the DOS and Windows 3.1 code base. Sure, there are many great new features in Windows 95; I'll be describing them here and throughout the book. For the purpose of truly understanding what Windows 95 is, however, it's important to set aside the hype and take an honest look at the foundations of Windows 95.

I've just now asserted that Windows 95 has evolved from the combination of DOS and Windows 3.1. It's time for me to put up or shut up. For our first experiment, let's take a look at what happens when you turn on the machine. (I'm assuming you have Windows 95 installed already.) Before rebooting your machine though, let's make a small change. In your boot drive's root directory is a hidden system file called MSDOS.SYS. If you run the dir /AH command, you'll see it:

```
C:\> dir /ah MSDOS.SYS
 Volume in drive C is MS-DOS_5
 Volume Serial Number is 1CDE-9CF5
 Directory of C:\
MSDOS    SYS         1,641 07-17-95  9:40p MSDOS.SYS
         1 file(s)          1,641 bytes
         0 dir(s)      71,696,384 bytes free
```

Now, this file is no big surprise if you've been using PCs for awhile. However, in Windows 95, the file has changed quite a bit. In fact, it's now an ASCII text file. Let's change the attributes to make it accessible to a text editor:

```
C:\> ATTRIB -r -h -s MSDOS.SYS
RHSA_ -> ___A_  C:\MSDOS.SYS
```

Bringing up MSDOS.SYS in an editor will show you something like this:

```
[Paths]
WinDir=C:\WINDOWS
WinBootDir=C:\WINDOWS
HostWinBootDrv=C
[Options]
BootMulti=1
BootGUI=1
Network=0
;
;The following lines are required for compatibility with other programs.
;Do not remove them. (MSDOS.SYS needs to be >1024 bytes.)
;xxxxxxxxxxxxxxxxxxxxxxxxxxxxxxxxxxxxxxxxxxxxxxxxxxxxxxxxxxxxxxxxxxxxxa
... rest of file omitted...
```

Your file may differ slightly, but you get the point. Now, let's add a line ("Logo=0") to the [Options] section:

```
[Options]
Logo=0
BootMulti=1
```

Next, save the file. While you're at it, you might want to change the attributes back to the way they were before (+r +h +s). Now reboot. Assuming you still have a CONFIG.SYS or AUTOEXEC.BAT files after installing Windows 95, you should see the contents of these files being processed before the Windows 95 user interface comes up. What's missing from the equation is the logo that Windows 95 usually displays during your bootup sequence. It's pretty obvious that the logo is primarily an attempt to hide those messy *technical* details involved in booting up the computer — the kind of details that can confuse end users. What they don't see can't concern them, right? With a single line, we just dismissed a big part of the Windows 95 "user friendliness."

It certainly looks like DOS may still be involved here somewhere. To check this out, I deleted my CONFIG.SYS and AUTOEXEC.BAT file and rebooted. Perhaps the DOS-like behavior we just saw is for backward compatibility. After booting without CONFIG.SYS or AUTOEXEC.BAT, I ran the MEM /DEBUG command to see what's in memory below 1MB. The abbreviated output is as follows:

```
Conventional Memory Detail:

Segment          Total        Name        Type
-------      ---------------   -----------  ------------------------
 00000        1,024   (1K)                 Interrupt Vector
 00040          256   (0K)                 ROM Communication Area
 00050          512   (1K)                 DOS Communication Area
 00070        1,344   (1K)    IO           System Data
                             CON          System Device Driver
                             AUX          System Device Driver
                             PRN          System Device Driver
                             CLOCK$       System Device Driver
                             A: - D:      System Device Driver
                             COM1         System Device Driver
                             LPT1         System Device Driver
                             LPT2         System Device Driver
                             LPT3         System Device Driver
                             CONFIG$      System Device Driver
                             COM2         System Device Driver
                             COM3         System Device Driver
                             COM4         System Device Driver
 000C4        5,072   (5K)    MSDOS        System Data
 00201       11,584  (11K)    IO           System Data
              1,152   (1K)    XMSXXXX0     Installed Device=HIMEM
              2,848   (3K)    IFS$HLP$     Installed Device=IFSHLP
                688   (1K)    SETVERXX     Installed Device=SETVER
                544   (1K)                 Sector buffer
                400   (0K)                 Block device tables
              1,488   (1K)                 FILES=30
                256   (0K)                 FCBS=4
                512   (1K)                 BUFFERS=24
                448   (0K)                 LASTDRIVE=E
              3,072   (3K)                 STACKS=9,256
 004D5           80   (0K)    MSDOS        System Program
 004DA          192   (0K)    WIN          Environment
 004E6        3,312   (3K)    WIN          Program
 005B5           32   (0K)    vmm32        Data
 005B7           16   (0K)    MSDOS        — Free —
 005B8        1,152   (1K)    vmm32        Program
 00600          208   (0K)    COMMAND      Data
 0060D        5,728   (6K)    COMMAND      Program
 00773        1,312   (1K)    COMMAND      Environment
 007C5          240   (0K)    MEM          Environment
 007D4       90,400  (88K)    MEM          Program
 01DE6      532,896 (520K)    MSDOS        — Free —
```

■Figure 2-1
The MEM /DEBUG command shows these fragments of DOS (even though DOS is supposedly gone in Windows 95).

If Windows 95 really does away with DOS, we shouldn't be seeing any vestiges of DOS. Yet two lines from the output in Figure 2-1 stick out:

```
000C4              5,072   (5K)   MSDOS        System Data
00201             11,584  (11K)   IO           System Data
```

Hmm . . . There's a 5K area labeled as MSDOS, and an 11K area with the name IO. Perhaps this is somehow related to the IO.SYS file from the days when we ran DOS and Windows 3.1 rather than the *integrated* Windows 95. Let's check this out. Another dir /AH command in the root directory confirms this:

```
C:\> dir /AH IO.SYS
 Volume in drive C is MS-DOS_5
 Volume Serial Number is 1CDE-9CF5
 Directory of C:\
IO      SYS      223,148  07-11-95  9:50a IO.SYS
        1 file(s)         223,148 bytes
        0 dir(s)       71,688,192 bytes free
```

Yes indeed, IO.SYS is a big file. Although it's close to 220K, when loaded on my system it takes up only the 11K of DOS memory we saw earlier. While 11K isn't much memory these days, it's still pretty good proof that there's at least some DOS-like code residing on every Windows 95 system.

Here are a couple of other interesting lines from the MEM /DEBUG output in Figure 2-1:

```
004DA                192   (0K)   WIN          Environment
004E6              3,312   (3K)   WIN          Program
```

These two lines sure make it look like a program called WIN was loaded into memory. Hey, wait a minute! When I started Windows 3.1 from my DOS prompt, didn't I type WIN, which invoked WIN.COM? Let's go have a look and see if WIN.COM is still hanging around in Windows 95:

```
C:\>dir c:\windows\win.com
 Volume in drive C is MS-DOS_5
 Volume Serial Number is 1CDE-9CF5
 Directory of C:\WINDOWS
WIN     COM       22,487  03-14-95  6:44p WIN.COM
        1 file(s)          22,487 bytes
        0 dir(s)       68,542,464 bytes free
```

Sure enough. It looks like WIN.COM is still there in Windows 95. Seeing as how the next thing in memory after the WIN program is something called vmm32, it looks like WIN.COM plays the same role in Windows 95 that it did in Windows 3.1. Namely, WIN.COM is what kicks off the whole process that takes the machine from real (or Virtual 8086) mode into the protected mode Windows environment.

Let's do one final experiment in this DOS area to confirm that theory. In the CONFIG.SYS file, let's change the DOS command processor (COMMAND.COM) to something else. I happen to prefer 4DOS, which is a COMMAND.COM-compatible replacement from JP Software that offers features above and beyond COMMAND.COM. To switch to 4DOS (assuming you have a copy), add the following line to your CONFIG.SYS file:

```
SHELL=C:\4DOS.COM
```

When I did this, I rebooted and found myself sitting at a 4DOS prompt rather than in the nice, cozy Windows 95 Explorer environment. It seems that my version of 4DOS.COM didn't know to invoke WIN.COM at the end of its processing of the AUTOEXEC.BAT file. Yet the COMMAND.COM that comes with Windows 95 does. Oops! It looks like another part of this seamless integration just fell away. The *transparent* boot straight into Windows 95 that most end users experience turns out to be nothing more than the moral equivalent of putting the following as the last line of your AUTOEXEC.BAT file:

```
WIN
```

Since we're at a 4DOS prompt (which presumably knows nothing about Windows), let's ask it what version of DOS we're running:

```
C:\>ver
4DOS 5.0   DOS 7.00
```

DOS 7, eh? I guess this shouldn't be a surprise. The previous version of DOS was 6.*x*, right? If you fire up the Windows 95 COMMAND.COM and ask it the same question, you'll get the following response:

```
Microsoft(R) Windows 95
   (C)Copyright Microsoft Corp 1981-1995.
C:\>ver
Windows 95. [Version 4.00.950]
```

That's strange, there's no mention of DOS anywhere. Microsoft really doesn't want the nontechnical end user to know that DOS is mixed in with Windows 95.

I could go on and present other examples and technical demonstrations that show the existence of DOS-like code in Windows 95. However, *Unauthorized Windows 95* covered this topic in much greater detail. If you have further interest in this particular subject, check out *Unauthorized Windows 95*.

Now let's look at what happens after Windows 95 begins firing up. If you were to load Windows 95 under versions of WINICE that were written for Windows 3.1, you could pop into WINICE and see much that would lead you to believe you were looking at Windows 3.1. For example, Windows 95 (like Windows 3.*x*) is still based heavily on VxDs. Many of the familiar VxDs are still there in Windows 95: VMM, VPICD, VTD, VDMAD, V86MMGR, and so on. (There are also many new VxDs, but we'll talk about those later.) In addition, you can continue to load your own VxDs via the [386enh] section of the SYSTEM.INI files. (However, Microsoft would prefer you to add VxDs through the registry, something I'll describe later.)

Doing a MOD command in WINICE would also take you back to the days of Windows 3.1:

```
:mod
hMod PEHeader     Module Name      .EXE File Name
0117              KERNEL           C:\WINDOWS\SYSTEM\KRNL386.EXE
01C7              SYSTEM           C:\WINDOWS\SYSTEM\system.drv
01BF              KEYBOARD         C:\WINDOWS\SYSTEM\keyboard.drv
01CF              MOUSE            C:\WINDOWS\SYSTEM\mouse.drv
01E7              DISPLAY          C:\WINDOWS\SYSTEM\atim32.drv
036F              DIBENG           C:\WINDOWS\SYSTEM\DIBENG.DLL
023F              SOUND            C:\WINDOWS\SYSTEM\mmsound.drv
02EF              COMM             C:\WINDOWS\SYSTEM\comm.drv
042F              GDI              C:\WINDOWS\SYSTEM\gdi.exe
17FF              FONTS            C:\WINDOWS\fonts\vgasys.fon
1807              FIXFONTS         C:\WINDOWS\fonts\vgafix.fon
17F7              OEMFONTS         C:\WINDOWS\fonts\vgaoem.fon
17CF              USER             C:\WINDOWS\SYSTEM\user.exe
```

All these DLLs were present in Windows 3.1 and continue to serve active roles in Windows 95. Likewise, a WINICE HEAP command would show you that the 16-bit global heap hasn't changed either. Again, I could continue with examples in which I show that vast portions of Windows 95 look and work identically to the way things worked in Windows 3.1. The fact that Windows 95 has evolved from Windows 3.1 is indisputable. Yes, the evolution was dramatic in some cases. The fact remains, though, that if you understand Windows 3.1, you've got a good head start on understanding Windows 95. Chapter 7 describes in more detail how the Win16 components of Windows 95 are similar but not identical to the Windows 3.1 components.

Let me clarify something I've said in this section. I think Microsoft made the right choice in evolving Windows 95 rather than starting from scratch. Backward compatibility was an absolute requirement. Although Windows 95 won't be 100-percent compatible with Windows 3.1, it will be significantly more compatible than Windows NT or OS/2 Warp can ever be. Starting from a fresh code base for Windows 95 would have been a nightmare for compatibility. Likewise, a fresh code base would have bloated the code, and a mass market operating system that doesn't run on the average PC doesn't make sense. You have to give Microsoft credit for facing the harsh reality that most end-user systems are limited when compared to the souped-up hardware most developers work on.

If you're an operating-system purist who turns your nose up at the compromises of Windows 95, do something about it. Run Windows NT, OS/2, or UNIX. Just don't complain when some program that you really need to run doesn't work on those platforms. To be honest, I'm guilty of doing my share of complaining about the Windows 95 architecture. However, I also run Windows NT regularly as a matter of course. My point is, both Windows 95 and Windows NT are valid operating-system platforms. You have to decide what's more important to you (memory consumption and compatibility or robustness and security), and choose the appropriate platform.

My philosophy is that both Windows 95 and Windows NT will be very important over the next several years. As such, I devote my efforts to both platforms. So why is this book about Windows 95? Because I feel that the programming market for Windows 95 will be larger than that for Windows NT in the near term.

IMPROVEMENTS OVER WINDOWS 3.1

Even if you don't care about the new features in Windows 95 (pre-emptive multithreading, protected process address spaces, and so on), it's worth upgrading from Windows 3.1 to Windows 95 just for the improvements it offers. In this section, I'll go over what these improvements are in broad strokes, deferring more detailed descriptions to subsequent chapters.

DOS is dead (almost)

Although you might never notice it, the biggest improvement in Windows 95 over the DOS/Windows 3.1 combination might be the placement of what we used to call DOS into VxDs. In Windows 3.*x*, the Virtual Machine Manager (VMM) acted as a DOS extender. When a program called DOS to do something, such as read from a file, the INT 21h was first bounced up to the ring 0 WIN386, which then reflected the interrupt down to the 16-bit DOS running underneath Windows. In Windows 95, once VMM32.VXD is up and running, almost all calls to DOS functions are handled entirely in VMM32 with all new 32-bit code. (VMM32 is the master collection of VxDs that comprise the ring 0 component of Windows 95. VMM32 is equivalent to WIN386.EXE in Windows 3.1.)

One of the most marked benefits of putting code formerly found in DOS into VxDs is that file I/O can be handled entirely in 32-bit ring 0 code, dramatically improving performance. When I say DOS, I'm not limiting the scope of the improvements to just DOS programs. A Windows program that calls _lread eventually ends up in the same VxD code for doing file I/O that a DOS program calling INT 21h would.

For backward compatibility with old hardware devices and drivers, Windows 95 continues to reflect certain critical interrupts to the small bit of real mode (actually V86 mode) DOS code that sits underneath Windows 95. (This is the DOS code I described in the previous section.) For example, when VMM32 sees that a DOS device driver is expecting to be used, it can fall back to the old behavior of reflecting interrupts down to a 16-bit DOS virtual machine so that the device driver can do its thing. Other interrupts, such as the DOS Get Time function (INT 21h, fn. 2Ch), are always reflected to the real mode (V86 mode) DOS code. The important thing to remember is that the majority of DOS's functionality has been moved to 32-bit code residing in Windows itself. With a little work, Microsoft could make Windows 95 entirely rid itself of the real mode DOS code. Although this might appeal to some operating-system purists, it would come at the expense of compatibility with existing software. If you want that, run Windows NT.

The windowing system

For some programmers, the biggest relief provided by Windows 95 is the introduction of 32-bit heaps to the windowing and graphics components. In Windows 3.0 and earlier, all windows and related data structures were crammed into the USER DGROUP, which was limited to a maximum of 64K. In Windows 3.1, some of the windowing system's data was moved out into other 64K segments, but this alleviated only certain limitations. In Windows 95, the windowing code in USER knows about and uses two separate 32-bit heaps to store items like the HWND data structures. As a result, you're no longer limited to a maximum of a couple hundred windows or to only 8160 entries in a listbox. (Having a listbox with eight thousand entries is usually not an example of good program design. However, if you *really* need that many entries for some reason, Windows 95 will be an improvement over Windows 3.1.)

Although the Windows 95 windowing system uses 32-bit data, you shouldn't confuse this with 32-bit code. All the windows in Windows 95 (yes, even windows created by 32-bit applications) are managed by the 16-bit USER.EXE that you've come to know and love. In contrast, the Windows NT team had the opportunity to write their USER components in brand new Win32 code. (Compatibility isn't nearly as important as robustness in NT.) There's been quite a bit of debate among programmers about whether the Windows 95 team made a wise decision in updating with the existing 16-bit USER code. However, there are two important factors that make this approach the only logical choice. I discussed this issue in Chapter 1 but the following paragraphs recap my main points.

The first reason for keeping the windowing system code in the 16-bit USER.EXE is the size issue. Having two copies of the windowing system code, one 16-bit and the other 32-bit, would add several hundred kilobytes to the memory footprint of Windows 95. Given Microsoft's goal of running on a 4MB system, this was unacceptable. Remember, Windows 95 isn't intended only for developers with moderate- to high-end hardware. Windows 95 needs to run on all those ancient 386s in companies that just recently took the plunge and upgraded them to 4MB. You might be thinking, so why doesn't Windows 95 put the windowing system code in a 32-bit DLL and call up into it?

That leads me to the second reason: To put things bluntly, the 16-bit USER.EXE is not tremendously portable. Important sections are written in optimized assembly language. In addition, USER.EXE is legacy code — it's been modified, tinkered with, and otherwise tweaked for close to a decade. It no doubt contains peculiarities that applications have come to rely on as normal behavior. It's unlikely that one person can keep an entire working model of USER and all its assumptions and quirks in his or her head. If USER's code was ported to completely 32-bit code, existing applications would break.

In addition to the size constraints, Windows 95 has its hands further tied by the need to be 99.44 percent backward compatible. The windowing system in NT is 32 bit, and was written to be as compatible as reasonably possible with its 16-bit predecessor. Still, Microsoft doesn't claim 100 percent backward compatibility with Win16. Windows 95 is being held to a higher standard of backward compatibility. In this light, the decision to keep the windowing system in 16-bit code makes sense.

Having dispensed with the high-level philosophizing, let's get down to the details of how the windowing system has changed to accommodate 32-bit applications. I've already mentioned that USER uses two different 32-bit heaps, but that's only part of the story. Windows 95's USER actually uses a combination of 16- and 32-bit heaps in a somewhat unusual memory layout. As in Windows 3.1, the 16-bit USER.EXE continues to have a 16-bit DGROUP segment with a local heap within it. Stored inside the local heap are items such as atoms, windows classes, and properties. All the normal things you'd expect in USER's 16-bit DGROUP. Conspicuously absent, however, are windows (or more accurately, WND structures). Where the heck did they go? At this point, 32-bit heaps come into play. Ahhh . . . USER must have created a special 32-bit heap for holding windows, right? Right. But that's not the end of the story.

If you look closely at the selector assigned to USER's DGROUP, you'll find that its limit isn't even close to 64K in length. Its limit is much greater that 64K. In Windows 95, the USER DGROUP selector's limit is 2MB+128K. The 32-bit window heap in Windows 95 actually encompasses the USER DGROUP segment at its low end. Consider the ramifications of this. All the various data structures that USER uses can be accessed with one selector. The USER code that deals with items still in the normal DGROUP local heap can continue to use 16-bit offsets as it did in Windows 3.1. Only the code that manipulates items in the 32-bit heap, such as the WND data structures, needs to be changed to use 32-bit offsets. Remember, though, that these 32-bit offsets as relative to the start of USER's data segment, not to 32-bit linear addresses.

In addition to the new 32-bit heap used to store windows, Windows 95's 16-bit USER has another 32-bit heap to store menus and their strings. Unlike the 32-window heap, there isn't a 16-bit local heap sitting in the bottom 64K of the menu heap. Incidentally, the idea of breaking out menu-related items into a separate heap isn't new to Windows 95. Windows 3.1 had a separate menu heap, albeit only 16 bits. Chapter 4 describes the 32-bit heaps in Windows 95 in more detail.

One immediate result of Windows 95's shift to a 32-bit window heap relates to window handles (HWNDs). In Windows 3.*x*, an HWND was a local heap handle of a block in USER's DGROUP. Since the WND structures were stored in LMEM_FIXED blocks, the local handle was nothing more than an offset. Therefore, by combining the selector of USER's DGROUP with an HWND, a program could get a far pointer to a WND structure and peek and poke at it directly. In Windows 95, this no longer works. Windows 95 HWNDs are small values like 0x80, 0x84, and 0x8C. These values aren't offsets. Instead, they're handles for blocks in the 32-bit window heap. Internally, USER can convert from one of these handles to a 32-bit offset and back again. Chapter 4 describes how HWNDs can be converted from their 16-bit HWND form to a 32-bit pointer, and back again.

As part of the move toward each application knowing only about itself, USER has changed the way it maintains the list of window classes. In Windows 3.1, all window classes were stored in a linked list. You could walk through the list and obtain the class names and owning module with the TOOLHELP ClassFirst and ClassNext functions. In Windows 95, ClassFirst and ClassNext still work, but they return information only about the standard system classes (such as buttons) that USER registers at startup time. Classes that are registered by applications are kept in a private list. At least part of the information for each of these private classes is kept in USER's 16-bit DGROUP, but again, TOOLHELP.DLL knows nothing of them. Chapter 4 covers the changes to window classes in Windows 95.

Changes to the messaging system

In Windows 95, Microsoft has finally stopped the insanity and provided separate input message queues for each process. Actually, there are separate message queues for each thread, but the important thing is that there's no longer a single system input queue shared by all tasks in the system. Why is a single input queue so bad? The short answer is that forcing all tasks to get their user input (for example, mouse and keyboard messages) from a single source leaves them vulnerable to a badly written task that doesn't yield. When a given task is active, it effectively has a lock on the user input system. Until it yields, no other task can retrieve input messages.

Windows 95 (like Windows NT) throws away this antiquated model and allows messages to be delivered immediately to the input queue of the appropriate task. Unfortunately, the controversial Win16Mutex (described later in "The Win16Mutex" section) causes Windows 95 to continue to act like Windows 3.1 if a 16-bit task doesn't yield by calling GetMessage or PeekMessage in a timely manner. Win32 processes don't have this problem and can dawdle in their message processing without affecting other processes.

Windows 95's method of delivering input messages to programs is an extension to the Windows 3.1 model. The raw mouse and keyboard messages are delivered to a single system queue by the interrupt handler code in the mouse and keyboard drivers. In Windows 3.x, all programs read their input from this single queue, and one program could lock out other programs from reading from the queue. In Windows 95, a dedicated thread, the Raw Input Thread (RIT) monitors the queue and as input messages come in, delivers them to a separate input queue for the appropriate thread. Thus, even if one program doesn't yield, other programs can continue to get input messages intended for them. Of course, there still remains the problem of the Win16Mutex and 16-bit programs. The benefits of this separate input system thread are primarily for 32-bit pre-emptively scheduled programs.

Along with separate input queues for each thread, the Win32 philosophy dictates that a process shouldn't be able to change values or states that another process is using. In Windows 3.1, USER maintained many windowing system states as systemwide values. A prime example of this is the focus window. In Windows 3.1, USER had a single global variable called HWndFocus. Any task could call SetFocus whenever it felt like it, thereby taking away the focus from another application (and causing the HWndFocus variable to change). The same was true for the window capture and other windowing system states. This is unacceptable in the Win32 model. In Windows 95, every thread (not just every process) has its own set of windowing system state variables. When you call an API function like SetFocus, you're acting on the current thread's state, not on a single global state. Beneath the surface, USER takes care of the onscreen representation so that everything looks kosher. The states that are definitely stored on a per-queue basis are the capture window, the focus window, the active window, and the cursor. Chapter 4 describes the per-queue windowing system states in detail.

Besides just storing windowing states on a per-thread basis, Windows 95's USER generally doesn't allow one thread to modify the windowing states of other threads. For instance, if you call SetFocus, passing it an HWND that's owned by a different thread/queue, you'll receive a warning message from the debug version of USER, and the operation won't succeed. From the HWND passed to SetFocus, USER can obtain the queue that owns the window. By comparing the current queue to the handle of the queue that owns the HWND passed to SetFocus, USER can tell if an inter-thread focus change is being attempted. Judging from other messages that appear in the debug version of USER.EXE, inter-queue window activations aren't allowed either.

Speaking of message queues and such, when someone posts a message to a window in Windows 95, that message doesn't immediately appear in the queue associated with the target window. Instead, the messaging system saves up a list of messages and distributes them to the appropriate queues only when their presence might affect a decision that USER makes. For example, whenever a task enters the 16-bit scheduler (via GetMessage, PeekMessage, Yield, and so on), Windows 95 first distributes the messages in the saved-up list to the appropriate thread's message queue. If the scheduler didn't do this, the scheduler wouldn't see that the task had a message, so it wouldn't choose it to run next. Likewise, calling GetQueueStatus forces USER to flush the temporary message list since the messages must be in the destination queue in order for GetQueueStatus to return an accurate set of flags. From an application programming level, you don't have to worry about this beneath the surface change in messaging behavior. USER assumes the responsibility of making sure that things look consistent and act just as they do in Windows 3.1.

The interaction between 16- and 32-bit processes

An area where the windowing system implementation of Windows 95 gets interesting is the interaction of windows from 16- and 32-bit applications. Even though the window procedure for a 32-bit program's window is written in 32-bit code, existing 16-bit applications don't know or care about this. These programs expect any window, regardless of its bit size, to act just as it would in Windows 3.*x*. Now, consider something like window subclassing. Imagine that a 16-bit program gets hold of an HWND for a 32-bit program's window. The 16-bit program then subclasses the 32-bit program's window by saving its original WNDPRC address and dropping in a new 16-bit WNDPROC address. If Windows 95 had originally stored a 32-bit linear address in the 32-bit windows WND structure, things would go up in smoke rather quickly. To prevent problem scenarios such as this, Windows 95 goes to great lengths to make all windows behave as if they were 16-bit windows.

Another area where USER does extra work behind the scenes is with message numbers. In Win16, the message numbers for private control messages start at WM_USER and go up. Additionally, some of these private message numbers overlap with message numbers for other controls. For instance, in Win16, the BM_GETSTATE message is defined as WM_USER+2, which is the same as EM_SETRECT, LB_INSERTSTRING, and CB_SETEDITSEL. In these cases, a message number by itself is meaningless unless you know what type of control it's being used with. Perhaps in an attempt to make things more consistent, the Win32 implementors reassigned the message numbers for certain controls so that they fall below WM_USER and don't overlap with other private message numbers. The remapped message groups are as follows:

```
Message group    Use                Win32 starting message
EM_              Edit controls      0x00B0
SBM_             Scroll bars        0x00E0
BM_              Buttons            0x00F0
CB_              Combo boxes        0x0140
STM_             Static controls    0x0170
LB_              List boxes         0x0180
```

If the same message has a different value in Win16 and Win32 programs, how are 16- and 32-bit windows able to communicate? Inside the thunking layer between 16- and 32-bit code, USER converts these messages to the appropriate value for the target window of the message. Messages sent between 16-bit programs don't incur the overhead of determining whether the message needs to be remapped.

The complexity involved in making 16- and 32-bit windows work together seamlessly doesn't stop at simple message translation, however. Many messages use the WPARAM and LPARAM parameters to convey additional information. Often the LPARAM of a Win16 message contains a far pointer to some data or a buffer to fill in. What happens when a 16-bit program sends a message to a 32- bit program and passes a far 16:16 pointer in the LPARAM? Again, the USER thunking layer needs to step in and make the message usable by the code in the 32-bit window procedures. In this example, the thunk layers convert the 16:16 far pointer into the equivalent 32-bit linear address that it passes to the 32-bit window procedure. In the opposite case, where a 32-bit process sends a message to a 16-bit window, a 32-bit linear address must be converted to a 16:16 far pointer. In this situation, USER keeps a selector around for this very purpose; it changes the base address of the selector to match the 32-bit linear address. The limit of this selector is set to 0xFFFF bytes.

Beyond the additional work with 16-bit far pointers versus 32-bit linear addresses, Windows 95's windowing system also needs to do parameter conversions when messages are exchanged between 16- and 32-bit applications. Earlier I mentioned that certain messages needed to be translated between Win16 and Win32 programs. The WPARAM parameter in a message also needs conversion. In Win32, the WPARAM parameter is 32 bits, while in Win16 it's 16 bits. In the general case, when converting a 16-bit message to be usable by a 32-bit window, USER puts a 0 in the high word of the 32-bit WPARAM. When going in the opposite direction (a 32-bit message converted for a 16-bit window), USER throws away the top WORD of the 32-bit WPARAM. There are a few exceptions to these rules, but we don't need to go into them in this overview chapter.

The Win16Mutex

Although the Windows 95 thread scheduler is pre-emptive, scheduling in Windows 95 is still affected by the single threaded, one at a time, 16-bit code in modules like USER.EXE. A Win32 process can create threads that don't call GetMessage or otherwise deal with user input. An example would be a thread that calculates the value of pi (3.14159265 . . .) to 50 places. These 32-bit threads that don't do user-interface activities are governed only by the 32-bit thread scheduler in VMM32. The thread scheduler continues to pre-emptively switch between these threads, even if things are jammed up and not moving because of clogged user-interface threads. Unfortunately, 16-bit tasks can't spawn additional threads, so they can't partake in the pre-emptive multitasking.

A second ago, I mentioned jammed up user-interface threads. Just what was I talking about? Aren't threads pre-emptively switched? The answer to this question leads to the infamous and unpopular Win16Mutex. At this point, the fact that Windows 95 is a mixture of old 16-bit and new 32-bit code is probably pounded into your head. The problem that resulted in the Win16Mutex solution is that the 16-bit USER and GDI code isn't written with pre-emptive multitasking in mind. The code assumes that it won't be interrupted for any reason, and that switches to other tasks will occur at a few well-defined places. There are also numerous global variables through-out the USER and GDI code. If Windows 95 ignored the problem entirely, a thread could be switched away from while it's in the middle of a USER or GDI call. Since the old 16-bit code isn't expecting this, the system would crash in very short order.

The problem of existing 16-bit code not being ready for pre-emptive multitasking isn't limited to the code in Windows. There are thousands of third-party DLLs that were also written without pre-emption in mind. Even if Microsoft came up with a magic bullet solution for the USER and GDI code, those other DLLs would still make the system vulnerable to a thread switch at an inopportune time.

One solution to this problem of pre-emptive switching would be to identify all the vulnerable areas in USER and GDI and protect them with synchronization mechanisms such as critical sections. Doing this in something as large and complex as USER.EXE would be error prone and time-consuming. More importantly, spreading synchronization code throughout USER and GDI would bloat the size of these modules. Code size ("4 megs or bust") was one of the mantras of the Windows 95 development team, so adding critical sections or mutexes throughout the code wasn't an acceptable solution. In NT, where resource requirements aren't so tough, the windowing and graphics systems are protected with critical sections, so they are re-entrant.

Microsoft's solution to the pre-emptive thread problem is known as the Win16Mutex. The Win16Mutex is essentially a mutual exclusion semaphore that covers all 16-bit areas of the system that would have trouble if they were executing when a thread switch occurred. The Win16Mutex covers all 16-bit code. Since much of the 32-bit windowing and graphics systems are implemented as calls to their 16-bit counterparts, even Win32 threads are affected when they perform user-interface-related actions or otherwise thunk down to 16-bit code. When 32-bit programs aren't doing any user-interface-related actions or thunking to 16-bit land, they don't own the Win16Mutex and they continue to be pre-emptively scheduled.

Whenever a thread is executing in 16-bit code, it owns the Win16Mutex. The Win16Mutex prevents other threads from entering code like the 16-bit USER and GDI code until the lock has been released. The 16-bit thread releases the Win16Mutex when the thread yields to another thread by calling a yielding function such as GetMessage. The thread that was yielded to then grabs the Win16Mutex and continues execution. The important thing to remember is that a 16-bit thread owns the Win16Mutex for the entire time that it's actively executing, not just while it has called into the operating system.

While Win32 threads own the Win16Mutex only when they call into certain operating-system functions, all Win16 programs own the Win16Mutex the entire time they're running. (Even if they're calculating pi to 50 places.) As a result, a 16-bit task that doesn't yield the Win16Mutex will prevent other threads from being able to acquire the Win16Mutex. These other threads, regardless of whether they belong to a 16- or 32-bit process, will effectively be hung until the thread holding the Win16Mutex gives it up. Thus, a 16-bit program that doesn't yield can lock out other programs, both 16- and 32-bit, from executing.

The basic situation of an application that doesn't promptly process messages and yield in a timely manner has always been a problem in Windows. What's new in Windows 95 is that there is finally pre-emptive multitasking. However, the Win16Mutex acts as a bottleneck for any code that has to execute through old 16-bit code like USER.EXE. The fact that a badly written 16-bit task can adversely affect 32-bit programs has made the Win16Mutex an incredibly unpopular design decision among those users who don't have to implement Windows 95 themselves.

While obnoxious, nonyielding 16-bit programs can bring the user input system to a halt, the Win16Mutex is almost never a problem for a system containing only 32-bit programs. (Granted, Windows 95 always has one or two 16-bit programs running, but they're background processes and don't grab the Win16Mutex and hang onto it.) Threads for a 32-bit program will need to acquire the Win16Mutex, but only when they thunk down to 16-bit code such as USER or GDI to perform user-interface actions. The USER and GDI code will theoretically execute quickly and then release the Win16Mutex. In general, no 32-bit thread will ever hold and hog the Win16Mutex for any significant period of time (of course, you can always concoct perverse exceptions to this rule). If you're worried about the Win16Mutex affecting your Win32 program, you can create additional threads that don't call down to 16-bit code such as USER and GDI. These threads will continue to be scheduled and run regardless of whether a 16-bit thread is hogging the Win16Mutex.

The Win16Mutex's effect on the system is simple to describe. If there are 16-bit applications running, the multitasking of application user interfaces in Windows 95 will continue to be similar to that of Windows 3.1. If there are no (nonsystem) 16-bit programs running, the user interface should multitask smoothly, like NT. The moral here should be obvious: Write all new programs as Win32 programs and port existing 16-bit applications to Win32 as soon as possible. Just say No to 16-bit code and Hello to smooth multitasking.

The Windows 95 GDI

The Windows 95 graphics system (GDI) is a hybrid of the Windows 3.1 16-bit GDI and new graphics functions implemented in the 32-bit GDI32.DLL. In general, if a given GDI function existed in Windows 3.1, it has remained in GDI.EXE in Windows 95. New functions like Beziers, paths, and enhanced metafile support were added to the existing GDI.EXE. Other new functions like the TrueType font rasterizer and the printing subsystem are in GDI32.DLL.

Like USER.EXE, the Windows 95 GDI has 16-bit code that uses a 32-bit heap immediately above it. The Windows 95 GDI uses the 32-bit heap to store regions and fonts. Also like USER.EXE, the 32-bit GDI heap contains the 16-bit GDI DGROUP within its first 64K. GDI objects other than regions are still held in the 16-bit GDI DGROUP, meaning that you can't go hog wild and create tons of GDI objects.

One of the most well-known limitations of Windows 3.*x* was that there was a limit of five screen device contexts (DCs) available systemwide. If a buggy application grabbed those five DCs, other applications couldn't do their painting, and the system often became unstable. In Windows 95, the limitation on screen DCs appears to have been lifted.

Since a large portion of Windows 95's GDI remains in 16-bit code, Windows 95's GDI coordinate system is still limited to 16 bits. Even though the Win32 API and NT specify that 32-bit coordinates are the norm, the Windows 95 GDI pays attention to only the bottom 16 bits of any coordinates passed in to it.

Another place where the Windows 95 GDI sticks to its 16 bit past is with device drivers. When it comes time for the GDI to display something on the screen or some other device, the GDI calls into a 16-bit device driver DLL. Although all new portions of Windows 95 expect 32-bit Portable Executable (PE) drivers, the GDI must remain backward compatible with existing 16-bit display and printer drivers. This isn't to say that all 16-bit device drivers confine themselves to 16 bits. Many high-performance drivers use 32-bit instructions even though the driver remains a 16-bit New Executable (NE) format DLL.

System resource cleanup

Windows 95 implements each 16-bit task as a separate process. One reason for this is resource cleanup. For whatever odd reason (space considerations, probably), prior versions of Windows didn't tag their USER objects such as icons with an owner. When a task terminated, USER didn't have any idea what owned the resource, so it couldn't clean up after the task. Repeatedly running a program that was sloppy about freeing its resources could cause the system to run out of room in its heaps; the result was that subsequent programs were unable to run. This problem has been an Achilles' heel for Windows and is one of the main reasons Windows hasn't gained acceptance in certain areas of the market. Windows 95 takes a major step forward (albeit a long overdue step) and associates each resource with the process that allocated it. When a process terminates, Windows 95 iterates through the resources and frees up those that the terminated process didn't release itself.

There's one twist to this improved model for resource usage. In Windows 3.1, one task could allocate a resource and pass the resource handle to another task to use. Even if the allocating task exited, the second task could continue to use the resource. The new Windows 95 method of freeing up resources when the allocating process exits could backfire in this situation. To retain backward compatibility, when Windows 95 is about to free a resource that belonged to a terminated process, it checks to see what kind of process it is. If the process was a 16-bit task and wasn't marked as being Windows 4.0-compatible, Windows 95 doesn't delete the resource until there are no more running 16-bit applications. This eliminates the possibility that Windows 95 will yank a resource out from under a 16-bit task that is using the resource.

If Windows 95 is much better about cleaning up after sloppy programs, how does this affect the infamous Free System Resources? In Windows 3.1, the magical System Resources number reported in About boxes was found by looking at the free space in four heaps: three 16-bit USER heaps and the 16-bit GDI heap. Of these four heaps, the heap with the lowest percentage free is what USER reports as the free system resources. Since Windows 95 has 32-bit heaps (such as the heap used to store WNDs), the calculation needs to change. In most cases, the reported free system resources isn't changed by the presence of 32-bit heaps, since these heaps almost invariably have a higher percentage free than the 16-bit USER or GDI DGROUPs. However, by moving certain space-consuming objects out of the 16-bit USER and GDI DGROUPs, Windows 95 makes the available system resources decrease at a slower rate. Chapter 4 contains a more complete discussion of exactly how free system resources are computed in Windows 95.

Decreased memory consumption below 1MB

Finally, we come to the infamous "insufficient memory to load this program" message. The good news is that the Microsoft coders have fixed the "below 1MB" problem! In Windows 3.x, FIXED segments in DLLs and GlobalPageLock()'d segments ended up at the low end of the heap. Often this meant that they ended up below 1MB. These segments could eat up all the memory below 1MB, thus preventing Windows from starting additional tasks (each task needs at least 512 bytes below 1MB for its task database). See my Questions & Answers column in the May 1995 *Microsoft Systems*

Journal for a more detailed description of the problem. In Windows 95, FIXED and GlobalPageLock'd segments still come from the low end of memory, but they stop short of going below 1MB. While it's still possible in perverse cases to create a scenario where applications can't run because of insufficient memory below 1MB, I think this will rarely be the case in normal use.

BRAND-NEW FEATURES

Up to this point, I've been discussing the ways in which Windows 95 is either the same as Windows 3.1 or improves on Windows 3.1 features. Now it's time to examine the Windows 95 features that are completely new. Of course, many of these areas are very similar to Windows NT. However, for the majority of programmers and end users, Windows 95 is the first exposure to these topics.

The Windows 95 Win32 implementation

From a programming perspective, the biggest news about Windows 95 is the addition of the Win32 API. It's Microsoft's hope that the Win32 API will enable applications to be written in a portable manner. Theoretically, an application written to the Win32 API can run unmodified on different operating systems (for example, Windows NT), as long as they also support the Win32 API and the underlying CPU is the same. A properly written Win32 application can also simply be recompiled and run on other CPUs — again, as long as they're running an operating system that supports the Win32 API. How effective the Win32 API is in glossing over operating-system differences will be the subject of discussion for years to come.

When I first heard of the Win32 support in Windows 95, the big question in my mind was, "Is it implemented like NT or like Win32s?" After working with it for over two years, my conclusion is that the best description of Windows 95 is "Win32s done properly." Like Win32s, Windows 95 has 32-bit system DLLs that thunk down to the equivalent 16-bit DLLs. Most calls to the Win32 windowing and messaging API functions go through thunks down to the 16-bit USER.EXE. Likewise, many calls to Win32 graphics functions thunk down to the 16-bit GDI.EXE. In contrast, Windows NT has fully 32-bit USER and GDI modules. 16-bit applications run under NT and have their calls thunked up to the 32-bit USER32 and GDI32 by the Windows On Windows (WOW) layer.

While Windows 95 is closer to Win32s than to NT in its implementation, Windows 95 is light years beyond Win32s. The implementors of Win32s were constrained by the necessity of building it atop the existing Windows 3.1 code. The Win32s developers couldn't make changes to Windows 3.1 since Windows 3.1 was already installed on millions of machines. Upgrading them to a newer version of Windows just for Win32 support was not an option. As such, Win32s is severely limited relative to Windows 95 or Windows NT.

The Windows 95 developers, on the other hand, had the luxury of being able to modify and adapt the underlying foundation in order to best implement the Win32 API on top of it. Starting from the Windows 3.1 code base, both the ring 0 components (the Virtual Machine Manager and VxDs in VMM32.VXD) and the ring 3 components (such as KRNL386, USER, and GDI) have been extensively modified to support the Win32 system DLLs (for example, KERNEL32.DLL, USER32.DLL, and GDI32.DLL). In essence, Windows 95 has most of NT's feature set but uses an implementation much closer to Win32s. For the average user, Windows 95 provides the best tradeoffs between speed, memory usage, features, and system stability.

Just because there are still 16-bit components in Windows 95 doesn't mean that they're unaware of the new 32-bit additions. For instance, KRNL386.EXE makes many calls up into KERNEL32.DLL, primarily for things like 32-bit heap and process management on behalf of the 16-bit USER and GDI. Chapter 6 contains more information about this.

The Windows 95 Win32 system DLLs

The Windows 95's Win32 API layer is implemented using a mixed collection of 16- and 32-bit DLLs. Table 2-1 lists some common Win32 API DLLs and how they're implemented. In the table, the pattern that emerges is that, wherever reasonable, Microsoft tried to reuse existing 16-bit code by thunking to it.

This approach has two benefits. First, 16-bit code is smaller on average than the 32-bit equivalent. Second, the 16-bit Windows 3.*x* code has already been shaken out and tested in the real world. A rewritten 32-bit version of a system DLL like USER would need to undergo much more extensive bug fixing and testing, possibly delaying the release of Windows 95. The windowing system implemented in the 16-bit USER.EXE is mature and most of its quirks are well understood. If Microsoft had recoded the windowing system in 32-bit code, it would have had to reproduce all the subtle behaviors of the 16-bit version, including bug fixes and workarounds.

The NT developers chose to write a 32-bit version of USER, sacrificing some compatibility with existing 16-bit applications. The NT design criteria allowed this. Windows 95's doesn't. Backward compatibility is essential in Windows 95.

Table 2-1

The implementation of selected Windows 95 32-bit system DLLs

Name of DLL	Purpose of DLL	How DLL is implemented
KERNEL32.DLL	Win32/Windows 95 kernel services	Mostly Win32 code, but makes many calls into VxDs, and some calls down to KRNL386.EXE.
USER32.DLL	Window Manager functions	Mostly thunks to 16-bit USER.EXE, but some functions are implemented in USER32.DLL.
GDI32.DLL	Graphics functions	Mostly thunks down to 16-bit GDI.EXE. However, TrueType rasterizer- and printing-related code are in GDI32.DLL.
ADVAPI32.DLL	Windows registry	Mostly Win32 code, but calls into VMM.VXD for registry functions.
OLE32.DLL	OLE 2.0 bBase DLL	All 32-bit code.
COMDLG32.DLL	Common Windows dialogs	Mostly 32-bit code, but does some thunks.
SHELL32.DLL	Windows 95 shell (32-bit) library	Mostly 32-bit code, but does some thunks to 16-bit code.
LZ32.DLL	LZA file decompression	Thunks to 16-bit code.
VERSION.DLL	Version-stamping library	Thunks to 16-bit code.
WINMM.DLL	Multimedia functions	Mix of 16- and 32-bit code.

The ring 0 components of Windows 95

Moving down to the level below the system DLLs, we encounter the ring 0 components of Windows 95. These are the Virtual Machine Manager and virtual device drivers (VxDs). In Windows 3.x, these components were all lumped into the WIN386.EXE file. In Windows 95, these components are still lumped together, but the file is now called VMM32.VXD. Tables 2-2 and 2-3 show the changes to the standard VxDs in VMM32.VXD as compared to WIN386.EXE.

Table 2-2

New VxDs in Windows 95's VMM32.VXD file

Name of VXD	Purpose of VXD
CONFIGMG	Configuration manager (Plug&Play)
DYNAPAGE	Paging manager
IFSMGR	Installable File System Manager
IOS	I/O Supervisor (replaces BLOCKDEV)
PERF	Configuration/status info
SHELL	Shell support
SPOOLER	Local spooler
VCACHE	Disk cache
VCDFSD	CD file system
VCOMM	COMM device driver
VCOND	Console device
VDD	Display device
VDEF	(Unknown)
VFAT	File Allocation Table helper
VFBACKUP	For backup apps
VFLATD	Flat Memory device
VMM	Virtual Manager Manager
VMOUSE	Mouse device
VPD	Printer device
VSHARE	File SHARE support
VTDAPI	Virtual Timer Device API
VWIN32	Win32 device
VXDLDR	VxD loader

Table 2-3

VxDs removed from Windows 95's VMM32.VXD file

Name of VXD	Purpose of VXD
BLOCKDEV	Block device (replaced by IOS)
CDPSCSI	SCSI CD device
PAGEFILE	Pagefile device (replaced by DYNAPAGE)
QEMMFIX	Fix for QEMM
VDDVGA	VGA display device
VFD	Floppy device
VNETBIOS	Netbios device
WDCTRL	Western Digital fastdisk
WIN386	Replaced by VMM
WSHELL	Old shell device

The most interesting addition to the VMM32 collection of VxDs is the VWIN32 device. Actually, VWIN32 isn't really a device. Instead, it's ring 0 code that the 16-bit KRNL386.EXE and 32-bit KERNEL32.DLL use to perform certain low-level primitives. The closest equivalent to VWIN32 in Windows NT is NTDLL.DLL, which isn't documented, but obviously contains a lot of the low-level operating-system goodies.

Both VWIN32.VXD and VMM.VXD (along with a few other VxDs) provide ring-3–callable functions that are known as Win32 VxD services. Much of KERNEL32's operations rely heavily on Win32 VxD service calls to VWIN32, and to a lesser extent, to VMM. These calls include operating-system primitives like thread creation, blocking on a synchronization object, creating a new memory context, and so on. I'll be describing VWIN32 and Win32 VxD services in Chapter 6.

One way the Windows 95 developers helped keep memory consumption down was through advances in the VxD architecture. Windows 95 supports dynamically loadable VxDs. In Windows 3.*x*, a VxD had to be loaded when Windows booted, and it remained in the system for the entire session. Windows 95 programs can load and unload VxDs only when they're needed, much like existing programs load printer drivers only when printing. The new VxD architecture also supports pageable VxDs. Portions of your VxD that aren't used often can be made pageable so that they're only loaded into memory when they're needed.

A porting issue for those of you with existing Win16 code concerns interrupts and interrupt handlers. Win32 programs under Windows 95 aren't allowed to install interrupt handlers in their code. Nor can they use interrupts to communicate with other code, even if it's an interrupt handler in a Win16 DLL. Most code that uses interrupts is for communicating with hardware devices. Microsoft recommends that you write a VxD to implement the interrupt code. Your program can communicate with the VxD through the DeviceIoControl function. If you need to call certain interrupt functions (such as INT 21h or INT 31h) the VWIN32 VxD provides routines for invoking those interrupts.

Process management

In Win16, an executing program is known as a *task*. At any given point in time, a task is executing at only one spot in its code. (This may seem obvious until you understand the notion of threads, which I'll describe next.) The Windows 16-bit KERNEL keeps information about each Win16 task in a segment called a Task Database (or TDB). The selector of a task database is known as an HTASK and can be passed as an argument to APIs that need to know which task you're referring to.

How does all this change for 32-bit programs in Windows 95? For starters, a running program is known as a *process* rather than a task. Each process runs in its own address space, which can have serious implications for programmers who are bringing existing Win16 code to the Win32 environment. I'll describe the ramifications of separate address spaces in "The Windows 95 address space" section. For now, it's sufficient to think of processes as being unaware of the existence of any other processes. They can see their own memory and operating-system resources, but they can't see other processes or the memory of other processes. The underlying reason for keeping processes apart from each other is so that a buggy or malicious process can't have an adverse effect on other processes.

This separation of processes is so complete that, in Win32 programs, the hPrevInstance parameter to WinMain is always 0, even if other copies of the program are running. In general, a process can consider itself to be the only running program in the system. Of course, if you really need to communicate with or manipulate another process, there are facilities to do so. However, you need to specifically plan ahead when writing your code to do this.

Each Windows 95 process is associated with a unique value in the system; this value is informally known as a *process ID*. A program can obtain its own process ID via the GetCurrentProcessId function. The process ID is the closest thing to a Win16 HTASK. In NT, process IDs definitely do not map to system data structures, since typical process ID values are numbers like 74, 77, 84, and so on. In Windows 95, process IDs have much higher values that are seemingly random. However, as you'll see in Chapter 3, a process ID can be put through a magical transformation to get a pointer to the actual process database structure that KERNEL32.DLL uses to keep track of the process.

When working with Windows 95 processes, you usually don't use a process ID. Instead, most process-related API functions expect a HANDLE parameter, informally known as an *hProcess*. An hProcess has no direct correlation to something like a Win16 task database. Unlike process IDs, there can be multiple distinct hProcess values, each of which refers to the same process.

KERNEL32 object handles

Handles permeate the Win32 API. A handle is a magic value that you obtain from the operating system and pass back to API functions when you need something done. Theoretically, a HANDLE value is meaningless to the application program. Only the operating system knows how to interpret it. (However, as you Win16 programmers probably know, almost all the handle values in Win16 programs can be interpreted as selector values or near pointers.)

When working with the KERNEL32 APIs, most handles you work with belong to a small group of handles that I call KERNEL32 handles. KERNEL32 handles have special attributes, such as being able to be passed to functions like WaitForSingleObject. KERNEL32 object handles include process and thread handles, file handles, mutex handles, and many more. Chapter 3 describes the various KERNEL32 handle types.

A KERNEL32 HANDLE is valid only within the process that owns it. Attempting to use a HANDLE from one process in another process is meaningless. Although handles are theoretically opaque, with enough underlying knowledge of the process-related data structures, it's possible for an application program to convert a handle into a usable object pointer. Chapter 3 shows how you can convert a KERNEL32 handle into a usable pointer.

The most fundamental process function in Windows 95 is CreateProcess, which is analogous to the Win16 WinExec and LoadModule functions. WinExec and LoadModule still exist in Windows 95, but under the surface they're a wrapper around a call to CreateProcess. If you need to query or manipulate the spawned process later, you'll want to use CreateProcess because it returns an hProcess HANDLE to you.

Since WinExec and LoadModule have no notion of an hProcess HANDLE, they can't return an hProcess. In fact, after these two functions call CreateProcess, they immediately close the hProcess that CreateProcess returned. They do this to prevent system resources allocated for that process from being tied up unnecessarily. It's important to remember that closing a handle doesn't mean that you're terminating the process. Rather, you're giving up access to the process via that particular handle. The operating system takes care of cleaning up its process-related resources when the process terminates and all outstanding handles to the process have been closed.

Besides creating a process, another way to get an hProcess is to call OpenProcess with a valid process ID. With an hProcess in hand from either method, you can do some basic process querying and manipulation. Under the category of process control, a program can terminate another process with TerminateProcess and affect the execution priority of other processes with SetPriorityClass.

It's interesting to learn that Windows mirrors certain KERNEL objects like tasks and modules on both the 16- and 32-bit side of the fence. In the area of processes and tasks, each Win32 process has a 16-bit task database (TDB) that's linked into the TDB chain. If you walk the task list with TOOLHELP, you'll see that in addition to the 16-bit tasks, there's also a TDB for each Win32 program that's running. You may recall that a TDB has 8 bytes near the end that stores the module name of the file that created the task.

In addition to TDBs for 16- or 32-bit processes, there's also a PSP for *all* TDBs in Windows 95, including TDBs for Win32 processes. Unlike Windows 3.*x*, the PSP in a Windows 95 TDB does not necessarily immediately follow the TDB in memory. Between the 100h-byte–long TDB and the PSP is a region that holds the current directory. This area is sufficiently large to hold a directory using the long filename and pathnames that Windows 95 supports. In Windows 3.*x*, the current directory was stored in an area only 65 bytes long inside the TDB. Chapter 7 describes this in more detail.

Thread management

Threads are an exciting new feature that Windows 95 brings to the party. A *thread* is an instance of execution through program code. In simpler terms, threads allow a program to be executing in more than one place in its code simultaneously. It's like having multiple CPUs, each executing a different part of the program. On a single-processor system (Windows 95 supports only uniprocessor systems), threads only appear to execute simultaneously. Under the hood, the Windows 95 scheduler switches the CPU between all the various threads in the system. This is known as *timeslicing*, since the hardware's built-in timer notifies the operating system at regular intervals, whereupon the operating system may choose to schedule a different thread. Incidentally, although 16-bit programs show up as a thread in the list of system threads, only Win32 applications can create additional threads in their process.

A thread can be switched away from for two reasons. The first reason is that the thread might do something that needs another thread to execute first. In this case the thread yields the CPU to another thread. (This happens transparently down inside the system DLLs, so you don't need to worry about it.) The second reason occurs when a thread has executed long enough and it's time to give other threads a chance. The Windows 95 thread scheduler uses a sophisticated algorithm that gives the most CPU time to the threads that need it the most. The CPU uses the hardware clock to interrupt the operating system at periodic intervals. Inside the hardware timer interrupt handler, the scheduler decides if another thread should run; if so, it switches to the other thread. In Windows 95, the timeslice is 20 milliseconds, meaning the scheduler code could theoretically switch between 50 threads in one second. This is close enough to simultaneous for most people.

Every thread is associated with a process. When the operating system creates a new process, it also sets up an initial thread for it. Threads execute in the memory context of the process they're associated with. All threads in a process share the process's resources. For the remainder of this discussion, I'll use the word "resource" to mean something provided by the operating system rather than the much narrower definition of resource as a dialog, a cursor, and the like. Process resources include a memory context, file handles, and a current directory.

Processes generally don't alter or use the resources of another process. However, multiple threads within a process can conflict in their use of a process resource. Thus, resource sharing can be a mixed blessing. For example, your program may have a code sequence that modifies several global variables. If a thread is switched away from in the middle of the sequence, the next thread would be using those global variables while they're in an inconsistent state. Doing multithreaded programming successfully requires you to identify all the resources within a process that could get messed up if a thread switch occurred while in the middle of manipulating them. These resources need to be guarded by synchronization mechanisms such as critical sections to make sure they aren't corrupted by an ill-timed thread switch. Critical sections and other thread synchronization mechanisms are discussed in the following section.

Although threads share process resources, each thread also has certain resources that are private to itself. The most important of these is a stack. No, each thread doesn't have its own SS register and stack segment. Instead, each thread has a dedicated region of address space within the address space of the process that owns the thread. By default, each thread is assigned 1MB of address space for its stack. This size can be overridden either in the executable file's .DEF file STACK line or by specifying a nonzero stack size when the thread is created by a call to CreateThread. I mentioned earlier that Windows 95 doesn't actually use up a whole megabyte of RAM for each thread stack. Instead, Windows 95 uses a mechanism known as a "guard page" to know when to commit additional memory in the stack's address range. Guard pages are an example of structured exception handling, which is discussed later in this chapter in the "Structured exception handling" section.

Another vital per-thread resource is the thread's register set. Whenever the scheduler switches away from a thread, the operating system saves a copy of the thread's register values at the time of the interruption. The useful but little known GetThreadContext API allows you to retrieve and modify a thread's registers. While normal programs usually don't need to do this, reading and modifying registers is the lifeblood of debuggers.

Inside the operating system, each thread has a unique value known as a thread ID. As with process IDs, Windows 95 thread IDs have relatively high values but definitely aren't 32-bit linear addresses. However, most thread API functions don't work with thread IDs. Instead, these functions expect a HANDLE, commonly known as an hThread. An hThread is meaningful only within the process that owns the thread. There can be multiple hThread values, each of which refers to the same thread. The same thread can be referred to by multiple hThread handles; some of these handles are valid in that thread's process, whereas others are valid in the context of a different process.

If you're starting to notice a parallel between threads and processes, that's good. Remember: Process and thread IDs are unique values within the system. No two threads or processes can have the same ID value. Handles are a different story. Each process and thread can be referred to by multiple hProcess or hThread handles. The handles might refer to a different process or a thread within in a different process. Or, the handle might be self-referential, and refer to its own process or thread.

Process and thread synchronization

One aspect of Win32 programming that will be new to programmers coming from DOS or Win16 programming is process and thread synchronization. *Synchronization* is the means by which a program prevents problems that would occur if the program were switched away from at an inopportune time. Although Win16 had multitasking, there were no real synchronization primitives since the multitasking was cooperative multitasking. A Win16 program will not be switched away from until it gives up control voluntarily. It does this by calling API functions such as GetMessage and PeekMessage. If a program calls GetMessage or PeekMessage, it's implicitly saying, "I'm now in an interruptable state."

Win32 programs, on the other hand, don't have the luxury (or the curse, depending on how you look at it) of cooperative multitasking. They must expect and prepare for the CPU to be switched away from at the worst possible moment. In a related vein, a proper Win32 program shouldn't burn up CPU time by spinning in a polling loop, waiting for some expected event to happen. The Win32 API has four main synchronization objects that allow for both of these needs to be met:

- Events
- Semaphores
- Mutexes
- Critical sections

With the exception of critical sections, the synchronization objects are system global objects and will work with threads that are in different processes, as well as within the same process. Thus, these synchronization mechanisms can also be used to synchronize the actions of separate processes, in addition to threads within the same process.

Events

The first type of synchronization object is an event. Events, as their name implies, are centered around some specific action occurring in another process or thread. You use an event when you want your thread to block until the desired action occurs. The term *block* means to suspend execution of the thread until some specified condition or conditions are met. Blocking is efficient because the scheduler doesn't waste any CPU cycles on threads that are blocked.

A program obtains a handle to an event object with CreateEvent or OpenEvent. The program then calls WaitForSingleObject, passing it the event handle and an optional timeout period. The thread will then block until some other thread in the current process or another process signals that the event has occurred. The other thread indicates that the desired actions have occurred by calling SetEvent or PulseEvent. After the event has been signaled, the thread that is blocked wakes up and continues execution.

You might want to use an event, for example, when one thread will be using the results of a sort being performed by another thread. A bad way to implement this would be to have the sorting thread set a global variable flag when the sort completes. The other thread spins in a loop, constantly checking the flag to see if it's been set yet. This wastes a lot of CPU cycles in the polling thread. Doing the same thing using events is simple. The sorting thread creates an event to represent when the sort is finished. The other thread calls WaitForSingleObject, passing it the event handle created earlier.

This causes the thread to block and not waste any CPU cycles. When the sorting thread completes the sort, it calls SetEvent, causing the other thread to wake up and resume execution. Not only has the CPU been used efficiently, we've avoided concurrency problems by preventing a thread from using data that may not be sorted yet.

This example used the simplest cases of the synchronization APIs. Besides WaitForSingleObject, there's also WaitForMultipleObjects, which allows a thread to block until a list of event handles has been signaled. In calling WaitForMultipleObjects, a thread can block until either any event in the list has been signaled or all the events have been signaled. Getting even more elaborate, a thread can use MsgWaitForMultipleObjects, which blocks until either the event conditions have been satisfied or there's a waiting window message. Other functions block until the blocking conditions are satisfied or a file I/O operation has completed. No doubt about it, there's a lot of flexibility here.

Semaphores

The second type of synchronization object is the semaphore. Semaphores are useful when you want to restrict access to a particular resource or restrict a section of code to a certain number of threads. A good analogy for a semaphore is the hall pass that most of us remember from school. At any given time there can only be a few students in the hall. If you want to go somewhere and all the hall passes are in use, you have to wait until one of the outstanding hall passes comes back. Then you can acquire the hall pass and leave. In Win32 programming, acquiring a semaphore is like taking control of one of the hall passes.

To use a semaphore, one thread calls CreateSemaphore to get a HANDLE to the semaphore. The call to CreateSemaphore includes a count of how many threads can be using the resource or code simultaneously. If the semaphore will be used within only one process, other threads can get at the HANDLE via a global variable. If the other threads are in another process, they'll call OpenSemaphore to get a HANDLE they can use. When a thread needs access to the shared resource, it passes the resource to WaitForSingleObject (or one of its variations such as WaitForMultipleObject). If the semaphore hasn't been claimed by the maximum number of threads already, the wait function simply bumps up the usage count of the semaphore and the thread continues. On the other hand, if the semaphore is already maxed out, the thread that called the wait function will block until some other thread releases its claim to the semaphore. A thread indicates that it's done using a semaphore by passing its handle to ReleaseSemaphore.

Mutexes

The third type of synchronization object is the mutex. The term "mutex" is a contraction of the term "mutual exclusion." A program or set of programs uses a mutex when it wants only one thread at a time to access a resource or section of code. If one thread is using the resource, other threads are excluded from that same resource. One way to view a mutex is as a semaphore with a usage count of one. Using a mutex is very similar to using a semaphore. Each of the create, open, and release semaphore functions has mutex counterparts. When a thread needs to acquire a mutex, it calls one of the functions in the WaitForXXX family.

Critical sections

The fourth type of Win32 synchronization objects are critical sections. Unlike the other types of synchronization objects, critical sections can be used only by threads within the same process. Critical sections are for preventing multiple threads from executing through the same section of code simultaneously. Relative to the other synchronization mechanisms, critical sections are relatively cheap and easy to use. A critical section can be thought of as a lightweight mutex that's only valid within a single process. To use a critical section, a program either allocates or declares a global variable of type CRITICAL_SECTION. Before a critical section can be used for the first time, its fields need to be initialized by calling InitializeCriticalSection. Afterwards, a thread enters the critical section by calling EnterCriticalSection. A call to LeaveCriticalSection tells the operating systems that it's okay for another thread to enter the critical section.

As I just mentioned, critical sections are relatively cheap to use. In Windows 95, if a thread calls EnterCriticalSection while no other threads are in it, EnterCriticalSection only needs to adjust and set some fields in the CRITICAL_SECTION structure. Only if another thread is already in the critical section will EnterCriticalSection call up into the VWIN32 VxD to cause the thread to block.

The WaitForXXX Functions

Now that I've covered the four primary methods of thread and process synchronization, I want to mention a few other ways to synchronize threads. Besides event, semaphore, and mutex handles, the WaitForXXX family of functions will accept several other handles. (These handles are the KERNEL32 handles described in the "KERNEL32 object handles" sidebar.) Passing a process HANDLE to one of the WaitForXXX functions causes the thread to block until the process specified by the HANDLE terminates. If the process has already terminated, the Wait function returns immediately. Likewise, passing a thread HANDLE to a WaitForXXX function suspends the thread until the HANDLE's thread terminates.

Another HANDLE that the WaitForXXX functions can block on is the file change notification HANDLE. A file change HANDLE can be used to determine when a specified change is made to a given directory and, optionally, in its subdirectories. Yet another HANDLE that the WaitForXXX functions accept is a file HANDLE for the console input device. Once there is unread input in the console input buffer, the Wait function returns and the calling thread resumes execution.

Module management

After processes and threads, the remaining key KERNEL concept that I'll mention is the module. A *module* is the in-memory version of the code, data, and resources of an executable file or DLL. Each process has a module for the EXE file. Every DLL used by a process is also a separate module. If two or more processes use the same DLL, they share the same DLL module. Likewise, if two copies of a process are running, both copies share the same EXE module.

In Win16, each task is created from the code and data in a New Executable (NE) format executable file. Win16 keeps a copy of the executable's header in a segment known as a module database. The selector of this segment is called an HMODULE. Each Win16 DLL also has a module database because Win16 executables and DLLs share the same file format. Win16 programs pass HMODULEs to API functions that need to know which particular executable or DLL file you're referring to.

Windows 95 creates 32-bit processes from a Portable Executable (PE) file. The PE format is an updated version of the old UNIX Common Object File Format (COFF) format. Chapter 8 goes over the PE format in exquisite detail, so I'll skip a detailed discussion here.

The closest equivalent to a Win16 module database in Windows 95 is the header portion of a program or DLL's PE file. The header of each EXE or DLL appears in memory because Windows 95 uses memory mapped files to load the program's code and data. I discuss memory mapped files in the "Memory mapped files" section later in this chapter. For now, think of a memory mapped file as a place in memory where the operating system has read in portions of a file (or possibly an entire file).

A Windows 95 HMODULE value is nothing more than the linear memory address to where the loader memory mapped the file. Given an HMODULE and a small amount of calculation, you can convert the HMODULE into a pointer to the PE header. With a pointer to the header address, a program can do some additional lookups to find the address of the code, data, and resources for that module in memory.

Win16 is somewhat sloppy about the difference between an HMODULE and an HINSTANCE, although they really are different. A Win16 HINSTANCE is the selector value of a task's or DLL's DGROUP segment. However, in Win16, an HINSTANCE is also frequently used to differentiate between two different tasks. In 32-bit Windows 95 processes, an HMODULE and an HINSTANCE are the same thing — the base address of the module in memory.

As with Win32 processes and Win16 tasks, Windows 95 stores information about a module on both sides of the 16- and 32-bit fence. Each 32-bit process module has a corresponding 16-bit NE module database. However, the 16-bit representation of these modules is minimal. Not all fields in these special 16-bit HMODULE segment are filled in. I call these minimal HMODULEs "pseudo-HMODULEs." Pseudo-HMODULEs don't appear in the normal linked list of 16-bit modules. If you walk the list of modules with TOOLHELP, the pseudo-HMODULEs don't show up. The SHOW16.EXE program from Chapter 7 shows how to find the 16-bit module databases for Win32 EXEs and DLLs.

The Windows 95 address space

A major architectural difference between Windows 95 and NT is that in Windows 95, 16- and 32-bit applications play in the same virtual machine and address space. To increase system stability, NT runs 16-bit Windows applications in a separate virtual machine called Windows on Windows (known informally as WOW). (NT 3.5 and later can also run each 16-bit Windows program in its own distinct virtual machine if desired.) The downside to NT's implementation is that it separates 32-bit processes from 16-bit processes, address-space–wise. This makes it harder to thunk between 32- and 16-bit code. In an ideal world you wouldn't need to use thunks. Unfortunately, the reality is that a lot of useful 16-bit Windows DLLs won't be immediately available in a 32-bit version.

From the perspective of a 16-bit application, the address space is unchanged from Windows 3.1. All 16-bit applications continue to use ring 3 16-bit selectors from a common local descriptor table (LDT). These programs can continue to access and share memory with other 16-bit applications through selector values. This works because all addresses used by 16-bit programs are within regions of the address space shared by all programs. One 16-bit task can always see the memory of another 16-bit task, assuming it has a valid selector that points to the other task's memory. A page of memory might be marked not present by the virtual memory manager, but touching that memory will bring it back in transparently to the task that touches it. Although Microsoft recommends allocating memory with GMEM_SHARE when you intend to share it between tasks, Windows 3.*x* programs habitually ignored this advice; 16-bit programs under Windows 95 can continue to do so.

The address space story for 32-bit processes is vastly different. As in Windows NT, the private memory of each 32-bit Windows 95 process is in the CPU's page mapping tables only when that process is the current process. When the scheduler switches to another 32-bit process, the private memory of the first process is no longer accessible to any other process. Doing this makes it almost impossible for one task to scribble on another task's memory, either accidentally or intentionally.

Because Win16 tasks allocate their code and data in the shared memory region, at any given time the current 32-bit Windows 95 process can see all the memory in use by 16-bit programs. However, a 32-bit process can't see the memory of other 32-bit processes. There's only one process memory context mapped in at one time. Looking through the opposite end of the telescope, 16-bit code can see all of the shared system memory, as well as the memory of the current Win32 process. (It would be rather difficult to thunk between 16- and 32-bit code if this weren't the case.)

Protecting processes from one other is generally a good idea, but sometimes you really do need shared memory. The primary way to share memory between processes is with memory mapped files. The name *memory mapped files* is somewhat of a misnomer since you can use them without involving any disk files. An interesting architectural difference between NT and Windows 95 involves the visibility of file mappings. In NT, a memory mapped file is accessible only to processes that have called CreateFileMapping and MapViewOfFile for that particular file. In addition, the file's memory region can be based at different virtual addresses in different processes. In Windows 95, once a program creates a memory mapped file, that memory region is accessible to all programs. Thus, a Windows 95 memory mapped file is always at the same virtual address in all processes. This no doubt simplifies the virtual memory management code in Windows 95. I'll talk more about memory mapped files later, in the section titled (would you believe?) "Memory mapped files."

Native Windows 95 applications dispense with the use of selectors in application code. Windows 95 initializes all 32-bit programs with the same code and data selectors at startup. The application itself never needs to change the segment registers. (The Windows 95 system DLLs change the segment registers temporarily during thunks down to 16-bit code.) For instance, when I run Win32 applications, each program uses a ring 3 LDT code selector with a value of 0x013F. This selector has a base address of 0 and a limit of 0xFFFFFFFF (4GB). The data selector that all Windows 95 applications have in the DS, ES, and SS registers is somewhat unusual. It's an expand-down selector with a limit of less than 1 MB.

Until Windows 95, expand-down selectors were rarely encountered, so a bit of explanation is in order. The limit of an expand-down selector (or descriptor) is the lowest offset that a program can use with that selector. The highest usable offset is the end of memory addressable with that selector. In Windows 95, the data segment selector is a 32-bit LDT selector with a base address of 0. This means that the valid address range when using that selector is between a value less than 1 MB and 4GB. Windows 95 makes the lowest addresses in 4K of a virtual machine inaccessible because it causes programs with NULL pointer errors to GP fault rather than silently overwrite memory.

The use of the same selectors for all 32-bit processes often confuses programmers coming from a 16-bit background. How can you use the same code selector with two different programs? As I mentioned previously, Windows 95 uses the CPU's page mapping features to map physical RAM to linear addresses. Each process has its own set of page mapping tables. Whenever Windows 95 switches tasks, it changes the CPU's page mapping tables to reflect the new process's memory layout. Thus, even though two programs have the same selector, they will have entirely different code at the same linear address. That's why an address by itself is useless without knowing which process it refers to.

Windows 95 memory management

In most regards, Windows 95's 32-bit memory management architecture is very similar to NT's on the surface. Under the hood, KERNEL32 relies heavily on services provided by VMM32.VXD to implement the Win32 memory management APIs. On the 16-bit side of the fence, KRNL386 now also calls directly into the VWIN32 VxD in VMM32 for low-level services such as allocating large memory regions and pagelocking. In Windows 3.1, KRNL386 used DPMI functions from WIN386 for many (but not all) of the same services.

At the level where most programmers work every day, the big news in Win32 and Windows 95 is *no more segments*! By moving to 32-bit programming, you can finally forget all about near and far pointers. You can also forget about GlobalLock, LocalLock, and anything related to memory models. Everything in a Windows 95 32-bit program is small model. That is, the *32-bit* small model. Of course, if you want to perform tricks with the memory manager, the Win32 API and Windows 95 have a whole new set of functions to delight the low-level hacker.

In Windows 95, the lowest level of memory manipulation is provided by the VirtualXXX functions, which are described in detail in Chapter 5. VirtualAlloc lets you allocate large chunks of address space with 4K granularity (the size of an 80386 page). Although there are important differences, the closest equivalent to VirtualAlloc in Windows 3.1 programming is GlobalAlloc. Both functions are intended for allocating large blocks of memory. Also, the granularity of both functions makes their system overhead relatively high. You probably wouldn't want to use either function in place of malloc or new.

At the same time you allocate address space with VirtualAlloc, you can optionally bind that address space to physical RAM by using the MEM_COMMIT flag. Why wouldn't you want an address space allocation to be backed up by memory immediately? Sparse memory is the main reason you wouldn't want to do this. For example, your program might need a great deal of memory for storage (on the order of megabytes). You don't know how much memory you need beforehand. In this situation, you could VirtualAlloc a chunk of address space large enough to be confident you won't need more memory. As your program uses up more and more of the address range, you can commit memory as needed by making additional calls to VirtualAlloc. See the "Structured exception handling" section later in this chapter for more details on automating this procedure. Incidentally, this commit-only-when-needed algorithm is precisely how Windows 95 implements large program stacks while not wasting memory on pages that are never touched.

Higher-level Windows 95 memory management comes in the form of heap functions (which are described in Chapter 5). When Windows 95 creates a new 32-bit process, it creates a heap default for it within its address space. The 32-bit heap is roughly equivalent to a 16-bit Windows local heap, since every process has one. However, the 32-bit heap certainly isn't limited to

64K! Windows 95 supports multiple heaps, so you need to pass a handle to the heap function when you want to allocate, free, or otherwise manipulate a heap memory block. A program retrieves the handle to its default process heap with the GetProcessHeap API. This heap handle is nothing more than the starting address of the heap.

Unlike the VirtualXXX functions, allocations from the Win32 heap functions have a much smaller granularity (4 bytes in the retail build rather than 4KB). The overhead for each allocation appears to be only 4 bytes as well. This makes the HeapAlloc function a suitable replacement for malloc (or a quick way to implement your own malloc). The 4-byte overhead comes from a DWORD immediately preceding the address returned by HeapAlloc(). Ignoring the bottom 2 bits, this DWORD holds the size of the block immediately following it.

While Win32 presses forward, there are still issues of backward compatibility. Thousands of 16-bit programs use GlobalAlloc and LocalAlloc. Can they be ported easily? Yes! Microsoft kept most of the important global and local heap functions in the Win32 API so that calls to those functions wouldn't need to be changed in the transition to 32 bits. However, the meaning of the APIs and their underlying implementation has changed. First and foremost, the global and local heap functions are essentially identical. You can use GlobalAlloc to allocate a block of memory and use LocalFree to release it. Second, the global and local heap functions are implemented using the 32-bit process heaps I mentioned earlier. Because of this, calling

```
HeapAlloc( GetProcessHeap(),    // Heap Handle
           0,                   // Flags
           0x100 );             // bytes requested
```

should return the same pointer as if you had called

```
Loc>alAlloc( LMEM_FIXED, 0x100 );
```

HeapAlloc always returns a usable pointer when successful, so all blocks allocated with HeapAlloc are equivalent to LMEM_FIXED. Fixed heap blocks can sometimes lead to fragmentation. As in Win16, you need to call LocalLock with a moveable block handle to get a usable pointer. It's a little-known fact that in Win16, moveable block handles always have bit 1 set, so their handle values always end in 2, 6, 0xA, or 0xE. Also, if you treat a moveable handle as a pointer to a pointer, you can dereference it to get the current address of the block associated with the handle. Microsoft's commitment to backward compatibility can be seen here because these same rules apply to the 32-bit heaps.

The mappings between the local heap functions and the new Win32 HeapXXX functions are very simple. HeapAlloc and HeapFree replace LocalAlloc and LocalFree. Likewise, HeapReAlloc and HeapSize take over from LocalReAlloc and LocalSize. HeapCreate corresponds roughly to using GlobalAlloc to grab a global heap block, followed by a call to LocalInit to set up a heap inside that block. There is no direct Win16 equivalent to HeapDestroy. In Win16, if you're done with a heap you created, you'd likely just get rid of the heap segment with GlobalFree. Chapter 5 describes memory management in much more detail.

Memory mapped files

One of the coolest features in Win32 and Windows 95 is memory mapped files. There is no Win16 equivalent to memory mapped files, and 16-bit tasks under Windows 95 can't use them. Memory mapped files have three main uses in Windows 95. The first and most obvious use is to enable you to use pointers to easily read and write data from a disk file. The file mapping assigns a section (or all) of a file on disk to a range of memory in the virtual address space. When you read or write to a memory address within that address space region, the operating system reads or writes the equivalent byte within the disk file.

The second use of memory mapped files is as a way to share memory between different Win32 processes. A process can set up a file mapping for a NULL file to reserve a block of address space without assigning it to a particular disk file. Other processes can then open up their own view of this file mapping. The physical memory that's connected to the mapping's range of addresses can be made visible to other processes. A process that wants to share memory with the first process merely needs to request a view into the same file mapping. No disk files need be involved for this memory sharing to occur.

The third use of memory mapped files is for module loading. When the Windows 95 32-bit loader needs to load an executable or DLL, it uses memory mapped files to map regions of the executable into the process's address space. Since memory mapped files can be made visible in other processes, it's relatively easy and efficient for Windows 95 to share an EXE or DLL's code, data, and resources between two or more processes. Working from values stored in the PE file, the Windows loader maps various sections of the executable to specific starting addresses in memory. Chapter 8 describes this in more detail.

Structured exception handling

One of the most useful but misunderstood components of the Win32 and Windows 95 architecture is structured exception handling. Before Windows 3.1, there was no formal mechanism in the Windows API for a program to handle interrupts. Windows 3.1 introduced TOOLHELP.DLL, which was a great step forward, but calling it structured is a bit of a stretch. TOOLHELP.DLL intercepts a small but useful set of interrupts such as the breakpoint interrupt (INT 3) and the GP fault (exception 13 (0dh)). When an exception occurs, TOOLHELP's internal handler gets control. The handler sets up a consistent stack frame and then calls handler functions installed by tasks that want an interrupt callback.

While TOOLHELP.DLL allows a lot of flexibility, it also leaves a lot of room for problems. Each task with an interrupt callback can see all the interrupts and exceptions that come through TOOLHELP. The callback function can indicate to TOOLHELP whether TOOLHELP should call the other interrupt callback functions that come later in the list. Thus, one task can prevent another task from seeing interrupts that it might be depending on. In addition, if the interrupt callback handler is buggy, it can cause nested GP faults and other system-crashing behavior. For 32-bit processes, Windows 95 replaces this "every task for itself" way of doing things with a much more well-defined way for a process to handle exceptions.

Other than debuggers, why would a process want to handle exceptions? One example is a process that needs to do an operation that might cause a GP fault or a division by zero. If the process knows how to recover from that situation, it shouldn't be terminated by the operating system. Another example is a process using sparse memory. A program might need to use a large amount of memory, but not know exactly how much memory beforehand. Using the VirtualAlloc function, the program can reserve a large enough range of virtual address space. When the process accesses a page of memory in that range that isn't backed up by physical RAM, the CPU generates a page fault. Using structured exception handling, a Win32 process can handle the page fault by assigning RAM to that page of memory, and then telling the operating system to restart the faulting instruction.

Technically, structured exception handling is built in to the operating system and is independent of any particular language. However, structured exception at the operating-system level is very messy and complex. In fact, at the time of this writing, I'm not aware of any formal documentation on this topic that's generally available. For these reasons, most programmers let their compiler and its runtime libraries put a pretty face over structured exception handling. For more information about the details of the Windows 95 implementation of structured exception handling here, see Chapter 3.

When a process doesn't handle an exception in any of its handlers, the exception gets passed to a default operating-system handler. This handler's action is to terminate the program and clean up unfreed resources and open handles. In a move to improve robustness, Windows 95 implements this sequence using a separate thread. The idea is that when a thread has unexpectedly blown up (with an access violation, for instance), the thread's context might be in an unstable state. By doing the cleanup in a separate thread with a known good context, the Windows 95 developers hope to cut down on the number of hard system crashes.

The registry

Before Windows NT, both the system and programs stored their persistent information in a morass of .INI files. (Remember those huge WIN.INI files? Remember having no idea how most of those entries got there?) Windows 95 uses a registry to take a big step toward moving this mass of information into a central location.

In Windows 95, information that you would have put into an .INI file in Windows 3.1 should instead be stored in the registry. The registry is a hierarchical database of information. (The Windows 95 REGEDIT program, in Figure 2-2, shows the registry hierarchy.) The top level has a small set of predefined "key" nodes; each key node has named subkeys below it. At any point in the hierarchy, a subkey can have one or more values (text or binary data) or additional subkeys. There's an extensive set of APIs (for example, RegCreateKeyEx, RegQueryValue, and so on) for adding, deleting, modifying, and searching the registry.

The six predefined, top-level keys in Windows 95 are as follows:

- HKEY_CLASSES_ROOT
- HKEY_CURRENT_USER
- HKEY_LOCAL_MACHINE
- HKEY_USERS
- HKEY_CURRENT_CONFIG
- HKEY_DYN_DATA

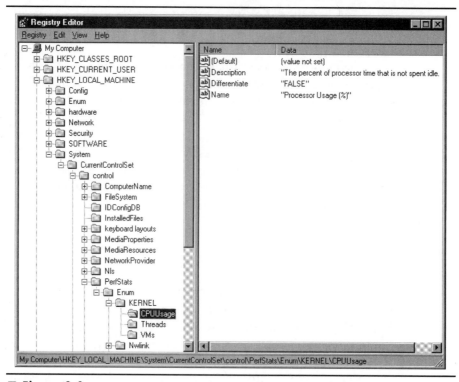

Figure 2-2
The Windows 95 REGEDIT program shows the registry hierarchy.

Of particular interest is the HKEY_DYN_DATA key (see Figure 2-2). Chasing this key down several nodes leads to quite a bit of useful information. For example, the subkey HKEY_DYN_DATA\PerfStats\StartStat\ leads you to a value with the name KERNEL\CPUUsage. Another value under that same key is VFAT\ReadsSec.

Note that the registry is actually implemented in VMM.VXD. By putting the registry code in the first VxD that's loaded (VMM.VXD), the information in the registry can be accessed and used by VxDs themselves. You can see this for yourself by looking in the VMM.H file from the Windows 95 DDK. In the file, you'll find that the following VxD services are available for use by other VxDs:

```
// Registry APIs for VxDs
/*MACROS*/
VMM_Service (_RegOpenKey)
VMM_Service (_RegCloseKey)
VMM_Service (_RegCreateKey)
```

```
VMM_Service (_RegDeleteKey)
VMM_Service (_RegEnumKey)
VMM_Service (_RegQueryValue)
VMM_Service (_RegSetValue)
VMM_Service (_RegDeleteValue)
VMM_Service (_RegEnumValue)
VMM_Service (_RegQueryValueEx)
VMM_Service (_RegSetValueEx)
```

At the Win32 API level, the registry functions are implemented in ADVAPI32.DLL. In Windows 95, that file is relatively small. Digging under the covers to find out why, you'll see that all the registry functions are just wrappers around calls to the VMM registry functions. Of course, since ADVAPI32.DLL is in ring 3 code, it can't call the VMM functions directly. Instead, it uses the same Win32 VxD services (described earlier) that KERNEL32 uses for other purposes. (These VxD services are described in Chapter 6.)

Additions to USER

What's new in the windowing system in Windows 95? For starters, there are now numerous new extended window styles that give Windows 95 programs that sculpted, three-dimensional look. Some of the new styles include

Style	Purpose
WS_EX_MDICHILD	Creates an MDI child window.
WS_EX_TOOLWINDOW	For toolbar windows.
WS_EX_CLIENTEDGE	Window has a sunken edge.
WS_EX_RIGHT	Window text is aligned on the right.
WS_EX_LEFTSCROLLBAR	The scrollbar is on the left.

Another exciting new addition for many developers is a new set of controls. The new control types are as follows:

Control type	Purpose
Animate	Displays .AVI files
DragListBoxes	Drags listbox items between lists
Header	Header bar

Control type	Purpose
HotKey	HotKey control
ImageList	List of images
ListView	List view
Progress	Progress gauge
Property Sheets	Edit item properties
RichEdit	Rich format text
StatusWindow	Status window
TabControl	Tabbed dialog
ToolBar	Customizable bitmap-button toolbar
Tooltips	Balloon-style help
TrackBar	Customizable column-width tracking
TreeView	Tree view
UpDown	Up and Down arrow increment/decrement

Unlike the standard controls (that is, those that existed in Windows 3.1), these new controls aren't implemented in USER.EXE. Instead, they're implemented in COMCTL32.DLL and COMMCTRL.DLL. As a result, these new controls are available only to 32-bit processes, leaving 16-bit programs excluded from the party.

System information and debugging

The Win32 debugging API that Windows 95 implements is much more formal than what's available for Win16. A 16-bit debugger under Windows 3.1 or Windows 95 will typically use TOOLHELP to install interrupt and notification callbacks. By watching the interrupt and notification streams, the debugger can sense what the debuggee is doing. However, the debugger's callbacks need to filter out events that were for other processes or that aren't of interest to a debugger. In addition, when the debuggee hits a breakpoint or causes an exception, the debugger's exception handler needs to spin in some sort of loop until the debugger wants the child to resume execution again. In short, 16-bit debuggers are messy.

The Windows 95 debug API is centered around the WaitForDebugEvent function. After creating or attaching to a process, the debugger calls WaitForDebugEvent, passing in a pointer to a DEBUG_EVENT structure.

This function blocks until something occurs in the debuggee that the debugger cares about. The debug events that WaitForDebugEvent can return are shown in Table 2-4.

Table 2-4
Debug events that WaitForDebugEvent can return

Debug event	Description
EXCEPTION_DEBUG_EVENT	Tells the debugger of breakpoints, access violations, and other exceptions.
CREATE_THREAD_DEBUG_EVENT and EXIT_THREAD_DEBUG_EVENT	Enable the debugger to keep track of the debuggee's threads.
LOAD_DLL_DEBUG_EVENT and UNLOAD_DLL_DEBUG_EVENT	Keep the debugger informed of which DLLs the child is using. A debugger can use these notifications to load and unload symbol tables for the DLLs on the fly.
OUTPUT_DEBUG_STRING_EVENT	Enables you to see your OutputDebugString messages. (In fact, it's the only way to see these messages.)
	For more details, refer to the discussion of OUTPUT_DEBUG_STRING_EVENT and the WaitForDebugEvent function in this section.
CREATE_PROCESS_DEBUG_EVENT and EXIT_PROCESS_DEBUG_EVENT	Tells the debugger that the program being debugged has spawned another process, or has terminated.
RIP_EVENT	This message doesn't appear to ever be generated.

Associated with each debug event is a structure containing detailed information about the event. A debugger can use these notifications to do things such as load and unload symbol tables for the DLLs on the fly. The OUTPUT_DEBUG_STRING_EVENT should be of interest to more than just debugger developers. Under Win32, this is the only way to see your OutputDebugString messages. Put another way, you must be running your program under a debugger (or something similar) that uses the WaitForDebugEvent function. In Win16, any program could see all the OutputDebugString messages in the system by simply tapping in to the TOOLHELP NotifyRegister stream. That's all that the Win16 DBWIN program does.

Whenever WaitForDebugEvent returns to the debugger with an event, all activity in the child process is frozen. The debugger doesn't need to worry about suspending all the child's threads. Instead, it does whatever processing it needs to with the event and eventually calls the ContinueDebugEvent function, which lets the debuggee process resume execution. The heart of a Win32 debugger is a loop that calls WaitForDebugEvent and ContinueDebugEvent in a loop until the debugger receives an EXIT_PROCESS_DEBUG_EVENT.

In addition to knowing about events in the debuggee, the debugger also needs a way to poke and prod at the debuggee's registers and memory. The ReadProcessMemory and WriteProcessMemory functions (see Chapter 5) fill the bill for accessing the debuggee's memory. Likewise, GetThreadContext and SetThreadContext (see Chapter 3) let the debugger read or write the register set of a particular thread in the debuggee.

Besides providing information about interrupt and system events, the Windows 3.1 TOOLHELP.DLL also provided a convenient way to iterate through various system data structures, such as modules, tasks, and heaps. In Windows 95, these data structures have changed significantly for 32-bit programs. To its credit, Microsoft implemented a 32-bit version of TOOLHELP. These TOOLHELP32 functions are defined in TLHELP32.H, and are listed here:

CreateToolhelp32Snapshot

Heap32ListFirst

Heap32ListNext

Heap32First

Heap32Next

Toolhelp32ReadProcessMemory

Process32First

Process32Next

Thread32First

Thread32Next

Module32First

Module32Next

These API functions are similar, but certainly not identical, to the Win16 TOOLHELP.DLL functions. Therefore, if your 16-bit code uses these TOOLHELP functions, you'll have a bit of porting to do. Also, unlike the Win16 TOOLHELP.DLL, which is separate from KRNL386, the TOOLHELP32 functions are implemented in KERNEL32.DLL, which is where they belong.

One problem with implementing these system information functions in Windows 95 is that Windows 95's pre-emptive multitasking will screw things up unless special care is taken. For example, in the middle of walking through the thread list, the enumerating thread might get switched away from. Before that thread gets back control, the thread list may have changed. To prevent this and similar problems, the TOOLHELP32 functions have the concept of a *snapshot*. When you want to walk through a list (such as the process list), you first create a snapshot by calling CreateToolhelp32Snapshot, which fills in a buffer with a completely consistent set of information about the system state. You then pass the snapshot handle to the TOOLHELP32 enumeration functions, which extract the relevant information from the buffer filled by CreateToolhelp32SnapShot.

Noticeably missing from the TOOLHELP32 functions (when compared to the Win16 TOOLHELP.DLL) are functions for walking the window classes, obtaining information on system heap usage, and performing a stack trace for another process. However, there are other ways of doing these things in Windows 95. My article on the new TOOLHELP32 functions in the September 1995 *Microsoft Systems Journal* describes the TOOLHELP32 functions in more detail and suggests other ways of accomplishing things that the TOOLHELP32 functions don't provide.

"DIRTY LITTLE SECRETS" ABOUT WINDOWS 95

Before finishing this chapter, I thought I'd throw in a list of bad design decisions and embarrassing information that Microsoft probably won't be publicizing anytime soon.

Many issues that I could talk about in this section have already been discussed elsewhere in this chapter or in other books or articles. Into this category, I put things like the following:

- Remnants of real mode DOS code are still being used.
- The shared memory address spaces (below 4MB, above 2GB) are almost completely unprotected. Both Win16 and Win32 applications can scribble all over sensitive system data areas.

- The Win16Mutex in conjunction with badly behaved 16-bit tasks can affect the overall system multitasking.

- Despite claims to the contrary, KERNEL32 does call KRNL386. (However, the magnitude of the number of calls down to KRNL386 is worth noting and is discussed in Chapter 6.)

Instead of talking about these topics again, I'd like to focus on some other interesting issues in Windows 95 — issues that until now have gone largely unnoticed. The following list gives you a brief preview of each topic discussed in this section:

- New anti-hacking code tries to prevent you from accessing undocumented KERNEL32 functions.

- The lack of cooperation and communication between the Windows NT and Windows 95 teams results in fewer Win32 functions in both NT and Windows 95.

- The free system resources calculation changed to make it look like Windows 95 has dramatically more USER and GDI heap space, even though it doesn't.

- Additions to 16-bit code were quietly made even though Microsoft publicly states that 32-bit code is the way to go.

Anti-hacking code

Unauthorized Windows 95 made extensive use of undocumented functions in KERNEL32.DLL. Although there obviously weren't header files for these functions, the functions appeared in the import library for KERNEL32.DLL. Calling these functions was as simple as providing a prototype and linking with KERNEL32.LIB.

In subsequent builds of Windows 95—after *Unauthorized Windows 95* came out—these functions disappeared from the import library for KERNEL32.DLL. (Surprise! Surprise!) At the same time, these function names disappeared from the exported names of KERNEL32.DLL. These undocumented functions were still exported, however. The difference is that they were exported by ordinal only.

Now, normally this would have been only a small nuisance to work around. You should be able to simply call GetProcAddress and pass in the desired function ordinal as the function name (0 in the HIWORD, the ordinal in the LOWORD) and get back the address. In a normal, sane world, this would work. However, at some point during the beta, Microsoft added code to GetProcAddress to see if it's being called with the ordinal form of the function. If so, *and* if the HMODULE passed to GetProcAddress is that of KERNEL32.DLL, GetProcAddress fails the call. In the debugging version of KERNEL32.DLL, the code emits a trace diagnostic: "GetProcAddress: kernel32 by id not supported."

Now, let's think about this. Since the undocumented functions aren't exported by name, you can't pass the name of a KERNEL32 function to GetProcAddress to get its entry point. And GetProcAddress specifically refuses to let you pass it an ordinal value. The Microsoft coder responsible for this abomination really didn't want people calling these undocumented KERNEL32 functions. Apparently, the only way you can call these functions is if you have the magic KERNEL32 import library, which Microsoft isn't supplying with the Win32 SDK. (Instead a stripped version of the library is being included.)

Never fear. As you'll see later in the book, I make extensive use of the KERNEL32 undocumented functions (for good, not evil). With a little bit of work, I was able to coerce the Visual C++ tools to create a KERNEL32 import library that contains these "documentation-challenged" functions. Appendix A contains information about these functions and an import library for them.

Another instance of anti-hacking code put into Windows 95 is the Obsfucator flag. In early versions of Windows 95, GetCurrentProcessId and GetCurrentThreadId returned pointers to the relevant process and thread database structures, which are described in Chapter 3. Shortly after *Unauthorized Windows 95* came out, these functions started returning values that most definitely weren't pointers. A bit of investigative work revealed that the return value was the original pointer value, but XOR'ed with a seemingly random value. Where does this random value come from? Each time the system boots up, it uses the system clock to compute a random value. Interestingly, in the debug build of KERNEL32.DLL, this random value is named "Obsfucator." Seeing as how the KERNEL32 coders misspelled "obfuscator" as "obsfucator," it's doubtful whether the KERNEL32 sources were subjected to a spell check.

As with the GetProcAddress code, there's no reason for this XOR trick in GetCurrentThreadId and GetCurrentProcessId, other than to attempt to prevent people from getting at system data structures. While Microsoft is certainly allowed to try and hide these things, they shouldn't complain when users who really need this information go in and dig it out anyway. Chapter 3 describes a technique for calculating the Obsfucator value at runtime so you can access the thread and process database structures.

The Win32 API farce

While Microsoft would like you to believe that there's one big happy Win32 API, internally the NT and Windows 95 teams don't communicate too well. One result of this lack of coordination is that the number of Win32 functions available both in NT and Windows 95 suffered needlessly. The following three "exhibits" serve to prove my point.

Exhibit 1 consists of the new Toolhelp32 functions. I've heard from many sources that the NT management team has vowed never to implement them. Yet if you look closely at the TOOLHELP32 functions, you'd find there's just a handful of functions. Of primary interest are the process and thread enumeration functions. This information can be extracted from the Windows NT registry, as the PVIEW program from the Win32 SDK plainly shows. The question in my mind is: Why didn't the Windows 95 team simply implement the same registry keys that NT provides so that PVIEW could work on both? Or, why couldn't the NT team write a layer on top of the registry functions and put the Toolhelp32 functions on Windows NT? If either side really wanted to, it could come up with a portable Win32 API way to do system information enumeration. As I'm finishing this book, I've heard rumblings from a member of the NT team that the TOOLHELP32 functions might appear in a future version of Windows NT.

Exhibit 2 consists of the heap functions. There are several Win32 heap functions that Windows 95 left unimplemented, although implementing them probably wouldn't have been more than an hour's worth of work. The prime example is the HeapWalk function from Windows NT. This function isn't implemented in Windows 95. Yet, if you look in TLHELP32.H, you'll find two functions that do exactly the same thing: Heap32First and Heap32Next. Rather than simply implementing an existing Win32 API, the Windows 95 coders went off and implemented two entirely new functions. The NT team will no doubt say that they're not going to support those functions. Lunacy!

Exhibit 3 consists of the HeapLock function. In Windows NT, this function simply acquires the mutex of a specified Win32 heap. As you'll see in Chapter 5, Windows 95 has a function that does exactly that. However, the KERNEL32 development team didn't export that function. Thus, the most likely reason the HeapLock function isn't implemented in Windows 95 is because somebody didn't feel like renaming the existing function to HeapLock and exporting it from KERNEL32.DLL.

The point is, while Microsoft is trying to convince everybody to write to the standard Win32 API, two teams at Microsoft are implementing only what they feel like. This will only hurt Microsoft in the long run. I've filed my share of WINBUG reports and sent numerous e-mails. It's now up to the market to see what happens to the supposedly unified Win32 API.

Free system resource fudging

If, after booting Windows 95, you immediately bring up the Windows 95 Explorer and then go to the Help|About Windows 95 dialog box, you'll see a free system resources value that's quite high; a typical value is 95 percent. This is a much higher value than you'd see under Windows 3.1. Did Windows 95 suddenly gain a whole bunch of free memory in the 16-bit USER and GDI heaps from which the free system resources are calculated? No! In fact, many new items were added to USER's DGROUP segment. If anything, the free system resources should have gone down or stayed about the same in Windows 95.

So what's the story? As I describe in Chapter 4, during the Windows 95 startup sequence, the Explorer causes the desktop window to calculate correct, Windows 3.1-like values for the free system resources. All future calls to GetFreeSystemResources are then biased by these initial values. Thus, when the Explorer says that there's 95 percent of the system resources available, it means 95 percent of the resources *after* the Explorer and other programs have started. This change in the way free system resources are calculated is a blatant attempt to make Windows 95 look better than Windows 3.1 in the eyes of the nontechnical user.

Win16 isn't dead

Although Microsoft is strongly pushing everybody to move to Win32, much of the underlying support for the Win32 APIs is in 16-bit code. That's no secret and not worth bringing up again. However, Microsoft isn't making much noise about all the new API functions that were added to the 16-bit DLLs. In many cases, these functions are 16-bit equivalents to documented Win32 APIs. I'm talking about useful functions like CreateDirectory and GetPrivateProfileSection. In some cases, these functions were silently added to the 16-bit WINDOWS.H without fanfare. In other cases, the functions are exported from the 16-bit DLL, but no prototype is given in the appropriate .H file. In these cases, the Win32 documentation and some common sense can usually get you through.

If Microsoft isn't publicizing these 16-bit additions, just who's supposed to be using them? If everyone should be writing Win32 code, why is Microsoft adding new Win16 APIs? It certainly looks like Microsoft knows that Win16 will continue to have a fairly long life even after Windows 95 ships. Yet it's telling developers that Win16 is a dead end and that Win32 is the only way to go. Personally, I agree that users should focus on Win32 programming if possible. But trying to force them toward Win32 programming in this manner seems like a bad way to go.

SUMMARY

Windows 95 is most definitely its own operating system. While a large part of Windows 95's code is derived from the Windows 3.1 code base, Windows 95's 16-bit code has been reworked to remove many 16-bit restrictions as well as to handle the demands of Win32 multithreading. Windows 95 is not Win32s, either. Windows 95 has threads and multiple address spaces and is much more architecturally sound than Win32s. Nor is Windows 95 an NT Lite. Windows 95's code is optimized for performance and minimal memory consumption on the Intel X86 CPUs. NT's focus is on portability and robustness. Although the Windows 95 and NT architectures differ by quite a bit in some key areas, they're both equally important in Microsoft's operating system strategy — and they'll continue to be important for several years to come.

MODULES, PROCESSES, AND THREADS

3

*M*ost people have a favorite color. Call me sick, but I have a favorite data structure. Actually, to be more precise, I have a favorite collection of three tightly connected data structures that make up the very core of ring 3 Windows 95. The structures I'm referring to are the module, the process, and the thread. When these structures are taken as a whole, it's hard to find any significant Windows API function that doesn't come into contact with them. Don't believe me? Take the ShowScrollBar function. The first parameter is the HWND of the window with the scrollbar. Every HWND is associated with a specific message queue. And, as you'll see later, in Windows 95, every message queue is associated with a thread. Thus, at some point during the ShowScrollBar code, the information in a thread data structure will be needed.

In this chapter, we'll be going over the core data structures of modules, threads, and processes. As we look at these structures, we'll often encounter auxiliary data structures that bear further investigation. For example, each process contains a pointer to a handle table (much like the handle table in a DOS Program Segment Prefix [PSP]). While looking at handle tables, we'll come across the all-important KERNEL 32 object. Likewise, when looking at threads, it's hard to ignore the presence of the Thread Information Block (TIB). The TIB turns out to play a vital part in structured exception handling.

This chapter is just brimming with information: Besides describing the three key data structures, I also throw in pseudocode for various Win32 functions that directly relate to the data structures. This will give you an opportunity to see these data structures in action, as well as to see how KERNEL32 deals with issues like thread synchronization. As a final bonus, I provide a discussion of the WIN32WLK program at the end of this chapter. WIN32WLK, which is a program I wrote to help me study the key data structures in a live situation, allows you to easily browse through all the processes, threads, and modules in the system and examine the individual data fields. Plus, wherever reasonable, WIN32WLK also lets you follow references. For instance, a thread database contains a pointer to its owning process. Double-clicking on that field updates the display to show the fields of the owning process database.

If you're a Windows 3.x programmer, you're probably already familiar with the concepts of modules and tasks. In Win32, the concept of a task has been broken up into two components, the process and the thread. Other than that, the concepts of Win16 and Win32 modules and tasks/processes seem very similar on the surface. Under the hood, though, they're quite different. A Win32 module database has no resemblance to a Win16 module database, and a Win16 task structure doesn't look anything like a Win32 thread or process data structure.

An interesting part of the Windows 95 architecture not found in Windows NT is the "mirroring" of information on both sides of the Win16/Win32 fence. In Windows 95, every program that starts up (be it 16- or 32-bit) shows up as both a Win16 task and a Win32 process. That's right, you can walk the task list with the Win16 TOOLHELP.DLL and see Win32 programs in the list. Likewise, you can walk the process list with the Win32 TOOLHLP32 functions and see Win16 programs in the list. Besides the task/process mirroring, Windows 95 also maintains Win16 module information for every EXE or DLL loaded, regardless of whether it's 16- or 32-bit. Unfortunately, the Win16 TOOLHELP.DLL is unable to "see" the Win16 module databases that Windows 95 creates for Win32 modules. However, the SHOW16.EXE program in Chapter 7 is able to find them. While this chapter and WIN32WLK concentrate on the Win32 side of things, Chapter 7 and SHOW16.EXE give the perspective from the Win16 side.

Before plunging into the details of modules, processes, and threads, I'm obligated to point out that this information isn't sanctioned by Microsoft. Microsoft would prefer that you not embed information about these data structures in your own code. Their solution for applications that simply must deal with modules, threads, and processes is the TOOLHELP32 API defined in TLHELP32.H.

The TOOLHELP32 functions provide limited access to certain fields of information within the module, thread, and process data structures that Microsoft has deemed it "safe" for you to know. It's important to stress that the access is read-only access. As is often the case, what Microsoft deems to be "safe" is sufficiently less than what system-level programmers like me need to know. For example, TOOLHELP32 provides no way to enumerate through a processes handle table. If you need that level of detail, you'll have to go in and get the information directly, as the WIN32LWLK programs does. Still, if it's at all possible for you to use TOOLHELP32 instead of grabbing the data directly, do so. Remember, partying on system data structures is something that should be left to trained chimpanzees (um . . . I mean professionals!).

WIN32 MODULES

As in Win16, a Win32 module represents the code, data, and resources for an EXE or DLL that's been loaded by the Win32 loader. Thus, every module in memory directly correlates to a file somewhere on disk. An EXE or DLL by itself isn't a module. Rather, the loader reads the information from a file into memory and creates the module from that information. One of the nice features of Win32 Portable Executable (PE) files is that loading them into memory is relatively simple. The loader creates a module by using memory mapped files to map selected regions of the PE file into linear memory. (Important point: Despite popular belief, the loader doesn't simply map the entire PE file into memory in one big chunk.) The operating system keeps all the top-level information about a loaded module in a structure that I call a *module database*. Chapter 8 describes the PE header and the module database in great detail.

When referring to loaded modules, applications use HMODULEs (handles to modules). In Win16, an HMODULE is just the global heap handle of the segment containing a 16-bit module database. (Chapter 7 describes the Win16 modules in detail.) In Win32, there are no segments (at least not that the program knows about), so some other way of referring to a loaded module is needed. The scheme that Microsoft uses is to make an HMODULE one and the same as the starting linear address in memory where the Win32 loader memory mapped the PE file. For example, most EXE programs are loaded at address 0x400000 (4MB) by the Win32 loader, so their HMODULE is 0x400000. Yes, this does mean that multiple EXEs can have the same

HMODULE when running at the same time. This situation isn't a problem, however, because Windows 95 and NT maintain separate address spaces for each process. A Win32 HMODULE is valid only in the process context in which the module is loaded. (Chapter 5 will discuss process contexts in detail.)

A module database falls very near the beginning of where the EXE or DLL was loaded into memory, and contains information such as where the code and data sections in the file were loaded into memory. The code and data in a module are more than just what a compiler generates from your program code. Other data areas in the module are the imports table, the exports table, and the resource directory. The imports table (usually the .idata section) tells the loader not only which DLLs the module needs to load, but also which individual functions should be imported. The exports table is the inverse of the imports table, and tells the operating system the addresses (and possibly the names) of the functions that the module exports. The resource section contains a directory-like hierarchy that the system uses to quickly find where a specific resource can be found in memory. The module database contains the information for finding these tables, as well as the required version of the operating system, whether it's a console mode application, and so forth.

Putting on our eye shields and firing up the acetylene torches, let's cut into the module database and see what Microsoft is trying to hide from us. Surprise, surprise! The format of a module database turns out to be documented, and right under our nose.

In Win32, a module database is nothing more than the PE header from an EXE or DLL. Looking in WINNT.H, you'll find the IMAGE_NT_HEADERS structure, which is composed of a DWORD and two substructures. The information in an IMAGE_NT_HEADERS struct is exactly what Windows 95 uses internally to find the code, data, and resources in a loaded EXE or DLL file.

While I could spill out the details of every field in an IMAGE_NT_HEADERS struct for several pages, I'm not going to. Why not? Because the details of the IMAGE_NT_HEADERS struct and PE files are sufficiently important to warrant their own chapter. (If you've already read the table of contents and decided to skip over Chapter 8, the PE format chapter, you might think again. I didn't include that chapter simply because I like dissecting file formats.)

The Win32 philosophy dictates that each process has its own list of modules. If a process hasn't implicitly linked to DLL or loaded the DLL via the LoadLibrary, then the process is unable to see the DLL module in memory, even if another process has loaded it. This is quite a difference from Win16, where a loaded module is visible to all tasks, even if they don't have any references to the DLL. Although the idea of each Win32 process having its own list of modules is good in terms of security and robustness, it isn't practical from the standpoint of attempting to save space with shared code and resources. After all, if you have three instances of WINHELP running, the WINHELP code shouldn't be loaded three times, right?

KERNEL32 is faced with a tough choice. From the application's perspective, each process is supposed to have its own module list. From KERNEL32's point of view, it's easier to share code and data by maintaining a single global list of modules (like Win16 does). Whenever a new process starts up, or a new DLL is requested to be loaded, KERNEL32 can quickly check the single global list and see if the EXE or DLL has already been loaded. If so, KERNEL32 can simply implement the module's reference count. If not, KERNEL32 needs to create a new module in memory.

Two data structures provide the solution that KERNEL32 uses to maintain a global list of modules while making it appear that each process has its own module list. The first data structure, the IMTE (Internal Module Table Entry), is used by the KERNEL32 code that needs to treat the module list as a global list. The other data structure, the MODREF, is used by the KERNEL32 code that deals with each process having its own module list. MODREFs are discussed in "The MODREF structure" section a bit later in the chapter.

IMTEs (Internal Module Table Entries [?])

As shown in Figure 3-1, the global KERNEL32 module list is really nothing more than an array of pointers to IMTEs. In the pseudocode that comes later in the chapter, I've given the name pModuleTableArray to this array of pointers to IMTEs. The block of memory holding the pointer array is allocated from the KERNEL32 heap, which is a regular HeapAlloc style heap (as I describe in Chapter 5). As new modules are loaded or unloaded from the memory, KERNEL32 dynamically grows or shrinks the block of memory holding pModuleTableArray via the HeapReAlloc function. When KERNEL32 creates a new IMTE, it looks for a free element in pModuleTableArray. If KERNEL32 finds one, it sticks the pointer to the IMTE into that free element. The index of that array element becomes important later, when we look at MODREFs. The first element in pModuleTableArray (array index 0) is for the KERNEL32.DLL module.

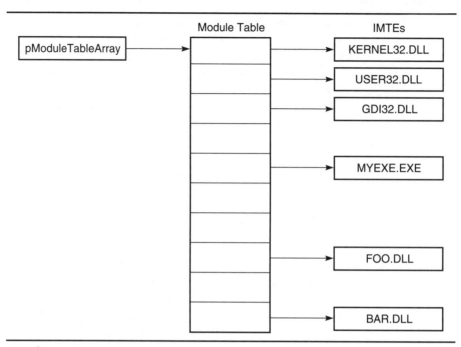

▌ Figure 3-1
The global module list is an array of pointers to IMTEs.

To quickly recap, each nonzero element in the pModuleTableArray represents a loaded EXE or DLL in the system. Each of these nonzero elements is a pointer to an IMTE (or a PIMTE, as I'll use throughout the pseudocode). While the format of an actual module database is documented (it's just an IMAGE_NT_HEADERS struct), the format of an IMTE isn't (at least not until now).

The IMTE structure

The MODULE32.H file from the WIN32WLK sources contains a C-style definition for an IMTE struct. Each IMTE has the following fields:

00h   *DWORD*   *un1*
This field appears to hold some sort of flags.

04h   *PIMAGE_NT_HEADERS*   *pNTHdr*

This pointer points to an IMAGE_NT_HEADERS structure in memory. However, the structure it points to is simply a copy of the IMAGE_NT_ HEADERS structure that appears just above the module's base address in memory. The memory for the structure pointed to by this field is allocated from the KERNEL32 heap, so it's always visible in the contexts of all processes. In contrast, the primary IMAGE_NT_HEADERS that's located near the module's base address may be below 2GB, so it's accessible only to processes that have loaded that module. By making a copy of the IMAGE_NT_HEADERS that's accessible in all contexts, KERNEL32 can easily locate the information for any loaded module without calling up into ring 0 to switch memory contexts.

08h   *DWORD*   *un2*

The meaning of this WORD is unknown. It appears to always be set to –1.

0Ch   *PSTR*   *pszFileName*

The pszFileName field contains a pointer to the complete filename for the EXE or DLL the module was created from. For example, the string C:\WINDOWS\ SYSTEM\KERNEL32.DLL is returned by the GetModuleFileName function. The GetModuleHandle function compares this string to the search string passed to it as a parameter. The memory holding this filename string is allocated out of the KERNEL32 heap.

10h   *PSTR*   *pszModName*

This PSTR points to a string with the module's module name. In Win32, a module name is just the name of the EXE or DLL with any path information stripped off. For example, the module name for the C:\WINDOWS\CALC.EXE program when loaded into memory is CALC.EXE. The GetModuleHandle function also compares this string to its parameter string. This pszModName PSTR actually points inside the pszFileName string (see offset 0Ch). For instance, in the previous example, it would point to the CALC.EXE after the second \.

14h   *WORD*   *cbFileName*

This WORD is the number of characters in the pszFileName string from offset 0Ch. It's used inside GetModuleHandle to quickly see if the pszFileName string could match the input search string.

16h   WORD   cbModName

This WORD is the number of characters in the pszModName string from offset 10h. It's also used inside GetModuleHandle to quickly see if the pszFileName string could match the input search string.

18h   DWORD   un3

The meaning of this DWORD is unknown.

1Ch   DWORD   cSections

This field is the number of sections (.text, .idata, and so on) that this module contains. This value can also be extracted from the IMAGE_NT_HEADERS structure pointed to by offset 04h (described previously in this list of fields).

20h   DWORD   un5

The meaning of this field is unknown. It's usually 0, but in one instance (COMCTL32.DLL), it contains a pointer to a block in the KERNEL32 heap.

24h   DWORD   baseAddress/Module Handle

The baseAddress DWORD contains the base address where the module was loaded. In Win32, the base address for a module is the same as its HMODULE and HINSTANCE, so this field can also be interpreted as the module's HMODULE or HINSTANCE. For EXEs, the base address is almost always 0x400000. For system DLLs, the base address is above 2GB, in the shared memory region. See Chapter 8 for a detailed description on base addresses and locating the module database from them.

28h   WORD   hModule16

This WORD contains a selector whose linear address points to a Win16 NE module database. (The format of an NE module database is described in Chapter 7.) The NE module database for Win32 applications contains important information about where the resources can be found in the Win32 module in memory. This is most likely necessary because the resource manipulation code is in the Win16 KRNL386 and USER.EXE. It's important to note that the hModule16 selector was not allocated via Win16 GlobalAlloc functions, so this selector won't appear like a Win16 global memory handle. For this and other reasons, the Win16 TOOLHELP is unable to see the NE modules created to mirror each Win32 module.

2Ah   WORD   cUsage
This field contains the reference count for the module. For instance, the module database for CALC.EXE would contain the value 3 if there were three copies running.

If there were a GetModuleUsage function in Win32, it almost certainly would report the value of this field. However, here's what the Win32 SDK documentation has to say about this topic:

> *The GetModuleUsage function is obsolete. It is provided to simplify porting of 16-bit Windows-based applications. Each Win32-based application runs in its own address space.*

Which are you gonna believe? The documentation, or what KERNEL32 really does?

2Ch   DWORD   un7
The meaning of this DWORD is unknown. However, it typically contains a valid pointer to a KERNEL32 heap block.

30h   PSTR   pszFileName2
This PSTR (and the following three fields) are somewhat of a mystery. They appear to serve the same function as do offsets 0Ch through 16h. This field (pszFileName2) points to a different copy of the complete path for the associated EXE or DLL. The strings pointed to by pszFileName (offset 0Ch) and pszFileName2 appear to always be the same.

34h   WORD   cbFileName2
This field contains the length of the string pointed to by pszFileName2. It should always have the same value as cbFileName (offset 14h).

36h   DWORD   pszModName2
This field points to the module name (that is, the base filename) portion of the pszFileName2 string. This field is the equivalent of the pszModName field (offset 10h).

3Ah   WORD   cbModName2
This field contains the length of the string pointed to by pszModName2. It should always have the same value as cbModName (offset 16h).

The fact that an IMTE maintains two separate pointers to the module's filename and module name is strange. I'm not sure what purpose this serves. Still, there is a bit of good news in the area of module names: In Win16, an EXE or DLL's module name is the first entry in the resident names table, and is set in the linker .DEF file. Even here, though, there's a problem because the Win16 loader assumes that the module name is the same as the base filename when determining if a module is already loaded. An EXE or DLL whose module name differs from its EXE or DLL filename can screw up the Win16 loader and cause strange problems such as module name space collisions, in which two or more completely unrelated DLLs have the same module name. For example, if you have two DLLs with the same name, but in different directories, the Win16 loader will load only one of them. An attempt to load the other DLL causes the loader to merely increment the reference count of the first module. Bad move!!! Since the Win16 loader can't distinguish between like-named DLLs in different directories, this situation can cause strange crashes — most often on a poor, unsuspecting end-user's machine.

Luckily, in Win32, the module name problem is mostly gone. A Win16 module name that you would pass to GetModuleHandle is one and the same as the EXE or DLL's filename. Thus, program A can load FOO.DLL from the \BAR directory, while program B can load its FOO.DLL from the \BAZ directory.

One situation Microsoft hasn't addressed, however, occurs when a program attempts to use two different DLLs with the same name at the same time. For example, program A implicitly links to FOO.DLL, and the loader finds FOO.DLL in the \BAR directory. Later, the program does a LoadLibrary on C:\BAZ\FOO.DLL. Does C:\BAZ\FOO.DLL get loaded, or does the reference count for C:\BAR\FOO.DLL go up? Microsoft's documentation doesn't say. However, in discussions I've had with the coder of the Windows 95 loader, he claims that two distinct copies of FOO.DLL are loaded in memory. I've seen this behavior myself while browsing the module list in SoftIce/W.

The MODREF structure

Now that you've seen how KERNEL32 maintains a global array of modules (pointers to IMTEs), we can bring the rest of the puzzle together. Earlier, I described how each process has its own list of modules and is unaware of other modules loaded by other processes. The glue that connects the per-process module lists to the global module table is the MODREF structure.

The per-process module list is just a linked list of MODREF structures. The MODREF list for each process (with the exception of the strange KERNEL32 process) contains a MODREF for the process's EXE, as well as MODREFs for each Win32 DLL used by the process. The memory for each MODREF comes from the KERNEL32 heap, which is in the shared memory area above 2GB. Thus, even though MODREFs enforce the notion that the module list is per-process, the MODREF lists themselves are actually globally accessible. The fact that the WIN32WLK program can walk the module list for each process is proof of this.

The head of the MODREF list is kept in the process database (which we'll discuss later). Each MODREF structure contains an index into the pModuleTableArray table. Figure 3-2 shows the relationship between MODREFs and IMTEs.

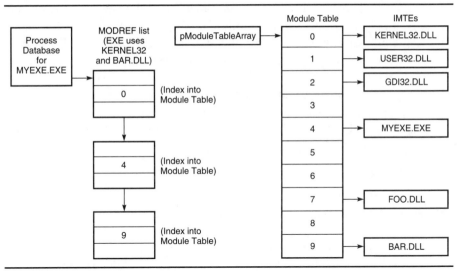

Figure 3-2
Per-process MODREFs and the global IMTE table.

The MODULE32.H file from the WIN32WLK source includes a C structure definition for the known fields of a MODREF structure. The following fields are known:

00h   PMODREF   pNextModRef

This pointer points to the next MODREF structure in the current process's list of MODREFs. The end of the list is indicated by a NULL pointer in this field. Enumerating the list of modules that a process knows about is as simple as getting the head MODREF node from the process database and then walking through the list. The WIN32WLK program on the disk that accompanies this book shows an example of how to do this.

10h   WORD   mteIndex
This WORD is a zero-based index into the global array of pointers to IMTEs. (In the pseudocode in this chapter, this array is referred to as pModuleTableArray.)

18h   PVOID   ppdb
This pointer is a PPROCESS_DATABASE (a pointer to a PROCESS_ DATABASE struct). It provides a "back link" from a MODREF to the process that owns the MODREF. We'll look at PROCESS_DATABASEs later in the chapter.

Since Windows 95 has to make it look like each process has its own unique module list, the module-related APIs like GetModuleHandle don't immediately start with the global module table (pModuleTableArray). Instead, they work only with those global module table entries that are referenced in the process's MODREF list. For example, the GetProcAddress function looks only at modules that are in the MODREF list of the current process. Even if the module was already loaded by another process, GetProcAddress won't attempt to locate the function in that module unless that module is also in the MODREF list of the current process.

MODULE-RELATED API FUNCTIONS

Now that you've seen how KERNEL32 manages a global list of loaded modules while still keeping a per-process module list, let's look at a few Win32 functions that involve module databases.

GetProcAddress and IGetProcAddress

GetProcAddress is a key function in Win32 programming because it's the method by which you dynamically hook up to DLLs loaded on the fly (as opposed to DLLs linked-to implicitly). Given a module identifier (an HMODULE) and a function identifier (either its name or export ordinal), GetProcAddress returns the entry point address for that function. To do this,

GetProcAddress must first locate the specified module database in memory and then walk through the exported function table to find the address.

The actual GetProcAddress code is nothing more than a parameter validation layer. It verifies that the lpszProc parameter is either a string or an import ordinal. The code distinguishes between the two types of function specifiers by looking at the high WORD of the lpszProc parameter. If the high word is 0, then the low WORD is the export ordinal and no further validation can be done. If the high WORD is nonzero, the lpszProc is assumed to be a PSTR and the code scans the string, looking for a NULL terminator. If the PSTR is bad, an exception occurs during this scanning, and a structured exception handler catches the exception and returns 0 (failure) to the caller. (We'll look at structured exception handling later in this chapter, in the discussion of threads.) If the execution successfully makes it through the tests, control jumps to the IGetProcAddress routine, which is where the real meat of the GetProcAddress code resides.

Pseudocode for GetProcAddress

```
// Parameters:
//      HMODULE  hModule
//      LPCSTR   lpszProc

    Set up structured exception handling frame.

    if ( lpszProc > 0x10000 )   // Values < 0x10000 contain ordinals in the
    {                           // low WORD, so they aren't valid LPSTRs.

        AL = 0
        EDI = lpszProc          // Touch all the bytes in the lpszProc routine
        REPNE SCASB             // up to a NULL. If it faults, the exception
    }                           // handler will catch it and return FALSE.

    Remove structured exception handling frame.

    goto IGetProcAddress
```

IGetProcAddress directs the steps of finding an exported function at a high level, leaving the grunge work to two lower-level functions I'll describe next. IGetProcAddress first does some thread synchronization to make sure the current thread won't get interrupted at an inopportune moment. Next, the routine calls MRFromHLib to get back a pointer to a MODREF. MRFromHLib is a KERNEL32 internal routine that scans through the process's list of MODREFs, looking for a module with an HMODULE matching what was passed to MRFromHLib. IGetProcAddress then uses the module table index in the MODREF structure to look up the IMTE of the associated module.

Phase two of IGetProcAddress is where KERNEL32 looks up the desired function address. Since IGetProcAddress can be passed either an export ordinal (in the low WORD) or a string pointer, it determines which form was passed and calls the appropriate lower-level routine to look up the function. If an export ordinal was passed, IGetProcAddress calls x_FindAddressFromExportOrdinal; if a string pointer was passed, it calls x_FindAddressFromExportName. In either case, if the lower-level functions don't find the specified function, IGetProcAddress spits out an error diagnostic and returns 0.

Up until the beta 3 of Windows 95, IGetProcAddress didn't make any special exceptions to looking up functions in a module. In beta 3 (a.k.a. the "Windows Preview Program" release), IGetProcAddress acquired a truly distasteful snippet of code. The new code can't be construed as anything other than anti-hacking code.

Specifically, IGetProcAddress won't allow you to obtain a function's address by its export ordinal *if and only if* you're looking for a KERNEL32.DLL function. Why would Microsoft do such a ghastly thing? In KERNEL32.DLL there are a good many undocumented functions that are exported by ordinal only (see Appendix A for some of their names). Since these function names aren't in KERNEL32.DLL, they won't be in the KERNEL32 import library. Thus, applications can't call these supposedly Microsoft-reserved functions directly. In *Unauthorized Windows 95*, Schulman wrote several programs that called undocumented KERNEL32 functions — in later builds of Windows 95, those programs broke. Was this breakage intentional on Microsoft's part? You decide for yourself.

Since beta 3, the direct approach to calling undocumented KERNEL32 functions no longer works. However, there are lots of smart programmers out there. They know that you can get a function's address with GetProcAddress and call it through the returned function pointer. If you know the export ordinal of the undocumented function, you're set, right? Nope! The horrible section of code in IGetProcAddress blocks attempts to use undocumented KERNEL32 functions by disallowing GetProcAddress to be used with a KERNEL32.DLL export ordinal. Thus, even if Schulman were to try to use GetProcAddress to fix his broken programs, he wouldn't get far. The plot thickens . . .

Personally, I think this munged-up IGetProcAddress is childish. Any Windows 95 system programmers worth their salt could write their own version of GetProcAddress, given the information on the PE module format in Chapter 8. An alternative approach I took was to use a .DEF file with the Visual C++ LIB.EXE to create a KERNEL32 import library with the undocumented functions. The WIN32WLK program later in the chapter uses this import library. Appendix A describes my Windows 95 undocumented KERNEL32 functions import library.

Let's return to a discussion of the rational code in IGetProcAddress. After successfully finding the specified function address, you'd think that IGetProcAddress would be done. Not so fast. For some odd reason, when a process is loaded for debugging under Windows 95, calls to system DLLs (those DLLs loaded above 2GB) first go through special code stubs that the loader builds on the fly. The purpose of these stubs is to prevent application debuggers from stepping into ring 3 system DLLs. For functions that are implicitly linked to, the loader handles everything behind the scenes. However, a program that calls GetProcAddress and then calls through the pointer would ordinarily bypass these stubs. Therefore, GetProcAddress checks to see if the program is being debugged; if the address that IGetProcAddress would ordinarily return is above 2GB, IGetProcAddress looks up the corresponding stub address and returns that address instead.

The final bit of IGetProcAddress checks to see if the specified function was found. If not, it sets the error value that GetLastError returns to ERROR_PROC_NOT_FOUND. Finally, IGetProcAddress leaves the critical section that it entered at the beginning of the function.

Pseudocode for IGetProcAddress

```
// Parameters:
//      HMODULE   hModule
//      LPCSTR    lpszProc
// Locals:
//      PTHREAD_DATABASE    ptdb
//      FARPROC             pfnProc // Return value
//      PMODREF             pModRef
//      PIMTE               pimte

    pfnProc = 0;        // Initial return value

    // Synchronization stuff
    _EnterSysLevel( ppCurrentProcessId->crst );
```

```
// Get a pointer to the MODREF that represents the module
// specified by the hModule param. MRFromHLib() just scans
// through the MODREF list, looking for a MODULE whose HMODULE
// matches the HMODULE passed in.

pModRef = MRFromHLib( hModule );

if ( !pModRef ) // If the MODREF wasn't found, bail out.
{
    InternalSetLastError( ERROR_INVALID_HANDLE );

    _DebugOut( SLE_MINORERROR, "GetProcAddress: %x not a Module handle",
                hModule );

    if ( x_LoaderDiagnosticsLevel > 2 )
        dprintf("On ..\peldr.c Failure Path line %d\n", linenumber);

    goto done;
}

// Get a pointer to the IMTE for the specified module by looking
// it up in the pModuleTableArray.
pimte = pModuleTableArray[ pModRef->mteIndex ];

if ( lpszProc < 0x10000 )   // Looking for a specified export ordinal.
{
    if ( hModule == hModuleKERNEL32 )
    {
        InternalSetLastError( ERROR_NOT_SUPPORTED );
        _DebugOut( "GetProcAddress: kernel32 by id not supported",
                    SLE_MINORERROR );

        if ( x_LoaderDiagnosticsLevel > 2 )
            dprintf( "On ..\peldr.c Failure Path line %d\n", line num );

        goto done;
    }

    // Scan through the module database, looking for the function
    // with the specified export ordinal.
    pfnProc = x_FindAddressFromExportOrdinal( pimte->pNTHdr, lpszProc );

    if ( !pfnProc ) // Function not found? Spit out an error message.
    {
        pModRef = MRFromHLib( hModule, lpszProc )
```

```
                _DebugOut(  SLE_MINORERROR,
                            "GetProcAddress(%s, %d) not found"
                            pModuleTableArray[pModRef->mteIndex]->pszModName,
                            lpszProc );
            }
        }
        else        // Looking for a specified function name.
        {
            // Scan through the module database, looking for the function
            // with the specified name.
            pfnProc = x_FindAddressFromExportName( pimte->pNTHdr, 0, lpszProc );

            if ( !pfnProc ) // Function not found? Spit out an error message.
            {
                pModRef = MRFromHLib( hModule, lpszProc )

                _DebugOut(  SLE_MINORERROR,
                            "GetProcAddress(%s, %s) not found"
                            pModuleTableArray[pModRef->mteIndex]->pszModName,
                            lpszProc );
            }
        }


        // If the function is in a shared, system DLL (i.e., it's above 2GB),
        // *AND* if the process is being debugged, change the returned
        // function address to point to the bizarre pre-API stubs that
        // KERNEL32 sets up. These stubs sit between the call to the
        // API and the actual API code.

        if ( (pfnProc >= 0x80000000) && (pfnProc != &DebugBreak) )
        {
            if ( ptdb->pProcess2->WaitEventList
                && !ppCurrentTDBX->MustCompleteCount )
            {
                pfnProc = DEBCreateDIT( ppCurrentTDBX->TopOfStack, pfnProc )
            }
        }

        // If the function is going to return a failure, set the GetLastError code.
        if ( pfnProc == 0 )
            InternalSetLastError( ERROR_PROC_NOT_FOUND );

done:
    // Undo the synchronization stuff.
    LeaveSysLevel( ppCurrentProcessId->crst );

    return ESI;
```

x_FindAddressFromExportOrdinal

The x_FindAddressFromExportOrdinal function (my name, not Microsoft's) is one of the core routines of KERNEL32. Not only is it called from GetProcAddress, but it's also called by the PE loader when fixing up calls to functions in implicitly loaded DLLs. Simply put, this routine is *the* one-stop shop for looking up exported function addresses in KERNEL32.DLL.

The x_FindAddressFromExportOrdinal function relies heavily on information found in the IMAGE_NT_HEADERs and .edata section of the PE file that was mapped into memory to make the module. (Again, I'll stress that this is why Chapter 8 on PE files is very important reading, even if you don't intend to directly work with PE files.)

Although there's a fair amount of code in x_FindAddressFromExport-Ordinal, the function is conceptually pretty simple. In the export table (the .edata section) of a module, you'll find an array of RVAs (relative virtual addresses) for the exported functions in the module. This array is known as the *export address table*. The first element in the array contains the RVA for export ordinal 1, the second element contains the address for export ordinal 2, and so on. The only thing x_FindAddressFromExportOrdinal should have to do is index into the array to get an RVA, then add the module's load address to make the RVA into a usable linear address. There are two twists to the above scenario, however.

The first (and unobvious) twist is that x_FindAddressFromExportOrdinal needs to account for the ordinal base. In PE files, the export ordinal with the lowest number is used as a base value. This allows the export address table to be smaller than it would ordinarily be. For example, let's say a DLL exports functions with ordinal 100 through 109. In a simple implementation, there would be 110 entries in the export address table, but only the last 10 would be used. To save space in the above scenario, the linker sets the ordinal base to 100, so it can create an export address table with only 10 elements. When looking up an exported function, x_FindAddressFrom-ExportOrdinal has to remember to bias the export ordinal value by the ordinal base to get a true array index.

The other twist in x_FindAddressFromExportOrdinal has to do with forwarded functions. Forwarded functions are explained in more detail in Chapter 8. For now, it's sufficient to know that a forwarded function is a sort of alias for an exported function in another DLL. For example, in Windows NT, the HeapAlloc function in KERNEL32.DLL is forwarded to RtlAllocateHeap in NTDLL.DLL. The address that the export address table contains for a forwarded function is always inside the .edata section. The address isn't that of the exported function. Rather, the address points to a string such as NTDLL.RTLAllocateHeap. If x_FindAddressFromExportOrdinal sees this happen, it breaks the string into its module name and function name components and calls GetProcAddress with those values. In case you're wondering, yes, this does make GetProcAddress recursive if called to search for a forwarded function.

Pseudocode for x_FindAddressFromExportOrdinal

```
// Parameters:
//      PIMAGE_NT_HEADERS pNTHdr
//      DWORD            ordinal
// Locals:
//      char    szForwardedModule[ MAX_PATH ]   // 0x260
//      PIMAGE_EXPORT_DIRECTORY pExpDir;
//      PDWORD              pFunctionArray;
//      DWORD               imageBase;
//      DWORD               retAddr;
//      DWORD               exportDirSize

    // Get the size of the export table out of the NT header.
    exportDirSize =
        pNTHdr->OptionalHeader.
                DataDirectory[IMAGE_DIRECTORY_ENTRY_EXPORT].Size

    // If no functions are exported, bail out immediately.
    if ( exportDirSize == 0 )
    {
        InternalSetLastError( ERROR_MOD_NOT_FOUND );
        if ( x_LoaderDiagnosticsLevel > 2 )
        {
            dprintf("On ..\peldr.c Failure Path line %d\n", line number );


        }

        return 0;
    }

    // Get the address where the module is loaded in memory.
    imageBase = pNTHdr->OptionalHeader.ImageBase;

    // Get a pointer to the export table.
    pExpDir = pNTHdr->OptionalHeader.
                DataDirectory[IMAGE_DIRECTORY_ENTRY_EXPORT].VirtualAddress
            + imageBase;
```

```
    // Get a pointer to the array of exported function addresses.
    pFunctionArray = imageBase + pExpDir->AddressOfFunctions

    // If the ordinal requested is greater than the number of exported
    // functions, bail out. Make sure to take the ordinal base into account.
    if ( pExpDir->NumberOfFunctions <= (ordinal - pExpDir->Base) )
        return 0;

    // Read RVA of the exported entry out of the array (again, taking
    // the ordinal base into account).
    retAddr = pFunctionArray[ ordinal - pExpDir->base ];

    // Bias the RVA extracted from the table by the image base to convert the
    // RVA into a usable linear address.
    if ( retAddr )
        retAddr += imageBase;

    // See if the found address is within the export directory. If so,
    // it's a forwarded DLL, and the address is a pointer to the name
    // of the function that it's forwarded to.
    //
    // If the address isn't within the export directory, we're done.  Return
    // the found address to the caller.
    if ( ( retAddr < pExpDir) || (retAddr >= (pExpDir + exportDirSize) )
    {
        PSTR pszForwardedFunctionName
        HMODULE hForwardedMod;

        Copy the DLL name pointed at by retAddr into the szForwardedModule
        local variable, stopping when a '.' is reached. Point
        pszForwardedFunctionName at the character after the '.'

        hForwardedMod = IGetModuleHandleA( szForwardedModule )
        if ( !hForwardedMod )
        {
            _DebugOut( SLE_MINORERROR, "Unable to find forwarded DLL %s",
                       szForwardedModule );
            retAddr = 0;
            goto done;
        }

        // Call GetProcAddress to get the real address of the forwarded
        // function in the DLL that contains it. Yes, this does make
        // GetProcAddress recursive if it's a forwarded function.
        retAddr = IGetProcAddress( hForwardedMod, pszForwardedFunctionName );
```

```
        if ( !retAddr ) // Oops! Didn't find the forwarded function.
        {
            _DebugOut( SLE_MINORERROR, "Unable to find forwarded export %s.%s",
                    szForwardedModule, pszForwardedFunctionName);
        }
    }

done:
    return retAddr;
```

x_FindAddressFromExportName

The x_FindAddressFromExportName function is a companion to the x_FindAddressFromExportOrdinal function. The primary difference between the two functions is that x_FindAddressFromExportName starts with a function name rather than with its import ordinal. The first part of the routine is similar to the x_FindAddressFromExportName code because both functions need to set up the same pointers to various locations in memory.

The meat of the x_FindAddressFromExportName code is where it searches through the array of exported names, looking for a match with lpszProc parameter. If the function finds a matching string, the code uses the AddressOfNameOrdinals array to convert the string array index to an export address table index. At this point, x_FindAddressFromExportName could simply go and look up the RVA of the exported function and return it to the caller. However, doing this would cause it to skip over the special-case code in the x_FindAddressFromExportOrdinal function (that is, the code that handles the ordinal base and the debugging stubs). Therefore, the routine passes the export ordinal it found to the x_FindAddressFromExportOrdinal function to let it do its thing. Whatever x_FindAddressFromExportOrdinal returns is what x_FindAddressFromExportName returns.

To put all this in simpler terms, a function address can be looked up either by name or by ordinal value. However, under the hood, the address always ends up being located using the export ordinal. When you pass a string name to GetProcAddress, or import a function by name, KERNEL32 merely injects an extra step to convert the string name to its export ordinal.

Pseudocode for x_FindAddressFromExportName

```
// Parameters:
//      PIMAGE_NT_HEADERS    pNTHdr
//      DWORD                hintNameOrdinal
//      PSTR                 lpszProc
// Locals:
//      PIMAGE_EXPORT_DIRECTORY pExpDir;
//      DWORD                   imageBase;
//      PDWORD                  pNamesArray;
//      PWORD                   pNameOrdinalsArray;
//      DWORD                   cbProcName
//      DWORD                   numNamesMinus1
//      DWORD                   nameOrdinal
//      DWORD                   curTestingNameOrdinal

    if ( hintNameOrdinal != some number )   // ???
    {
        CheckDll();
    }

    // If no functions are exported, bail out immediately.
    if ( 0 == pNTHdr->OptionalHeader.
             DataDirectory[IMAGE_DIRECTORY_ENTRY_EXPORT].Size )
    {
        if ( x_LoaderDiagnosticsLevel > 2 )
        {
            dprintf("On ..\peldr.c Failure Path line %d\n", line number);
        }

error_return:
        InternalSetLastError( ERROR_MOD_NOT_FOUND );
        if ( x_LoaderDiagnosticsLevel > 2 )
        {
            dprintf("On ..\peldr.c Failure Path line %d\n", line number);
        }

        return 0;
    }

    // Get the address where the module is loaded in memory.
    imageBase = pNTHdr->OptionalHeader.ImageBase;

    // Get a pointer to the export table.
    pExpDir = pNTHdr->OptionalHeader.
                DataDirectory[IMAGE_DIRECTORY_ENTRY_EXPORT].VirtualAddress
              + imageBase;
```

```
// Get a pointer to the array of PSTRs for the exported function names.
pNamesArray = imageBase + pExpDir->AddressOfNames;

// Get a pointer to the array that correlates names array indices
// to indices in the export address table.
pNameOrdinals = imageBase + pExpDir->AddressOfNameOrdinals;

// If no names were exported, bail out.
if ( pExpDir->NumberOfNames == 0 )
{
    if ( x_LoaderDiagnosticsLevel > 2 )
    {
        dprintf("On ..\peldr.c Failure Path line %d\n", line number);
    }

    return 0;
}

// Calculate how many names are exported.
numNamesMinus1 = pExpDir->NumberOfNames - 1;

curTestingNameOrdinal = 0;

cbProcname = strlen( lpszProc )

// It appears that the function can be passed a "hint" ordinal
// that may or may not be the ordinal of the actual function
// we're looking for. Check to see if the name of the function that
// corresponds to the hint ordinal is the same string as was passed
// in the lpszProc parameter. If so, we know the ordinal, and we
// can skip the linear search through all the function names that comes
// later.
if ( numNamesMinus1 >= hintNameOrdinal )
{
    // Uses CompareStringA() with SystemDefaultLangID as the LCID to
    // see if the strings match.
    if (!GlorifiedStringCompare(imageBase + pNamesArray[hintNameOrdinal]))
    {
        ordinal = hintNameOrdinal;
        goto FoundOrdinal
    }
}

if ( numNamesMinus1 < 0 )
    goto error_return;
```

```
            // Scan through the array of function names PSTRs, looking for a
            // string that matches the passed-in lpszProc parameter.

            A nasty little piece of code iterates through the entries in the
            "AddressOfNames" array. Each entry is compared (REP CMPSB) with the
            lpszProc string.

            if a match is found
            {
                set nameOrdinal to the index of the matching string in the
                AddressOfNames array

                goto to FoundOrdinal
            }

            if a match isn't found
                goto error_return:

        FoundOrdinal:

            return x_FindAddressFromExportOrdinal(
                    pNTHdr, pNameOrdinalsArray[nameOrdinal] + pExpDir->Base );
```

GetModuleFileName and IGetModuleFileName

The GetModuleFileName function takes an HMODULE as input, and returns the complete path to the EXE or DLL that the module was created from. The GetModuleFileNameA code itself is very small, and is just a parameter validation stub. After verifying that the lpszPath parameter (where the file name will be returned) is valid, GetModuleFileName jumps to IGetModuleFileName.

IGetModuleFileName would be simpler if it didn't have to concern itself with ANSI versus OEM filenames. The SetFileApisToANSI and SetFileApisToOEM functions in KERNEL32 let the caller specify whether the filenames should use ANSI characters or OEM characters. Internally, Windows 95 stores all the filenames in their ANSI form, and converts them to and from the OEM character set as needed. The meat of the IGetModuleFileName function is flanked by code that does this conversion.

Aside from the issue of filenames, the core of IGetModuleFileName is fairly simple. All it needs to do is copy the complete filename from the correct IMTE into the output buffer. However, because each process thinks it has its own module list, IGetModuleFileName can't simply go search the pModuleTableArray to find the module it's looking for. Instead, IGetModule-FileName uses the MRFromHLib function to find the MODREF for the module. (I briefly described the MRFromHLib function earlier in the discussion of GetProcAddress.) With the MODREF for the desired module, IGetModuleFileName uses the MODREF's mteIndex field to index into the pModuleTableArray and get the IMTE pointer. Once it has the IMTE pointer, all that remains is to copy the string pointed to by the IMTE's pszFileName field into the buffer passed to GetModuleFileName.

Pseudocode for GetModuleFileNameA

```
// Parameters:
//      HMODULE  hinstModule
//      LPTSTR   lpszPath
//      DWORD    cchPath


    Set up structured exception handling frame

    *lpszPath += 0;      // Harmlessly write to lpszPath. If a fault occurs,
                         // the exception handler will catch us and return
                         // failure.

    Remove structured exception handling frame

    goto IGetModuleFileNameA
```

Pseudocode for IGetModuleFileNameA

```
// Parameters:
//      HMODULE  hinstModule
//      LPTSTR   lpszPath
//      DWORD    cchPath
// Locals:
//      DWORD    fOem
//      DWORD    retValue
//      PMODREF  pModRef

    retValue = 0;

    EnterSysLevel( ppCurrentProcessId->crst );

    // Deal with OEM stuff (if SetFileApisToOEM is somehow involved).
    fOem = x_AreFileApisOEM();
```

```
       if ( fOem )
       {
           // Calls k32CharToOemA and some other things.
           SomeFunction( lpszPath, 1 );
       }

       if ( cchPath )      // Null out the return path string.
           *lpszPath = 0;

       if ( hInstModule == 0 )     // The HMODULE was 0. We want the EXE's name.
       {
           pModRef = ppCurrentProcessId->pExeMODREF
       }
       else                // We were passed a specific HMODULE to look for.
       {
           // Scan through the process's MODREF list, looking for a module
           // with an HMODULE that matches the hInstModule parameter.
           pModRef = MRFromHLib( hInstModule );
       }

       if ( pModRef == 0 ) // Oops! Didn't find the module.
       {
           InternalSetLastError( ERROR_INVALID_PARAMETER );

           if ( x_LoaderDiagnosticsLevel > 2 )
               dprintf("On ..\peldr.c Failure Path line %d\n", line number);
       }
       else                // We found the module.
       {
           PIMTE pimte;

           // Get a pointer to the IMTE by looking it up in the global module
           // table array.
           pimte = pModuleTableArray[ pModRef->mteIndex ];

           if ( cchPath )  // Are we supposed to write anything out?
           {
               retValue = pimte->cbFileName;
               if ( retValue >= cchPath )
                   retValue = cchPath - 1;

               // Copy the path name to the output buffer.
               memmove( lpszPath, pimte->pszFileName, retValue )
               lpszPath[ retValue ] = 0;       // Null terminate it.
           }
       }
```

```
    if ( fOem ) // If fOEM'ing, convert the output buffer to OEM.
    {
        ppCurrentProcessId->flags &= ~fOKToSetThreadOem;    // Turn off flag.

        if ( cchPath )
        {
            // Also calls k32CharToOemA and some other things.
            SomeOtherFunction( lpszPath, 1 );
        }
    }

    LeaveSysLevel( ppCurrentProcessId->crst );

    return retValue;
```

GetModuleHandle and IGetModuleHandle

The GetModuleHandle function performs the inverse operation of the
GetModuleFileName function. Given a module name, the function returns
the HMODULE (or base address, if you prefer) of that module. Unfortunately,
the Microsoft documentation is somewhat vague about what the module name
consists of. However, the pseudocode that follows will clear that problem all
up. In a nutshell, the module name can be either a base filename or a complete
path name to the EXE or DLL file. Also, in either case, the name can optionally omit the extension if the file's extension is .DLL. Thus, the following are
all valid module names for C:\WINDOWS\SYSTEM\USER32.DLL:

USER32

USER32.DLL

C:\WINDOWS\SYSTEM\USER32

C:\WINDOWS\SYSTEM\USER32.DLL

The actual GetModuleHandle code is very short; it just validates the
lpszModule parameter to make sure it's a valid string pointer. If it is,
GetModuleHandle jumps to IGetModuleHandle. Like IGetModuleFileName,
the core of IGetModuleHandle is bracketed by code that performs the ANSI
to OEM string conversions (if necessary). The core portion of the code first
uppercases the module name that was passed to it so that the code can do

faster case-sensitive compares later on. Next, IGetModuleHandle checks to see if the filename has a file extension (for example, .EXE or .DLL). If not, the code tacks on a .DLL extension.

The remaining core code consists of calls to two helper functions: x_GetMODREFFromFilename and x_GetHMODULEFromMODREF. First, x_GetMODREFFromFilename scans through the list of MODREFs for this process until it finds one with a matching file name, and then returns a pointer to that MODREF. Next, x_GetHMODULEFrom-MODREF takes the PMODREF and returns the associated HMODULE for it. These helper functions are described in the following two sections.

Pseudocode for GetModuleHandleA

```
// Parameters:
//      LPCTSTR   lpszModule;

    Set up structured exception handling frame

    if ( lpszModule )                       // Read each byte of the name to
        REPNE SCASB till a zero is found    // make sure it's valid. The
                                            // exception handler will catch
                                            // us if something's wrong.

    Remove structured exception handling frame

    goto IGetModuleHandleA
```

Pseudocode for IGetModuleHandleA

```
// Parameters:
//      LPCTSTR   lpszModule;
// Locals:
//      DWORD     myLocal
//      BOOL      fOem
//      DWORD     retValue
//      char      szBuffer[260]
//      PMODREF   pModRef

    pszFileExtension = 0;

    fOem = x_AreFileApisOEM();

    if ( fOem )
```

```
    {
        // Calls k32OemToCharA and some other things.
        lpszProc = SomeFunction( lpszModule, 0 );
    }

    if ( lpszModule == 0 )    // Asking for the EXE.
    {
        retValue = x_GetHModuleFromMODREF( ppCurrentProcessId->pExeMODREF );
    }
    else    // Caller specified a module name.
    {
        strcpy( szBuffer, lpszModule );

        x_UppercasePathName( szBuffer, &pszFileExtension );

        if ( pszFileExtension == 0 )    // If no extension found, tack
        {                               // on ".DLL".
            strcat( szBuffer, ".DLL" )
        }
        else
        {
            if ( *pszFileExtension == 0 )   // Strip off a trailing '.' if
                *(pszFileExtension-1) = 0;  // present.
        }

        pModRef = x_GetMODREFFromFilename( szBuffer );

        retValue = x_GetHMODULEFromMODREF( pModRef );

        if ( retValue == 0 )
            InternalSetLastError( ERROR_MOD_NOT_FOUND );
    }

    if ( fOem )
    {
        ppCurrentProcessId->flags &= ~fOKToSetThreadOem;    // Turn off flag.

        // Also calls k32CharToOemA and some other things.
        SomeOtherFunction( lpszPath, 0 );
    }

    return retValue
```

x_GetMODREFFromFilename

The x_GetMODREFFromFilename function (my name) scans through the linked list of MODREFs for a process, comparing the filename of each module to the lpszModName parameter passed to the function. If a match is found, x_GetMODREFFromFilename returns a PMODREF. Otherwise, it returns NULL.

It's interesting to discover that x_GetMODREFFromFilename can do not just one, not just two, but up to *four* string comparisons between the input string and the MODREF's filenames. In the first comparison, x_GetMODREF-FromFilename compares the input string to just the base filename for the MODREF (for example, to KERNEL32.DLL). If that fails, x_GetMODREF-FromFilename compares the input string to the complete path pointed at by the MODREF. If that fails, the function will do up to two more comparisons: the third to the secondary copy of the base filename, and the fourth to the secondary copy of the complete path name stored in the MODREF. If any of these comparisons succeed, the function returns a pointer to the matching MODREF.

To speed up the comparisons, x_GetMODREFFromFilename first calculates the length of the input string. Because the lengths of the strings pointed at by the MODREF struct are also stored in the MODREF, x_GetMODREFFromFilename first compares the input string length to the MODREF string length. If they don't match, the function doesn't have to bother doing a string comparison for that particular MODREF string.

Pseudocode for x_GetMODREFFromFilename

```
// Parameters:
//      PSTR    lpszModName
//      PMODREF pModRef;
//      PIMTE   pimte;
//      DWORD   nameLen;

    nameLen = strlen( lpszModName );

    pModRef = ppCurrentProcessId->MODREFlist;

    if ( !pModRef )
        return 0;

    while ( pModRef )
    {
        pimte = pModuleTableArray[ pModRef->mteIndex ]
```

```
            if ( nameLen == pimte->cbModName )
            {
                if ( 0 == strcmp(lpszModName, pimte->pszModName) )
                    break;      // Found it!!!
            }

            if ( nameLen == pimte->cbFileName )
            {
                if ( 0 == strcmp(lpszModName, pimte->pszFileName) )
                    break;      // Found it!!!
            }

            if ( nameLen == pimte->cbModName2 )
            {
                if ( 0 == strcmp(lpszModName, pimte->pszModName2) )
                    break;      // Found it!!!
            }

            if ( nameLen == pimte->cbFileName2 )
            {
                if ( 0 == strcmp(lpszModName, pimte->pszFileName2) )
                    break;      // Found it!!!
            }

            // We didn't find it in any of the above comparisons. Try
            // the next module in the list.
            pModRef = pModRef->pNextModRef;
        }

        // When we get here, we've either found a PMODREF with the right name,
        // or pModRef == 0;

        return pModRef;
```

x_GetHModuleFromMODREF

The x_GetHModuleFromMODREF function takes a PMODREF as an input parameter, and returns the HMODULE (or base address) of the corresponding module. The work required to do this is minimal. From the MODREF structure it was passed, the function extracts a pointer to the module database (an IMAGE_NT_HEADERS struct). One of the fields in an IMAGE_NT_HEADERS is the base load address of the module, which, as we now know, is the same as the HMODULE.

Pseudocode for x_GetHModuleFromMODREF

```
// Parameters:
//      PMODREF      pModRef
// Locals:
//      PIMAGE_NT_HEADERS pNTHdr
//      PIMTE        pimte;

    if ( pModRef == 0 )
        return 0;

    pimte = pModuleTableArray[ pModRef->mteIndex ];

    pNTHdrs = pimte->pNTHdr

    return pNTHdr->ImageBase;        // The load address (image base) is
                                     // the same as the HMODULE.
```

KERNEL32 OBJECTS

At this point I'd like to jump headfirst into the discussion about processes and threads, but I can't do that until I explain the concept of objects. I'm talking about what I call KERNEL32 objects (or K32 objects for short). Although just about anything for which KERNEL32 allocates memory from its heap could be considered "an object," I have a specific definition in mind here.

K32 objects are key system data structures that come from KERNEL32's heap. There are numerous types of K32 objects, and they all start with a common header. One way to determine whether or not something is a K32 object is to ask, "Do applications have handles to these objects?" For example, applications can have file handles or event handles, so files and events are K32 objects. On the other hand, I've seen no evidence that application code ever has handles to things like MODREFs or IMTEs. Thus, MODREFs and IMTEs aren't K32 objects.

Every K32 object starts out with a common header that has the following format:

00h   DWORD
The type of the object. This value determines how subsequent members of the structure should be interpreted.

04h   DWORD

The reference count of the object. This value determines how many times other code is referencing an object. For example, when you call GetFile-InformationByHandle(), the reference count of the file object that you're asking about goes up by one upon entry to the function. Before the function returns, it decrements the file object's reference count.

By now, you're probably dying to know what type of K32 objects there are. So, without further adieu, here's the list:

K32OBJ_SEMAPHORE (0x1)

K32OBJ_EVENT (0x2)

K32OBJ_MUTEX (0x3)

K32OBJ_CRITICAL_SECTION (0x4)

K32OBJ_PROCESS (0x5)

K32OBJ_THREAD (0x6)

K32OBJ_FILE (0x7)

K32OBJ_CHANGE (0x8; see FindFirstChangeNotification)

K32OBJ_CONSOLE (0x9)

K32OBJ_SCREEN_BUFFER (0xA)

K32OBJ_MEM_MAPPED_FILE (0xB; see CreateFileMapping()

K32OBJ_SERIAL (0xC)

K32OBJ_DEVICE_IOCTL (0xD; see DeviceIoControl)

K32OBJ_PIPE (0xE)

K32OBJ_MAILSLOT (0xF)

K32OBJ_TOOLHELP_SNAPSHOT (0x10; see CreateToolhelp32Snapshot)

K32OBJ_SOCKET (0x11)

For the remainder of this chapter, our primary focus is on the process and thread objects (IDs 5 and 6). A process database is just a K32_PROCESS object, and a thread database is just a K32_THREAD object. As you'll see in the "What's a Process Handle? What's a Process ID?" section, a process handle table is simply an array of pointers to various K32 objects of the types shown above. Throughout KERNEL32 and VWIN32.VXD, the code checks the first DWORD of a supposed object to make sure that it's really dealing with an object of the type it thinks it's dealing with.

If you're familiar with the Win16 kernel, you might notice that unlike Win16 tasks and modules, the 8-byte Win32 object headers don't have any fields for storing linked list pointers. In Win16, once you find the first task or module in the list, you have everything you need to walk the rest of the list. In Windows 95, KERNEL32 has its own section of code (LSTMGR.C) that maintains lists of K32 objects.

WINDOWS 95 PROCESSES

At this point in the book, it's time to drag out the usual hackneyed definition of what a process is, so let's get it over with. A *process* is a unit of ownership. That is, processes own things. A process owns memory (actually, it owns a memory context). A process owns file handles that the application code can use to read and write files. Processes own threads (which I'll define fully in the "Threads" section later in this chapter). Processes own a list of DLL modules that have been loaded into the process's memory context. I could go on, but I think you get the idea.

Note that a process does not represent execution (threads represent the execution of code), and a process is not an EXE file. Before it's loaded, an EXE file on disk is just a program. Only when it's loaded into memory does Windows 95 create a process. On the other hand, every process is associated with a disk file (although there is the strange case of the KERNEL32.DLL process, which you'll see in the WIN32WLK section at the end of this chapter).

When Windows 95 creates a new process, it also creates a new memory context for the process's threads to execute in. In addition, Windows 95 creates an initial thread of execution for the process. If needed, the process can create additional threads. The system also creates a file handle table in which the process can keep a list of open handles. Finally, and most importantly for the discussion in the next couple of paragraphs, Windows 95 creates a process database to represent the process.

A *process database* is a K32 object that contains a vast quantity of information about the process. (We'll look at the fields in "The Windows 95 Process Database (PDB)" section.) The process database memory is allocated out of KERNEL32's heap, so all process databases are visible to all tasks (assuming they know where to look; that's the tricky part that I'll show how to do in the WIN32WLK source).

Process database highlights include a list of threads, a list of loaded modules, the heap handle of the default process heap, a pointer to the process handle table, and a pointer to the memory context that the process runs in (see Chapter 5). And those are just a few of the highlights; there are many, many more. In fact, if you buy now, we'll also throw in a list of memory mapped files, a pointer to the parent process, a list of available thread local storage slots, and a pointer to the environment block. Just send $49.95 to KERNEL32.DLL at 1 Microsoft Way . . .

WHAT'S A PROCESS HANDLE?
WHAT'S A PROCESS ID?

Before I go one step further, I want to clear up the widespread confusion regarding process handles versus process IDs. Two similar sounding Win32 routines — GetCurrentProcess and GetCurrentProcessId — tend to confuse a fair number of programmers. The difference between the two functions is actually rather simple, once you understand what's going on.

A process handle is essentially the same thing as a file handle. It's an "opaque" value with no significance as a pointer to anything. Internally, the system uses K32 object handles (such as process or file handles) as an index into the process handle table. The value returned by indexing into the process handle table array is an actual pointer to a K32 object. However, since applications aren't given direct access to their handle tables, a process handle is useless, except as a magic cookie to pass to certain routines that expect it.

Remember that since each application has its own handle table, it's entirely possible that different processes will have the same process handle within their own process context. For example, normally each process has a process handle open for itself, and that handle value is 1. The implication that should be drawn is that a process handle is *not* a way to differentiate between different processes. Another example: If an application opens another process handle for its own process, it would then have two different handle values that both identified the same process.

Further proof that a process handle is not suitable for identifying which process you're working with can be found in the GetCurrentProcess code:

Pseudocode for GetCurrentProcess

```
// Normally this function does nothing. It appears to be there
// for the benefit of the KERNEL32 developers.
x_LogSomeKernelFunction( function number for GetCurrentProcess );

return 0x7FFFFFFF;
```

That's it! Ignoring the call to the logging function, GetCurrentProcess does nothing more than return a fixed value (0x7FFFFFFF). No matter what process calls GetCurrentProcess, it'll always get back 0x7FFFFFFF. The value 0x7FFFFFFF is a "magic" value that KERNEL32 interprets to mean "use the current process." In routines where KERNEL32 expects a process handle, it checks for the value 0x7FFFFFFF and substitutes whatever the current process is. Need any more proof that process handles are useless except when used within their own context? I didn't think so.

Let's now turn to the process IDs. As noted in *Unauthorized Windows 95*, early versions of Windows 95 up through beta 1 used the address of the process database as a process ID. Since process databases are kept in shared memory accessible by all processes, the address of a process database is guaranteed to be a unique value throughout the system. *Unauthorized Windows 95* made extensive use of the GetCurrentProcessId function to get a pointer to the current processes database, from which it then extracted key fields. Unfortunately, the Microsoft KERNEL32 coders crashed that particular party as we can see in a more recent version of GetCurrentProcessId:

Pseudocode for GetCurrentProcessId

```
x_LogSomeKernelFunction( function number for GetCurrentProcessId );

return PDBToPid( ppCurrentProcess );
```

Again, ignoring the logging function, GetCurrentProcessId boils down to passing a global variable (ppCurrentProcess) to the PDBToPID function. Let's stop and examine this point closely, since it's extremely important for understanding the rest of the chapter. The ppCurrentProcess global variable is a pointer to a pointer to the current process database. Put in C notation, this means that **ppCurrentProcess points to the current process database.

The reason you have to indirect through this pointer twice is one of the fascinating things you'll find out in Chapter 6. For now, just remember that the ppCurrentProcess pointer is a global variable in KERNEL32.DLL that allows KERNEL32 to find the process database of the current process. (To keep things simple, when I show the ppCurrentProcess variable being used in the pseudocode, I pretend that it's just a pointer to the process database, not a pointer to a pointer.)

So, if KERNEL32 has a pointer to the current process database handy, why doesn't GetCurrentProcessId just return it? For an answer, let's look at the PidToPDB function:

Pseudocode for PDBToPid

```
// Parameters:
//      PROCESS_DATABASE * ppdb

    if ( ObsfucatorDWORD == FALSE )
    {
        _DebugOut( "PDBToPid() Called too early! Obsfucator not yet"
                    " initialized!" );
        return 0;
    }

    if ( ppdb & 1 )
    {
        _DebugOut( "PDBToPid: This PDB looks like a PID (0%1xh) Do a"
                    " stack trace BEFORE reporting as bug." );
    }

    // Here's the key! XOR the obsfucator DWORD with the process database
    // pointer to make the PID value.

    return ppdb ^ ObsfucatorDWORD;
```

Oh really? Yes. The term "Obsfucator" comes straight from the Microsoft binaries (and yes, "Obsfucator" is misspelling; it should be "Obfuscator"). Other than checking to make sure that a valid process database pointer was passed, the only essential thing PDBToPID does is XOR the current process database pointer with the ObsfucatorDWORD. This is an obvious attempt on Microsoft's part to keep hackers from prying into the internals of system data structures. However, as I'll show in the WIN32WLK code at the end of this chapter, this is only a small, temporary obstacle (hint: think about the transitive properties of a binary XOR).

Incidentally, if you're wondering where the ObsfucatorDWORD value comes from, you'll be dismayed to know that it's calculated at runtime each time the system starts up. This prevents a simple attack on the problem of getting a real pointer to a process database. To compound matters, not only are process databases "guarded" by this obsfucator DWORD, but so are thread databases. I'll show you later how the GetCurrentThreadId function is uncannily similar to the GetCurrentThreadId function.

To sum up, a process handle is like a file handle. It's opaque, and meaningless outside the process context in which it's defined. A process ID, on the other hand, is a unique value across all processes. It's essentially a pointer to a process database structure, even though Microsoft has taken steps to "obsfucate" that fact (their choice of words, not mine). The WIN32WLK program at the end of the chapter shows the magic translation formula to convert a process ID into a usable pointer.

If you've seen the TOOLHELP32 Process32First and Process32Next functions, you may have noticed the th32ProcessID fields in the PROCESSENTRY32 structure. Are these related in any way to the values returned by GetCurrentProcessId? Fortunately, the answer is yes! The WIN32WLK program takes advantage of this to let TOOLHELP32 handle some of the dirty work of iterating through the system's processes and threads.

THE WINDOWS 95 PROCESS DATABASE (PDB)

In Windows 95, each process database is a block of memory allocated from the KERNEL32 shared memory heap. KERNEL32 often uses the acronym PDB instead of the longer term "process database." Unfortunately, in Win16, PDB is a synonym for the DOS PSP that all programs have. Is this confusing? Yes! For the purposes of this chapter, I'll use PDB in the KERNEL32 sense of the term. Each PDB is considered to be a KERNEL32 object as evidenced by the value 5 (K32OBJ_PROCESS) in the first DWORD of the structure. The PROCDB.H file from the WIN32WLK program gives a C-style view of the PDB structure. Let's look at the fields in detail:

00h   DWORD   Type
This DWORD contains 5, the KERNEL32 object type for a process.

04h   DWORD   cReference
This DWORD is the reference count for the process. This is the number of things that are currently using the process structure for something (for example, they have an open handle for the process).

08h   DWORD   un1
The meaning of this DWORD is unknown. It may be a standard part of a KERNEL32 object header. It appears to always be 0.

0Ch   DWORD   pSomeEvent
This DWORD is a pointer to an event object (K32OBJ_EVENT). Event objects are passed to functions like WaitForSingleObject. It appears that this event is what is actually waited on when you pass a process handle to one of the WaitForSingleEvent family of functions.

10h   *DWORD*   *TerminationStatus*

This DWORD is the value that would be returned by calling
GetExitCodeProcess. The process exit code is the value returned from the
main or WinMain functions. Alternatively, it can be specified when a
process calls ExitProcess or TerminateProcess. While a process is still
actively running, its exit code is 0x103 (STILL_ACTIVE).

14h   *DWORD*   *un2*

The meaning of this DWORD is unknown. It appears to always be 0.

18h   *DWORD*   *DefaultHeap*

This DWORD contains the address of the default process heap.
GetProcessHeap returns this value for the current process.

1Ch   *DWORD*   *MemoryContext*

This DWORD is a pointer to the process's memory context. A memory
context contains the page directory mappings necessary to provide a process
with its own private region in the 4GB address space. Chapter 5 describes
memory contexts in more detail.

20h   *DWORD*   *flags*

These flags are described in the following table:

Flag name and bit value	Description (when available)
fDebugSingle 0x00000001	Set if process is being debugged.
fCreateProcessEvent 0x00000002	Set in debugged processes after starting.
fExitProcessEvent 0x00000004	Might be set in debugged processes at exit time.
fWin16Process 0x00000008	A 16-bit program.
fDosProcess 0x00000010	A DOS program.
fConsoleProcess 0x00000020	A console (text mode) Win32 process.
fFileApisAreOem 0x00000040	See SetFileApisToOEM() in the API documentation.
fNukeProcess 0x00000080	

Flag name and bit value	Description (when available)
fServiceProcess 0x00000100	For example, MSGSRV32.EXE.
fLoginScriptHack 0x00000800	Might be a Novell network login process.
fSendDLLNotifications 0x00200000	
fDebugEventPending 0x00400000	For example, stopped in a debugger.
fNearlyTerminating 0x00800000	
fFaulted 0x08000000	
fTerminating 0x10000000	
fTerminated 0x20000000	
fInitError 0x40000000	
fSignaled 0x80000000	

24h   DWORD   pPSP

This DWORD holds the linear address of the DOS PSP created for this process. This field is set for both Win16 and Win32 processes. The linear addresses in this field are always below 1MB (the maximum address that real mode DOS code can reach). See also field 28h.

28h   WORD   PSPSelector

This WORD is a selector that points to the DOS PSP for this process. Both Win16 and Win32 applications have DOS PSPs. See also field 24h.

2Ah   WORD   MTEIndex

This WORD contains an index into the global module table (pModuleTable-Array). The IMTE referenced by indexing into the module table is the IMTE for this module. IMTEs and the global module table were discussed earlier in the chapter.

2Ch   WORD   *cThreads*

This field is the number of threads belonging to this process.

2Eh   WORD   *cNotTermThreads*

This field holds the number of threads for this process that haven't yet been terminated. In all instances seen to date, this WORD always has the same value as field 2Ch.

30h   WORD   *un3*

The meaning of this WORD is unknown. It appears to always be 0.

32h   WORD   *cRing0Threads*

This WORD holds the number of ring 0 threads as managed by VMM.VXD. For normal applications, this value is the same field 2Ch (cThreads). However, in the case of the special KERNEL32.DLL process, this field is one more than the cThreads field.

34h   HANDLE   *HeapHandle*

This DWORD holds the handle of the HEAP that handle tables (and possibly other things) belonging to this process should be allocated from. This field appears to always contain the KERNEL32 shared heap handle.

38h   HTASK   *W16TDB*

This DWORD holds the Win16 Task Database (TDB) selector associated with this process. Both Win16 and Win32 applications have Task Database selectors and maintain valid task databases.

3Ch   DWORD   *MemMapFiles*

A pointer to the head node in the list of memory mapped files in use by this process. Each memory mapped file is represented by a node in the list. The format of each node is:

      DWORD   Base address of the memory mapped region

      DWORD   Pointer to next node, or 0

40h   PENVIRONMENT_DATABASE   *pEDB*

This DWORD is a pointer to the environment database. The environment database contains the current directory, the environment, the process command line, the "standard" handles (for example, stdin), and other items. I'll describe the format of the environment in "The Environment Database" section later in this chapter.

44h   PHANDLE_TABLE   pHandleTable

This field is a pointer to a process handle table. All handles (be they file handles, event handles, process handles, or so on) go into the handle table. The DOS/Win16 equivalent of a Win32 handle table is the DOS System File Table (SFT). (See Schulman et al.'s *Undocumented DOS,* 2nd ed.)

However, the DOS SFT applies to the entire system, whereas a Win32 process handle table applies only to its owning process. The Win32 handle table layout is described in the "Process Handle Tables" section.

48h   PPROCESS_DATABASE   ParentPDB

This DWORD is a pointer to the PROCESS_DATABASE for the process that created this process. Typically the parent process is EXPLORER for applications launched via the GUI. MSGSRV32 is the parent of the initial "service" processes and EXPLORER.EXE.

4Ch   PMODREF   MODREFlist

This field points to the head of the process's module list. This is the linked list of MODREFs described earlier in "The MODREF structure" section.

50h   DWORD   ThreadList

A pointer to the list of threads owned by this process. This list is a listmgr.c-style list. (The exact format of this type of list is unknown to me.)

54h   DWORD   DebuggeeCB

This DWORD appears to be a debuggee context block. When a process is being debugged, this field points to a block of memory above 2GB. This block includes a pointer to the debuggee's process database.

58h   DWORD   LocalHeapFreeHead

This DWORD points to the head of the free list in the default heap for the process. Chapter 5 describes the format of process heaps and the free list.

5Ch   DWORD   InitialRing0ID

The meaning of this DWORD is unknown. It appears to always be 0.

60h   CRITICAL_SECTION   crst

This field is a CRITICAL_SECTION used by various API functions for synchronizing threads within the same process. Much of the pseudocode you'll see later on shows this critical section in action.

78h   DWORD   un4[3]

These three DWORDS appear to always be set to 0, and their meaning is currently unknown.

84h   DWORD   pConsole

If this process uses the console (that is, if it's a text mode process), this DWORD points to the console object (K32OBJ_CONSOLE) used for output.

88h   DWORD   tlsInUseBits1

These 32 bits represent the status of the lowest 32 TLS (Thread Local Storage) indexes. If a bit is set, the TLS index is in use. Each successive TLS index is represented by successively greater bit values; for example:

TLS index: 0 = 0x00000001

TLS index: 1 = 0x00000002

TLS index: 2 = 0x00000004

Thread local storage is discussed in detail in the "Thread Local Storage" section later in this chapter.

8Ch   DWORD   tlsInUseBits2

This DWORD represents the status of TLS indices 32 through 63. See the previous field description (88h) for more information.

90h   DWORD   ProcessDWORD

The meaning of this field is currently unknown, although there is an undocumented API (GetProcessDword) that retrieves its value.

94h   PPROCESS_DATABASE   ProcessGroup

This field is either 0 or points to the master process in a process group. Process groups are collections of processes that belong together. When the group is destroyed, all processes in that group are destroyed. Normally, each process is considered to be in its own group, and this field points to the process's own PDB (a circular reference). If a process is being debugged, it belongs to the debugger's process group.

98h   DWORD   pExeMODREF

This field points to EXE's MODREF (module list entry). MODREFs were described earlier. Typically, the EXE's MODREF is the head MODREF in the list, so this field usually matches field 4Ch unless the process has loaded additional DLLs via LoadLibrary or LoadModule.

9Ch   DWORD   TopExcFilter

This DWORD holds the "Top Exception Filter" for the process. This is the routine that will be called if no other exception handlers choose to handle an exception. This value is set via the SetUnhandledExceptionFilter function. Structured exception handling is discussed later in the chapter.

A0h   DWORD   BasePriority

This DWORD holds the scheduling priority for this process. Windows 95 supports 32 priority levels, grouped into four classes. The following priority classes are supported in Windows 95, shown with the normal priority level for that class:

Idle	4
Normal	8
High	13
Realtime	18

Within each class, the priority can vary both below and above the default priority level. Priority levels are described in more detail later in this chapter.

A4h   DWORD   HeapOwnList

This field points to the head of the linked list of heaps for the process. By default, each process has a single heap; the handle for that heap is retrieved by calling GetProcessHeap. However, a process can create additional heaps by calling HeapCreate. These heaps are put into the linked list of heaps for the process when they're created. Chapter 5 discusses this topic in much more detail.

A8h   DWORD   HeapHandleBlockList

Moveable memory blocks in the process heap are managed via moveable handle tables embedded within the heap. This field is a pointer to the head of the moveable handle table list within the default process heap. Chapter 5 describes moveable handle tables in detail.

ACh   DWORD   pSomeHeapPtr

The exact meaning of this field is unknown. It's normally 0, but when not, it's a pointer to a moveable handle table block in the default process heap. See also field A8h.

B0h   DWORD   pConsoleProvider
This field is either 0, or a pointer to a KERNEL32 console object
(K32OBJ_CONSOLE). It appears to always be 0 for console mode Win32
processes but is nonzero for the WINOLDAP process. WINOLDAP is the
Windows process for managing DOS programs within Windows.

B4h   WORD   EnvironSelector
This WORD holds a selector that points to the process's environment.
This selector's base address is the same value as the linear address in the
pszEnvironment field in the Environment Database (see field 40h).

B6H   WORD   ErrorMode
This field contains the value set by the SetErrorMode function. SetErrorMode
in KERNEL32 thunks down to KRNL386's SetErrorMode, so this field
merely reflects the Win16 error mode value for the process. The documented
error mode values are:

    SEM_FAILCRITICALERRORS

    SEM_NOALIGNMENTFAULTEXCEPT

    SEM_NOGPFAULTERRORBOX

    SEM_NOOPENFILEERRORBOX

B8h   DWORD   pevtLoadFinished
This DWORD points to a KERNEL32 Event object (K32OBJ_EVENT). It
appears that this event is signaled when the process has finished loading.

BDh   WORD   UTState
The meaning of this field is unknown, but based on the name, it probably
has something to do with Universal Thunks. It's usually set to 0.

Of special note in all these process database fields is the number of
DOS-related fields. There's both a PSP selector and a linear address for the
DOS PSP (which just happens to always be below 1MB). Given the number
of occasions that windows reflects INT 21hs down into Virtual 86 mode
DOS- style code, this isn't entirely surprising. (See *Unauthorized Windows 95*,
Chapter 8, for a thorough proof that dispatching INT 21hs to DOS isn't
entirely surprising.) It's unlikely that the Windows NT process database
equivalent contains PSP information for all processes. It sure looks like DOS
just won't die, at least not on platforms evolved from Windows 1.*x* code.
Now that we've seen what a process database looks like, let's look at some
pseudocode for some process-related functions.

GetExitCodeProcess and IGetExitCodeProcess

GetExitCodeProcess retrieves the termination status of the process specified by the hProcess handle passed in. The main function is just a validation layer that verifies that a valid pointer was passed as the second parameter. The real code is IGetExitCodeProcess. After some standard thread synchronization and logging code germane to many process-related functions, the code takes the hProcess parameter and looks up the associated pointer to a PROCESS_DATABASE. Since hProcess is a handle, this means indexing into the process's handle table and retrieving the process pointer. x_Convert-HandleToK32Object handles this chore along with incrementing the usage count of the process database.

With a PPROCESS_DATABASE pointer in hand, the function extracts the value of the TerminationStatus field and stores it to the caller-specified buffer. To clean up, IGetExitCodeProcess decrements the usage count of the process object and leaves the "must complete" state it entered previously.

Pseudocode for GetExitCodeProcess

```
// Parameters
//      HANDLE  hProcess;
//      LPDWORD lpdwExitCode;

    Set up structured exception handling frame

    if ( lpdwExitCode )          // If a non-null pointer was passed, verify
        EAX = *lpdwExitCode;     // that the DWORD it points to can be written.

    Remove structured exception handling frame

    goto IGetExitCodeProcess;
```

Pseudocode for IGetExitCodeProcess

```
// Parameters
//      HANDLE  hProcess;
//      LPDWORD lpdwExitCode;
// Locals:
//      PPROCESS_DATABASE ppdb;
//      BOOL    retValue;

    retValue = TRUE;          // Assume successful return.

    x_EnterMustComplete();    // Prevent us from being interrupted.
                              // Increments ptdbx->MustCompleteCount.
```

```
    x_LogSomeKernelFunction( function number for GetExitCodeProcess );

    // Get a pointer to the PROCESS_DATABASE struct
    ppdb = x_ConvertHandleToK32Object( hProcess, 0x80000010, 0 );

    if ( ppdb )
    {
        // Save away exit status.
        *lpdwExitCode = ppdb->TerminationStatus;
        x_UnuseObjectWrapper( ppdb );    // Decrement usage count.
    }
    else....                  // Opps! No process database.
    {
        retValue = FALSE;
    }

    // Call the API logging function again (???).
    x_LogSomeKernelFunction( function number for GetExitCodeProcess );

    LeaveMustComplete();    // Decrements ptdbx->MustCompleteCount.

    return retValue;
```

SetUnhandledExceptionFilter

SetUnhandledExceptionFilter sets the address of the function that KERNEL32's
UnhandledExceptionFilter function calls when no other exception filters
have elected to handle an exception (what a mouthful!). The function
stashes away the current value of the TopExcFilter field in the process database, then replaces that value with the value of the parameter passed in. The
function returns the previous value of TopExcFilter.

Pseudocode for SetUnhandledExceptionFilter

```
// Parameters:
//      LPTOP_LEVEL_EXCEPTION_FILTER  lpTopLevelExceptionFilter
// Locals:
//      LPTOP_LEVEL_EXCEPTION_FILTER prevValue;

    // Save old value.
    prevValue = ppCurrentProcess->TopExcFilter;

    // Stuff in new value.
    ppCurrentProcess->TopExcFilter = lpTopLevelExceptionFilter;

    return prevValue;       // Return old value.
```

OpenProcess

OpenProcess takes a process ID and returns a handle that refers to that process. This handle can then be passed to functions like ReadProcessMemory and VirtualQueryEx. When you combine this function with TOOLHELP32's ability to give you a process ID for any process in the system, you have a potent combination. It's somewhat strange that Windows 95 allows you to open a process handle but not a thread handle. Perhaps Microsoft thought that the havoc that could be created with a thread handle was just too great to allow.

OpenProcess first converts the process ID parameter to a PPROCESS_DATABASE. Because the algorithm for converting a process ID to a process pointer is identical to converting a thread ID to a thread pointer, OpenProcess checks to make sure it has a PPROCESS_DATABASE pointer. (Some knucklehead might otherwise pass in a thread ID and screw things up.) The next part of OpenProcess is where the flags parameter is tweaked to ensure that it has only legal and/or required flags set. Finally, OpenProcess calls an internal function that allocates a slot in the current process's handle table and places the PPROCESS_DATABASE pointer into that slot.

Pseudocode for OpenProcess

```
// Parameters:
//   DWORD    fdwAccess;
//   BOOL     fInherit;
//   DWORD    IDProcess;
// Locals:
//   PPROCESS_DATABASE ppdb;
//   DWORD    flags;

    x_LogSomeKernelFunction( function number for OpenProcess );

    // Convert the process ID to a PPROCESS_DATABASE.
    ppdb = PidToPDB( IDProcess )

    if ( !ppdb )
        return 0;

    if ( ppdb->Type != K32OBJ_PROCESS ) // Make sure thread ID not passed.
    {
        InternalSetLastError( ERROR_INVALID_PARAMETER );
        return 0;
    }
```

```
flags = fdAccess & 0x001FFFBF;   // Turn off all non-allowed flags.
                                 // Flags like PROCESS_QUERY_INFORMATION
                                 // and PROCESS_VM_WRITE are allowed.

if ( fInherit )
    flags |= 0x80000000;

flags |= PROCESS_DUP_HANDLE;     // Always pass. PROCESS_DUP_HANDLE

// Allocates a new slot in the handle table of the current process.
// The slot contains the ppdb pointer.
return x_OpenHandle( ppCurrentProcess, ppdb, flags );
```

SetFileApisToOEM

The SetFileApisToOEM function changes the way the file-related KERNEL32 functions interpret filenames. By default, KERNEL32 uses ANSI strings for the filenames. By calling SetFileApisToOEM, a program can change this to use OEM character strings. For an example of this in action, see the GetModuleFileName and GetModuleHandle functions earlier in this chapter.

Internally, the function couldn't be much simpler. It grabs a pointer to the process database for the current process and turns on the fFileApisAreOem flag in the flags field.

Pseudocode for SetFileApisToOEM

```
x_LogKernelFunction( function number for SetFileApisToOEM )

ppCurrentProcess->flags |= fFileApisAreOem;
```

THE ENVIRONMENT DATABASE

At offset 40h in the process database is a pointer to a vital data structure that also contains process-related information. The name that KERNEL32 uses internally for this pointer is pEDB, which I interpret to mean "pointer to Environment Database." As with the PROCESS_DATABASE structure, I've given the layout of an ENVIRONMENT_DATABASE in the PROCDB.H file. Let's look at these fields now:

00h   *PSTR*   *pszEnvironment*

This field points to the process environment. The environment is the standard DOS-style environment (string=value, with semicolons between multiple items, as in string=value;string=value). The process environment is in a block of memory in the per-process data area, and usually resides just above where the EXE module loads.

04h   *DWORD*   *un1*

The meaning of this DWORD is currently unknown. It appears to always have a value of 0.

08h   *PSTR*   *pszCmdLine*

This field points to the command line passed to CreateProcess to start this process. In most cases, the command line is just the complete filename for the process's EXE. In several cases, though, it's a pointer to an empty string (\0).

0Ch   *PSTR*   *pszCurrDirectory*

This field is a pointer to the current directory of the process.

10h   *LPSTARTUPINFOA*   *pStartupInfo*

This pointer points to the process's STARTUPINFOA structure, which is defined in WINBASE.H. A STARTUPINFOA structure is passed to CreateProcess to specify the process's window size, title, standard file handles, and so forth. This field points to a copy of that structure.

14h   *HANDLE*   *hStdIn*

This is the file handle the process uses for the standard input device. If not used (for instance, if this is a GUI application), the handle value is –1.

18h   *HANDLE*   *hStdOut*

This is the file handle the process uses for the standard output device. If not used (for instance, if this is a GUI application), the handle value is –1.

1Ch   *HANDLE*   *hStdErr*

This is the file handle the process uses for the standard error device. If not used (for instance, if this is a GUI application), the handle value is –1.

20h   *DWORD*   *un2*

The meaning of this field is unknown. It seems to always be 1.

24h   DWORD   InheritConsole

Presumably this field indicates whether the process is inheriting the console from its parent process (as opposed to getting its own console). See the CREATE_NEW_CONSOLE flag to the CreateProcess function. In my observations, this field was always 0.

28h   DWORD   BreakType

This field most likely indicates how console events (CTRL+C, and so on.) should be handled. In the programs I ran, it was usually 0, but it's occasionally set to 0xA.

2Ch   DWORD   BreakSem

Normally this field is 0, but if an application calls SetConsoleCtrlHandler, this DWORD points to a KERNEL32 semaphore object (K32OBJ_SEMAPHORE).

30h   DWORD   BreakEvent

Normally this field is 0, but if an application calls SetConsoleCtrlHandler, this DWORD points to a KERNEL32 EVENT object (K32OBJ_EVENT).

34h   DWORD   BreakThreadID

Normally this field is 0. However, if an application calls SetConsoleCtrlHandler, this DWORD points to the thread object (K32OBJ_THREAD) of the thread that installed the handler.

38h   DWORD   BreakHandlers

Normally this field is 0. However, if an application calls SetConsoleCtrlHandler, this DWORD points to a data structure allocated from the KERNEL32 shared heap. This data structure is a list of the installed console control handlers.

Let's now look at some more pseudocode for a few process functions, this time related to the ENVIRONMENT_DATABASE we've just looked at.

GetCommandLineA

There's really not much to comment on in the GetCommandLineA code. The function returns the command-line pointer that's stored in the environment database.

Pseudocode for GetCommandLineA

```
return ppCurrentProcess->pEDB.pszCmdLine
```

GetEnvironmentStrings

There's not much to say about GetEnvironmentStrings, either. Like GetCommandLineA, it just returns the relevant pointer from the environment database. However, it's interesting to note that the actual implementation and the SDK documentation say two different things. The SDK documentation says:

> When GetEnvironmentStrings is called, it allocates memory for a block of environment strings. When the block is no longer needed, it should be called FreeEnvironmentStrings.

Although this may be the case for Windows NT, it's certainly incorrect for Windows 95.

Pseudocode for GetEnvironmentStrings

```
return ppCurrentProcess->pEDB.pszEnvironment
```

FreeEnvironmentStringsA

The FreeEnvironmentStringsA function is a bit more interesting. Since GetEnvironmentStrings doesn't really allocate any memory, there's nothing that FreeEnvironmentStringsA *has* to do. However, just for sport, the function checks the input parameter string to see if it matches the pointer to the environment from the environment database. If they don't match, FreeEnvironmentStringsA sets the LastError value to ERROR_INVALID_PARAMETER.

Pseudocode for FreeEnvironmentStringsA

```
// Parameters:
// LPSTR  lpszEnvironmentBlock;

    x_LogSomeKernelFunction( function number for FreeEnvironmentStringsA );

    if ( ppCurrentProcess->pEDB.pszEnvironment != lpszEnvironmentBlock )
    {
        InternalSetLastError( ERROR_INVALID_PARAMETER );
        return FALSE;
    }

    return TRUE;
```

GetStdHandle

GetStdHandle is just as straightforward as you probably imagine it to be. Given a device ID to look for (stdin, stdout, or stderr), the function retrieves the associated file handle from the environment database. If a bogus device ID was passed, the function fails and sets the last error code.

Pseudocode for GetStdHandle

```
// Parameters:
//      DWORD    fdwDevice
// Locals:
//      PENVIRONMENT_DATABASE pEDB;

    pEDB = ppCurrentProcess->pEDB;

    if ( fdwDevice == STD_INPUT_HANDLE )
        return pEDB->hStdIn;
    else if ( fdwDevice == STD_OUTPUT_HANDLE )
        return pEDB->hStdOut;
    else if ( fdwDevice == STD_ERROR_HANDLE )
        return pEDB->hStdErr;

    InternalSetLastError( ERROR_INVALID_FUNCTION );

    return 0xFFFFFFFF;
```

SetStdHandle

SetStdHandle is just a tad more interesting than GetStdHandle. The code first verifies that the handle is a valid KERNEL32 object handle. How does it do this? By calling x_ConvertHandleToK32Object, which returns a pointer to the associated KERNEL32 object if the handle is a valid handle. SetStdHandle never uses the K32 object pointer, though — a simple test for a NULL value is all that's required. After verifying the hHandle parameter, the remaining code stuffs the hHandle into the appropriate field in the environment database structure.

Pseudocode for SetStdHandle

```
// Parameters:
//      DWORD   IDStdHandle
//      HANDLE  hHandle
// Locals:
//      PVOID                   pK32Object;
//      PENVIRONMENT_DATABASE pEDB;

    if ( hHandle == STD_INPUT_HANDLE )
    {
        pK32Object =
            x_ConvertHandleToK32Object( hHandle, 0x00002140, 0x00000020 );
    }
    else if ((hHandle == STD_OUTPUT_HANDLE) || (hHandle == STD_ERROR_HANDLE))
    {
        pK32Object =
            x_ConvertHandleToK32Object( hHandle, 0x00002140, 0x00000110 );
    }
    else
    {
        InternalSetLastError( ERROR_INVALID_FUNCTION );
        return FALSE;
    }

    if ( pK32Object )
    {
        pEDB = ppCurrentProcess->pEDB;

        if ( IDStdHandle == STD_INPUT_HANDLE )
            pEDB->hStdIn = hHandle;
        else if ( IDStdHandle == STD_OUTPUT_HANDLE )
            pEDB->hStdOut = hHandle;
        else
            pEDB->hStdErr = hHandle;
    }

    return TRUE;
```

PROCESS HANDLE TABLES

At offset 44h in a PROCESS_DATABASE is a pointer to the handle table for that process. In this section, I use the term *handle* to indicate things that can be referenced via the process handle table. Besides file handles, Windows 95 also creates handles to other system objects. Processes, threads, events, and mutexes are just a few examples. In fact, there can be handles for any of the KERNEL32 objects listed in the "KERNEL32 Objects" section earlier in this chapter.

A handle value is theoretically "opaque." That is, the handle value can't tell you anything about what it's referring to. For instance, given the handle value 5, you can't tell whether it's a file handle or a mutex handle. However, once you understand process handle tables in Windows 95, you can easily correlate a handle value to what it's referring to.

A handle table for a Windows 95 process is quite simple. The first DWORD of the table is the maximum number of handle table entries in the current table. The default at process startup is 0x30 (48) handles. This doesn't mean, however, that a process is limited to 48 open handles. When a process opens more handles than will fit in the current handle table, KERNEL32.DLL reallocates the handle block of memory so the handle table can be grown. The increments appear to be in multiples of 0x10. For example, after outgrowing the initial 0x30 handle entries, the reallocated handle table has 0x40 entries. There doesn't appear to be a significant upper limit on the number of handles. I wrote a small program to open file handles in a loop, and it allocated well over 255 handles (the old DOS limit) before I stopped it.

Immediately following the first DWORD of the handle table is an array of 8-byte structures. Each structure consist of two DWORDS:

DWORD   flags

DWORD   pK32Object

The second field (pK32Object) is a pointer to one of the 17 possible types of KERNEL32 objects that I described earlier in the "KERNEL32 Objects" section. The first DWORD is access control flags for that object. The meaning of the flags depends on what type of object the entry points to. For instance, if the entry points to a process object (K32OBJ_PROCESS), the flags are the PROCESS_xxx flags from WINNT.H (PROCESS_TERMNATE, PROCESS_VM_READ, and so forth).

At this point, you might be suspecting what a handle value represents. If you're guessing that the value of a handle is an index into the process handle table, you're right. Once you know that, you can easily match up a handle value with the type of KERNEL32 object that it refers to. An unused handle table entry is filled with 0's in both DWORDs. When allocating a new handle, KERNEL32 uses the index of the first empty slot in the table. Although browsing through a process handle table isn't suggested programming practice, the WIN32WLK program provides this capability. When using Win32Wlk, note the number and type of handles used by KERNEL32.

THREADS

Now that you've seen modules and processes, we can complete our tour of fundamental KERNEL32 data structures by looking at threads. Although processes primarily represent ownership of things like file handles, an address space, and so on, threads represent the execution of code through modules. You see how all the pieces are interrelated? It's hard to isolate just one and not drag in the others. For example, in the earlier description of processes, I had to have forward references to threads and synchronization objects.

At an abstract level, threads are a convenient way to keep various portions of your program running while other portions are waiting for some external action to occur. By splitting up the various tasks that a process performs into threads, you can usually eliminate things like polling loops. Polling loops waste much of the CPU's time executing the same code repeatedly while waiting for some event (like a key press) to occur.

At any given time, a thread is in one of three basic states. The first state is when the thread is actually running. The actual CPU registers are where the thread's registers are kept. When a thread is in the running state, all other threads in the system are suspended.

The second state is the "ready to run" state. In this state, there's no reason why the thread couldn't be running — except that some other thread is currently using the CPU. In due time, the ready-to-run thread will get control of the CPU.

The third state is the blocked state. When a thread is blocked, it's waiting for something to happen. Until that thing happens, the scheduler won't allow the thread to execute. The things that a thread blocks on are called *synchronization objects*. The Windows 95 synchronization objects are critical sections, mutexes, events, and semaphores.

I described the basic functionality of the Windows 95 synchronization objects in Chapter 2, so I won't repeat myself here. In this book, I don't give the same full treatment to the inner workings of synchronization objects that I give to processes, threads, and modules. There are many good books, such as Jeffrey Richter's *Advanced Windows*, that go over the details of using synchronization objects; consult them if you'd like more information on this topic. In this book, however, you'll just have to assume that synchronization objects exist and that they work as described.

Initially, every process starts out with one thread. If the process wants, it can create additional threads so that the CPU can execute through different sections of the process's code at the same time. The standard example that's wheeled out at this point is that of a word processor. When it comes time for a word processor to print, the program spins off another thread that handles all the printing chores. This allows the primary thread to continue interacting with the user, so he or she can continue working while the printing takes place in the background.

Of course, if you're familiar with basic CPU architecture, you know that a machine with just one CPU can't really execute in more than one location at the same time. The illusion of multiple threads running simultaneously is provided by the VMM scheduler, which uses a hardware timer and a complex set of rules to very quickly switch between different threads.

Microsoft claims that Windows 95 uses a timeslice of 20 milliseconds for scheduling. That is, in the absence of other factors (like thread priorities), each thread will run for 20 milliseconds before the system suspends it and starts up a different thread. I'll talk a little bit more about thread scheduling in the "Thread Priorities" section. However, I'll state up front that this book doesn't provide an in-depth discussion of thread scheduling and the VMM scheduler. As with synchronization objects, this is a topic for another book and another time.

Like processes, every thread is represented internally in KERNEL32.DLL by a block of memory allocated from the shared KERNEL32 heap. This memory block holds all the information KERNEL32 needs to maintain for a thread. (Actually, the block contains a few pointers to information outside the block, but you get the idea.) This memory block is called a thread database (TDB) in this book. (Note that, at different times, Microsoft has used TDB to mean Task Database and Thread Database.) As with process databases, a thread database is a KERNEL32 object. Its first DWORD contains the value 6, branding the block as a K32OBJ_THREAD object.

If you're an advanced programmer who's poked around in the DDK or used WDEB386 or SoftIce/W, you may have encountered another thread-related data structure called a *THCB* (Thread Control Block). THCBs are the ring 0 representation of threads. In Windows 95, threads are represented by separate ring 0 and ring 3 data structures. The ring 0 components, such as VMM.VXD, work with threads primarily via thread control blocks. The ring 3 components, such as KERNEL32.DLL, primarily use the thread database that I'll discuss in the upcoming section called "The Thread Database." This chapter describes ring 3 thread behavior and mechanics, and doesn't attempt to cover the ring 0 side of threads.

Although processes are the primary K32 object that owns things, threads also own (or are associated with) certain items. The first thing that springs to mind when asked, "What would a thread own?" is a register set. As I mentioned earlier, at any given time a thread is either executing or not executing (pretty obvious, huh?). When a thread is executing, its register set is stored in the CPU's registers. That is, the thread's EIP value *is* the value in the EIP register. When a thread isn't executing, its registers need to be stored off into memory somewhere. Therefore, each thread has a pointer to a memory buffer where the thread's register values are stored when it's not executing.

Another thing every thread is associated with is a process. All the threads in a process share access to the things that a process owns. For instance, a process owns a memory context and has a private address space. All the threads in the process run in the same address space. A process also has a handle table for referring to files, events, consoles, memory mapped files, and so on. All threads in the process share the same handle values. For example, if handle value 3 refers to a memory mapped file, any thread in the process can use handle value 3 to refer to that memory mapped file.

Threads also own many other things. Each thread has its own stack area, its own window message queue, its own set of Thread Local Storage values, and its own structured exception handling chain. (In case you don't know what the latter two items are, I'll be describing them shortly.) In addition, a thread also acquires and releases ownership of the various synchronization objects that the thread uses during its execution. We'll go through all the things a thread owns when we look at the layout of a thread database a bit later.

WHAT'S A THREAD HANDLE? WHAT'S A THREAD ID?

Earlier in the chapter, I described the difference between a process handle and a process ID. It turns out that the description I gave could easily be repeated for thread and handles and thread IDs. Just replace the word "process" with the word "thread" and you're all set. If you're at all unsure about the difference between a process handle and a process ID, go back and reread the "What's a Process Handle? What's a Process ID?" section, since I'm going to give just the summarized version for threads here.

The GetThreadHandle function returns a constant value (a "pseudohandle" in Microsoft-speak) that can be used wherever a true thread handle can be used:

Pseudocode for GetCurrentThread

```
x_LogSomeKernelFunction( function number for GetCurrentThread );

return 0xFFFFFFFE;
```

Like GetCurrentProcessId, the GetCurrentThreadId would return a pointer to the current thread database, except that the KERNEL32 coders intentionally obfuscate (or obsfucate, which is the Microsoft misspelling) the return value:

Pseudocode for GetCurrentThreadId

```
return TDBToTid( ppCurrentThread );
```

How does KERNEL32 obfuscate the thread return value? Let's look:

Pseudocode for TDBToTid

```
// Parameters:
//      THREAD_DATABASE * ptdb

    if ( ObsfucatorDWORD == FALSE )
    {
        _DebugOut( "TDBToTid() Called too early! Obsfucator not yet"
                    " initialized!" );
        return 0;
    }

    if ( ptdb & 1 )
    {
        _DebugOut( "TDBToTid: This TDB looks like a TID (0%1xh) Do a"
                    " stack trace BEFORE reporting as bug." );
    }

    // Here's the key! XOR the obsfucator DWORD with the thread database
    // pointer to make the TID value.

    return ptdb ^ ObsfucatorDWORD;
```

If this looks amazingly similar to the PDBToPID function earlier in the chapter, you're right. KERNEL32 uses a single ObsfucatorDWORD to "convert" process and thread database pointers into IDs. Once you figure out what the ObsfucatorDWORD value is (and keep in mind that Microsoft misspelled it), you can use it to convert either process or thread IDs into useful pointers. Again, this isn't recommended programming practice, but for the purpose of understanding how the system works, there's not much of an alternative.

THE THREAD DATABASE

The thread database is a KERNEL32 object (type K32OBJ_THREAD) that's allocated from the KERNEL32 shared heap. Like process databases, the thread databases aren't directly linked together in a linked-list fashion. The THREADB.H file from the WIN32WLK sources has a C-style structure definition for a thread database. The format of a thread database is as follows:

00h   DWORD   Type
This DWORD contains 6, the KERNEL32 object type for a thread.

04h   DWORD   cReference
This DWORD contains the reference count for the thread. This is the number of things that are currently using the thread structure for something (for example, they have an open handle for the thread).

08h   PPROCESS_DATABASE   pProcess
This PROCESS_DATABASE is a pointer to the process this thread belongs to.

0Ch   DWORD   pSomeEvent
This DWORD is a pointer to an event object (K32OBJ_EVENT). Event objects are passed to functions like WaitForSingleObject. It appears that this event is what's actually waited on when you pass a thread handle to one of the WaitForSingleEvent family of functions.

10h   DWORD   pvExcept
This DWORD is a pointer to the head of the structured exception handling chain. (Structured exception handling is a whole topic unto itself, so I'll defer a discussion of it until later in the chapter.) Note that this field also marks the beginning of a TIB (thread information block) structure nested within the task database. The TIB structure is also described later in this chapter.

14h   DWORD   TopOfStack

This DWORD holds the maximum (topmost) address in the stack area allocated for this thread. The typical amount of address space reserved for each thread's stack is 1MB.

18h   DWORD   StackLow

This DWORD holds the lowest page aligned address in the stack area that this thread's stack is using. In a sense, this field is a low water mark — by subtracting this field from the TopOfStack field, you can get a sense of how much stack the thread uses.

1Ch   WORD   W16TDB

This WORD holds the Win16 global memory handle (essentially, a selector) for the Win16 task database. As Chapter 7 explains, each process (be it Win16 or Win32) has both a 16-bit task database segment and a Win32 process database.

1Eh   WORD   StackSelector16

Win32 code needs to switch to a 16-bit stack before it can thunk down to 16-bit code. This WORD in the thread database holds the selector that KERNEL32 sets up as the 16-bit stack selector when thunking down to 16-bit code.

20h   DWORD   SelmanList

A pointer to the SelmanList for this thread. (Selman is short for "Selector Manager.") The Selman component of KERNEL32 seems to be responsible for managing lists of selectors that threads can allocate for various uses (for instance, thunking between 16- and 32-bit code).

24h   DWORD   UserPointer

The precise meaning of this DWORD is unclear. However, the documentation for the TIB structure says this field is available for use by application programs. Remember, the TIB structure is nested within the thread database structure.

28h   PTIB   pTIB

This field points to the thread information block (TIB) for this thread. In Windows 95, the TIB is within the thread database, so this pointer points to another field in this thread database (the pvExcept field at offset 10h, to be exact).

2Ch *WORD* *TIBFlags*

This WORD contains flags for this TIB. These flags are known:

Flag name and bit value	Description
TIBF_WIN32 0x0001	This thread is from a Win32 application.
TIBF_TRAP 0x0002	Some sort of exception handling.

2Eh *WORD* *Win16MutexCount*

This field is somehow related to the Win16Mutex (which is also known as the Win16Lock). Normally, this field is –1 for Win32 threads and 0 for Win16 threads.

30h *DWORD* *DebugContext*

If the process associated with this thread is being debugged, this field points to a debug context structure. The format of this structure is unknown, but it appears to have register values for the debuggee process in it. If the process isn't being debugged, this DWORD is 0.

34h *PDWORD* *pCurrentPriority*

This field points to a DWORD that contains the current priority level of the thread. The DWORD that this field points to is above address 0xC0000000, which places it squarely in VxD land.

38h *DWORD* *MessageQueue*

The low WORD of this DWORD holds a Win16 global heap handle for the thread's message queue. Message queues are how window messages move through the system; they are described in Chapter 4. This field is closely related to the W16TDB field at offset 1Ch.

3Ch *PDWORD* *pTLSArray*

This pointer points to the thread's TLS array. The entries in this array are used by the TlsSetValue family of functions. TLS is described later in this chapter. The actual memory for the TLS array comes a bit later in the thread database.

40h *PPROCESS_DATABASE* *pProcess2*

This DWORD contains a pointer to the process that this thread is associated with. It seems to always be a duplicate of the pointer at offset 08h in the thread database.

44h   DWORD   *Flags*

This DWORD holds various flags for the thread. The following values are known:

Flag name and bit value	Description
fCreateThreadEvent 0x00000001	Set if the thread is being debugged.
fCancelExceptionAbort 0x00000002	
fOnTempStack 0x00000004	
fGrowableStack 0x00000008	
fDelaySingleStep 0x00000010	
fOpenExeAsImmovableFile 0x00000020	
fCreateSuspended 0x00000040	CREATE_SUSPENDED flag to CreateProcess.
fStackOverflow 0x00000080	
fNestedCleanAPCs 0x00000100	APC = Asynchronous Procedure Call
fWasOemNowAnsi 0x00000200	ANSI/OEM file functions
fOKToSetThreadOem 0x00000400	ANSI/OEM file functions

48h   DWORD   *TerminationStatus*

This is the value that would be returned by calling GetExitCodeThread. The thread exit code is the value returned from the function where thread execution begins. Alternatively, it can be specified when a thread calls ExitThread or TerminateThread. While a thread is still actively running, its exit code is 0x103 (STILL_ACTIVE).

4Ch   WORD   *TIBSelector*

This WORD is an extremely important field. It contains a selector that references the current thread's TIB (thread information block). The TIB contains vital information, such as the head of the exception handler chain for the thread. As Windows 95 switches between threads, it updates the FS register to contain this value. By doing this, the current thread can always look up information about itself by using the memory pointed at by the FS register.

4Eh   *WORD*   *EmulatorSelector*
This WORD might be a selector that points to a block of memory with information about the current 80387 emulator state for the thread. This data area probably includes an FSAVE-style structure. On machines using a math coprocessor, this field is always 0.

50h   *DWORD*   *cHandles*
The meaning of this DWORD is unknown. It appears to always be 0.

54h   *DWORD*   *WaitNodeList*
If the thread is waiting for one or more events to be signaled, this field points to a linked list of event nodes stored up in VxD land. Each node holds a pointer to an event object and a pointer to the thread that's waiting on the event.

58h   *DWORD*   *un4*
The meaning of this DWORD is unknown. It's typically either 0 or 2.

5Ch   *DWORD*   *Ring0Thread*
This DWORD holds a pointer to the ring 0 Thread Control Block (THCB) for this thread.

60   *PTDBX*   *pTDBX*
This field points to a TDBX structure. The TDBX structure is VWIN32.VXD's representation of a thread. The TDBX structure is described in more detail in Chapter 6.

64h   *DWORD*   *StackBase*
For Win32 threads, this DWORD holds the lowest possible address that the thread's stack can use. By subtracting this value from the maximum stack address (offset 14h), you can calculate how much address space has been reserved for the stack. For Win16 threads, this field is 0.

68h   *DWORD*   *TerminationStack*
Based on its name, this field contains the ESP value that the thread's termination should initially use. For Win32 threads, this value is the same as the TopOfStack value (offset 14h). For Win16 threads, this field holds an address just below the shared KERNEL32 heap.

6Ch   DWORD   *EmulatorData*

Presumably, this field is a 32-bit linear address for the thread's 80387 emulator data. If so, this field is related to the EmulatorSelector field (offset 4Eh).

70h   DWORD   *GetLastErrorCode*

This DWORD holds the value that GetLastError returns for the current thread. This value can be set by calling SetLastError.

74h   DWORD   *DebuggerCB*

If a thread is acting as a debugger thread (that is, if it's calling WaitForDebugEvent), this field contains a pointer to a block of information used by the debugger. The information in this field includes pointers to the debugger's process database, thread database, and the debuggee's thread database.

78h   DWORD   *DebuggerThread*

If this thread is being debugged, this field contains a non-NULL value. The meaning of the value isn't known because it's too low to be a valid pointer.

7Ch   PCONTEXT   *ThreadContext*

This pointer points to an Intel CONTEXT structure as defined in WINNT.H. This structure holds the register values for the thread when the thread isn't the currently running thread. This structure is read from and written to with the GetThreadContext and SetThreadContext functions. This field is only non-zero when the process is being debugged.

80h   DWORD   *Except16List*

The exact meaning of this DWORD is unknown, although from the name, it would appear to have something to do with exception handling. In my tests, it was always 0.

84h   DWORD   *ThunkConnect*

The exact meaning of this DWORD is also unknown. From the name, you might think it has something to do with thunking. In my tests, it was always 0.

88h   DWORD   *NegStackBase*

If you add the value of this field to the StackBase field (offset 64h), you'll get FFEF9000. Don't ask me why.

8Ch   DWORD   *CurrentSS*

This DWORD holds a 16-bit stack selector for thunking from 32-bit code down to 16-bit code. This field appears to be related to the very similar StackSelector16 field (offset 1Eh). The difference in usage between the two fields is currently unknown.

90h   DWORD   SSTable

This field is a pointer to a memory block containing information about the 16-bit stack to be used when thunking down to 16-bit code.

94h   DWORD   ThunkSS16

This DWORD contains yet another selector value used for thunking. In some threads, it matches the value in the StackSelector16 field (offset 1Eh), while in other threads it has the same value as the CurrentSS field (offset 8Ch).

98h   DWORD   TLSArray[64]

The TLSArray field is an array of 64 DWORDs. Each DWORD holds the value that TLSGetValue returns for a given TLS ID. For instance, the first DWORD in the array is returned by TLSGetValue(0). The second DWORD is returned by TLSGetValue(1), and so on. TLS is described in a subsequent section of this chapter.

198h   DWORD   DeltaPriority

This DWORD holds the difference in priority of this thread as compared to the priority class of the owning process. Typical values for this field would be:

THREAD_PRIORITY_LOWEST	−2
THREAD_PRIORITY_BELOW_NORMAL	−1
THREAD_PRIORITY_NORMAL	0
THREAD_PRIORITY_HIGHEST	1
THREAD_PRIORITY_ABOVE_NORMAL	2

19Ch   DWORD   un5[7]

This stretch of DWORDs appears to always be 0. The meanings are unknown.

1B8h   DWORD   pCreateData16

If nonzero, this field points to a structure with two 32-bit pointers:

    00h pProcessInfo — a PPROCESS_INFORMATION
    04h pStartupInfo — a PSTARTUPINFO

In all my testing, however, the pCreateData16 pointer was always 0.

1BCh   DWORD   APISuspendCount

This field is incremented each time SuspendThread is called and decremented each time ResumeThread is invoked.

1C0h   DWORD   un6

The meaning of this DWORD field is unknown.

1C4h   DWORD   WOWChain

This field presumably has something to do with WOW (Windows On Windows) support in Windows 95. WOW is the method by which Windows NT runs 16-bit applications in their own protected address space, which keeps them from potentially crashing 32-bit applications. The field was always 0 during testing.

1C8h   WORD   wSSBig

Based on the name, this field contains a flat 32-bit selector for use as a stack segment. However, the field was always 0 during testing.

1CAh   WORD   un7

The meaning of this WORD is unknown. It may be just filler to keep the subsequent fields DWORD aligned.

1CCh   DWORD   lp16SwitchRec

The meaning of this DWORD is unknown, but based on the name, it probably has some connection to Win16 thunking.

1D0h   DWORD   un8[5]

These five DWORDS appear to always be 0. Their meaning is unknown.

1E4h   DWORD   pSomeCritSect1;

This field points to a critical section object (K32OBJ_CRITICAL_SECTION). The critical section is different for each process. The purpose of this particular critical section is unknown. This field seems to always have the same value as pSomeCritSect2 (described below).

1E8h   DWORD   pWin16Mutex;

This pointer points to the Win16Mutex in KRNL386.EXE.

1ECh   DWORD   pWin32Mutex;

This pointer points to the Krn32Mutex in KERNEL32.DLL.

1F0h   DWORD   pSomeCritSect2;

This field points to a critical section object (K32OBJ_CRITICAL_SECTION). The critical section is different for each process. This field seems to always have the same value as pSomeCritSect1 (described earlier in the structure).

1F4h   DWORD   un9;

This DWORD's meaning is currently unknown. It appears to always be set to 0.

1F8h   DWORD   ripString

From the name, you might think this field is a PSTR for a string that will be used during a FatalAppExit RIP. However, in almost all cases, this field is 0, and when nonzero, it doesn't point to a character string.

200h   DWORD   LastTlsSetValueEIP[64]

This array of 64 DWORDs is a parallel array to the primary TLS array at offset 98h in the thread database. Each DWORD in this array corresponds to a TLS index value, and each contains the EIP where the corresponding TLS indexed value was last set from. The EIP value is retrieved from the stack frame set up by TlsSetValue.

A final note on the thread database: There's more than one way to get a pointer to a thread database. Besides the XOR'ing trick I alluded to earlier, each Win16 task database also contains a pointer to a thread database. At offset 54h in a Win16 task database is the linear address of the thread database for the task/process's first thread.

THE THREAD INFORMATION BLOCK (TIB)

Within the thread database, certain fields are immensely useful to running programs. In fact, they're so useful that the Win32 architecture makes them immediately accessible without looking them up in the thread database structure. These fields are encompassed in a structure called the Thread Information Block (or TIB, as KERNEL32 refers to it). The fields of a Windows 95 TIB encompass offsets 10h through 3Ch in a thread database.

How does application code access the TIB? If you've looked at much assembly language output for compiled Win32 code, you've probably noticed that the FS segment register is used quite a bit. Wait a minute! Isn't Win32 supposed to remove segments from the programming picture? Although the answer is yes, under the hood the Win32 architecture (Windows NT, Windows 95, and Windows Win32s) dedicates the FS register to pointing at the thread information block for the current thread. As it turns out, Win32 wasn't the first operating system to do this. OS/2 2.0 did it long before Win32 arrived on the scene. As you might suspect, when Windows 95 switches threads, the scheduler has to update the FS register to contain the selector that points to the new thread's TIB.

The primary use of the FS register and the TIB is to add entries to the structured exception handling chain (which I'll describe later in the chapter). The head of the structured exception handling chain is at offset 0 in the TIB, so when you see assembler code using FS:[0], you know it's doing something related to structured exception handling.

Two other fields in the Windows 95 TIB that are used quite extensively are the pvQueue and pvTLSArray fields (offsets 28h and 2Ch, respectively). The pvQueue field contains the queue handle for the current thread's message queue. This field is used frequently by USER.EXE's windowing system code, because in Windows 95 things like the focus window are stored on a per-thread basis. The pvTLSArray field points to the thread local storage array in the thread databases. The compiler vendors use it in conjunction with the .tls section in the executable file to provide transparent per-thread global variables.

Although the layout of the TIB structure can be inferred from the thread database structure, it bears a brief summarization here. A C structure definition can be found in TIB.H from the WIN32WLK sources. A formal Microsoft definition for the first couple of items is in the NTDDK.H file from the Windows NT 3.5 DDK (along with a stern warning that the fields must be compatible with OS/2 2.0). This is apparently a remnant from the early days of NT, when Microsoft was still trying to give the impression that it cared about OS/2. (See Z. Pascal Zachary's book *Showstopper* for some interesting stories on this particular topic.)

The TIB fields in Windows 95 are as follows:

00h	DWORD	pvExcept
04h	DWORD	TopOfStack
08h	DWORD	StackLow
0Ch	WORD	W16TDB
0Eh	WORD	StackSelector16
10h	DWORD	SelmanList
14h	DWORD	UserPointer
18h	PTIB	pTIB
1Ch	WORD	TIBFlags
1Eh	WORD	Win16MutexCount
20h	DWORD	DebugContext
24h	PDWORD	pCurrentPriority
28h	DWORD	MessageQueue
2Ch	PDWORD	pTLSArray
30h	DWORD	pProcess (process database pointer)

For a description of each of the fields, add 10h to the offset and look up that offset in "The Thread Database" section earlier in the chapter. Note that only some of these fields are common across all Win32 platforms.

THREAD PRIORITIES

The core scheduler in the Windows 95 Virtual Machine Manager (VMM) has no real knowledge of processes. Instead, it concentrates on scheduling the threads with the highest priority, without regard to what process they're in. Put another way, processes don't *really* have a priority. Still, to the end-user of these thread scheduling services (that is, to the application programmer), it's a useful abstraction to think of processes as having a priority. The SetPriorityClass and SetPriorityClass functions act as interpreters between the two views of process/thread priorities.

At any given time, the thread with the highest priority that isn't waiting on something is the thread that's going to be run. To ensure a smoothly running system and prevent many problems, the system changes the priority of threads on the fly. For instance, a thread's priority may be temporarily boosted when an I/O operation it's waiting for completes. Going into thread scheduling in any more detail than this could easily require a large chapter of its own. Therefore, I'm going to put off a detailed discussion of thread priorities for another book (or perhaps a future magazine article).

Within the Windows 95 VMM scheduler, there are 32 distinct priority levels. These 32 levels are broken into four groups, known as priority classes. Each priority class is associated with a specific priority level that is the default priority for threads of that priority class. Within the priority class, threads can vary from two below the default priority to two above. (There are also some special cases such as THREAD_PRIORITY_LEVEL, where a thread's priority can be bounced entirely out of its priority class.) Unless specifically instructed to do otherwise, when the operating system creates a process, the new process is given the NORMAL_PRIORITY_CLASS.

The four priority classes, their default priority values, and their range of priority values are as follows:

Priority	Default value	Range of priority level
IDLE_PRIORITY_CLASS	4	2 – 6
NORMAL_PRIORITY_CLASS	9 or 7 (9 if foreground process; 7 otherwise)	6 – 10
HIGH_PRIORITY_CLASS	13	11 – 15
REALTIME_PRIORITY_CLASS	24	16 – 31

The thread priority of 1 is a special case. Threads that are nominally of the IDLE_PRIORITY_CLASS, NORMAL_PRIORITY_CLASS, or HIGH_PRIORITY_CLASS can be set to priority level 1 via the SetPriorityClass function.

As a side note on Windows 95 priority levels, the 32 levels in the Windows 95 scheduler don't correspond numerically to the values for the priority classes in WINBASE.H. For example, NORMAL_PRIORITY_CLASS is 0x20 in WINBASE.H. Windows 95's KERNEL32.DLL maps these values to the appropriate Windows 95 thread scheduler priority value.

GetThreadPriority

GetThreadPriority is a simple function. Given a thread handle (which can be for any thread in any process), the code converts the handle into a pointer to the process database for that thread. Assuming the handle conversion went smoothly, GetThreadPriority returns the value of the DeltaPriority field (offset 198h) in the thread database. All this code is wrapped by an EnterSysLevel and LeaveSysLevel to prevent problems with an inopportune thread switch.

Pseudocode for GetThreadPriority

```
// Parameters:
//      HANDLE  hThread;
// Locals:
//      PTHREAD_DATABASE ptdb;
//      DWORD   retValue;

    x_LogSomeKernelFunction( function number for GetThreadPriority );

    _EnterSysLevel( pKrn32Mutex );
```

```
    retValue = 0x7FFFFFFF;

    ptdb = x_ConvertHandleToK32Object( hThread, 0x20, 0 );

    if ( ptdb )
        retValue = ptdb->DeltaPriority;

    _LeaveSysLevel( pKrn32Mutex );
```

SetThreadPriority

The SetThreadPriority code is broken up into four parts. First, the function
converts the thread handle into a thread database pointer. Second,
SetThreadPriority validates the passed-in new priority to see if it's within the
allowable range. Third, the code uses the internal CalculateNewPriority function to convert the input priority parameter into one of the 32 thread priorities used by the Windows 95 scheduler. We'll look at CalculateNewPriority
in the next section.

Finally, SetThreadPriority calls VWIN32.VXD to inform the ring 0
components of the new priority. The mechanism by which KERNEL32
calls into ring 0 is the VxDCall functions (for example, VxDCall0). Ring 3
components invoke Win32 VxD services by using VxDCall. In this case,
VWIN32.VXD provides a ring 3 callable service to set a thread's priority.
Win32 VxD services are new in Windows 95 and play a key part in the ring
0–ring 3 interactions. In fact, the new Windows 95 Win32 VxD services
are so important that much of Chapter 6 is devoted to describing them.
Because Win32 VxD services will be covered thoroughly a bit later in the
book, I won't dwell on the actual mechanics of VxDCall in this chapter.

Pseudocode for SetThreadPriority

```
// Parameters:
//     HANDLE  hThread
//     int     nPriority;
// Locals:
//     PTHREAD_DATABASE ptdb;
//     DWORD   retValue;

    x_LogSomeKernelFunction( function number for SetThreadPriority );

    _EnterSysLevel( pKrn32Mutex );
```

```
    ptdb = x_ConvertHandleToK32Object( hThread, 0x20, 0 );
    if ( ptdb )
    {

        if (    (nPriority < THREAD_BASE_PRIORITY_MIN)
            && (nPriority > THREAD_BASE_PRIORITY_MAX) )
        {
            if (    (nPriority != THREAD_BASE_PRIORITY_LOWRT)
                && (nPriority != THREAD_BASE_PRIORITY_IDLE) )
            {
                InternalSetLastError( ERROR_INVALID_PRIORITY );
                goto error;
            }
        }

        ptdb->DeltaPriority = nPriority;

        if ( ptdb->Ring0Thread )
        {
            DWORD newAbsPriority = CalculateNewPriority(ptdb, ptdb->pProcess2);

            // Call into VWIN32 to do the real work.
            // Set_Thread_Win32_Pri == 0x002A0021
            VxDCall0(Set_Thread_Win32_Pri, ptdb->Ring0Thread, newAbsPriority);
        }

        retValue = TRUE;
    }
    else
    {
error:
        retValue = FALSE;
    }

    _LeaveSysLevel( pKrn32Mutex );

    return retValue;
```

CalculateNewPriority

The CalculateNewPriority function encapsulates the rules for thread priorities in the Windows 95 scheduler. Given a process and a thread, it calculates the priority level (within the range of 1 – 31) that the thread should have. From the process database, the function extracts the priority class for the thread (normal, idle, high, or realtime). To this base priority, it adds the thread's delta priority. The delta priority is typically in the range of +– 2. After adding the priority class priority to the thread's delta priority, the code makes sure the new priority is within the expected bounds. It's worth noting that realtime priority threads get special handling here; that's because the range of realtime priority levels is greater than the ranges of the other priority classes.

Pseudocode for CalculateNewPriority

```
// Parameters:
//   PTHREAD_DATABASE ptdb;
//   PPROCESS_DATABASE ppdb;
// Locals:
//      DWORD baseProcPri
//      DWORD sum
//      DWORD upperLimit, lowerLimit

    baseProcPri = ppdb->BasePriority;

    if ((baseProcPri != 4) &&
        (baseProcPri != 8) &&
        (baseProcPri != 13) &&
        (baseProcPri != 24))
    {
        x_Assertion2( "..\priority.c" );
    }

    sum = ptdb->DeltaPriority + ppdb->BasePriority;

    if ( ppdb->BasePriority == 24 ) // Real time class thread?
    {
        upperLimit = 31
        lowerLimit = 16
    }
    else                            // Other priority class.
    {
        upperLimit = 15
        lowerLimit = 1
    }

    if ( upperLimit >= sum )
        upperLimit = sum

    if ( lowerLimit <= upperLimit )
        return upperLimit;
    else
        return lowerLimit;
```

SetPriorityClass

The SetPriorityClass function lets the caller change the priority class for all the threads of a process. The function starts by converting its hProcess parameter into a PPROCESS_DATABASE pointer. Using the pointer, the function determines the process's current priority class. If it's the same as the new priority class, the function bails out because there's nothing to be done.

If the new priority class is different from the previous class, SetPriorityClass plugs the default value for the new priority class into the BasePriority field of the process database. But wait, there's more! Earlier, I mentioned that the notion of process priority classes is just an illusion, since the VMM scheduler concerns itself only with threads, and not with processes. To bridge the two views of priority levels, SetPriorityClass loops through each of the threads in the process and calls into VWIN32.VXD to set the new priority for each thread.

There's one slight twist to note here. Threads can have priorities that differ slightly from the default class priority. This difference is kept in the "DeltaPriority" field of the thread database (we'll look at this field later). SetPriorityClass has to take into account each thread's priority delta when calculating the new priority value for the thread. The CalculateNewPriority function (just described) does this calculation.

Pseudocode for SetPriorityClass

```
// Parameters:
//      HANDLE  hProcess
//      DWORD   fdwPriority
// Locals:
//      BOOL    retValue
//      PPROCESS_DATABASE ppdb;
//      PTHREAD_DATABASE ptdb;
//      DWORD   newPriority
//      PK32OBJECTLISTENTRY pK32Object;

    x_LogSomeKernelFunction( function number for SetPriorityClass );

    _EnterSysLevel( pKrn32Mutex );

    ppdb = x_ConvertHandleToK32Object( hProcess, 0x10, 0 );

    if ( ppdb )
    {
        retValue = TRUE;
```

```
        if ( fdwPriority == NORMAL_PRIORITY_CLASS )
            goto SetNormal;

        if ( fdwPriority == IDLE_PRIORITY_CLASS )
            goto SetIdle;

        if ( fdwPriority == REALTIME_PRIORITY_CLASS )
            goto SetHigh;

        if ( fdwPriority == HIGH_PRIORITY_CLASS )
            goto SetRealTime;

        // None of the allowable priorities was specified, so bomb out.
        retValue = FALSE;
        InternalSetLastError( ERROR_INVALID_PRIORITY );
        goto done;

SetNormal:
        if ( ppdb->BasePriority == 8 )  // No change from previous state?
            goto done;
        ppdb->BasePriority = 8;
        goto SetIt;

SetIdle:
        if ( ppdb->BasePriority == 4 )  // No change from previous state?
            goto done;
        ppdb->BasePriority = 4;
        goto SetIt;

SetHigh:
        if ( ppdb->BasePriority == 13 ) // No change from previous state?
            goto done;
        ppdb->BasePriority = 13;
        goto SetIt;

SetRealTime:
        if ( ppdb->BasePriority == 24 ) // No change from previous state?
            goto done;
        ppdb->BasePriority = 24;

SetIt:
        // Start looping through all the threads for this process.
        pK32object = x_GetNextObjectInList( ppdb->ThreadList, 0 );

        while ( pK32object )
        {
            ptdb = pK32object->pObject;
```

```
                    if ( ptdb->Ring0Thread )
                    {
                        // Calculate the new priority, taking into account the
                        // process's base priority and the thread's relative priority.
                        newPriority = CalculateNewPriority( ptdb, ppdb );

                        // Call into VWIN32 to do the Dirty Deed (Done Dirt Cheap).
                        // VxDCall ID == 0x002A0021
                        VxDCall0(Set_Thread_Win32_Pri, ptdb->Ring0Thread, newPriority);
                    }

                    pK32Object = x_GetNextObjectInList( ppdb->ThreadList, 1 );
                }
            }
            else
            {
                retValue = FALSE;
            }

    done:

        _LeaveSysLevel( pKrn32Mutex );

        return retValue;
```

GetPriorityClass

The GetPriorityClass function returns the priority class for the specified
process. After changing the hProcess parameter into a PPROCESS_
DATABASE, the function retrieves the priority class from the process
database. This priority level should be in the range of 1 – 31, which is
different from the xxx_PRIORITY_CLASS #define's in WINBASE.H.
Therefore, GetPriorityClass converts the VMM scheduler priority level
into the corresponding xxx_PRIORITY_CLASS flag.

Pseudocode for GetPriorityClass

```
// Parameters:
//   HANDLE   hProcess
// Locals:
//   DWORD    retValue;

    x_LogSomeKernelFunction( function number for GetPriorityClass );
```

```
        retValue = 0;

        _EnterSysLevel( pKrn32Mutex );

        ppdb = x_ConvertHandleToK32Object( hProcess, 0x10, 0 );

        if ( ppdb )
        {
            if ( ppdb->BasePriority == 4 )
                retValue = IDLE_PRIORITY_CLASS;
            else if ( ppdb->BasePriority == 8 )
                retValue = NORMAL_PRIORITY_CLASS;
            else if ( ppdb->BasePriority == 13 )
                retValue = HIGH_PRIORITY_CLASS;
            else if ( ppdb->BasePriority == 24)
                retValue = REALTIME_PRIORITY_CLASS;
        }

        _LeaveSysLevel( pKrn32Mutex );

        return retValue;
```

THREAD EXECUTION CONTROL

The Win32 API provides a small set of APIs for modifying and querying the execution status of other threads. At a low level, one thread can read and write the registers of another thread (assuming the first thread has a valid handle for the other thread). On a broader level, there are Win32 functions that let you freeze and thaw the execution of other threads. Let's look at these thread control functions now.

GetThreadContext and IGetThreadContext

GetThreadContext enables one thread to obtain a copy of the register values of another thread. At any given time, a thread is either executing or is suspended. While a thread is in the suspended state, its register values are kept in a data structure known as a *thread context*. The GetThreadContext function lets you read the values in a suspended thread's thread context structure. As input, SetThreadContext takes a copy of a thread context structure (a CONTEXT in WINNT.H).

The actual GetThreadContext is just a parameter validation layer. It verifies that the pointer passed in points to memory of sufficient size to hold a CONTEXT structure. If so, the code jumps to the internal IGetThreadContext routine.

IGetThreadContext is a convoluted routine. It starts by converting the hThread parameter into a thread database pointer. Then, it calls the x_ThreadContext_CopyRegs to copy the input register set into the ring 3 CONTEXT structure for the thread. (x_ThreadContext_CopyRegs is described in the next section.) In addition to copying the register in the ring 3 CONTEXT structures, IGetThreadContext also calls into VWIN32.VXD to get the ring 0 version of these register. The reasons why there are both ring 0 and ring 3 versions of the registers isn't entirely clear.

After filling in the input CONTEXT structure, GetThreadContext verifies that the CS and flags registers contain valid values. (In this case, *valid* means that the CS register is set to the selector used to execute ring 3 code.) The flags register test is a simple check to make sure the V86 mode flag isn't on.

Pseudocode for GetThreadContext

```
// Parameters:
//      HANDLE      hThread
/       LPCONTEXT   lpContext

    Set up structured exception handling frame

    Touch the first and last bytes that lpContext point to.
    If a fault occurs, it's considered a bad pointer, and the exception
    handler returns FALSE;

    Remove structured exception handling frame

    goto IGetThreadContext;
```

Pseudocode for IGetThreadContext

```
// Parameters:
//      HANDLE      hThread
//      LPCONTEXT   lpContext
// Locals:
//      PTHREAD_DATABASE ptdb;
//      BOOL    retValue
//      DWORD   errCode;
```

```
retValue = TRUE;

x_CheckNotSysLevel_Win16_Krn32_mutexes();

x_LogSomeKernelFunction( function number for GetThreadContext );

_EnterSysLevel( pKrn32Mutex );

ptdb = x_ConvertHandleToK32Object( hThread, 0x20, 0 );

if ( !ptdb )
{
    retValue = FALSE;
}
else    // Found a valid process database.
{
    // Is there a valid ThreadContext field in the thread database?
    if ( ptdb->ThreadContext )
    {
        x_ThreadContext_CopyRegs( lpContext->ContextFlags,
                                  pdtb->ThreadContext, lpContext );
    }
    else    // ThreadContext is 0 in the thread database.
    {
        if ( ptdb->DebugContext && ptdb->DebugContext.SomeField )
        {
            // Are floating point or debug regs specified?
            if ( lpContext->ContextFlags
                & (CONTEXT_FLOATING_POINT | CONTEXT_DEBUG_REGISTERS) )
            {
                ptdb->DebugContext.ThreadContext.ContextFlags
                    = (CONTEXT_FLOATING_POINT | CONTEXT_DEBUG_REGISTERS);

                // Call VWIN32 to do the copying.
                // _VWIN32_Get_Thread_Context == 0x002A0014
                retValue = VxDCall0( _VWIN32_Get_Thread_Context,
                                     ptdb->Ring0Thread,
                                     &ptdb->DebugContext.ThreadContext );

                if ( retValue == 0 )
                    goto error;
            }

            x_ThreadContext_CopyRegs( lpContext->ContextFlags,
                                      &ptdb->DebugContext.ThreadContext,
                                      lpContext );
        }
```

```
            else    // ptdb->DebugContext.SomeField == 0
            {
                if ( lpContext->ContextFlags == 0xFFFFFFFF )
                {
                    x_Assertion2( line number, "..\deb.c" );
                }

                // Call VWIN32 to do the copying.  _VWIN32_Get_Thread_Context
                // == 0x002A0014
                retValue = VxDCall0( _VWIN32_Get_Thread_Context,
                                     ptdb->Ring0Thread, lpContext );
            }
        }
    }

    if ( retValue == FALSE )
        goto error;

    if ( lpContext->CONTEXT_CONTROL & 1 )    // Were CONTEXT_CONTROL regs
    {                                        // requested?

        // Make sure the right CS is in the context buffer.
        if ( lpContext->SegCs != Ring3_flatCS )
            x_Assertion2( line number, "..\deb.c" );

        // Make sure the VM (V86 mode) flag isn't set in the EFlags field.
        if ( lpContext->EFlags & 0x20000 )
            x_Assertion2( line number, "..\deb.c" );
    }

    errCode = ERROR_SUCCESS;        // = 0

error:
    if ( retValue == FALSE )
        retValue = GetLastError();

    SomeOutputFunction( "GetThreadContext ptdb %08x lpContext %08x eip %08x "
                        "esp %08x ebp %08x erc %d\n",
                        ptdb, lpContext, lpContext->Eip, lpContext->Esp,
                        lpContext->Ebp, errCode );

    _LeaveSysLevel( pKrn32Mutex );

    return retValue;
```

x_ThreadContext_CopyRegs

The x_ThreadContext_CopyRegs routine (my name) copies selected sets of registers from a source CONTEXT record into the corresponding fields of a destination CONTEXT. The CONTEXT record is defined for the $x86$ chips in WINNT.H, and the first field is a DWORD of flags indicating which registers should be copied within the CONTEXT.

The grouping of registers set up for the $x86$ chips is as follows:

CONTEXT_DEBUG_REGISTERS	Debug registers 0 – 3,6,7
CONTEXT_FLOATING_POINT	Math coprocessor state
CONTEXT_SEGMENTS	DS, ES, FS, GS
CONTEXT_INTEGER	EAX, EBX, ECX, EDX, ESI, EDI
CONTEXT_CONTROL	SS:ESP, CS:EIP, EFLAGS, EBP

The x_ThreadContext_CopyRegs function is straightforward. It dutifully checks each of the flags in the source context, and if set, copies the corresponding register values into the destination context. No surprises to be found in this code.

Pseudocode for x_ThreadContext_CopyRegs

```
// Parameters:
//      DWORD      flags
//      PCONTEXT   pSrcCtx;
//      PCONTEXT   pDestCtx;

    if ( flags & 0x00000010 )        // CONTEXT_DEBUG_REGISTERS
    {
        // Copy the debug registers over.
        pDestCtx->Dr0 = pSrcCtx->Dr0;
        pDestCtx->Dr1 = pSrcCtx->Dr1;
        pDestCtx->Dr2 = pSrcCtx->Dr2;
        pDestCtx->Dr3 = pSrcCtx->Dr3;
        pDestCtx->Dr6 = pSrcCtx->Dr6;
        pDestCtx->Dr7 = pSrcCtx->Dr7;
    }

    if ( flags & 0x00000008 )        // CONTEXT_FLOATING_POINT
    {
        // Copy the FLOATING_SAVE_AREA. See WINNT.H for the
        // layout of a FLOATING_SAVE_AREA struct.
        memcpy( &pDestCtx->FloatSave, &pSrcCtx->FloatSave,
                sizeof(FLOATING_SAVE_AREA) );
    }
```

```
if ( flags & 0x00000004 )        // CONTEXT_SEGMENTS
{
    pDestCtx->SegGs = pSrcCtx->SegGs;   // Copy the non-control-related
    pDestCtx->SegFs = pSrcCtx->SegFs;   // segments over.
    pDestCtx->SegEs = pSrcCtx->SegEs;
    pDestCtx->SegDs = pSrcCtx->SegDs;
}

if ( flags & 0x00000002 )        // CONTEXT_INTEGER
{
    pDestCtx->Edi = pSrcCtx->Edi;
    pDestCtx->Esi = pSrcCtx->Esi;
    pDestCtx->Edx = pSrcCtx->Edx;
    pDestCtx->Ecx = pSrcCtx->Ecx;
    pDestCtx->Ebx = pSrcCtx->Ebx;
    pDestCtx->Eax = pSrcCtx->Eax;
}

if ( flags & 0x00000001 )        // CONTEXT_CONTROL
{
    pDestCtx->Ebp = pSrcCtx->Ebp;
    pDestCtx->Eip = pSrcCtx->Eip;
    pDestCtx->SegCs = pSrcCtx->SegCs;
    pDestCtx->EFlags = pSrcCtx->EFlags;
    pDestCtx->Esp = pSrcCtx->Esp;
    pDestCtx->SegSs = pSrcCtx->SegSs;
}
```

SetThreadContext and ISetThreadContext

SetThreadContext enables one thread to change the register values of another thread. In this way, the function complements the GetThreadContext function. Depending on which flags you've set in the input context struct, SetThread-Context copies certain fields into the actual thread context that Windows 95 uses to keep the suspended thread's registers.

The actual SetThreadContext is just a parameter validation layer. It verifies that the pointer passed in points to memory of sufficient size to hold a CONTEXT structure. If so, the code jumps to the internal ISet-ThreadContext routine.

ISetThreadContext (like IGetThreadContext) is convoluted. It begins by converting the input hThread into a thread database pointer. Then, depend-

ing on external conditions, it makes calls to the x_ThreadContext_
CopyRegs (described in the previous section), as well as to VWIN32.VXD.
Again, as with IGetThreadContext, the reason for mucking about with both
the ring 0 and ring 3 versions of the registers isn't entirely clear.

Pseudocode for SetThreadContext

```
// Parameters:
//      HANDLE     hThread
//      LPCONTEXT  lpContext

    Set up structured exception handling frame

    Touch the first and last bytes that lpContext point to.
    If a fault occurs, it's considered a bad pointer, and the exception
    handler returns FALSE;

    Remove structured exception handling frame

    goto ISetThreadContext;
```

Pseudocode for ISetThreadContext

```
// Parameters:
//      HANDLE     hThread
//      LPCONTEXT  lpContext
// Locals:
//      PTHREAD_DATABASE ptdb;
//      BOOL    retValue
//      DWORD   errCode;
//      PCONTEXT pDestCtx;

    retValue = TRUE;

    x_CheckNotSysLevel_Win16_Krn32_mutexes();

    x_LogSomeKernelFunction( function number for GetThreadContext );

    _EnterSysLevel( pKrn32Mutex );

    ptdb = x_ConvertHandleToK32Object( hThread, 0x20, 0 );

    if ( !ptdb )
    {
        retValue = FALSE;
    }
```

```
    else    // Found a valid thread database.
    {
        if ( ptdb->Flags & 0x20000000 )
        {
            retValue = 0;
            InternalSetLastError( ERROR_INVALID_PARAMETER );
            goto doneCopying;
        }

        if ( ptdb->ThreadContext )
        {
            x_ThreadContext_CopyRegs( lpContext->ContextFlags,
                                    lpContext, pdtb->ThreadContext );
        }
        else
        {
            if ( ptdb->DebugContext && ptdb->DebugContext.SomeField )
            {
                x_ThreadContext_CopyRegs(lpContext->ContextFlags,
                                        lpContext,
                                        &ptdb->DebugContext.ThreadContext);

                if ( !(ptdb->DebugContext.ThreadContext.ContextFlags
                    & (CONTEXT_FLOATING_POINT | CONTEXT_DEBUG_REGISTERS)) )
                    goto doneCopying;

                pDestCtx = &ptdb->DebugContext.ThreadContext
            }
            else
            {
                pDestCtx = lpContext;

                if ( lpContext->ContextFlags == 0xFFFFFFFF )
                    x_Assertion2( line number, "..\deb.c" );
            }

            // Call VWIN32 to do the copying.  _VWIN32_Set_Thread_Context
            // == 0x002A0015
            retValue = VxDCall0( _VWIN32_Set_Thread_Context,
                                ptdb->Ring0Thread, pDestCtx );
        }
    }

doneCopying:

    errCode = ERROR_SUCCESS;        // = 0
```

```
if ( retValue == FALSE )
    errCode = GetLastError();

SomeOutputFunction( "SetThreadContext ptdb %08x lpContext %08x eip %08x "
                    "esp %08x ebp %08x erc %d\n",
                    ptdb, lpContext, lpContext->Eip, lpContext->Esp,
                    lpContext->Ebp, errCode );

_LeaveSysLevel( pKrn32Mutex );

return retValue;
```

SuspendThread and VWIN32_SuspendThread

SuspendThread bumps up the suspend count of the specified thread. If the suspend count is nonzero, the ring 0 scheduler won't allow that thread to execute. The SuspendThread code is really just a wrapper around an internal routine that I call VWIN32_SuspendThread. The VWIN32_Suspend-Thread function expects a thread database pointer, so before calling it, SuspendThread first converts the hThread into a thread database pointer. If VWIN32_SuspendThread succeeds, SuspendThread also increments the suspend count in offset 1BCh of the thread database.

However, it's important to remember that when it comes to deciding which threads are runnable, the thread database suspend count isn't used. Rather, VWIN32 keeps the real suspend count in the TDBX structure, described in Chapter 6. The VWIN32_SuspendThread routine is itself really just a wrapper around a lower-level routine. In this case, VWIN32_SuspendThread sets things up and calls into VWIN32.VXD via the undocumented VxDCall function. The Win32 VxD service ID passed in this instance is 0x002A001A.

Pseudocode for SuspendThread

```
// Parameters:
//      HANDLE  hThread
// Locals:
//      PTHREAD_DATABASE ptdb;
//      DWORD   retValue

    retValue = 0xFFFFFFFF;
```

```
        _EnterSysLevel( pKrn32Mutex );

        ptdb = x_ConvertHandleToK32Object( hThread, 0x20, 0 );

        if ( ptdb )
        {
            if ( !ptdb->Flags & fCreateSuspended )
            {
                retValue = VWIN32_SuspendThread( ptdb );

                if ( retValue != 0xFFFFFFFF )
                    ptdb->APISuspendCount++;
            }
        }

done:
        _LeaveSysLevel( pKrn32Mutex );

        return retValue;
```

Pseudocode for VWIN32_SuspendThread

```
// Parameters:
//      PTHREAD_DATABASE ptdb;
// Locals:
//      DWORD   retValue

        retValue = 0xFFFFFFFF;

        // Make sure _EnterSysLevel was called earlier.
        _ConfirmSysLevel( pKrn32Mutex );

        if ( !(ptdb->Flags & 0x10000000) && ptdb->Ring0Thread )
        {
            // Call VWIN32 to suspend it. "SuspendThread" == 0x002A001A.
            retValue = VxDCall ( SuspendThread, ptdb );
        }

        if ( retValue = 0xFFFFFFFF )
            SetLastError( ERROR_NO_MORE_ITEMS );    // ???

        return retValue;
```

ResumeThread

The ResumeThread complements the SuspendThread function. It decrements the suspend count of a specified thread (both the ring 0 suspend count in the thread's TDBX structure and offset 1BCh in the thread database). When the suspend count is 0, the ring 0 scheduler considers the thread to be eligible for execution.

ResumeThread begins by converting the passed-in hThread into a thread database pointer. It then checks the ring 3 version of the suspend count to make sure it's nonzero. (If it's 0, ResumeThread has nothing to do.) Next, the function calls another VWIN32.VXD service to decrement the suspend count. In this instance, the Win32 service ID is 0x002A001B (which is one greater than the 0x002A001A used to bump up the suspend count). If VWIN32 was able to successfully decrement the ring 0 version of the suspend count, ResumeThread also decrements the ring 3 version stored in the thread database.

Pseudocode for ResumeThread

```
// Parameters:
//     HANDLE   hThread
// Locals:
//     PTHREAD_DATABASE ptdb;
//     DWORD    retValue

    retValue = 0xFFFFFFFF;

    _EnterSysLevel( pKrn32Mutex );

    ptdb = x_ConvertHandleToK32Object( hThread, 0x20, 0 );

    if ( ptdb && ptdb->APISuspendCount )
    {
        if ( ptdb->Flags & fCreateSuspended )
        {
            ptdb->APISuspendCount-;
        }
        else
        {
            // Call VWIN32 to wake up the thread.  VWIN32_ResumeThread
            // is identical to VWIN32_SuspendThread, except that it
            // calls VWIN32 service 0x002A001B instead of 0x002A001A.
            retValue = VWIN32_ResumeThread( ptdb );
```

```
            if ( retValue != 0xFFFFFFFF )
                ptdb->APISuspendCount-;
        }
    }

    _LeaveSysLevel( pKrn32Mutex );

    return retValue;
```

STRUCTURED EXCEPTION HANDLING

Structured Exception Handling (typically abbreviated to SEH) is a much hyped and often misunderstood topic in modern operating systems such as OS/2, Windows NT, and Windows 95. Most books and articles on structured exception handling cover it at the compiler level. Compilers use keywords like _ _try, _ _except, catch, throw, and so on to put a nice wrapper around what is fundamentally a messy operating system interface. To date, I've never seen a good overview of how SEH is implemented at the operating system level, so I'm going to attempt to remedy that here.

Since numerous books and articles describe how to use SEH in application code, I'm not going to give yet another rendition of that topic. Chapter 2 gives a quick overview of how you might use _ _try and _ _except in your C/C++ code. Other than that, this discussion assumes that you're familiar with SEH basics. If you're not, I'd suggest that you read something like Brian Meyer's *Mastering Windows NT Programming* or Jeffrey Richter's *Advanced Windows*.

Whenever an exception (such as a page fault) occurs, the CPU immediately transfers control to the ring 0 exception handler whose address is stored in the interrupt descriptor table. It's up to this ring 0 handler to decide what should be done with the exception. If it's an exception that the system is expecting and knows how to deal with (for example, a page fault when more stack space is needed), the ring 0 handler does whatever is necessary and restarts the instruction. These exceptions are essentially invisible to ring 3 applications and system DLLs, and we're not concerned with them here.

What we *are* concerned with here is what happens to an exception that the first line system exception handler doesn't know what to do with. A typical response in older operating systems (such as Windows 3.0) was to terminate the process that caused the exception. This is what you're seeing when a buggy application causes the system to display the UAE dialog box in Windows 3.0 or the GPF dialog box in Windows 3.1.

While the philosophy of "terminate anything that causes an unexpected fault" works, it's not very flexible. A better way to do things is to inform the application (or perhaps other applications) that a fault has occurred and let them decide what should be done. If you've used the 16-bit TOOLHELP InterruptRegister function, you've seen this strategy in action. Applications can register interrupt and exception callbacks with TOOLHELP (but only one handler per installing process). When one of a select group of exceptions or interrupts occurs, TOOLHELP calls back the installed callback functions and uses their return values to determine how the exception should be handled. For instance, programs like WinSpector or Dr. Watson use the exception callback function to log information about the machine state at the time of the exception. Afterward, they tell TOOLHELP to pass the exception on to the next handler. Assuming no TOOLHELP callback function restarts the faulting instruction, the default operating system exception handler gets invoked. The default handler terminates the faulting task.

Although the TOOLHELP callback scheme was a big step forward (as opposed to having no control at all), it still wasn't good enough. When the 32-bit PC operating systems like OS/2 and NT came on the scene, they introduced a much more flexible method of handling exceptions. This new scheme is what we now call *structured exception handling*. Structured exception handling is much a much better way to deal with multiple threads and the demands of implementing the C++ language catch and throw exception mechanism. In C++ exceptions, code itself can cause an exception that has nothing to do with a CPU exception. For instance, if the C++ new operator fails, it throws an exception with a code indicating an out-of-memory condition. The structured exception handing mechanism in the 32-bit operating systems is flexible enough to handle both hardware exceptions and language "exceptions" with the same code.

Before proceeding, I want to reemphasize that the structured exception handling I'm describing here is how it's implemented at the OS level. The following discussion will probably sound *completely different* from what you learned about in your C/C++ training.

In systems with structured exception handling, each thread has its own private linked list of exception handlers. When an exception occurs, the operating system walks the list of installed exception handlers and calls the handlers. This continues until a handler function returns a code indicating that it wants to handle the exception. This is phase 1 (finding a handler that wants to handle the exception). If no user-installed handler chooses to handle the exception, the system handler at the end of the chain terminates the process. We won't concern ourselves with this particular scenario, which is simply the operating system terminating the process that faulted.

Once a handle has elected to handle the exception, the next phase of handling an exception consists of walking the exception handler list from the head again. The undocumented RtlUnwind function does this, and is called from within the exception handler that decided to handle the exception. When the exception handlers are invoked via RtlUnwind, the system passes a different flag to the handler functions. The flag tells the handler functions that the thread's stack is being unwound. Unwinding the stack is a controlled way to restore the program state at the time that the handling exception handler was installed. Rather than just resuming execution in the _ _except block, the system gives each of the installed handlers that didn't handle the function a chance to clean up. By giving them this opportunity, important things like calling the destructors for stack based C++ objects can be accomplished in an orderly manner.

Enough theoretical talk! What are the actual structures and interfaces that Windows 95 uses? As I mentioned in the earlier description of the TIB, the pointer at FS:[0] always points to the head of the list of installed exception handlers for the current thread. The exception handler list is a linked list of EXCEPTIONREGISTRATIONRECORD structures. (The long structure name is from the OS/2 2.0 BSEXCPT.H file. For some reason, Microsoft seems intent on hiding the details of OS-level structured exception handling from mere mortals.) The layout of an EXCEPTIONREGISTRATION-RECORD looks like this:

```
DWORD prev_structure    // A pointer to the previously installed
                        // EXCEPTIONREGISTRATIONRECORD.
DWORD ExceptionHandler  // Address of the exception handler function.
```

The end of the exception handling list is indicated by a –1 in the prev_structure field.

In normal use, program code creates each EXCEPTIONREGISTRATION-RECORD structure on the stack as it's needed. In C/C++ code, each EXCEPTIONREGISTRATIONRECORD corresponds to one _ _try/_ _except sequence. As _ _try blocks are entered, the compiler builds a new EXCEPTION-REGISTRATIONRECORD on the stack and puts it at the head of the chain. After exiting the block, the compiler sets FS:[0] to point at the next EXCEPTIONREGISTRATIONRECORD in the chain. Figure 3-3 shows these linked records.

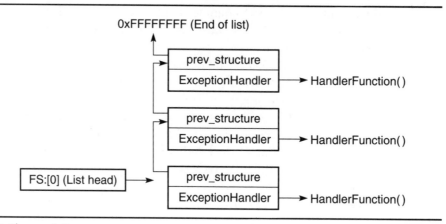

Figure 3-3
A structured exception handling chain at the operating system level.

Remember that the 8-byte structure given above is only the minimum required by the operating system. Nothing prevents compilers from creating larger structures on the stack and putting the EXCEPTIONREGISTRTION-RECORD come at the beginning of the structure. The additional fields that the compilers obtain from the structure provide enough contextual information so that a single exception handler function can be used for all __try blocks. You'll see that both the Microsoft and Borland compilers use exception record structures that are supersets of the required EXCEPTION-REGITRATIONRECORD structure.

Speaking of the exception handler function, what does it look like? Again, Microsoft seems to be trying to hide this information, but at least there's a prototype in the Win32 header files for what an exception handler function should look like. In the EXCPT.H file, you'll find the following:

```
EXCEPTION_DISPOSITION __cdecl _except_handler (
    struct _EXCEPTION_RECORD *ExceptionRecord,
    void * EstablisherFrame,
    struct _CONTEXT *ContextRecord,
    void * DispatcherContext
    );
```

At first glance, this prototype looks more complex than it really is. The EXCEPTION_DISPOSITION return value is just an enum, and tells the system how the handler function has chosen to deal with the exception:

```
typedef enum _EXCEPTION_DISPOSITION {
    ExceptionContinueExecution,
    ExceptionContinueSearch,
    ExceptionNestedException,
    ExceptionCollidedUnwind
} EXCEPTION_DISPOSITION;
```

The last two enums are rarely encountered. The ExceptionContinue-Execution return code tells the system that the exception handler function has handled the exception and wants execution to continue. The Exception-ContinueSearch return code tells the system that the handler function doesn't want to handle the exception, and that the system should continue walking the EXCEPTIONREGISTRATIONRECORD list, searching for a handler that returns ExceptionContinueExecution.

Rewriting the _except_handler prototype to make it look a little more accessible, we get:

```
int _except_handler (
            PEXCEPTION_RECORD ExceptionRecord,
            PVOID EstablisherFrame,
            PCONTEXT ContextRecord,
            PVOID DispatcherContext );
```

Translated into English, this means that an exception handler function takes four pointers to information about the exception and the machine state at the time of the exception. The function returns an integer telling the system whether this handler handled the exception or not. The EXCEPTION_RECORD structure contains the exception code (among other things); it is documented in the WINNT.H file. The CONTEXT structure contains the register set at the time of the exception, and is also described in WINNT.H. The EstablisherFrame parameter contains a pointer to the stack frame where the associated EXCEPTIONREGISTRATIONRECORD was set up, and the DispatcherContext parameter appears to be unused.

Earlier, I mentioned that handler functions are called twice in a typical exception scenario. The first time they're called, the system is searching for a handler that will handle the exception. The second time they're called, the system is unwinding from the exception, and the handler is supposed to do any cleanup it deems necessary (such as invoking destructors for stack-based objects). How does the exception handler differentiate between these invocations? The ExceptionRecord structure (pointed to by the first parameter) contains an ExceptionFlags field. If both the EH_UNWINDING

(0x2) or EH_EXIT_UNWIND (0x4) flags are clear, the exception handler is being invoked to check if the handler wants to handle this exception. If either of the bits is set, the handler is being invoked to unwind from the exception.

Although what I've just described isn't enough to go write your own OS-level exception handling code, it should be enough for you to get a general sense of how SEH works. To prove that I'm not blowing smoke with all this, I wrote the SHOWSEH program, which you can find on the accompanying disk. SHOWSEH uses __try blocks to set up an exception handling chain with multiple entries. Once they're all set up, the program walks through the SEH list and prints out information about each of the nodes.

The output from running SHOWSEH is shown in Figure 3-4. There are several things I'd like you to note about this figure. First, note that the address in the next rec column always increases. These addresses are within SHOWSEHss stack area, which is consistent with the compiler putting each EXCEPTIONREGISTRATIONRECORD on the stack. The first four entries were created in direct response to the __try blocks in the SHOWSEH.C code. Second, notice how the first four addresses in the next rec address column correlate by a constant value to the ESP value in the various SHOWSEH functions. (The end of the output shows the ESP value inside each of the functions in SHOWSEH.C.)

```
offset of __except_handler3: 00401468

next rec   handler
========   ========
0063FD90   00401468
0063FDC0   00401468
0063FDF0   00401468
0063FE30   00401468
0063FF68   00401468
FFFFFFFF   BFFC2D18

in    c(), ESP = 0063FD48
in    b(), ESP = 0063FD78
in    a(), ESP = 0063FDA8
in main(), ESP = 0063FDD8
```

Figure 3-4

Output from SHOWSEH.EXE.

The last thing to notice is that the first five addresses in the handler column are the same address. This address is within SHOWSEH's code area, and shows that compiler-generated code uses the same exception handler function for all _ _try blocks. Again, the first four entries in the list are from the _ _try blocks in SHOWSEH.C. The fifth exception handler (but with the same handler address) is an exception handler installed by the runtime library code before calling the main() function. These handler addresses are all for _ _except_handler3, a runtime library function in Visual C++. The last exception handler is the default system exception handler, which is located in KERNEL32.DLL.

Structured exception handling and parameter validation

One of most important uses of structured exception handling in Windows 95 is as a fast and easy way to validate parameters to the exported API functions. The basic idea is to assume the parameters are correct, and then run a series of sanity tests on them. However, before doing the sanity tests, the code first adds a new structured exception handling frame to the head of the exception handler list. If the parameters are valid, nothing bad happens during the sanity tests, and the exception handler is subsequently removed. There's very little execution time overhead in this case.

In the other scenarios, the parameters turn out to be incorrect during the execution of the sanity test code. This causes a CPU exception to be generated, which the newly installed exception handler handles. The exception handler tells the operating system to resume normal thread execution in a spot that causes the API function to return a failure value (for example, FALSE). Let's look at some pseudocode for a KERNEL32 API that illustrates this in action. In other API descriptions in this book, I've brushed lightly over the role of SEH in parameter validation. For the GetCurrentDirectoryA function, I present detailed pseudocode that shows SEH in use by the operating system.

Besides showing SEH concepts, the GetCurrentDirectoryA pseudocode also illustrates in detail what a typical parameter validation layer stub looks like. The code for functions that have a parameter validation layer stub is broken up into two parts. The code at the address where the function is exported from is just a small chunk of code that tests the parameters for validity. If the parameters are correct, stub code jumps to the real code elsewhere in the module. In Windows 3.1, the real version of the code for a parameter-validated function had the name of the exported function with an *I* prepended. For example, as we saw earlier in the chapter, the GetProcAddress code is broken up into two parts:

```
GetProcAddress stub
    Validate the procedure name string parameter
    JMP IGetProcAddress

IGetProcAddress
    Meat of the code that looks up a function address
```

To keep things consistent, I carried forward the Windows 3.1 convention of prepending the internal version of a function's code with an *I*.

GetCurrentDirectoryA

GetCurrentDirectoryA is a typical parameter-validation layer stub. It begins by creating a new EXCEPTIONREGISTRATIONRECORD on the stack (using PUSH instructions). The prev_structure member of the struct is placed on the stack by pushing FS:[0] (the current head of the exception chain). The exception handler function placed into the EXCEPTIONREGISTRATIONRECORD is a routine I named x_invalid_param_2_params. All functions that have two parameters and have parameter-validation stubs use x_invalid_param_2_params as their exception handler during the validation stage.

After the EXCEPTIONREGISTRATIONRECORD is on the stack, the code then moves a pointer to the structure into FS:[0]. This puts the new EXCEPTIONREGISTRATIONRECORD at the head of the exception handler chain (making it the first one called in the event of an exception). With the exception handler for this function finally in place, the code can safely touch and inspect the passed-in lpszCurDir pointer without caring whether it's valid or not. The validation of the parameters in this case is to verify that the entire block of memory described by the lpszCurDir and length parameters is writeable.

If an exception occurs during this checking, the x_invalid_param_2_params function gets control. (The x_invalid_param_2_params function is described in the next section.) If the parameters were proper, execution continues along the expected path. The next-to-last bit of the GetCurrentDirectory code removes the exception handler frame. A POP FS:[0] restores the previous pointer to the head of the exception handler list, and an ADD ESP,4 removes the exception handler address.

Assuming everything went well (that is, assuming that no exception occurred), the last thing in GetCurrentDirectoryA is a jump to the IGetCurrentDirectory code. Somewhat surprisingly, KERNEL32 doesn't appear to use the current directory pointer it stores in the environment database. Instead, it pokes around in the Win16 task database and uses VWIN32's Int 21h dispatch mechanism to call INT 21h, function 19h (Get Current Directory), and function 7147h (the long filename version of Get Current Directory).

Pseudocode for GetCurrentDirectoryA

```
// Parameters:
//      DWORD   cchCurDir
//      LPTSTR  lpszCurDir

    // Set up structured exception handling frame. We do this by creating
    // the exception record on the stack. An exception record looks like this:
    //
    // prev_structure;      // Pointer to previous record.
    // ExceptionHandler     // Address to call on an exception.
    //

    push    offset x_invalid_param_2_params     // Offset of handler.
    push    FS:[0]                              // Head of list in FS:0.
    mov     FS:[0], ESP                         // Point FS:0 at record
                                                // we just built.

    if ( lpszCurDir && cchCurDir )  // If both params are non-null...
    {
        LSPTR lpszEndPtr = lpszCurrDir + cchCurDir + 1;
        LPSTR lpszTemp;

        *lpszEndPtr += 0;       // Harmlessly write the last byte in the
                                // buffer. If a fault occurs, the exception
                                // handler will be invoked.

        if ( lpszEndPtr != lpszCurDir )
        {
            lpszTemp = lpszCurDir;

            // Go through each page between the start and end of the buffer
            // and touch it. If a fault occurs, the exception handler will
            // be invoked.
            while ( lpszTemp < lpszEndPtr )
            {
```

```
            *lpszTemp +=0;              // Harmlessly write to the page.
            lpszTemp += 0x1000;        // Advance pointer to next page.
        }
    }
}

// If we got here, everything went well. Clear off the exception
// record from the stack and restore the previous head pointer.

pop     FS:[0]      // Put the previous head of the list into FS:0.
add     esp,4       // Throw away the exception handler address we pushed.

goto    IGetCurrentDirectoryA
```

x_invalid_param_handler

The x_invalid_param_handler function is where the typical invalid parameter
exception ends up. This function isn't called directly, though. Instead,
KERNEL32 has a series of ten stubs, with each stub passing a different
parameter byte count to x_invalid_param_handler. The reason for having
ten different stubs is because the x_invalid_param_handler function has to
remove from the stack all the arguments to the function that had an invalid
parameter.

Inside x_invalid_param_handler, the code performs three main actions.
First, the function prints out the "Invalid parameter passed to: XXXXXXXX"
message that shows up on the debug terminal. Second, the function calls
RtlUnwind to clean up any exception handlers that were installed after the
exception handler that was installed by the parameter validation stub. Third,
and most important, the function calls what I've named the ReturnFailureCode
function. ReturnFailureCode calculates the correct failure return value for the
original function (for example, GetCurrentDirectoryA), and then jumps to the
exit prologue of the original function.

The result of all these contortions is that the program that passed an
invalid parameter to a Win32 function simply sees that the function failed.
The program has no idea of all the SEH gyrations that went on under the
surface. In addition, if you were running the debug Windows 95, you'll
have an invalid parameter diagnostic.

Pseudocode for x_invalid_param_X_param

```
x_invalid_param_1_param proc
    x_invalid_param_handler( 0x04 );

x_invalid_param_2_params proc
// parameters:
//   struct _EXCEPTION_RECORD *ExceptionRecord,
//   void *EstablisherFrame,
//   struct _CONTEXT *ContextRecord,
//   void *DispatcherContext

    x_invalid_param_handler( 0x08 );

x_invalid_param_3_params proc
    x_invalid_param_handler( 0x0C );

x_invalid_param_4_params proc
    x_invalid_param_handler( 0x10 );

x_invalid_param_5_params proc
    x_invalid_param_handler( 0x14 );

x_invalid_param_6_params proc
    x_invalid_param_handler( 0x18 );

x_invalid_param_7_params proc
    x_invalid_param_handler( 0x1C );

x_invalid_param_8_params proc
    x_invalid_param_handler( 0x20 );

x_invalid_param_9_params proc
    x_invalid_param_handler( 0x24 );

x_invalid_param_special proc
    x_invalid_param_handler( 0x80000000 );
```

Pseudocode for x_invalid_param_handler

```
// Parameters:
//   DWORD    cbParams
//   DWORD    caller_retAddr
//   struct _EXCEPTION_RECORD *ExceptionRecord,
//   void *EstablisherFrame,
```

```
//  struct _CONTEXT *ContextRecord,
//  void *DispatcherContext
// Locals:
//      DWORD   faultEBX
//      DWORD   faultEBP
//      DWORD   faultESI
//      DWORD   faultEDI
//      DWORD   fSomeFlag

    // If the unwinding flags aren't set (TRUE the first time through),
    // then handle the exception...
    if ( 0 == (pExcRec->ExceptionFlags & (EH_UNWINDING | EH_EXIT_UNWIND) ))
    {
        if ( cbParams == 0 )
        {
            fSomeFlag = -1
            if ( !(pEstablisherFrame->8 &0x100) )
                fSomeFlag = 0;
        }
        else
            fSomeFlag = 0;

        dprintf( "Invalid parameter passed to:\n" );

        // Send the EIP out via the debugger INT 41h interface.
        x_INT41_DS_printf( "%pLNS", pContext->Eip );

        dprintf( " (%04x:%08x)\n", pContext->SegCS, pContext->EIP );

        push    EBX, ESI, EDI   // Preserve across the RTLUnwind call.

        RtlUnwind( pEstablisherFrame, FFC00BAD, 0, 0 );

        pop     EDI, ESI, EBX

        SetLastError( ERROR_INVALID_PARAMETER );

        // Restores EBX, ESI, EDI, ESP, and returns to original code.
        return ReturnFailureCode(    cbParams,
                                     fSomeFlag,
                                     pEstablisher,
                                     faultEBX
                                     faultESI
                                     faultEDI
                                     faultEBP );
    }

    return XCPT_CONTINUE_SEARCH;
```

THREAD LOCAL STORAGE

Thread Local Storage (TLS) is a nice Win32 feature that makes multithreaded programming easier. Thread local storage is a mechanism by which a program can have global variables, but on a per-thread basis. That is, all threads in a process can have data that acts like it's global in scope, but is actually specific to that thread. For example, you might have a multithreaded program, with each thread writing to a separate file (and therefore using a separate file handle). In this situation, it's convenient to store the file handle that each thread uses in thread local storage. When the code for a thread needs to know the handle to use, it retrieves the value from thread local storage. Here's the important part: The code that the file-writing threads use to retrieve the file handle code is identical in all cases. However, the file handle returned by the TLS mechanism is different for each thread. Neat, huh? All the convenience of global variables, but on a per-thread basis.

Sure, you could simulate thread local storage in this case with a linked list that associates a thread ID with a file handle, with one node per thread. When a thread needed to know which file handle to write with, it could look up the file handle in the linked list. Alternatively, you could store the file handle for each thread in true local variables in the thread's stack. But then you'd have to pass around the file handle from function to function. What a pain! Thread local storage eliminates these hassles with a simple alloc/set/get/free API.

While TLS is convenient, it's not unlimited. In both Windows NT and Windows 95, there are 64 DWORD slots available for use by each thread. That means that a process can store up to potentially 64 unique DWORDs on a per-thread basis. To reserve a slot in each thread, a program calls TlsAlloc. Each call to TlsAlloc returns a single index value used by each thread. This index is usually stored in a true global variable. When a thread wants to store a value in one of the allocated slots, it calls TlsSetValue, passing in the TLS index value, as well as the value to store in the slot. Later, when the thread needs to use the per-thread value it saved away, the code calls TlsGetValue, again passing in the index specifying a particular TLS slot. Finally, when a program is finished with a TLS slot, it passes the TLS index to TlsFree. This, of course, makes that slot unusable by all threads, since a TLS index applies across all threads in a process.

Although TLS can certainly store single values such as file handles, a more common use of TLS is to store pointers to per-thread data. In many cases, a multithreaded program needs to store a collection of variables, each on a per-thread basis. What many programmers do in this case is bundle the per-thread variables into a C-style struct and then keep a pointer to the structure in a TLS slot. As new threads are created, the program mallocs some memory for the structure and stores the pointer into the TLS slot reserved for it. When the thread terminates, the code frees the allocated block.

A good example of this programming style is in the APISPY32 program in Chapter 10. The APISPY32.DLL needs to keep a stack of return addresses from functions that it's intercepted. (In this case, I'm using the term *stack* in the classical computer science sense; that is, I'm using it to refer to an array of structures and a stack *pointer*.) Since the program being spied on may have multiple threads, APISPY32.DLL needs to keep separate return address stacks for each thread.

If each thread in a process has 64 slots for storing per-thread data, where do these slots come from? As I showed earlier in this chapter, each thread database contains an array of 64 DWORDs for use by the TLS functions. When you set or retrieve a value using a TLS function, you're actually reading or writing into the thread database of the current thread. It's worth pointing out here that the TlsGetValue and TlsSetValue functions implicitly operate on the current thread's TLS data. There is no documented way for one thread to access the TLS data of another thread. Let's now take a closer look at the TLS functions to see this in action.

TlsAlloc

Since TLS makes up to 64 slots available for use by each thread, there needs to be some means of keeping track of which TLS slots are in use. KERNEL32 uses two DWORDs (totaling 64 bits) to keep track of which TLS slots are available and free. These two DWORDS can be thought of as a 64-bit array. If a given bit is on, the TLS index associated with that bit is in use.

The 64-bit TLS slot array is stored in the process database (not in the thread database, as you might initially guess). Remember, when you allocate a TLS slot, that slot is accessed using the slot's index value in all threads of the process. The 64-bit TLS slot array is found in the DWORDs at offsets 0x88 and 0x8C in the process database. Although the following TlsAlloc pseudocode may look complex, it's really not. All the code actually does is to scan through bits in the 64-bit array, looking for a bit with a value of 0. When TlsAlloc finds a zero bit, it turns that bit on and returns the bit's position within the array. Thus, if the fifth bit in the 64-bit array is 0, TlsAlloc flips on that bit and returns a TLS index of 4 (TLS indices are 0-based).

Pseudocode for TlsAlloc

```
// Locals:
//      DWORD    i;
//      PDWORD   pTlsInUseBits;
//      DWORD    newFlag;

    x_LogSomeKernelFunction( function number for TlsAlloc );

    i = 0;

    _EnterSysLevel( x_TlsMutex );

    pTlsInUseBits = &ppCurrentProcess->tlsInUseBits1;

    // Position pTlsInUseBits so that it points at the first of the two
    // tls bit DWORDs that has a free bit available.
    while ( *pTlsInUseBits == 0xFFFFFFFF && (i < 2) )
    {
        i++;
        pTlsInUseBits++;          // Point at next DWORD of tlsInUseBits.
    }

    if ( i < 2 )    // If a free bit-slot was found, i is 0 or 1.
    {
        i *= 32;    // 'i' starts at either 0 or 1, so the end result is
                    // either 0 or 32. There are 32 "inUse" bits in each
                    // of the TlsInUseBits DWORDs.

        newFlag = 1;

        if ( *pTlsInUseBits & newFlag )
        {
            // Blast through the bits in this DWORD until we find one that's
            // 0 (available). Keep incrementing 'i' so that when we're
            // done, it's a TLS index.
            do
            {
                i++;
                newFlags << 1;
            } while ( *pTlsInUseBits & newFlag )
        }
```

```
            *pTlsInUseBits |= newFlag;  // Turn on the newly allocated bit to
                                        // indicate that the corresponding TLS
                                        // index is in use.
        }
        else    // No free bits were found.
        {
            // If we get here, all the TLS indices were in use. Return -1 and
            // set the last error code.

            i = TLS_OUT_OF_INDEXES; // 0xFFFFFFFF

            InternalSetLastError( ERROR_NO_MORE_ITEMS );
        }

        _LeaveSysLevel( x_TlsMutex );

        return i;
```

TlsSetValue

TlsSetValue is the method by which a thread stores a value into a previously
allocated TLS slot. As you'd expect, the two parameters are the TLS slot to
write into and the value to be written. The code starts out by verifying the
TLS index passed in is less than the maximum TLS index value (64). In beta
builds of Windows 95, the TlsSetValue function verified that the passed-in
TLS index had been previously allocated. Starting in beta 3, TlsSetValue
does only the minimal index checking I just described. If the passed-in TLS
index was less than 64, TlsSetValue stuffs the value you want to store into
the appropriate element in the array of 64 DWORDs from the current
thread database.

In addition (and this is a little-known fact), TlsSetValue also updates a
second array of 64 DWORDS that parallels the TLS data array. This array
contains the EIP value where TlsSetValue was last called from for the current
thread. No doubt this EIP array is for debugging purposes. Alas, Microsoft
doesn't appear to have provided a means for programs to access this information, short of poking through the thread database yourself (a big no-no,
remember?).

Pseudocode for TlsSetValue

```
// Parameters:
//      DWORD   dwTlsIndex;
//      LPVOID  lpvTlsValue;
// Locals:
//      PTHREAD_DATABASE    ptdb

    // The thread database starts 0x10 bytes before the TIB pointed to by
    // the FS register. Make a pointer to the thread database.
    ptdb = FS:[ptibSelf] - 0x10;

    if ( dwTlsIndex < TLS_MINIMUM_AVAILABLE (64) )
    {
        ptdb->TLSArray[ dwTlsIndex ] = lpvTlsValue;

        // Grab return EIP off the stack and store in the other TLS
        // array that runs parallel to the main array.
        ptdb->LastTlsSetValueEIP[ dwTlsIndex ] = [EBP+04];

        return TRUE;
    }
    else    // The TLS index passed in was >= TLS_MINIMUM_AVAILABLE.
    {
        ptdb->GetLastErrorCode = ERROR_INVALID_PARAMETER ;

        return 0;
    }
```

TlsGetValue

TlsGetValue is nearly a mirror image of TlsSetValue, with the obvious difference that it retrieves a value rather than stores it. Like TlsSetValue, the TlsGetValue function first verifies that the TLS index passed to it is valid. If so, the function uses the TLS index value to index into the array of 64 DWORDS in the current thread's thread database. TlsGetValue returns whatever is there.

Pseudocode for TlsGetValue

```
// Parameters:
//      DWORD   dwTlsIndex;
// Locals:
//      PTHREAD_DATABASE    ptdb
```

```
// The thread database starts 0x10 bytes before the TIB pointed to by
// the FS register. Make a pointer to the thread database.
ptdb = FS:[ptibSelf] - 0x10;

if( dwTlsIndex < TLS_MINIMUM_AVAILABLE (64) )
{
    // Set last error value to 0.
    ptdb->GetLastErrorCode =  ERROR_SUCCESS;

    return ptdb->TLSArray[ dwTlsIndex ];
}
else    // The TLS index passed in was >= TLS_MINIMUM_AVAILABLE.
{
    ptdb->GetLastErrorCode = ERROR_INVALID_PARAMETER ;
    return 0;
}
```

TlsFree

The TlsFree function undoes the effect of previous TlsAlloc and TlsSetValue calls. As you'd expect, TlsFree takes the TLS index value you passed in and verifies that it was previously allocated. If so, TlsFree turns off the corresponding bit in the array of 64 TLS slot bits. TlsFree doesn't stop there, however. To prevent programs from using potentially invalid values stored in a previously allocated TLS slot, TlsFree loops through each thread in the process. For each thread it encounters, TlsFree stores a 0 into the TLS slot that was just freed. As a result, if a particular TLS index is subsequently reallocated, all threads that use that index are guaranteed to get back a 0 value until they call TlsSetValue.

Pseudocode for TlsFree

```
// Parameters:
//      DWORD    dwTlsIndex;
// Locals:
//      DWORD    retValue
//      PDWORD   pTlsInUseBits;
//      PTHREAD_DATABASE ptdb;
//      PK32OBJECTLISTENTRY pK32Object;

    x_LogSomeKernelFunction( function number for TlsFree );
```

```
    _EnterSysLevel( pKrn32Mutex );

    _EnterSysLevel( x_TlsMutex );

    point pTlsInUseBits to either ppCurrentProcess->tlsInUseBits1 or
    ppCurrentProcess->tlsInUseBits2 as appropriate.

    if ( dwTlsIndex < TLS_MINIMUM_AVAILABLE (64) )
    {
        DWORD turnOffFlag;

        // Create a DWORD with the appropriate flag set that represents the
        // TLS index to be freed.
        turnOffFlag = 1 << ( dwTlsIndex & 0x1F );

        // If that bit is already turned off in the process database's
        // tlsInUseBits field, the TLS index isn't allocated. This is
        // a bad thing, so go report an error.
        if ( 0 == turnOffFlag & *pTlsInUseBits )
            goto error;

        // Turn off the correct bit in the tlsInUseBits field of the process
        // database.
        *pTlsInUseBits = ~turnOffFlag;

        // Now walk through each of the threads of the process, putting the
        // value 0 into the DWORD assigned to the TLS index we're freeing.

        pK32Object = x_GetNextObjectInList(ppCurrentProcess->ThreadList, 0);

        while ( pK32Object )
        {
            ptdb = pK32Object->pObject;

            ptdb->TLSArray[dwTlsIndex] = 0;
            ptdb->AnotherTLSArray[dwTlsIndex] = 0;

            pK32Object=x_GetNextObjectInList(ppCurrentProcess->ThreadList,1);
        }

        retValue = 1;
    }
    else
    {
error:
        retValue = 0;
        InternalSetLastError( ERROR_INVALID_PARAMETER );
    }
```

```
done:
    _LeaveSysLevel( x_TlsMutex );

    _LeaveSysLevel( pKrn32Mutex );

    return retValue;
```

MISCELLANEOUS THREAD FUNCTIONS

The functions described in this section don't fall into any of the previous function categories. Nonetheless, they're all important functions that highlight KERNEL32.DLL's use of the thread database.

GetLastError

The GetLastError function is a mechanism that applications can use to determine why a particular system call failed. When a Windows 95 function fails, it can optionally set the last error code in the current thread to indicate why the function failed. These error codes are found in the WINERROR.H file. In a sense, the GetLastError function is similar to the C runtime library errno variable.

Besides the system functions, applications can join the party and call SetLastError themselves. Ideally, these error codes will be outside the range of the system-defined error values.

The GetLastError function is simple in its implementation. After checking that there's a current thread to query, the code returns the GetLastErrorCode field (offset 70h) from the thread database of the current thread. If there is no current thread, the function returns whatever is in the KERNEL32 global variable shown in the following pseudocode. (I haven't come up with a name for that global variable.)

Pseudocode for GetLastError

```
if ( ppCurrentThread )
    return ppCurrentThread->GetLastErrorCode
else
    return x_LastErrorIfNoCurrentThread;    // A global variable.
```

SetLastError

SetLastError is also very simple in its implementation. If there's a current thread, this function returns the value of the GetLastError field in the thread database.

Pseudocode for SetLastError

```
// Locals:
//     DWORD    fdwError

    if ( ppCurrentThread )
        ppCurrentThread->GetLastErrorCode = fdwError;
```

GetExitCodeThread and IGetExitCodeThread

The GetExitCodeThread function returns the current exit status of the thread specified by the hThread parameter. The thread's exit status is kept in the TerminationStatus field (offset 48h) of the thread database. During normal execution, the exit status is 0x103 (STILL_ACTIVE).

The GetExitCodeThread function is just a parameter-validation wrapper. After verifying that a valid pointer to store the exit status into was passed, it jumps to the IGetExitCodeThread.

IGetExitCodeThread begins by entering a "must-complete" section. It then converts the hThread parameter into a thread database pointer. After retrieving the value of the TerminationStatus field in the thread database, the code leaves its must-complete state.

Pseudocode for GetExitCodeThread

```
// Parameters:
//     HANDLE  hThread;
//     LPDWORD lpdwExitCode;

    Set up structured exception handling frame

    *lpdwExitCode += 0;      // Verify that lpdwExitCode can be written to.

    Remove structured exception handling frame

    goto IGetExitCodeThread;
```

Pseudocode for IGetExitCodeThread

```
// Parameters:
//      HANDLE  hThread;
//      LPDWORD lpdwExitCode;
// Locals:
//      PTHREAD_DATABASE ptdb;
//      BOOL    retValue;

    retValue = TRUE;        // Assume successful return.

    x_EnterMustComplete();

    x_LogSomeKernelFunction( function number for GetExitCodeThread );

    ptdb = x_ConvertHandleToK32Object( hThread, 0x80000020, 0 );

    if ( ptdb )
    {
        *lpdwExitCode = ptdb->Status;

        x_UnuseObjectWrapper( ptdb );
    }
    else
    {
        retValue = FALSE;
    }

    LeaveMustComplete();

    return retValue;
```

THE WIN32WLK PROGRAM

To help ferret out the numerous data structures and concepts that I've discussed in this (way too long) chapter, I wrote the Win32Wlk program. With its original mission completed, it still remains a useful tool for spelunking around in the KERNEL32 data structures that I've described in this chapter.

As you can see in Figure 3-5 (made up of three separate screenshots), Win32Wlk is a GUI Win32 program. The three primary data structures that Win32Wlk shows are the process database, the thread database, and the IMTE (modules). In addition, Win32Wlk shows three additional data structures when called upon: The process handle table, the process module list, and the Thread Information Block (TIB).

The process list

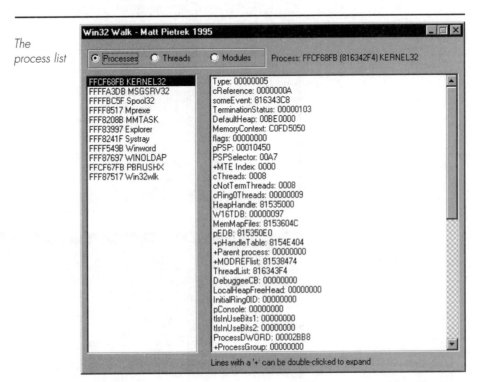

continued

The
thread list

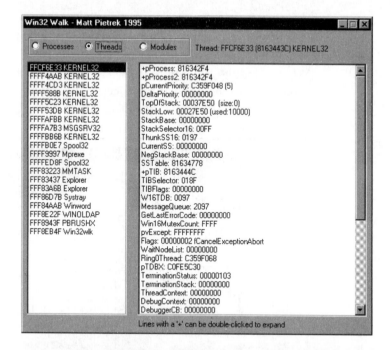

The
module list

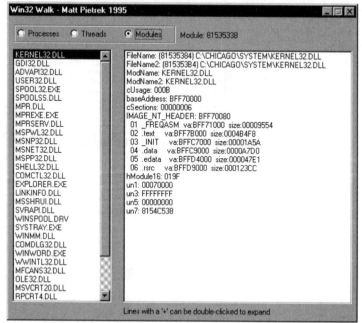

Figure 3-5

The Win32Wlk program is made up of three primary data structures: the process list, the thread list, and the module list.

Win32Wlk is oriented around two listboxes. The listbox at left always shows a current list of either processes, threads, or modules. You can switch between the three lists by clicking on the appropriate radio button (Processes, Threads, or Modules) in the top left of the window. It's important to remember that the lists in the left listbox don't update dynamically as new processes, threads, or modules enter or leave the system. If at any time you want to update the list, simply click on the corresponding radio button and Win32Wlk recomputes the list.

The listbox at the right is the details window. At any given time, it shows the fields of a process database, a thread database, an IMTE, a process handle table, a process MODREF list, or a TIB. The contents of the details window are updated and changed in two ways. First, when you click on a line in the listbox on the left, the details window updates to show all the meaningful fields of the selected process, thread, or module. The other way to change the details window is via hot links. In some of the details window displays, you'll see lines that are preceded by a + (a plus sign) indicating a hot link. For instance, when displaying the process details, the pHandleTable line is actually +pHandleTable. If you double-click lines with a +, the details window shows pertinent details about that item. So, for example, if you double-click the +pHandleTable line, the details window changes to the process handle table list for that process. It's important to remember that the fields shown in the details pane aren't presented in the same order in which they appear in the associated data structure. Nor do I show every field in some data structures. When laying out the details windows, I tried to sort the information by its relative interest. Obscure fields that almost no one would care to see are therefore presented toward the bottom of the list. In cases where the meaning of a particular field was unknown, and always appeared to be 0, I don't display the value. Instead, I use an assertion with this field so that if the field is ever nonzero, I'll immediately know it. If you're using Win32Wlk and come across one of these assertions (currently, the assertion action is to just abort the program), you'll want to track down which field asserted and remove it from the list of assertions.

Under the hood of Win32Wlk

A couple of technical hurdles and implementation details in Win32Wlk bear closer examination. When I set out to write Win32Wlk, I wanted to walk all the data structures myself without using any TOOLHELP32 functions. For the most part, Win32Wlk achieves this goal. However, in two cases, I wimped out and used TOOLHELP32 functions. Both the process and thread lists in KERNEL32 are difficult to walk in Windows 95. This is primarily because these structures aren't simple linked lists like the Win16 KRNL386 uses. Luckily, the TOOLHELP32 th32ProcessID and th32ThreadID values are nothing more than the PID and TID values returned by GetCurrentProcessId and GetCurrentThreadId. Thus, I was able to get away with using the Process32First, Process32Next, Thread32First, and Thread32Next functions to obtain a list of process and thread IDs. From that point on, Win32Wlk uses its knowledge of the data structures to find everything else.

Finding where KERNEL32 kept its array of pointers to IMTEs (a.k.a., the system module list) presented another challenge. A pointer to the array of IMTE pointers is kept in KERNEL32.DLL. (This is the pModuleTableArray that I referred to earlier.) The trick was finding pModuleTableArray. After some searching through KERNEL32.DLL, I came across the undocumented GDIReallyCares function (KERNEL32 export #23). After this function is called, the ECX register contains the pModuleTableArray pointer. Yes, this is a horrifically disgusting coding practice. Read the standard list of dire warnings before you rely on something like this. On the other hand, you gotta do what you gotta do. There are other ways to find the pModuleTableArray list, but they're equally lousy. It's really too bad that Microsoft didn't just make a TOOLHELP32 API to return the entire list of system modules so that we didn't have to turn to hacks like this.

The other disgusting hack-o-rama in Win32Wlk is how it converts process and thread IDs to process and thread database pointers. Much earlier in the chapter, I described how process and thread IDs are just K32 object pointers that have been XOR'ed with the KERNEL32 Obsfucator DWORD. A well known property of binary XORs is that they're commutative. That is, if:

    (A XOR B) == C

then

    (A XOR C) == B

Put another way, if you know any two values of an XOR operation, you can calculate the third value.

Now, let's use actual KERNEL32 values in the above equation:

    (PTHREAD_DATABASE XOR Obsfucator) == ThreadId

In the case of Win32Wlk, we initially have only one of the three values in the equation (the ThreadId returned by GetCurrentThreadId). We don't know the value of the Obsfucator DWORD, nor can we use a hard-coded value because it changes from boot to boot. However, if we can somehow get a pointer to a THREAD_DATABASE, we can rearrange the equation like this:

(ThreadID XOR PTHREAD_DATABASE) == Obsfucator

As it turns out, there are several ways to get a pointer to the current process's THREAD_DATABASE. The solution I chose as the simplest is to get the address of the current Thread Information Block (TIB) and subtract 0x10. The current TIB is always pointed to by the FS segment register. At offset 18h in the TIB you'll find the linear address of that TIB. The algorithm is basically:

pTIB = FS:[18h]

pThreadDatabase = pTib - 0x10

You can see this done in a small bit of inline assembler in the Init-Unobsfucator function in WIN32WLK.C. Once you get the Unobsfucator value, you're set for both processes and threads. Both process and thread IDs are calculated using the KERNEL32 Obscfucator DWORD. The Win32Wlk Unobsfucator DWORD works equally well in retrieving both process and thread database pointers.

As a final note on Win32Wlk, it will be interesting to see if Win32Wlk continues to work in the inevitable bug-fix upgrades to Windows 95. Seeing how easy it was for Win32Wlk to find and decode these data structures, the Windows 95 coders could easily intentionally break Win32Wlk. For instance, they could apply a second XOR to the PID and TID value. Likewise, they could slightly tweak GDIReallyCares so that the pointer to the array of IMTE pointers isn't in ECX when the function returns. Of course, if Win32Wlk does break in the future, you can bet I'll be there to find out if it's a faulty assumption in Win32Wlk or a deliberate attempt to break it.

If Microsoft chooses to gratuitously break programs that do "non-approved" things, such as Win32Wlk, I have secondary methods for finding the necessary information. My hope is that rather than degrading into a spy versus spy situation, Microsoft will realize that in some cases, people outside Microsoft can use this information to write better products. In the case of Win32Wlk, the code doesn't attempt to change any system behavior, and exists solely to help programmers have a better understanding of the system. The "black box" approach to programming that Microsoft wants us to take is nice when writing "Hello World" programs, but it fails miserably when attempting to write anything other than toy applications.

If the Windows 95 team was truly concerned about security and making the system data structures opaque, they would have designed Windows 95 to be more like Windows NT. If smart programmers want information badly enough, they'll find a way to get it. Why add layers of garbage to the operating system to try to prevent these efforts? Windows 95 isn't Windows NT, and isn't supposed to be. Why pile kludge on top of kludge to try to make life more difficult for people who really do need the information, and who use it responsibly?

SUMMARY

Modules, processes, and threads form the nucleus around which the rest of Windows 95 is built. In this chapter, we've examined their data structures and seen how various KERNEL32 functions use them. Chapter 8 on the PE file format will have more to say about modules. However, in nearly all the chapters that follow, you'll encounter some aspect of modules, processes, or threads. Understanding them is the magic key that unlocks the door to truly understanding Windows 95.

USER AND GDI SUBSYSTEMS

*I*t's a bit strange to start out a chapter with an apology, but that's exactly what I'm about to do. As the chapter title implies, I'm going to dig into and describe various facets of the Windows 95 USER and GDI components. The USER module contains all the code responsible for passing messages around the system and for managing windows. GDI is the core of the Windows graphics system. Putting a window on the screen requires an intense amount of cooperation between USER and GDI. Therefore, as you can probably imagine, describing just the topmost layer of the USER and GDI modules could easily encompass two books. That's why I'm going to beg off even attempting to describe how USER and GDI do much of their magic. Instead, this chapter focuses on how the Windows 95 USER and GDI modules have evolved from their 16-bit Windows 3.1 roots and have drawn from the Windows NT USER and GDI components.

Windows 95 features significant new USER and GDI-like functionality (such as the new common controls) that I can't even hope to cover in this book. I even half-jokingly suggested to my technical reviewer that there's probably a market for a book titled something like *WndProc Internals*. In that (purely hypothetical) book, there'd be detailed pseudocode listings for all the standard system window procedures (for example, the button window, the tooltips windows, and so on). The closest we'll come to that topic in this chapter is the desktop window procedure, for which I'll show pseudocode a bit later on.

So, given that you now know what's *not* going to be covered, what exactly *is* there to talk about? Lots, as it turns out. Just reimplementing the basic code of the Windows 3.1 USER and GDI to accommodate the demands of the Win32 API put these modules through gut-wrenching changes. If you're basically comfortable in your understanding of the way things worked under Windows 3.1, this chapter should help you make a transition in your mental model to the new way things work in Windows 95. I'm going to partition the chapter into two major parts (yes, you guessed it: USER and GDI). The USER portion of this chapter turned out to be much larger because USER's changes were more dramatic. Plus, once you understand Windows 95's changes to USER, it's not much harder to grasp how GDI has changed.

THE WINDOWS 95 USER MODULE

Throughout the writing of this book, I've struggled to categorize the changes to USER into neat compartments. As it turns out, the changes to the USER subsystem can't easily be placed into one or two specific categories. The Windows 95 USER component is neither fish nor fowl. The vast majority of the code for the messaging system resides in the 16-bit USER.EXE file, yet there is 32-bit code scattered throughout this 16-bit module. Some parts of the 16-bit USER.EXE are virtually identical to Windows 3.1, while other pieces have been radically reworked and bear no resemblance to the 3.1 USER.

The USER component of Windows 95 also includes the 32-bit USER32.DLL that Win32 EXEs and DLLs interface with. You may have heard that USER32.DLL is just a bunch of thunks down to the 16-bit USER.EXE. Although the vast majority of functions in USER32 are just thunks to 16-bit code, there are also nontrivial functions implemented in USER32.DLL with nary a thunk in sight. We'll see several examples of this later on.

Trying to put neat boxes around the design and implementations of the 16-bit USER.EXE and 32-bit USER32.DLL just doesn't seem possible. The best that I can say is that the Windows 95 coders did their best to balance the twin goals of backward compatibility and adherence to the Win32 specification as set forth by Windows NT. In many cases, backward compatibility and Win32 API adherence are at odds with one another. This resulted in the inevitable design compromises and decisions that nobody is particularly happy with. ("Class, can you say Win16Mutex?") All things considered, though, I think the Windows 95 USER team did an admirable job of balancing the twin requirements of compatibility and the Win32 API. I doubt many programmers would want to take on such a task for themselves, nor would they do as good a job.

To get a feel for the Windows 95 USER component, it helps to look at USER in Windows 95's Win32 siblings. The Windows NT USER is fully 32 bit, and its primary requirement is to properly implement the Win32 API. Backward compatibility is nice but not absolutely essential. The 16-bit USER.EXE component in Windows NT is implemented by thunks up to the real USER code in NT's USER32.DLL.

On the other side of Windows 95, the (mostly forgotten) Win32s attempts to provide as much of the Win32 API as possible while residing atop the relentlessly 16-bit Windows 3.1 USER.EXE. No changes to the 16-bit USER.EXE are allowed for Win32s. The poor Win32s coders had to live with the majority of their base code being frozen a year before the initial version of Win32s shipped. (Talk about requirements being cast in stone!)

So where does the Windows 95 USER system fall between these two points? While the Win32 purists (myself included) would have liked to have seen Windows 95 go the Windows NT route, it wasn't an option. Windows 95 is intended as the mass-market successor to Windows 3.1, and sacrificing backward compatibility simply wasn't an option. There are just too many existing programs out there that rely on the idiosyncrasies and quirks of the 16-bit USER.EXE. (A typical Microsoft comment at this point would be "See, we told you not to use undocumented stuff!")

Besides introducing incompatibilities with existing programs, Microsoft makes another case for keeping the core of USER's functionality in the 16-bit USER.EXE. Specifically, code size. In general, 32-bit code takes up more space because of the increased size of the operands for many instructions. (To be fair, this particular issue has been hotly debated, and one can come up with numerous examples where a particular operation can be implemented in fewer bytes by using 32-bit instructions.) On the whole, however, the Microsoft coders felt that reimplementing USER's functionality in pure 32-bit code would bloat the code size by something like 40 percent. Given that Windows 95 is supposed to run just as badly on a 4MB machine as Windows 3.1 (oops, the Microsoft marketeers would want me to say "just as well"), redoing USER as pure Win32 code (as Windows NT did) wasn't an option for Windows 95.

So, given that a real Win32 USER subsystem was out, the Windows 95 team did the next best thing. They started with the Windows 3.1 USER.EXE code and, unlike the Win32s team, were allowed to modify it. Since Windows 95's design necessitates at least an 80386, the Windows 95 USER team went hog wild with USER.EXE. There are 32-bit instructions all throughout USER.EXE's 16-bit code segments. (That's why you find so many size-override opcodes (66h) in the Windows 95 USER.EXE code segments.)

The fact that USER.EXE uses 32-bit data offsets throughout much of its 16-bit code bears a closer look. Much of USER's code is written in C, and, as you probably know, C compilers for the PC use memory models when generating their code. A regular 16-bit C compiler like Borland C++ emits 16-bit code instructions, which use segments and access data with 16-bit offsets. Even if the 16-bit compiler is allowed to generate 32-bit instructions, the generated code still won't generate instructions that index more than 64K into a segment.

In contrast, 32-bit compilers use the flat memory model. In the flat model, PC C compilers forget that segments exists. The code they generate never explicitly references the code selector, data selector, or stack selectors (the CS, DS, and SS registers). The code in Windows 95's USER.EXE looks like a hybrid of the 16-bit and flat memory models. That is, USER.EXE's code resides in 16-bit segments, and the code explicitly uses segment registers. On the other hand, the USER code also contains instructions that address more than 64K into a segment. Consider the following code snippet from USER.EXE:

```
1ACA:    MOV     AX,SEG 0021:0000
1ACD:    MOV     ES,AX
1ACF:    MOV     EAX,ES:[062E]
1AD4:    CMP     WORD PTR ES:[EAX+46],BX
1AD9:    JNE     1ADC
1ADB:    RET
```

The size of the instructions (such as the 3-byte first instruction) prove that this is 16-bit code. The first two instructions explicitly set up a segment register to grab a global variable at offset 062Eh in USER's DGROUP. But then the fourth instruction uses the EAX register as part of an address calculation. In actual execution of this code, EAX does in fact contain a value greater than 128K. Never before have I seen a compiler that can generate what is fundamentally 16-bit code at the same time it uses 32-bit offsets to data. It makes me wonder if the Windows 95 USER team used a special compiler developed by the languages division of Microsoft. (Update: An unnamed source told me after I had already written this chapter that such a compiler actually exists at Microsoft.)

Although many changes to the 16-bit USER.EXE were made simply to provide increased capacity (since running out of heap space was a chronic Windows 3.1 problem), many of the changes in the 16-bit USER.EXE were made solely to support the demands of the Win32 API. (Put another way, the Windows 95 team had to catch up to the NT team.) For example, the Win32 AttachThreadInput function, which associates the input state of one thread with that of another thread, has no Win16 counterpart. There simply wasn't anything even remotely like it in any prior 16-bit version of Windows. Yet Windows 95's 16-bit USER.EXE dutifully contains code that implements AttachThreadInput. USER.EXE is a modest DLL and doesn't export AttachThreadInput, yet USER32.DLL does support it. If you look closely, though, the AttachThreadInput code in USER32.DLL is little more than a thunk down to USER.EXE. USER32.DLL gets all the glory for providing its part of the Win32 API, while the Cinderella 16-bit USER.EXE does all the work.

Yet another example of where the 16-bit USER.EXE acts on behalf of its Win32 counterpart is with resources. As you'll see in Chapter 8, the resources stored in a Win32 Portable Executable (PE) file are organized in a completely different format than in the 16-bit New Executable (NE) file layout. Yet, as Chapter 7 shows, the 16-bit NE module database that Windows 95 creates for 32-bit modules contains a pointer to the base of the resources within the Win32 module in memory. Here's why: The 16-bit USER.EXE has taken on the burden of supporting both the old 16-bit NE format resources as well as the new Win32 PE format resources. The resources-related functions in USER32.DLL are relegated to the role of thunking down to USER.EXE.

USER32 thunking example

Since I'm on the subject of thunking, now is a good time to explain how thunking works in Windows 95. Windows 95 relies heavily on thunks between 16- and 32-bit code, so to really understand the Windows 95 architecture, there's no avoiding thunks. Let's look at an example of a typical function that USER32 uses to thunk down to the 16-bit USER.EXE. The function I've chosen to show is SetFocus. SetFocus takes one parameter, and this parameter (an HWND) doesn't require any translation of its value to be used by the 16-bit code. (In Windows NT, this is a different story altogether, but that's a subject for some future book.)

The SetFocus function

The SetFocus function in USER32 is similar to many other USER32 functions that thunk down to USER.EXE. In the debug version of USER32, the code starts out by calling a logging function. If a particular flag is set somewhere in USER32's data area, this function emits the string "[F] SetFocus" to the debug port. The important part of the USER32 SetFocus code is loading the CL register with an index into what is essentially a jump table of 16:16 addresses. In the case of SetFocus, the index value is 0x7E. That means that the 0x7E'th entry in the table is a 16:16 pointer to the 16-bit version of SetFocus.

After loading CL with 0x7E, SetFocus JMPs to a small routine that I've named ThunkToUSER16_One_Param. This small code is a common entry point for USER32 routines that take one parameter and thunk down to the 16-bit USER.EXE. All that ThunkToUSER16_One_Param does is push the calling function's parameters and thunk index onto the stack and then call another routine that I've named CommonThunk (and described next).

Pseudocode for SetFocus (32 -> 16)

```
LogWin16ThunkFunction1( "[F] SetFocus" );

CL = 0x7E   // Thunking index for SetFocus.

goto ThunkToUSER16_One_Param
```

Pseudocode for ThunkToUSER16_One_Param

```
// Parameters:
//  DWORD   param1
//  DWORD   thunkIndex  // Actually in CL register.

    return CommonThunk( param1, thunkIndex );
```

The CommonThunk code is so simple that trying to express it in C pseudocode would actually obscure its operation. For some unknown reason, the code for this routine resides in USER32's data area. Perhaps this code is built on the fly during startup. In any event, the routine's operation is extremely simple. First, it takes the thunk index (for example, 0x7E for the SetFocus function) and uses it as an array index into a table of 16:16

pointers. The routine retrieves the appropriate 16:16 address out of the array and places that into the EDX register. Finally, CommonThunk JMPs to the QT_Thunk routine in KERNEL32.DLL (which is described next).

Code for CommonThunk

```
// This code actually resides in USER32's data area.

XOR     ECX,ECX                      ;; 0 out ECX.
MOV     CL,[EBP-04]                  ;; Grab the thunk index (pushed by
                                     ;; ThunkToUSER16_One_Param).

MOV     EDX,[8014E264+4*ECX]         ;; Index into the array of 16:16 pointers
                                     ;; into the 16-bit DLLs. Put the appropriate
                                     ;; 16:16 pointer (e.g., SetFocus) into EDX.

MOV     EAX,offset KERNEL32!QT_Thunk ;; Jump to the QT_Thunk routine
JMP     EAX                          ;; in KERNEL32.DLL.
```

The QT_Thunk function

The QT_Thunk function is exported from KERNEL32.DLL. QT_Thunk is a general-purpose function that's used by Win32 code that needs to thunk down to Win16 code. In other words, its use isn't restricted to just KERNEL32 or USER32. In fact, if you look at the assembler output from the Win32 SDK's thunk compiler (THUNK.EXE), you'll see that it references and uses the QT_Thunk routine.

The QT_Thunk routine is quite obviously coded in assembler and is optimized for both space and speed. I briefly debated showing the raw assembler version of the function in this section. However, it quickly became obvious that the code would be impenetrable except to a very small group of assembler hackers. Therefore, what you'll see in the following pseudocode is a mix of C pseudocode and assembler. I did my best to convey the intent of a fairly complex routine. If you really want to see what goes on, by all means, set a breakpoint on QT_Thunk in SoftIce/W (or some other system debugger) and step through it. I guarantee that you won't wait long for the breakpoint to be hit.

Looking at the routine from orbit (as a certain Microsoft employee would say), the job of QT_Thunk is simple: Take the 16:16 address passed into it in the EDX register and transfer control to that address. Of course, nothing is ever that simple, and there are other issues that need to be taken care of. For starters, saving away the address that execution should return to after the 16-bit code finishes would be very helpful. Likewise, it's a very good idea to switch the stack from a flat 32-bit stack selector to a 16-bit selector.

Moving in a bit closer to the routine (a "helicopter view," if you will), QT_Thunk is divided into five distinct phases. First, in the debug version, the code calls a routine that logs the call (assuming the right logging flag is set, which it usually isn't). This section of code also verifies that the Thread Information Block (TIB) selector (see Chapter 3) is the same as the FS register. If not, the routine complains (in the debug version, that is).

Phase 2 of QT_Thunk pushes the 16:16 address that's the ultimate target of the thunk onto the stack. (We'll come back to this in phase 5.) Phase 2 also handles the preservation of the return address and the 32-bit register variables. The 32-bit return address that control returns to after the 16-bit code completes is stored in an area of the stack that won't be touched. The register variables that are saved away are ESI, EDI, and EBX. These are the commonly used register variables that Win32 compilers expect will be preserved (see Chapter 3).

Phase 3 of QT_Thunk relates to acquiring the Win16Mutex. As almost everybody knows by now, whenever 32-bit code thunks down to 16-bit code, the operating system needs to acquire the Win16Mutex. The Win16Mutex is just a run-of-the-mill mutex semaphore that happens to reside in KRNL386.EXE's data segment. By forcing all Win32 code that thunks down to 16-bit land to acquire the Win16Mutex, Windows 95 can guarantee that only one thread at a time is executing through the Win16 system DLLs (as well as other 16-bit bit DLLs).

This is how Microsoft got around the problem of the 16-bit system DLLs being written without multithreading in mind. The whole subject of the Win16Mutex has been highly controversial, and I could easily write an entire chapter on just this topic. I'll talk a bit more about this in the "Messaging System Changes" section, but here I'm simply going to say that the QT_Thunk routine is one of the places where Windows 95 acquires the Win16Mutex.

Phase 4 of QT_Thunk is where the routine switches from the flat 32 stack used by the Win32 code to a 16:16 stack for use by the Win16 code. Since Win32 threads typically have 1MB stacks, and the ESP at the time of the thunk could be anywhere within that 1MB, you can see that switching to a 16:16 stack could be tricky. It's not sufficient to just allocate a 16-bit stack selector during the thread's startup and set its base address at that time. Instead, during the thunk to 16 bits, the QT_Thunk routine may need to adjust the base address of the stack selector used by the thread when executing in 16-bit code. The base address of the 16-bit selector is set so that it points to the same general linear address region that the ESP register was using prior to the thunk. After fiddling with the stack selector as necessary, QT_Thunk figures out an appropriate 16-bit SS:SP combination and loads those values into the SS and SP registers.

Phase 5, the final phase of QT_Thunk, is to transfer control to the intended 16:16 address that's the target of the thunk. As I showed in phase 2, the 16:16 target address was stored in EDX upon entry to QT_Thunk and was subsequently pushed on the stack. QT_Thunk jumps to the 16:16 address via the standard RETF trick. Before transferring control to that address, though, the QT_Thunk code zeros out all the nonessential segment registers (DS, ES, FS, and GS). It wouldn't do to hand the target 16:16 function a DS register set up with a nice, juicy flat 32 selector for the function to scribble on. It's expected that the 16:16 function will set up the segment registers however it needs to.

Pseudocode for QT_Thunk

```
// On entry, EDX contains the 16:16 address to transfer control to.

//
// Phase 1: logging and sanity checking
//
if ( bit 0 not set in FS:[TIBFlags] )
    goto someplace else;              // Not interested in that here.

PUSHAD          // Save all the registers.

SomeTraceLoggingFunction( "LS", EDX, 0 );   // EDX is 16:16 target.

// Make sure that the FS register agrees with the TIB register stored
// in the current thread database.

if ( (ppCurrentThread->TIBSelector != FS)
      && (ppCurrentThread != SomeKERNEL32Variable) )
{
    _DebugOut( SLE_MINORERROR,
               "32=>16 thunk:  thread=%lx, fs=%x, should be %x\n\r",
               ppCurrentThreadId, FS, ppCurrentThread->TibSelector );

}

POPAD           // Restore all the registers.
```

```
//
// Phase 2: saving away the return address and register variable registers
//
POP     DWORD PTR [EBP-24]        // Grab return address off the stack
                                  // and store it away for later use.


PUSH    DWORD PTR [someVariable]    // ???
PUSH    EDX     // Push 16:16 address on the stack. The RETF
                // at the end will effectively JMP to it.

MOV     DWORD PTR [EBP-04],EBX  // Save away the common
MOV     DWORD PTR [EBP-08],ESI  // compiler register variables.
MOV     DWORD PTR [EBP-0C],EDI


//
// Phase 3: Acquiring the Win16Mutex
//
PUSHAD, PUSHFD                   // Save all registers.
_CheckSysLevel( pWin16Mutex )
POPFD, POPAD                     // Restore all registers.

FS:[Win16MutexCount]++;
if ( FS:[Win16MutexCount] == 0 )
    GrabMutex( pWin16Mutex );

PUSHAD, PUSHFD                   // Save all registers.
_CheckSysLevel( pWin16Mutex )
POPFD, POPAD                     // Restore all registers.

//
// Phase 4: Saving off the old SS:ESP and switching to the 16:16 stack
//
Calculate the 16:16 stack ptr. Set EBX for the SUB EBP,EBX instruction below.

MOV     DX,WORD PTR [EDI->currentSS]     // Load DX with 16-bit SS.

MOV     DI,SS     // Save away the flat SS value into DI.
                  // (The callee is expected to preserve it.)

MOV     SS,DX     // Load SS:(E)SP with the 16-bit stack ptr.
MOV     ESP,ESI

SUB     EBP,EBX   // Adjust EBP for the thunk.
MOV     SI,FS     // Save away FS (TIB ptr) register into SI.
                  // (The callee is expected to preserve it.)
```

```
//
// Phase 5: Jumping to the 16:16-bit code
//
GS = FS = ES = DS = 0;   // Zero out the segment registers.

RETF                     // Effectively does a JMP 16:16 to the address
                         // passed in the EDX register.
```

After the 16-bit code does its stuff, it needs to return to the 32-bit code. There's a whole other section of code that goes through those motions. Although I could go through it here, it's not terribly exciting. It's also important to note that during this example of thunking to 16-bit code, there weren't any flat 32 pointer parameters that would have needed conversion to 16:16 addresses. The thunking code for that is understandably more complex, and we won't get into it here.

32-bit heaps

Perhaps the biggest and most drastic change to the USER subsystem is the addition of 32-bit heaps. You're probably aware that any Win32 program can access and use 32-bit heap services provided via the Win32 HeapXXX API (for example, HeapAlloc, HeapFree, and so on). What you may not know is that the 16-bit USER.EXE and 16-bit GDI.EXE also use 32-bit heaps to store certain items. You heard that right. The 16-bit USER.EXE and GDI.EXE actually thunk up to 32-bit KERNEL32.DLL to allocate memory from special 32-bit heaps set up especially for the use of the 16-bit USER and GDI components. Although these particular heaps are intended solely for USER's and GDI's use, they share the exact same format as a Win32 program's GetProcessHeap heap. For instance, you can use the WALKHEAP program from Chapter 5 to walk the USER or GDI 32-bit heaps (although you would have to locate them first, which I'll show how to do later).

Why go to all this trouble with 32-bit heaps? In versions of Windows prior to Windows 95, all allocated memory used by USER and GDI came out of a standard LocalAlloc style heap with a maximum size of 64K. Needless to say, this put quite a crimp on how many windowing and graphics system objects could be kept around at any given time. By moving these large objects to 32-bit heaps, Windows 95 significantly improves the capacity of the system. Each of these specially created heaps is 2MB, so capacity shouldn't be a problem for awhile.

USER.EXE actually uses two separate 32-bit heaps. One of these heaps stores WND structures. There's a WND structures for every window in the system. (We'll look at WND structures a bit later in this chapter.) The other USER 32-bit heap is for storing menus. GDI.EXE has just one 32-bit heap, which it uses to store fonts and regions. Like WNDs and MENUs on the USER side, fonts and regions are relatively large, so moving them out of the 16-bit heaps makes sense.

If the addition of 32-bit heaps to the 16-bit components of Windows 95 is big news, then the location of those heaps is even more interesting. You see, when accessing data in the 32-bit heaps, USER and GDI don't use the flat model linear addresses of the items. Instead, USER and GDI continue to use the same DS selector that they use to access their regular 128K DGROUP. How do they get away with that? By using a rather interesting arrangement, the 32-bit WND heap and 32-bit GDI heaps start exactly 128K past the 16-bit DGROUP area. If this sounds a bit weird, perhaps Figure 4-1 will make it clearer.

As I mentioned earlier, USER and GDI don't use 32-bit flat pointers to items in their 32-bit heaps. Rather, they store offsets relative to the base address of the USER or GDI DGROUP selector. These offsets are, of course, 32 bits. For example, USER's 16-bit (128K) DGROUP area has a maximum size of 64K. The 32-bit WND heap starts 128K past the end of the 16-bit DGROUP area. That means that the lowest possible WND structure offset that you would find in Windows 95 is 0x20000. In actual use (as you'll see in Chapter 5), the first couple of paragraphs of a Win32 heap are used for bookkeeping, so a more typical WND structure offset would be something like 0x20924. Since this offset isn't a flat linear address, the offset is meaning-less unless the selector (that is, USER or GDI's DGROUP) is also known. Of course, if you know the linear address of USER's or GDI's DGROUP segment, you can add that value to the offset of an object in a 32-bit heap and access the data object with a flat linear address. The SHOWWND program introduced later in this chapter does just that.

Let's prove that the 32-bit WND heap really starts 128K above the reg-ular DGROUP and that it's really a standard Win32-style heap. To do this, we'll use SoftIce/W. To start out, we need to find the base address of USER's DGROUP segment. And to find this information, we need to first find USER's DGROUP handle/selector. As Chapter 7 will show, the DGROUP for a module can be extracted from the 16-bit module database.

The SoftIce/W MOD command applied to USER yields the following:

```
:mod user
hMod PEHeader     Module Name     EXE File Name
17CF              USER            C:\WINDOWS\SYSTEM\user.exe
1857 0147:81537DB8 USER32         C:\WINDOWS\SYSTEM\USER32.DLL
```

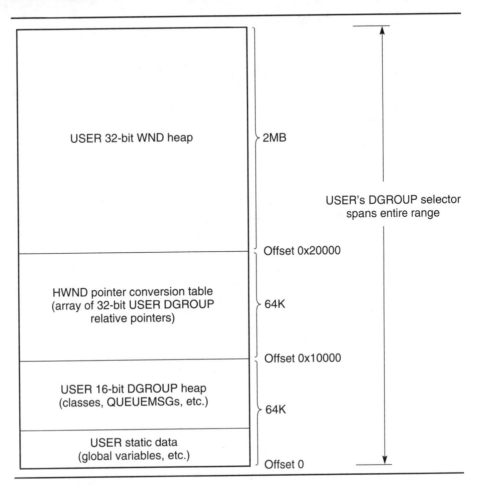

Figure 4-1

USER.EXE's 16- and 32-bit heap configuration.

We now know that USER's module handle is 17CF. At offset 8 in a module database is a near pointer to the 10-byte segment record for the DGROUP segment, so let's dump that out:

```
:dw 17cf:8
17CF:00000008 0180 10D9 C341 0021 157C 0000 1F42 0015    ....A.!.|...B...
....
```

Okay. At 17CF:180 is the 10-byte segment record for USER's DGROUP. The last WORD of the segment record is the handle assigned to that segment. Dumping that segment record gives us:

```
:dw 17cf:180
17CF:00000180 4042 0B02 0177 157C 16C6 0005 800C 000F     B@..w.|.........
```

So, now we know that USER's DGROUP handle is 16C6 (and that the corresponding selector is 16C7). Let's get the linear address of that selector with the SoftIce/W LDT command (also, note that the limit of the segment is greater than 64K):

```
:ldt 16c6
16C7  Data16    Base=81D09000  Lim=0021FFFF  DPL=3  P   RW
```

Knowing that USER's DGROUP is at linear address 0x81D09000, we can add 0x20000 to it to obtain the starting address of the USER32 window heap. Let's test this out by feeding the address to the SoftIce/W "Heap 32" command:

```
:heap 32 81d29000
Heap: 81D29000  Max Size: 2048K  Committed: 16K  Segments: 1
Address   Size        EIP       TID    Owner
81D290E0  00000088  BFFA0A27  0001   hpWalk+082D
81D29178  00000058  BFF71AA6  0001   IGetLocalTime+0942
81D291E0  00000058  BFF71AA6  0001   IGetLocalTime+0942
81D29248  0000005C  BFF71AA6  0001   IGetLocalTime+0942
81D292B4  00000058  BFF71AA6  0004   IGetLocalTime+0942
81D2931C  00000058  BFF71AA6  0007   IGetLocalTime+0942
81D29384  00000060  BFF71AA6  000A   IGetLocalTime+0942
81D293F4  0000005C  BFF71AA6  000A   IGetLocalTime+0942
81D29460  00000058  BFF71AA6  000A   IGetLocalTime+0942
81D294C8  0000005C  BFF71AA6  000A   IGetLocalTime+0942
81D29534  0000005C  BFF71AA6  000A   IGetLocalTime+0942
81D295A0  0000005C  BFF71AA6  000A   IGetLocalTime+0942
81D2960C  0000005C  BFF71AA6  000A   IGetLocalTime+0942
81D29678  00000058  BFF71AA6  000A   IGetLocalTime+0942
... rest of output omitted...
```

As you can see, SoftIce/W certainly didn't complain about the address we fed it, and, in fact, it printed out results that look quite reasonable. In particular, notice how all the blocks are somewhere in the neighborhood of 0x58 bytes. As we'll see later, 0x58 is the minimum size of a WND structure. The blocks that are slightly bigger can be explained by their use of window extra words (see the cbWndExtra field in the WNDCLASS structure, which is used to register a class). By all accounts, it looks like there really is a Win32 heap residing 128K above the start of USER's DGROUP segment.

At this point, you're probably wondering why the 32-bit heaps start 128K past the end of the USER or GDI DGROUP segments. (You were wondering, weren't you?) Why not start the heap right after the 16-bit 128K DGROUP area ends? Here's the answer in a nutshell: Handles! Although the WND structures themselves are accessed using 32-bit offsets from USER's DGROUP, this pesky backward compatibility thing means that HWNDs must be 16 bits.

In Windows 3.*x* and earlier, an HWND was nothing more than an offset into USER's DGROUP segment. Clearly that won't work when the WND structures are at least 128K into USER's combined 16-/32-bit DGROUP. To allow a 16-bit value (such as an HWND) to be mapped to a 32-bit offset, USER and GDI use the 64K region between their 16-bit DGROUP and the 32-bit heaps as a handle table. Specifically, a handle value (like an HWND) is just an offset into the handle table region. As Figure 4-2 shows, at the offset pointed to by a handle, you'll find the 32-bit offset (relative to the appropriate DGROUP) of the actual data.

To prove this point about handle tables, let's again turn to SoftIce/W. Let's pick the desktop HWND and look it up through the handle table. The SoftIce/W WND command provides a hierarchical view of the window list, with the desktop window at the top. In the following output, the desktop window's HWND is 0x80:

```
:hwnd
Window Handle    hQueue   SZ  QOwner     Class Name        Window Procedure
0080(0)          1437     32  MSGSRV32   #32769            17B7:571C
   00B4(1)       1A4F     32  EXPLORER   Shell_TrayWnd     1457:0140
     00B8(2)     1A4F     32  EXPLORER   Button            1457:01AE
     00BC(2)     1A4F     32  EXPLORER   TrayNotifyWnd     1457:01C4
... rest of windows omitted...
```

Now, if what I said earlier is true, we should be able to add the HWND value to 0x10000 and, at that offset in USER's DGROUP, find a DWORD with the WND struct's address. 0x10000 + 0x0080 == 0x10080, so let's dump memory at 16C7:10080:

```
:dd 16c7:10080
16C7:00010080 0002:0178 0002:01E0 0002:0248 0002:02B4    x.......H.......
```

Ignoring the ":" (colon) that SoftIce/W stuck in (it's trying to show the value as a 16:16 pointer), the offset of the WND struct appears to be at 0x20178. Since USER's DGROUP is at linear address 0x81d09000, this would place the WND struct at linear address 81D29178. Looking back at SoftIce/W's walk of the 32-bit user heap that I showed earlier, you can see that 0x81D29178 is indeed the address of a block in the heap. Once again, it looks like everything checks out.

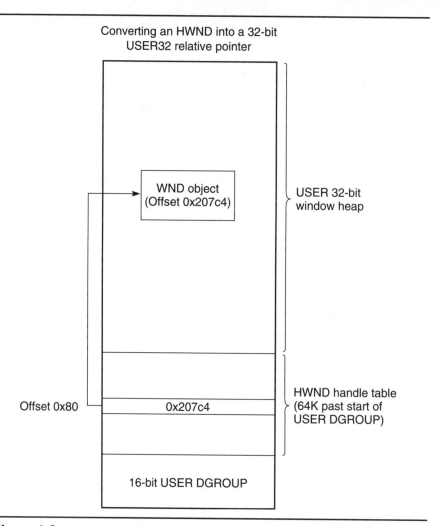

Converting an HWND into a 32-bit
USER32 relative pointer

WND object
(Offset 0x207c4)

USER 32-bit
window heap

Offset 0x80

0x207c4

HWND handle table
(64K past start of
USER DGROUP)

16-bit USER DGROUP

▌ Figure 4-2
The 32-bit offset (relative to the appropriate DGROUP) of the actual data is found at the offset pointed to by a handle.

When it comes to GDI's 32-bit heap, this same handle table mechanism is essentially the same for objects that GDI keeps in the 32-bit heap. For instance, regions are kept in a 32-bit heap and are referred to by an HRGN structure. You could apply a similar set of steps to the HRGN to find the actual linear address of the region structure.

If the handle table region is 64K and each handle is really a pointer to a 4-byte DWORD, that would make the maximum number of handles equal to 16384 (65,536/4 == 16,384). Microsoft claims that you can now have up to 32,767 windows and 32,767 menus, so I don't know how they're coming up with these numbers. Regardless, what's not mentioned is that other system limitations will most likely be hit before you manage to create 16 thousand (or 32 thousand) windows.

Earlier, I mentioned that USER also has a 32-bit menu heap. The menu heap area and the handle table region are operationally identical to the USER window heap (although at a different address, obviously). The only thing missing is a 64K 16-bit DGROUP sitting beneath the handle table. While you might think it was nice of Microsoft to break menus out into their own separate 32-bit heap, this isn't as big a change as you might imagine. In Windows 3.1, menus were already broken out into their own 16-bit heap. In Windows 95, the only change is that the size of the menu heap increased. Incidentally, the selector to the base of the menu heap can be found by one of the UserSeeUserDo subfunctions that I'll describe later in this chapter.

If the 32-bit heaps used by USER and GDI are functionally the same as the heaps of Win32 applications, it makes sense that the KERNEL32 functions for operating on Win32 heaps would be used for the USER and GDI heaps as well. Indeed, this turns out to be the case. When USER allocates memory for a WND structure, the code that implements the HeapAlloc function in KERNEL32.DLL is called via a thunk. However, USER and GDI don't thunk up to KERNEL32 directly. Rather, KRNL386.EXE provides a set of undocumented exported functions that take care of calling the KERNEL32 heap code. The KRNL386 functions are the following:

KRNL386.209 — Local32Alloc

KRNL386.210 — Local32ReAlloc

KRNL386.211 — Local32Free

KRNL386.213 — Local32Translate (Translate a handle into a
            16:16 address)

KRNL386.214 — Local32FreeQuickly

Although the function names start with Local32, they really call into the equivalent HeapXXX function (for instance, Local32Alloc calls HeapAlloc). Chapter 5 shows that the Win32 local heap functions are just a thin wrapper around the Win32 HeapXXX functions. Of special note in the list of KRNL386 32-bit heap functions is function 214. This function appears to create the net effect of marking a block as free, without actually thunking up to KERNEL32. However, certain key things aren't done by this routine, such as adding the block to the free list.

The mysterious GetFreeSystemResources issue

Having covered 32-bit heaps, we now have enough background information to look at the mysteriously growing FreeSystemResources issue. I say mysterious, because the average FreeSystemResource number seems to have jumped in Windows 95, although under the hood there doesn't seem to be any reason for it. We'll look at free system resources early on in this chapter, since to most nonprogrammers, the "free system resources" are the only notion they have of USER and GDI. If the free system resources go up, it must be good, right? Not so fast!

The free system resource number is really just a fancy term for the amount of memory left in various systems heaps, specified as a percentage. In Windows 3.1, the free system resources was the smallest value of several percentages. The percentages in question were the amount of free space in the USER DGROUP heap, the USER menu heap, the USER string heap (which is apparently gone or not important in Windows 95), and the GDI DGROUP heap. Out of those heaps, the heap with the smallest percentage free became the free system resources.

In Windows 95, the calculation for FreeSystemResources starts out on a somewhat similar track, but toward the end it takes an unexpected turn. In a nutshell, the FreeSystemResources in Windows 95 starts out looking like it's the lowest percentage free among five separate heaps:

1) The USER 16-bit DGROUP heap

2) The 32-bit window heap

3) The 32-bit menu heap

4) The 16-bit GDI heap

5) The 32-bit GDI heap

Since the three 32-bit heaps are all 2MB in size, their percentage free is usually a ridiculously high value, like 99 percent. Therefore, for all intents and purposes, they don't count toward the free system resource calculation. That leaves only the 16-bit USER and GDI DGROUP heaps. Whichever one has the smaller percentage will dictate the free system resource percentage. Since there's still quite a few items floating around in the USER and GDI DGROUPs, they shouldn't have values anywhere near 96 percent free (which is a typical value you might see in the Explorer About box after you first start Windows 95).

At this point, I'd suggest you try a small experiment. Boot up Windows 95 and immediately start up CALC, or Explorer, or some standard application that comes with the system. Choose Help|About to get the About dialog that displays the free system resource value. Typically, under Windows 95 you'll have a value like 96 percent. If that sounds a little high, you're right. As you'll see in the pseudocode for GetFreeSystemResources later on, neither USER nor GDI have anywhere near 96 percent free in their heaps.

So just what exactly is going on here? To make a long story short, Windows 95 is "cooking the books." Rather than simply report the lowest percentage free among the heaps, the Windows 95 free system resources is a relative number. You're no doubt asking, "Relative to what?" The Windows 95 free system resources value that is reported is a percentage relative to how much was free after the system booted. Specifically, after the system has booted and Explorer has done its thing, Windows 95 takes a snapshot of what the real percentage free is. Subsequently, when you query the system for the free system resources, it reports the percentage free, relative to the original snapshot value.

Let's look at an example. Say that Windows 95 is up and running and the true free system resource value (à la Windows 3.1) is 75 percent. Let's also say that, at some later point, you've started some applications, and there's now only 50 percent free in one of the heaps. Windows 95 will report the free system resources as 66 percent (50/75) rather than as the true 50 percent. If this isn't an attempt to put a positive spin on things, I don't know what is. Perhaps Microsoft feels the need for its customers to believe that Windows 95 really has eliminated the free system resources problem. Sure, Windows 95 improves the situation with its 32-bit heaps, but not *that* much.

Lest I be accused of Microsoft-bashing, here's an alternative explanation for why Microsoft changed the way that the free system resource value is calculated: There's a well-defined maximum amount of memory that's available for system resources. The act of starting up and creating windows like the desktop and the tray window consumes some of this memory. Since there's no way to reclaim this memory, why report it to the unsuspecting end users? The new free system resource value can be viewed as being more accurate from the end users' perspective. If the end users have 50 percent resources free, then they've used up about half of the available capacity. The end users don't know (and probably don't care) that the system itself takes up some of the free system resources.

The GetFreeSystemResources function

Now that we know basically what's up (pun intended) with the new free system resource calculation, let's look at the details of how Windows 95 comes up with that value. The GetFreeSystemResources is implemented in the 16-bit USER.EXE (when necessary, SHELL32.DLL thunks down to it to get the value it displays in the system utility About boxes). The function itself is just a standard parameter-validation layer stub like I described in Chapter 3. After checking that a correct argument was passed to it, GetFreeSystemResources JMPs to the IGetFreeSystemResources code.

IGetFreeSystemResources has three distinct sections of code. The first section consists of coming up with percentage-free values for the USER and GDI components. The USER percentage free is the lowest percentage free of the USER 16-bit DGROUP, the 32-bit window heap, and the 32-bit menu heap. The GDI percentage free is done by calling a 16-bit GDI.EXE function called GDIFreeResources. At the end of this section of code, the function has one free resource value for USER and another for GDI.

The second section of IGetFreeSystemResources is where the function does the adjustments that take into account how much USER and GDI heap space was taken up by system components at startup. The key to this section of code is two USER.EXE global variables; I've named the variables base_USER_FSR_percentage and base_GDI_FSR_percentage. These two values initially start out with a value of 0 in USER.EXE's data segment. If they're 0 when IGetFreeSystemResources is called, the function doesn't do any adjustment to the USER and GDI percentage free values it calculated earlier. However, if these two global variables are nonzero, they contain the percentage free in the USER and GDI heaps after Windows 95 booted. If they're nonzero, IGetFreeSystemResources divides the boot-up time version of these values by the current USER and GDI percentage free values to get a relative percentage.

When I first saw these global variables, my first question was, "Who the heck sets them?" Would you believe the Explorer process? (Even if you don't see the Explorer window on the screen, Explorer is still there as a running process.) Now mind you, Explorer doesn't reach down into USER's DGROUP segment and set the base_USER_FSR_percentage and base_GDI_FSR_percentage values directly. Rather, it lets USER.EXE do it itself. How does it do this? At some point when Explorer decides that it's sufficiently set up, it sends a window message with a MSG number of 0x400 (WM_USER) to the desktop window procedure. As you'll see later, the desktop WNDPROC handler for the WM_USER message sets these two global variables. The ramifications of this are mind boggling. If you have a process or a DLL that calls GetFreeSystemResources before the desktop WM_USER message is sent, you'll get a distinctly different value than after the message is sent.

The third section of IGetFreeSystemResources is where the function uses the parameter passed in. If you specifically request the USER or GDI free resources (GFSR_USERRESOURCES or GFSR_GDIRESOURCES), the code returns the appropriate value calculated earlier. If you ask for GFSR_SYSTEMRESOURCES, the function returns the smaller of the USER and GDI percentages.

Pseudocode for GetFreeSystemResources

```
// Parameters:
//   UINT    fuSysResource

    // Is the input parameter within range?
    if ( (fuSysResource < 0) || (fuSysResource > 2) )
    {
        // Calls LogParamError.
        HandleParamError( ERR_BAD_VALUE );
    }

    // JMP to the real code.
    return IGetFreeSystemResources( fuSysResource );
```

Pseudocode for IGetFreeSystemResources

```
// Parameters:
//   UINT    fuSysResource
//   WORD    gdiResourcePercentage, userResourcePercentage

    //
    // Phase 1:  Getting USER and GDI's percentage free
    //
    if ( UserTraceFlags & 0x200 )
        _DebugOutput( DBF_USER, "GetFreeSystemResources" );

    userResourcePercentage =
        GetPercentFree16BitHeap(hInstanceWin);  // Get 16-bit DGROUP % free.

    // Call GDI and let it do its heap free calculations.
    gdiResourcePercentage = GDIFreeResources( 0 );
```

```
// Take the lesser of the USER's DGROUP and the 32-bit menu heap.
// (Gee, I wonder which one it will be???)
if ( GetPercentFree32BitHeap(hMenuHeap) < userResourcePercentage )
    userResourcePercentage = GetPercentFree32BitHeap(hMenuHeap);

// Now take the lesser value of the previous calculation and the
// percentage free in the 32-bit window heap.
if ( GetPercentFree32BitHeap(hWindowHeap) < userResourcePercentage )
    userResourcePercentage = GetPercentFree32BitHeap( hWindowHeap );

//
//  Phase 2: Cooking the books
//

// Adjust the percentages so that they're relative to the percent
// free after booting. This might be an attempt to make Windows 95 look
// like it has more free system resources than Windows 3.1.
if ( base_USER_FSR_percentage )
{
    userResourcePercentage = MulDiv( userResourcePercentage, 0x100,
                                     base_USER_FSR_percentage );

    gdiResourcePercentage  = MulDiv( gdiResourcePercentage, 0x100,
                                     base_GDI_FSR_percentage );
}

if ( userResourcePercentage > 99 )
    userResourcePercentage = 99;

if ( gdiResourcePercentage > 99 )
    gdiResourcePercentage = 99;

//
// Phase 3
//
switch ( fuSysResources )
{
    case GFSR_SYSTEMRESOURCES:
        return min( userResourcePercentage, gdiResourcePercentage );

    case GFSR_GDIRESOURCES:
        return gdiResourcePercentage;

    case GFSR_USERRESOURCES:
        return userResourcePercentage;

    default: return fuSysResources;
}
```

The GetPercentFree16BitHeap and GetPercentFree32BitHeap functions

The GetPercentFree16BitHeap and GetPercentFree32BitHeap functions are two helper routines used by IGetFreeSystemResources. Both functions expect a parameter specifying the heap of interest. The GetPercentFree16BitHeap function uses the undocumented GetHeapSpaces function described in Chapter 5 of *Undocumented Windows* (Schulman, Maxey, and Pietrek). It considers the ratio of free space (in K) to total space (also in K) to be the percentage free.

The GetPercentFree32BitHeap is a little more sophisticated. It uses the same basic code that the Windows 95 16-bit TOOLHELP function exports as the Local32Info function. This code returns dwMemCommitted, dwTotalFree, and dwMemReserved fields for the heap in question. The dwMemCommitted and dwMemReserved fields seem to always be the same, and the dwTotalFree value is usually right up there in value. After subtracting the dwTotalFree field from the dwMemCommitted field, the function divides the result by the dwMemReserved field. Since these values are all nearly equal, the GetPercentFree32BitHeap function typically returns values such as 98 or 99 percent.

Pseudocode for GetPercentFree16BitHeap

```
// Parameters:
//   HGLOBAL hHeap
// Locals:
//   DWORD    freeK, totalK
//   DWORD    myDWORD

    myDWORD = GetHeapSpaces( hHeap );    // See Undocumented Windows,
                                         // Chapter 5.

    freeK = LOWORD(myDWORD) / 1024;

    totalK = HIWORD(myDWORD) / 1024;

    return (freeK * 100) / totalK
```

Pseudocode for GetPercentFree32BitHeap

```
// Parameters:
//   HGLOBAL hHeap
// Locals:
//   LOCAL32INFO local32Info;
//   WORD percentUsed;
```

```
// Call the same function that TOOLHELP.DLL's Local32Info uses.
local32Info.dwSize = sizeof( LOCAL32INFO );
if ( KRNL386_Local32Info( &local32Info, hHeap ) == 0 )
    return 0;

if ( local32Info.dwMemReserved == 0 )    // Some problem here officer???
    return 0;

percentUsed =
    CalculatePercentage(
        100 * (local32Info.dwMemCommited - local32Info.dwTotalFree),
        local32Info.dwMemReserved );

// percentUsed is typically some ridiculously low value, like 1%. Thus
// this function usually returns 99% free for 32-bit heaps.

return 100 - percentUsed;
```

Getting Free System Resources from 32-Bit Code: Thunking Without the Thunk Compiler

Believe it or not, Windows 95 doesn't provide a way for 32-bit applications to get the Free System Resources (FSR) value easily from a 32-bit program. Even when the standard Windows 95 utilities display the FSR in their About box, they're getting the value from a 32-to-16-bit thunk in SHELL32.DLL. If you're writing a 32-bit program and want to call an existing 16-bit system bit function (such as GetFreeSystemResources), you could spend a couple of hours (or days) learning the Windows 95 thunk compiler, and then write a pair of thunking DLLs. Ugh. There's got to be a better way.

As I discuss in "The SetFocus function" section, USER32.DLL thunks down to USER.EXE all the time, yet it doesn't have separate 16- and 32-bit DLLs for thunking. Instead, the 32-bit SetFocus code uses the QT_Thunk function, which I described earlier in "The QT_Thunk routine" section. You can use this very same routine in your own programs, although it's a bit trickier to use than your standard Win32 API function. It's an undocumented function (although you'll see that the THUNK.EXE thunk compiler emits references to it), and it requires that you use a bit of assembler to call it.

Calling QT_Thunk in your code requires you to do two things. First, you have to put the 16:16 address to call into the EDX register. Second, you need to ensure that the code you're calling QT_Thunk from has an EBP stack frame set up and has at least 0x3C bytes of local storage that you're not relying on. This second requirement is because QT_Thunk builds the convoluted stack frame for calling the 16-bit code in the region below where your EBP register points at.

To show calling QT_Thunk from your own program, I wrote the FSR32 program, which uses QT_Thunk to get the free USER and GDI system resources. The code for FSR32 is a single source file, FSR32.C, and is short enough to show here. To compile FSR32, use the following Visual C++ command line:

```
cl fsr32.c k32lib.lib thunk32.lib
```

Alternatively, you can use the BUILDFSR.BAT file included on this book's source disk.

```c
//==================================
// FSR32 - Matt Pietrek 1995
// FILE: FSR32.C
//==================================
#define WIN32_LEAN_AND_MEAN
#include <windows.h>
#include <stdio.h>
#pragma hdrstop

typedef int (CALLBACK *GFSR_PROC)(int);

// Steal some #define's from the 16-bit WINDOWS.H.
#define GFSR_GDIRESOURCES       0x0001
#define GFSR_USERRESOURCES      0x0002

// Prototype some undocumented KERNEL32 functions.
HINSTANCE WINAPI LoadLibrary16( PSTR );
void WINAPI FreeLibrary16( HINSTANCE );
FARPROC WINAPI GetProcAddress16( HINSTANCE, PSTR );
void __cdecl QT_Thunk(void);

GFSR_PROC pfnFreeSystemResources = 0;   // We don't want these as locals in
HINSTANCE hInstUser16;                   // main(), since QT_THUNK could
WORD user_fsr, gdi_fsr;                   // trash them...

int main()
{
    char buffer[0x40];

    buffer[0] = 0;  // Make sure to use the local variable so that the
                    // compiler sets up an EBP frame.
```

Continued

Continued from previous page

```
        hInstUser16 = LoadLibrary16("USER.EXE");
        if ( hInstUser16 < (HINSTANCE)32 )
        {
            printf( "LoadLibrary16() failed!\n" );
            return 1;
        }

        FreeLibrary16( hInstUser16 );    // Decrement the reference count.

        pfnFreeSystemResources =
            (GFSR_PROC) GetProcAddress16(hInstUser16,
    "GetFreeSystemResources");
            if ( !pfnFreeSystemResources )
        {
            printf( "GetProcAddress16() failed!\n" );
            return 1;
        }

        __asm {
            push    GFSR_USERRESOURCES
            mov     edx, [pfnFreeSystemResources]
            call    QT_Thunk
            mov     [user_fsr], ax

            push    GFSR_GDIRESOURCES
            mov     edx, [pfnFreeSystemResources]
            call    QT_Thunk
            mov     [gdi_fsr], ax
        }

        printf( "USER FSR: %u%%  GDI FSR: %u%%\n", user_fsr, gdi_fsr );

        return 0;
    }
```

The output from FSR32.C looks like this:

```
C:\NEWBOOK\USERGDI>FSR32.EXE
USER FSR: 90%  GDI FSR: 90%
```

A couple of things in the FSR32.C code need to be discussed. First, how is FSR32.C getting the address of the 16-bit GetFreeSystemResources function from 32-bit code? FSR32.C uses three undocumented KERNEL32 functions (LoadLibrary16, FreeLibrary16, and GetProcAddress16) to work with the 16-bit system DLLs. Appendix A provides a fairly complete list of the undocumented functions in KERNEL32. In order for FSR32 to successfully link to these undocumented functions, it needs the K32LIB.LIB import library that you first saw in Chapter 3. (This library is discussed in Appendix A.)

To ensure that there's enough space on the stack for QT_Thunk to play its funny games with, FSR32.C declares a local array of 0x40 characters that it doesn't use for anything. The QT_Thunk code can bash this memory with impunity. Any variables that are important to FSR32.C are declared as globals, and so can't be trashed by QT_Thunk. (I learned this lesson the hard way!)

FSR32.C makes the actual call to QT_Thunk using inline assembler code. The reason FSR32.C doesn't make a regular C call to QT_Thunk is because EDX needs to be set up with the 16:16 addresses to call beforehand. You could theoretically just load EDX with one line of inline assembler before calling QT_Thunk normally. However, you'd be relying on the compiler to not trash the EDX register before the CALL instruction executes.

As a final note, be advised that this code doesn't do anything tricky like passing pointers to 16-bit code. The Win32 API functions that thunk down to 16-bit code, and that pass pointers to 16-bit DLLs, have elaborate code for setting up alias selectors and so forth. The main point here is that if you're going to do anything at all tricky, I suggest that you use the thunk compiler, which really is the proper way of doing things. The above example passes only one parameter, and that parameter doesn't require any translation to be used by the 16-bit code. Examples of parameters that would need to be translated include pointers and window message values. In short, think carefully before you decide to bypass the thunk compiler, and use Windows 95 thunks directly.

The mixed 16-/32-bit nature of the windowing system

Earlier, I said that WND structs are stored in 32-bit heaps and that their offsets, relative to USER's DGROUP, are therefore greater than 64K. I also said that HWNDs are limited to 16-bit values, so that the region between the 16-bit DGROUP and the window heap is used as a handle table to convert HWNDs to usable pointers to WND structures.

At this point, it's important to stress the bi-modality of the windowing system with regards to this mixing of 16- and 32-bit code/data. The first thing that needs to be clarified is that the 16-bit HWND values are used *throughout* the system. It doesn't matter whether or not a Win16 or a Win32 application is running; the HWNDs being passed around are 16-bit values and are offsets into the window heap handle table. Let me state this again to make it perfectly clear: An HWND is an HWND is an HWND. It doesn't matter whether you're in Win16 or Win32 code: HWNDs are 16-bit values, and they are not simply offsets into USER's DGROUP as they were in Windows 3.1.

Now that you know that HWNDs are truly 16-bit handles *everywhere*, I can tell you that internally, USER.EXE often converts these HWNDs into 32-bit pointers and passes those around. These 32-bit pointers are pointers relative to the USER's DGROUP selector, not flat 32-bit pointers. A perfect example of where USER uses these special 32-bit pointers is in the WND struct itself. The first four fields of a WND structure are the window's parent, owner, child, and sibling windows. In these four fields, USER stores 32-bit pointers (not 16-bit HWND values) to the appropriate parent, owner, child, and sibling windows. This is most likely for performance reasons, since USER would need to convert the HWNDs to a pointer anyhow to traverse through the window hierarchy. I'll come back to the window hierarchy later on.

Of course, while USER may internally use 32-bit pointers to WND structures, it still has to use 16-bit HWNDs when interfacing to the outside world. Therefore, there has to be a quick and easy method to go from a 16-bit HWND to a 32-bit pointer, and vice versa. Indeed, there is. You'll see this a bit later when we look at some pseudocode for selected windowing functions (both 16- and 32-bit).

A tough issue that comes up when trying to support both Win16 and Win32 applications in the same system is the differences in the window procedures. A Win16 application has a window procedure that, when all the typedef names have been stripped away, looks like this:

```
WndProc16(  unsigned short hWnd,
            unsigned short wMsg,
            unsigned short wParam,
            unsigned long  lParam );
```

A Win32 application on the other hand, has a WNDPROC that looks like this:

```
WndProc32(  unsigned long hWnd,
            unsigned long wMsg,
            unsigned long wParam,
            unsigned long lParam );
```

So the $128,000 question is: What happens when a Win32 application does a SendMessage to a window in a 16-bit program? Obviously, there's going to be some problem unless the parameters are rearranged and/or truncated. Likewise, if a 16-bit application sends a message to a Win32 application, most of the parameters pushed on the stack will need to be widened (the hWnd, wMsg, and wParam parameters). Since applications can't be expected to handle these details, the job falls to USER.EXE.

Another related problem is window subclassing. Windows programs have long subclassed the windows of other applications. The basic idea of subclassing is that a program uses GetWindowLong(GWL_WNDPROC) to retrieve the current WNDPROC callback address for a window and store that value away. Next, the program uses SetWindowLong(GWL_WNDPROC) to change the window's WNDPROC address to the application's subclass procedure. Now, here's the problem: The WNDPROC of a window created by a 32-bit application is a 32-bit linear address. If a 16-bit application were to change the WNDPROC address of a 32-bit window to a 16:16 address, there's obviously going to be a sticky situation. The 32-bit code for calling the WNDPROC is expecting a flat 32 linear address, and calling a 16:16 segmented address as a flat 32 linear address is certainly not going to work.

To prevent these obvious problems, USER.EXE creates a small code stub for each window that's created with a 32-bit WNDPROC. This stub is 16-bit code and contains the 32-bit linear address for the real WNDPROC that the Win32 application uses as its WNDPROC. For example, here's the stub for Explorer's tray window:

```
:u 1457:140
1457:00000140   PUSH    00401DFA    ; A 32-bit WNDPROC address.
1457:00000146   PUSH    00030000
1457:0000014C   JMP     0127:7555
```

And a bit later on in the segment:

```
:u 1457:156
1457:00000156   PUSH    0040180D    ; A 32-bit WNDPROC address.
1457:0000015C   PUSH    00030000
1457:00000162   JMP     0127:7555
```

As you can imagine, the address 0127:7555 is some sort of thunk routine (in KRNL386.EXE) that converts the parameters for the Win16 WND-PROC call into parameters of the form that a Win32 WNDPROC expects, and then calls the address specified in the thunk. As for the segment that these thunks reside in, the segment was allocated from the global heap by USER.EXE, and a code segment alias selector (0x1457) was created for it.

So what does all this mean? If you look in the WND structure of any window, you'll always find a 16:16 address given for the WNDPROC. However, if you look at the memory contents at that 16:16 address, you can determine whether this is a regular Win16 WNDPROC or a thunk up to a Win32 WNDPROC. Of course, this has ramifications for the GetWindowLong(GWL_WNDPROC) function: Depending on whether it's called from a Win16 program or a Win32 program, it has to respond with the appropriate address.

Messaging system changes

One of the more dramatic changes in the USER subsystem of Windows 95 (as compared to prior versions) is how window messages are passed around. I call the code that posts, sends, and processes messages the *messaging system*. The best news about the Windows 95 messaging system is that it eliminates the synchronous nature of messaging for Win32 applications. In 16-bit Windows, only one task at a time can execute. That task has to explicitly give up control by calling one of the messaging APIs. Typically, a task yields by calling GetMessage or PeekMessage in its main loop, although SendMessage can also cause a task to yield.

The problem with this model is that a task that doesn't regularly yield (that is, pump messages) prevents other tasks from executing. This has the effect of hanging the input system. As long as the Win16 task isn't calling GetMessage or PeekMessage, nobody else can execute. The task that takes a long time to finish some processing renders the rest of the system useless.

When Windows NT came along, the NT team reworked the USER component so that yielding and scheduling weren't affected by whether a task calls GetMessage or PeekMessage. A Win32 program can take its sweet time processing a message without adversely affecting other processes. After Windows NT had this functionality, there was no way that Windows 95 could go out the door without also having the same improved behavior.

Of course, if 16-bit applications are to continue to run correctly on Windows 95, these messaging system changes couldn't be made to apply to Win16 applications. Too many Win16 applications rely on the cooperative multitasking model, where an application doesn't yield until it's ready to. Therefore, only Win32 programs are allowed to process messages at their own pace (or not process them at all) without affecting the rest of the system.

One of the ways that Windows 95 creates this dual mode behavior (Win16 applications cooperatively multitask, while Win32 applications pre-emptively multitask) is via the Win16Mutex and thread scheduling. At any given time, the Windows 95 thread scheduler has scheduled the highest priority thread that is ready to run. One of the things that can make a thread not ready to run is when it's waiting to acquire a mutex semaphore (such as the Win16Mutex).

Whenever a Win16 task is executing, it owns the Win16Mutex (actually, to be more accurate, when any 16-bit code is executing, the Win16Mutex is owned). When there's a Win16 task running, all the old-style rules about requiring the task to call GetMessage or PeekMessage still apply in order for another 16-bit task to be able to run. However, just because a Win16 task is holding the Win16Mutex doesn't mean that the thread scheduler won't switch away from it. When a Win32 thread is executing through regular 32-bit code, it doesn't need to own the Win16Mutex. Therefore, even if a Win16 task isn't pumping messages in a timely manner, at least 32-bit threads can continue to run. Other 16-bit applications are of course blocked.

Now, here's the problem with this setup. Since the messaging system code is in the 16-bit USER.EXE, a 32-bit application that's using a message processing loop needs to acquire the Win16Mutex before it can get down to the Win16 USER.EXE. Therefore, this pre-emptive multitasking is only partial. If a thread is doing calculations or other work that doesn't require thunking down to 16-bit DLLs like USER.EXE, the thread is pretty much impervious to badly behaved applications that don't pump messages. However, if a Win32 thread needs to call down into USER, GDI, or some other 16-bit component, it needs to acquire the Win16Mutex, and that thread is blocked until the Win16Mutex becomes available. Thus, a badly behaved 16-bit application can still effectively block other applications from executing (assuming those applications are using messaging system or related functions).

What we have here in Windows 95 is a pre-emptive multitasking system with a potential army of Achilles' heels. That heel is Win16 applications that don't pump messages in a timely manner. Although you can't get rid of the Win16Mutex altogether, you can work to eliminate as many Win16 tasks from your system as possible. By minimizing the time spent with the Win16Mutex acquired, you're also minimizing the chance that a badly behaved application will hang the input system.

One of the design improvements that Microsoft claims to have made in Windows 95 is the addition of a "Raw Input Thread" (a.k.a., the RIT). In all the Microsoft diagrams that depict messaging coming into the system, interrupt handlers are shown depositing messages into a central system queue.

Then, a separate thread (the RIT) continually monitors that thread, retrieves messages, and distributes the message to the appropriate thread's message queue. (I'll get to the details of message queues in just the next section.)

Although the RIT sounds nice in theory (and is supposedly the way Windows NT does things), I've been unable to conclusively verify its existence in Windows 95. I have found a function in KERNEL32.DLL called DispatchRITInput. However, setting a breakpoint on this routine and checking the current thread when the breakpoint is hit reveals that it's not called by a single thread. Rather, a wide variety of application threads are the current thread when DispatchRITInput is called. Ultimately, DispatchRITInput thunks down to the DispatchInput routine in the 16-bit USER.EXE. I tried setting a breakpoint there, and although the breakpoint went off nearly constantly, it was still called in a variety of different thread contexts. I tried similar experiments on other internal messaging system functions in USER and was unable to find a particular routine that was called only in the context of a single system thread. Eventually, I broke down and asked one of the Windows 95 developers about the RIT, and he had this to say:

> There is a real RIT but if we can process common stuff on some random thread, we do that for speed/efficiency instead of scheduling the RIT. That's why you see DispatchInput being called in a variety of contexts. We only defer things to the RIT as a last resort.

Unauthorized Windows 95 and the Win16Mutex Problem

On page 552 of *Unauthorized Windows 95*, Schulman takes some of my *PC Magazine* and *Microsoft Systems Journal* articles to task for being somewhat incorrect about the Win16Mutex. He quotes several statements I made, including this one from *PC Magazine*:

. . . the sooner you move your applications to 32 bits, the better. If a system doesn't have any 16-bit programs running, the Win16Mutex can't be a source of trouble . . .

He then goes on to say, "a Windows 95 system (at least Windows 95 Beta-1) always has two running Win16 tasks, TIMER and MSGSRV32."

From *Microsoft Systems Journal*, Schulman quotes something I wrote in *Microsoft Systems Journal*:

The USER and GDI code will execute quickly and release the Win16Mutex. No 32-bit thread will ever hold and hog the Win16Mutex for any significant period of time.

He then goes on to show a small Win32 program (W16LOCK) that in fact does acquire the Win16Mutex and hold on to it for as long as desired.

These are both valid points, and deserve a response. The first point (wherein a Windows 95 system always has at least two Win16 tasks) has changed slightly. In more recent builds, Windows 95 really uses only one 16-bit task, MSGSRV32. (You may have a 16-bit MMTASK task on your system, but it's not required, and I have terminated it without adverse system effects.) The one important Win16 task (MSGSRV32) is the task that allows you to start programs from the DOS prompt. To see if MSGSRV32 could really be a problem, I used SoftIce/W to set a hardware write breakpoint on the CurTDB variable in KRNL386.EXE. The breakpoint was further qualified to go off only when the HTASK of MSGSRV32 was written to it. By doing this, whenever MSGSRV32 (the lone 16-bit task in the system) became the active task, the breakpoint would be hit. In the majority of cases, the only way I was able to get MSGSRV32 to consistently become the current task was by starting applications from a command prompt. MSGSRV32 also became the current task very sporadically at other times.

In looking at the code for MSGSRV32, I didn't notice anything that would indicate a desire for MSGSRV32 to hang around and not process messages in a timely manner. The only thing even close to this that I saw was when MSGSRV32 fired up another program via WinExec. The Win16Mutex is held the entire time that the WinExec call executes. The point here is that, yes, it's true that you can't entirely eliminate 16-bit applications from Windows 95. On the other hand, MSGSRV32 looks like it can be trusted to not acquire the Win16Mutex and hold on to it for unduly long periods of time.

As for the second point (the W16LOCK program that holds and acquires the Win16Mutex from a Win32 program), my feeling is that W16LOCK is a perverse case. Yes, it does expose a hole in the way that Windows 95 allows access to system functions and synchronization objects. However, W16LOCK had to explicitly work to grab the Win16Mutex and hold onto it from a Win32 program. This scenario isn't something that Win32 applications will just happen to inadvertently do if they're not careful. (If they thunk down to 16-bit DLLs, that's another story.) I concede that the Win16Mutex can be a source of trouble and of system hangs. On the other hand, if you eliminate nonsystem Win16 applications and don't intentionally try to hack the system, you'll probably never notice the effect of the Win16Mutex. In other words, be aware of the Win16Mutex, but don't lose any sleep over it.

Per-thread message queues

In Windows 95, each thread can have its own *message queue*. In a nutshell, a message queue is the data structure that controls which messages a particular thread's calls to GetMessage or PeekMessage will retrieve. In Windows 3.1 and earlier, each Win16 task had its own message queue. The message queue was created shortly after program startup. In Windows 95, each thread has its own message queue, and the queues are created only when a thread actually needs one for the first time. Since each Win16 task in Windows 95 has an associated thread, each Win16 task continues to have a single message queue.

Let's look at message queues a little more closely, since they're one of the primary data structures that permeate the USER subsystem. When a thread calls GetMessage or PeekMessage, it's looking for messages within the queue of the current thread. The notion of the current thread is implicit within the GetMessage and PeekMessage code. You can't ask for messages from another thread's queue. Message queues are also used as part of sending a message to another program. From USER's perspective, the SendMessage call is from one message queue to another message queue (although the source and destination queues may be the same).

I'm not going to go into all the details of GetMessage, PeekMessage, or SendMessage here. I covered those topics pretty thoroughly in *Windows Internals*. While there are some changes in Windows 95 from Windows 3.1, I didn't feel that repeating much of the same information here would be beneficial. Instead, I'm going to focus on what changed in Windows 95 from Windows 3.1.

Message queue format

For starters, let's look at what the format of a message queue looks like. Each message queue is kept in a segment allocated from the 16-bit global heap by USER.EXE. Each thread database (Chapter 3) and task database (Chapter 7) contains the selector for the associated message queue. The known fields of a message queue are given in the MSGQUEUE.H file included with the SHOWWND program. The details of these fields follow (note that the three items at the beginning of each entry are the offset, the type, and the name):

00h   *WORD*   *nextQueue*
This WORD contains the next queue in the list. All the message queues are kept in a linked list, with the end indicated by a 0 in this field.

02h   *WORD*   *hTask*

This WORD holds the HTASK that this queue is associated with. As I show in Chapter 7, even Win32 processes have a 16-bit task database associated with them.

04h   *WORD*   *headMsg*

This WORD holds a near pointer (relative to USER's DGROUP) to the head of a linked list of QUEUEMSGs. (QUEUEMSGs are described in the next section.)

06h   *WORD*   *tailMsg*

This WORD holds a near pointer (relative to USER's DGROUP) to the end of a linked list of QUEUEMSGs.

08h   *WORD*   *lastMsg*

This WORD holds a near pointer (relative to USER's DGROUP) to a QUEUEMSG that has been retrieved by a call to GetMessage or PeekMessage. Exactly which message is undetermined at this time.

0Ah   *WORD*   *cMsgs*

This WORD is the number of messages in this queue waiting to be processed. (That is, it's the number of QUEUEMSG structures in the linked list pointed to by offset 04h.)

0Dh   *BYTE*   *sig[3]*

For queues of Win32 application threads, these three bytes hold the ASCII representation for "MJT" (which perhaps stands for Jon Thomason, a Microsoft programmer). For the queues of most Win16 applications, these three bytes are 0.

10h   *WORD*   *npPerQueue*

This WORD is a near pointer (relative to USER's DGROUP) to a PERQUEUEDATA structure. This structure holds the per-thread active, focus, and capture windows. I'll describe these concepts and this structure in the "Per-queue system windows" section.

16h   *WORD*   *npProcess*

This WORD is a near pointer (relative to USER's DGROUP) to a QUEUE-PROCESSDATA structure. If a process has multiple threads and queues, this field in all the queues will point to the same QUEUEPROCESSDATA structure. The QUEUEPROCESSDATA structure contains information such as the process ID associated with this queue, and will be described later.

24h *DWORD* *messageTime*

This DWORD holds the value that will be retrieved by a call to GetMessage-Time (that is, the time that the message was posted). This value is set by copying it out of the QUEUEMSG structure as each message is retrieved by GetMessage/PeekMessage.

28h *DWORD* *messagePos*

This DWORD holds the value that will be retrieved by a call to GetMessagePos (that is, the X,Y coordinates of the cursor at the time of the message). This value is set by copying it out of the QUEUEMSG structure as each message is retrieved by GetMessage/PeekMessage.

2Eh *WORD* *lastMsg2*

This field holds a near pointer (relative to USER's DGROUP) to the last retrieved QUEUEMSG structure.

30h *DWORD* *extraInfo*

This DWORD holds the value that will be retrieved by a call to GetMessage-ExtraInfo. This value is set by copying it out of the QUEUEMSG structure as each message is retrieved by GetMessage/PeekMessage.

3Ch *DWORD* *threadId*

This is thread ID of the thread that is associated with this queue. The relationship between thread IDs and the thread database is described in Chapter 3.

42h *WORD* *expWinVer*

This is the version of Windows this application expects. This is usually either 0x300, 0x30A, or 0x400 to represent Windows 3.0, 3.1, or 4.0. This value is extracted from the program's executable header at startup. It's used by USER in certain cases to determine how messages should be processed or which messages should be sent. In other words, it allows USER to be compatible with the behavior of multiple versions of Windows.

48h *WORD* *ChangeBits*

This value is comprised of various QS_XXX flags representing the various types of message events that have occurred since the last call to GetQueueStatus. The following QS_xxx flags are given in WINUSER.H:

```
QS_KEY           0x0001
QS_MOUSEMOVE     0x0002
QS_MOUSEBUTTON   0x0004
QS_POSTMESSAGE   0x0008
```

```
QS_TIMER          0x0010
QS_PAINT          0x0020
QS_SENDMESSAGE    0x0040
QS_HOTKEY         0x0080
```

The GetQueueStatus returns this field in the low-order word of its returned DWORD. Chapter 7 of *Windows Internals* contains much more information about the QS_xxx flags and their meaning.

4Ah   WORD   WakeBits

This value is comprised of various QS_XXX flags representing the various types of messages that are in the queue. The QS_xxx flags are listed in the previous field's description. The GetQueueStatus returns this field in the high-order word of its returned DWORD.

4Ch   WORD   WakeMask

If a thread is blocked, waiting for a message inside a call to GetMessage or PeekMessage, this WORD hold the QS_XXX flags for the message types it's waiting for. Typically, applications are blocked inside a call to GetMessage, so this field would hold QS_ALLINPUT, which is the combination of all the QS_XXX flags.

50h   WORD   hQueueSend

If this thread is processing a message that was sent to it by another thread, this WORD holds the queue handle of the sending thread.

56h   WORD   sig2

This WORD holds 0x5148, which is the ASCII representation for HQ (which perhaps stands for Handle Queue?). Each message queue is associated with a particular thread. Each thread in turn is associated with a process. Therefore, there can be a many-to-one relationship between message queues and a process. The messaging system information that's common between all queues in a process is stored in a structure that I call a QUEUEPROCESSDATA structure. The QUEUEPROCESSDATA structure is kept in a block allocated from the 16-bit USER heap. The pointer to the QUEUEPROCESSDATA structure is kept at offset 0x16 in a message queue. In the Windows 95 16-bit TOOL-HELP.H file, this data structure is marked with the LT_USER_PROCESS (0x1D) identifier. (Only the debug version of USER.EXE tags the blocks with a type identifier.)

The known fields in the QUEUEPROCESSDATA structure can be found in the MSGQUEUE.H file from the SHOWWND program written for this chapter. The details of these fields follow (note that the three items at the beginning of each entry are the offset, the type, and the name):

00h   WORD   *npNext*
This field is a near pointer (relative to USER's DGROUP) to the next
QUEUEPROCESSDATA in the system.

02h   WORD   *un2*
What this field points to is unknown. However, in the debug version of
Windows, its block is given the type of LT_USER_SUBSYSTEM.

04h   WORD   *flags*
Some sort of flags WORD. The meanings are unknown.

08h   DWORD   *processId*
This DWORD holds the process ID associated with this queue.

0Eh   WORD   *hQueue*
This WORD holds an hQueue value. Its exact significance is not known,
although it may be a back-pointer to the queue created for the thread in
the process.

The QUEUEMSG structure

In Windows 3.1 and earlier, a message queue actually contained the messages
that had been posted to it. A large area toward the end of the queue structure
was basically just an array of MSG structures. Two WORD fields near the
beginning of the queue structure acted as head and tail pointers. Because the
messages were stored in an array, there was a maximum number of messages
that could be stored at any given time in a queue. By default, this value was
eight messages, but it could be upped by calling SetMessageQueue with a
new message count.

Windows 95 totally changes the way messages are stored for a queue. In
a Windows 95 message queue, there's a near pointer to the head of a linked
list of structures, one structure per message. I've dubbed these structures
with the name QUEUEMSG. The QUEUEMSG structures are allocated out
of the 16-bit USER DGROUP. This is rather surprising, since a lot of work
went into moving things out of USER's DGROUP in Windows 95, so
putting message structures in there seems counterproductive. Incidentally,
the Windows 95 16-bit TOOLHELP.H refers to these structures by the
name LT_USER_QMSG (0x1A).

In case you find it hard to believe that the messages for a queue are no
longer kept in an array at the end of the queue, consider the following code
for Windows 95's SetMessageQueue function:

```
SETMESSAGEQUEUE proc
C0ED:   XOR     AX,AX
C0EF:   INC     AX
C0F0:   RETF    3702
```

For those of you who don't read assembler (for shame!), the function simply returns 1. That's because there's no longer an array of MSG structures in a queue. In contrast, the Windows 3.1 SetMessageQueue calculated how big the new queue would have to be (taking into account the number of messages to be held) and allocated a new global heap block for the queue.

The layout of a QUEUEMSG structure is given in C-style format in the MSGQUEUE.H file from the SHOWWND program. The details of the known QUEUEMSG fields follow (note that the three items at the beginning of each entry are the offset, the type, and the name):

00h   WORD   HWND
This WORD is the window handle (HWND) that this message will be delivered to.

02h   WORD   msg
This WORD is the message number. Only the bottom 16 bits of a message number are stored. This isn't a problem in Win16, where messages are only 16 bits, but for a Win32 application, a message is a DWORD value, so the top WORD of a Win32 program's message value is lost.

04h   WORD   wParamLow
For Win16 applications, this field holds the WPARAM value for the message. For Win32 programs, this field holds the low WORD of the WPARAM value.

06h   DWORD   lParam
This field contains the LPARAM of the message.

0Ah   DWORD   messageTime
This DWORD is the time that the message was deposited into the queue. According to the SDK documentation, the message time is the number of milliseconds since the system started. This field's value is ultimately returned by the GetMessageTime function. As part of retrieving this message, GetMessage and/or PeekMessage copies this value into offset 24h of the message queue, which is where GetMessageTime retrieves it from.

0Eh   DWORD   messagePos

This DWORD contains the X,Y coordinates of the cursor at the time the message was generated. This field's value is ultimately returned by the GetMessagePos function. As part of retrieving this message, GetMessage and/or PeekMessage copies it into offset 28h of the message queue, which is where GetMessagePos retrieves it from.

12h   WORD   wParamHigh

For Win32 applications, this WORD holds the high WORD of the WPARAM. For Win16 programs, this WORD is ignored.

14h   DWORD   extraInfo

This DWORD contains the extra information that's sometimes associated with a message. This field's value is ultimately returned by the GetMessageExtraInfo function. As part of retrieving this message, GetMessage and/or PeekMessage copies it into offset 30h of the message queue, which is where GetMessage-ExtraInfo retrieves it from.

18h   WORD   nextQueueMsg

This is a near pointer (relative to USER's DGROUP) to the next QUEUEMSG structure in the list. The end of the list is indicated by a 0 in this field.

Per-queue system windows

One of the design concepts espoused in Windows NT is that one process shouldn't be able to adversely affect the behavior of another process (at least not without the permission of the other process). Windows 3.1 and earlier didn't follow this philosophy, especially when it came to the state of the windowing system. At any given time in Windows 3.1 and earlier, there was just one active window, one focus window, and one capture window. Any application could steal the focus away from another by calling SetFocus. Likewise, a call to SetActiveWindow could change the active window out from underneath a task that thought it was the active window.

Windows NT solved this problem by giving each application its own copy of the active, focus, and capture HWNDs. (Actually, this is a bit of a simplification, but it will suffice for now.) By making these system-state windows per-application in scope, Win32 programs don't have to worry about other programs (malicious or not) affecting their behavior. As with the decoupled messaging system, the idea of per-application system state windows was such a good idea that it was brought over to Windows 95 as well. (The fact that this behavior is prescribed by the Win32 API didn't hurt matters either.)

The per-queue information is kept in (yet another) structure allocated from USER's DGROUP segment. (Hey! I thought Windows 95 was supposed to move things *out* of USER's DGROUP, not add new items.) The pointer to the per-queue data area is found at offset 0x10 in a message queue. I've given the per-queue information structure the name PERQUEUEDATA. The Windows 95 16-bit TOOLHELP.H refers to this structure as an LT_USER_VWININFO (type ID = 0x1B).

Incidentally, during the final Windows 95 beta (M8), the March 27th *InfoWorld* ran a story with the headline, "Win95 beta lays an egg." Much of the ensuing controversy arising from that article ultimately ended up related to the PERQUEUEDATA structure. At the time of the final Windows 95 beta, each PERQUEUEDATA was several hundred bytes in length. As a result, starting up a large number of threads would quickly fill up USER's 64K DGROUP. Subsequently, Microsoft restructured the PERQUEUEDATA structure to take up significantly less space, and the controversy died down.

A C-style structure definition for PERQUEUEDATA is given in the MSGQUEUE.H file from the SHOWWND sample program. The details of the known fields follow (note that the three items at the beginning of each entry are the offset, the type, and the name):

00h   *WORD*   *npNext*
This field is a near pointer (relative to USER's DGROUP) to the next PERQUEUEDATA structure in the system. Apparently, the PERQUEUE-DATA are kept in a linked list.

06h   *WORD*   *npQMsg*
This WORD is a near pointer (relative to USER's DGROUP) to a QUEUEMSG structure. (QUEUEMSGs is described in the preceding section.)

14h   *WORD*   *somehQueue1*
This WORD is a message queue handle. Its exact significance is currently unknown.

16h   *WORD*   *somehQueue2*
This WORD is a yet another message queue handle. Its exact significance is currently unknown.

| 18h | DWORD | hWndCapture |

This DWORD holds a 32-bit pointer (relative to USER's DGROUP) to the current window with capture for this queue.

| 1Ch | DWORD | hWndFocus |

This DWORD holds a 32-bit pointer (relative to USER's DGROUP) to the current focus window of this queue.

| 20h | DWORD | hWndActive |

This DWORD holds a 32-bit pointer (relative to USER's DGROUP) to the current active window of this queue.

Changes to (H)WND structures in Windows 95

The WND structure is perhaps the most commonly used system data structure in Windows 95. For each window in the system (visible or not), there is a corresponding WND structure. In Windows 3.1, an HWND was a near pointer to a WND structure in USER's DGROUP. As I described earlier, a Windows 95 HWND is an offset into an array of 32-bit USER32 relative pointers to WND structures.

Because each WND structure contains a pointer to its parent window, its sibling window, and its first child window, you can easily see that windows are kept in a tree hierarchy. Figure 4-3 shows the tree hierarchy and describes a little about each "level." At the root of the WND tree hierarchy is the desktop window. The first level of windows immediately below the desktop window have styles of WS_OVERLAPPED or WS_POPUP. These are what what most developers think of as "top-level" or "main" windows. Windows that are lower in the hierarchy have the WS_CHILD style. The prototypical child window is a control window in a dialog box (for example, a button). Because of the window hierarchy, you can start at the desktop window and enumerate through all the windows in the system, as the SHOWWND.C program shows. (See "The SHOWWND Program" section later in this chapter.)

Although this fact isn't commonly known, the Z-order of windows is determined by their relative positions within the hierarchy. Within a given group of sibling windows, the window that's first in the list is highest in the Z-order. The second window in the list is next in the Z-order, and so forth. For example, all top-level windows (WS_OVERLAPPED and WS_POPUP) are siblings of one another, and are all children of the desktop window. The desktop window's first child window (that is, the first WS_OVERLAPPED or WS_POPUP window) holds the highest rank in the Z-order.

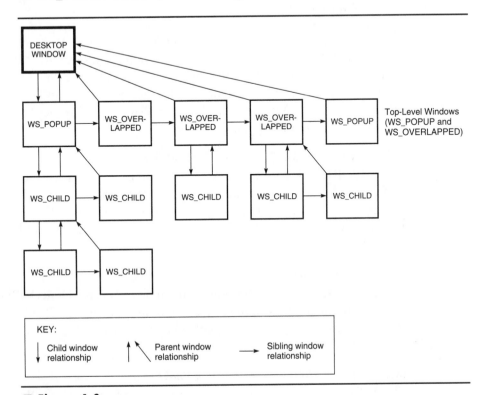

Figure 4-3
The tree hierarchy of WND structures lets you start at the desktop window and enumerate through all the windows in the system.

WND structure details

Although there are definite changes to the WND structure in Windows 95 (relative to Windows 3.1), they're not very dramatic. For the most part, the ordering of the fields didn't change (although the sizes of certain fields certainly did). Also, the WND structure has a few new fields in Windows 95. The primary new field is the WORD that holds the 16-bit HWND value for that window. This WORD is what allows windows to be easily referred to by either a 16-bit HWND or a 32-bit USER DGROUP relative pointer.

The HWND32.H file from the SHOWWND sources has a C-style definition for a Windows 95 WND structure. The details of the WND follow (note that the three items at the beginning of each entry are the offset, the type, and the name):

00h   *struct _WND32 **   *hWndNext*
This DWORD holds a 32-bit pointer (relative to USER's DGROUP) to the sibling of this window. The sibling window is the next window at this level of the hierarchy that has the same parent window as this window. You can obtain the 16-bit HWND of the sibling window by calling GetWindow with the GW_HWNDNEXT parameter.

04h   *struct _WND32 **   *hWndChild*
This DWORD holds a 32-bit pointer (relative to USER's DGROUP) to the first child window of this window. You can obtain the 16-bit HWND of the first child window by calling GetWindow with the GW_CHILD parameter. By calling GetWindow(GW_HWNDNEXT), you can obtain child windows for each subsequent child window.

08h   *struct _WND32 **   *hWndParent*
This DWORD holds a 32-bit pointer (relative to USER's DGROUP) to the parent window of this window. You can obtain the 16-bit HWND of the parent window by calling GetParent. The only window that truly does not have a parent window is the desktop window.

0Ch   *struct _WND32 **   *hWndOwner*
This DWORD holds a 32-bit pointer (relative to USER's DGROUP) to the owner window for this window. The owner window is the window that receives notification messages (for example, the BN_CLICKED message). For WS_OVERLAPPED and WS_POPUP windows, the owning window and the parent window don't have to be the same, although they often are. For WS_CHILD windows, the parent window always also acts as the owner window (that is, it receives all notification messages). By calling GetWindow(GW_OWNER), you can obtain the 16-bit HWND of a window's owning window.

10h   *RECTS*   *rectWindow*
This field is a 16-bit RECT structure (four short integers) that define the boundaries of the window (including the nonclient area).

18h   RECTS   rectClient

This field is a 16-bit RECT structure (four short integers) that defines the boundaries of the client area of the window. The client area is the portion of window that the application is allowed to draw in using a device context obtained from BeginPaint or GetDC.

20h   WORD   hQueue

This field contains the 16-bit global heap handle for the queue that handles messages for this particular window. The existence of this field proves that in Win32, windows are bound to a single queue and, hence, to a single thread. Thus, there is a Win32 GetWindowThreadProcessId function.

22h   WORD   hrgnUpdate

If a portion of this window needs repainting, this field holds an HRGN that describes the region needing to be updated. Regions are GDI data structures, and are stored in a 32-bit heap in Windows 95.

24h   WORD   wndClass

This WORD holds a near pointer (relative to USER's DGROUP) to a USER_DGROUP_WNDCLASS structure. A USER_DGROUP_WNDCLASS structure is just the minimum amount of window-class–related information that USER needs to access frequently. The less frequently accessed class information is kept in another structure that's kept in a 32-bit heap. We'll look at the format of the USER_DGROUP_WNDCLASS and this other structure in the "Changes to Windows 95 window classes" section. To sum up, this field in the WND structure gives the class type of the window.

26h   WORD   hInstance

In most cases, this WORD contains the 16-bit hInstance (DGROUP) for the application that created the window. However, for edit controls that need to contain very large buffers (up to 64K), this field holds the DS value that will be used in the edit control's WNDPROC. Before calling a window procedure, USER loads this field into the AX register. In some Win16 exported function prologues, the code expects that AX contains the DS value to be used by the function. Normally, the DS that a program will want to use is the DGROUP segment, but in the case of an edit control holding significant amounts of text, a separate segment can be used.

28h   WNDPROC   lpfnWndProc

This DWORD holds the window procedure address associated with the window. It appears to always be a far 16:16 address. If the window's declared window procedure is in Win32 code, this field holds a pointer to a 16:16 thunk up to the Win32 window procedure.

2Ch   DWORD   dwFlags

This DWORD holds flags specific to the internal state of the window. The meanings of individual bits aren't documented.

30h   DWORD   dwStyleFlags

This DWORD holds the WS_XXX-style flags given in the 16-bit WINDOWS.H and 32-bit WINUSER.H.

34h   DWORD   dwExStyleFlags

This DWORD holds the WS_EX_XXX extended-style flags given in the 16-bit WINDOWS.H and 32-bit WINUSER.H. Windows 95 added several new extended style flags, which I'll talk more about in the "Other windowing system changes (or lack thereof)" section.

38h   DWORD   moreFlags

This field appears to be used as flags. The meanings are unknown.

3Ch   HANDLE   ctrlID (or hMenu)

For top-level (WS_OVERLAPPED or WS_POPUP) windows, this field holds the hMenu for the window. Its value is retrieved by the GetMenu function. For WS_CHILD windows, this field holds the control ID. You're probably most familiar with control IDs in the context of the controls in a dialog box. If this window is a WS_CHILD window, this field's value can be retrieved by GetDlgCtrlId.

40h   DWORD   some32BitHandle

This WORD is a 32-bit handle for the window's text. The handle is similar to an HWND, but applies a heap that is neither the window heap nor the menu heap.

42h   WORD   scrollBar

This WORD holds information relating to the window's scrollbar attributes.

44h   WORD   properties

This WORD is the handle for the first window property in the linked list of properties. Properties are really just atoms, and allow you to bind named 16-bit values to a window. See the GetProp and SetProp functions in the SDK documentation for more information.

46h   *WORD*   *hWnd16*

This WORD is one of the key fields in the WND structure. It contains the
16-bit HWND value for this window. When the USER code has a 32-bit
pointer to a WND structure, it can grab the contents of this field to return
to code that expects a real 16-bit HWND. This allows USER to internally
pass around 32-bit pointers to WND structures without also passing around
the corresponding 16-bit HWND. Whenever it's needed, the HWND can be
looked up in the WND structure.

48h   *struct _WND32 **   *lastActive*

This DWORD holds a 32-bit pointer (relative to USER's DGROUP) to the last
active popup window associated with this window. The GetLastActivePopup
function grabs this value to get a pointer to a WND structure, and then
returns the 16-bit HWND stored at offset 46h in the structure.

4Ch   *HANDLE*   *hMenuSystem*

This field is a handle to the system menu associated with this window. See
the GetSystemMenu function in the SDK documentation for details.

56h   *WORD*   *classAtom*

This WORD holds the atom associated with the class name for this window.
It can either be a regular atom (that is, > 0xC000), or it can be one of the
predefined window class types:

```
0x8000  (PopupMenu)
0x8001  (Desktop)
0x8002  (Dialog)
0x8003  (WinSwitch)    // The ALT-TAB window.
0x8004  (IconTitle)    // In Win 3.X, the title window below an icon.
0x002A  ???            // The class associated with MMTASK.TSK.
```

This field (offset 56h) is usually the same as the field at offset 2 in the structure pointed to by the wndClass pointer (offset field 24h of the WND class).

58h   *DWORD*   *alternatePID*
5Ch   *DWORD*   *alternateTID*

These two fields don't appear to actually contain a process ID or a thread
ID. However, there is a path through the GetWindowThreadProcessId code
which indicates that these fields could contain a PID and a TID.

    As a final note on Windows and the WND structure, it often surprises
people when I tell them that creating a window takes absolutely no space
from USER's 64K DGROUP. If you're creating a window from an existing

class, the only data that needs to be allocated is the WND structure itself. Since WND structures come from a 32-bit heap, there's absolutely no impact on USER's 16-bit DGROUP from creating a window. To prove this to myself, I've written programs that created several thousand windows and checked the free space in USER's DGROUP at various points during the creation of the windows. In all cases, no memory was allocated during USER's DGROUP in the course of this process.

Other windowing system changes (or lack thereof)

For some users, one of the biggest disappointments in Windows 95 is that the maximum of 64K of text in a standard window didn't go away. Given Windows 95's design goals, this shouldn't be surprising. The code that manipulates and displays the text for a window is resolutely 16 bit. A good chunk of the 16-bit USER would have had to have been converted to 32-bit code to break the 64K limit. Given the size and compatibility risks involved, it's understandable that the Windows 95 team didn't jump to do this. On the other hand, Windows NT, which has a fully 32-bit USER and GDI, doesn't have this limitation. Thus, the limit of 64K of window text is one of the major end-user discernible differences between NT and Windows 95.

On a positive note, Windows 95 defines numerous new window styles to give Win32 applications that cool Windows 95 look. The new styles in WINUSER.H are:

```
#define WS_EX_MDICHILD          0x00000040L
#define WS_EX_TOOLWINDOW        0x00000080L
#define WS_EX_WINDOWEDGE        0x00000100L
#define WS_EX_CLIENTEDGE        0x00000200L
#define WS_EX_CONTEXTHELP       0x00000400L
#define WS_EX_RIGHT             0x00001000L
#define WS_EX_LEFT              0x00000000L    (The default in Win 3.1)
#define WS_EX_RTLREADING        0x00002000L
#define WS_EX_LTRREADING        0x00000000L    (The default in Win 3.1)
#define WS_EX_LEFTSCROLLBAR     0x00004000L
#define WS_EX_RIGHTSCROLLBAR    0x00000000L    (The default in Win 3.1)
#define WS_EX_CONTROLPARENT     0x00010000L
#define WS_EX_STATICEDGE        0x00020000L
#define WS_EX_APPWINDOW         0x00040000L
```

I won't bore you by reciting the SDK documentation on what all these new styles do. However, there's something quite interesting going on regarding these new styles — something that's not immediately obvious. If you dig through the 16-bit WINDOWS.H for Windows 95, you won't find any of these new WS_EX_XXX styles listed. The new WS_EX_XXX styles appear only in the 32-bit WINUSER.H file. Now, I've been stressing throughout this chapter that almost all the USER subsystem functionality (including the windowing system) is implemented in the 16-bit USER.EXE. Something should be rattling around in the back of your mind here. If the 16-bit USER.EXE is what implements the windowing system, the 16-bit USER.EXE must implement these styles — which are supposedly for 32-bit applications only. Why the heck can't 16-bit applications use these same new WS_EX_XXX styles? As it turns out, there isn't a good reason. In fact, in some informal testing, I turned up some 16-bit Windows 95 utilities that did in fact use these new extended styles.

Changes to Windows 95 window classes

Before jumping into a discussion of the changes made to Windows 95 window-class management, a brief review of window classes is in order. A window class is a collection of attributes used when creating a window. These attributes include items such as the window procedure callback address, the window's style bits, the number of extra data bytes the window needs for auxiliary storage, and so on. While USER could theoretically get by without using classes, it would be a real pain to have to specify all those attributes each time you wanted to create a window. This is especially true for windows that programs create numerous instances of, such as buttons.

Window classes serve as templates from which specific instances of windows can be created. After the window has been created, some of the class attributes that were copied to the WND structure can be modified. The prime example of this is the window procedure address. All windows created from the same class initially have the same window procedure address. Later on, a program can use SetWindowLong to change the window procedure of a specific window. This is exactly what subclassing is.

When Windows starts up, it creates a small collection of a dozen standard classes:

Button	ListBox
ComboBox	MDIClient
ComboLBox	PopupMenu
Desktop	ScrollBar
Dialog	Static
Edit	WinSwitch

Most of these classes will be heavily used by various applications, so it makes sense to make them common system classes. Additional application-specific classes can be created by calling RegisterClass. Regardless of whether you use a standard system class or your own class that you've created, you must pass a class identifier (typically its name) to the CreateWindow or CreateWindowEx functions.

In Windows 3.1 and earlier, USER kept all the registered window classes in the system in a linked list. There were even TOOLHELP functions (ClassFirst and ClassNext) for enumerating through all the registered classes. In Windows 95, the linked list of all registered classes is no more. Sure, there's still a small set of classes that you can get information on via ClassFirst and ClassNext. However, these classes are only the standard set of system classes (for example, buttons, listboxes, and so forth). These are the standard system classes registered by USER during its startup phase (see Chapter 1 of *Windows Internals*).

As in Windows 3.*x* and earlier, the Windows 95 USER still allocates the space for classes out of its 16-bit heap (so, yes, each new class uses up a small amount of the available system resources). In the debug version of USER, the memory allocated for a class structure is preceded by an LT_USER_CLASS (1) signature.

As part of the move toward the Win32 philosophy of letting processes know as little as possible about other processes, each Windows 95 32-bit process now has its own private class list. This private class list includes classes registered by system DLLs such as COMCTL32.DLL. Each time a new process uses COMCTL32.DLL, roughly a dozen new classes are registered. These classes are application-private copies of the classes provided by COMCTL32.DLL. If you're thinking that all these application-private classes can quickly suck up space in USER's 64K heap, you're right!

Given that there are application-private class lists, it would be nice to be able to enumerate them. Unfortunately, neither the 16- nor 32-bit TOOLHELP APIs provide a method for walking the private class list of a process. To date, the only way I've been able to find the private class list is to enumerate through all the windows in the system and retrieve the class pointers from the WND structures. The class pointer is at offset 24h in each WND structure. Using the SHOWWND program, you can walk a process's class list by hand (that is, you have to find the head of the class list and then double-click on the "next" field of each class in the list).

A C-style definition for a Windows 95 window class structure is given in the WNDCLASS.H file from the SHOWWND program (see the following section). I've named this structure a USER_DGROUP_WNDCLASS.

This structure contains the minimal set of fields that the 16-bit USER needs to access frequently. The less frequently used fields of a window class have moved off into a separate structure in a 32-bit heap. The known fields of a USER_DGROUP_WNDCLASS follow (note that the three items at the beginning of each entry are the offset, the type, and the name):

00h   *DWORD*   *lpIntWndClass*

This field is a far (16:16) pointer into the window heap. The pointer points to an INTWNDCLASS structure that I'll describe next. Basically, the INTWNDCLASS contains the class information that USER doesn't need immediate access to.

04h   *WORD*   *hcNext*

This WORD holds a near pointer (in USER's DGROUP) to the next class. The next class is either one of the system registered classes or the next application private class.

06h   *ATOM*   *classNameAtom*

This WORD holds the atom that describes the class name. It's either a regular atom (for example, > 0xC000) or a standard class atom (0x8000, 0x8001, and so on). The GetClassNameFromAtom function in the SHOWWND.C source file on the accompanying disk shows how to decode these atoms to class names.

08h   *DWORD*   *style*

This DWORD holds the CS_xxx styles (for example, CS_VREDRAW) for the class. This field is widened from Win 3.1, where it was only a WORD.

Summing up the fields in USER_DGROUP_WNDCLASS structure, you'll find that it takes up about 0x0C bytes in USER's DGROUP for each class. In Windows 3.1, all the information about the WNDCLASS was stored in USER's DGROUP. In an attempt to free up additional USER DGROUP memory, Microsoft moved most of the fields in a window class out into a separate 32-bit heap. The first field of the USER_DGROUP_WNDCLASS contains a far pointer into this heap, and what it points at is a structure that I call an INTWNDCLASS (INTernal WNDCLASS). The INTWNDCLASS is similar to, but not identical with, the WNDCLASS structure that you pass to the RegisterClass function. The format of an INTWNDCLASS is also given in the WNDCLASS.H header file; the details are as follows:

00h   *WORD*   *cClsWnds*

This field contains the number of current windows that are of this class.

04h   DWORD   lpfnWndProc

This WORD holds the window procedure address for windows of this class.
The act of superclassing involves using SetClassLong to change this field.

08h   WORD   cbClsExtra

This WORD holds the number of extra bytes that are allocated at the end of
this INTWNDCLASS structure. Applications can use these bytes to store application-specific data. These extra bytes are accessed with SetClassWord/Long
and GetClassWord/Long.

0Ah   WORD   hModule

This WORD holds the 16-bit version of the HMODULE that registered the
class. Note that this differs from the SDK documentation, which refers to
this as an HINSTANCE. USER gets away with this because it routinely
converts HINSTANCE to HMODULEs using the 16-bit GetExePtr routine
described in Chapter 7.

0Ch   WORD   hIcon

This is the icon associated with windows of this class.

1Eh   WORD   hCursor

This is the cursor to be used when the mouse is over windows of this class.

10h   WORD   hBrBackground

This is the brush to be used when refreshing the window's background.

12h   DWORD   lpszMenuName

This is the name of the menu to be used for windows of this class. This field
is usually 0, but it occasionally contains a valid 16:16 pointer.

16h   DWORD   hIconSm

The small icon associated with windows of this class. If nonzero, this is the
icon used for such things as representing the window on the Explorer
taskbar.

18h   WORD   cbWndExtra

This WORD holds the number of extra bytes that are allocated at the end of
each window created from this class. Applications can use these bytes to store
per-window data. These extra bytes are accessed with SetWindowWord/Long
and GetWindowWord/Long.

The SHOWWND program

To illuminate most of the data structures I've been talking about up to this point, I wrote the SHOWWND program. (Of course, I used SHOWWND myself when ferreting out certain details of the data structures I've described.) The central focus of SHOWWND is the window hierarchy. You can click on each window in the system to show the details of that window's various fields. If a field is a link to another important data structure, you can double-click on that line to switch to a detailed listing of that data structure. In this way, the SHOWWND program on the accompanying disk shows the fields of WND structures, window classes, and message queues. Since all three of these structures contain links (pointers) to other instances of their structure type, you can easily follow linked lists of windows, classes, and message queues.

To demonstrate that the data structures really are as I've described them, SHOWWND uses as few USER functions as possible. Wherever possible, it directly accesses the data structures. For example, SHOWWND could have used the EnumWindows and EnumChildWindows to display the window hierarchy. But that strategy wouldn't have proved that the WND struct looks the way I've described it. Of course, going into system data structures and poking around yourself isn't good programming practice, and it should be avoided if possible. However, for the purpose of showing what's going on under the hood in USER, it's the only way to prove that I'm not just hand-waving here.

Like several of the other programs from this book, SHOWWND is a dialog box with two listboxes. As you can see in Figure 4-4, the listbox on the left contains a nested hierarchical view of the current windows in the system. At any point, you can refresh the list by clicking the Refresh button. The listbox on the right is a "details pane" — when you select a window in the left pane, the right listbox updates to show the contents of the selected window's WND struct.

If you look closely within the righthand listbox, you'll see that several of the lines are preceded by a + (a plus sign). The + indicates that the line can be double-clicked to cause the details pane to show the details of whaever you've clicked on. From within a WND details pane, you can go to another WND, to the window's class, or to the window's queue. From the class details pane, you can follow the hcNext pointer to the next class in the list. The message queue pane works in a similar manner, and lets you walk the list of message queues.

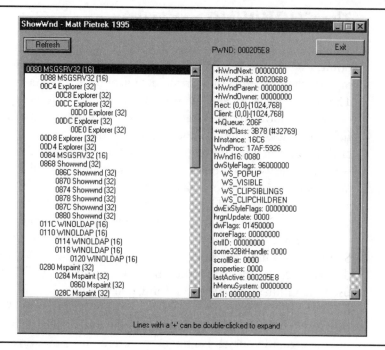

Figure 4-4
The SHOWWND program is a dialog box containing two listboxes that show the hierarchical structure of the current windows and details about each window.

For the most part, the SHOWWND.C code is pretty straightforward, so I won't bore you with descriptions of the code or a code listing here. However, there is one important detail in the code that bears mentioning. SHOWWND is a Win32 program. And as you no doubt know by now, Win32 programs can be pre-empted by other threads. As a result, SHOWWND could be in the middle of its window hierarchy walk and another thread could come along and change the window hierarchy. Although this would probably be a rare occurrence, it could happen.

To prevent this from happening, SHOWWND acquires and holds on to the Win16Mutex during its walk of the window hierarchy. SHOWWND.C does this by using three undocumented functions: GetpWin16Lock, EnterSysLevel, and LeaveSysLevel. The GetpWin16Lock function fills in a DWORD with the address of the Win16Mutex (which is actually in KRNL386.EXE). By passing this address to EnterSysLevel, a program can acquire the Win16Mutex and release the mutex with LeaveSysLevel. This technique is somewhat similar to what the W16LOCK program from *Unauthorized Windows 95* does. The key difference is that W16LOCK is

using these functions to prove that the system can be deadlocked from a
Win32 application, while SHOWWND uses them to properly handle thread
synchronization issues.

Pseudocode for select 16-bit USER.EXE functions

Now that we've looked at some of the key 16-bit USER data structures and
USER's use of the new Win32 heaps, let's look at some pseudocode for
some functions in USER.EXE. The following sections are practical in
nature, because I want to show you how these data structures and concepts
are actually put to use.

The IsWindow and IsWindow16 functions in USER.EXE

The IsWindow function takes a 16-bit HWND as a parameter and verifies
whether it's really a valid HWND. The IsWindow code in the debug
USER.EXE is just logging code that emits the name of the function to the
debug port if a certain USER trace mode flag (not documented) is enabled.
The real verification of the HWND happens after IsWindow falls through
into the IsWindow16 code.

IsWindow16 starts out by quickly throwing out HWND values that
can't possibly be valid. As I described earlier, HWNDs in Windows 95 are
always a multiple of four, so IsWindow16 returns FALSE for any value that
has either of its lowest two bits set. IsWindow16 also immediately throws
out values that are less than 0x80. Why 0x80? Because the first 0x80 bytes
of the handle table area (at USER's DGROUP base address + 0x10000) are
used for storing other information related to the 32-bit window heap. The
first available window pointer slot in the handle table area is at offset 0x80,
and this slot appears to always be taken by the desktop window. (This
makes sense, because the desktop window is the first window created.)

IsWindow16 next throws out HWND values that are too high. At offset
0x70 in the handle table area is a DWORD that contains the maximum
handle table offset in use. If the HWND passed into IsWindow is bigger
than that value, it can't be a valid HWND, so IsWindow16 returns FALSE.

The final part of IsWindow16 is to use the 16-bit HWND value to look
up the 32-bit pointer to the WND structure. (Remember, the 32-bit pointer
to the WND struct is relative to USER's DGROUP, and isn't a flat 32
pointer.) IsWindow16 does two checks with the pointer that the HWND

value dereferences to. First, the pointer must be greater than 0x10000. (In the USER32 version of IsWindow, the test is for 0x20000, which is more accurate.) Second, the pointer that the HWND dereferences to must be nonzero. If both conditions are met, IsWindow16 returns TRUE, indicating that the 16-bit HWND is valid.

Pseudocode for IsWindow

```
// In 16-bit USER.EXE
// Parameters:
//      HWND    hWnd    // The 16-bit version.

    Push DS

    Load DS with USER's DGROUP

    Grab UserTraceFlags WORD from USER's DGROUP

    restore USER's DGROUP

    if ( UserTraceFlags & 0x2000 )
        _DebugOutput( DBF_USER, "IsWindow" );

    // Execution falls through to IsWindow16...

IsWindow16 proc
// Parameters:
//      HWND    hWnd    // The 16-bit version.
// Locals:
//      PWND32  pWnd32  // 32-bit USER DGROUP relative pointer to HWND32.
//      PVOID   USER_dgroup_base    // Base address of USER's DGROUP.

    // Pops return address and HWND off the stack, then pushes them
    // back on. Supposedly saves space on stack frames.

    if ( hWnd & 3 )     // HWND16s must be a multiple of 4.
        return 0;

    if ( hWnd < 0x80 )  // HWND16s are always >= 0x80.
        return 0;
```

```
// At offset 0x10070 in the USER DGROUP seg is a DWORD with the
// maximum HWND value.
if ( hWnd > *(PDWORD)(USER_dgroup_base + 0x10070) )
    return 0;

// Use the HWND as an offset into the handle table area at
// offset 0x10000 in USER's DGROUP. Grab the pointer stored there.
pWnd32 = *(PDWORD) (USER_dgroup_base + 0x10000 + hWnd);

if ( pWnd32 <= 0x10000 )     // All HWND structs are above 0x10000.
    return 0;                // Actually, they're above 0x20000, but...

if ( pWnd32 )                // if the HWND ptr table contains a nonzero
    return TRUE;             // entry, we'll say it's a valid HWND.
```

The GetCapture, GetFocus, and GetActiveWindow functions

As I mentioned earlier, in Windows 95 the capture, focus, and active windows are stored on a per-queue basis. Thus, unlike in Windows 3.*x*, GetCapture, GetFocus, and GetActiveWindow can't merely scoop the relevant value out of USER's DGROUP segment. On the other hand, the three HWNDs (actually USER 32-bit pointers) are stored side by side in the PERQUEUEDATA structure that I described earlier. This means that the code for retrieving the three HWNDs can share common code.

The three functions each load a register (called perQueueOffset in the pseudocode) with the offset of their desired window pointer within the PERQUEUEDATA structure. The functions then all jump to a common spot (called Get_XXX_common in the pseudocode). The common code first calls into KRNL386 to get a pointer to the current thread's message queue. Within the queue is a pointer to the PERQUEUEDATA structure. With the pointer to the PERQUEUEDATA in hand, the code adds in the appropriate offset set earlier by the GetCapture, GetFocus, or GetActiveWindow functions. At the calculated location is a 32-bit pointer (relative to USER's DGROUP) to the desired window. All that remains for the common code to do is go to that WND struct and extract the 16-bit HWND value at offset 46h. This work is represented in the pseudocode by the call to HWnd32ToHWnd16.

Pseudocode for GetCapture, GetFocus, GetActiveWindow

```
// In 16-bit USER.EXE
// Locals:
//  PMSGQUEUE    pQueue;
//  WORD         perQueueOffset
//  BOOL         flag
//  PWND32       pWnd

GetCapture proc
    perQueueOffset = 0x0018 // Offset of the capture WND in the PERQUEUEDATA.
    flag = FALSE
    goto Get_XXX_common

GetFocus proc
    perQueueOffset = 0x001C // Offset of the focus WND in the PERQUEUEDATA.
    flag = FALSE
    goto Get_XXX_common

GetActiveWindow proc
    perQueueOffset = 0x0020 // Offset of the active WND in the PERQUEUEDATA.
    flag = TRUE

Get_XXX_common:

    pQueue = GetCurrentThreadQueue();   // KERNEL.625
    if ( !pQueue )
        INT 3;      // Oops! No queue. Break into the debugger.

    if ( pQueue->npPerQueue == 0 )
        INT 3;      // Oops! No per-queue data. Break into the debugger.

    // Using the perQueueOffset value (in the BX register), index into the
    // per-queue area and extract a USER relative pointer to the desired WND.
    pWnd = *(PWND32 *)(pQueue->npPerQueue + perQueueOffset);

    if ( !pWnd && flag )    // If pWnd is 0, but "flag" is set (which
    {                       // only happens for GetActiveWindow)...

        // Try a second approach to getting the active window. If
        // the conditions are right, try calling GetForegroundWindow.
        // npCurrentPerQueueData is a USER.EXE global variable.
        if ( pQueue->npPerQueue == npCurrentPerQueueData )
            return GetForegroundWindow();
    }

    // Convert from the 32-bit HWND form to the 16-bit form, and return it.
    return HWnd32ToHWnd16( pWnd );
```

The GetWindowThreadProcessId and IGetWindowThreadProcessId functions

The GetWindowThreadProcessId function is new to the Win32 API. (The closest equivalent in Windows 3.*x* was GetWindowTask.) Although the GetWindowThreadProcessId function is exported by the 32-bit USER32.DLL, it falls to the 16-bit USER.EXE to implement it. (Will the indignity never end?) The GetWindowThreadProcessId function is essentially just a parameter validation layer. The real work is in the IGetWindowThreadProcessId function. However, before calling IGetWindowThreadProcessId, the code first converts the 16-bit HWND into a USER32-relative 32-bit pointer, and passes that along.

IGetWindowThreadProcessId has to extract the process ID and thread ID from two different places. The thread ID that a window is associated with is stored in the thread's message queue. Since queues are per-thread (and not per-process as you might think), the process ID isn't stored in the message queue. Instead, the process ID is stored in the QUEUEPROCESSDATA structure that I described earlier. IGetWindowThreadProcessId uses the message queue to get a pointer to the QUEUEPROCESSDATA data, and extracts the process ID from that structure.

The IGetWindowThreadProcessId code does have a strange bit of code that I'm at a loss to explain. Apparently, if some flag is set in the QUEUE-PROCESSDATA structure, the thread ID and processID for the window are actually stored at the end of the WND structure itself. I was never able find an example where this was the case.

Pseudocode for GetWindowThreadProcessId

```
// In USER.EXE (believe it or not)
// Parameters:
//     HWND    hWnd           // 16-bit version
//     LPDWORD lpdwProcessId  // Pointer at which to store the process ID.
// Locals:
//     PWND32  pWnd32;

    pWnd32 = HWnd16toHWnd32( hWnd ); // Convert the 16-bit HWND value into
                                     // the 32-bit pointer version.

    // Verify that a valid pointer to at least 4 bytes was passed.
    VerifyPtr( lpdwProcessId, sizeof(DWORD) )

    return IGetWindowThreadProcessId( pWnd32, lpdwProcessId );
```

Pseudocode for IGetWindowThreadProcessId

```
// Parameters:
//      PWND32  pWnd;
//      LPDWORD lpdwProcessId
// Locals
//      LPMSGQUEUE lpMsgQueue;
//      DWORD   threadId;

    lpMsgQueue = MAKELP( pWnd->hQueue, 0 ); // Get a pointer to the window's
                                            // message queue.
    if ( UserTraceFlags & 0x00042000 )
        _DebugOutput( DBF_USER, "GetWindowThreadProcessId" );

    if ( lpMsgQueue->npProcess->flags & 2 ) // This is rarely the case.
    {
        processId = pWnd->alternatePID; // Grab the PID/TID from the WND
        threadId = pWnd->alternateTID;  // struct.
    }
    else    // Execution most often comes through here.
    {
        processId = lpMsgQueue->npProcess->processId;
        threadId = lpMsgQueue->threadId;
    }

    if ( SELECTOROF(lpdwProcessId) )
        *lpdwProcessId = processId;

    return threadId;
```

The DesktopWndProc function

When deciding what functions were worth looking into for this chapter, I quickly gravitated to the DesktopWndProc function. There were two reasons for this. First, this function is relatively simple, and I wanted to show a working system-provided window procedure. Second, DesktopWndProc contains the code for enabling the free system resource fudging that I talked about earlier in the chapter.

The first thing to notice about DesktopWndProc is that it's a semi–32-bit WNDPROC. That is, the hWnd and msg fields are 16 bits, but the WPARAM is 32 bits (like a WNDPROC in a Win32 program would be). Another important thing to notice is that the function immediately converts the 16-bit

HWND into a USER32 relative 32-bit pointer. It uses this 32-bit pointer for all its accesses to the WND structure. All the other standard system WNDPROCs do the same thing in this regard (that is, they use USER DGROUP-relative 32-bit pointers).

The core of the DesktopWndProc code is a switch statement (no, the Windows 95 team hasn't switched Windows over to use MFC yet). The windows messages that DesktopWndProc handles are listed here:

- **The WM_USER message:** The WM_USER message is the dark horse of the messages handled by DesktopWndProc. When the desktop receives this message for the first time (and only for the first time), it calls GetFreeSystemResources to get the percentage free in both the USER and GDI heaps. Subsequent calls to GetFreeSystemResources make their return value relative to the percentage-free values determined here. Who sends the WM_USER message to the desktop? The Explorer process itself, after it's done its initialization. The idea of this WM_USER message is apparently to establish a baseline system resource usage, from which subsequent calls to GetFreeSystemResources can be compared. While this sounds reasonable enough, it is a big change from Windows 3.1, and it would be nice if Microsoft were to describe the change to its users. As it stands now, the free system resources numbers for the typical system will look like they've jumped way up when the machine was updated to Windows 95. Under the hood, though, the change isn't really that dramatic.

- **The WM_ERASEBKGND message:** This messages erases the background and validates the specified rectangle. Nothing exciting here.

- **The WM_CANCELMODE message:** If there isn't a system modal window, this handler falls through to the default handler.

- **The WM_NCCREATE message:** This message handler seems to be used primarily as a sanity check. The code checks to make sure that there are no other windows of class desktop. It also verifies that the desktop window doesn't have a parent window.

- **The WM_LBUTTONDBLCLK message:** This message handler changes the message being processed into a WM_SYSCOMMAND message with SC_TASKLIST as the high WORD of the WPARAM. In Windows 3.1, a double-click on the desktop would bring up the task manager. In Windows 95, when DefWindowProc receives the SC_TASKLIST command, it calls into the shell, which in turn brings up Explorer's start menu.

- **The WM_QUERYNEWPALETTE and WM_PALETTECHANGED messages:** These two functions call some function in USER that (you guessed it) probably has something to do with the palette. Any messages that come through the DesktopWndProc and which aren't handled by the above handlers fall through the switch statement, and call DefWindowProc. (And the inner workings of DefWindowProc is probably a book unto itself.)

Pseudocode for DesktopWndProc

```
// In 16-bit USER.EXE
// Parameters:
//     HWND    hWnd
//     UINT    msg
//     WPARAM  wParam      // 32 bits, not 16.
//     LPARAM  lParam
// Locals:
//     PWND32  pWnd32      // 32-bit pointer, relative to USER DGROUP.

    pWnd32 = HWnd16ToHWnd32( hWnd )

    if ( UserTraceFlags & 0x4 )
        _DebugOutput( DBF_USER, "DesktopWndProc" );

    switch ( msg )
    {
        case WM_ERASEBKGND:
            // Erase the desktop. The function calls:
            // FILLRECT, GETCLIPBOX, GETDCORG, GETTEXTEXTENT, LOADSTRING
            // LSTRCATN, LSTRLEN, OFFSETRECT, SETBKMODE, SETBRUSHORG,
            // SETTEXTCOLOR, SETVIEWPORTORG, and TEXTOUT.
            SomeFunction( wParam );      // wParam == HDC to paint with.

            ValidateRect( pWnd32->hWnd16, 0 );
            return 1;

        case WM_CANCELMODE:
            if ( HWndSysModal == SomeUserGlobalVar )
                return 0;
            break;
```

```
    case WM_NCCREATE:
        // This is the first message through the WND proc.
        if ( pWnd32->wndClass->cClsWnds != 1 )
        {
            _DebugOutput( DBF_FATAL | DBF_USER, "USER: Assertion failed" );
        }

        pWnd32->classAtom = DesktopClassAtom;   // USER global variable.

        if ( 0 == DefWindowProc32( pWnd32->hWnd16, msg, wParam, lParam ) )
            return 0;

        // The desktop window better not have a parent!!!
        if ( 0 == pWnd32->hWndParent )
            return 1;

        _DebugOutput( DBF_FATAL | DBF_USER, "USER: Assertion failed" );
        return 1;

    case WM_LBUTTONDBLCLK:
        msg = WM_SYSCOMMAND;
        HIWORD( wParam ) = SC_TASKLIST
        break;

    case WM_QUERYNEWPALETTE:
    case WM_PALETTECHANGED:
        if ( wParam == hWnd )   // wParam == HWND that changed the palette.
            SomeFunction();     // Same basic actions as 3.1, including
                                // calling RedrawWindow().

        return 0;

    case WM_USER:    // 0x0400 (sent by Explorer)
        if ( base_USER_FSR_percentage == 0 )
        {
            base_GDI_FSR_percentage
                = GetFreeSystemResources( GSFR_GDIRESOURCES );

            base_USER_FSR_percentage
                = GetFreeSystemResources( GSFR_USERRESOURCES );
        }

        return 0;
}

return DefWindowProc32( pWnd32->hWnd16, msg, wParam, lParam );
```

USER32 isn't just thunks to USER.EXE

Throughout this chapter, I've emphasized that the real work of the Windows 95 USER subsystem is handled by the 16-bit USER.EXE. It is indeed true that large portions of USER32 are just thunks down to USER.EXE. However, it would be wrong to think that USER32 consists of nothing but thunks. In looking at the USER32 listings, it's readily apparent that Microsoft took some time to determine which USER routines are heavily called and could easily be implemented without thunking down to USER.EXE. In a few cases (such as the ones I'll show next), the Windows 95 team decided that the additional speed gain from eliminating a thunk warranted using a little extra code in USER32.DLL. The functions I'll describe in the following sections are by no means a complete list — rather, they're a representative sample of the windowing system functions.

The IsWindow function in USER32.DLL

The USER32 version of IsWindow is only slightly more complicated than the USER.EXE version. Since USER32's IsWindow function could be called by a Win32 thread that doesn't currently hold the Win16Mutex, the function uses two helper functions (GrabWin16Mutex and ReleaseWinMutex) to bracket the call to the core of the routine. The GetWndPtr32 function (which is described next) is used throughout USER32.DLL. If GetWndPtr32 returns 0, IsWindow returns FALSE, indicating that the passed-in HWND isn't valid. Otherwise, IsWindow returns TRUE on any nonzero return value from GetWndPtr32.

Pseudocode for IsWindow

```
// in USER32.DLL
// Parameters:
//   HWND    hWnd        // The 16-bit version.
// Locals:
//   BOOL    retValue;

    GrabWin16Mutex();

    retValue = GetWndPtr32( hWnd );      // Pass 16-bit HWND version.

    ReleaseWin16Mutex();
```

Pseudocode for GrabWin16Mutex

```
EnterSysLevel( pWin16Mutex );    // Call KERNEL.97 to acquire the Win16.
```

Pseudocode for GrabWin16Mutex

```
LeaveSysLevel( pWin16Mutex );    // Call KERNEL.98 to release the Win16
                                 // mutex semaphore.
```

The GetWndPtr32 function in USER32

The GetWndPtr32 function is a general-purpose USER32 internal routine. Given a 16-bit HWND, it returns a USER32-relative 32-bit pointer to the WND structure. In terms of how it verifies the 16-bit HWND and looks up the WND struct, the GetWndPtr32 function is nearly identical to the IsWindow function in the 16-bit USER.EXE. The only real difference is at the end of the function: The 16-bit IsWindow returns TRUE or FALSE, while GetWndPtr32 returns a USER32 DGROUP relative pointer to the WND.

Pseudocode for GetWndPtr32

```
// Parameters:
//     HWND    hWnd       // The 16-bit version.
// Locals:
//     DWORD   retValue;

    ConfirmSysLevel( pWin16Mutex );        // Make sure we already have acquired
                                           // the Win16Mutex.

    if ( !hWnd )                           // Filter out the 0 HWND case.
        return 0;

    if ( hWnd & 3 )                        // HWNDs are always multiples of 4.
        return 0;

    if ( hWnd < 0x80 )                     // The lowest HWND value is 80.
        return 0;

    // At offset 0x10070 in the USER DGROUP seg is a DWORD with the
    // maximum HWND value.
    if ( hWnd > *(PDWORD)(USER_dgroup_base + 0x10070) )
        return 0;
```

```
// Dereference the DWORD at 0x10000 + the HWND value to get a pointer.
retValue = *(PDWORD) (USER_dgroup_base + 0x10000 + hWnd);

if ( retValue < 0x20000 )    // The HWND(32) heap starts 0x20000 bytes
    return 0;                // into USER's DGROUP. Note the different
                             // comparison than the one IsWindow16 uses.

// Return a flat PTR to the WND32 structure. The value in the HWND
// table is a USER DGROUP 32-bit relative offset.
return (PWND32) (retPtr + UserDgroupBase);
```

The GetCapture, GetFocus, and GetActiveWindow functions in USER32.DLL

Earlier, I presented pseudocode for the GetCapture, GetFocus, and GetActiveWindow functions as implemented in USER.EXE (see the "Pseudocode for select 16-bit USER.EXE functions" section). The 32-bit versions in USER32 are essentially identical in their core implementation. Two differences bear mentioning, though. The first difference is that the USER32 versions all acquire and release the Win16Mutex around their access to the USER data structures. The 16-bit equivalents don't have to do this, since they're in 16-bit code and, by definition, the Win16Mutex has already been acquired. The second difference is the absence of error checking in the USER32 versions. The 16-bit versions of these functions check to make sure there's a queue present before they start rooting around in the PERQUEUEDATA structure.

Pseudocode for GetCapture, GetFocus, GetActiveWindow

```
// Locals:
//      DWORD    perQueueOffset;

GetActiveWindow proc
    perQueueOffset = 0x20;  // Offset of the active WND in the PERQUEUEDATA.
    goto GetWndXXX_common

GetCapture proc
    perQueueOffset = 0x18;  // Offset of the capture WND in the PERQUEUEDATA.
    goto GetWndXXX_common

GetFocus proc
    perQueueOffset = 0x1C;  // Offset of the focus WND in the PERQUEUEDATA.
    // Fall though...
```

```
GetWndXXX_common:
// Locals:
//    PMSGQUEUE pQueue;
//    PWND32 pWnd;

    pQueue = GetCurrentQueuePtr();

    GrabWin16Mutex();

    if ( pQueue->npPerQueue == 0 )
        goto SuckHWND16_release_Win16Mutex; // Oops! No per-queue data.

    // Extract the USER DGROUP relative 32-bit PWND32 pointer out of the
    // per-queue data structure.
    pWnd = *(PWND32 *) (UserDgroupBase + pQueue->npPerQueue + perQueueOffset );

    goto SuckHWND16OutOfUserDGROUP;

SuckHWND16OutOfUserDGROUP:

    // Execution arrives here with a pointer to actual WND32 struct (in EAX).

    if ( pWnd )
    {
        pWnd = (WORD)( UserDgroupBase + pWnd->hWnd16 );
        // pWnd is now really a 16-bit HWND, not a pointer.
    }

SuckHWND16_release_Win16Mutex:

    ReleaseWin16Mutex();
    return pWnd;    // Either 0, or a 16-bit HWND.
```

The GetMessagePos, GetMessageTime, and GetMessageExtraInfo functions in USER32.DLL

The GetMessagePos, GetMessageTime, and GetMessageExtraInfo functions in USER32 are essentially identical to their 16-bit equivalents in USER.EXE. Since the three functions each just grab a single variable from the current thread's message queue, they all start with a small stub that loads the desired offset into a register before jumping to a common location. At the common location, the code gets a pointer to the current thread's queue and extracts the relevant DWORD from it. Interestingly, these functions don't bother to acquire the Win16Mutex like the USER GetCapture, GetFocus, and GetActiveWindow functions do.

Pseudocode for GetMessagePos, GetMessageTime, GetMessageExtraInfo

```
// In USER32.DLL
// Locals:
//   DWORD   infoOffset
GetMessagePos proc
    infoOffset = 0x28;
    goto GetMsgXXX_common

GetMessageTime proc
    infoOffset = 0x24;
    goto GetMsgXXX_common

GetMessageExtraInfo proc
    infoOffset = 0x30;
    // Fall through...

GetMsgXXX_common:
// Locals:
//   PMSGQUEUE pQueue;

    // Note that this code doesn't grab the Win16Mutex like the GetWndXXX
    // functions do.

    pQueue = GetCurrentQueuePtr();

    // Add the infoOffset to the base address of the queue, and return
    // the DWORD stored therein.
    return *(PDWORD)( pQueue + infoOffset );
```

The SendMessage function in USER32.DLL

You might be somewhat surprised to discover that I've provided pseudocode for USER32's SendMessage routine. After all, SendMessage is one of the most complicated routines in all of the USER subsystem, so it surely must thunk down to the 16-bit USER.EXE, right? In many cases, that assumption is correct. However, SendMessage is a heavily used routine, and if the right conditions are met, it can do its work without ever thunking down to 16-bit code. We're talking major performance improvement here.

The USER32 SendMessage starts out by acquiring the Win16Mutex. The code then goes through a long series of tests to see whether this particular message can be sent safely without getting the real SendMessage (in USER.EXE) involved. Among the conditions that can disqualify the attempt and force a thunk down to USER.EXE are the following:

- The HWND is 0.
- The queue of the destination window is different from the current thread's queue.
- Certain variables in USER.EXE's DGROUP are nonzero.

If the particular message being sent makes it through the gauntlet of tests that would force it to thunk down, SendMessage begins setting things up for the call to the destination WNDPROC. In particular, SendMessage needs the address of the WNDPROC it'll be calling.

As I've mentioned earlier, the WND structures themselves don't ever store an actual 32-bit flat pointer to a WNDPROC. Instead, if a WND structure is a 32-bit window, the WNDPROC address in the WND structure points to a 16-bit code stub that ultimately transfers control up to 32-bit land. Part of that code stub is the actual 32-bit WNDPROC. The SendMessage code knows about these special stubs, and reads the 32-bit WNDPROC address out of the stub itself. Finally, before JMP'ing to the target WNDPROC, SendMessage releases the Win16Mutex. This whole sequence smacks of being a big kludge, but if it works and improves performance, why not?

Pseudocode for SendMessage

```
// 32-bit version in USER32.DLL
// Parameters:
//   HWND     hWnd
//   UINT     uMsg
//   WPARAM   wParam
//   LPARAM   lParam
// Locals:
//   PWND32   pWnd
//   PMSGQUEUE pQueue;
//   LPVOID   lpvMsgProcThunk // A 16:16 pointer.
//   WNDPROC  wndProc32

    GrabWin16Mutex();

    pWnd = GetWndPtr32( hWnd );
    if ( !pWnd )                        // No HWND... gotta thunk.
        goto ThunkToSendMessage16;

    if ( !pWnd->flags & 0x02000000 )    // Some flag ain't set... gotta thunk.
        goto ThunkToSendMessage16
```

```
        if ( pCurrentTIB->pvQueue != pWnd->hQueue )  // Sending a message to a
            goto ThunkToSendMessage16                 // different queue. Gotta
                                                      // thunk.

        if ( SomeVariableInUserDgroup != 0 )          // USER's in some funky state.
            goto ThunkToSendMessage16                 // Gotta thunk.
        if ( SomeOtherVariableInUserDgroup != 0 )
            goto ThunkToSendMessage16

        // Get a flat pointer to the message queue.
        // MapSL takes a selector and an offset, and returns a linear address.
        pQueue = MapSL( pCurrentTIB->pvQueue, 0 );

        if ( pQueue->(0x6A+0xA) != 0 )        // ??? Gotta thunk.
            goto ThunkToSendMessage16;

        if ( pQueue->(0x6A+0x1A) != 0 )       // ??? Gotta thunk.
            goto ThunkToSendMessage16;

        // Get a pointer to the thunk code that USER.EXE created for this
        // window. Index 2 bytes into the USER message thunk, and grab the
        // linear address of the window procedure.
        lpvMsgProcThunk = pWnd->lpfnWndProc;
        wndProc32 = *(LPWORD)(lpvMsgProcThunk+2)

        ReleaseWin16Mutex();   // Don't need this no more.

        // If all went well, jump to the 32-bit window procedure.
        // We've successfully avoided the intertask SendMessage contortions,
        // and have also avoided thunking down to 16-bit USER.EXE.
        goto wndProc32;

ThunkToSendMessage16:        // Well, it looks like we gotta thunk down to
                             // USER.EXE.
        ReleaseWin16Mutex();

        pop return address into EAX
        pop hWnd into ECX

        push    0
        push    hWnd          // in ECX
        push    0
        push    returnAddress // in EAX

        goto    common thunking code
```

The GetDlgItem function in USER32.DLL

The GetDlgItem function is another of the heavily used functions in Win32, especially with dialog-related code. Given an HWND and a child control ID, the function needs to return the HWND of the child control. If you remember back when I was describing the WND structure, you can see how GetDlgItem doesn't need to do anything more sophisticated than walk a section of the WND hierarchy, looking for a window with the right control ID.

The USER GetDlgItem function begins by grabbing the Win16Mutex (after all, we don't want the WND hierarchy changing beneath us as we're walking it!). Dialog controls are simply child windows of the dialog window. Therefore, all GetDlgItem has to do is walk the list of child windows for the specified dialog and compare the control ID of each window it finds to the idControl input parameter. This is exactly what GetDlgItem does. When it finds a WND structure with a controlID field that matches the input parameter, the code looks up and returns the 16-bit HWND value found elsewhere in the WND structure. Of course, before returning, the function remembers to release the Win16Mutex.

Pseudocode for GetDlgItem

```
// 32-bit version in USER32.DLL
// Parameters:
//   HWND     hwndDlg
//   int      idControl
// Locals:
//   PWND32   pWnd

    GrabWin16Mutex();

    pWnd = GetWndPtr32( hwndCtl );  // Get a flat pointer to the WND struct.

    if ( pWnd )
    {
        pWnd = pWnd->hWndChild; // Start at the first child window.

        while ( pWnd )  // While there are child windows...
        {
            pWnd += UserDgroupBase; // convert USER DGROUP relative pointer
                                    // to a flat pointer.

            // Is the control ID of this window what we're looking for?
            if ( idControl == pWnd->ctrlID )
            {
```

```
                pWnd = pWnd->hWnd16;
                break;
            }

            pWnd = pWnd->hWndNext;  // Advance to next child window.
        }
    }

    ReleaseWin16Mutex();

    return pWnd;    // This is always either 0 or a 16-bit HWND value.
```

The GetDlgCtrlID function in USER32.DLL

The GetDlgCtrlID function is the complement of the GetDlgItem function.
Given a 16-bit HWND value, it merely needs to return the control ID stored
in the corresponding windows WND struct. As with GetDlgItem, the code
does all its work while holding on to the Win16Mutex.

    The GetDlgCtrlID function couldn't be much simpler. It passes the 16-bit
HWND input parameter to GetWndPtr32 and gets back a USER32-relative
32-bit WND pointer. Assuming it gets back a non-null pointer, the function
retrieves the control ID value from the appropriate offset in the WND struct
and returns it. (And don't forget to free the Win16Mutex!)

Pseudocode for GetDlgCtrlID

```
// 32-bit version in USER32.DLL
// Parameters:
//   HWND     hwndCtl
// Locals:
//   PWND32   pWnd
//   DWORD    retValue;

    GrabWin16Mutex();

    pWnd = GetWndPtr32( hwndCtl );  // Get a flat pointer to the WND struct.

    if ( !pWnd )
        retValue = 0;
    else
        retValue = pWnd->ctrlID;    // Grab the ctrlID field out of the WND.

    ReleaseWin16Mutex();

    return retValue;
```

Unicode support in Windows 95 (Huh?)

Believe it or not, Windows 95 does have a smidgen of actual, usable Unicode support. If you don't believe me, check out the following short program, which I've titled WIN95UNI.C:

```
#define UNICODE
#include <windows.h>

int main()
{
    MessageBox( 0,
                TEXT("Yes! Really!"),
                TEXT("Unicode in Windows 95?"),
                MB_ICONQUESTION );
    return 0;
}
```

When compiled, this code produces a Unicode program. We can even verify it by dumping out the EXE file using PEDUMP from Chapter 8:

```
Imports Table:
  USER32.dll
  Hint/Name Table: 00006084
  TimeDateStamp:   00000000
  ForwarderChain:  00000000
  First thunk RVA: 000060D4
  Ordn  Name
   395  MessageBoxW

  KERNEL32.dll
  Hint/Name Table: 0000603C
  TimeDateStamp:   00000000
  ..... rest omitted....
```

There's definitely a call to the Unicode version of MessageBox in there. What happens when we run it? Check out Figure 4-5.

Just what the heck's going on in Figure 4-5? Windows 95 supposedly doesn't support Unicode, but as you can plainly see, the WIN95UNI program proves that there's some form of Unicode support in there. Here's a call chain for an invocation of the Unicode MessageBoxW in Windows 95:

```
MessageBoxW
    MessageBoxExW
        WideCharToMultiByte // Convert the 2nd parameter to ASCII.
        WideCharToMultiByte // Convert the 3rd parameter to ASCII.
        MessageBoxExA       // Invoke the ASCII MessageBoxEx.
```

Figure 4-5
The WIN95UNI program proves that Windows 95 supports Unicode.

So why does Windows 95 go to the trouble of supporting Unicode (at least in this minimalist fashion)? One of Microsoft's requirements for its Windows 95 logo is that programs should degrade gracefully on a system that doesn't support the full set of capabilities required by the program. One of the things a program could do is throw up a MessageBox and say "Sorry, I can't run." By providing a somewhat reasonable implementation of the MessageBoxW function, Windows 95 lets programs compiled for Unicode at least get the word out that they may not work (or may not work properly).

The UserSeeUserDo function (USER.EXE)

I couldn't finish this chapter's discussion of the USER subsystem without describing UserSeeUserDo. This function was introduced in Windows 3.1 as an undocumented back door to various USER variables and functions. In Windows 95, the volume of things that can slip through that back door has been increased. In a way, examining what UserSeeUserDo provides is a good way to get a handle on the key things the USER architects feel are important.

UserSeeUserDo is implemented in the 16-bit USER.EXE, and takes four input parameters. The first parameter indicates what UserSeeUserDo should do, or what variable's value it should return. The interpretation of the remaining three parameters depends on what the first parameter is requesting.

The first three subfunctions allow the caller to allocate, free, or compact memory from USER's 16-bit DGROUP heap. The next five subfunctions are for returning the values of various important USER global variables: the menu heap handle, the head of the system class list, USER's DGROUP handle, the head of the device context entry chain (see Chapter 6 of *Undocumented Windows*), and a pointer to the desktop window. This last variable isn't the 16-bit HWND of the desktop window. Rather, it's a USER32-relative 32-bit pointer to the desktop window's WND structure.

The final two subfunctions made available by UserSeeUserDo are for allocating and freeing memory from the new 32-bit heaps that USER uses.

Subfunction 10 allocates memory, while subfunction 11 frees it. If the second parameter to UserSeeUserDo is nonzero, the code allocates memory from the 32-bit menu heap. Otherwise, it allocates the memory from the 32-bit window heap.

Pseudocode for UserSeeUserDo

```
// Parameters:
//   WORD    wReqType
//   WORD    param1, param2, param3

    if ( UserTraceFlags & 0x1000 )
        _DebugOutput( DBF_USER, "UserSeeUserDo" );

    switch ( wReqType )
    {
        case 1:
            // Call LocalAlloc, using USER's DGROUP.
            return UserLocalAlloc(LT_USER_USERSEEUSERDOALLOC, param1, param3);

        case 2:
            // Call LocalFree, using USER's DGROUP.
            return UserLocalFree( param1 );

        case 3:
            // Call LocalCompact, using USER's DGROUP.
            return LocalCompact( param3 );

        case 4:
            return hMenuHeap;    // Handle to the 32-bit menu heap.

        case 5:
            return PClsList;     // Near pointer to first class in list of
                                 // system classes registered by USER.EXE.
        case 6:
            return DS;           // USER's DGROUP.

        case 8:
            return PDCEFirst;    // Head of DCE (Device Context Entry) list.
                                 // See "DCE" in Chapter 5 of Undocumented
                                 // Windows.
        case 9:
            return HWndDesktop;  // The USER-DGROUP-relative 32-bit version.

        case 10:
            // Allocate memory from either the 32-bit menu or window heaps.
            if ( param1 )
            {
```

```
                    return Local32Alloc( MenuHeapHandleTableBase, param3, 0, 0, 0);
                }
                else
                {
                    return Local32Alloc(WindowHeapHandleTableBase, param3, 0,0,0);
                }

            case 11:
                // Free memory from either the 32-bit menu or window heaps.
                if ( param1 )
                {
                    return Local32Free( MenuHeapHandleTableBase, param3, 0 );
                }
                else
                {
                    return Local32Free(WindowHeapHandleTableBase, param3, 0 );
                }

            case 7:
            default:
                return -1;
    }
```

THE WINDOWS 95 GDI MODULE

After all the new things I've described in Windows 95's USER subsystem, my
coverage of Windows 95's GDI side will probably be anticlimactic if you're
one of those pixel pushers who love GDI. It's not that GDI isn't important.
There are actually many new and exciting things on the graphics side of
Windows 95. Rather, it's just the plain and simple truth that I'm first and
foremost a KERNEL person who doesn't mind digging into USER. Graphics
and the GDI simply aren't as interesting to me. Now that I've provided full
disclosure on my GDI experience, let's move on.

If I could impart only one piece of information about Windows 95's
GDI.EXE and GDI32.DLL, it would be this: These two subsystems are parallel
to the equivalent USER subsystems. Both GDI and USER manage objects
allocated from their heaps. In the case of USER, the primary objects are
windows, menus, and classes. For GDI, the equivalent objects are pens,
brushes, bitmaps, and so on. In Windows 3.1, both USER and GDI were
constrained by their respective 64K heap (although USER.EXE did break
out menus into a separate 64K heap). In Windows 95, both USER and GDI

are still heavily dependent on data structures allocated from their DGROUP heaps. At the same time, though, both USER and GDI gained access to Win32 heaps with 2MB of memory in which to stuff large data items. The layout of the USER DGROUP, handle table area, and 32-bit window heap translates exactly over to the GDI equivalents, as shown in Figure 4-6.

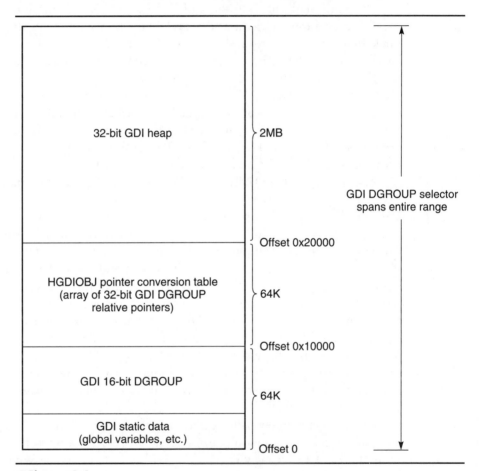

Figure 4-6

In Windows 95, GDI and USER have a generally parallel structure. Here, you can see that the layout of the DGROUP and handle table area of GDI is similar to that of USER.

Just as you access USER's objects with handles (HWNDs and HMENUs), you also use handles to access GDI objects (HPENs, HBRUSHs, and so on). Earlier, I described how 16 HWNDs are used to look up 32-bit pointers in an array to find the actual offset to a WND structure. For GDI objects that are stored in the 32-bit GDI heap, the translation from 16-bit handle to 32-bit pointer works exactly as it does for HWNDs on the USER side. If the GDI object that a handle references is allocated from GDI's DGROUP, then the handle is a regular 16-bit heap local handle, and can easily be dereferenced to an offset into GDI's 16-bit DGROUP.

The point of all this is to think of USER and GDI as being somewhat parallel in operation, at least at the level where they manipulate data structures. If you really understand how the USER code works with regards to handles and pointers, you can probably dive into GDI code and know what's going on without too much difficulty.

So what items did the Windows 95 GDI feel compelled to move up into its 32-bit heap? Well, according to the HEAPWALK program from the Win32SDK, there are fonts and regions floating around up there. There are also some additional objects that HEAPWALK (and I, being a relative neophyte regarding GDI issues) are unable to identify.

Another area where USER and GDI are parallel involves thunking. The vast majority of the USER subsystem code is implemented in the 16-bit USER.EXE, and USER32 serves primarily (but not entirely) as thunks down to that code. The situation with the GDI subsystem is similar, but not identical. Vast portions of GDI remain implemented in the 16-bit GDI.EXE code. However, Microsoft added many new GDI-related features having to do with Win32 support to the GDI subsystem. Some of this new code was done in the 16-bit GDI.EXE. However, Microsoft claims that some of GDI's new functionality was put into GDI32.DLL and that GDI.EXE thunks up to it. The areas that Microsoft says are in GDI32 are the TrueType rasterizer, the spooler and printing subsystem, and the DIB engine. I haven't yet conclusively proved that this is true. However, from looking at what goes in GDI32.DLL, it appears that there is quite a bit of code in GDI32 that's unrelated to simply thunking down to GDI.EXE.

One especially noteworthy addition to the 16-bit GDI.EXE is 32-bit code within the 16-bit module. In Chapter 7, I describe a bit in the segment table entries of 16-bit New Executable (NE) files that tells the Windows 95 loader to make the selector for the segment a 32-bit code selector. That is, when the CPU loads that selector into its CS register, it's interpreting the code as 32-bit code rather than as the 16-bit code used by most Win16 applications and DLLs. The 16-bit GDI.EXE uses four such 32-bit segments. Although there were no exported functions in these 32-bit segments, I examined the code around the calls to these 32-bit segments from GDI.EXE, and came to the following conclusions:

GDI.EXE Segment 0x20:	Bezier stuff
GDI.EXE Segment 0x23:	Paths, Enhanced Metafile (EMF) support
GDI.EXE Segment 0x24:	??? (unknown)
GDI.EXE Segment 0x26:	The string "engine font" appears in this segment

Microsoft's description of the relationship between the 16- and 32-bit components of Windows 95 states that Beziers, paths, and enhanced metafiles are in the 16-bit GDI.EXE. This is consistent with what I found.

GDI objects

One of the keys to being a GDI expert is understanding GDI objects. The GDI subsystem deals with a dozen or so different object types. Most of them have their own unique handle name (which you're undoubtedly already familiar with). For example, a device context (DC) is one type of GDI object, and you pass an HDC (handle to a DC) to various GDI functions. Likewise, a pen is a GDI object, and you refer to a specific pen via an HPEN (handle to a PEN). Functions that accept any particular type of GDI object take HGDIOBJ parameters. An HGDIOBJ can be considered a base class for more specific GDI objects like HDCs, HBRUSHs, and so forth. You can find the list of GDI objects in Windows 3.1 from examining the LT_GDI_xxx #defines in TOOLHELP.H. Unfortunately, those #defines don't appear to have been updated for the new GDI object types in Windows 95.

You can tell that GDI tries to deal with its objects in a uniform manner because it has functions like SelectObject and DeleteObject that don't need to be told what they're being passed. GDI inspects the object, determines what type it is, and acts accordingly. How does GDI know the type of a particular object that's passed to it? Each GDI object starts out with a standard header that includes a WORD that marks the object as a particular type. The Windows 95 GDI object list (including the corresponding marker values) is as follows:

```
PEN        0x4F47 (1)
BRUSH      0x4F48 (2)
FONT       0x4F49 (3)
PAL        0x4F4A (4)
BITMAP     0x4F4B (5)
REGION     0x4F4C (6)
```

```
DC              0x4F4D (7)
IC              0x4F4E (8)

// Beyond this point, the markers get a bit sketchy, but here's my
// best guess...

METADC          0x4F4F
METAFILE        0x4F50
ENHMETADC       0x4F51
ENHMETAFILE     0x4F52
```

The IsGDIObject function in GDI.EXE

The IsGDIObject function is documented as returning FALSE if the input
GDI object handle (an HGDIOBJ) isn't a valid handle. Interestingly, the
documentation says that if IsGDIObject returns TRUE, the input handle
may not actually be a real GDI object handle. Nonetheless, the documented
purpose of the function is to determine if an HGDIOBJ is invalid. What the
documentation doesn't tell you is that if the input HGDIOBJ parameter is
valid, the return value identifies what type of object was passed in. This can
come in handy for applications like Bounds-Checker/W that need to verify
handles such as HDCs, HBRUSHs, and so forth.

As I mentioned earlier, GDI stores some objects in its 16-bit DGROUP
heap and other objects (fonts and regions) in its 32-bit heap. The first thing
IsGDIObject needs to do is figure out where it should look for the object so
that it can read in the object type WORD (for example, 0x4F47). Luckily,
this isn't hard for GDI to do. GDI objects that are allocated out of the 16-bit
DGROUP heap are allocated with the LMEM_MOVEABLE attribute. To
make a long story short, 16-bit LMEM_MOVEABLE handles always end in
2, 6, 0xA, or 0xE. As you may recall from earlier in the chapter, the handles
for objects in 32-bit USER or GDI heap are always multiples of 4.

Knowing this key distinction between the two types of objects, IsGDIObject
merely needs to examine the second to last bit. If it's set, the handle ends in
2, 6, 0xA, or 0xE and the object was allocated from GDI's 16-bit DGROUP.
If the second to last bit is 0, the handle value ends in 0, 4, 8 or 0xC, so the
object was allocated in the 32-bit GDI heap. In either case, IsGDIObject calculates the address where the object can be found and constructs a pointer
to the object. Using the pointer, IsGDIObject extracts the block type WORD.

With the block type WORD in hand, IsGDIObject then masks off a couple
of the bits, which apparently mean something elsewhere in GDI. The result

of the masking should be a value between 0x4F47 and 0x4F52. If this isn't the case, this isn't a valid GDI object, so IsGDIObject returns 0. If the block type WORD is within range, IsGDIObject subtracts 0x4F46 from the value to make it a one-based value. This is the number that IsGDIObject returns.

Pseudocode for IsGDIObject

```
// In 16-bit GDI.EXE
// Parameters:
//   HGDIOBJ hObj
// Locals:
//   PGDIOBJ pObj;
//   WORD    retValue;   // The doc says a BOOL, but it's really an obj type.

    // Note that the doc says that this function can return TRUE without
    // it really being a GDI object.

    if ( hObj == 0 )    // Check for the bonehead case.
        return 0;

    if ( (hObj & 2) == 0 )  // Object handles in 32-bit heap are
    {                       // multiples of 4.

        // Use the handle as an offset into the GDI object table that
        // starts 0x10000 from GDI's DGROUP. The DWORD there is a PGDIOBJ.
        // Actually dereferences through ES. ES points to GDI's DGROUP.
        pObj = *(PGDIOBJ)( 0x10000 + hObj );
    }
    else    // Object handles that end in 2, 6, A, or E are GDI 16-bit
    {       // heap local handles.

        // Since the hObj is a moveable handle, it's a pointer to a 16-bit
        // local heap handle table entry. The WORD at offset 2 in a
        // handle table entry is 0xFF if the block is free. Check for
        // this case, and bail out if so.
        if ( *(NPWORD)(hObj+2) == 0xFF )
            return 0;

        // If we get here, it's (theoretically) an in-use handle.
        // Dereference the first WORD of the handle table entry to get
        // a near pointer to the GDI object within the 16-bit GDI heap.
        pObj = *(NPWORD)(hObj);

        // If LMEM_DISCARDED (???) flag set in handle flags, then
        // the pObj is really a 32-bit heap handle. Go dereference it
        // in the table starting 64K into GDI's DGROUP.
```

```
        if ( *(NPWORD)(hObj+2) & 0x40 )
            pObj = *(PGDIOBJ)( 0x10000 + pObj );
    }

    retValue = pObj->ilObjType
    retValue &= 0x5FFF;          // Mask off the 0x8000 and 0x2000 bits.

    retValue -= 0x4F46           // Make the object type value 1-based.
    if ( retValue <= 0 )
        return 0;

    if ( retValue > 13 )         // Is the object type out of range?
        return 0;                // Yes? Sorry, you lose. Do not pass Go.

    return retValue;    // Return value indicates the object type.
```

The GetObjectType function in GDI32.DLL

In the Win32 API, there is no IsGDIObject function. Luckily, the Win32 API goes one step further and actually provides a function that returns the type of an HGDIOBJ handle passed into it. The GetObjectType is quite a bit more sophisticated than IsGDIObject in its probing for the correct type of the HGDIOBJ passed in.

GetObjectType starts out by probing the HGDIOBJ handle to see if it's really a selector. The handle for metafile objects is apparently an actual selector for the data in the metafile. If the HGDIOBJ looks like a selector value, GetObjectType gropes around inside the segment, and if it finds that certain fields are what it thinks they should be, it returns the value OBJ_METAFILE.

With this initial selector monkey business out of the way, GetObjectType enters a section of code that looks remarkably similar to what IsGDIObject in GDI.EXE does. If the handle value ends in 2, 6, 0xA, or 0xE, GetObjectType assumes that it's a 16-bit local heap handle for an object in USER's 16-bit DGROUP. If this turns out to be the case, GetObjectType grabs the Win16Mutex to prevent a thread from potentially changing the state of the USER heap or the object being examined. If the HGDIOBJ doesn't end in 2, 6, 0xA, or 0xE, GetObjectType figures the object is a font or a region in the 32-bit heap. In either case, the code creates a 32-bit pointer to the GDI object.

With the pointer to the object, GetObjectType extracts the object type WORD and goes through the similar masking and subtraction process that IsGDIObject performs on the object type value. GetObjectType then checks the object type value to make sure it's within the allowable range, and if not, returns 0. If the object type at this point is 6 (an HDC), GetObjectType probes further into the object's data to see if it might be an enhanced metafile DC or a memory DC. If this is the case, the function returns the appropriate OBJ_XXX value from WINGDI.H.

The final phase of GetObjectType is to convert the 16-bit object type values (such as the LT_GDI_xxx values from TOOLHELP.H) into their 32-bit OBJ_XXX equivalents. For some strange reason, the OBJ_XXX values don't map one-to-one to the object type values stored in the object itself. (This is probably because the OBJ_XXX values were originally defined by the Windows NT GDI team, which wasn't basing its code around the Windows 3.1 GDI.EXE.) In any event, the object types need to be converted from the values that GDI.EXE uses to the OBJ_XXX values that WINGDI.H defines. This translation step is performed via a lookup array. The final section of GetObjectType releases the Win16Mutex if it was previously acquired.

Pseudocode for GetObjectType

```
// in GDI32.DLL
// Parameters:
//   HGDIOBJ hObj;
// Locals:
//   BYTE fHaveWin16Mutex
//   DWORD retValue;
//   PGDIOBJ pObj;

    fHaveWin16Mutex = FALSE;     // We'll only grab the Win16Mutex if we
                                 // absolutely have to.

    Set up a structured exception handling frame in case all this monkey
    business goes bad on us.

    if ( LAR (load access rights) succeeds on hObj )
    {
        if ( access rights indicate a non-system, ring 3 descriptor )
        {
            WORD MetaFileType;

            Use hObj as a selector, and grab the first WORD of the
            segment it points to. Call this value MetaFileType.

            if ( MetaFileType < 1 )
            {
                Grab the WORD at offset 2 in the segment.
                if ( this WORD == OBJ_METAFILE )
                {
```

```
                        Grab the WORD at offset 4 in the segment.
                        if ( (this WORD == 0x100)  || (this WORD == 0x300) )
                        {
                            retValue = OBJ_METAFILE
                            goto done;
                        }
                    }
                }
            }
        }

    // Figure out where the object resides (in GDI.EXE's DGROUP? or in
    // the 32-bit GDI heap?).

    if ( hObj & 2 ) // Object handles that end in 2, 6, A, or E are GDI
    {               // 16-bit heap local handles.
        EnterSysLevel( pWin16Mutex );
        fHaveWin16Mutex = TRUE;

        pObj = ConvertHGDIOBJToPtr32( hObj );
    }
    else    // Object handles in a 32-bit heap are multiples of 4.
    {
        // Index into the handle table and grab out the GDIOBJ pointer.
        pObj = *(PGDIOBJ) ( hGDIHeapHandleTableBase + hObj );

        // The GDIOBJ pointer is relative to GDI's DGROUP, so go add the
        // offset of GDI's DGROUP to make it a flat pointer.
        pObj += GDIDGroupBase;
    }

    retValue = pObj->ilObjType; // Get the object type WORD.
    retValue  &= 0x5FFF;        // Mask off the 0x8000 and 0x2000 bits.

    retValue -= 0x4F47          // Make the value 0 based (so that we
                                // can do an array-based translation later).

    if ( retValue >= 12 )   // Out of range? You lose. Do not pass Go.
    {
        SetLastError( ERROR_INVALID_HANDLE );
        retValue = 0;
        goto done;
    }
```

```
// If the object is a DC, it could be one of several different subtypes.
// Peek inside the DC structure and see if we can figure out what it is.
if ( retValue == 6 )        // 6 == DC
{
    if ( pObj[102] != 0 )   // Is WORD at offset 102 in DC != 0 ?
    {                       // Yes? Then it's an enhanced metafile.
        retValue = OBJ_ENHMETADC;
        goto done;
    }

    if ( pObj[0xE] & 1 )    // Is bit 1 in the BYTE at offset 0xE turned
    {                       // on? If so, it's a memory DC.
        retValue = OBJ_MEMDC;
        goto done;
    }
}

// Convert the 16-bit object type stored in the object into its
// equivalent OBJ_xxx value as given in WINGDI.H.
retValue = ObjectTypeConversionArray[ retValue ]

// The array conversions are as follows:

Win16 (TOOLHELP.H)        Win32 (WINUSER.H)
------------------        -----------------
LT_GDI_PEN(1)             OBJ_PEN
LT_GDI_BRUSH(2)           OBJ_BRUSH
LT_GDI_FONT(3)            OBJ_FONT
LT_GDI_PALETTE(4)         OBJ_PAL
LT_GDI_BITMAP(5)          OBJ_BITMAP
LT_GDI_RGN(6)             OBJ_REGION
LT_GDI_DC(7)              OBJ_DC
LT_GDI_DISABLED_DC(8)     OBJ_DC
LT_GDI_METADC(9)          OBJ_DC
LT_GDI_METAFILE(10)       0
??? (11)                  OBJ_METADC
??? (12)                  OBJ_ENHMETAFILE

done:
    if ( fHaveWin16Mutex )               // If we grabbed the Win16Mutex
        LeaveSysLevel( pWin16Mutex );    // earlier, release it now.

    remove structured exception handling frame

    return retValue;
```

New Win32 GDI functions available to Win16 applications

As a final note on GDI, I was curious to see how much of the new Win32 API GDI functionality bled over to the 16-bit side. (It's only natural to wonder this, seeing as how so many GDI functions new for Win32 are implemented in the 16-bit GDI.) To figure out if any supposedly Win32-only GDI functions are available for calling by 16-bit code, all I had to do was dump the exports from the Windows 95 GDI.EXE and compare it to the exports from the Windows 3.1 GDI.EXE. After filtering out undocumented functions, what's left over are GDI functions that were added to the Win32 specification, yet are callable by Win16 code. The task of comparing the two versions of GDI.EXE was made almost effortless by the excellent EXEUTIL program from *Undocumented Windows*. The command:

```
EXEUTIL -diff C:\WIN31\SYSTEM\GDI.EXE C:\WINDOWS\SYSTEM\GDI.EXE
```

gave me a nice delta of the exports between the two versions of GDI. (Only three undocumented functions were removed from Windows 95's GDI.EXE.) There were quite a few new exported 16-bit GDI functions that showed up as being added in Windows 95's GDI.EXE. I filtered out all the undocumented functions and other exports that don't have equivalents in the Win32 API. After some rearranging and grouping, I came up with the 16-bit GDI functions shown in Table 4-1. These functions are exported and presumably are safe to be called from Win16 code.

Table 4-1
New GDI functions that are callable from Win16 code

Function Type	Function Names
Printing (These functions are all thunks up to GDI32.DLL.)	ABORTPRINTER, CLOSEPRINTER, ENDDOCPRINTER, ENDPAGEPRINTER, OPENPRINTERA, STARTDOCPRINTERA, STARTPAGEPRINTER, WRITEPRINTER
Device-Independent Bitmaps (These functions appear to be implemented in GDI.EXE	CREATEDIBSECTION, GETDIBCOLORTABLE, SETDIBCOLORTABLE

Function Type	Function Names
Enhanced Metafiles (These functions appear to be implemented in GDI.EXE with the aid of 32-bit code segments.)	CLOSEENHMETAFILE, COPYENHMETAFILE, CREATEENHMETAFILE, DELETEENHMETAFILE, GDICOMMENT, GETENHMETAFILE, GETENHMETAFILEBITS, GETENHMETAFILEDESCRIPTION, GETENHMETAFILEHEADER, GETENHMETAFILEPALETTEENTRIES, PLAYENHMETAFILERECORD, SETENHMETAFILEBITS, SETMETARGN
Line drawing (These functions appear to be implemented in GDI.EXE with the aid of 32-bit code segments.)	GETARCDIRECTION, POLYBEZIER, POLYBEZIERTO, SETARCDIRECTION
Paths (These functions appear to be implemented in GDI.EXE with the aid of 32-bit code segments.)	ABORTPATH, BEGINPATH, CLOSEFIGURE, ENDPATH, FILLPATH, FLATTENPATH, GETMITERLIMIT, GETPATH, PATHTOREGION, SELECTCLIPPATH, SETMITERLIMIT, STROKEANDFILLPATH, STROKEPATH, WIDENPATH
Miscellaneous (These functions appear to be implemented in GDI.EXE.)	CREATEHALFTONEPALETTE, ENUMFONTFAMILIESEX, EXTCREATEPEN, EXTCREATEREGION, EXTSELECTCLIPRGN, GETCHARACTERPLACEMENT, GETFONTLANGUAGEINFO, GETREGIONDATA

SUMMARY

Throughout this chapter, I've shown the strange, hybrid nature of the Windows 95 USER and GDI components. While they are quite obviously derived from their Windows 3.1 predecessors, the Windows 95 USER and GDI have significant amounts of 32-bit code. The end result is many improvements that programmers can take advantage of, both in 16- and 32-bit programs. In addition, moving many of the heavily used data structures (such as WNDs) out of 16-bit heaps makes Windows 95 a worthwhile upgrade from Windows 3.1, even if you're not interested in the snazzy new features. While the Windows 95 USER and GDI components aren't anywhere near as full-featured and robust as their Windows NT equivalents, the improvements Windows 95 offers are a welcome relief to frustrated Windows 3.1 programmers.

MEMORY MANAGEMENT

5

*J*ust as programmers were beginning to get used to the idiosyncracies and gotchas of memory management under Windows 3.*x*, Microsoft rolled out the Win32 API, which presents a different set of challenges for the overwhelmed programmer.

Theoretically, Win32 memory management should be similar under the three incarnations of Win32: NT, Windows 95, and Win32s. Given Microsoft's track record in this area, however, you would expect Windows 95 memory management to have numerous differences (both subtle and not so subtle) from NT and Win32s. This is indeed the case. In this chapter, I dissect Windows 95's implementation of Win32 memory management. To be fair to Microsoft, note that many of the general concepts described here also apply to NT and Win32s.

I've divided the various subtopics of memory management into two categories. The first set of topics relates to issues such as the process address space, memory contexts, and paging behaviors (for example, copy on write). Later, I move to the other set of memory management subtopics: the APIs that the operating system provides for allocation and manipulation of memory.

If you're looking for information on 16-bit or DOS virtual machine memory management, this chapter is not what you're looking for. I've chosen to keep this chapter resolutely 32-bit based with only a few exceptions where absolutely necessary. If you're interested in Windows 95's 16-bit memory management, see Chapter 2 of my previous book, *Windows Internals*. Windows 95's 16-bit memory management is almost completely unchanged (except for bug fixes) from Windows 3.1. With these preliminaries out of the way, let's jump into . . .

WINDOWS 95 PAGE-BASED MEMORY MANAGEMENT

If you want to have any hope of really understanding the memory architecture of Windows 95, there's simply no way to avoid understanding memory paging on the Intel 80386 class of CPUs. Although the technique of memory paging far predates the 80386, we're interested only in how Windows 95 uses paging on the 80386, so I'll speak in 80386-specific terms. If you already know paging cold, you can skip this section. If memory paging is mysterious to you or if you need a quick refresher, read on.

Memory paging

The primary reason for paging is to provide a method for the operating system to collaborate with the CPU to fake programs into thinking that there's more memory available than is actually installed in the computer. When a program reads or writes a byte of memory, it may or may not be accessing a byte of physical RAM. If a program touches an address that doesn't map directly to a byte of physical RAM, the CPU informs the operating system of this event. The operating system in turn takes the steps necessary to associate physical memory to the address that the program attempted to use.

If the total memory usage of all the running programs exceeds the amount of memory installed in the computer, the operating system may need to yank a block of RAM away from some other program that's using the memory. Blindly stealing memory out from underneath a program that's using it is a recipe for disaster, so Windows 95 arranges for the original contents of RAM to be saved elsewhere before reassigning the block of RAM. The "elsewhere" in this case is the computer's hard drive. At any given time, all memory in use by the operating system and running programs is stored either in RAM or on a hard drive. (This is a bit of simplification, but it will suffice for now.)

Virtual memory is the commonly used term to refer to this method of simulating memory using paging and space on a secondory storage device such as a hard drive. One of the fundamental jobs of the Virtual Machine Manager in Windows 95 (the VMM module in VMM32.VXD) is to provide virtual memory with a minimum of fuss to application programs.

What confuses many people is that paging affects the CPU's memory addressing. Without paging, the address that a program tells the CPU to use will be the same address that goes out on the computer's memory bus. For example, in a real mode program, you can easily calculate a physical address from a segment:offset combination by multiplying the segment value by 16 and adding the offset. With paging enabled, a memory address that a program uses may not be the same address that the CPU sends out to the memory bus. Paging introduces a level of indirection (actually two levels) to all addresses. When a program passes an address to the CPU to access, the CPU uses certain bits of the 32-bit address to look up the physical RAM address that it should send out to the machine's bus. The tables that the CPU uses to translate addresses are under the operating system's control. Putting the address translation tables under the control of the operating system allows the operating system to tell a program to use addresses anywhere in the 4GB range of memory addressable by a 32-bit address, even though there may not be physical RAM at a given address.

The term *paging* comes into play because the CPU doesn't provide this indirection for each address on a byte-by-byte basis. Rather, the translation of memory addresses affects 4K chunks of memory. For example, if you use paging to assign physical RAM address 0x1000 to program address 0x400000, then RAM address 0x1001 will appear to the program to be at address 0x400001, and RAM address 0x1FFF will be at program address 0x400FFF. However, the next program address (that is, 0x401000) is the start of a new 4K page, so physical address 0x2000 does not necessarily have to be mapped to program address 0x401000. Program address 0x401000 may be mapped to a different physical RAM address (for example, 0x6000), or it may not have any physical RAM mapped to it. All decisions about which pages will have RAM mapped to them are made by the operating system's paging code.

Besides allowing the operating system to provide virtual memory, the CPU's support for paging also allows the operating system a great deal of flexibility in how it should arrange various objects in memory. By *objects,* I mean things such as the operating system code, the program's code, the program's data areas, and memory mapped files. The memory layout that an operating system uses is known as its *address space layout.* I'll describe the Windows 95 address space shortly.

The benefit of paging is that the operating system can spread operating system objects throughout the entire addressable range of the CPU (in the case of Intel 386 class CPUs, a 4 billion byte range). The entire addressable range of memory that the CPU can theoretically access is known as its *address space*. Addresses that the CPU will translate because it has enabled paging are called *linear addresses*. This differentiates them from the addresses after the CPU has translated them. These are actual addresses that will go out on the CPU's bus to the physical RAM. These addresses are known as *physical addresses*. The important thing to remember is that in almost all cases, program and API calls deal with linear addresses, not physical addresses.

With paging support, the operating system can assign various sections of the address space to particular items and leave room for those items to grow or to be added to as necessary. For example, when a program starts up, by default Windows 95 reserves a 1MB range of the CPU's address space for the program stack. This doesn't mean that Windows 95 will map 1MB of physical RAM to the stack's range of memory addresses. Rather, it means that the maximum size of the stack is 1MB. Windows 95 will only map physical memory to those 4KB regions in the stack area that the program uses.

Paging provides the operating system with the capability to reserve vast ranges of memory addresses without having to pay for those addresses (with physical RAM) until they're used. It's like reserving twelve seats for a concert without knowing how many of your friends will show up. If only three are in your group, you have to pay for only three seats.

At any given time, every 4KB section (page) in the CPU's 4GB address space is in one of four possible states:

- *State 1: Available.* This page of memory hasn't been reserved for use by anybody, and is theoretically available to be allocated. An attempt to access this memory by reading or writing to it will result in a page fault exception (exception 14 (0Eh)). I'll describe page faults shortly.

- *State 2: Reserved.* The page is part of a range of memory that somebody has requested. However, physical RAM is not currently mapped to this address, nor is any hard drive space reserved to save a copy of its contents. An attempt to access this memory by reading or writing to it will result in a page fault exception (exception 14 (0Eh)). Note, though, that the operating system gives the owner of the page an opportunity to change the page state to Committed and Present (state 3).

■ *State 3: Committed and present.* This range of addresses has been allocated by somone, and a program is using it to store information. The CPU's paging mechanism has mapped a 4KB physical block of RAM to this page's address. Reading or writing to this address will cause the physical RAM mapped to the page to be read or written. A substate to the committed and present state is known as pagelocked. A pagelocked page is committed, present, and guaranteed to never be swapped out. There will always be physical RAM associated with a pagelocked page until the page is unpagelocked.

■ *State 4: Committed and not-present.* This is similar to the preceding state (committed and present). The program has allocated the memory and is using the memory to store information. The difference is that the operating system has decided that the RAM mapped to the page was needed more urgently elsewhere. Therefore, the CPU has copied the contents of this memory to the hard disk drive and marked the page as "Not Present."

Like states 1 and 2, a page fault will occur if a memory address within the page is accessed. The difference is that when a program accesses this memory, the operating system transparently handles the page fault exception and remaps a 4KB block of physical RAM to the page. Next, the operating system reads in the original contents of the page from the hard disk, and then finally reexecutes the instruction that page faulted. The result is that the program doesn't have any idea that a page fault happened. This transparent simulation of RAM using space on a hard drive is the essence of virtual memory.

Windows 95 provides application-level APIs that enable you to allocate ranges of memory pages and to change them to have the attributes that I just described. These are the VirtualXXX (VirtualAlloc, VirtualFree, and so on) functions, which I describe later in the chapter.

Memory paging versus selectors

If you've programmed for Windows 3.*x*, you're probably wondering how paging can be reconciled with selectors. Programs that run in 16-bit protected mode on the Intel CPU invariably must use selectors to access a section of memory in the CPU's address space. Each of a Win16 program's code segments is associated with a selector, as are its data segments and any memory blocks it allocates with the global heap functions (for example, GlobalAlloc). It's impossible to do application-level Win16 programming without encountering selectors.

The most fundamental information associated with each selector is where in memory it points to (that is, its base address). On a 386, the base address of a selector can be anywhere between 0 and 4GB minus 1. In other words, the selector can potentially point anywhere in the CPU's address range. However, the base address of a selector is specified as a linear address, not a physical address. Therefore, the paging mechanism of the CPU operates underneath the selectors. In both Windows 3.1 and Windows 95, 16-bit code doesn't think about paging and virtual memory support. Instead, it just assumes that there will be large regions of memory available to it. The 16-bit global heap management code allocates large pieces of memory from the ring 0 operating system components and then subdivides the memory into smaller pieces that it makes accessible to programs through selectors. The base addresses of selectors do not have to start on a 4KB page boundary, nor does every page beneath a given memory segment need to be physically present.

As mentioned, the selector/segment management code doesn't sweat the details at the paging level. It lets the underlying paging system code provide virtual memory and assumes that memory will be there when it needs to access it. Chapter 2 of *Windows Internals* describes the 16-bit selector/segment management code in Windows 3.1. This particular aspect of memory management hasn't changed much in Windows 95.

If you're executing in protected mode, you can't avoid selectors. They're absolutely required to access memory. The great thing about Windows 95 is that it requires at least a 386 CPU, and one of the key features of the 386 is that you can make segments that span the entire 4GB of the CPU's address space. It's therefore possible to create selectors with base address of 0 and limits of 4GB. If you load these selectors into the CS and DS registers, you can effectively forget that segmentation exists. Programs can refer to addresses in memory with just a 32-bit offset value. In this scenario, the 32-bit offset is the same as a linear address. The mode of using selectors with a 0 base address and a 4GB limit has been dubbed the *flat memory model* (as opposed to the small, medium, compact, and huge memory models from 16-bit programming). Remember, however, that although flat model programs make it appear that segments no longer exist for Win32 programs, the CPU is still using segmentation under the hood. This is especially important to remember if you're going to mix 32-bit code with 16-bit code (which cannot hide the ugly reality of segments).

With wide open segments that let a program touch any address in the CPU's address range, you might be wondering how the operating system protects its internal data structures and other areas of memory that application code shouldn't be mucking with. This wasn't hard to do in 16-bit programming because a selector defined a specific starting and ending address that a program could touch. Theoretically, the operating system would never hand out a selector with a base address that would allow an application program to get at memory that it shouldn't have access to. (However, Windows 3.1 and Windows 95 don't prevent you from creating your own selectors and going to town with them. I'll take advantage of this "hole" later in the chapter.)

If a Win32 program uses flat segments, how can the operating system restrict access to areas that it doesn't want programs to touch? In this case, instead of relying on segment limits, the operating system sets the attributes of the pages as appropriate. For example, a program shouldn't be able to blindly write to and corrupt its code areas. The operating system therefore sets the page attributes of the code areas to read only. Programs can read those pages, but attempts to write to them will cause a page fault. Likewise, a program that gets hold of a trashed pointer will likely write to a page of memory that's not allocated by anybody.

The operating system marks all pages that aren't specifically owned by somebody as not-present. Trying to touch one of these addresses also results in a page fault. In addition, the operating system can mark a range of pages with the supervisor attribute. Pages with the supervisor attribute can be accessed only by code running at a high privilege level (that is, certain parts of the operating system and VxDs). An attempt to access a supervisor page by a low-life application program results in a page fault. As you can see, even without segments, Windows 95 can use paging to effectively protect sensitive areas of memory. The only downside is that the granularity of memory allocations at the lowest level is in 4KB pages rather than in single bytes like 16-bit segments.

THE ADDRESS SPACE OF A WINDOWS 95 WIN32 PROCESS

In versions of Windows before Windows 95, all running programs ran in the same address space. That is, any program could easily read the memory of another program. More importantly, a program could modify another program's memory, a potential ticket to a disaster if buggy programs are involved. For example, a 16-bit Windows program (even on Windows 95) can get hold of the selector for the 16-bit USER's DGROUP and write random garbage. Bye-bye windowing system.

Windows 95 is the first mass-market version of Windows that runs each process (at least each Win32 process) in its own address space. By *its own address space*, I mean that a program can see memory owned only by itself. Memory in use by other processes is not physically accessible. Specifically, the Windows 95 memory manager uses the CPU's page-based memory management capabilities to ensure that only memory owned by the current process is mapped somewhere in the 4GB address range of the CPU. Physical RAM in use by other processes simply does not show up in the page tables for the current process. The huge benefit of this is that theoretically a buggy program can screw up only itself, and won't affect other programs. Each program gets its own sandbox to play in; if it kicks sand, the only harmful effect is to itself.

Lest you become too excited by this advance in Windows, this method of isolating programs from one another for their mutual protection is nothing new. Operating systems such as UNIX have been doing this for decades. Windows NT also keeps each Win32 process in its own address space. It was about time that the desktop operating system that Microsoft was pushing on the masses obtained this most basic feature of a decent operating system. (Win32s, the forgotten stepsister in the Win32 family, doesn't use separate address spaces for each process.)

Although it's important to keep the memory of all programs separate, certain ranges of memory need to be shared across all processes. That is, certain pages in the linear address spaces of all processes should map to the same physical page of RAM. Why would you want this? A perfect example is for the systems DLLs that each process uses. For instance, every process at the very minimum requires the use of KERNEL32.DLL. It would be incredibly wasteful to load a fresh copy of KERNEL32.DLL into memory for every running process. Therefore, KERNEL32.DLL (and other system DLLs such as USER32) reside in shared memory. When the operating system switches around the CPU's page tables because it's about to run a new process, it leaves the page table mapping for the shared memory regions alone. I'll describe other examples and needs for shared memory later.

Because Windows 95 keeps the memory for different processes separate from one another, any discussion of how Windows 95 lays out the 4GB address space must necessarily include the concept of memory contexts. A *memory context* is essentially a list of RAM pages and what linear address they will be be mapped to when a given process is active. Phrased another way, a memory context is the view of the CPU's linear address that the operating system gives to a process.

Each process has its own memory context. When the Windows 95 scheduler suspends one process and lets another process execute, Windows 95 must also switch the memory contexts from the original process to that of the newly scheduled process. Because memory contexts are maintained on a per-process basis, they're sometimes referred to as a *process context*. Memory contexts are also known as *address contexts*. Whatever you call them, the important thing to remember is that a memory address by itself is meaningless unless you specify which memory context it's in.

At the topmost level, the memory layout Windows 95 uses for Win32 processes is simple. In the 4GB address range, Windows 95 reserves the bottom 2GB (addresses 0h through 7FFFFFFFh) for the application's memory. Addresses above 2GB (addresses 80000000h through FFFFFFFFh) are intended for use by the operating system. Within these two halves of the address space are several subdivisions. Figure 5-1 shows the breakdown of the various regions in the 4GB address space. If you have the Windows 95 DDK, you might also want to read the "Page Mapping and Address Spaces" section under the "Arenas" heading in the online help.

The first 4MB of the address space is shared between all processes in the system virtual machine (VM). Part of this region is the memory below 1MB, which includes the memory image of MS-DOS that was loaded as part of the Windows 95 bootstrap process. Also of interest below 1MB is the lower portion of the 16-bit global heap. As I described in Chapter 2 of *Windows Internals*, all 16-bit heap segments in Windows 3.1 have a linear address that's either below 1MB or above 2GB. 16-bit heap allocations with the GMEM_FIXED attribute are allocated from the lowest available address in the global heap, so the allocated block often ends up with a linear address below 1MB. You'll find the memory for numerous 16-bit system DLLs in this first 4MB range of the address space because many of them (such as KRNL386) need fixed and pagelocked memory. This is an important point that I'll come back to shortly.

The next region in the 4GB address space is the range from 4MB to 2GB. This is the per-process address space that each Win32 process uses. Each Win32 process has its code, data, and resources mapped into this nearly 2GB region. When you switch memory contexts, the effect is to apply a different set of page mappings to this range of memory. Except in special cases that the programmer specifies, the physical RAM pages mapped in this region for use by one process are not accessible by any other processes. Besides the executable's code and data, this region also contains the code and data for any application-specific DLLs used by the process. Also in this region, you'll find the application's heap and stacks for each of its threads.

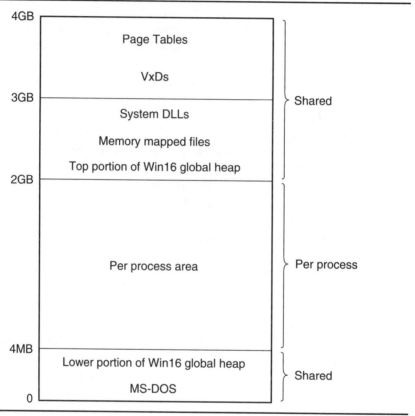

Figure 5-1
The Windows 95 linear address space.

The default load address for Win32 programs in the per-application area is at the very bottom (4MB). Unless you really understand paging, this idea can be disconcerting. How can more than one program be loaded at the same address in memory? The answer is that they share the same linear address, but not the same physical address. In general, a linear address in one process will not be mapped to the same physical address in RAM. Because of paging, each process can assume that it has the entire 4MB to 2GB range of addresses all to itself. It can't see the memory of other processes, nor can they see its memory, even though they may be sharing the same linear addresses. The magic of paging keeps them physically distinct.

The exception to the preceding rule of keeping separate 4MB to 2GB regions for each process is when Windows 95 has determined that it's safe to share the same page of RAM between multiple copies of a program. A prime example of this is program code because a program usually doesn't modify its code. If you're running more than one copy of a program, Windows 95 conserves available RAM by mapping the RAM containing program code into the address space of all the instances of the processes.

From an operating system purist point of view, it would be ideal if each 16-bit process was kept in its own address space, similar to the way 32-bit processes are. Unfortunately, a huge number of 16-bit programs rely on the capability to see the memory of other programs. To remain compatible with existing 16-bit code, Windows 95 has to allow 16-bit programs to have greater access to one another than it lets Win32 processes have. Windows NT 3.5 introduced the capability of running each Win16 process in its own address space, but it consumes more memory and introduces more complexity. The designers of Windows 95 apparently felt the benefits weren't worth the price.

A question that intrigued me from the first time I saw Windows 95 was how 16-bit tasks were able to share their address space while still running as separate processes. As it turns out, the memory used by 16-bit tasks always comes from the shared memory regions below 4MB and above 2GB.

Moving now to the the upper half of the 4GB address space, you can see that Figure 5-1 shows it subdivided into two regions. The range of memory between 2GB and 3GB is shared across all processes, and is intended for use by the ring 3 (user level) operating system code. At the lowest addresses in this range, you'll find the remainder of the 16-bit global heap. Above the global heap, you'll find the location for memory mapped files. This is interesting, and bears a further look.

If memory mapped files are in a range of memory shared by all processes, it would appear that any process can see the memory mapped file, even if that process hasn't explicitly mapped a view for it. That assumption is indeed correct. In Windows 95, the act of using a memory mapped file makes that file accessible to all processes. In this aspect, Windows 95 differs from Windows NT. Windows NT uses a more sophisticated paging model, thereby causing memory mapped files to be visible only in the memory context of processes that open up a view into the memory mapped file.

The uppermost portion of the 2GB to 3GB range is where you'll find the 32-bit system DLLs (KERNEL32, USER32, and so on). To free up as much space as possible for memory mapped files before running into the ring 3 system DLLs, Windows 95 adds DLLs to the system from the 3GB line downward in memory. The following excerpt from the SoftIce/W MOD command shows this very clearly:

```
:mod
hMod Base     PEHeader        Module Name    EXE File Name
019F BFF70000 0147:BFF70080   KERNEL32

                                             C:\WINDOWS\SYSTEM\KERNEL32.DLL
01A7 BFF20000 0147:81525AF4   GDI32          C:\WINDOWS\SYSTEM\GDI32.DLL
186F BFEF0000 0147:81525E98   ADVAPI32

                                             C:\WINDOWS\SYSTEM\ADVAPI32.DLL
1827 BFC00000 0147:815270F0   USER32         C:\WINDOWS\SYSTEM\USER32.DLL
```

The number in the second column is the load address of the module. KERNEL32.DLL is the first 32-bit system DLL to load, and loads as close to 3GB as possible (address BFF70000h) while keeping all of its contents in the 2GB to 3GB range. Next lower in memory is GDI32.DLL at address BFF20000, which butts up as close as possible to KERNEL32.DLL. Although it might seem like these load address are calculated as the DLLs load, they're not. Microsoft has a program (REBASE.EXE from the Win32 SDK) that determines how much address space each DLL requires, and then figures out the load address that will cause the system DLLs to be packed together as closely as possible. After compiling and linking the system DLLs, the Windows 95 build procedure modifies the DLLs so that they have the preferred load address that was calculated by REBASE.EXE. The effect is that these system DLLs load as fast as possible and don't need to have any relocations applied by the Windows 95 loader.

The final portion of the Windows 95 address space is the range from 3GB to 4GB (C0000000h to FFFFFFFFh). This final gigabyte is the domain of the ring 0 system components of Windows 95 (that is, the VxDs). This can be seen by looking at this abbreviated (believe it or not) output from the SoftIce/W VXD command:

```
:vxd
```

VxD Name	Address	Length	Seg	ID	DDB	Control	PM	V86	VxD	Win32
VMM	C0001000	00FDC0	0001	0001	C000E990	C00024F8	Y	Y	402	41
WINICE	C001A9C8	04D0FC	0001	0202	C0042418	C001A9CD	Y	Y	2	0
NWLINK	C0067AC4	007C78	0001	0487	C006D1F4	C006C538	N	N	7	0
VNetSup	C006F73C	00121C	0001	0480	C0070814	C006F798	Y	Y	7	0
CONFIGMG	C0070958	0003F8	0001	0033	C0070CF4	C0070958	Y	Y	91	0
VSHARE	C0070D50	001864	0001	0483	C0071130	C007100B	Y	Y	1	0
VWIN32	C00725B4	00277C	0001	002A	C0073DA0	C00725B4	Y	N	29	79
VFBACKUP	C0074D30	0004D0	0001	0036	C0075174	C0074D34	Y	Y	6	0
VCOMM	C0075200	000434	0001	002B	C00754F4	C0075200	Y	Y	35	27
COMBUFF	C0075634	000264	0001	0000	C00757D8	C0075634	N	N	0	0
IFSMgr	C0075898	007140	0001	0040	C007A964	C0075964	N	N	117	0
IOS	C007C9D8	002264	0001	0010	C007E8DC	C007C9D8	Y	Y	17	0
SPOOLER	C007EC3C	000140	0001	002C	C007ED20	C007EC3C	N	N	17	0
VFAT	C007ED7C	00A410	0001	0486	C0089064	C0086FD8	N	N	0	0
VCACHE	C008918C	0016A0	0001	048B	C0089A2C	C00893FA	Y	Y	25	0
VCOND	C008A82C	0000A0	0001	0038	C008A870	C008A82C	Y	Y	2	53
VCDFSD	C008A8CC	00019C	0001	0041	C008A938	C008A8CC	N	N	4	0
VXDLDR	C008AA68	0000F0	0001	0027	C008AAF8	C008AA68	Y	Y	18	0
VDEF	C008AD68	0004EC	0001	0000	C008B204	C008AFB8	N	N	0	0
VPICD	C008B254	002314	0001	0003	C008CCCC	C008B690	Y	Y	25	0
VTD	C008DD9C	000570	0001	0005	C008E238	C008DED1	Y	Y	11	0
REBOOT	C008E744	0002F0	0001	0009	C008E9AC	C008E744	Y	N	4	2
VDMAD	C008EA34	002164	0001	0004	C009083C	C008EBF4	N	N	34	0
VSD	C0091364	000220	0001	000B	C0091524	C0091364	N	N	4	0
V86MMGR	C0091584	001334	0001	0006	C0092730	C0091B13	Y	N	25	0
PAGESWAP	C00928B8	0000D8	0001	0007	C0092938	C00928B8	N	N	10	0
DOSMGR	C0092990	000324	0001	0015	C0092B34	C0092990	N	Y	19	0
VMPOLL	C0094350	00018C	0001	0018	C0094470	C0094350	N	N	4	0
SHELL	C0094630	000C24	0001	0017	C0094FE0	C0094CD2	Y	Y	28	0
PARITY	C00953DC	000118	0001	0008	C009549C	C00953DC	N	N	0	0
BIOSXLAT	C00954F4	00009C	0001	0013	C009553C	C00954F4	N	N	0	0
VMCPD	C0095590	0006A0	0001	0011	C0095BC8	C0095590	Y	N	9	0
VTDAPI	C0095C30	0002F0	0001	0442	C0095EB8	C0095E71	Y	N	0	0
PERF	C0096190	000140	0001	0048	C0096274	C0096190	N	N	5	0
VREDIR	C00962D0	005A50	0001	0481	C009B188	C0099E8C	N	N	17	0
NDIS	C009BD20	0071BC	0001	0028	C00A0190	C009C6E7	Y	Y	96	0
VNETBIOS	C00A2EDC	001B78	0001	0014	C00A4818	C00A376F	N	N	8	2
EBIOS	C00A4A54	000078	0001	0012	C00A4A7C	C00A4A54	N	N	2	0
PAGEFILE	C00A4ACC	0000F8	0001	0021	C00A4B6C	C00A4ACC	Y	N	10	0
VCD	C00A4BC4	000430	0001	000E	C00A4F2C	C00A4BD8	Y	N	13	0
VPD	C00A4FF4	000A30	0001	000F	C00A5860	C00A4FF4	Y	N	0	0
INT13	C00A5A24	0009F8	0001	0020	C00A62D8	C00A5A5A	N	N	5	0
VKD	C00A641C	001540	0001	000D	C00A75D8	C00A641C	Y	N	21	0
VDD	C00A795C	000FD8	0001	000A	C00A7F08	C00A795C	Y	Y	23	0
VFLATD	C00A8934	000330	0001	011F	C00A8BDC	C00A8934	Y	N	2	0
VMOUSE	C00A8C64	0008B4	0001	000C	C00A92A0	C00A8C64	Y	Y	12	0
MSMINI	C00A9518	00056C	0001	0000	C00A998C	C00A9518	N	N	0	0

```
------------------------- Dynamically Loaded VxDs -------------------------
 LPTENUM    C0FD7DB8   0005C8   0001   0000   C0FD8328   C0FD7DB8   N   N     0     0
 SERENUM    C0FD616C   00007C   0001   0000   C0FD6194   C0FD616C   N   N     0     0
 ESDI_506   C102AA7C   001388   0001   008D   C102BD94   C102AA7C   N   N     0     0
 HSFLOP     C1029CEC   000808   0001   0000   C102A4A4   C1029CFE   N   N     0     0
 VSERVER    C1013A10   014C98   0001   0032   C10268E8   C101C8D0   Y   N     4     0
 NETBEUI    C1007CB0   007E18   0001   0031   C100E9FC   C1007CB0   N   N     0     0
 SPAP       C1002880   001D74   0001   0000   C1002B4C   C1002880   Y   Y     0     0
 PPPMAC     C0FE8840   01961C   0001   0499   C0FE9100   C0FE8928   Y   Y    10     0
 voltrack   C0FE4088   0005C8   0001   0090   C0FE45C4   C0FE4088   N   N     0     0
 DiskTSD    C0FD85F8   0002B0   0001   0000   C0FD8850   C0FD85F8   N   N     0     0
 SB16       C0FD8920   0092BC   0001   32A5   C0FE10A4   C0FE1794   Y   Y     0     0
 VJOYD      C0FD6240   0016EC   0001   0449   C0FD7510   C0FD7560   Y   N     2     0
 MMDEVLDR   C0FD5088   000090   0001   044A   C0FD50A0   C0FD50F0   Y   Y     6     0
 ATI        C0FD4E28   0001AC   0001   0000   C0FD4F54   C0FD4E28   N   N     0     0
 ISAPNP     C0FD51AC   00007C   0001   003C   C0FD51CC   C0FD51AC   N   N     0     0
```

The full output from the SoftIce/W VxD command ran over 360 lines. On a whim, I totaled the sizes of all the blocks to see roughly how much memory is consumed by the VxD components. After subtracting the memory consumed by SoftIce/W, the number of VxD components was in the neighborhood of a megabyte. Although some of this memory most likely was pageable, a good chunk of operating system code is hidden at ring 0, out of the reach of most programmers.

You might think that Windows 95 would use the paging attributes to protect the VxD region of memory above address 0xC0000000 from prying or clumsy ring 3 system code. However, this is not the case. Many places in KERNEL32 keep pointers to variables in the ring 0 components. Likewise, many places in the VxD code keep pointers to KERNEL32 variables or, even worse, KRNL386 variables. The worst offender here may be VWIN32.VXD, which, as Chapter 6 will show, even exports two Win32 VxD service functions for this purpose. One service passes pointers to places in VWIN32 down to ring 3, and the other receives ring 3 addresses in KERNEL32 and KRNL386.

SHARING MEMORY

In Win16, the memory of all programs and DLLs is accessible to all other programs and DLLs. (Win16 uses the same local descriptor table for all processes.) As a result, it's very easy to share memory between multiple processes: You simply arrange for two or more programs to get hold of the same selector. Despite Microsoft's dire warnings, using the GMEM_SHARE attribute when allocating memory isn't a requirement in Win16.

Now contrast this to Windows 95's Win32 memory management, which keeps all the memory of a Win32 process separate from other processes unless you specifically take steps to share the memory. Unfortunately, these steps aren't as simple as specifying GMEM_SHARE. Specifying GMEM_SHARE to GlobalAlloc won't buy you memory that's shared across multiple memory contexts. (This is typical of Microsoft. GMEM_SHARE has no effect on memory sharing in Win16 or in Win32. In the 16-bit case, it isn't necessary because everything is shared, and in the 32-bit case, it's ignored.)

You may have heard some Win32 pundits say that the only way to share memory in Windows 95 (or NT for that matter) is with memory mapped files. Although you can share memory with memory mapped files, they're certainly not the only solution. If all you want to share is a small amount of data between a few instances of the same program, using memory mapped files is overkill. In this book, I'll focus on sharing readable/writeable data between applications. Don't forget, however, that the entire upper half of the 4GB address space is reserved for system usage and is always visible and shared between all processes.

At the lowest level, sharing memory between memory contexts is nothing more than including pages of RAM in the page table mappings of more than one process. The shared memory pages can map to the same linear address in each process, or they might map to different linear addresses.

In Windows 95, memory shared through memory mapped files is always at the same linear address in each process. (The PHYS program, presented later in the chapter, shows that this is the case.) However, it's dangerous to make this assumption in your code. One reason is that Windows NT doesn't guarantee that memory mapped files will be at the same address in each context. Since sharing with memory mapped files is covered in many texts on Win32 programming, I won't dwell on the details here.

The easiest way to share memory in Win32 programs is not mentioned in many discussions on Win32 memory management. Specifically, giving the SHARED attribute to your program's data sections when you link lets you easily share memory between multiple copies of an EXE or between multiple users of a DLL. Giving the SHARED attribute to a DLL's data section makes it functionally the same as the data segment in a Win16 DLL. Luckily, Windows 95 gives you the flexibility to share some of your data, while still having other data that is per-process. You can create multiple data sections in your EXE or DLL. Put all the data you want to share in one section and give that section the SHARED attribute. The remainder of your data goes into another section that you leave with the default attributes (nonshared).

The PHYS program does exactly what I've described to show the difference between shared and nonshared memory.

Normally, the Microsoft compiler puts all your initialized data into a section of the executable called .data, and leaves the IMAGE_SCN_MEM_SHARED attribute out of the section's attributes. This causes a new copy of that data to be created for each process that uses the data. To share memory, you'll tell the compiler to create a new section. This section can have any name you want (although only the first 8 characters will be used in the EXE section table.) For instance:

```
#pragma data_seg("SHAREDAT")
```

After the #pragma, declare any variables that you want to be shared. The variables should be initialized; otherwise, the compiler puts them into the uninitialized data section. You probably weren't intending to make your uninitialized data shared, so just initialize them and bypass some of the hair-pulling I went through.

After declaring the variables, if you want to go back to putting data into the default data section, throw this in at the end of your shared variable declarations:

```
#pragma data_seg()
```

Once you've declared all the data you want to be shared, the final step is to convey your desires to the linker. You can do this in two ways. The traditional way is to put that section and its attributes into the .DEF file. For instance:

```
SECTIONS
    SHAREDAT READ WRITE SHARED
```

Another way is to specify the attributes on the linker command line:

```
LINK /SECTION:SHAREDAT,RWS <other linker options and files>
```

In this example, the RWS is interpreted as "Read, Write, and Shared."

I should mention a "buyer beware" warning about sharing your DLL's data sections. If you initialize your data with the address of another code or data symbol, you're in for an interesting time if the DLL loads at different linear addresses in two or more processes. For example, consider this seemingly innocent data declaration in a shared data section:

```
int i;
int * AddressOf_i = &i;
```

The problem is that the AddressOf_i can't be known until the DLL loads. Therefore, the DLL contains a fixup record telling the loader to patch in the correct value in the AddressOf_i variable. The first time the DLL loads, there's no problem. Now, consider what happens if another process loads the DLL, but the DLL can't load at the same linear address in the second process. Because the AddressOf_i variable is already in use by the first process (it's shared, remember?), the loader can't go in and patch in the correct value for the second process. The value of AddressOf_i is wrong in the second process. When I encountered this problem in my own code, I was able to work around it by using pointers. In my per-process data variables, I included a pointer to the shared memory area. Because the pointer was in the per-process area, the loader always fixed up the pointer value so that it was correct for the current process.

Beyond explicitly sharing your data, Windows 95 shares other regions of memory. I've already mentioned that all the memory above a linear address of 2GB is shared between Windows processes. However, Windows 95 also silently shares certain ranges of memory below 2GB. If you run multiple copies of an EXE file, or use a DLL in more than one process, it would be wasteful to load all the code sections for each user of the code. Although code sections don't have the IMAGE_SCN_MEM_SHARED attribute, Windows 95 loads only one copy of the code, and uses the CPU's page table to map the code into the memory contexts of all users of the code.

An exception to this sharing of code sections between multiple processes occurs when a DLL cannot load at the same base address in each process. For example, suppose FOO.DLL is used by two different processes. When process A loads the DLL, it is brought into memory at linear address X. Process B may use a different group of DLLs (but including FOO.DLL). When process B loads, some other DLL may be assigned to linear address X before the loader gets around to loading FOO.DLL. Because address X isn't available in process B's memory context, FOO.DLL has to be loaded elsewhere. If you have control over programs that run into a situation like this, you can usually solve it by rebasing the DLL to a base address that's not used in either process.

"Copy on Write" in Windows 95 (or the Lack Thereof)

Knowing that Windows 95 shares code across processes (where possible), a reasonable question concerns how debuggers handle this. Why is this an issue? Debuggers set breakpoints by writing breakpoint instructions (INT 3, opcode 0xCC) into the code. If a debugger writes a breakpoint into a code page that's shared by two processes, there's a potential problem. The debugger is debugging only one of the processes, and won't see the breakpoint interrupt if another process hits the breakpoint instruction. When the operating system sees the INT 3 in the other process and determines that the process isn't being debugged, it terminates the process because there was an unhandled exception. If the memory management code in Windows 95 were to work the way I described in the last section, you wouldn't be able to debug through DLLs used by more than one process at the same time — at least not without causing all the other processes to terminate abruptly. Nor would you be able to debug one copy of a program while another copy runs.

Advanced operating systems such as UNIX handle this problem with a mechanism called "copy on write." In a system with copy on write (such as Windows NT), the memory manager uses the CPU's paging to share memory wherever possible, and duplicates a page of memory in RAM only when necessary.

An example will make this much clearer. Suppose that two copies of a program are executing and sharing the same code pages (which have the read-only attribute). One of the processes is being debugged, and the user tells the debugger to set a breakpoint somewhere in the code. When the debugger attempts to write out the breakpoint instruction, it triggers a page fault (the page is read-only). When the operating system sees the page fault, it first determines that a debugger is trying to read the memory, and that the request is legitimate. However, the operating system doesn't just let the write go through to the shared code page. Instead, the system makes a copy of the affected page, and changes the page table of the debuggee to use the copy of the original page. Once the page has been copied and mapped, the system lets the write go through. The write operation affects only the copied page and leaves the original page alone.

Copy on write isn't limited to shared code. In Windows NT, writeable data pages start out with the read-only attribute. When the program writes to one of these page, the CPU generates a page fault. The operating system handler then marks those pages as read/write. Why go through this trouble? When a second copy of the EXE or DLL is loaded, the memory manager can share all the data pages that still have the read-only attribute. If these shared pages are then written to, the copy on write mechanism kicks in and provides separate RAM pages to each process wherever necessary.

The benefit of copy on write is that memory is shared as efficiently as possible. The system makes a new copy of a shared page only when necessary. Unfortunately, copy on write requires a sophisticated memory and page table management scheme. Apparently, Windows 95's memory manager isn't sophisticated enough because Windows 95 doesn't directly support copy on write through paging. This has caused a lot of anguish among the early adopters of Windows 95. After all, Microsoft is pushing for all Win32 programs to run on Windows NT as well as Windows 95. It's a pain to do so when major architectural features such as copy on write are missing from Windows 95.

In defense of Windows 95, it isn't blindly stupid about the problem of writing to shared memory. Because something had to be done to make debuggers usable, Windows 95 supports a pseudo copy on write scheme. In this scheme, the WriteProcessMemory function takes the place of a page fault on a shared page. Way down inside WriteProcessMemory, the operating system determines whether the address range you're attempting to write lies in shared memory. If so, the system copies the original page(s) to a new set, maps the new page(s) to the same linear address in the current process, and then does the write operation. The PHYS program proves that this pseudo copy on write is at work.

Although the WriteProcessMemory function is sufficient to allow debuggers to debug through most DLLs, it unfortunately doesn't work on the shared region above 2GB. (It's intentionally crippled.) Because the system DLLs such as KERNEL32 lie above 2GB in Windows 95, regular application debuggers can't step through the system DLLs like they can in Windows NT. Go ahead and try it. Fire up your favorite application debugger under Windows 95 and try to step into an operating system call. Both the Visual C++ debugger and Turbo Debugger silently step over these calls even if you're in the disassembly pane and tell them to step into the call. If you want to step through the system code in Windows 95, you'll need a debugger that doesn't rely on WriteProcessMemory, for example, a system-level debugger such as SoftIce/W or WDEB386.

THE PHYS PROGRAM

To demonstrate all the Windows 95 memory management details I've discussed, I wrote the PHYS program. PHYS doesn't have a fancy user interface, but it effectively shows the layout of memory, shared memory, and Windows 95's pseudo copy on write support.

The concept behind PHYS is simple. It finds and displays the linear addresses of various items in memory (for example, a code section or a memory mapped file). When just one copy of PHYS is run, it's a crude but useful demonstration of the Windows 95 process memory layout. The program's functionality doesn't stop there, however. Besides showing the linear addresses of memory objects, it also shows the physical RAM address mapped to the linear address as well as the page's protection attributes. By running two or more copies of PHYS, you can see which memory regions are shared by multiple processes. In addition, PHYS shows writes to a code page in memory and shows the before and after addresses, proving that WriteProcessMemory effectively performs a copy on write.

The complete source for PHYS is included in the accompanying disk. The main workhorse routine is shown in Listing 5-1. ShowPhysicalPages calculates the linear and physical addresses of various memory objects and prints them, one to a line. However, PHYS makes no attempt to show every memory object in its address space. Rather, it shows selected items that I consider important when indicating the memory layout of a process.

The ShowPhysicalPages functions from the PHYS.EXE program

```
void ShowPhysicalPages(void)
{
    DWORD linearAddr;
    MEMORY_BASIC_INFORMATION mbi;

    //
    // Get the address of a 16-bit DLL that's below 1MB (KRNL386's DGROUP).
    //
    linearAddr = Get_KRNL386_DGROUP_LinearAddress();
    printf( "KRNL386 DGROUP    - Linear:%08X  Physical:%08X  %s\n",
            linearAddr,
            GetPhysicalAddrFromLinear(linearAddr),
            GetPageAttributesAsString(linearAddr) );

    //
    // Get the starting address of the code area. We'll pass VirtualQuery
    // the address of a routine within the code area.
    //
```

```
VirtualQuery( ShowPhysicalPages, &mbi, sizeof(mbi) );
linearAddr = (DWORD)mbi.BaseAddress;
printf( "First code page    - Linear:%08X  Physical:%08X  %s\n",
        linearAddr,
        GetPhysicalAddrFromLinear(linearAddr),
        GetPageAttributesAsString(linearAddr) );


//
// Get the starting address of the data area. We'll pass VirtualQuery
// the address of a global variable within the data area.
//
VirtualQuery( &callgate1, &mbi, sizeof(mbi) );
linearAddr = (DWORD)mbi.BaseAddress;
printf( "First data page    - Linear:%08X  Physical:%08X  %s\n",
        linearAddr,
        GetPhysicalAddrFromLinear(linearAddr),
        GetPageAttributesAsString(linearAddr) );


//
// Get the address of a data section with the SHARED attribute.
//
MySharedSectionVariable = 1;    // Touch it to force it present.
linearAddr = (DWORD)&MySharedSectionVariable;
printf( "Shared section     - Linear:%08X  Physical:%08X  %s\n",
        linearAddr,
        GetPhysicalAddrFromLinear(linearAddr),
        GetPageAttributesAsString(linearAddr) );


//
// Get the address of a resource within the module.
//
linearAddr = (DWORD)
        FindResource(GetModuleHandle(0), MAKEINTATOM(1), RT_STRING);
printf( "Resources          - Linear:%08X  Physical:%08X  %s\n",
        linearAddr,
        GetPhysicalAddrFromLinear(linearAddr),
        GetPageAttributesAsString(linearAddr) );


//
// Get the starting address of the process heap area.
//
linearAddr = (DWORD)GetProcessHeap();
printf( "Process Heap       - Linear:%08X  Physical:%08X  %s\n",
        linearAddr,
        GetPhysicalAddrFromLinear(linearAddr),
        GetPageAttributesAsString(linearAddr) );
```

```
        //
        // Get the starting address of the process environment area.
        //
        VirtualQuery( GetEnvironmentStrings(), &mbi, sizeof(mbi) );
        linearAddr = (DWORD)mbi.BaseAddress;
        printf( "Environment area    - Linear:%08X  Physical:%08X  %s\n",
                linearAddr,
                GetPhysicalAddrFromLinear(linearAddr),
                GetPageAttributesAsString(linearAddr) );


        //
        // Get the starting address of the stack area. We'll pass
        // the address of a stack variable to VirtualQuery.
        //
        VirtualQuery( &linearAddr, &mbi, sizeof(mbi) );
        linearAddr = (DWORD)mbi.BaseAddress;
        printf( "Current Stack page  - Linear:%08X  Physical:%08X  %s\n",
                linearAddr,
                GetPhysicalAddrFromLinear(linearAddr),
                GetPageAttributesAsString(linearAddr) );


        //
        // Show the address of a memory mapped file.
        //
        linearAddr = (DWORD)PMemMapFileRegion;
        printf( "Memory Mapped file  - Linear:%08X  Physical:%08X  %s\n",
                linearAddr,
                GetPhysicalAddrFromLinear(linearAddr),
                GetPageAttributesAsString(linearAddr) );


        //
        // Show the address of a routine in KERNEL32.DLL.
        //
        linearAddr = (DWORD)
            GetProcAddress( GetModuleHandle("KERNEL32.DLL"), "VirtualQuery" );
        printf( "KERNEL32.DLL        - Linear:%08X  Physical:%08X  %s\n",
                linearAddr,
                GetPhysicalAddrFromLinear(linearAddr),
                GetPageAttributesAsString(linearAddr) );
    }
```

The memory objects that PHYS shows are a routine in a 16-bit DLL, a
memory mapped file, and a routine in a 32-bit DLL. In addition, the routine
also displays the address of PHYS.EXE's heap and its code, data, shared data,
resource, and stack regions. I chose KRNL386's DGROUP to show that the

Win16 DLLs are in fact mapped into the address space of a Win32 process.
(It would be hard to thunk down to them if they weren't.) By showing the
addresses of a memory mapped file and a routine in KERNEL32, I can
demonstrate that they're in the shared ring 3 region between 2GB and 3GB.

Figure 5-2 shows the output from running two copies of PHYS. To
show memory sharing between processes and have meaningful results, it's
important to use the correct sequence, as follows. Run the first instance of
PHYS. When it's paused at the *Press any key...* prompt, start the second
copy of PHYS. This guarantees that the second instance will be running at
the same time as the first instance. Finally, switch back to the first instance
and press a key to get the second half of the first instance's output.

For now, let's concentrate on the first set of addresses shown for the
first instance. The addresses are sorted by their linear addresses. Examinine
the correlation betwen physical and linear addresses. Can't find a corre-
spondence? Don't try too hard because there isn't one. Windows 95 keeps a
pool of available RAM pages, and doesn't try to match physical RAM pages
to any particular linear address.

The first item in the list of addresses is the KRNL386 DGROUP. The
next four items are memory sections in the PHYS.EXE executable. Earlier, I
mentioned that in Windows 95, the default load address for a 32-bit process
is 4MB (0x400000). If you dump out PHYS.EXE's header with PEDUMP
from Chapter 8, you'll find that the code section starts at a relative virtual
address (RVA) of 0x1000. Adding 0x1000 to 4MB yields 0x401000, which
is the address shown in PHYS's output. You can go a step further and
obtain the RVAs of the data section, the shared data section, and the
resource section and verify that adding their RVAs to 4MB gives the same
linear address shown in PHYS's information.

The next item in PHYS's sorted output is the default process heap. At
address 0x410000, it's not too far past the last linear address used by the
code and data sections in the PHYS.EXE module. It looks like KERNEL32
allocates linear memory in a bottom-up fashion. The default size for the initial process heap in Windows 95 is 1MB+4K. This would make the next
available linear address in the address space appear to be somewhere
around 0x511000. Windows 95 starts each new virtual memory allocation
at a 64K boundary, however, so the next available region would be at
address 0x520000. Surprise, surprise — that happens to be the address
where the process's environment area starts. It looks like the bottom-up
allocation theory is still holding up.

```
//
// First instance output:
//

***** FIRST INSTANCE *****
KRNL386 DGROUP      - Linear:00036F60   Physical:00245F60   Read/Write USER
First code page     - Linear:00401000   Physical:00BBE000   ReadOnly USER
First data page     - Linear:00408000   Physical:006E2000   Read/Write USER
Shared section      - Linear:0040B000   Physical:0041D000   Read/Write USER
Resources           - Linear:0040D088   Physical:00B3F088   ReadOnly USER
Process Heap        - Linear:00410000   Physical:0082A000   Read/Write USER
Environment area    - Linear:00520000   Physical:00A2E000   Read/Write USER
Current Stack page  - Linear:0063F000   Physical:00ADD000   Read/Write USER
Memory Mapped file  - Linear:8233A000   Physical:0099D000   Read/Write USER
KERNEL32.DLL        - Linear:BFFAF09C   Physical:004F609C   ReadOnly USER
Press any key...


Now modifying the code page
KRNL386 DGROUP      - Linear:00036F60   Physical:00245F60   Read/Write USER
First code page     - Linear:00401000   Physical:00CA1000   Read/Write USER
First data page     - Linear:00408000   Physical:006E2000   Read/Write USER
Shared section      - Linear:0040B000   Physical:0041D000   Read/Write USER
Resources           - Linear:0040D088   Physical:00805088   ReadOnly USER
Process Heap        - Linear:00410000   Physical:0082A000   Read/Write USER
Environment area    - Linear:00520000   Physical:00A2E000   Read/Write USER
Current Stack page  - Linear:0063F000   Physical:00ADD000   Read/Write USER
Memory Mapped file  - Linear:8233A000   Physical:0099D000   Read/Write USER
KERNEL32.DLL        - Linear:BFFAF09C   Physical:004F609C   ReadOnly USER


//
// Second instance output:
//

***** SECONDARY INSTANCE *****
KRNL386 DGROUP      - Linear:00036F60   Physical:00245F60   Read/Write USER
First code page     - Linear:00401000   Physical:00BBE000   ReadOnly USER
First data page     - Linear:00408000   Physical:002FF000   Read/Write USER
Shared section      - Linear:0040B000   Physical:0041D000   Read/Write USER
Resources           - Linear:0040D088   Physical:00B3F088   ReadOnly USER
Process Heap        - Linear:00410000   Physical:00704000   Read/Write USER
Environment area    - Linear:00520000   Physical:00809000   Read/Write USER
Current Stack page  - Linear:0063F000   Physical:00B95000   Read/Write USER
Memory Mapped file  - Linear:8233A000   Physical:0099D000   Read/Write USER
KERNEL32.DLL        - Linear:BFFAF09C   Physical:004F609C   ReadOnly USER
Press any key...
```

Figure 5-2

Combined output from two instances of PHYS.EXE running simultaneously.

Most environments don't contain 64KB of strings, but a rule's a rule, so the next available address region should be 64KB after the start of the environment (that is, at 0x530000.) Looking at the PHYS output, we see the program's current stack page starts at 0x63F000. At first glance, this would appear to shoot a hole in my bottom-up theory for address space allocation. However, a bit more consideration shows that a bottom-up allocation scheme could still be at work here. Remember, a stack grows from a higher address to a lower one, so we have to subtract the length of the stack area from the top of the stack to get the starting address of the stack region. If the current program stack page is at 0x63F000, and if we haven't used too much stack space, the end of the stack region should be at 0x640000. The default program stack size for PHYS.EXE is 1MB, so subtracting 1MB from 0x640000 gives us 0x540000. This is 64KB higher than the 0x530000 my bottom-up allocation theory would suggest. However, if I call VirtualQuery for an address within the stack, the AllocationBase value returned by VirtualQuery is 0x530000. It appears that when the loader calculates the size needed for the program stack, it is rounding up by 64KB; therefore, a range of size 1MB+64KB (rather than just 1MB) is allocated. From what I can see, the bottom-up allocation theory still appears to hold.

After items directly related to program data areas, PHYS shows a memory mapped file that it creates. The base address of this memory mapped file at offset 0x8233A000 is well over 32MB into the shared ring 3 region between 2GB and 3GB. Because the 2GB to 3GB region is mapped by all processes, any program can view (and potentially trash) any memory mapped files. Yes, even memory mapped files that the process hasn't created a view of. This is a potential source of bad pointer overwrites in Windows 95. Windows NT has a more sophisticated memory manager and doesn't allow this serious breach of address space privacy.

The remaining item in PHYS's output is the address of the VirtualQuery routine in KERNEL32.DLL. The address (0xBFFAF09C) is pretty close to the end of the shared 2GB to 3GB region. Why so high an address? Windows 95 sets the base address of the system DLLs so that they'll be as high up and as close together as possible. The goal is to keep as much free space as possible in the 2GB to 3GB region for use by memory mapped files. You can see this yourself by examining the base address of some system DLLs such as KERNEL32.DLL, USER32.DLL, and GDI32.DLL.

Examining shared memory with PHYS

To see what regions of memory that Windows 95 shares between processes, we can run two copies of PHYS and compare their output. That's why Figure 5-2 has output from two instances of PHYS. Let's compare the first set of addresses from the first instance of PHYS to the addresses given by the second instance. In the two sets of addresses, memory blocks that have the same physical address are shared between the two instances. To make things easier, I've broken the items into the shared and unshared lists in Figure 5-3.

In shared memory	In nonshared memory
KRNL386 DGROUP	First data page
First code page	Process heap
Shared section	Environment area
Resources	Current stack page
Memory mapped file	
KERNEL32.DLL	

Figure 5-3
Shared and nonshared regions of memory between two simultaneous instances of a 32-bit process.

The shared list shouldn't be too surprising. KRNL386's DGROUP and KERNEL32.DLL are both part of system DLLs, which you would certainly hope to be shared. PHYS.EXE's code and resources are shared, which means that Windows 95 is trying to be efficient about using memory. PHYS explicitly created the two remaining shared items (the shared section and the memory mapped file) to share memory with other instances. The items in the nonshared list aren't too surprising either. All of the items are read/write program data. If Windows 95 were to try and share these memory regions, running multiple instances of PHYS would quickly cause a crash.

Examining copy on write with PHYS

The final demonstration in PHYS is the pseudo copy on write provided by WriteProcessMemory. Look at the three lines for the first code page (condensed in the following):

```
***** FIRST INSTANCE *****
First code page    - Linear:00401000  Physical:00BBE000  ReadOnly USER
...
Now modifying the code page
First code page    - Linear:00401000  Physical:00CA1000  Read/Write USER

***** SECONDARY INSTANCE *****
First code page    - Linear:00401000  Physical:00BBE000  ReadOnly USER
...
```

To make sense of the output, it's vital to remember the sequence of events while the two copies of PHYS ran. The first and third address lines are from two different processes, and happened before the code page was written to. The physical address of the code page in both processes is 0x00BBE000, proving that the page is shared between the two instances. The middle address line was output after the first instance wrote to the code page with WriteProcessMemory. Notice how it now has a different physical address? This shows that WriteProcessMemory changed the underlying physical RAM page to a different page of memory. Although it's not shown here, the physical address of the first code page remains at 0x00BBE000 in the second instance.

Cool stuff in the PHYS program (for advanced readers)

Lurking under the surface of the PHYS program is some low-level system code that Microsoft would probably prefer that you didn't know about. In a well-designed operating system, programs shouldn't be able to access the mappings between physical memory and linear addresses. Normally, there's no need for a program to determine these mappings, but this capability is at the heart of the PHYS program's functionality. Because Windows 95 doesn't provide a supported way to get at the page mappings, PHYS has to circumvent the operating system. Part of PHYS's sidestepping around the operating system involves executing code at ring 0 (the highest privilege level of the CPU). Application programs run at ring 3 (the least privileged level), and are generally kept from getting up to ring 0, except in a precise manner controlled by the operating system. Because the ring 0 code that PHYS needs to execute isn't sanctioned by the operating system, I had to write a general-purpose mechanism to call into ring 0 code from a ring 3 Win32 application. You can easily modify the PHYS ring 0-related code and drop it into your own code.

To map linear addresses to physical addresses, the GetPhysicalAddr-FromLinear function needs to party with the page tables. (*Party* is apparently an official Microsoft term for doing something you're not supposed to.) Page tables are a complicated topic, and I discuss them briefly in the following section, "Memory Contexts." If you don't know what page tables are, for now just think of them as data structures that describe the mapping between physical RAM addresses and linear addresses used by programs. The page tables are maintained by the operating system and used by the CPU. Turning to the trusty CPU manual, you'll find that the page directory is pointed to by the CR3 register. Unfortunately, the instruction that retrieves the value of the CR3 register is privileged. Attempting to call it from ring 3 results in the CPU generating a general protection fault (exception 0Dh). When Windows 95 sees this fault, it analyzes the instruction and sees that it's a privileged instruction. Rather than terminating the application, Windows 95 silently returns control to the application without retrieving the CR3 register value.

What does this mean? Windows 95 is preventing a direct assault on the page tables from application programs. Sure, I could write a VxD (which runs at ring 0) to get the CR3 value, but I dislike lots of VxDs floating around my system. Besides, even if I could get the CR3 value, there's still a big problem. The CR3 register tells the *physical* address of the page tables. There's no good way to convert a physical address into a linear address that PHYS can use. Short of turning off paging while I use the physical address, there's not much I can do with the CR3 value.

The next approach is to see whether Windows 95 maps the page tables to a linear address that ring 3 code can see. As it turns out, Windows 95 does. The full 4MB range of page table entries is always mapped to linear address 0xFF800000 (8MB before the end of linear memory.) With that little bit of information, we would seem to be all set. Simply create a pointer to the page tables and start reading whatever information you want. Because ring 3 Win32 programs use 32-bit linear addresses, you should even be able to read the page tables from any arbitrary Win32 program, right? Not so fast! Although the Windows 95 coders seemingly made the page tables very susceptible to overwrites from wild pointers, the tables are not as unprotected as they might appear. Both the page directory and each page table entry keep a bit (the user/supervisor bit) that indicates whether the page should be accessible to code at any privilege level or just at ring 0. The page directory entry that maps the 4MB region used by the page tables has the user/supervisor bit cleared. This means that the entire 4MB memory range used for page tables is off-limits to ring 3 code.

Because the Windows 95 page tables are off-limits to ring 3 applications, we have to execute our code at ring 0 to access the page table. For my May 1993 *Microsoft Systems Journal* article on ring privilege levels, I wrote RING0.EXE. RING0 uses some holes in how Windows manages memory to call 16-bit code at ring 0 from a ring 3 Windows program. The gist of how RING0 works is with CPU call gates, which provide a method for less privileged code to call into more privileged code (for instance, from ring 3 to ring 0). Because Windows won't hand you a call gate just for the asking, RING0 goes into the LDT and creates a call gate itself. To get at the LDT, RING0 uses the same INT 2Fh subfunction that KRNL386 calls to obtain a selector pointing at the LDT. (Yes, even in Windows 95!)

After RING0 appeared, Alex Schmidt wrote an excellent article (in *Dr. Dobb's,* March 1994) that extended the premise of RING0 to call 32-bit ring 0 code. Alex went so far as to write a method for dynamically loading VxDs using these call gate tricks. (Luckily, Windows 95 now supports dynamically loading VxDs without these horrible hacks that Alex and I use.) When I saw that the PHYS program needed to call ring 0 code, I saw a chance to update the original RING0 code to be usable from Win32 programs. Among other things, this meant making a 32-bit call gate rather than a 16-bit call gate. The results of the effort are in the PHYS program on this book's disk.

Using this generic mechanism of calling ring 0 code from a Win32 application is a little tricky, but not overly so. The code in GetPhysicalAddress-FromLinear in Figure 5-4 is a good example. First, you need to create a call gate selector by calling the GetRing0Callgate function. This function is just the front-end portion of a Windows 95 thunk down to 16-bit code. Down in the 16-bit portion of GetRing0Callgate, the code creates the 32-bit call gate that will be used later up in 32-bit land. There are two parameters to GetRing0Callgate. The first is the 32-bit linear address of the code that you want executed at ring 0. The second parameter is the number of DWORD parameters to pass on the stack to the code that executes at ring 0.

Once you have the call gate selector, the next step is to store it into a 6-byte far pointer (a.k.a. an FWORD). Six bytes? Yes. In 32-bit mode, a far call is made through a 16-bit selector combined with a 32-bit offset. Because the offset is 32 bits, it's implicit that the selector will be for a 32-bit segment, much like the flat selectors used by Win32 programs. Getting back to the subject at hand, we need to make a far call using the call gate selector in order for the CPU to switch to ring 0. In Figure 5-4, the code stores the call gate selector into the high WORD of a 6-byte array (3 WORDs). The offset portion of the pointer isn't important because the CPU ignores it and instead loads EIP from the offset in the call gate descriptor. After creating the pointer, the code uses inline assembler to call through an fword pointer (because the C compiler knows only about 32-bit near calls). I bracketed the call gate call with cli and sti to prevent interrupts in the ring 0 code. This eliminates the problem of switching to a safe stack once we're in ring 0 code.

```
DWORD GetPhysicalAddrFromLinear(DWORD linear)
{
    if ( !callgate1 )
        callgate1 = GetRing0Callgate( (DWORD)_GetPhysicalAddrFromLinear, 1
);

    if ( callgate1 )
    {
        WORD myFwordPtr[3];

        myFwordPtr[2] = callgate1;
        __asm    push    [linear]
        __asm    cli
        __asm    call    fword ptr [myFwordPtr]
        __asm    sti
```

Figure 5-4
PHYS.EXE calling through a callgate in 32-bit

Because of the contortions required to get to ring 0 from a Win32 program, there are a few reasons why I wrote the ring 0 PAGETABL.ASM code in assembler. First, the 16:32 far call to the ring 0 code caused the CPU to put 8 bytes on the stack, rather than the normal 4. Therefore, after setting up an EBP frame, the first parameter is at EBP+0Ch rather than at EBP+08. More importantly, when the code returns to ring 3, it needs to do a 16:32 RETF rather than a 32-bit near return. Like a 16:32 far call, a 16:32 RETF is something that the compiler doesn't know how to generate.

To sum up calling ring 0 code from a Win32 application, first write the ring 0 code (most likely in assembler), taking into account the caveats just mentioned. Next, in your program, call GetRing0Callgate, passing it the name of your ring 0 routine and the number of arguments. Then create a 16:32 far pointer with the call gate, and call through the pointer. Finally, when you no longer need to call the ring 0 routine, delete the call gate by calling FreeRing0Callgate. It's not elegant, but it's better than being at the mercy of the operating system.

MEMORY CONTEXTS (ADVANCED STUFF)

Although it's fine to talk abstractly about memory contexts, at some point the rubber must meet the road. Windows 95 needs to maintain data structures that keep track of which pages of RAM should be mapped to linear addresses in a given process. To understand memory contexts in Windows 95, you need to understand the CPU's paging mechanism at a low level. I'll give a warp speed overview of 80386 paging that omits some of the more advanced details. If you're interested in a precise description of paging, refer to the Intel manuals or other books on the 386 architecture.

The 80386 class of CPU uses two levels of lookup tables to translate a linear address to a physical address that goes out on the address bus. The first lookup table is the *page directory*. It is 4KB and can be viewed as an array of 1024 DWORDs. Each DWORD in the page directory array contains the physical address of another 4KB block known as as a *page table*. Like the page directory, the page table is an array of 1024 DWORDs. Each DWORD in the page table array contains the physical address of a 4KB block of memory.

To use the page directory and page tables, the CPU breaks up a 32-bit linear address into the three components shown in Figure 5-5. The CPU uses the top 10 bits of the address as an index into the page directory. The next lower 10 bits of the address are an index into a 4KB page table. Which page table do these bits index? None other than the page table pointed to by the page directory that the CPU found in the previous step. The address in the page table is a physical address aligned on a 4KB boundary. The final part of the calculation is to take the bottom 12 bits of the linear address and use them as an offset into the memory pointed to by the page table.

In simpler terms, the top 10 bits of the address index into an array that contains 1024 pointers to other arrays. The second 10 bits of the address index this secondary array to get a physical address. The low 12 bits of the linear address are added to this physical address to get the final physical address.

How does the CPU know where to find the page directory? The page directory is pointed at by the CR3 register, one of the special registers introduced on the 80386. A brute force method of implementing memory contexts would be to simply create a page directory and 1024 associated page tables for each processs, changing the CR3 register to point at each process's page directory as needed.

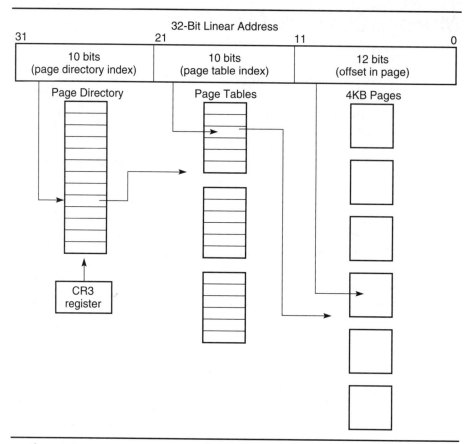

Figure 5-5
How the CPU converts a linear address to a physical address.

The problem with this approach is that to map the entire 4GB address space would require 1024 page tables, each 4KB in size. This would take up 4MB of memory per process, obviously not an effective use of RAM. Therefore, to change memory contexts, Windows 95 sets up a single 4MB region of memory, and modifies the entries within the page directory to quickly change the page mappings.

If you're concerned that 4MB still sounds like a lot of memory to use just for paging, don't be. At the page directory level, the operating system can tell the CPU that an entire 4KB page table isn't present in memory, thereby eliminating the need to map a 4KB block of physical memory to the page table. Windows 95 doesn't use anywhere near 4MB of memory to manage paging. The Windows 95 page directory and page tables are mapped into a 4MB region of memory that's 8MB from the end of the 32-bit address space. Put another way, they don't use the last 4MB of the address space, but they do use the 4MB before that. This range of memory starts at FF800000h, and can be viewed in SoftIce/W. The page directory itself is stored in a page within this 4MB range.

You can easily find the linear address of the page directory by dumping out the CR3 register with the SoftIce/W CR command. On my machine, CR3 contains 6EE000h. The CR3 register contains a physical address, so you'll need to find the associated linear address if you want to view it. The SoftIce/W PHYS command is handy for this purpose. The PHYS command searches the page tables to find all linear addresses that correspond to a given physical address. The command PHYS 6EE000 yields two linear addresses. The second of these addresses is FFBFE000h, which is in the 4MB range of memory reserved for page tables.

Given that we can find the page directory in SoftIce/W, we should be able to prove or disprove what I said about context switching by setting a hardware write breakpoint in the page directory. If the breakpoint doesn't go off, context switching is probably accomplished some other way. If it does go off, it's a strong indicator that context switching is accomplished by manipulating the page tables. Also, the location of the write should give us a clue as to what's responsible for switching contexts.

Running this simple experiment in SoftIce/W confirms that the page directory is being written to on a regular basis. To see this, back up a few instructions from where the write occurs, as shown in the following SoftIce/W code window output:

```
        _ContextSwitch
        0028:C0004856  MOV      EAX,[C001084C]
        0028:C000485B  MOV      EDX,[ESP+04]
        0028:C000485F  CMP      EAX,EDX
        0028:C0004861  JZ       C0004893
        0028:C0004863  PUSH     ESI
        0028:C0004864  PUSH     EDI
        0028:C0004865  MOV      EDI,FFBFE000
        0028:C000486A  MOV      ECX,[EDX+04]
        0028:C000486D  MOV      ESI,[EDX]
        0028:C000486F  REPZ MOVSD
        0028:C0004871  MOV      ECX,[EAX+04]
        0028:C0004874  SUB      ECX,[EDX+04]
        0028:C0004877  JBE      C0004880
        0028:C0004879  MOV      EAX,[C00107E0]
        0028:C000487E  REPZ STOSD
        0028:C0004880  XCHG     EDX,[C001084C]
```

```
0028:C0004886  MOV    EAX,EDX
0028:C0004888  MOV    ECX,[C0010CDC]
0028:C000488E  MOV    CR3,ECX
0028:C0004891  POP    EDI
0028:C0004892  POP    ESI
0028:C0004893  RET
```

The core of the _ContextSwitch routine is the REPZ MOVSD and REPZ STOSD instructions. The three MOV instructions leading up to the REPZ MOVSD are setting up things to copy a region of memory from one location to another. The fact that the destination address is FFBFE000h (which as we saw earlier is in the page directory) is a tip-off that the routine is blasting a new set of page table mappings into the page directory. Each DWORD it copies corresponds to one of the 1024 possible page tables.

It's also interesting that the number of DWORDs moved isn't a hard-coded number. Rather, the code loads ECX with the number of DWORDs (page table mappings) each time. The effect of the second REPZ STOSD isn't as obvious. It's comparing how many DWORDs were just copied with the number of DWORDs copied the previous time _ContextSwitch was called. If the number of DWORDs just copied is less than the previous time, there will be extra page table entries for the previous memory context, which the new context shouldn't be allowed to see. Therefore, if necessary, the REPZ STOSD blast over these remaining page directory entries with a value indicating a non-present page table.

SoftIce/W helpfully put the label _ContextSwitch at the top of the code listing. It turns out that the _ContextSwitch routine is one of the VMM services in the VMM VxD. Its address appears in the table of VMM services that are pointed to by a field in VMM's Device Descriptor Block. So where did SoftIce/W come up with this name? See the VMM.INC file from the Windows 95 DDK. Each line that starts with VMM_Service is service routine provided by the VMM VxD. Near the end of the list you'll find the routine _ContextSwitch. Also of interest in the vicinity of _ContextSwitch in VMM.INC are the _PageModify and _PageModifyPermissions functions.

Having found the _ContextSwitch routine in VMM, we can see that Windows 95 must be keeping a set of page mappings for each memory context, as well as a count of the number of pages. As luck would have it, we can verify this with the SoftIce/W Addr command:

```
:addr
Handle    PGTPTR   Tables  Min Addr   Max Addr   Mutex     Owner
C0FE5D04  C103C6F8  0004   00400000   7FFFF000   C0FD83B4  KERNEL32
C103C9B0  C103E274  0200   00400000   7FFFF000   C103C9E4  MSGSRV32
C1040854  C10416D0  0200   00400000   7FFFF000   C1040898  Explorer
C1045808  C1046190  0200   00400000   7FFFF000   C104584C  Winword
C10483C4  C10402F4  0002   00400000   7FFFF000   C104A220  HEAPWALK
C1048BEC  C0FE38E4  0002   00400000   7FFFF000   C1048C20  WINMINE
C1048850  C104921C  0002   00400000   7FFFF000   C1048884  FREECELL
C1040304  C1042534  0200   00400000   7FFFF000   C10406BC  Systray
C1041398  C104031C  0002   00400000   7FFFF000   C10413CC  MMTASK
C103EA78  C103EF2C  0200   00400000   7FFFF000   C103EAAC  Mprexe
C103CE70  C103D344  0200   00400000   7FFFF000   C103CEB4  Spool32
C10CD00C  C10CD024  0002   00400000   7FFFF000   C10CD050
```

In this list, the FREECELL, WINMINE, MMTASK, and HEAPWALK programs are all Win16 programs. Interestingly, even though Win16 programs can always see one another, Windows 95 treats them as separate processes and memory contexts. However, this is academic because the code and data segments in Win16 programs are always loaded in the shared memory areas (0 – 4MB and above 2GB). Thus, Win16 programs can always see each other, even though they technically have different address contexts.

All the remaining processes in the ADDR list are either 32-bit or unknown. The column labeled "Tables" is misleading because it's the number of page directory entries that make up the memory context. Each page directory maps 1024 page tables, each of which maps a 4K region. Thus, each page directory entry corresponds to 4MB of linear address space. Notice how the 16-bit programs use only two page table entries. This is because 16-bit programs have no need for memory in the Win32 per-process data area (0x00400000 – 0x7FFFFFFF). Win32 processes, on the other hand, need separate page mappings for that entire range, even if most of the pages are marked not-present.

The "handles" for each memory context looks suspiciously like a linear address. Let's dump out memory at the location given by a handle value. For this test, I arbitrarily chose the first context (handle C0FE5D04 for KERNEL32):

```
:dd c0fe5d04
0030:C0FE5D04 C103C6F8  00000004  C0FD4D1C  C103C9B0      .........M......
```

Hmmm . . . We can easily match up the first and second DWORDs to the SoftIce/W ADDR output. The first DWORD (C103C6F8) is what the ADDR command reports for the PGTPTR (Page Table Pointer) value. The second DWORD (00000004) matches up with the value in the Tables column. If you go back and study the _ContextSwitch code, you can see that _ContextSwitch is expecting a pointer to a data structure in the format we're seeing here: a pointer to the page directory entries to copy, followed by the number of entries to copy.

The fourth DWORD found when dumping out our memory context handle (in the preceding example, C103C9B0) can also be found easily in the ADDR output. It happens to be the context handle of the next context in the ADDR list. (Further exploration confirms that the contexts are kept in a linked list.) What about the third DWORD (C0FD4D1C)? It looks like it could be a pointer, so let's dump it:

```
:dd c0fd4d1C
0030:C0FD4D1C 00000400  0007FFFF  C0E0E310  C0E0E31C      ...............
```

Interesting! If you multiply the first and second DWORDs by 0x1000 (the size of a page), you get the values that the ADDR command reports as the minimum and maximum address for the memory context. It looks like we've found the core of Windows 95's context management.

If you're interested in digging deeper into Windows 95 memory contexts, the DDK is indispensible. Unlike the SDK documentation, the DDK doesn't try to hide much from the programmer. The DDK says that memory contexts are created by _ContextCreate in VMM.VXD and destroyed by _ContextDestroy. By writing VxD code, you can actually create, switch to, and destroy your own memory contexts. Of course, hooking things up so that the rest of Windows 95 knows what you're doing is a bit more work!

Some other cool VMM functions to check out are _CopyPageTable and _PageAttach. _CopyPageTable lets you obtain the logical-to-physical mappings for a memory context without going into the page tables as I did in the PHYS program. The _PageAttach function documentation describes how it's used to make memory in one context map to the same linear address in another context. This is the mechanism by which Windows 95 shares code and data between multiple copies of a process.

THE WINDOWS 95 MEMORY APIs

The Windows 95 memory management functions are built in layers. At each level (other than the bottom layer), the functions depend on the functions in a lower layer. I've come to think of Windows 95's memory management as consisting of four levels of code. At the lowest level, the Virtual Machine Manager (VMM) provides functions for allocating large regions of memory and manipulating pages within those regions. Application programs don't call these APIs directly. Rather, KERNEL32.DLL uses the VMM memory functions on behalf of the higher-level memory API functions.

The next layer up contains the VirtualXXX functions provided by KERNEL32: VirtualAlloc, VirtualFree, and VirtualProtect. These functions are implemented in terms of the lower-level VMM functions. The VirtualXXX functions provide applications with the capability to manage large regions of memory on the page granular level.

Moving up another notch, we come to the KERNEL32 HeapXXX functions. The HeapXXX functions include HeapAlloc, HeapFree, and HeapCreate. They are roughly equivalent to the C runtime library memory functions (malloc, free, and so on). In fact, in the Windows NT SDK runtime library DLL, malloc is just a wrapper around the HeapAlloc function. The topmost layer of memory management functions contains the LocalXXX and GlobalXXX functions. Unlike in Win16 programs, the LocalXXX and GlobalXXX functions are essentially identical. For instance, GlobalAlloc and LocalAlloc are the same function; KERNEL32 exports both functions using the same address in its code. The LocalXXX and GlobalXXX functions are really just a layer atop the lower-level HeapXXX functions. There's not much of a reason to keep GlobalAlloc and LocalAlloc around in Win32. The memory functions no longer work with selectors like the Win16 GlobalAlloc does. Nor is memory allocated out of the application's data segment as it is with the Win16 LocalAlloc. The main reason why the GlobalXXX and LocalXXX functions are in Win32 is to ease existing Win16 applications to Win32. The rest of this chapter is mostly an in-depth look at the Windows 95 Win32 memory management API, divided into four layers. With the exception of the lowest level of functions in the VMM VxD, I'll give pseudocode for every memory management function. In some cases, a Win32 function may not be implemented in Windows 95 or may just map to another function. I'll note these cases as well.

THE VMM FUNCTIONS

The lowest level memory management code in Windows 95 lies in VMM.VXD. Within VMM are VxD functions that reserve, commit, decommit, and free pages of the linear address space. VMM also contains VxD functions for querying the status of pages, managing memory contexts, and installing page fault handlers, and it provides heap functions for use by VxDs. Table 5-1 contains the DDK description for the majority of the VMM memory management-related functions.

Table 5-1
DDK Descriptions of VMM Memory Management Functions

VMM Function Name	Purpose
_PageReserve	Reserves a range of linear addresses in the current context without allocating any physical storage.
_PageFree	Frees the specified memory block.
_PageCommit	Commits physical pages to a range of linear addresses.
_PageDecommit	Decommits physical storage from a specified range of linear addresses.
_PageAttach	Maps a range of linear pages in the current memory context to the same physical storage that those pages are mapped to in a specified context (the source context).
_PageFlush	Writes a range of committed pages to the backing file by calling the appropriate pager function. This service does not mark the pages as not-present.
_PageModifyPermissions	Modifies the permissions for pages in the specified range.
_PageQuery	Retrieves information about a range of virtual pages. The information is in the same format that VirtualQuery returns.
_PagerRegister	Informs the system of a new type of pager.
_PagerQuery	Retrieves information about a registered pager.
_ContextCreate	Creates a new memory context. The tasking and scheduling components of Windows 95 use this service to create a private linear address space for a new Win32 application.
_ContextDestroy	Destroys a memory context created by the _ContextCreate service.
_ContextSwitch	Changes the current memory context. The current memory context determines the mapping of pages in the private arena.
_GetCurrentContext	Determines the current memory context.
_HeapAllocate	Allocates a block of memory from the system heap.
_HeapReAllocate	Reallocates or reinitializes a memory block in the system heap.
_HeapFree	Frees an existing memory block in the system heap.

If you're familiar with VxDs, you're probably thinking that this table of VMM memory-related functions is nice, but what does it have to do with ring 3 application code? After all, regular ring 3 programs can't just call any VxD function that happens to come along. I've shown Table 5-1 for a good reason: Each of the functions *is* callable by ring 3 applications, just not directly.

It turns out that the Windows 95 coders felt that this set of functions was vital to KERNEL32.DLL. As such, they implemented Win32 VxD services for each of the functions. Win32 VxD services are a new mechanism in Windows 95 that allows ring 3 application code to call into VxDs using a C-style calling convention (no registers need apply). They are *not* related to Windows NT services, which are really just special-purpose processes.

Chapter 6 describes Windows 95 Win32 VxD services in more detail. Here, it's sufficient to know that each Win32 VxD service provided by a VxD such as VMM is identified by a unique number. The high WORD is the VxD device ID, and the low WORD is an index into the device's Win32 VxD service table. Figure 5-6 shows the Win32 VxD service IDs for the VMM functions listed in Table 5-1. Chapter 6 describes Win32 VxD services, and has a more complete list of service IDs.

```
0x00010000 _PageReserve
0x00010001 _PageCommit
0x00010002 _PageDecommit
0x00010003 _PagerRegister
0x00010004 _PagerQuery
0x00010005 _HeapAllocate
0x00010006 _ContextCreate
0x00010007 _ContextDestroy
0x00010008 _PageAttach
0x00010009 _PageFlush
0x0001000A _PageFree
0x0001000B _ContextSwitch
0x0001000C _HeapReAllocate
0x0001000D _PageModifyPermissions
0x0001000E _PageQuery
0x0001000F _GetCurrentContext
0x00010010 _HeapFree
```

Figure 5-6

VMM's Win32 VxD service IDs for calling ring 0 VMM functions.

To call one of these VMM functions through a Win32 service, KERNEL32 simply pushes the arguments on the stack, followed by the Win32 VxD service number. It then calls the VxDCall function (referred to as VxDCall0 in *Unauthorized Windows 95*). For example, the _PageReserve function in VMM.VXD is prototyped like this:

```
ULONG EXTERNAL _PageReserve(ULONG page, ULONG npages, ULONG flags);
```

The following KERNEL32 loader code shows how _PageReserve would be called from ring 3:

```
BFFA00A6:   PUSH    10                      ;; PR_STATIC from VMM.INC

BFFA00A8:   MOV     EAX,DWORD PTR [EBP-000000F4]
BFFA00AE:   ADD     EAX,00000FFF
BFFA00B3:   SHR     EAX,0C                  ;; Round up to 4K boundary
BFFA00B6:   PUSH    EAX

BFFA00B7:   PUSH    80000400                ;; PR_PRIVATE from VMM.INC

BFFA00BC:   PUSH    00010000                ;; VWIN32 call 00010000 = _PageReserve

BFFA00C1:   CALL    VxDCall0
```

I haven't provided pseudocode for these VMM functions, as I did for the higher-level memory management APIs. Application programs don't call them directly. Instead, think of them as the fundamental building blocks that the ring 3 memory management functions are built upon. I've listed them here because some readers don't have the Windows 95 DDK, which lists and describes these functions. I also didn't want to ignore them entirely, and handwave over the VxD functions in the following sections.

THE WIN32 VIRTUAL FUNCTIONS

At the lowest level of memory management in the Win32 API, you'll find the virtual functions (such as VirtualAlloc and VirtualProtect). The virtual functions are for allocating and managing memory in large chunks. In Windows 95, the granularity of the virtual functions is 4KB, making them unsuitable for replacing malloc and new in the C/C++ runtime library. For the most part, the virtual functions are a thin layer over the VMM functions. You'll see this momentarily when I present pseudocode for the virtual functions.

The closest equivalent to the virtual functions in Win16 is the global heap functions (for instance, GlobalAlloc). Both the Win16 global heap functions and the Win32 virtual functions let you allocate vast regions of memory that you manage however you want. Unlike the global heap functions, though, the virtual functions don't use selectors to reference memory. Instead, the virtual functions deal with memory in 4KB chunks and don't use selectors. Also, the Win16 global heap functions let you allocate memory regions as small as 20h bytes.

VirtualAlloc

VirtualAlloc is several functions in one. At any given time, the VMM memory manager considers each page of linear memory to be either free, reserved, or committed. The VirtualAlloc function enables you to change the state of a range of pages in one direction (from free toward committed). VirtualAlloc can change pages from free to reserved, or from free to committed. In addition, it can change previously reserved pages to the committed state.

The last state change — from reserved to committed — is particularly valuable for implementing sparse memory and stacks. In this scenario, a program first uses VirtualAlloc to reserve a block of memory sufficiently large to meet any demands made on the program. The program then sets up a structured exception handler that looks for page faults in the reserved memory range. As these page faults occur, the program calls VirtualAlloc a second time. This time, the VirtualAlloc call changes the page that caused the fault from the reserved state to the committed state. In this way, a program can "allocate" huge amounts of memory without requiring physical RAM to back it up at the time of the allocation. Only the memory pages that end up being touched have physical RAM mapped to them.

Normally, VirtualAlloc is used by the operating system and programs to allocate memory in the application's address space (that is, below 2GB). However, VirtualAlloc has an undocumented flag (0x8000000) that allows it to grab regions of memory above 2GB. Memory above 2GB is shared by all applications, so this is an undocumented method of sharing memory across processes. You can do the same thing with the documented memory mapped file functions. In fact, from a cursory examination, it appears that the address range used for memory mapped files is equivalent to what VirtualAlloc returns with the 0x8000000 flag.

The Win32 VirtualAlloc rounds down to the nearest 64K boundary when reserving memory. Indeed, memory blocks allocated from VirtualAlloc always appear to be aligned. However, VirtualAlloc's code doesn't do this rounding. Instead, the rounding occurs in the _PageReserve function used by VirtualAlloc.

VirtualAlloc begins by checking whether the requested memory range is too large. Too large in this context means 2GB to 4MB. This is the size of the linear address reserved for per-application memory. VirtualAlloc then calculates the number of pages needed to span the memory region. When determining how many pages are needed, VirtualAlloc rounds the starting address down to the nearest 4KB and the ending address up to the next 4KB. Thus, if you request a 2-byte region that covers the last byte of one page and the first byte of the next, VirtualAlloc will try to reserve two pages.

Next up for VirtualAlloc is to handle the various flags it was passed in the fdwProtect parameter. First, the code looks for the undocumented 0x8000000 flag, which tells it to allocate the memory in the shared region above 2GB. VirtualAlloc ignores the MEM_TOP_DOWN flag, and turns it off if passed. Afterward, the function tests to see whether you passed only the MEM_COMMIT or MEM_RESERVED flag. Any bits besides those two flags trigger a debug version warning. Finally, the code calls the mmPAGEToPC function, which is a helper function (described in the next section) that converts the fdwProtect parameter flags to the flags used by VMM's _PageReserve.

At this point in the code, the function splits into two pieces. One section executes if the user doesn't care at which address the memory is reserved. The other section handles the case where the user specified a specific address to reserve or commit to. In either case, if memory is to be reserved, VirtualAlloc calls Win32 service 00010000, which is a wrapper around the VMM _PageReserve function. After reserving the memory (if necessary), and if the caller specified the MEM_COMMIT flag, VirtualAlloc calls Win32 service 00010001, which is a wrapper around VMM's _PageCommit routine. If the caller specified a specific address to commit memory to, VirtualAlloc checks to make sure the address is below 0xC0000000, which is the start of VxD land.

Throughout all this code, VirtualAlloc conscientiously checks the return values from _PageReserve and _PageCommit. If anything fails, the code emits a debugging diagnostic, then falls through to a single exit point. This exit point executes only in the failure case, and frees the pages previously reserved.

Pseudocode for VirtualAlloc

```
// Parameters:
//  LPVOID  lpvAddress
//  DWORD   cbSize
//  DWORD   fdwAllocationType
//  DWORD   fdwProtect
```

```
// Locals:
// DWORD   address, startPage
// DWORD   sizeInPages;
// DWORD   pcFlags;                    // Returned from mmPAGEToPC
// BOOL    fReserve;

    if ( cbSize > 0x7FC00000 )  // 2GB - 4MB
    {
        _DebugOut( "VirtualAlloc: dwSize too big\n\r",
                   SLE_WARNING + FStopOnRing3MemoryError );
        InternalSetLastError( ERROR_NOT_ENOUGH_MEMORY );
        return 0;
    }

    address = lpvAddress;

    // Calculate how many pages will be spanned by this memory request.
    sizeInPages = lpvAddress & 0x00000FFF;
    sizeInPages += cbSize
    sizeInPages += 0x00000FFF;
    sizeInPages = sizeInPages >> 12;

    startPage = PR_PRIVATE; // 0x80000400h from VMM.INC This value can
                            // be either an actual page number or a PR_ equate.

    if ( fdwAllocationType & 0x8000000 )     // Undocumented shared mem flag.
    {
        startPage = PR_SHARED;               // 0x80060000 in VMM.INC.
        fdwAllocationType &= ~0x8000000;     // Don't need this flag anymore.
    }

    fdwAllocationType &= ~MEM_TOP_DOWN;      // Ignore the MEM_TOP_DOWN flag.

    // You can specify MEM_COMMIT and/or MEM_RESERVE, but no other flags
    // (the undocumented one above notwithstanding).
    if (    (fdwAllocationType != MEM_COMMIT)
         && (fdwAllocationType != MEM_RESERVE)
         && (fdwAllocationType != (MEM_RESERVE | MEM_COMMIT)) )
    {
        _DebugOut( "VirtualAlloc: bad flAllocationType\n\r",
                   SLE_WARNING + FStopOnRing3MemoryError );
        InternalSetLastError( ERROR_INVALID_PARAMETER );
        return 0;
    }

    // Convert the fdwProtect flags into the PC_ flag values used by
    // VMM.VXD. Pseudocode follows this function.
    pcFlags = mmPAGEToPC(fdwProtect);
```

```
if ( pcFlags == -1 )    // Something wrong?
    return 0;

if ( lpvAddress == 0 )  // Don't care where the memory is allocated.
{
    // Reserve the memory block. startPage should be either
    // PR_PRIVATE or PR_SHARED.
    lpvAddress = VxDCall( _PageReserve, startPage, sizeInPages, pcFlags );

    if ( lpvAddress == -1 )
    {
        _DebugOut( "VirtualAlloc: reserve failed\n",
                    SLE_WARNING + FStopOnRing3MemoryError );
        InternalSetLastError( ERROR_NOT_ENOUGH_MEMORY );
        return 0;
    }

    // If caller is just reserving, we're finished.
    if ( !(fdwAllocationType & MEM_COMMIT) )
        return lpvAddress;

    // Caller has specified MEM_COMMIT.
    if ( VxDCall(_PageCommit,lpvAddress>>12, sizeInPages, 1, 0, pcFlags))
        return lpvAddress;      // Success!

    // Oops. Something went wrong. Tell the user, then fall through
    // to the code to free the pages.
    _DebugOut( "VirtualAlloc: commit failed\n",
                SLE_WARNING + FStopOnRing3MemoryError );
    InternalSetLastError( ERROR_NOT_ENOUGH_MEMORY );
}
else    // Caller specified a particular address to allocate/commit at.
{
    if ( address > 0xBFFFFFFF )
    {
        _DebugOut( "VirtualAlloc: bad base address\n\r",
                    SLE_WARNING + FStopOnRing3MemoryError );
        InternalSetLastError( ERROR_INVALID_ADDRESS );
        return 0;
    }

    fReserve = fdwAllocationType & MEM_RESERVE;
    if ( fReserve )
    {
        // Call VMM _PageReserve to allocate the memory. Note that
        // the caller-specified lpvAddress is rounded down to the
```

```
                    // nearest 4KB page. Note that it's not down to 64KB like
                    // the doc says. However, _PageReserve still rounds it down.
                    lpvAddress=VxDCall(_PageReserve,address>>12, sizeInPages,pcFlags);
                    if ( lpvAddress == -1 )
                    {
                        _DebugOut( "VirtualAlloc: reserve failed\n",
                                    SLE_WARNING + FStopOnRing3MemoryError );
                        InternalSetLastError( ERROR_NOT_ENOUGH_MEMORY );
                        return 0;
                    }

                    // Hmmm...It turns out that KERNEL32 will complain if you
                    // didn't specify an address aligned on a 64KB boundary!
                    if ( lpvAddress != (address & 0xFFFF0000) )
                        _DebugOut("VirtualAlloc: reserve in wrong place 1\n\r",
                                    SLE_ERROR);
                }

            if ( !(fdwAllocationType & MEM_COMMIT) )
                return lpvAddress;

            lpvAddress &= 0xFFFFF000;

            if ( VxDCall(_PageCommit,lpvAddress>>12, sizeInPages, 1, 0, pcFlags) )
                return lpvAddress;
            else
            {
                _DebugOut( "VirtualAlloc: commit failed\n",
                            SLE_WARNING + FStopOnRing3MemoryError );
                InternalSetLastError( ERROR_NOT_ENOUGH_MEMORY );
                if ( !fReserve )
                    return 0;
            }
        }

    // Unreserve the memory allocated earlier.
    VxDCall( _PageFree, lpvAddress & 0xFFFF0000, 0 );

return_0:
    lpvAddress = 0;

return_lpvAddress:
    return lpvAddress;
```

mmPAGEToPC

The mmPageToPC function is used by VirtualAlloc, VirtualProtectEx, and, by extension, VirtualProtect. The function converts the PAGE_ flags from WINNNT.H (such as PAGE_READONLY) into the equivalent PC_ flags. The PC_ (Page Commit) flags are defined in VMM.INC, and are used with VMM's _PageCommit function.

One of the flags used by Windows 95 indicates that a particular page is a guard page. When the operating system receives a page fault when accessing a guard pages, the operating system needs to commit additional memory at the bottom of the stack to allow the stack to grow downward. However, you apparently can't request a guard page with VirtualAlloc, because mmPageToPC filters out the PAGE_GUARD bit. The function also ignores the PAGE_NOCACHE flag by turning it off. The bulk of mmPageToPC is a simple mapping of the various PAGE_ flags. In all cases except for PAGE_NOACCESS, the converted flags contain the PC_USER bit, which means the page will be accessible by ring 3 (user level) code. If the page should be writeable, the PC_WRITEABLE flag is OR'ed into the returned flags. Put another way, with the exception of PAGE_NOACCESS, all the PAGE_ flags map to PC_USER or PC_USER|PC_WRITEABLE. Any bits other than those corresponding to the PAGE_ flags cause mmPageToPC to complain in the debug version and cause the VirtualAlloc or VirtualProtect(Ex) call to fail.

Pseudocode for mmPAGEToPC

```
// Parameters:
//   DWORD   PAGE_flags;
// Locals:
//   DWORD   retValue;

    if ( PAGE_flags & PAGE_GUARD )
    {
        _DebugOut( "mmPAGEToPC: PAGE_GUARD flag not supported\n",
                    SLE_WARNING + FStopOnRing3MemoryError );
        InternalSetLastError( ERROR_CALL_NOT_IMPLEMENTED );

        return -1;
    }

    PAGE_flags &= ~PAGE_NOCACHE;        // Turn off the PAGE_NOCACHE flag.
    if ( PAGE_flags == PAGE_NOACCESS )
        return 0;
```

```
if ( PAGE_flags == PAGE_READONLY )
    return PC_USER;

if ( PAGE_flags == PAGE_READWRITE )
    return PC_USER | PC_WRITEABLE;

if ( PAGE_flags == PAGE_EXECUTE )
    return PC_USER;

if ( PAGE_flags == PAGE_EXECUTE_READ )
    return PC_USER;

if ( PAGE_flags == PAGE_EXECUTE_READWRITE )
    return PC_USER | PC_WRITEABLE;

if ( PAGE_flags == PAGE_EXECUTE_WRITECOPY )
    return PC_USER;

_DebugOut( "mmPAGEToPC: extra fdwProtect flags\n",
           SLE_WARNING + FStopOnRing3MemoryError );
InternalSetLastError( ERROR_INVALID_PARAMETER );
return -1;
```

VirtualFree

VirtualFree performs the mirror image functionality of VirtualAlloc. (No kidding. Really?) It can change pages from committed to reserved, commited to free, or reserved to free. The first portion of VirtualAlloc checks to ensure that it was passed valid address and size parameters. The address must be below 3GB, and the size must be smaller than the value 2GB minus 4MB (the size of the private application area).

You can pass either the MEM_RELEASE or MEM_DECOMMIT flag to VirtualFree, but not both. MEM_RELEASE causes VirtualFree to call VMM's _PageFree function to decommit (if necessary) and unreserve the entire range of pages. In this mode, you must pass 0 as the size, which causes _PageFree to free the entire block allocated earlier through VirtualAlloc. Passing MEM_DECOMMIT makes VirtualFree call VMM's _PageDecommit to decommit the specified block of pages.

Pseudocode for VirtualFree

```
// Parameters:
//  LPVOID  lpvAddress
//  DWORD   cbSize
//  DWORD   fdwFreeType
// Locals:
//  DWORD   decommitPageSize

    // Is range to free bigger than 2GB-4MB? Fail if so.
    if ( cbSize > 0x7FC00000 )
    {
        _DebugOut( "VirtualFree: dwSize too big\n\r",
                   SLE_WARNING + FStopOnRing3MemoryError );
        InternalSetLastError( ERROR_INVALID_ADDRESS );
        return 0;
    }

    // Are pages in VxD land? If so, something's wrong.
    if ( lpvAddress > 0xBFFFFFFF )
    {
        _DebugOut( "VirtualFree: bad base address\n\r",
                   SLE_WARNING + FStopOnRing3MemoryError );
        InternalSetLastError( ERROR_INVALID_ADDRESS );
        return 0;
    }

    if ( fdwFreeType == MEM_RELEASE )
    {
        if ( cbSize != 0 )
        {
            _DebugOut( "VirtualFree: dwSize must be 0 for MEM_RELEASE\n\r",
                       SLE_WARNING + FStopOnRing3MemoryError );
            InternalSetLastError( ERROR_INVALID_PARAMETER );
            return 0;
        }

        // Unreserve the range of memory.
        return VxDCall( _PageFree, lpvAddress, 0 );
    }

    if ( fdwFreeType == MEM_DECOMMIT )
    {
        if ( cbSize == 0 )
        {
```

```
            _DebugOut( "VirtualFree: dwSize == 0 not allowed with
MEM_DECOMMIT\n\r",
                            SLE_WARNING + FStopOnRing3MemoryError );
            return 1;
        }

        // Calculate how many pages will be affected.
        decommitPageSize = lpvAddress & 0x00000FFF;
        decommitPageSize += cbSize;
        decommitPageSize += 0x00000FFF;
        decommitPageSize = decommitPageSize >> 12;

        return VxDCall( _PageDecommit, lpvAddress >> 12, decommitPageSize, 0);
    }

    _DebugOut( "VirtualFree: bad dwFreeType\n\r",
            SLE_WARNING + FStopOnRing3MemoryError );
    InternalSetLastError( ERROR_INVALID_PARAMETER );
    return 0;
```

VirtualQueryEx

VirtualQueryEx is perhaps one of the niftiest functions in Windows 95. It
provides a wealth of information about the type of memory at a particular
address. For instance, given an arbitrary address in a process's address
space, VirtualQueryEx can tell you which EXE or DLL owns that memory.
VirtualQueryEx is at the heart of the Windows NT PWALK program,
which shows a memory layout map for a given process.

VirtualQueryEx wasn't originally slated to be in the Windows 95 Win32
subset. This came as a shock to developers of system-level programming tools
such as debuggers. Luckily, the Windows 95 developers took heart, perhaps in
part due to persistent whining by yours truly and others, and included
VirtualQueryEx in the Windows 95 API.

VirtualQueryEx fills in a MEMORY_BASIC_INFORMATION structure
with information about a particular address. The structure looks like this:

```
PVOID BaseAddress;
PVOID AllocationBase;
DWORD AllocationProtect;
DWORD RegionSize;
DWORD State;
DWORD Protect;
DWORD Type;
```

The fields of this structure are described in the Win32 documentation. However, one field requires further explanation here. The AllocationBase field sounds pretty dry, but it's usually the most important field of the lot. Technically, it contains the base address of the original memory range allocated by VirtualAlloc. More importantly, when the lpvAddress parameter to VirtualQueryEx falls anywhere within an EXE or a DLL module, AllocationBase is the base address of the EXE or DLL. That is, AllocationBase is the same as the EXE or DLL's HMODULE/HINSTANCE. The PWALK program from the NT SDK uses this bit of knowledge to walk the address space of a process and label the various regions with the name of their owning EXE or DLL. Debuggers can use this capability to figure out which EXE or DLL is associated with a fault address.

VirtualQueryEx is essentially just a call to VWIN32.VXD's Win32 service 40h (VxDCall 0002A0040). This service in turn calls the VMM _PageQuery function. In the DDK, _PageQuery is described as taking a parameter to a MEMORY_BASIC_INFORMATION structure. Perhaps to prevent an inopportune thread switch from returning inconsistent values in the MEMORY_BASIC_INFORMATION structure, VirtualQueryEx grabs the Krn32Mutex upon entry and releases the mutex on exit. It does this with the undocumented KERNEL32 _EnterSysLevel and _LeaveSysLevel functions.

The VWIN32 service 43h, which fills the MEMORY_BASIC_INFORMATION structure, is more than just a wrapper around a _PageQuery call. At this writing, I can't tell exactly what it's doing. However, it appears that this wrapper code needs to know the address of the ring 0 stack for the current thread in the process that's being queried. Therefore, before calling the VWIN32 service, VirtualQueryEx uses the hProcess parameter to get a pointer to the process structure (see the section titled "The Process Database" in Chapter 6). From there, VirtualQueryEx extracts the thread database of the process's current thread to pass to the VWIN32 service. Interestingly, in several step-throughs of VWIN32 service 43h, I never found a case where the code did anything other than call _PageQuery.

Pseudocode for VirtualQueryEx

```
// Parameters:
//  HANDLE  hProcess;
//  LPCVOID lpvAddress; // Address of region.
//  PMEMORY_BASIC_INFORMATION pmbiBuffer;  // Address of information buffer.
//  DWORD   cbLength;   // Size of buffer.
// Locals:
//  DWORD   pProcess;   // Pointer to process structure.
//  DWORD   ptdb;       // Per-thread database.
//  DWORD   retValue;
```

```
// Function that emits function names and parameters to the KERNEL
// debugger if a KERNEL32 global variable is TRUE (off by default).
x_LogKernelFunction( number indicating the VirtualQueryEx function );

_EnterSysLevel( Krn32Mutex );

retValue = 0;

pProcess = x_GetObject( hProcess, 0x80000010, 0 );

if ( pProcess )
{
    if ( ppCurrentProcessId == pProcess )
        ptdb = ppCurrentThreadId;
    else
        ptdb = SomeFunction( pProcess->threadList, 0 );

    if ( ptdb && (lpvAddress < 0xC0000000) )
    {
        // Call into the VWIN32 VxD to do the real work.
        // VWIN32 ultimately calls the VMM _PageQuery function.
        retValue = VxDCall( 0x002A0040, ptdb->ring0_hThread,
                            lpvAddress, pmbiBufer, cbLength );
    }

    x_UnuseObjectSafeWrapper( pProcess );
}

_LeaveSysLevel( Krn32Mutex );

return retValue;
```

VirtualQuery and IVirtualQuery

The VirtualQuery function is just a special case of the VirtualQueryEx function. VirtualQuery retrieves information about a specific addresss in the current process context, whereas VirtualQueryEx works on any process.

The VirtualQuery code does almost nothing of value; it's just a parameter validation layer. VirtualQuery's code merely checks that a pointer to a buffer large enough to hold a MEMORY_BASIC_INFORMATION was passed in. Assuming the test succeeds, VirtualQuery jumps to the start of the IVirtualQuery code. VirtualQuery's validation of the parameters before jumping to an internal routine that does the real work is typical of many functions in the system DLLs (for instance, VirtualProtect, described later).

Other than some logging code in the debug version, IVirtualQuery is nothing more than a call to VirtualQueryEx with the current process's pseudohandle as the first parameter. Note that in Windows 95, IVirtualQuery calls VirtualQueryEx. Contrast this to Win32s, where VirtualQueryEx is just a call to VirtualQuery. The key difference is that all processes share the same address space in Win32s, so VirtualQuery should be equivalent to VirtualQueryEx.

Pseudocode for VirtualQuery

```
// Parameters:
//   LPCVOID lpvAddress; // Address of region.
//   PMEMORY_BASIC_INFORMATION  pmbiBuffer;  // Address of information buffer.
//   DWORD   cbLength;   // Size of buffer.

    Set up structured exception handler frame

    // Make sure that the beginning and end of the MEMORY_BASIC_INFORMATION
    // structure is acccessible.
    *(PBYTE)pmbiBuffer += 0;
    *(PBYTE)(pmbiBuffer+0x1B) += 0;

    Remove structured exception handler frame

    goto IVirtualQuery;
```

Pseudocode for IVirtualQuery

```
// Parameters:
//   LPCVOID lpvAddress; // Address of region.
//   PMEMORY_BASIC_INFORMATION  pmbiBuffer;  // Address of information buffer.
//   DWORD   cbLength;   // Size of buffer.

    // Function that emits function names and parameters to the KERNEL
    // debugger if a KERNEL32 global variable is TRUE (off by default).
    x_LogKernelFunction( number indicating the VirtualQuery function );

    // Let VirtualQueryEx do the real work. 0x7FFFFFFF is the process
    // pseudohandle that GetCurrentProcess() would return.
    return VirtualQueryEx( 0x7FFFFFFF, lpvAddress, pmbiBuffer, cbLength );
```

VirtualProtectEx

The VirtualProtectEx function changes the access protection of a committed page or range of pages. It acts on any process for which you have a process handle. The key difference between VirtualProtectEx and VirtualAlloc is that VirtualProtectEx assumes you've already committed the pages that you're changing access to. VirtualAlloc, on the other hand, allows you to allocate, commit, and specify the access of a page or pages in one shot.

VirtualProtectEx's code is straightforward. Just as with the other virtual functions I've described, it starts out with some error checking. The code verifies that the range to be modified is less than 2GB minus 4MB, and that the starting address is below 0xC0000000. The heart of VirtualProtectEx is the call to VWIN32 service 0x3F. This service ultimately calls VMM.VXD's _PageModifyPermission service. As in VirtualQueryEx, the VWIN32 call for some reason expects a pointer to the ring 0 stack of the current thread for the specified process. There's a chunk of code for determining this ring 0 stack that's identical to what we found in VirtualQueryEx. Also as with VirtualQueryEx, VirtualProtectEx grabs and holds on to the Krn32Mutex during the VWIN32 call.

The VWIN32 service 0x3F call returns the previous state of the altered pages when the call succeeds. However, the state is given in terms of VMM's PC_ flags, rather than the PAGE_ style flags that the caller expects. VirtualProtectEx therefore does a quick conversion. Finally, if the caller specified a pointer to store the old page attributes, the code copies the PAGE_ flags to that location.

Pseudocode for VirtualProtectEx

```
// Parameters:
//  HANDLE  hProcess;
//  LPVOID  lpvAddress;      // Address of region of committed pages.
//  DWORD   cbSize;          // Size of the region.
//  DWORD   fdwNewProtect;   // Desired access protection.
//  PDWORD  pfdwOldProtect;  // Address of variable to get old protection.
// Locals:
//  DWORD   pcFlags;         // Returned from mmPAGEToPC.
//  DWORD   pProcess, ptdb;
//  DWORD   oldProtectFlags

    // Function that emits function names and parameters to the KERNEL
    // debugger if a KERNEL32 global variable is TRUE (off by default).
    x_LogKernelFunction( number indicating the VirtualProtectEx function );
```

```
if ( cbSize > 0x7FC00000 )
{
    _DebugOut( "VirtualProtect: dwSize too big\n\r",
               SLE_WARNING + FStopOnRing3MemoryError );
    InternalSetLastError( ERROR_INVALID_ADDRESS );
    return 0;
}

if ( lpvAddress > 0xBFFFFFFF )
{
    _DebugOut( "VirtualProtect: bad base address\n\r",
               SLE_WARNING + FStopOnRing3MemoryError );
    InternalSetLastError( ERROR_INVALID_ADDRESS );
    return 0;
}

pcFlags = mmPAGEtoPC( fdwNewProtect );
if ( pcFlags == -1 )                    // Were invalid flags passed?
    return 0;

_EnterSysLevel( Krn32Mutex );

pProcess = x_GetObject( hProcess, 0x80000010, 0 );
if ( !pProcess )
{
    _LeaveSysLevel( Krn32Mutex );
    _DebugOut( "VirtualProtectEx: Invalid process handle\n",
               SLE_WARNING + FStopOnRing3MemoryError );
    InternalSetLastError( ERROR_INVALID_PARAMETER );
    return 0;
}

if ( pProcess == ppCurrentProcessId )
    ptdb = ppCurrentThreadId;
else
    ptdb = SomeFunction( pProcess->threadList, 0 );

if ( ptdb && (lpvAddress < 0xC0000000) )
{
    // Call into the VWIN32 VxD to do the real work. The VWIN32
    // service calls VMM's _PageModifyPermissions.
    oldProtectFlags = VxDCall( 0x002A003F, ptdb->ring0_hThread,
                               lpvAddress, cbSize, 0, pcFlags );
}
else
{
```

```
        oldProtectFlags = some uninitialized local variable;  // ???
    }

    x_UnuseObjectSafeWrapper( pProcess );

    _LeaveSysLevel( Krn32Mutex );

    if ( oldProtectFlags == -1 )
    {
        _LeaveSysLevel( Krn32Mutex );
        _DebugOut( "VirtualProtect: ModifyPagePermission failed\n",
                   SLE_WARNING + FStopOnRing3MemoryError );
        InternalSetLastError( ERROR_INVALID_PARAMETER );
        return 0;
    }

    // This section is sort of a quick-and-dirty "PCPAGETomm". It converts
    // the PC_ flags returned by the VWIN32 service into MEM_ flags.
    if ( oldProtectFlags & PC_USER )    // PC_USER flag set
    {
        if ( oldProtectFlags & PC_WRITEABLE )
            oldProtectFlags = PAGE_READWRITE;
        else
            oldProtectFlags = PAGE_READONLY;
    }
    else                                    // PC_USER flag not set
        oldProtectFlags = PAGE_NOACCESS;

    // If the caller specified a pointer to a DWORD as the last param,
    // fill it in with the old flag's value.
    if ( pfdwOldProtect )
        *pfdwOldProtect = oldProtectFlags;
```

VirtualProtect and IVirtualProtect

VirtualProtect is a simplified version of VirtualProtectEx that works with only the current process. The VirtualProtect code is just the validation layer, with the real code in IVirtualProtect. The only validation performed in VirtualProtect (as opposed to the checks in VirtualProtectEx) is to determine whether the pfdwOldProtect pointer is either a valid DWORD pointer or 0.

The IVirtualProtect code is just a wrapper around a call to Virtual-ProtectEx. The hProcess it passes is the pseudohandle that represents the current process (0x7FFFFFFF). In the debug version, IVirtualProtect also calls a function that logs certain API calls to the debug terminal.

Pseudocode for VirtualProtect

```
// Parameters:
//   LPVOID   lpvAddress;     // Address of region of committed pages.
//   DWORD    cbSize;         // Size of the region.
//   DWORD    fdwNewProtect;  // Desired access protection.
//   PDWORD   pfdwOldProtect; // Address of variable to get old protection.

    Set up structured exception handler frame

    // If nonzero, verify that the pointer to DWORD where the previous
    // protection flags will be stored is valid.
    if ( pfdwOldProcect )
        EAX = *pfdwOldProtect;

    Remove structured exception handler frame

    goto IVirtualProtect;
```

Pseudocode for IVirtualProtect

```
// Parameters:
//   LPVOID   lpvAddress;     // Address of region of committed pages.
//   DWORD    cbSize;         // Size of the region.
//   DWORD    fdwNewProtect;  // Desired access protection.
//   PDWORD   pfdwOldProtect; // Address of variable to get old protection.

    // Function that emits function names and parameters to the KERNEL
    // debugger if a KERNEL32 global variable is TRUE (off by default).
    x_LogKernelFunction( number indicating the VirtualProtect function );

    // Let VirtualProtectEx do the real work. 0x7FFFFFFF is the value that
    // GetCurrentProcess() would return.
    return VirtualProtectEx( 0x7FFFFFFF, lpvAddress, cbSize, fdwNewProtect,
                            pfdwOldProtect );
```

VirtualLock and VirtualUnlock

The VirtualLock and VirtualUnlock functions aren't implemented in
Windows 95. In Win32 platforms that do support them (that is, Windows
NT), they allow a process to pagelock a range of pages. The system guarantees

that physical RAM will always be assigned to those pages. This is useful for situations where you can't afford a page fault (such as a time-critical device driver).

In Windows 95, both VirtualLock and VirtualUnlock jump to the CommonUnimpStub code. CommonUnimpStub is a short section of code that all unimplemented Win32 APIs are supposed to go through. The effect of CommonUnimpStub is twofold. First, in the debug version, KERNEL32 emits a diagnostic to the debug terminal. For instance:

```
*** Unimplemented Win32 API: VirtualLock
```

The second thing CommonUnimpStub does is to clear the appropriate number of parameters off the stack. In the case of VirtualLock/Unlock, it's 8 bytes. Because CommonUnimpStub handles APIs that have various numbers of parameters, the number of bytes to be popped off needs to be given to CommonUnimpStub. This is accomplished through a value placed in the CL register. The value placed in CL is a bitfield encoding, rather than the number of bytes to pop off.

Pseudocode for VirtualLock

```
EAX = "VirtualLock"
CL = 12
JMP CommonUnimpStub
```

Pseudocode for VirtualUnlock

```
EAX = "VirtualUnlock"
CL = 12
JMP CommonUnimpStub
```

THE WIN32 HEAP FUNCTIONS

In Win32, Microsoft has finally put fairly decent heap management code in the operating system. The DOS memory allocation scheme created blocks that were often too big, and was too slow for general use as a heap. In Win16, the GlobalAlloc function has a minimum allocation size of 20h bytes, and runs out of the 8192 selectors too quickly. The Win16 LocalHeap functions are somewhat suited for small allocations, but are limited to allocating at most 64KB from a heap. In addition, there's no support for leak tracking or memory overrun detection in these functions.

The Win32 heap functions are far superior to the allocation schemes of prior Microsoft operating systems. In the retail build of Windows 95, the overhead per-block is only 4 bytes, and you can create a heap up to a theoretical maximum size of 2GB minus 4MB. In addition, Windows 95's Win32 heaps maintain four separate free lists for blocks of varying sizes to prevent excessive fragmentation. Yet another advantage of Windows 95's Win32 heaps occurs only in the debug version. In this mode, each allocated block is tagged with additional information that enables you to easily find overruns, memory leaks, and who allocated the memory. See the description for in-use blocks in the debug version of Windows 95 later for more information on how this additional information is used. Unfortunately, the only way to enable heap block overrun checking is by using an obscure, Windows 95-only function called HeapSetFlags. At the time of this writing, this function doesn't appear in any Microsoft documentation that I've seen, but I've been told it will be forthcoming. I described the HeapSetFlags function in my October 1995 *Microsoft System's Journal* column. (I found out about the HeapSetFlags function too late to include a description of it in this chapter.)

In addition to these nifty features, Windows 95 allows applications to support multiple heaps in the same process. This makes it convenient to group all your memory allocations of a certain type in one heap. (This is often a good strategy for avoiding heap fragmentation.) Because Windows 95 supports multiple heaps, you always have to pass a heap handle to the Win32 heap functions. The heap handle identifies which heap you want to operate on. This heap handle turns out to be nothing more than the linear address of the start of the specified heap.

Yet another nice feature of Windows 95's heaps is that they can grow beyond their initial reserved size if you want them to. In this situation, KERNEL32 allocates additional blocks of linear address space and associates the block with the heap. I call these additional memory blocks *subheaps*. Figure 5-7 shows an admittedly complex process heap setup that contains multiple heaps, with some of the heaps using subheaps.

The list of Win32 heap functions include HeapAlloc, HeapFree, and HeapReAlloc. You'd think that just these basic functions would be a natural choice for compiler vendors who need to implement the malloc, realloc, free, new, and delete functions. This isn't the case though. Both Borland and Microsoft bypass the Win32 heap functions in their runtime libraries in favor of their own heap implementations. One notable exception is the Win32 SDK runtime library (CRTDLL.DLL). The malloc and free functions in CRTDLL.DLL use HeapAlloc and HeapFree, respectively. Different versions of CRTDLL ship with Windows NT and Windows 95.

Update: As this book was going to press, I found that Visual C++ 4.0 uses the Win 32 heap functions for its C/C++ runtime heap.

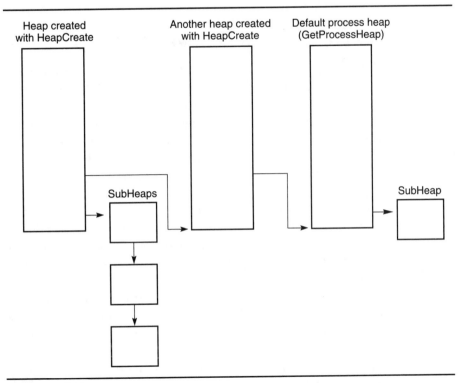

Heap created with HeapCreate

Another heap created with HeapCreate

Default process heap (GetProcessHeap)

SubHeaps

SubHeap

Figure 5-7
A process with multiple Win32 heaps.

In the layer above Windows 95's Win32 heap services, you'll find the GlobalAlloc and LocalAlloc functions. GlobalAlloc and LocalAlloc are implemented in terms of the HeapAlloc family of functions. LocalAlloc isn't just a wrapper around HeapAlloc though. The reason for this is that Win16 programmers played some nasty games with LocalAlloc'ed blocks such that the Windows 95 Win32 version of LocalAlloc needs to remain backward compatible. I'll describe this in detail in the upcoming section, "The Win32 Local and Global Heap Functions." Moving downward to the layer below Windows 95's Win32 heap function, the code directly uses the memory management Win32 VxD services provided by VMM. However, I didn't see anything in these functions that couldn't have been implemented with the virtual functions I've already described. For this reason, I think of the Win32 heap functions as being a layer atop the Win32 virtual memory functions. Interestingly, the VMM _HeapXXX functions that provide heap functionality to VxDs use the same format for the heap structures that KERNEL32 uses for ring 3 processes.

The Win32 heap header and heap arenas

All the components of a Windows 95 heap are created from regions of memory reserved through the VMM _PageReserve WIN32 VxD service. The heap region is divided into two sections. At the start of the heap region is a header. This header (which we'll get to shortly) contains the information for managing the heap, such as the free lists, the size of the heap, and the heap creation flags. Immediately following the heap header are the heap's memory blocks. Each heap block begins with an arena structure that contains information about the block that follows. The start of each heap block is contiguous with the end of the preceding block. The blocks extend to the end of the allocated heap region, although not every page in the heap region needs to be physically committed. Figure 5-8 shows a typical heap layout.

As mentioned, every heap block, be it free or in-use, starts with a standard arena structure. The format of the arena differs between the debug and release builds of Windows 95. In addition, additional fields are present if the block is a free block. This leads to four variations in the arena layout: retail free, retail in-use, debug free, and debug in-use. The first field, however, is common to all arenas.

Every heap arena starts with a DWORD that contains the size of the block. The size includes the space taken up by the arena itself. However, you can't simply take the first DWORD in an arena and use it as the block size. Why not? Because some of the bits in the arena's first DWORD are used for items unrelated to the block's size. The high byte of this DWORD is always 0xA0. The meaning of 0xA0 isn't clear. My guess is that it's a bit pattern that allows KERNEL32 to tell whether an arena has been overwritten. The other bits not used for holding the block size come about because the size of all heap blocks is always a multiple of 4 bytes. This frees up the bottom 2 bits (values 1 and 2) for use as flags. The meaning of these flags are:

1 — The block is free. A 0 value for this bit indicates that the block is allocated.

2 — The block preceding this block is free. This bit should end up being set only in allocated blocks. When the current block is freed, it can be coalesced with the preceding free block. If this bit isn't set, the preceding block isn't free, so there's no need to attempt to coalesce the blocks.

Taking all these bits into consideration, it's easy to figure out the size of a heap block. Simply do a bitwise AND of the arena's first DWORD with the value 0x5FFFFFFC. This turns off all the bits in the DWORD not used for the size. An easier way to think of this in C notation is to do a logical AND of the first arena DWORD with ~0xA0000003. To figure out how much memory in the block is available for use by the calling program, simply subtract the size of the arena from the size of the block.

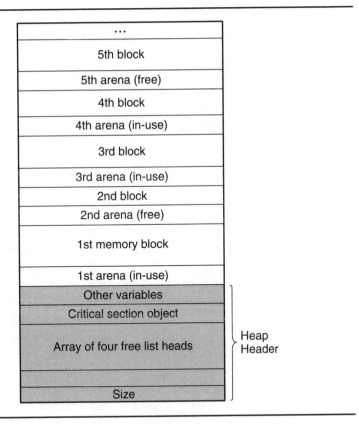

Figure 5-8
A typical Win32 heap.

In-Use Blocks in the Retail Version of Windows 95

In-use blocks in the retail build of Windows 95 have the simplest format of four arena types:

```
DWORD    size             // OR'ed with 0xA0000000 or 0xA0000002.
```

In other words, the arena is nothing more than the initial size/flags DWORD.

Free Blocks in the Retail Version of Windows 95

Free blocks in the retail build of Windows 95 start out the same as the in-use arena, but they add previous and next fields:

```
DWORD    size             // OR'ed with 0xA0000001.
DWORD    prev             // Pointer to the previous heap arena.
DWORD    next             // Pointer to the next heap arena.
```

In-Use Blocks in the Debug Version of Windows 95

An in-use heap arena starts out like the retail version, but then adds additional fields:

```
DWORD    size             // OR'ed with 0xA0000000 or 0xA0000002.
DWORD    allocating EIP   // The EIP value that called HeapAlloc/HeapReAlloc.
WORD     thread number    // The thread number (not ID) that allocated the block.
WORD     signature        // 0x4842 == "BH"
DWORD    checksum         // A checksum of the previous three DWORDSs.
```

The additional fields aid in tracking down memory overrun and heap corruption bugs. The allocating EIP field stores the program address where the block was allocated. This can be used to pinpoint where a block of code that somehow wasn't free was allocated. The thread number field serves a similar purpose, but identifies which thread allocated it. Note that the thread number isn't the same as a thread ID (which is what GetCurrentThreadId returns). Rather, the thread number is an index into the current list of threads. You can see the thread numbers with the SoftIce/W THREAD command. The signature WORD should always be 0x4842 for an in-use block. If it's not, the arena has probably been corrupted.

The final field of the arena provides a more powerful heap corruption fighter. This field contains a checksum of the preceding three DWORDs in the arena. The algorithm is detailed in the description for ChecksumHeapBlock later in the chapter. Although the checksums are alway maintained, the debug KERNEL32 doesn't automatically verify the checksum — you have to tell it to do so. This feature, called "paranoid heap corruption checking," is toggled on and off by the HeapSet Flags function. In a simple test I wrote, I received the following output after enavling heap checking:

```
hpWalk: bad busy block checksum trashed addr between 560014 and 560020
heap handle=460000
```

Free Blocks in the Debug Version of Windows 95

The Windows 95 free block arenas are a hybrid of the free retail arena and the in-use debug arena. Like the free retail arena, there are previous and next fields. From the debug in-use arena, there's the thread number, signature, and checksum fields. The signature field changes slightly (from 0x4842 to 0x4846), as does the checksum algorithm. There's one DWORD more than the in-use version, so when KERNEL32 checksums the arena, it uses the first four (rather than three) DWORDs.

```
DWORD   size            // OR'ed with 0xA0000000 or 0xA0000002.
DWORD   prev            // Pointer to the previous heap arena.
WORD    thread number   // The thread number (0xFEFE for free blocks).
WORD    signature       // 0x4846 == "FH"
DWORD   next            // Pointer to the next heap arena.
DWORD   checksum        // A checksum of the previous four DWORDS.
```

The Windows 95 heap header

At the start of every heap is a heap header structure. A heap handle such as the one you get back from GetProcessHeap is nothing more than a pointer to the heap header. The primary job of the HeapCreate function (besides reserving memory for the heap) is to initialize the structure. The heap header structure varies in size (but not much in format) in the retail and debug versions of Windows 95. Immediately following the heap header is the first heap block arena. Arena blocks are described in the preceding section.

The Heap Header in the Retail Version of Windows 95

00h   WORD   dwSize

The total size of memory reserved for this heap. The default process heap created for every process has 1MB + 4KB in this field.

04h   DWORD   nextBlock

If HeapCreate is called with the dwMaximum size parameter set to 0, the heap can grow beyond the allocation size specified in the preceding dwSize field. In this case, if the caller requests a block that's too big for the current heap region, KERNEL32 reserves additional regions of memory and sets up subheaps. The subheaps use heap arena blocks, but don't have an entire heap header structure. To keep track of these subheaps, KERNEL32 stores them in a linked list. The head of the list is kept in this field (offset 4) in the primary heap structure. A pointer to the next reserved region is kept at offset 4 in each subheap. When the heap is destroyed, KERNEL32 walks the list of subheaps and frees their pages back to the system.

08h   FREE_LIST_HEADER_RETAIL   freeListArray[4]

To minimize fragmentation and speed up searching for free blocks, each heap header maintains four free lists. There are free lists for blocks less than 0x20 bytes, less than 0x80 bytes, less than 200h bytes, and less than 0xFFFFFFFF. When searching for a new memory block, KERNEL32 begins its search at the start of the best fitting free list. For example, when searching for a block 0x18 in size, KERNEL32 searches the 0x20 bytes and under list first. While looking for a 0x100h byte block, it seaches the 0x200h byte free list first.

The four free lists are represented as an array of four simple structures. Each structure has the following format:

DWORD	maxBlockSize for this list. Contains 0x20, 0x80, 0x200 or 0xFFFFFFFF.
free arena	This arena is for all intents a regular retail free arena, except that the block size is given as 0 bytes (after removing the 0xA0000001 bits). The prev pointer in this arena points to the first free arena. Because the block size is 0 for this arena, the searching algorithm can be very simple yet never select this arena for allocation.

48h   *PVOID*   *nextHeap*

Offset 48h in a retail Windows 95 heap is a pointer to the next heap created with HeapCreate for this process. Note that the next heap is different than the next subheap given in the field at offset 4. The region pointed to by a nonzero pointer in this field (offset 0x48) is a full-fledged heap. This field will be 0 unless the process calls HeapCreate.

4Ch   *HCRITICAL_SECTION*   *hCriticalSection*

This field holds the handle of the critical section used by the heap functions to synchronize access to the heap. Note that this field is not a CRITICAL_ SECTION itself (see the next field). Rather, it's a pointer to an internal data structure that KERNEL32 uses for critical sections. The handle value seems to always match the DWORD at offset 0Ch in the field described next.

50h   *CRITICAL_SECTION*   *criticalSection*

This portion of a heap header contains a CRITICAL_SECTION structure (defined in WINBASE.H). When entering code that needs access synchronization, KERNEL32 passes a pointer to this region to EnterCriticalSection. The structure members of this field are initialized by a call to InitializeCriticalSection during the program startup phase. If you don't need synchronization (for instance, you have only one thread), you can bypass it by passing the HEAP_NO_SERIALIZE flags to HeapAlloc, or HeapCreate, or both.

68h   *DWORD*   *unknown1[2]*

The meaning of this field is unknown.

70h   *BYTE*   *flags*

This BYTE contains the HEAP_ flags that can be passed to HeapCreate:

```
HEAP_NO_SERIALIZE
HEAP_GROWABLE
HEAP_GENERATE_EXCEPTIONS
HEAP_ZERO_MEMORY
HEAP_REALLOC_IN_PLACE_ONLY
HEAP_TAIL_CHECKING_ENABLED
HEAP_FREE_CHECKING_ENABLED
HEAP_DISABLE_COALESCE_ON_FREE
```

The Windows 95 documentation mentions only HEAP_NO_SERIALIZE and HEAP_GENERATE_EXCEPTIONS.

71h   BYTE   *unknown2*

The meaning of this byte is unknown. It may be reserved in case additional
HEAP_ flags are needed.

72h   WORD   *signature*

This WORD contains the signature used to identify a heap. In a valid
Windows 95 heap, it contains 0x4948 ("HI").

The Heap Header in the Debug Version of Windows 95s

The debug version of a Win32 heap header is fairly close to the retail version.
However, the embedded free arena structures are bigger, and there are a few
additional fields. Following is the layout of the debug heap header.

00h   DWORD   *dwSize*

See the description in the preceding section.

04h   DWORD   *nextBlock*

See the description in the preceding section.

08h   FREE_LIST_HEADER_DEBUG   *freeListArray[4]*

The array of four free list headers is the same as the retail version, except
that the free arena portion is a debug arena, rather than a retail arena. The
structure layout is as follows:

DWORD   maxBlockSize for this list. Contains 0x20, 0x80,
                0x200 or 0xFFFFFFFF.

free arena   This arena is for all intents a regular debug free
                arena, except the block size is given as 0 bytes (after
                removing the 0xA0000001 flags).

68h   PVOID   *nextHeap*

See the description in the preceding section.

6Ch   HCRITICAL_SECTION   *hCriticalSection*

See the description in the preceding section.

70h   CRITICAL_SECTION   *criticalSection*

See the description in the preceding section.

88h   DWORD   unknown1[14]

See the description in the preceding section.

C0h   DWORD   creating EIP

This DWORD holds the EIP of the routine that called the internal HPInit function to initialize the heap. It appears to always be set to the location where HeapCreate calls HPInit.

C4h   DWORD   checksum

This field holds the result of XOR'ing the first DWORD of the heap header (the size field) with 0x17761965. Presumably, this helps KERNEL32 detect overwrites in the heap header.

C8h   WORD   creating thread number

The thread number (not the thread ID) of the thread that created this heap. See the description of debug block arenas in the preceding section for a description of thread numbers.

CAh   WORD   unknown2

This WORD appears to be unused.

CCh   BYTE   flags (HEAP_xxx flags)

See the description in the preceding section.

CDh   BYTE   unknown3

See the description in the preceding section.

CEh   WORD   signature (0x4948)

See the description in the preceding section.

The WALKHEAP program

To show the Windows 95 Win32 heap headers and arenas in action, I wrote the WALKHEAP program. Source code for WALKHEAP is on the accompanying disk. WALKHEAP consists of two program files: WALKHEAP.C, which contains code to walk and display a Win32 heap, and HEAPW32.H, which contains structure definitions for the heap headers and arenas. The WALKHEAP program needs to run under the debug version of Windows 95. A similar program on the disk (WALKHP2.EXE) walks the Win32 heaps of the retail build. Yes, I could have walked the heap using the 32-bit TOOL-HELP32 functions, but that wouldn't have been as much fun. Nor would it have been as informative. The TOOLHELP32 functions tend to hide some of the interesting details.

When run without any command line parameters, WALKHEAP walks and displays all its heaps. To make things interesting, WALKHEAP first makes a series of allocations and deletions using the default heap, and also creates a second heap. WALKHEAP can iterate through all the process's Win32 heaps by using the Next Heap field in the header.

If you know the address of a specific heap you want to walk (which must be accessible by the WALKHEAP process), you can pass the address (a.k.a. the handle) of the heap on the WALKHEAP command line. This number should be specified in hex, without any 0x's or h's. For example, I can walk USER's 32-bit window heap like this:

WALKHEAP 81CEC000 (The address will probably be different on your machine.)

Figure 5-9 shows the output from running WALKHEAP without any parameters. The numbers in the Block column are the linear address of the block. Note that the first four blocks shown in a heap are the free list headers and have a size of 0. Also, note that you can walk the free list by following the prev pointers, starting with one of the first four blocks (the free list headers).

```
Heap at 00B60000
size:                          00100000
next block:                    00000000
Free lists:
  Head:00B6000C  size: 20
  Head:00B60024  size: 80
  Head:00B6003C  size: 200
  Head:00B60054  size: FFFFFFFF
Next heap:                     00410000
CritSection:                   1066F7C6
Creating EIP:                  BFF8BAE0
checksum:                      17661965
Creating Thread:               0040
Flags:                         05
                               HEAP_NO_SERIALIZE
                               HEAP_GENERATE_EXCEPTIONS
Signature:                     4948
```

```
Heap Blocks
Block      Stat  Size      Checksum  Thrd
--------   ----  --------  --------  ----
00B6000C   free  00000000  FF3009F6  1066  prev:00B60024  next:00B600D0
00B60024   free  00000000  FF30692B  707F  prev:00B6003C  next:00B6000C
00B6003C   free  00000000  FF30F214  EB00  prev:00B60054  next:00B60024
00B60054   free  00000000  FF438FBB  66F7  prev:00C5F014  next:00B6003C

00B600D0   free  000FEF34  FF4CF8B6  FEFE  prev:00B6000C  next:00C5F014
00C5F004   used  00000010  FF341977  0000  EIP: 00000000
00C5F014   free  00000FDC  FF30E8C2  FEFE  prev:00B600D0  next:00B60054


Heap at 00410000
size:                                     00101000
next block:                               00760000
Free lists:
   Head:0041000C  size: 20
   Head:00410024  size: 80
   Head:0041003C  size: 200
   Head:00410054  size: FFFFFFFF
Next heap:                                00000000
CritSection:                              8153C074
Creating EIP:                             BFF8BAE0
checksum:                                 17660965
Creating Thread:                          0040
Flags:                                    40
                                          HEAP_FREE_CHECKING_ENABLED
Signature:                                4948

Heap Blocks
Block      Stat  Size      Checksum  Thrd
--------   ----  --------  --------  ----
0041000C   free  00000000  FF201A5C  0000  prev:0051002C  next:00410314
00410024   free  00000000  FF3019DC  0000  prev:005100D8  next:00510060
0041003C   free  00000000  FF301A8C  0000  prev:005102A4  next:0051014C
00410054   free  00000000  FF30156C  0000  prev:00510850  next:00510458

004100D0   used  00000244  FF740EBC  0040  EIP: 004015DD
00410314   free  000FFCF0  FFD01B4E  FEFE  prev:0041000C  next:00AE0028
00510004   used  00000010  FF341977  0000  EIP: 00000000
00510014   used  00000018  FF740D41  0040  EIP: 0040147C
0051002C   free  00000018  FF20E7EE  FEFE  prev:00510060  next:0041000C
00510044   used  0000001C  FF740DA5  0040  EIP: 0040149E
00510060   free  00000020  FF20E7B2  FEFE  prev:00410024  next:0051002C
00510080   used  00000024  FF740DC3  0040  EIP: 004014C0
005100A4   used  00000034  FF740DC0  0040  EIP: 004014D1
```

```
005100D8  free  00000038  FF20E6CA  FEFE  prev:0051014C  next:00410024
00510110  used  0000003C  FF740DE8  0040  EIP: 004014F3
0051014C  free  00000040  FF20E73E  FEFE  prev:0041003C  next:005100D8
0051018C  used  00000044  FF740C76  0040  EIP: 00401515
005101D0  used  000000D4  FF740CD8  0040  EIP: 00401529
005102A4  free  000000D8  FF20E326  FEFE  prev:00510458  next:0041003C
0051037C  used  000000DC  FF740CAA  0040  EIP: 00401551
00510458  free  000000E0  FF20E58A  FEFE  prev:00410054  next:005102A4
00510538  used  000000E4  FF740CBA  0040  EIP: 00401579
0051061C  used  00000234  FF740E9C  0040  EIP: 0040158D
00510850  free  00000238  FF20E932  FEFE  prev:00510CC4  next:00410054
00510A88  used  0000023C  FF740EAE  0040  EIP: 004015B5
00510CC4  free  0000032C  FFD41CF2  FEFE  prev:00B5F014  next:00510850
```

Figure 5-9
Output from running the WALKHEAP program.

Now that we've seen the layout of the Win32 heap headers and block arenas, it's time to dive into some pseudocode. In the course of this discussion, we'll see how KERNEL32 creates, manages, and destroys heaps. This pseudocode is for the debug version of Windows 95. The retail build doesn't have nearly as much debugging and sanity checking code, and so it is much more efficient.

GetProcessHeap

The first thing you need to use a Win32 heap function is a heap handle. Most programs use the default process heap created by KERNEL32 when the application is created. You retrieve a handle to this heap by calling GetProcessHeap. The GetProcessHeap function is simple. The function retrieves a KERNEL32 global variable that points to the process database for the current process (see Chapter 6 for details). Inside a process database is the handle (that is, the starting address) of the process's default Win32 heap.

Pseudocode for GetProcessHeap

```
return  ppCurrentProcessId->lpProcessHeap;
```

HeapAlloc and IHeapAlloc

HeapAlloc, as its name implies, is the method by which you allocate a block of memory from a specified heap. The HeapAlloc code is part of the validation layer in KERNEL32.DLL. The real work of allocating the block is handled by IHeapAlloc and HPAlloc (described next). The only validity testing that HeapAlloc does is to check whether the hHeap handle points to a region of memory large enough to hold a heap header. Although the code could verify additional fields, including the signature and checksum fields, HeapAlloc strangely ignores these fields. Assuming the hHeap handle passes the (less than rigorous) test, the function jumps to IHeapAlloc.

Pseudocode for HeapAlloc

```
// Parameters:
//    HANDLE    hHeap
//    DWORD     dwFlags
//    DWORD     dwBytes

    Set up structured exception handler frame

    // Make sure that the hHeap is valid. A heap handle is just a
    // pointer to the beginning of the heap area.
    AL = *(PBYTE)hHeap;
    AL = *(PBYTE)(hHeap + 0xCF);

    Remove structured exception handler frame

    goto IHeapAlloc;
```

IHeapAlloc is just a wrapper around the HPAlloc function (that is, the "real" HeapAlloc). Before calling HPAlloc, though, IHeapAlloc does some manipulation of the dwFlags parameter before passing them on to HPAlloc. The only flags that survive this munging are the HEAP_ZERO_MEMORY and the HEAP_GENERATE_EXCEPTIONS flags. The HEAP_ZERO_MEMORY flag (if it survives) ends up 3 bits higher than it started out.

Pseudocode for IHeapAlloc

```
// Parameters:
//    HANDLE    hHeap
//    DWORD     dwFlags
//    DWORD     dwBytes
// Locals:
//    DWORD     modifiedFlags;
```

```
        // Apparently some apps need a little extra room...
        if ( 0x00400000 bit set in TDB AppCompatibility flags )
            if ( hHeap == ppCurrentProcessId->DefaultHeap )
                dwBytes += 0x10;

    modifiedFlags = dwFlags;
    modifiedFlags &= HEAP_ZERO_MEMORY;
    dwFlags &= HEAP_GENERATE_EXCEPTIONS;
    modifiedFlags << 3;
    modifiedFlags |= dwFlags;

    return HPAlloc( hHeap, dwBytes, modifiedFlags );
```

HPAlloc

HPAlloc is the real HeapAlloc function. The code starts out by checking
whether the size of the requested block is too big. In this case, too big
means 0x0FFFFF98 bytes (approximately 256MB). Next, HPAlloc calls
hpTakeSem, which causes the critical section in the heap header to be
acquired. From this point, no other threads in the process can proceed past
this spot in HPAlloc until the original thread returns from HPAlloc. In the
debug build, hpTakeSem also optionally verifies that the heap isn't corrupted.
Among other things, hpTakeSem can walk the heap and verify the arena
checksums as well as verify that the heap signature (0x4948) is still there.
You toggle this behavior with the HeapSetFlags function, which as I mentioned at the start of the "Win32 Heap Functions" section, was put into
Windows 95 too late in the game to include in this book.

HPAlloc next takes the requested block size parameter and rounds it up
to a multiple of 4 (after also taking into account the required arena size).
The minimum block size is 0x18 bytes, which translates to 8 bytes for the end
user after you subtract the arena. With the block size in hand, HPAlloc then
determines which of the four size-based free lists it should search. After finding the correct list, HPAlloc walks through the list (using the prev pointers
in the free blocks) to find the first block that's of sufficient size.

At this point, let's assume that HPAlloc finds a free block of sufficient
size. HPAlloc then calls hpCarve (which I'll show pseudocode for next). The
hpCarve function examines a block to see whether it's just big enough or
whether it needs to be split into two pieces. If the block needs to be split,
hpCarve handles all the work of creating new arenas, setting up previous

and next pointers, and so forth. One of the blocks hpCarve makes is just big enough to satisfy the needs of HPAlloc. The other block is whatever's left over, and goes into the free list.

After hpCarve returns, HPAlloc turns to the work of initializing the arena fields in the new block. This is a simple series of assignment statements, except for the call to get the EIP of HPAlloc's caller and the call to checksum the first three fields of the arena. Finally, HPAlloc releases the heap's critical section and returns a pointer to the first byte after the arena.

Now let's go back and see what happens when HPAlloc doesn't find a free block in the free list. If the heap is allowed to grow (that is, 0 was specified as the dwMaximumSize parameter when the heap was created), HPAlloc needs to create a subheap. As mentioned, a subheap is a region of memory separate from the original heap that contains additional heap blocks. KERNEL32 keeps track of all these subheaps by keeping them in a linked list. If a subheap needs to be created, KERNEL32 determines its initial size (typically 4MB), and calls VMM to reserve a range of pages. Next, HPAlloc calls HPInit to initialize the heap header of the new subheap. We'll look at HPInit in detail when I describe HeapCreate later. After initializing the subheap, HPAlloc inserts it into the linked list of subheaps. Finally, HPAlloc jumps back to the start of the code that searches the free lists. Presumably, this time a block of sufficient size will be found.

Pseudocode for HPAlloc

```
// Parameters:
//      HANDLE    hHeap        // ebp+0x08
//      DWORD     dwBytes      // ebp+0x0C
//      DWORD     dwFlags      // ebp+0x10
// Locals:
//      DWORD     newSubHeap
//      DWORD     temp;
//      HEAP_ARENA * pArena
//      DWORD     carvedSize;
//      DWORD     commitSizeBytes, commitSizePages;
//      FREE_LIST_HEADER *pFreeList;

    if ( dwBytes > 0x0FFFFF98 )
    {
        _DebugOut( "HPAlloc: request too big\n\r",
                   SLE_WARNING + FStopOnRing3MemoryError );
        InternalSetLastError( ERROR_NOT_ENOUGH_MEMORY );
        return 0;
    }
```

```
    // Grab the heap semaphore. This allows only one thread at a time to
    // be in the heap code so that the heap doesn't get corrupted.
    // In the debug version, with paranoid heap checking enabled, this is
    // where the heap would be walked and checked for corruption.
    if ( !hpTakeSem(hHeap, 0, dwFlags) )
        return 0;

    temp = dwBytes + 13;     // Round up to the next multiple of 4.
    temp &= 0xFFFFFFFC
    if ( temp <= 0x18 )      // Minimum allocation size is 0x18 bytes
        dwBytes = 0x18       // (or 8 bytes after subtracting the arena).

HPAlloc_find_free_block:

    // Figure out which of the four free lists should be searched
    // (based on the size of the requested block).
    pFreeList = hHeap->freeListArray;           // Point at first free list.
    while ( dwBytes > pFreeList->dwMaxBlockSize )
        pFreeList++;         // Advance to next free list.

    // Walk the free list looking for a block that's big enough. If one
    // is found, jump to HPAlloc_split_block. Otherwise, fall through.

    // Are there entries in the free list?
    if ( pFreeList->arena.prev != &hHeap.freeListArray[0].freeArena )
    {
        pArena = pFreeList->arena.prev; // Start at head of free list

        // Scan through the list, looking for a block that's big enough.
        // When we find one, go split it.
        while ( pArena != &hHeap.freeListArray[0].freeArena )
        {
            if ( (pArena->size & 0x0FFFFFFC) < dwBytes )
                goto HPAlloc_split_block;

            // Not big enough. Go on to next (previous) block in free list.
            pArena = pArena->prev;
        }
    }

    // If we get here, there's not enough room to satisfy the request.
    // If the HEAP_FREE_CHECKING_ENABLED flag wasn't specified when the
    // heap was created, display a message and then bail out. The
    // HEAP_FREE_CHECKING_ENABLED flag is set by specifying 0 as the
    // dwMaximumSize param to HeapCreate.
    if ( ! (hHeap->flags & HEAP_FREE_CHECKING_ENABLED) )
    {
```

```
        _DebugOut( "HPAlloc: not enough room on heap\n",
                    SLE_WARNING + FStopOnRing3MemoryError );
        InternalSetLastError( ERROR_NOT_ENOUGH_MEMORY );
        goto HPAlloc_error;
    }


    // If we get here, there wasn't enough room to satisfy the heap, but
    // HEAP_FREE_CHECKING_ENABLED was specified (the dwMaximumSize param
    // was 0). Therefore, KERNEL32 can try to extend the heap by
    // allocating more virtual memory. The normal size of these new
    // subheaps is 4MB.
    if ( dwBytes <= 0x400000 )
        commitSizeBytes = 0x400000;


    commitSizePages = commitSizeBytes >> 12;     // Convert bytes to pages.


    // Reserve the memory for the new subheap. Check the hHeap value
    // to see if it should be in app private memory or in shared memory.
    newSubHeap = VxDCall( _PageReserve,
                        hHeap > 0x80000000 ? PR_SHARED : PR_PRIVATE,
                        commitSizePages, PR_STATIC );


    if ( newSubHeap == -1 )              // Oops! The reserve failed.
    {
        _DebugOut( "HPAlloc: reserve failed\n",
                    SLE_WARNING + FStopOnRing3MemoryError );
        InternalSetLastError( ERROR_NOT_ENOUGH_MEMORY );
        goto HeapAlloc_error
    }


    // Go initialize the new subheap. If the init fails, free the memory.
    if ( !HPInit(hHeap, newSubHeap, commitSizeBytes, hHeap->flags & 0x0100) )
    {
        VxDCall( _PageFree, newSubHeap, 0x10 );
        goto HeapAlloc_error;
    }


    // Insert the newly allocated subHeap in the linked list of subHeaps.
    newSubHeap->next = hHeap->next;
    hHeap->next = newSubHeap;


    // Go back and start the search again.
    goto HPAlloc_find_free_block;

HPAlloc_split_block:
```

```
        // If we get here, we've found a free block that's either just big
        // enough or too big. If necessary, hpCarve splits the block into
        // two blocks, one of which is just big enough for the allocation.
        dwBytes = hpCarve( hHeap, pArena, dwBytes, dwFlags );
        if ( dwBytes == 0 )
            goto HPAlloc_error;

        // Start filling in the fields of the new block's arena.
        pArena->size = carvedSize | 0xA0000000;
        pArena->signature = "BH";                    // "BH" = 0x4842
        pArena->calling_EIP = x_GetCallingEIP();

        if ( ppCurrentThreadId )
            pArena->threadID = ppCurrentThreadId->processID->CurrentThreadOrdinal;
        else
            pArena->threadID = 0;

        pArena->checksum = ChecksumHeapBlock(pArena, 3);    // Checksum the block.

        x_hpReleaseSem( hHeap, dwFlags );   // Release the heap semaphore.

        return pArena+0x10; // Return first address following the arena struct.


HPAlloc_error:
        // If we get here, something went wrong.

        // Release the heap semaphore.
        x_hpReleaseSem( hHeap, dwFlags );

        // If the HEAP_GENERATE_EXCEPTIONS flag is set in the heap header
        // or dwFlags param, make a STATUS_NO_MEMORY exception.
        if ( (hHeap->flags | dwFlags) & HEAP_GENERATE_EXCEPTIONS )
            x_RaiseException( STATUS_NO_MEMORY, 0, 1, &dwBytes );

        return 0;
```

hpCarve

hpCarve takes a free block from the HPAlloc function and splits it into two pieces. The first of the two resultant blocks must be the size that the caller (HPAlloc) requested. hpCarve begins with some validity testing code that makes sure the block isn't smaller than the requested size. The second test is to make sure the block to be split isn't already in use.

The majority of the hpCarve code is straightforward and easy to follow. It is mostly a matter of setting up a new free block arena and making sure all the previous and next pointers are set up. The pseudocode shows all the details.

What's more interesting than the general hpCarve code is the memory committing code. As we saw previously in the HPAlloc code (and you'll see later in HeapCreate), the Win32 heaps are sparse. That is, all the memory in the limits of the heap is reserved but not committed. It would be wasteful to have a 1MB heap and commit 1MB of physical memory to it if 1MB wasn't needed. However, when a process touches a reserved but not committed page, a page fault results. Therefore, the heap functions need to make sure to commit all pages that an in-use block will use. hpCarve is where this happens.

When splitting a block into two, hpCarve has to commit all the pages that the first block spans. In addition, hpCarve creates (and writes to) a new arena for the second block (the "remainder"), so that page must be committed as well. The committing is performed by the hpCommit function. hpCommit determines the status of the memory pages and, if necessary, calls the VMM _PageCommit Win32 service. If you thought that Windows 95 used structured exception handling to commit pages in the heap as necessary, you guessed wrong! (At least in the debug build of Windows 95.)

After the "remainder" block's arena has been set up, hpCarve initializes the first of the split block pieces with a constant value. (That's why hpCarve didn't set its arena fields.) If the HEAP_ZERO_MEMORY was passed to HeapAlloc, hpCarve sets the block to 0's. Otherwise, hpCarve sets the block to 0xCC's, which are the breakpoint opcode. The caller of hpCarve is responsible for creating the arena structure at the beginning of the carved block.

Pseudocode for hpCarve

```
// Parameters:
//      HANDLE hHeap        // ebp+08
//      HEAP_ARENA * pArena // ebp+0c
//      DWORD   dwBytes     // ebp+10
//      DWORD   dwFlags     // ebp+14
// Locals:
//      DWORD   myLocal
//      DWORD   currBlockSize
//      DWORD   startCommitPage, endCommitPage, pagesToCommit
//      HEAP_ARENA *pNextArena

    // Get the size of the block that's about to be split. Mask
    // the 0xA0000003 bits to get the actual size.
    currBlockSize = pArena->size & 0x0FFFFFFC;
```

```
if ( dwBytes > currBlockSize )
{
    _DebugOut( "hpCarve: carving out too big a block\n", SLE_ERROR );
}

if ( 0 == (pArena->size & 1) )        // Check the "block in use" flag.
{
    _DebugOut( "hpCarve: target not free\n", SLE_ERROR );
}

endCommitPage1 = ((DWORD)pArena + currBlockSize - 4) >> 12;

startCommitPage = (pArena + 0x1013) >> 12;

// At this point, the code checks to see if the block being carved
// is the same size (or only slightly bigger) than the requested block
// size. If so, it doesn't make sense to make two separate blocks.
// The "if" portion of the following code handles the case where the
// block being split is large enough to warrant making two blocks.
// The first of the resulting two blocks will be the block of size
// dwBytes. The remaining memory will go into a new free block.

if ( (dwBytes + 0x18) <= currBlockSize )
{
    endCommitPage2 = (pArena + dwBytes + 0x13) >> 12;

    if ( endCommitPage2 == endCommitPage1 )
        endCommitPage2--;

    pagesToCommit = endCommitPage2 - startCommitPage + 1

    // hpCommit ultimately calls VMM's _PageCommit Win32 service
    // to commit the page.
    if ( !hpCommit(startCommitPage, pagesToCommit, hHeap->flags) )
        return 0;

    // Set up the new arenas.
    pArena->prev->next = pArena->next;
    pArena->next->prev = pArena->prev;
    pArena->prev->freeBlockChecksum = ChecksumHeapBlock( pArena->prev, 4 );
    pArena->next->freeBlockChecksum = ChecksumHeapBlock( pArena->next, 4 );

    // Make a new free block starting "dwBytes" into the block we're
    // splitting. hpFreeSub is the same routine used by HeapFree.
    hpFreeSub( hHeap, pArena + dwBytes, currBlockSize - dwBytes, 0 );
}
```

```
else    // The block isn't large enough to warrant making two blocks.
{
    // hpCommit ultimately calls VMM's _PageCommit Win32 service
    // to commit the page.
    if ( !hpCommit(startCommitPage, endCommitPage1-startCommitPage,
                   hHeap->flags))
        return 0;

    pArena->prev->next = pArena->next;
    pArena->next->prev = pArena->prev;
    pArena->prev->freeBlockChecksum = ChecksumHeapBlock( pArena->prev, 4 );
    pArena->next->freeBlockChecksum = ChecksumHeapBlock( pArena->next, 4 );

    // The next arena is for an in-use block. (If it weren't in use,
    // it would have been coalesced with this block.)
    pNextArena = pArena + currBlockSize;
    HIBYTE(pNextArena->size) &= 0xFD;
    pNextArena->checksum = x_ChecsumBlock( pNextArena, 3 );
}

if ( dwFlags & 0x40  )                    // 0x40 == HEAP_ZERO_MEMORY << 3
    memset( pArena, 0, dwBytes );         // Zero fill the block.
else
    memset( pArena, 0xCC, dwBytes );      // Fill the blocks with 0xCC's.

return dwBytes;
```

ChecksumHeapBlock

ChecksumHeapBlock is the last routine we're going to look at with regard
to HeapAlloc-related functions. ChecksumHeapBlock is used only in the
debug build of Windows 95. It takes a pointer to the start of an arena and
the number of DWORDS to use. ChecksumHeapBlock is told to process
three DWORDs for an in-use block, and four DWORDs for a free block.
Starting with an initial value of 0, ChecksumHeapBlock XOR's each successive DWORD into a checksum DWORD. Finally, ChecksumHeapBlock
XOR's the checksum DWORD with 0x17751965 and returns the result.

Pseudocode for ChecksumHeapBlock

```
// Parameters:
//      DWORD   count   // Number of contiguous DWORDs to checksum.
//      PDWORD  pBlock  // Starting address to checksum.
// Locals:
//      DWORD   accumulator, i;

    accumulator = 0;

    for ( i=0; i < count; i++ )
        accumulator ^= pBlock[i];    // XOR the accumulator with the next
                                     // DWORD in the block;

    accumulator ^= 0x17761965;    // 1776 == U.S. Independence?
                                  // 1965 == year of birth of an MS programmer?
    return accumulator;
```

HeapSize and IHeapSize

HeapSize takes a pointer to a previously-allocated block and returns the size of the block (not counting the arena).

The HeapSize code is just a parameter-validation layer that validates the passed-in parameter before JMPing to IHeapSize. The IHeapSize code starts by subtracting 0x10 from the lpMem pointer to get a pointer to the block's arena — or so we hope! Next, IHeapSize grabs the heap's critical section to prevent an untimely thread switch from giving invalid results. The meat of IHeapSize is simply to take the arena's size field, AND off the 0xA0000003 bits, and then subtract 0x10. Subtracting 0x10 takes into the account the arena size so that the return value is the amount of memory usable by the caller. Finally, IHeapSize gives up the heap's critical section and returns the block size (minus the arena).

Pseudocode for HeapSize

```
// Parameters:
//    HANDLE    hHeap
//    DWORD     dwFlags
//    DWORD     lpMem

    Set up structured exception handler frame
```

```
// Make sure that the hHeap is valid. A heap handle is just a
// pointer to the beginning of the heap area.
AL = *(PBYTE)hHeap;
AL = *(PBYTE)(hHeap + 0xCF);

// Verify that the lpMem parameter points to valid memory.
AL = *(LPBYTE)(lpMem+0x7)
AL = *(LPBYTE)(lpMem-0x10);

Remove structured exception handler frame

goto IHeapSize;
```

Pseudocode for IHeapSize

```
// Parameters:
//     HANDLE    hHeap
//     DWORD     dwFlags
//     LPCVOID   lpMem
// Locals:
//       HEAP_ARENA * pArena
//       DWORD size;

   pArena = lpMem - 0x10;

   // Grab the heap semaphore. This allows only one thread at a time to
   // be in the heap code so that the heap doesn't get corrupted.
   if ( hpTakeSem(hHeap, lpMem, dwFlags) )
       return 0;

   // Get the size field from the arena, get rid of the 0xA0000000 flags,
   // and subtract 0x10 (to subtract out the size of the arena).
   size = (pArena->size & 0x0FFFFFFC) - 0x10;

   x_hpReleaseSem( hHeap, dwFlags );

   return size;
```

HeapFree and IHeapFree

HeapFree is yet another function that's really just a parameter validation stub. HeapFree checks that the hHeap handle points at valid memory large enough to hold a heap header. The code also tests that the lpMem pointer points to what could be a valid heap block pointer. There should be a 0x10 byte arena preceding the lpMem parameter, and the lpMem block should be at least 8 bytes long (not counting the arena). HeapFree therefore verifies that memory can be accessed 0x10 bytes before and 0x7 bytes after lpMem. After these tests, HeapFree jumps to a strange routine I call x_HeapFree (described next).

Pseudocode for HeapFree

```
// Parameters:
//    HANDLE    hHeap
//    DWORD     dwFlags
//    LPVOID    lpMem

    Set up structured exception handler frame.

    // Make sure that the hHeap is valid. A heap handle is just a
    // pointer to the beginning of the heap area.
    AL = *(PBYTE)hHeap;
    AL = *(PBYTE)(hHeap + 0xCF);

    // Verify that the lpMem parameter points to valid memory.
    AL = *(LPBYTE)(lpMem+0x7)
    AL = *(LPBYTE)(lpMem-0x10);

    Remove structured exception handler frame.

    goto x_HeapFree;
```

The x_HeapFree routine sits between the HeapFree validation code and the IHeapFree function, which frees the block. It appears that for some reason, not every heap block can be passed straight to IHeapFree. Blocks released by a certain routine seem to need special handling. The job of x_HeapFree is to determine who called it. If not called from a particular address, x_HeapFree jumps to the IHeapFree code. (This is almost always the case.) If x_HeapFree is called from one particular routine (unknown to me at this time), it calls a function that seems to mess around with the block's arena. After this function returns, x_HeapFree jumps to IHeapFree.

Pseudocode for x_HeapFree

```
// Locals:
//      DWORD    returnAddress;

    returnAddress = *(LPWORD)ESP;

    if ( (returnAddress & 0x00000FFF) != some number )
        goto IHeapFree;

    if ( !someFunction( ) )
        goto IHeapFree;

    Munge the return address on the stack so that control returns to
    to x_HeapFreeRet when IHeapFree returns

    goto IHeapFree

x_HeapFree_ret:
```

IHeapFree has two functions. First, if the block immediately prior to the block being freed is itself free, IHeapFree coalesces the blocks. How does IHeapFree know whether the prior block is free? Bit 1 (value 2) in the size field of the block's arena is on if the prior block is free. So how does IHeapFree know how to find the prior block's arena? It turns out that the last DWORD of the prior block's memory is a pointer to the prior block's arena. Thus, IHeapFree just subtracts four from the arena being freed. At that address is a pointer to the prior block in the heap. IHeapFree coalesces the block by calling hpFreeSub for the prior block, telling hpFreeSub that the length of the block is the size of both blocks combined.

The second task of IHeapFree is to invoke hpFreeSub. hpFreeSub is the counterpart to the HPAlloc function. hpFreeSub does the real work of freeing a block back to the heap, and is described next. While this is going on, IHeapFree is holding onto the heap's semaphore, which it grabbed upon entry and released after calling hpFreeSub.

Pseudocode for IHeapFree

```
// Parameters:
//      HANDLE    hHeap
//      DWORD     dwFlags
//      LPVOID    lpMem
// Locals:
```

```
//      HEAP_ARENA * pArena
//      HEAP_ARENA * pPrevArena
//      DWORD   blockSize;

    pArena = lpMem - 0x10;

    // Grab the heap semaphore. This allows only one thread at a time to
    // be in the heap code so that the heap doesn't get corrupted.
    if ( !hpTakeSem(hHeap, pArena, dwFlags) )
        return 0;

    blockSize = pArena->size & 0x0FFFFFFC;

    // Is previous arena free? If so, we'll be coalescing this block
    // with the previous block. This is going to affect the arenas
    // of the previous block's previous/next blocks, so recalculate
    // the checksums.
    if ( pArena->size & 2 )
    {
        pPrevArena = *(PDWORD)(pArena-4);

        blockSize += (pPrevArena->size & 0x0FFFFFFC);

        pPrevArena->prev->next = pPrevArena->next
        pPrevArena->next->prev = pPrevArena->prev

        pPrevArena->prev.freeBlockChecksum
                = ChecksumHeapBlock(pPrevArena->prev, 4);
        pPrevArena->next.freeBlockChecksum
                = ChecksumHeapBlock(pPrevArena->next, 4);

        pPrevArena = pArena;
    }

    // Call hpFreeSub to do the real work.
    hpFreeSub( hHeap, pArena, blockSize, 0x200 );

    // Give up the heap critical section.
    x_hpReleaseSem( hHeap, dwFlags );

    return 1;
```

hpFreeSub

The hpFreeSub function frees a block back to the heap. It's passed the address of the arena to be freed and a length. The function is called from several places, including IHeapFree and hpCarve. The latter use of hpFreeSub is interesting, because the block being freed is part of an already free block.

The hpFreeSub pseudocode is fairly long, so I'll leave it to the pseudocode to show all the details. At a high level, hpFreeSub consists of two distinct portions. The first part of hpFreeSub takes care of decommitting memory if necessary. When a program frees a large block of memory back to the operating system, it doesn't make sense to keep all that memory committed. Thus, hpFreeSub determines whether any memory pages can be decommitted without messing up other blocks in the heap. If there are blocks that fit the criterion, hpFreeSub calls VMM's _PageDecommit Win32 service to free the block. The exception to this rule seems to be when hpFreeSub is called by hpCarve. In this case, hpFreeSub doesn't decommit any pages. Instead, it checks to see whether the affected pages are in a reserved state.

The second part of hpFreeSub takes care of updating the arenas. First, the block after this free block must be an in-use block; otherwise, it would already be part of the block being freed. hpFreeSub therefore turns on bit 1 (value 2) in the next arena's size field, telling the next arena that the previous arena is a free block. Next, hpFreeSub determines which of the size-based free lists the block being freed should go in. After finding the appropriate free list, hpFreeSub scans the list, looking for the right spot to insert the newly freed block. (The free list is kept sorted according to size.) Finally, hpFreeSub writes a new arena for the newly free block. This includes filling in the previous and next fields, and calculating the checksum.

Pseudocode for hpFreeSub

```
// Parameters:
//      HANDLE  hHeap
//      HEAP_ARENA * pArena
//      DWORD   size            // Size to make the free block.
//      DWORD   flags
// Locals:
//      HEAP_ARENA * pNextArena // Arena that immediately follows pArena.
//      HEAP_ARENA * pFreeListArena // Pointer to first arena in the free list.
//      DWORD nextArenaSize;
//      DWORD *myLocal
//      DWORD bytesToblast;
//      PSTR pszError
```

```
//      DWORD startDecommitPage, endDecommitPage1, endDecommitPage2;
//      FREE_LIST_HEADER *pFreeList;

    if ( size < 0x18 )
        _DebugOut( "hpFreeSub: bad param\n", SLE_ERROR );

    endDecommitPage1 = 0x00100000;

    pNextArena = &pArena + size;     // Get a pointer to the next arena.

    if ( pNextArena->size & 1 )
    {
        nextArenaSize = pNextArena->size & 0x0FFFFFFC;

        pNextArena->prev->next = pNextArena->next

        pNextArena->next->prev = pNextArena->prev

        pNextArena->prev->freeChecksumBlock
                = ChecksumHeapBlock( pNextArena->prev, 4 );

        pNextArena->next->freeChecksumBlock
                = ChecksumHeapBlock( pNextArena->next, 4 );

        endDecommitpage1 = (pNextArena + 0x1013) >> 12;

        pNextArena = pArena + size + nextArenaSize;
    }

    // Figure out how many bytes there are from the start of the arena
    // to the end of the containing page. Then round down to the size
    // of the block to free (if less).
    bytesToBlast = 0x1000 - (&pArena & 0x00000FFF);
    if ( bytesToBlast >= size )
        bytesToBlast = size;

    // Fill in the block to be freed with 0xFE's.
    memset( &pArena, 0xFE, bytesToBlast );

    if ( flags & 0x200 )    // True if called from IHeapFree; not true if
    {                       // called from hpCarve.

        startDecommitPage = (&pArena + 0x1013) >> 12;
        endDecommitPage2 = (&pNextArena - 4) >> 12;

        if ( endDecommitPage2 < endDecommitPage1 )
            goto hpFreeSub_modify_arenas;
```

```
        if ( VxDCall( _PageDecommit, startDecommitPage,
                    endDecommitPage2 - startDecommitPage, 0x20000000) )
            goto hpFreeSub_modify_arenas;

        pszError = "hpFreeSub: PageDecommit failed\n"
        goto hpFreeSub_error
    }
    else    // This code is hit when hpCarve is the caller.
    {
        MEMORY_BASIC_INFORMATION mbi;

        startDecommitPage = (&pArena + 0x1013) >> 12;
        endDecommitPage2 = &pNextArena >> 12;

        if ( endDecommitPage2 < startDecommitPage )
            goto hpFreeSub_modify_arenas;

        VxDCall( _PageQuery, startDecommitPage << 12,
                &mbi, sizeof(mbi) )

        // Check that the structure was filled in with values indicating
        // that the range of pages is all reserved.
        if ( (mbi.state == MEM_RESERVE) &&
            ((endDecommitPage2>> 12) <= someStruct[3]) )
                goto hpFreeSub_modify_arenas

        pszError = "hpFreeSub: range not all reserved\n"
    }

hpFreeSub_error:
    _DebugOutput( pszError, SLE_ERROR );

hpFreeSub_modify_arenas:
    *myLocal = pArena;

    // The next block must be an in-use block; otherwise, it would
    // been coalesced already. Turn on the "Previous block is free"
    // bit and redo its checksum.
    pNextArena->size |= 2;
    pNextArena->checksum = ChecksumHeapBlock( pNextArena, 3 );

    // Find the appropriate free list to insert this block into. The free
    // lists are kept as an array of FREE_LIST_HEADER structures starting
    // at offset 8 in the heap structure.
    pFreeList = hHeap->freeListArray;
    while ( size > pFreeList->dwMaxBlockSize )
        pFreeList++;        // Advance to next free list
```

```
// We found the right free list. Now go insert it into the list in
// size-sorted order.
pFreeListArena = &pFreeList->arena;

// Figure out where in the free list this block should go. The blocks
// are kept in size-sorted order.
while ( size > (pFreeListArena->prev.size & 0x0FFFFFFC) )
    pFreeListArena = pFreeListArena->prev;

pArena->prev = pFreeListArena->prev;
pFreeListArena->prev->next = pArena;
pArena->next = pFreeListArena;
pFreeListArena->prev = pArena;

pArena->prev->freeBlockChecksum = ChecksumHeapBlock( pArena->prev, 4 );

pFreeListArena->freeBlockChecksum = ChecksumHeapBlock( pFreeListArena, 4 );

pArena->signature = "FH";    // FH = 0x4846
pArena->freeBlockChecksum = ChecksumHeapBlock( pArena, 4 );
pArena->size = size | 0xA0000001;
```

HeapReAlloc and IHeapReAlloc

HeapReAlloc reallocates an existing block in a Win32 heap. The HeapReAlloc
code is just a parameter validation layer stub. The tests that HeapReAlloc
does are identical to the validations that HeapFree performs. The hHeap
parameter must point to a block of memory 0xD0 bytes in length. The
lpMem parameter must be valid 0x10 bytes before and 0x7 bytes after the
pointer. If the tests pass, HeapReAlloc jumps to IHeapReAlloc.

IHeapReAlloc is a bit odd. Before it calls the HPReAlloc function, the
code rearranges the dwFlags parameters to HPReAlloc's preferences. (Why
the original HEAP_xxx flags passed to HeapReAlloc aren't good enough is
a mystery to me . . .) The only flags that make it past the HeapReAlloc flag
masher are

HEAP_GENERATE_EXCEPTIONS

HEAP_NO_SERIALIZE

HEAP_ZERO_MEMORY

HEAP_REALLOC_IN_PLACE_ONLY

Pseudocode for HeapReAlloc

```
// Parameters:
//      HANDLE  hHeap
//      DWORD   dwFlags
//      LPVOID  lpMem
//      DWORD   dwBytes

    Set up structured exception handler frame

    // Make sure that the hHeap is valid. A heap handle is just a
    // pointer to the beginning of the heap area.
    AL = *(PBYTE)hHeap;
    AL = *(PBYTE)(hHeap + 0xCF);

    // Verify that the lpMem parameter points to valid memory.
    AL = *(LPBYTE)(lpMem+0x7)
    AL = *(LPBYTE)(lpMem-0x10);

    Remove structured exception handler frame

    goto IHeapReAlloc;
```

Pseudocode for IHeapReAlloc

```
// Parameters:
//      HANDLE  hHeap
//      DWORD   dwFlags
//      LPVOID  lpMem
//      DWORD   dwBytes
// Locals:
//      DWORD   modifiedFlags

    modifiedFlags = some contorted mess of calculations with dwFlags.

    HEAP_GENERATE_EXCEPTIONS and HEAP_NO_SERIALIZE are passed through
    unscathed.

    The HEAP_ZERO_MEMORY bit is shifted left by 3.

    If the HEAP_REALLOC_IN_PLACE_ONLY bit is off, bit 1 (value 2) is turned
    on.

    return HPRealloc( hHeap, lpMem, dwBytes, modifiedFlags );
```

HPReAlloc

HPReAlloc contains the core of the HeapReAlloc function. The code in HPReAlloc is fairly lengthy, but it's not hard to figure out. The pseudocode contains all the gory details. From a high-level perspective, HeapReAlloc has four cases to contend with:

- The new block size is smaller than the original block size.
- The new block size is roughly the same as the original block size.
- The new block size is bigger than the original. The next block in the heap is free and can be combined with the original block to make a block sufficiently big in size.
- The new block size is bigger than the original, and the next block isn't free. Alternatively, the next block is free, but isn't big enough to be combined with the original block to satisfy the allocation.

For the first case (the new block is smaller than the original), HPReAlloc uses hpFreeSub to split the original block into two pieces. The first portion is the new block, and the second portion is marked as a free block.

For the second case (the new and original blocks are roughly the same size), HPReAlloc simply leaves the existing block alone. The threshold appears to be around 8 bytes (0x18 bytes if you count the arena).

In the third case (the next block is free and big enough to combine), HPReAlloc figures out how much of the next block it needs. The code then uses hpCarve to split the next free block into two pieces. The first of the two pieces is big enough to combine with the original block to meet the new requested size. The remaining part of the free block becomes a smaller free block.

The final case is when all else fails. In this situation, HPReAlloc tries to allocate a new block of the requested size with HPAlloc. If the allocation succeeds, HPReAlloc copies the contents of the original block into the newly allocated block. Afterward, HPReAlloc calls the internal version of HeapFree to release the original block's memory.

Pseudocode for HPReAlloc

```
// Parameters:
//     HANDLE  hHeap
//     LPVOID  lpMem
//     DWORD   dwBytes
//     DWORD   dwFlags
```

```
// Locals:
//      DWORD     newSize;
//      HEAP_ARENA *pArena, *pNextArena
//      DWORD     nextBlockSize;
//      LPVOID    lpMem2;
//      DWORD     originalBlockSize;
//      PVOID     prevFreeArena

    newSize = dwBytes;

    // Make sure the new size isn't too big.
    if ( newSize > 0x0FFFFF98 )
    {
        _DebugOut( "HPReAlloc: request too big\n\r",
            SLE_WARNING + FStopOnRing3MemoryError );
        InternalSetLastError( ERROR_NOT_ENOUGH_MEMORY );
        goto HPReAlloc_failure;
    }

    // Point at the arena of the block to be reallocated.
    pArena = lpMem - 0x10;

    // Prevent any other threads from coming through here and
    // screwing up the heap.
    if ( !hpTakeSem( hHeap, pArena, dwFlags ) )
        goto HPReAlloc_failure;

    // Round up the requested size by 0x10 bytes (for the arena), and then
    // make sure it's a multiple of 4.
    if ( (newSize + 0x13) & 0xFFFFFFFC < 0x18 )
        newSize = 0x18;

originalBlockSize = pArena->size & 0x0FFFFFFC;

    // Is the new block size + 0x18 less than the original size? If so,
    // we can simply shorten the existing block.

    if ( (newSize + 0x18) <= originalBlockSize )
    {
        // Shorten the existing block by having hpFreeSub make a new arena
        // right past where the realloc'ed block will end.
        hpFreeSub(hHeap, pArena+newSize, originalBlockSize - newSize, 0x200);

        // Update the arena's size field to contain the new size. Leave
        // the high BYTE and bottom 2 bits of the size the way they were.
        // Yes, this is somewhat of a brain twister at first.
        pArena->size = (pArena->size & 0xF0000003) | newSize;

        pArena->checksum = ChecksumHeapBlock( pArena, 3 );
```

```
        goto HPReAlloc_success;
}

// If the new block size is only marginally smaller than the original
// size, just leave the block alone.
if ( originalBlockSize >= newSize )
    goto HPReAlloc_success;

// If we get here, the block is being reallocated to a size bigger than
// it was originally.

pNextArena = pArena + originalBlockSize;    // Get pointer to next arena.
nextBlockSize = pNextArena->size;           // Get size of next block.

// If the next arena is free, we can combine part of it with the
// existing block. Whatever's left over will remain a free block.
if ( nextBlockSize & 1 )        // Is next arena free?
{
    if ( (nextBlockSize & 0x0FFFFFFC) >= (newSize - originalBlockSize) )
    {
        DWORD extraNeeded = newSize-originalBlockSize;

        // Carve out a block big enough to tack onto the existing
        // block. The remainder becomes a new free block.
        if ( !hpCarve(hHeap, extraNeeded, pNextArena, , dwFlags))
            goto HPReAlloc_failure;

        pArena->size = (pArena->size & 0xF0000003) | extraNeeded;
        pArena->checksum = ChecksumHeapBlock( pArena, 3 );
        goto HPReAlloc_success;
    }
}

// If HEAP_REALLOC_IN_PLACE_ONLY wasn't specified, we can alloc a
// new block somewhere else, then copy the original block's contents
// over. Normally, HEAP_REALLOC_IN_PLACE_ONLY isn't specified.
if ( dwFlags & 2 )
{
    // Save some fields of the original arena, because we'll need to
    // copy them into the new block's arena.

    WORD threadID = pArena->threadID;
    prevFreeArena = pArena->prev

    if ( dwFlags & 0x20 )   // This doesn't seem to happen normally.
    {
        HeapFree_special( hHeap, HEAP_NO_SERIALIZE, lpMem );
```

```
            lpMem = HPAlloc( hHeap, newSize, dwFlags | HEAP_NO_SERIALIZE );
            if ( lpMem )
                goto HaveNewBlock;

            _DebugPrintf( "HPReAlloc: HPAlloc failed 1\n" );
            goto HPReAlloc_failure;
        }

        // Allocate a new block of the desired size from the heap.
        lpMem2 = HPAlloc( hHeap, newSize, dwFlags | HEAP_NO_SERIALIZE );
        if ( !lpMem2 )
        {
            _DebugPrintf( "HPReAlloc: HPAlloc failed 2\n" );
            goto HPReAlloc_failure;
        }

        // Copy the contents of the original block to the new block.
        // We subtract 0x10 because we don't need to copy the arena.
        memcpy( lpMem2, lpMem, originalBlockSize - 0x10 );

        // Free the original block.
        lpMem = HeapFree_special( hHeap, HEAP_NO_SERIALIZE, lpMem );

HaveNewBlock:
        // Fill in the arena header of the new block.
        pArena = lpMem - 0x10;

        lpMem->prev = prevFreeArena;
        lpMem->threadID = threadID;
        pArena->checksum = ChecksumHeapBlock( pArena, 3 );
        goto HPReAlloc_success;
    }

    // If we get here, HEAP_REALLOC_IN_PLACE_ONLY was specified, and there
    // wasn't enough memory. Display a warning to the debug terminal.
    _DebugOut( "HPReAlloc: fixed block\n",
            SLE_WARNING + FStopOnRing3MemoryError );
    InternalSetLastError( ERROR_LOCKED );

    // Fall through to failure.

HPReAlloc_failure:
    x_hpReleaseSem( hHeap, dwFlags );   // OK, safe for other threads now.
    return 0;

HPReAlloc_success:
    x_hpReleaseSem( hHeap, dwFlags );   // OK, safe for other threads now.
    return lpMem;
```

HeapCreate

The HeapCreate function is the origin of all Win32 heaps. Every Win32 program has a heap created for it before the application starts. In addition, programs can call HeapCreate to create heaps separate from the default program heap. Besides being used by programs, KERNEL32 itself calls HeapCreate to create heaps in shared memory. It uses these heaps for storing system data structures such as thread and process instance structures. Although not documented, application programs can use this same functionality to make a shared heap by specifing the 0x04000000 bit value in the fOptions flag when calling HeapCreate.

The process of creating a Win32 consists of two parts. HeapCreate handles the high-level details of reserving memory for the heap and linking the heap into the list of process heaps. The other portion of heap creation is initializing all the fields of the heap header. For this task, HeapCreate calls the HPInit function, which I'll describe next.

HeapCreate begins by examining and modifying the input size parameters (if necessary). First, it checks to see whether the dwInitialSize parameter is less than the maximum size parameter. Next, HeapCreate rounds the dwMaximumSize parameter up to the nearest 4KB page boundary. The case where dwMaximumSize equals 0 requires special handling. In this case, the heap can grow as necessary. If the HeapAlloc function can't find enough free memory in the current heap, it can reserve another large chunk of memory and set up a subheap within that block. The HeapCreate code checks whether dwMaximumSize is set to 0, and if so, sets the 0x40 bit (perhaps HEAP_FREE_CHECKING_ENABLED) in the fOptions parameters. The final bit of initial parameter testing is to see whether the 0x04000000 bit was set, indicating that the heap should be in shared memory above 2GB.

After HeapCreate has decided what it should create, it calls VMM's _PageReserve Win32 service to reserve enough linear address space to hold the heap. Assuming that the page reservation came through, HeapCreate calls HPInit to initialize the heap's header fields. After HPInit returns, HeapCreate checks to see whether it's creating the KERNEL32 shared heap and takes some necessary actions. The final part of the HeapCreate code adds the newly created heap to the list of heaps for this process. In the case of the first heap created for a process, the new heap is put at the head of the heap list, which is kept in the process database (see Chapter 6). If the new heap isn't the firstborn heap, HeapCreate puts the new heap at the beginning of the list.

Pseudocode for HeapCreate

```
// Parameters:
//      DWORD   fOptions
//      DWORD   dwInitialSize
//      DWORD   dwMaximumSize;
// Locals:
//      HANDLE  hHeap, hHeap2;
//      DWORD   retValue
//      DWORD   fShared

    retValue = 0;

    // If a nonzero maximum size was specified, make sure it's bigger
    // than the initial size.
    if ( dwMaximumSize && (dwMaximumSize < dwInitialSize) )
    {
        _DebugOut( "HeapCreate: dwInitialSize > dwMaximumSize\n",
                    SLE_WARNING + FStopOnRing3MemoryError );
        InternalSetLastError( ERROR_INVALID_PARAMETER );
        return 0;
    }

    // Round dwMaximumSize up to the nearest page boundary.
    dwMaximumSize += 0xFFF;
    dwMaximumSize &= 0xFFFFF000;

    // Specifying dwMaximumSize == 0 means that the heap is "growable."
    if ( dwMaximumSize == 0 );
    {
        fOptions |= HEAP_FREE_CHECKING_ENABLED;
        dwInitialSize &= 0xFFFFF000;
        dwMaximumSize = dwInitialSize + 0x100000;
    }

    fShared = fOptions & 0x04000000;    // Check for undocumented shared flag.

    // Reserve the memory for the heap.
    retValue = hHeap = VxDCall0(
                        _PageReserve,
                        fShared ? PR_SHARED : PR_PRIVATE,
                        dwMaximumSize >> 12,
                        ((fOptions & 0x80) >> 4) | PR_STATIC );
```

```
    if ( retValue == -1 )    // Did allocation succeed?
    {
        _DebugOut( "HeapCreate: reserve failed\n"
                    SLE_WARNING + FStopOnRing3MemoryError );
        InternalSetLastError( ERROR_INVALID_PARAMETER );

        return 0;
    }

    // Turn off all the flags that we don't care about.
    fOptions &= ( HEAP_FREE_CHECKING_ENABLED | HEAP_GENERATE_EXCEPTIONS |
                HEAP_NO_SERIALIZE );

    // Initialize the data fields of the heap header.
    retValue = HPInit( hHeap, hHeap, dwMaximumSize, fOptions );

    if ( retValue == 0 )     // Did the initialization fail?
    {
        // Unreserve the memory we just reserved.
        VxDCall0( _PageFree, hHeap, 0x10 );

        return retValue;
    }

    // If it's the KERNEL32 heap, make the critical section effective in
    // all processes.
    if ( fShared && HKernelHeap )
        MakeCriticalSectionGlobal( hHeap + 0x70 );

    if ( 0 == ppCurrentProcessId )  // If no current process, we're finished.
    {
        _DebugOut( "HeapCreate: private heap created too early",
                    SLE_ERROR );
    }

    // Insert the new heap at the head of the process's heap list.
    hHeap->nextHeap = ppCurrentProcessId->HeapOwnList;
    ppCurrentProcessId->HeapOwnList = hHeap;

    return retValue;
```

HPInit

The HPInit routine takes care of initializing the fields of a new heap. The heap that HPInit operates on can be either a main heap or a subheap off a main heap. In the latter case, the heap header is significantly smaller.

After some initial boundary condition checking, HPInit calls hpCommit to commit the first page of the heap. Why? Because the heap header will be written at the beginning of the heap's first page. Before this commit, the entire heap region is in the reserved (but not committed) state. HPInit then begins filling in the fields of the heap header. When initializing a normal heap, HPInit has to fill in numerous fields including the heap size, the signature WORD, and the allocating thread ID. If the HEAP_NO_SERIALIZE flag wasn't specified (normally it isn't), HPInit calls InitializeCriticalSection, passing in the address of the CRITICAL_SECTION object in the heap header. HPInit also sets up the array of free list headers at this point.

If HPInit is initializing a new subheap, the initialization is much smaller. In this instance, the heap header consists of only two DWORDs: the size of the heap region and a pointer to the next subheap.

After initializing the heap header fields, HPInit then creates an arena for a zero-length block 4KB from the end of the heap. Because the last page is also initially in the uncommitted state, HPInit calls hpCommit to commit the last page before writing to it. From this, we can deduce that each new heap takes a minimum of 8KB of physical RAM to be committed: 4KB for the first page and 4KB for the last page.

After creating the zero-length sentinel arena 4KB from the end of the heap region, HPInit makes one huge free block. This free block spans the entire range between the end of the heap header and the zero-length sentinel block. For this task, HPInit uses the hpFreeSub function (described earlier). You can see the initial layout of the blocks in a Win32 heap by examining the first heap in the WALKHEAP output shown earlier in the chapter.

Pseudocode for HPInit

```
// Parameters:
//     HANDLE hHeap
//     PVOID  pHeapRegion
//     DWORD  size
//     DWORD  flags
```

```
// Locals:
//      HEAP_HEADER pHeap;
//      DWORD startPage, lastPage;
//      HEAP_ARENA * pLastArena;
//      HEAP_ARENA * pArena, * pArena2;
//      FREE_LIST_HEADER * pFreeListEntry, pFreeListArrayEnd;
//      PVOID pFirstArena;  // Pointer to first byte after HEAP_HEADER.
//      PDWORD pFreeListSize;
// Statics:
//      DWORD freeListSizes[4] = { 0x20, 0x80, 0x200, 0xFFFFFFFF };

    // Make sure the heap base and size are page-aligned.
    if ( (pHeapRegion & 0x00000FFF) || ( size == 0 ) || (size & 0x00000FFF) )
    {
        DebugOut( "HPInit: invalid parameter\n", SLE_ERROR );
    }

    pHeap = pHeapRegion;

    startPage = pHeapRegion >> 12;

    // Commit the first page of the heap. We'll be writing a header there.
    if ( !hpCommit(startPage, 1, flags) )
        return 0;

    if ( !(flags & 0x100) )      // True if called from HeapCreate.
    {                            // Not true if called from HeapAlloc.
        pHeap->nextHeap = 0;
        pHeap->nextBlock = 0;

        pFirstArena = pHeap + sizeof(HEAP_HEADER);

        pHeap->signature = 0x4948;  // 0x4948 = "HI"
        pHeap->flags = flags;
        pHeap->size = size;
        pHeap->checksum = ChecksumHeapBlock( pHeap, 1 );
        pHeap->allocating_EIP = x_GetCallingEIP();

        if ( ppCurrentThreadId )
            pHeap->creating_thread_ordinal
                = ppCurrentThreadId->processID->CurrentThreadOrdinal;
        else
            pHeap->creating_thread_ordinal = 0;

        if ( !(flags & HEAP_NO_SERIALIZE) ) // TRUE if serialization needed.
        {
            if ( HKernelHeap )  // KERNEL heap has already been initialized.
```

```
    {                    // This is typically the case.
        InitializeCriticalSection( &pHeap->criticalSection );
        pHeap->pCriticalSection = a field in pHeap->criticalSection;
    }
    else     // We're creating the KERNEL heap (the first heap).
    {
        pHeap->pCriticalSection = &pHeap->criticalSection
        some critical section init function(&pHeap->criticalSection);
    }
}

pFreeListArrayEnd = &pHeap->freeListArray
                    + (4 * sizeof(FREE_LIST_HEADER));
pFreeListEntry = pHeap->freeListArray;

pFreeListSize = freeListSizes;  // Point to array of free list sizes.

// Build the array of free lists.
while ( pListFreeEntry < pFreeListArrayEnd )
{
    pFreeListEntry->dwMaxBlockSize = *pFreeListSize;
    pFreeListEntry->arena.size = 0xA0000001;
    pFreeListEntry->arena.signature = 0x4846;       // "FH"
    pFreeListEntry->arena.prev = previous free list entry;
    pFreeListEntry->arena.next = next free list entry;
    pFreeListEntry->freeBlockChecksum
        = ChecksumHeapBlock( &pFreeListEntry->arena, 4 );
    pFreeListEntry++;   // Point at next entry in free list array.
    pFreeListSize++;    // Point at next free list block size.
}

// Hook up the first and last free list arenas (the array of four
// arenas near the beginning of the heap that point to four separate
// free lists).

// Point at arena in the first FREE_LIST_HEADER structure.
pArena = &pHeap->freeListArray[0]->arena;

// Point at arena in the last FREE_LIST_HEADER structure.
pArena2 = &pHeap->freeListArray[3]->arena;

pArena->next = pArena2;
pArena2->prev = pArena;
pArena->freeBlockChecksum = ChecksumHeapBlock( &pArena, 4);
pArena->freeBlockChecksum = ChecksumHeapBlock( &pArena2, 4);


}
```

```
else    // TRUE if called from HeapAlloc. We're creating a subheap.
{
    pFirstArena = 8;
}


//
// At this point we're going to write the final arena at the
// end of the last page of this heap region.
//

pHeap->size = size;

pLastArena = pHeap + size - 0x10;
lastPage = pLastArena >> 12;

if ( size > 0x1000 )
{
    if ( !hpCommit( lastPage, 1, flags) )
    {
        // Decommit the starting page (we couldn't commit the last page).
        VxDCall0( _PageDecommit, startPage, 1, 0x20000000 );
        pHeap = 0;
        return 0;
    }
}

// Make the last block in the heap a zero-length in-use block.
pLastArena->size = 0xA0000000;
pLastArena->signature = 0x4842; // "BH"
pLastArena->checksum = ChecksumHeapBlock( pLastArena, 3 );

// Make an in-use block of length 0x10 bytes at the end of the heap.
if ( !(flags & 0x0400) && (size > 0x1000) )    // Comes through here in
{                                              // the typical case.
    size -= pFirstArena;
    size -= 0xFFC;

    pArena = pHeapRegion + size + pFirstArena;

    pArena->size = 0xA0000010;
    pArena->signature = 0x4842; // 0x4842 = "BH"

    pArena->checksum = ChecksumHeapBlock( pArena, 3);

    // Call hpFreeSub on this block.
    hpFreeSub( hHeap, pArena + 0x10, 0xFDC, 0);
}
else
{
```

```
        size -= pFirstArena;
        size -= 0x10;
}

// Make one huge free block out of the the region between the heap
// header and the end of the heap.
hpFreeSub( hHeap, pHeapRegion + pFirstArena, size, 0);

if ( FParanoidHeapChecking )        // Verify the heap?
    hpWalk( pHeap );

return pHeapRegion;
```

HeapDestroy and IHeapDestroy

HeapDestroy is just a parameter validation layer stub. The function that destroys a Win32 heap is in IHeapDestroy. The only validation that HeapDestroy does is the standard (bogus) hHeap validation: Does the heap handle point to a region of memory that's at least 0xD0 bytes long?

Pseudocode for HeapDestroy

```
// Parameters:
//      HANDLE hHeap

    Set up structured exception handler frame

    // Make sure that the hHeap is valid. A heap handle is just a
    // pointer to the beginning of the heap area.
    AL = *(PBYTE)hHeap;
    AL = *(PBYTE)(hHeap + 0xCF);

    Remove structured exception handler frame

    goto IHeapDestroy;
```

Contrary to what you might think, destroying a Win32 heap isn't as simple as freeing the heap's pages back to the operating system. Two things make it more complicated. First, all heaps created without the HEAP_NO_SERIALIZE attribute are in the possession of a critical section object. IHeapDestroy checks to see whether the heap owns such an object and frees it as appropriate.

The other complication in IHeapDestroy is the linked list of heaps. If IHeapDestroy were to simply free the heap's pages, the linked list of heaps for the process would be corrupted. IHeapDestroy handles this by walking through the list of heaps and updating the list as appropriate.

After the chain has been updated, IHeapDestroy calls the VMM _PageFree Win32 service to free the heap's pages. One call to _PageFree may not be sufficient to free all of a heap's pages. Why is this? If the user of the heap has made many allocations or very large allocations, HeapAlloc may have created additional subheaps and added them to the subheap list (offset 4 in a heap header). Therefore, IHeapFree uses a loop to free the primary heap as well as any subheap blocks.

As a final note on HeapDestroy, it's not called by the system when a program exits. Presumably all the heap's memory is freed when the process address space is swept away.

IHeapDestroy proc

```
// Parameters:
//      HANDLE hHeap
// Locals:
//      DWORD   nextSubHeap;
//      DWORD    retValue;
//      HEAP_HEADER_DEBUG pHeap;
//      HANDLE currentHeap;

    EnterMustComplete();    // Prevent us from being interrupted.

    // Grab the heap semaphore. This allows only one thread at a time to
    // be in the heap code so that the heap doesn't get corrupted.
    retValue = hpTakeSem( hHeap, 0, 0);
    if ( !retValue )
    {
        LeaveMustComplete();
        return 0;
    }

    pHeap = hHeap;

    x_hpReleaseSem( hHeap, 0 );

    if ( !(hHeap->flags & HEAP_NO_SERIALIZE) )
    {
        if ( hHeap == HKernelHeap )
        {
```

```
            DestroyCrst( pHeap->pCriticalSection );
            goto elsewhere
      }
      else          //Not the KERNAL32 heap.
      {
          if ( (pHeap->pCriticalSection->Type & 0x7FFFFFFF) != 4 )
              _assert( line number, "..\lmem.c" );

          if ( (pHeap->pCriticalSection->Type & 0x7FFFFFFF) == 4 )
              some critsect deletion function( pHeap->pCriticalSection );
      }
}

if ( ppCurrentProcessId == 0 )
    goto HeapDestroy_free_it;

if ( hHeap == HKernelHeap )          // Is this the KERNEL heap?
    goto HeapDestroy_free_it;

if ( ppCurrentProcessId == HKernelProcess ) // Is this the KERNEL process?
    goto HeapDestroy_free_it;

if ( hHeap > 0x80000000 )        // Is it a shared heap?
    goto HeapDestroy_free_it;

if ( 0 == ppCurrentProcessId->HeapOwnList )     // No heaps in this
    goto HeapDestroy_not_in_list;               // process? Oops!

//
// We have to walk through the list of heaps for this process. After
// we free the heap region, we need to update the linked list of heaps.
//

// Start at the first heap.
currentHeap = ppCurrentProcessId->HeapOwnList;

if ( currentHeap == hHeap ) // Are we destroying the default (main) heap?
{
    // Yes!
    ppCurrentProcessId->HeapOwnList = currentHeap->nextHeap;
    goto HeapDestroy_free_it;
}
```

```
        if ( !currentHeap->nextHeap )          // Hmmm...There are no other heaps.
            goto HeapDestroy_not_in_list;   // How can we free it? Complain!

        if ( ppCurrentProcessId->HeapOwnList->nextHeap == hHeap )
        {
            currentHeap->nextHeap = pHeap->nextHeap;
            goto HeapDestroy_free_it;
        }

        do
        {
            if ( currentHeap->nextHeap == hHeap )
            {
                currentHeap->nextHeap = pHeap->nextHeap;
                goto HeapDestroy_free_it;
            }

            currentHeap = currentHeap->nextHeap;
        } while ( currentHeap->nextHeap->nextHeap );

HeapDestroy_not_in_list:

    _DebugOut( "HeapDestroy: Heap not on list", SLE_ERROR );

HeapDestroy_free_it:

    nextSubHeap = hHeap->nextBlock; // Determine whether there's another
                                    // subheap block chained onto this one.

    // Free the range of memory.
    VxDCall0( _PageFree, hHeap, 0x10 );

    if ( nextSubHeap )        // If there is another block, loop back and
    {                         // unreserve it as well.
        hHeap = nextSubHeap;
        goto HeapDestroy_free_it;
    }

    LeaveMustComplete();     // We can now be interrupted. A lot of good
                             // it'll do though!

    return retValue;     // Value returned from hpTakeSem.
```

HeapValidate

HeapValidate is a Windows NT function that scans a Win32 and checks it for consistency. I see no excuse for it not being in the Windows 95 API when you consider that there is code in hpTakeSem that validates the heap.

See the VirtualLock description for details on how CommonUnimpStub works.

Pseudocode for HeapValidate

```
EAX = "HeapValidate"
CL = F3
JMP CommonUnimpStub
```

HeapCompact

HeapCompact is a Windows NT function that attempts to coalesce free blocks and decommit unused pages in a Win32 heap. It appears that Windows 95 does these things as part of its normal housekeeping, so this function may not be necessary.

See the VirtualLock description for details on how CommonUnimpStub works.

Pseudocode for HeapCompact

```
EAX = "HeapCompact"
CL = 2
JMP CommonUnimpStub
```

GetProcessHeaps

GetProcessHeaps is a Windows NT function that returns an array of heap handles for a process. Strangely, it's not in the Windows 95 API although it would be simple to implement. In fact, the TOOLHELP32 Heap32ListFirst and Heap32ListNext functions give you this information.

See the VirtualLock description for details on how CommonUnimpStub works.

Pseudocode for GetProcessHeaps

```
EAX = "GetProcessHeaps"
CL = 2
JMP CommonUnimpStub
```

HeapLock

HeapLock is a Windows NT function that grabs a Win32 heap's critical section object for the current thread. This is yet another function that was omitted from the Windows 95 API for no justifiable reason that I can think of. The hpTakeSem function that HPAlloc uses appears to do just what you'd expect the HeapLock function to do.

See the VirtualLock description for details on how CommonUnimpStub works.

Pseudocode for HeapLock

```
EAX = "HeapLock"
CL = 1
JMP CommonUnimpStub
```

HeapUnlock

HeapUnlock is a Windows NT function that releases a Win32 heap's critical section object. Like HeapLock, its omission from the Windows 95 API is a real head scratcher. (Class, can you say "Just enough to get by?")

See the VirtualLock description for details on how CommonUnimpStub works.

Pseudocode for HeapUnlock

```
EsAX = "HeapUnlock"
CL = 1
JMP CommonUnimpStub
```

HeapWalk

HeapWalk is a Windows NT function that iterates through all the blocks of a Win32 heap. This API is a wonderful example of the farce that the Win32 API has become. The Windows 95 coders ignored HeapAlloc when defining the Windows 95 API. They left it out because they didn't have time (or so they said). However, after making the decision to omit HeapWalk from the Windows 95 API subset, they added the TOOLHELP32 Heap32First and Heap32Next functions.

See the VirtualLock description for details on how CommonUnimpStub works.

Pseudocode for HeapWalk

```
EAX = "HeapWalk"
CL = 1
JMP CommonUnimpStub
```

THE WIN32 LOCAL AND GLOBAL HEAP FUNCTIONS

The local and global heap functions in Win32 are holdovers from the days of Win16 — there's no need for them in Windows 95. Local heaps were created in Win16 so that applications and DLLs could reach their heap data without requiring a selector change. Likewise, the global heap existed in Win16 because there was no way to allocate large areas of memory without dealing with selectors. Win32 programs under Windows 95 have neither of these limitations, so ideally the Win32 API would have dispensed with the global and local heaps.

As we all know, the Win32 API makes some compromises for the sake of backward compatibility. There are just too many Win16 programs out there that use the global and local heap functions. Removing them from the Win32 API would make porting those apps to Win32 a much more labor-intensive process. Therefore, Microsoft elected to keep these functions around and try to keep the same high-level semantics between the Win16 and Win32 versions of the heap functions.

For the most part, the Windows 95 local and global heap functions are identical. That is, GlobalAlloc and LocalAlloc are both exported, but are found at the same address in KERNEL32.DLL. Likewise, GlobalFree and LocalFree are the same function. Later, in the pseudocode for the functions, I'll point out any differences. In examining Windows 95's implementation, I've found that the common Global/Local functions are referred to by the Local name. I'll follow that convention as well.

One existing code base that makes extensive use of the Win32 local heap functions is the Win16 components of Windows 95. Windows 95's USER and GDI are still in 16-bit code segments, but in many cases use 32-bit pointers for items such as HWNDs, menus, and GDI objects. These objects are kept in Win32 local heaps that reside immediately above the USER and GDI DGROUP segments in memory. Chapter 4 contains more information about the exact layout. The important thing in terms of memory management is that KRNL386 exports 16-bit functions that call up into KERNEL32 to use the Win32 Local heap functions. For instance, the undocumented K209 function (KRNL386 export 209) thunks up to KERNEL32's LocalAlloc function. The 16-bit USER and GDI call K209 to allocate memory for windows, device contexts, and so forth. Likewise, a similar function (K211) calls KERNEL32's LocalFree function.

Win32 local heaps

Local heaps are simpler in Windows 95 than in Win16. The Win32 local heap functions use the underlying Win32 heap code I described earlier. This greatly simplifies the code in the local heap functions. For instance, calling LocalAlloc with the LMEM_FIXED flag is essentially the same as calling the HeapAlloc function. Under the hood, both LocalAlloc and HeapAlloc call the KERNEL32 HPAlloc function.

Another area where the Win32 local heap functions are simpler than their Win16 counterparts comes in the sheer number of local heaps. In Win16, the executable program has its own local heap, as does each of the DLLs it uses (the obvious exceptions are DLLs such as font files). By default Windows 95 processes have only one Win32 local heap. Allocations made through the Win32 local heap API functions come from the default process heap (described earlier). If it weren't for LMEM_MOVEABLE blocks, you could implement LocalAlloc as simply as this:

```
HLOCAL WINAPI LocalAlloc(UINT uFlags, UINT cbBytes)
{
    return (HLOCAL) HeapAlloc( GetProcessHeap(), 0, cbBytes );
}
```

As you'll see shortly in the pseudocode, LocalAlloc with the LMEM_FIXED flag isn't that much more complicated than this hypothetical implementation. The addition of LMEM_MOVEABLE blocks make Win32 local heaps more complicated. You might be asking, "So why implement LMEM_MOVEABLE? Why not just ignore that flag and do the same as the LMEM_FIXED case?" Memory allocated with LMEM_MOVEABLE can't be moved within the heap it was allocated from. Still, KERNEL32 can't just chuck the LMEM_MOVEABLE flag. A lot of apps (including Windows itself) took advantage of the fact that an LMEM_MOVEABLE handle was really a pointer to a pointer to the memory block:

```
pMemoryBlock = *(void *)_LMEM_MOVEABLE_handle;
```

By treating the handle as a pointer and dereferencing it, these apps could get a pointer to the associated memory block without the hassle of calling LocalLock. Although this isn't good programming practice, once it's in widespread use, you have to support it.

The Win32 local heap functions maintain semantic backward compatibility with their Win16 predecessor. If you dereference an LMEM_MOVEABLE handle, you'll get a pointer to the associated memory block. The key difference is that it's a 2-byte near pointer in Win16 but a 4-byte near pointer in Win32. To keep up this facade of Win16 compatibility, the Win32 local heap functions use handle tables, which are nothing new. As I described in Chapter 2 of *Windows Internals,* the Win16 local heap functions use them as well, although with a different format.

Each Win32 local heap handle table keeps information for up to eight local handles. When a program uses more than eight local handles at once, LocalAlloc allocates an additional local handle table for up to another eight handles. The handle tables are allocated from the same heap as the memory blocks they reference. These tables are kept in a linked list to facilitate finding a free handle table entry. The pointer to the head of the handle table list is kept in the process database. A handle table looks like this:

```
struct HANDLE_TABLE          // Size == 0x48 bytes
{
    WORD      signature;          // "LA" (0x414C)

    WORD      cHandleTables;       // Number of previously allocated
                                   // handle tables - 1.
    DWORD     pPrevHandleTable;    // Pointer to previous handle table.

    LOCAL_HANDLE_TABLE_ENTRY    handleEntries[8];
};
```

Each LOCAL_HANDLE_TABLE_ENTRY looks like this:

```
struct LOCAL_HANDLE_TABLE_ENTRY
{
    WORD    signature;   // "BS" (0x5342) if an in-use entry.
                         // "FS" (0x5346) for free entries.
    union
    {
        PVOID   pBlock;     // If in-use: pointer to data block.
        PVOID   pNextFree;  // If free: Points to next free
                            // LOCAL_HANDLE_TABLE_ENTRY.
    } x;

                            // These two fields are valid for in-use blocks.
    BYTE    flags;       // 0x02 == discardable
    BYTE    cLock;       // Lock count of the block.
}
```

When you allocate memory with LMEM_MOVEABLE (or GMEM_
MOVEABLE for that matter), LocalAlloc has to find an available LOCAL_
HANDLE_TABLE_ENTRY slot somewhere in the list of handle tables. After
finding a free entry, it allocates a block of the requested size and puts the block's
address into the pBlock field of the LOCAL_HANDLE_TABLE_ENTRY.
The "handle" that LocalAlloc returns is the address of the LOCAL_HANDLE_
TABLE_ENTRY.pBlock field.

Given that LMEM_FIXED blocks are just a pointer to memory but
LMEM_MOVEABLE blocks aren't, you may be wondering how KERNEL32
knows what type of handle you're using. For instance, you can pass either
LMEM_FIXED or LMEM_MOVEABLE handles to LocalFree. How does
KERNEL32 know which one is which? It's actually easy. Local heap handles
that end in 0, 4, 8 or 0xC are fixed blocks. Local handles that end in 2, 6,
0xA, or 0xE are moveable handles. This difference in handles is by design.
All memory blocks returned by HPAlloc have addresses that end in 0, 4, 8,
or 0xC. To make moveable handles always end in 2, 6, 0xA, or 0xE,
Microsoft put the pBlock pointer two bytes into the LOCAL_HANDLE_
TABLE_ENTRY structure. Incidentally, the Win16 local heap handle tables
have a similar design in this respect.

LocalAlloc and ILocalAlloc

The LocalAlloc code isn't much to look at. It's a call to a KERNEL32 internal function (HouseCleanLogicallyDeadHandles) followed by a jump to ILocalAlloc. The HouseCleanLogicallyDeadHandles appears to do something related to what its name implies. However, I never saw the meat of the function being executed, so the meaning of "logically dead handles" is unclear.

Pseudocode for LocalAlloc

```
HouseCleanLogicallyDeadHandles();
goto ILocalAlloc;
```

ILocalAlloc starts by looking up the address of the default process heap from the process database. Next, it acquires the heap semaphore for the process heap, allowing the code to pass the HEAP_NO_SERIALIZE flags to the lower-level functions that ILocalAlloc uses later. At this point, ILocalAlloc splits into two code paths, one for LMEM_MOVEABLE blocks and the other for LMEM_FIXED blocks.

If allocating an LMEM_MOVEABLE block, ILocalAlloc looks up the head of the free handle list in the process database. If the free handle list is empty, ILocalAlloc use HPAlloc to allocate memory for a new handle table, and then initializes the new table. One way or another, ILocalAlloc eventually gets a free handle table entry. With this entry, ILocalAlloc fills in the fields to indicate an in-use handle.

After filling in nearly all of the handle table entry, ILocalAlloc calls HPAlloc to obtain a memory block of the size requested from LocalAlloc. ILocalAlloc adds 4 bytes to the allocation size so that it can use the first DWORD of the allocation for its own purposes. What might ILocalAlloc put in this first DWORD? Nothing less than a pointer to the handle table entry. By doing this, the local heap functions can convert a pointer to a moveable memory block back to its handle. Because the first DWORD of the allocated block is used by the local heap functions, ILocalAlloc adds 4 to the block's address when storing the block's pointer into the handle table slot.

The other code path that ILocalAlloc can take is for LMEM_FIXED handles. In this case, the code calls HPAlloc to obtain the memory block. The address of the block is what ILocalAlloc returns as the handle. Put another way, the handle for an LMEM_FIXED block in the local heap is the same as its address. Once again, this is the same as the Win16 local heap functions.

Pseudocode for lLocalAlloc proc

```
// Parameters:
//      UINT uFlags;
//      UINT uBytes;
// Locals:
//      HANDLE hHeap;
//      DWORD retHandle;
//      LOCAL_HANDLE_TABLE_ENTRY *pFreeHandle, *pHandleEntry;
//      LOCAL_HANDLE_TABLE * pHandleTable;
//      PVOID pBlock;

    // Get the default process heap from the process database.
    hHeap = ppCurrentProcessId->lpProcessHeap;

    uFlags &= 0xFFFF8FFF;   // Turn off LMEM_INVALID_HANDLE bit if set.

    // Acquire the heap semaphore so that we're not interrupted.
    x_WaitForSemaphore( hHeap->pCriticalSection );

    if ( uFlags & 0xFFFF808D )  // Check for any invalid or undefined flags,
    {                           // e.g., LMEM_INVALID_HANDLE or LMEM_MODIFY.
        _DebugOut( "LocalAlloc: invalid flags\n",
                    SLE_WARNING + FStopOnRing3MemoryError );
        InternalSetLastError( ERROR_INVALID_PARAMETER );
        goto return_0;
    }

    if ( uFlags & LMEM_MOVEABLE )
    {
        // pNextFreeHandle is at offset 0x58 in Process Database.
        pFreeHandle = ppCurrentProcessId->pNextFreeHandle;
        if ( pFreeHandle )
            goto have_handle_table

        // Hmmm...There's no available LOCAL_HANDLE_TABLE_ENTRYs.
        // Go create a new handle table.
        pHandleTable = HPAlloc( hHeap, 0x48, HEAP_NO_SERIALIZE );
        if ( !pHandleTable )
            goto return_0;

        // Initialize the new handle table.
        pHandleTable->signature = "LA"; // "LA" = 0x414C
```

```
        // KERNEL32 keeps a linked list of LOCAL_HANDLE_TABLEs. Insert
        // the new table at the head of the list.

        if ( ppCurrentProcessId->pHandleTableHead )
        {
            pHandleTable->cHandleTables =
                    ppCurrentProcessId->pHandleTableHead->cHandleTables+1;
        }
        else
            pHandleTable->cHandleTables = 0;

        // Point to first entry in the array of LOCAL_HANDLE_TABLE_ENTRYs,
        // then initialize the 8 elements of the LOCAL_HANDLE_TABLE_ENTRY
        // array.
        pHandleEntry = pHandleTable + sizeof(LOCAL_HANDLE_TABLE);
        pFreeHandle = pHandleEntry;
        while ( pHandleTable2 < end of handle table )
        {
            pHandleEntry->signature = "FS"
            pHandleEntry->pNextFree = pHandleEntry + 8;
            pHandleEntry += sizeof( LOCAL_HANDLE_TABLE_ENTRY );
        }

        // Add the new handle table to the head of the list of handle
        // tables. The pointer to the list head is kept in the process
        // database.
        pHandleTable->pPrevHandleTable=ppCurrentProcessId->pHandleTableHead;
        ppCurrentProcessId->pHandleTableHead = pHandleTable;

have_handle_table:
        if ( pFreeHandle->signature != "FS" )
            _DebugOut( "LocalAlloc: bad handle free list 2\n", 1 );

        // Remove this handle entry from the list of free entries.
        ppCurrentProcessId->pNextFreeHandle = pFreeHandle->pNextFree;

        // Modify the handle entry to describe the new block.
        pFreeHandle->cLock = 0;
        pFreeHandle->signature = "BS";
        pFreeHandle->flags = 0;

        if ( ( uFlags & LMEM_DISCARDABLE) == LMEM_DISCARDABLE )
            pFreeHandle->flags |= 2;

        if ( uBytes == 0 )
            goto moveable_0_bytes;
```

```
            if ( uBytes > 0xFFFFFF98 )
            {
                _DebugOut( "LocalAlloc: requested size too big\n",
                           SLE_WARNING + FStopOnRing3MemoryError );
                InternalSetLastError( ERROR_NOT_ENOUGH_MEMORY );

                goto moveable_alloc_error;
            }

            // Call HeapAlloc to allocate the memory block of the requested size.
            // Add an extra 4 bytes, because the back pointer to the handle
            // table entry needs to be stored in the first 4 bytes.
            pBlock = HPAlloc( hHeap, uBytes+4, flags & HEAP_NO_SERIALIZE );
            if ( !pBlock )
                goto moveable_alloc_error;

            // Store the pointer to the data area in the handle table entry.
            pFreeHandle->pBlock = &pBlock + 4;

            // Store a pointer to the handle table entry in the first 4 bytes
            // of the allocated block.
            *(PDWORD)pBlock = pFreeHandle;

            retHandle = &pFreeHandle->pBlock;
            goto moveable_alloc_done

moveable_alloc_0_bytes:
    pFreeHandle->pBlock = 0;

moveable_alloc_done:

            if ( (retHandle & 2) == 0 )
                _DebugOut( "LocalAlloc: handle value w/o LH_HANDLEBIT set\n", 1);

            goto return_retHandle;
        }

    // This code allocates LMEM_FIXED blocks.

    // Call HeapAlloc to allocate the memory block of the requested size.
    pBlock = HPAlloc( hHeap, uBytes, flags & HEAP_NO_SERIALIZE );

    if ( pBlock )
    {
        // Verify that HeapAlloc returned a pointer that's a multiple of 4.
        // (LMEM_FIXED blocks must be a multiple of 4.
        if ( pBlock & 2 )
            _DebugOut("LocalAlloc: pointer value w/ LH_HANDLEBIT set\n", 1);
```

```
            retHandle = pBlock;
        goto return_retHandle;
    }

moveable_alloc_error:

    // Put the LOCAL_HANDLE_TABLE_ENTRY that we acquired earlier back
    // into the free list of LOCAL_HANDLE_TABLE_ENTRYs.
    pFreeHandle->pNextFree = ppCurrentProcessId->pNextFreeHandle;
    ppCurrentProcessId->pNextFreeHandle = pFreeHandle;
    pFreeHandle = "FS"; // (0x5346)

return_0:
    retHandle = 0;

return_retHandle:
    InternalLeaveCriticalSection( hHeap->pCriticalSection );
    return retHandle;
```

LocalLock and ILocalLock

In Win16, the LocalLock function serves two purposes: to prevent a block from moving and to return the memory address associated with the handle. In Win32, LocalLock is primarily a handle validation function, although it does return the address of the associated block. In Win32, local heap blocks don't move around, so there's no need to lock the blocks. And because you can't get truly moveable memory, there's no reason to allocate LMEM_MOVEABLE blocks in the first place. Still, KERNEL32 goes through the motions of maintaining a lock count.

The actual LocalLock function is part of the validation layer. It verifies that the hLocal passed to it is valid from 0x10 bytes before to 7 bytes after the pointer. Any handle — LMEM_FIXED or LMEM_MOVEABLE — should meet these criteria. Assuming the tests don't cause a fault, LocalLock jumps to ILocalLock.

If the handle passed to ILocalLock is an LMEM_MOVEABLE handle, the function subtracts two bytes from the handle to get a pointer to the block's LOCAL_HANDLE_TABLE_ENTRY structure. With this pointer, ILocalLock verifies the signature (BS) and retrieves the current lock count (a BYTE). If the lock count is 0xFE, ILocalLock refuses to increment the lock count any further. Otherwise, the function bumps up the lock count in the LOCAL_HANDLE_TABLE_ENTRY structure and returns the pointer to the associated memory.

If the handle given to lLocalLock is LMEM_FIXED, there's no lock count kept for it. Still, lLocalLock takes the opportunity to verify the handle. The handle in this case should be the same as if the block had been allocated through HeapAlloc. Thus, there should be a HPAlloc style arena 0x10 bytes before the handle/address. LocalAlloc grabs the size field from the arena and checks that the appropriate bits for an in-use block are set. The LocalAlloc return address for a valid LMEM_FIXED block is the same as the handle passed in.

Pseudocode for LocalLock

```
// Parameters:
//      HLOCAL  hLocal

    Set up a structured exception handler frame

    AL = *(PBYTE)(hLocal + 7 );     // If the pointer is bogus, these will
    AL = *(PBYTE)(hLocal - 0x10 );  // fault, and the exception handler
                                    // returns a failure value to the caller.
    Remove structured exception handler frame

        goto lLocalLock
```

Pseudocode for lLocalLock

```
// Parameters:
//      HLOCAL   hLocal
// Locals:
//      HANDLE hHeap;
//      PSTR pszError;
//      BYTE lockCount;
//      HEAP_ARENA pHeapArena;
//      LOCAL_HANDLE_TABLE_ENTRY *pHandleEntry
//      DWORD retValue;

    // Get the default process heap from the process database.
    hHeap = ppCurrentProcessId->lpProcessHeap;

    // Acquire the heap semaphore so that we're not interrupted.
    x_WaitForSemaphore( hHeap->pCriticalSection );

    // Verify that the local handle is even with the range of valid handles.
    if ( !x_IsHandleInRange(hHeap, hLocal) )
    {
```

```
        pszError = "LocalLock: hMem out of range\n";
        goto error;
    }

    if ( hLocal & 2 )        //A moveable block.
    {
        // The handle points 2 bytes into the LOCAL_HANDLE_TABLE_ENTRY
        // struct. Subtract 2 bytes to get a pointer to the
        // LOCAL_HANDLE_TABLE_ENTRY.
        pHandleEntry = hLocal - 2;

        if ( pHandleEntry->signature != "BS" )  // "BS" = 0x5342
        {
            pszError = "LocalLock: invalid hMem, bad signature\n";
            goto error;
        }

        lockCount = pHandleEntry->cLock;

        // Make sure the lock count isn't going to overflow.
        if ( lockCount == 0xFE )
        {
            _DebugPrintf("LocalLock: lock count overflow, handle "
                        "cannot be unlocked\n");
        }

        if ( lockCount != 0xFF )    // If lockCount != 0xFF, bump it up.
        {
            lockCount++;
            pHandleEntry->cLock = lockCount;
        }

        // Return the address of the associated data block.
        retValue = pHandleEntry->pBlock
        goto return_retValue;
    }
    else    // A fixed block.
    {
        // The hLocal parameter is just the pointer to the data.
        // Back up to the HEAP_ARENA structure.
        pHeapArena = hLocal - 0x10;

        // Are the bits indicating an in-use block set in the
        // HEAP_ARENA size field?
        if ( (pHeapArena->size & 0xF0000003) != 0xA0000001 )
        {
            pszError = LocalLock: hMem is pointer to free block\n;
            goto error;
        }
```

```
            retValue = hLocal;      // Just return the handle parameter, because
                                    // it points directly to the block's memory.
            goto return_retValue;
    }

error:
    _DebugOut( pszError, SLE_WARNING + FStopOnRing3MemoryError );
    InternalSetLastError( ERROR_INVALID_HANDLE );
    retValue = 0;

return_retValue:
    InternalLeaveCriticalSection( hHeap->pCriticalSection );
    return retValue;
```

LocalUnlock

The LocalUnlock function is part of the validation layer. It verifies that the
hLocal passed to it is valid from 0x10 bytes before to 7 bytes after the pointer.
Any handle — LMEM_FIXED or LMEM_MOVEABLE — should meet
these criteria. Assuming the tests don't cause a fault, LocalUnlock jumps to
ILocalUnlock.

The ILocalUnlock code is a replay of the ILocalLock code, but in reverse.
If the handle parameter is an LMEM_FIXED handle, ILocalUnlock doesn't
have anything to do. It doesn't even bother to validate the handle like
LocalLock does. If the handle is a possible LMEM_MOVEABLE handle,
ILocalUnlock checks the signature byte in the handle table entry to make
sure it's a valid handle. If so, ILocalUnlock checks the block's lock count to
see whether it's safe to decrement. If it is, ILocalUnlock decrements the lock
count and returns a BOOL indicating whether the block is still locked or not.

Pseudocode for LocalUnlock

```
// Parameters:
//      HLOCAL  hLocal

    Set up a structured exception handler frame

    AL = *(PBYTE)(hLocal + 7 );      // If the pointer is bogus, these will
    AL = *(PBYTE)(hLocal - 0x10 );   // fault, and the exception handler
                                     // returns a failure value to the caller.
    Remove structured exception handler frame

    goto ILocalUnlock
```

Pseudocode for lLocalUnlock

```
// Parameters:
//      HLOCAL  hLocal
// Locals:
//      HANDLE hHeap;
//      PSTR pszError
//      BYTE lockCount;
//      LOCAL_HANDLE_TABLE_ENTRY *pHandleEntry
//      DWORD retValue;

    retValue = 0;        // FALSE: the block isn't locked.

    // Get the default process heap from the process database.
    hHeap = ppCurrentProcessId->lpProcessHeap;

    // Acquire the heap semaphore so that we're not interrupted.
    x_WaitForSemaphore( hHeap->pCriticalSection );

    // Verify that the local handle is even with the range of valid handles.
    if ( !x_IsHandleInRange(hHeap, hLocal) )
    {
        pszError = "LocalUnlock: hMem out of range\n";
        goto error;
    }

    if ( (hMem & 2) == 0 )      // If it's a FIXED block, there's nothing to do.
        goto return_retValue;

    if ( pHandleEntry->signature != "BS" )  // "BS" = 0x5342
    {
        pszError = "LocalUnlock: invalid hMem, bad signature\n";
        goto error;
    }

    // The handle points two bytes into the LOCAL_HANDLE_TABLE_ENTRY struct.
    pHandleEntry = hLocal - 2;

    // A lock count of 0xFF seems to be some sort of error condition.
    if ( pHandleEntry->cLock == 0xFF )
        goto return retValue;

    // Make sure the lock count won't underflow.
    if ( lockCount == 0 )
    {
```

```
        _DebugOut( "LocalUnlock: not locked" );
        goto return_retValue;
    }

    // Decrement the lock count in the handle table entry.
    pHandleEntry->cLock--;

    if ( pHandleEntry->cLock )
        retValue = 1;        // Return TRUE (the block is still locked).

    goto return_retValue;

error:
    _DebugOut( pszError, SLE_WARNING + FStopOnRing3MemoryError );
    InternalSetLastError( ERROR_INVALID_HANDLE );
    EDI = 0;

return_retValue:
    InternalLeaveCriticalSection( hHeap->pCriticalSection );
    return retValue;
```

LocalFree and lLocalFree

The Win32 LocalFree function is an odd duck. Before it gets to the real code for freeing a LocalAlloc'ed handle, it first checks for a special case handle. Somehow, KERNEL32 and KRNL386 conspire to create and use handle groups. It's a mystery to me exactly what handle groups are because I was unable to to find one. Regardless, handle groups are some sort of three-way relationship between a Win16 Task database, a Win32 LocalAlloc'ed handle, and a handle group. When LocalFree detects that this special local handle is being freed, it calls the GlobalNukeGroup function to get rid of the handle group. The handle group list is maintained by KRNL386, so GlobalNukeGroup ends up calling down into KRNL386. This is yet another case that disproves Microsoft's assertion that KERNEL32 doesn't thunk down to KRNL386. The vast majority of the time that LocalAlloc is called, it's not for a handle group handle. In this situation, LocalFree reduces down to just a call to lLocalFree.

LocalFree proc

```
// Parameters:
//     HLOCAL hMem

    _CheckSysLevel( x_Another_Win16_mutext );

    CheckHGHeap();        // Check Handle Group Heap. Thunks down to KRNL386.

    _EnterSysLevel( x_Another_Win16_mutext );

    if ( *someGlobal )        // *someGlobal points to a Handle Group selector.
    {
        // This is a loop that iterates through a list. This list
        // associates a Win16 TDB with a Win32 LocalAlloc handle and a
        // "handle group" (whatever that is). The node is considered found
        // if the TDB and local handle match the current thread's TDB
        // and the handle passed to this function.
        while ( not at end of list )
        {
            if ( the node being searched for is found )
            {
                _LeaveSysLevel( x_Another_Win16_mutext )
                GlobalNukeGroup( EBX );
                HouseCleanLogicallyDeadHandles();
                return hMem;
            }
            go to next node in list
        }
    }

    _LeaveSysLevel( x_Another_Win16_mutext )

    CheckHGHeap();        // Check Handle Group Heap yet again.

    return lLocalFree( hMem );
```

The lLocalFree code is where a LocalAlloc'ed handle is freed. As with most of the other Win32 local heap functions, the code for handling LMEM_FIXED blocks is simple; it's essentially a call to the underlying HeapXXX function. In the case of LocalFree, the code merely calls lHeapFree.

Freeing an LMEM_MOVEABLE block in lLocalFree is considerably more complex. After verifying that a valid local heap handle was passed, lLocalFree checks the block's lock count. If the count is nonzero, lLocalFree complains that the block is still locked. Next, lLocalFree frees the block associated with the handle parameter back to the heap through the IHeapFree function. Finally, lLocalFree puts the handle table entry at the head of the list of available handle table entries.

It's interesting to note that the lLocalFree makes no attempt to delete a handle table when all eight of its entries are unused. That is, it's not a good recycler that returns its empties. To verify that I wasn't overlooking something, I modified a copy of the WALKHEAP program to make 50 LocalAllocs in a row and then free the 50 handles. The resulting output showed that all the handle tables remained in memory. As an added bonus (not!), the heap had a nice, regular pattern to its fragmentation. The only consolation is that the handle tables will be reused for future moveable memory allocations.

Pseudocode for lLocalFree

```
// Parameters:
//      HLOCAL hMem
// Locals:
//      HANDLE hHeap;
//      DWORD retValue;
//      LOCAL_HANDLE_TABLE_ENTRY *pHandleEntry;

    Set up structured exception handler frame

    // Get the default process heap from the process database.
    hHeap = ppCurrentProcessId->lpProcessHeap;

    // Acquire the heap semaphore so that we're not interrupted.
    x_WaitForSemaphore( hHeap->pCriticalSection );

    retValue = hMem;

    if ( hMem & 2 )      // A moveable block (bit 1 set)?
    {
        if ( !x_IsHandleInRange(hHeap, hMem) )
        {
            _DebugOut( "LocalFree: hMem out of range\n",
                        SLE_WARNING + FStopOnRing3MemoryError );
            InternalSetLastError( ERROR_INVALID_HANDLE );
            goto return_retValue;
        }

        // Back up two bytes to point at the handle table entry.
        pHandleEntry = hMem - 2;
```

```
        if ( pHandleEntry->signature != "BS" )   // 0x5342
        {
            _DebugOut( "LocalFree: invalid hMem, bad signature\n",
                       SLE_WARNING + FStopOnRing3MemoryError );
            InternalSetLastError( ERROR_INVALID_HANDLE );
            goto return_retValue;
        }

        // If the handle is still locked, complain.
        if ( pHandleEntry->cLock )
        {
            _DebugOut( "LocalFree: invalid handle\n",
                       SLE_WARNING + FStopOnRing3MemoryError );
            InternalSetLastError( ERROR_INVALID_HANDLE );
        }

        // If the memory block hasn't been discarded, free it with IHeapFree.
        // Note that the code subtracts 4 from the pBlock field to get
        // the original value returned by HeapAlloc.
        if ( pHandleEntry->pBlock )
            if ( IHeapFree(hHeap, HEAP_NO_SERIALIZE, &pHandleEntry->pBlock-4))
            {
                retValue = pHandleEntry;
                goto return_retValue;
            }

        // Insert the handle being freed at the head of the free handle list.
        pHandleEntry->pNextFree = ppCurrentProcessId->pNextFreeHandle;
        ppCurrentProcessId->pNextFreeHandle = pHandleEntry;

        // Set the handle table entry's signature back to the free version.
        pHandleEntry->signature = "FS"; // 0x5346
        retValue = 0;
    }
    else    // A fixed block.
    {
        if ( IHeapFree(hHeap, HEAP_NO_SERIALIZE, hMem) )
            retValue = hMem
        else
            retValue = 0;
    }

return_retValue:
    InternalLeaveCriticalSection( hHeap->pCriticalSection );

    Remove structured exception handler frame

    return retValue;
```

LocalReAlloc and ILocalRealloc

The LocalRealloc function is part of the validation layer. It verifies that the hLocal passed to it is valid from 0x10 bytes before to 7 bytes after the pointer. Any handle — LMEM_FIXED or LMEM_MOVEABLE — should meet these criteria. Assuming the tests don't cause a fault, LocalRealloc jumps to ILocalRealloc.

Pseudocode for LocalReAlloc

```
// Parameters:
//      HLOCAL  hLocal
//      UINT uBytes;
//      UINT uFlags;

    Set up a structured exception handler frame

    AL = *(PBYTE)(hLocal + 7 );    // If the pointer is bogus, these will
    AL = *(PBYTE)(hLocal - 0x10 ); // fault, and the exception handler
                                   // returns a failure value to the caller.
    Remove structured exception handler frame

    goto ILocalReAlloc
```

ILocalReAlloc is one of the longest and most complex of the heap functions in KERNEL32. As with the other local heap functions, the code divides nicely into a section for LMEM_FIXED blocks and a section for LMEM_MOVEABLE blocks. The LMEM_FIXED code is much simpler, and consists of calling HPReAlloc, which is the underlying function for HeapReAlloc as well. Before doing this, though, ILocalReAlloc checks to see whether the caller is trying to modify the flags for an LMEM_FIXED block. This is a no-no.

The ILocalReAlloc code for LMEM_MOVEABLE blocks starts by checking to see whether the caller simply wants to modify the flags. If so, the code modifies the flags in the handle's LOCAL_HANDLE_TABLE_ENTRY and gets out. Next, the code checks to see whether it was called with a size parameter of 0. If so, the caller wants the block to be discarded. ILocalReAlloc complies by passing the block's handle to the IHeapFree. Before doing this, though, ILocalReAlloc checks whether the block is locked, and complains if appropriate.

If the size parameter is nonzero, the caller is requesting the allocation of a new block. If the current memory block for the handle is 0, the block has been previously discarded. In this case, the function simply calls HPAlloc to get a block of the requested size. If a memory block is already associated with this handle, ILocalReAlloc passes the memory block's address to HPReAlloc to let it do the messy work of reallocating the block.

Pseudocode for ILocalReAlloc

```
// Parameters:
//      HLOCAL  hMem
//      UINT uBytes;
//      UINT uFlags;
// Locals:
//      DWORD fDiscardable;
//      HANDLE hHeap;
//      HANDLE hNewHandle;
//      LOCAL_HANDLE_TABLE_ENTRY * pHandleEntry;
//      PVOID pBlock;

    uFlags &= 0xFFFFDFFF;        // Turn off 0x00002000 bit, which has no
                                // meaning.

    HouseCleanLogicallyDeadHandles();   // ???

    // Get the default process heap from the process database.
    hHeap = ppCurrentProcessId->lpProcessHeap;

    // Acquire the heap semaphore so that we're not interrupted.
    x_WaitForSemaphore( hHeap->pCriticalSection );

    if ( uFlags & 0xFFFFD02D )              // Test for any flags that aren't
        goto LocalRealloc_invalid_flags // defined, or which shouldn't be
                                        // used (e.g., LMEM_INVALID_HANDLE).

    fDiscardable = uFlags & LMEM_DISCARDABLE;

    if ( (uFlags & LMEM_DISCARDABLE) && !(uFlags & LMEM_MODIFY) )
        goto LocalRealloc_invalid_flags;

    if ( hMem & 2 )     // If an LMEM_MOVEABLE block.
    {
        if ( !x_IsHandleInRange(hHeap, hMem) )
        {
            _DebugOut( "LocalReAlloc: hMem out of range\n",
                        SLE_WARNING + FStopOnRing3MemoryError );
            InternalSetLastError( ERROR_INVALID_HANDLE );
            goto LocalRealloc_error;
        }
```

```
    // Point to the HANDLE_TABLE_ENTRY for this handle.
    pHandleEntry = hMem - 2;

    if ( pHandleEntry->signature != "BS" )
    {
        _DebugOut( "LocalReAlloc: invalid hMem, bad signature\n",
                    SLE_WARNING + FStopOnRing3MemoryError );
        InternalSetLastError( ERROR_INVALID_HANDLE );
        goto LocalRealloc_error;
    }

    pBlock = pHandleEntry->pBlock;      // Get pointer to the data area.

    if ( uFlags & LMEM_MODIFY )
    {
        pHandleEntry->flags |= fDiscardable ? 2 : 0
        goto done;
    }

    if ( uBytes == 0 )  // Setting size to 0 is the same as discarding
    {                   // the block.
        if ( pHandleEntry->cLock )
        {
            _DebugOut( "LocalReAlloc: discard of locked block\n",
                        SLE_WARNING + FStopOnRing3MemoryError );
            InternalSetLastError( ERROR_INVALID_HANDLE );
            goto LocalRealloc_error
        }

        if ( pBlock == 0 )  // If no data area is associated with this
            goto done;      // handle, there's nothing else to do.

        // There is a data area associated with this handle. Go
        // free it.
        if ( IHeapFree( hHeap, HEAP_NO_SERIALIZE, pBlock - 4 ) )
            goto LocalRealloc_error;

        // Set the pointer to the data area to NULL, because we just
        // released the memory.
        pHandleEntry->pBlock = 0;
        goto done;
    }

    // If we get here, we're not setting the size to NULL. This
    // means that we'll need to HeapAlloc or HeapReAlloc a new block.

    uBytes += 4;    // Add space for back-pointer to HANDLE_TABLE_ENTRY.
```

```
        if ( pBlock == 0 )  // If there's no data area associated with this
        {                   // handle, we can just HeapAlloc a new area.
            if ( uBytes == 0 )
                goto new_moveable_handle

            hNewHandle = HPAlloc( hHeap, uBytes, uFlags & HEAP_NO_SERIALIZE );
            if ( !hNewHandle )
                goto LocalRealloc_error

            // Set the first DWORD of the HeapAlloc'ed area to be a pointer
            // to our HANDLE_TABLE_ENTRY struct.
            *(PDWORD)hNewHandle = pHandleEntry;
            goto new_moveable_handle;
        }

        // If we get here, there's already a data area associated with
        // this handle. Therefore, we'll use HeapReAlloc to get the new block.

        if ( pHandleEntry->cLock )
            uFlags |= HEAP_GROWABLE;

        hNewHandle = HPReAlloc( hHeap, hMem, uBytes,
                                uFlags | HEAP_NO_SERIALIZE );
        if ( hNewHandle )
        {
new_moveable_handle:
            // Set the pointer to the data area to be 4 bytes into the
            // block returned by HeapReAlloc/HeapAlloc. (The first DWORD
            // of this block is a pointer to our HANDLE_TABLE_ENTRY struct.)
            pHandleEntry->pBlock = hNewHandle+4;
            goto done;
        }
        else    // Oops! Something is wrong. Return 0.
        {
            hMem = 0;
            goto done;
        }
    }
    else    // An LMEM_FIXED block.
    {
        if ( uFlags & LMEM_MODIFY )
        {
            _DebugOut( "LocalReAlloc: can't use LMEM_MODIFY on fixed block\n",
                        SLE_WARNING + FStopOnRing3MemoryError );
            InternalSetLastError( ERROR_INVALID_PARAMETER );
            goto LocalRealloc_error;
        }
```

```
            // There's always memory associated with an LMEM_FIXED handle, so
            // we can just call HeapReAlloc without all the contortions
            // that an LMEM_MOVEABLE block needs to go through.
            hMem = HPReAlloc( hHeap, hMem, uBytes, uFlags & HEAP_NO_SERIALIZE );
            goto done;
        }

LocalRealloc_invalid_flags:

    _DebugOut( "LocalReAlloc: invalid flags\n",
               SLE_WARNING + FStopOnRing3MemoryError );
    InternalSetLastError( ERROR_INVALID_PARAMETER );

LocalRealloc_error:

    hMem = 0;

done:
    InternalLeaveCriticalSection( hHeap->pCriticalSection );
    return hMem;
```

LocalHandle and ILocalHandle

The LocalHandle function is part of the validation layer. It verifies that the pointer passed to it is valid from 0x10 bytes before to 7 bytes after the pointer. Any local heap block — LMEM_FIXED or LMEM_MOVEABLE — should meet these criteria. Assuming the tests don't cause a fault, LocalHandle jumps to ILocalHandle.

The ILocalHandle function takes the address of a memory block and returns the local heap handle associated with the block. This is a simple task for an LMEM_FIXED block because the block address and the handle are the same. However, ILocalHandle is at least kind enough to verify that the address is really that of a HPAlloc'ed block.

The other scenario that ILocalHandle has to contend with is LMEM_MOVEABLE handles. This is trickier, but not by much. In the pseudocode for ILocalAlloc, I showed that for LMEM_MOVEABLE blocks, ILocalAlloc adds 4 bytes to the allocation size. In the first 4 bytes of the allocation, ILocalAlloc stuffs in a pointer to the local handle table entry. It's in the ILocalHandle function that these 4 bytes come into play. ILocalHandle merely needs to subtract 4 bytes from the pointer passed to it, and then read in the DWORD at that spot. The DWORD should be a pointer to a handle table entry. ILocalHandle verifies that the pointer does in fact point to a handle table entry. If so, ILocalHandle returns the address of the handle table entry plus 2. As we saw earlier, at this spot the handle table entry is pointer to the memory block.

Pseudocode for LocalHandle

```
// Parameters:
//      PVOID   pMem

    Set up a structured exception handler frame

    AL = *(PBYTE)(hLocal + 7 );     // If the pointer is bogus, these will
    AL = *(PBYTE)(hLocal - 0x10 );  // fault, and the exception handler
                                    // returns a failure value to the caller.
    Remove structured exception handler frame

    goto ILocalHandle
```

Pseudocode for ILocalHandle

```
// Parameters:
//      PVOID   pMem
// Locals:
//      HANDLE hHeap;
//      HLOCAL hLocal
//      LOCAL_HANDLE_TABLE_ENTRY * pHandleEntry;
//      DWORD pLocalArena;
//      PSTR pszError;

    // Get the default process heap from the process database.
    hHeap = ppCurrentProcessId->lpProcessHeap;

    // Acquire the heap semaphore so that we're not interrupted.
    x_WaitForSemaphore( hHeap->pCriticalSection );

    // Verify that the local handle is even with the range of valid handles.
    if ( !x_IsHandleInRange(hHeap, pMem) )
    {
        pszError = "LocalHandle: pMem out of range\n";
        goto error;
    }

    // If the block is MOVEABLE, then 4 bytes before the block is a
    // pointer to the handle table entry. This pointer is sandwiched
```

```
        // between the HPAlloc arena and the block's data.
        pHandleEntry = *(PDWORD)(pMem-4);

        if ( x_IsHandleInRange(hHeap, pHandleEntry) )
        {
            // It's an LMEM_MOVEABLE handle. Verify the signature
            if ( pHandleEntry->signature == "BS" )  // "BS" = 0x5342
            {
                hLocal = pHandleEntry+2;
                goto return_hLocal
            }
            // Hmmm...it's not an LMEM_MOVEABLE handle. Fall through to
            // see if it's LMEM_FIXED.
        }
        else    // An LMEM_FIXED handle.
        {
            pLocalArena = pMem - 0x10;
            if ( (pLocalArena->size & 0xF0000001) == 0xA0000000 )
            {
                hLocal = pMem;
                goto return_hLocal;
            }
        }

        // If we get here, it's not a valid MOVEABLE or FIXED block.
        pszError = "LocalHandle: address not a heap block\n";

error:
    _DebugOut( pszError, SLE_WARNING + FStopOnRing3MemoryError );
    InternalSetLastError( ERROR_INVALID_HANDLE );
    hLocal = 0;

return_hLocal:
    InternalLeaveCriticalSection( hHeap->pCriticalSection );
    return hLocal;
```

LocalSize and ILocalSize

The LocalSize function is part of the validation layer. It verifies that the
hLocal passed to it is valid from 0x10 bytes before to 7 bytes after the
pointer. Any handle — LMEM_FIXED or LMEM_MOVEABLE — should
meet these criteria. Assuming the tests don't cause a fault, LocalSize jumps
to ILocalSize.

LocalSize returns the size of the memory block associated with the passed-in local handle. The real work of determining the size is performed by the HeapSize function toward the end of the code. If the local handle is LMEM_FIXED, LocalSize goes almost directly to HeapSize call.

If the handle is LMEM_MOVEABLE, LocalSize needs to first convert the handle to a pointer to the memory block before calling HeapSize. If this is the case, LocalSize first verifies that the local handle parameter is a valid local handle. If it is, LocalSize grabs the pointer to the memory block from the LOCAL_HANDLE_TABLE_ENTRY structure.

The final bit of code in LocalSize applies only to LMEM_MOVEABLE handles. As I showed in the ILocalAlloc code, LMEM_MOVEABLE memory blocks are 4 bytes bigger than the requested size. These 4 bytes are used to hold the pointer back to the handle table entry. To make LocalSize report values consistent with what was LocalAlloc'ed, LocalSize subtracts 4 from the value returned by HeapSize for LMEM_MOVEABLE blocks.

Pseudocode for LocalSize

```
// Parameters:
//     HLOCAL  hLocal

    Set up a structured exception handler frame

    AL = *(PBYTE)(hLocal + 7 );     // If the pointer is bogus, these will
    AL = *(PBYTE)(hLocal - 0x10 );  // fault, and the exception handler
                                    // returns a failure value to the caller.
    Remove structured exception handler frame

    goto ILocalSize
```

Pseudocode for ILocalSize

```
// Parameters:
//     HLOCAL  hLocal
// Locals:
//     HANDLE hHeap;
//     DWORD size;
//     PSTR pszError;
//     LOCAL_HANDLE_TABLE_ENTRY * pHandleEntry;

    // Get the default process heap from the process database.
    hHeap = ppCurrentProcessId->lpProcessHeap;
```

```
            // Acquire the heap semaphore so that we're not interrupted.
            x_WaitForSemaphore( hHeap->pCriticalSection );

            if ( hLocal & 2 )          // A moveable handle.
            {
                if ( !x_IsHandleInRange(hHeap, hLocal) )
                {
                    pszError = "LocalSize: hMem out of range\n";
                    goto error;
                }

                // The handle points 2 bytes into the LOCAL_HANDLE_TABLE_ENTRY
                // struct. Subtract 2 bytes to get a pointer to the
                // LOCAL_HANDLE_TABLE_ENTRY.
                pHandleEntry = hLocal - 2;

                if ( pHandleEntry->signature != "BS" )
                {
                    pszError = "LocalSize: invalid hMem, bad signature\n";
                    goto error;
                }

                hLocal = pHandleEntry->pBlock
                if ( !hLocal )
                {
                    size = 0;
                    goto return_size;
                }
            }

            size = IHeapSize( hHeap, HEAP_NO_SERIALIZE, hLocal );

            if ( hLocal is a MOVEABLE block )
                size -= 4;
            goto return_size;

    error:
        _DebugOut( pszError, SLE_WARNING + FStopOnRing3MemoryError );
        InternalSetLastError( ERROR_INVALID_HANDLE );
        size = 0;

    return_size;
        InternalLeaveCriticalSection( hHeap->pCriticalSection );

        return size;
```

LocalFlags

LocalFlags returns a local heap block's lock count in the low BYTE and the block's flags in the second lowest BYTE. The LocalFlags code starts out by checking the handle for validity. Next, the code splits into two paths. If the handle is an LMEM_FIXED handle (the low nibble ends in 0, 4, 0x8 ,or 0xC), the function returns 0 (flags = LMEM_FIXED, lock count = 0). However, LocalFlags does check to make sure the handle points to an HPAlloc'ed block. If it doesn't, LocalFlags returns LMEM_INVALID_HANDLE.

The other case LocalFlags contends with is LMEM_MOVEABLE handles. In this scenario, the function subtracts 2 from the handle to make a pointer to a LOCAL_HANDLE_TABLE_ENTRY. From this structure, the function extracts the cLock, flags, and pBlock fields. The lock count goes into the return value unmodified. The flags field, however, isn't made up of LMEM_xxx type flags. Therefore, LocalFlags has to synthesize the returned LMEM_xxx flags from information in the flags and pBlock field. If pBlock is 0, it means that the block has been discarded. (This should happen only if LocalReAlloc is called with a size of 0.) As with the LMEM_FIXED case, if the passed-in local handle looks incorrect, LocalAlloc returns LMEM_INVALID_HANDLE.

Pseudocode for LocalFlags

```
// Parameters:
//      HLOCAL   hMem
// Locals:
//      HANDLE hHeap;
//      DWORD flags;
//      PSTR pszError;
//      WORD retValue;
//      LOCAL_HANDLE_TABLE_ENTRY * pHandleEntry;
//      HEAP_ARENA * pArena;

    Set up structured exception handler frame

    retValue = LMEM_INVALID_HANDLE;

    // Get the default process heap from the process database.
    hHeap = ppCurrentProcessId->lpProcessHeap;

    // Acquire the heap semaphore so that we're not interrupted.
    x_WaitForSemaphore( hHeap->pCriticalSection );

    if ( !x_IsHandleInRange(hHeap, hMem) )
    {
```

```
        pszError = "LocalFlags: hMem out of range\n";
        goto error;
    }

    if ( hMem & 2)      // A moveable block.
    {
        // Back up two bytes to point at the LOCAL_HANDLE_TABLE_ENTRY.
        pHandleEntry = hMem - 2;

        // Look for signature at start of handle table entry.
        if ( pHandleEntry->signature != "BS" )
        {
            pszError = "LocalFlags: invalid hMem, bad signature\n";
            goto error;
        }

        retValue = pHandleEntry->cLock;

        if ( pHandleEntry->pBlock == 0 )    // Is address of real data 0?
            HIBYTE(retValue) |= LMEM_DISCARDED;

        // If the discardable (2) bit is set in the handle table entry flags,
        // turn on the LMEM_DISCARDABLE bits in the return value.
        if ( pHandleEntry->flags & 2 )
            HIBYTE(flags) |= LMEM_DISCARDABLE;

        goto return_flags;
    }
    else    // A fixed block.
    {
        // The hMem points to a HPAlloc block, so there should be an HPAlloc
        // style arena 0x10 bytes earlier.
        pArena = hMem - 0x10;

        // Check the arena's size field to make sure it's consistent with
        // an in-use block. If hMem is a bogus pointer, this will
        // fault, but the structured exception handler will catch it.
        if ( ( (pArena->size & 0xF0000001) == 0xA0000000 )
        {
            retValue = 0;
            goto return_flags
        }

        pszError = "LocalFlags: invalid hMem\n";
```

```
        // Fall through to error code.
    }

error:
    _DebugOut( pszError, SLE_WARNING + FStopOnRing3MemoryError );
    InternalSetLastError( ERROR_INVALID_HANDLE );

return_flags:

    InternalLeaveCriticalSection( hHeap->pCriticalSection );

    Remove structured exception handler frame

    return retValue;
```

LocalShrink

In Win32, LocalShrink has no effect on the heap itself because Win32 heap blocks aren't moveable. In the Win16 LocalShrink, however, the function returns the size of the heap. Therefore, for compatibility's sake, the Win32 LocalShrink returns the size of the default process heap.LocalShrink may have some usefulness for Win32 applications. For some strange reason, the Win32 API doesn't seem to have a good, documented method for getting the size of the default process heap. The LocalShrink function returns that value in Windows 95.

Pseudocode for LocalShrink

```
// Parameters:
//      HLOCAL hMem          // Neither of the two parameters is used.
//      UINT cbNewSize
// Locals:
//      HANDLE hHeap;

    // Get the default process heap from the process database.
    hHeap = ppCurrentProcessId->lpProcessHeap;

    return hHeap->size;     // Size field is first DWORD in heap region.
```

LocalCompact

Like LocalShrink, the Win32 LocalCompact function exists solely for backward compatibility with Win16. Because Win32 heap blocks don't move, the heap can't be compacted.

Pseudocode for LocalCompact

```
        return 0;        // Easy enough?
```

THE WIN32 GLOBAL HEAP FUNCTIONS

The global heap functions in Windows 95 are barely there. For the most part, they either jump directly to their local heap counterpart or, in the case of GlobalAlloc, share the same entry point. Most of the functions that accept HGLOBAL parameters make a token attempt to verify that a valid HGLOBAL was passed. This less than stringent test is the same test that some of the local heap functions use. Any block allocated with GlobalAlloc or LocalAlloc ultimately comes from the HPAlloc function. Thus, there should always be valid memory 0x10 bytes before and 7 bytes after the block.

Because the Global heap functions are so minimal, it's best to let the pseudocode speak for itself, rather than describe each individual function.

GlobalAlloc

GlobalAlloc shares the same entry point as LocalAlloc.

GlobalLock

Pseudocode for GlobalLock

```
  Set up a structured exception handler frame

      AL = *(PBYTE)(hGlobal + 7 );     // If the pointer is bogus, these will
      AL = *(PBYTE)(hGlobal - 0x10 );  // fault, and the exception handler
                                       // returns a failure value to the caller.
      Remove structured exception handler frame

      goto GlobalWire;                 // JMPs to ILocalLock.
```

GlobalUnlock

Pseudocode for GlobalUnlock

```
same tests as GlobalLock
    goto GlobalUnwire;              // JMPs to ILocalUnlock.
```

GlobalFree

Pseudocode for GlobalFree

```
same tests as GlobalLock
    goto LocalFree;
```

GlobalReAlloc

Pseudocode for GlobalReAlloc

```
// Parameters:
//      HGLOBAL hGlobal
    same tests as GlobalLock
        goto IGlobalReAlloc;        // JMPs to ILocalReAlloc.
```

GlobalSize

Pseudocode for GlobalSize

```
same tests as GlobalLock
    goto IGlobalSize;        ß    // JMPs to ILocalSize.
```

GlobalHandle

Pseudocode for GlobalHandle

```
same tests as GlobalLock
    goto IGlobalHandle;            // JMPs to ILocalHandle.
```

GlobalFlags and IGlobalFlags

Pseudocode for GlobalFlags

```
same tests as GlobalLock
    goto IGlobalFlags;
```

Pseudocode for IGlobalFlags

```
// Parameters:
//      HGLOBAL hMem

    // Pass through to LocalFlags, and then turn off any bits in the
    // high BYTE of the low WORD that aren't valid GMEM_xxx flags.
    return LocalFlags( hMem ) & 0xFFFFF1FF
```

GlobalWire

Pseudocode for GlobalWire

```
goto ILocalLock;
```

GlobalUnWire

Pseudocode for GlobalUnWire

```
goto ILocalUnlock;
```

GlobalFix

Pseudocode for GlobalFix

```
// Parameters:
//      HGLOBAL hMem

    if ( hMem != 0xFFFFFFFF )
        return GlobalLock( hMem );  // GlobalLock ultimately calls ILocalLock.
```

GlobalUnfix

Pseudocode for GlobalUnfix

```
// Parameters:
//      HGLOBAL hMem

    if ( hMem != 0xFFFFFFFF )
        return GlobalUnlock( hMem );    // GlobalUnlock ultimately
                                        // calls ILocalUnlock.
```

GlobalCompact

```
    goto LocalCompact;
```

MISCELLANEOUS FUNCTIONS

The last few functions I'll cover in this chapter don't fit into any of the previous categories, but are important nonetheless. I haven't included every possible memory function. Instead, I chose just a few interesting functions. (This chapter is long enough without going into a dozen additional routines!)

WriteProcessMemory and ReadProcessMemory

ReadProcessMemory and WriteProcessMemory are the approved method by which one process can read and modify the memory of another. To use these functions, you have to have a handle for the other process, and the Win32 API doesn't make it easy to get such a handle. WriteProcessMemory and ReadProcessMemory are two key functions for Win32 debuggers. Debuggers are in the small category of applications that need to read and write to the memory of another process (the debuggee to be specific).

Under the hood, WriteProcessMemory and ReadProcessMemory are similar. Therefore, I've decided to show pseudocode for just one, WriteProcessMemory. The only significant difference is that WriteProcessMemory calls VWIN32 service 0x002A0017, and ReadProcessMemory uses service 0x002A0016.

WriteProcessMemory starts out with some synchronization code. It makes sure that it doesn't hold either the Win16Mutex or the Krn32Mutex. The code then goes to a "must-complete" section, which means that it can't be switched away from. WriteProcessMemory follows this with checks to make sure that the source address is in the application private arena, which is what the VMM documentation calls the area above 4MB and below 2GB.

The next step for WriteProcessMemory is to get pointers to the process structures associated with the source address process. The code uses the process structure to find the thread list for the source address process. For some reason, the VWIN32 service that copies the memory wants the ring 0 stack address for the current thread in the target process. Once WriteProcessMemory has everything it needs to call into VWIN32, it acquires the Krn32Mutex and then calls VWIN32 service 0x002A0017. After VWIN32 does its magic with memory context, WriteProcessMemory releases the Krn32Mutex and exits the must-complete state by calling LeaveMustComplete. If something went wrong during these steps, WriteProcessMemory calls SetLastError to let the caller know what went wrong.

Pseudocode for WriteProcessMemory

```
// Parameters:
//   HANDLE  hProcess;        // Handle of the process whose memory is read.
//   LPCVOID lpBaseAddress;   // Address to start writing to.
//   LPVOID  lpBuffer;        // Address of buffer with data to write.
//   DWORD   cbRead;          // Number of bytes to write.
//   LPDWORD lpNumberOfBytesWritten;    // Actual number of bytes written.
// Locals:
//   DWORD   pProcess;
//   DWORD   ptdb;
//   DWORD   lastError;

    // Make sure we don't already have the Krn32Mutex or Win16Mutex.
    x_CheckNotSysLevel_Krn32_Win16_mutex();

    // Function that emits function names and parameters to the KERNEL
    // debugger if a KERNEL32 global variable is TRUE (off by default).
    x_LogKernelFunction( number indicating the WriteProcessMemory function );

    EnterMustComplete();

    if ( lpNumberOfBytesWritten )
        *lpNumberOfBytesWritten = 0;
```

```
if ( lpBuffer < 0x00400000 )
    goto set_invalidParam_lasterror_with_bp

if ( lpBuffer < 0xC0000000 )
    goto set_invalidParam_lasterror_with_bp

pProcess = x_GetObject( hProcess, 0x80000010, 0 );

if ( !pProcess )
{
    lastError = 1;
    goto emit_trace_info;
}

if ( some flag set in a certain pProcess field )
{
    lastError = ERROR_PROCESS_ABORTED;
    goto set_last_error;
}

myLocal1 = x_SomeListFunction(pProcess->threadList, 0);

if ( myLocal1 )
{
    do
    {
        ptdb = *(PDWORD)(myLocal1+8);
        if ( ptdb->ring0_hThread )
            break;
    } while ( myLocal1 = x_SomeListFunction( pProcess->threadList, 1) )
}
else
    ptdb = some unitialized local variable?

if ( !myLocal1 )
{
    InternalSetLastError( ERROR_PROCESS_ABORTED );
    goto done;
}

_EnterSysLevel( Krn32Mutex );

// Call the Win32 VxD service in VWIN32.VXD to copy the memory.
lastError = VxDCall( 0x002A0017, ptdb->ring0_hThread, lpBaseAddress,
                     lpBuffer, cbRead, lpNumberOfBytesWritten );
```

```
        if ( !lastError )
            InternalSetLastError( lastError );

        _LeaveSysLevel( Krn32Mutex );

done:
    x_UnuseObjectSafeWrapper( pProcess );
    goto emit_trace_info;

set_invalidParam_lasterror_with_bp:
    INT 3

    InternalSetLastError( ERROR_INVALID_PARAMETER );

emit_trace_info:

    x_SomeLoggingFunction( "WriteProcessMemory ptdb %08x Src %08x (%02x) "
                        "Dst %08x cb %d erc %d\n",
                        ptdb, lpBuffer, *(PWORD)lpBuffer,
                        lpBaseAddress, cbRead, lpNumberOfBytesWritten );

    LeaveMustComplete();

    return !lastError
```

GlobalMemoryStatus and IGlobalMemoryStatus

The GlobalMemoryStatus function is a convenient way to get some insight into the state of the machine's memory. The function fills in a MEMORY-STATUS structure with information such as how many pages of physical RAM are being used and the size of the swap file. In many ways, this function is the Win32 equivalent of the Windows 3.1 MemManInfo routine.

The actual GlobalMemoryStatus code is just a parameter validation layer stub. Its only test is to make sure that the pointer passed to the function points to enough memory to hold a MEMORYSTATUS structure. Despite what the documentation says, you don't have to initialize the dwLength field of the MEMORYSTATUS structure before calling GlobalMemoryStatus.

Pseudocode for GlobalMemoryStatus

```
// Parameters:
//   LPMEMORYSTATUS lpmstMemStat

    Set up structured exception handler frame

    // Make sure that the beginning and end of the MEMORYSTATUS
    // structure is accessible.
    *(PBYTE)lpmstMemStat += 0;
    *(PBYTE)(lpmstMemStat+0x1F) += 0;

    Remove structured exception handler frame

    goto IGlobalMemoryStatus;
```

The IGlobalMemoryStatus does nothing more than fill in a MEMORY-STATUS struct with an abreviated version of the information in a DemandInfoStruc structure. This structure is filled in by calling the _GetDemandPageInfo VxD function in VMM.VXD. Because ring 3 applications can't call VxDs directly, IGlobalMemoryStatus uses VMM Win32 service 0x0001001E as a surrogate for calling _GetDemandPageInfo. For the benefit of those who don't have the DDK documentation in front of you, a DemandInfoStruc looks like this:

DemandInfoStruc struc

DWORD	DILin_Total_Count	; Pages in linear address space.
DWORD	DIPhys_Count	; Specifies the total number of physical pages ; managed by the memory manager.
DWORD	DIFree_Count	; Specifies the number of pages currently in the ; free pool.
DWORD	DIUnlock_Count	; Specifies the number of pages that are currently ; unlocked. Free pages are always unlocked.
DWORD	DILinear_Base_Addr	; Always zero.
DWORD	DILin_Total_Free	; Total number of free virtual pages in the ; current memory context. This value includes only ; pages in the private arena.
DWORD	DIPage_Faults	; Total page faults.
DWORD	DIPage_Ins	; Calls to pagers to page in.
DWORD	DIPage_Outs	; Calls to pagers to page out.
DWORD	DIPage_Discards	; Calls to pagers to discard.
DWORD	DIInstance_Faults	; Instance page faults.
DWORD	DIPagingFileMax	; Current maximum size of the swap file, in pages. ; Zero if swapping is turned off.

```
DWORD    DIPagingFileInUse    ; Number of swap file pages currently in use. This
                              ; is the number of pages by which physical memory
                              ; is overcommitted. Zero if swapping is disabled
                              ; or if physical memory is available for all
                              ; swappable pages.
DWORD    DICommit_Count       ; Total committed pages.
DWORD    DIReserved[2]        ; Reserved; do not use.
DemandInfoStruc ends
```

No doubt, there will be many programs written that sit in the corner of the screen and tell the user what the "memory load" is. What exactly is the memory load? In the pseudocode, you can see that it's 50 times the committed page count divided by the number of physical pages managed by the Windows 95 memory manager. Put another way, it's half the percentage ratio of physical pages to committed pages. For example, a system with 8MB of RAM and 11MB of committed pages would have a memory load of 68 (out of a maximum 100):

$(11 \times 50) / 8 == 68.75$

And yes, you can have more committed pages than actual RAM. Committing a page doesn't mean that RAM will always be associated with it. Unless you pagelock the memory, Windows 95 is free to page it out.

IGlobalMemoryStatus proc

```
// Parameters:
//   LPMEMORYSTATUS lpmstMemStat
// Locals:
//   DemandInfoStruc dis;
//   DWORD    memLoad;

    Set up structured exception handler frame

    // Call the VMM Win32 VxD service to fill the struct
    VxDCall( _GetDemandPageInfo, &dis, 0 );

    memLoad = (dis.DICommit_Count * 50) / dis.DIPhys_Count
    if ( memLoad < 100 )
        lpmstMemStat->dwMemoryLoad = memLoad;
    else
        lpmstMemStat->dwMemoryLoad = 100;

    lpmstMemStat->dwTotalPhys = dis.DIPhys_Count * 4096;
```

```
lpmstMemStat->dwAvailPhys = dis.DIFree_Count * 4096;

lpmstMemStat->dwTotalPageFile = dis.DIPagingFileMax * 4096;

lpmstMemStat->dwAvailPageFile = 4096 *
    (dis.DIPagingFileMax - dis.DIPagingFileInUse)

lpmstMemStat->dwTotalVirtual = 0x7FC00000;  // Size of app private data
                                            // area (2GB - 4MB).

lpmstMemStat->dwAvailVirtual = dis.DILin_Total_Free * 4096;

lpmstMemStat->dwLength = sizeof( MEMORYSTATUS )

Remove structured exception handler frame
```

GetThreadSelectorEntry and IGetThreadSelectorEntry

When I saw the GetThreadSelectorEntry function, I was shocked that it was included in the Win32 API. GetThreadSelectorEntry has nothing to do with threads. In fact, the hThread parameter is checked for validity, but never used for anything. GetThreadSelectorEntry gives you read-only access to the system VM's local descriptor tables. This is the very descriptor table that contains the flat code and data segments for Win32 applications. It's also the descriptor table from which Win16 applications get their code and data segments, as well as GlobalAlloc'ed handles. This function is a valuable tool in any system spelunker's tool kit!

Assuming you pass a valid selector to GetThreadSelectorEntry, you'll get back an 8-byte structure that's the same as an LDT descriptor. Among the information in each descriptor is its base address and length. Because Win32 apps have a flat pointer that can reach anywhere, they can use this function to convert a 16:16 address to a flat 32 address that the Win32 app can read and write to. You can even construct your own Win32 versions of the Win16 GetSelectorBase and GetSelectorLimit function.

Speaking of GetSelectorLimit, on page 449 of *Unauthorized Windows 95*, there is code for obtaining the base address of a selector. This code used a VWIN32 VxD service call to invoke DPMI subfunction 6. This DPMI subfunction returns the base address of the specified selector. While this method is technically impressive, GetThreadSelectorEntry would have worked just as well and would have made the code simpler. Better yet, GetThread-SelectorEntry is a documented function, which should be used in preference to undocumented functions if at all possible.

Of primary interest in the GetThreadSelectorEntry code are the LDTAlias and LDTPtr variables. These are both global variables in KERNEL32.DLL. LDTPtr contains the linear address of the system VM's LDT. LDTAlias is a selector value with read and write access to the selector table's memory. This is the same LDT alias selector that KRNL386 uses to bash the selector table inside the global heap functions. (See Chapter 2 of *Windows Internals*.)

GetThreadSelectorEntry proc

```
// Parameters:
//      HANDLE  hThread;
//      DWORD  dwSelector;
//      LPLDT_ENTRY  lpSelectorEntry;

    Set up structured exception handling frame

    Touch the first and last bytes that lpSelectorEntry points to.
    If a fault occurs, it's considered a bad pointer, and the exception
    handler returns FALSE;

    Remove structured exception handling frame

    goto IGetThreadSelectorEntry;

IGetThreadSelectorEntry proc
// Parameters:
//      HANDLE  hThread;
//      DWORD  dwSelector;
//      LPLDT_ENTRY  lpSelectorEntry;
// Locals:
//      PTHREAD_DATABASE ptdb;
//      BOOL    retValue;
//      LPLDT_ENTRY pLDTAliasDesc;
//      LPLDT_ENTRY pDesiredDesc;


    retValue = TRUE;

    x_CheckNotSysLevel_Win16_Krn32_mutexes();

    x_LogSomeKernelFunction( function number for GetThreadSelectorEntry );
```

```
    _EnterSysLevel( Win16Mutex );

    _EnterSysLevel( Krn32Mutex );

    ptdb = x_ConvertHandleToK32Object( hThread, 0x20, 0 );
    if ( ptdb )                 // The hThread is okay.
    {
        if ( dwSelector & 0x4 ) // Check if it's a GDT selector. Bail if so.
        {
            InternalSetLastError( ERROR_INVALID_PARAMETER );
            goto error;
        }

        pDesiredDesc = dwSelector & 0x0000FFF8;     // Get offset in LDT.

        // Get a ptr to LDT alias selector's descriptor in the LDT.
        pLDTDesc = LDTPtr + (LDTAlias & 0x0000FFF8);

        // Check if the selector asked for is outside the upper limit
        // of in-use selectors in the LDT.
        if ( pDesiredDesc > pLDTDesc->limit )
        {
            InternalSetLastError( ERROR_INVALID_PARAMETER );
            goto error;
        }

        pDesiredDesc += LDTPtr;     // Make it point into the LDT now.

        // Copy the LDT descriptor into lpSelectorEntry.
        memcpy( lpSelectorEntry, pDesiredDesc, sizeof(LDT_ENTRY) );
    }
    else
    {
error:
        retValue = FALSE;
    }

    SomeOutputFunction( "GetThreadSelectorEntry sel %04x erc %d\n",
                        dwSelector, (retValue ? 0 : GetLastError()) );

    _LeaveSysLevel( Krn32Mutex );

    _LeaveSysLevel( Win16Mutex );

    return retValue;
```

The C/C++ compiler's malloc and new functions

In many cases, C/C++ programmers ignore all the operating systems memory management functions and use the C runtime library for their memory management, specifically, the malloc and free functions. But what if you use C++? In all PC compilers that I know of, the new operator maps directly to malloc, and delete maps to free. The question is, how are these functions implemented in terms of the underlying OS functionality?

In this chapter, I've shown how the heap functions (such as HeapAlloc and HeapFree) are fairly close in functionality to malloc and free. Does this mean that malloc and free in the C runtime libraries are just wrappers around HeapAlloc and HeapFree? Up until Visual C++ 4.0, the answer was no, with one exception: the CRTDLL.DLL version of the C runtime library from Microsoft. In CRTDLL.DLL, malloc and new simply call HeapAlloc, whereas free or delete call HeapFree. CRTDLL.DLL is used by many standard Windows NT and Windows 95 EXEs and DLLs. This is a great idea, because it prevents Microsoft from having to ship a separate copy of the C runtime library in every EXE and DLL.

Unfortunately, the C compiler vendors haven't cooperated enough to enable everyone to use the CRTDLL.DLL shipped with their operating systems. Thus, we're still stuck with separate copies of the C runtime library in every executable or (only slightly better) shipping C runtime DLLs with our programs. Because this scenario isn't likely to change soon, it's a good idea to know what's going on under the hood of these runtime libraries.

I'm not going to cover malloc and free from the C runtime libraries in the same detail as the operating system functions. Instead, I'll give enough of an overview that you can judge for yourself how you want to implement your memory management code.

As far as I've been able to determine, both Borland and Microsoft implement their runtime library heaps in a similar manner. In fact, other than the size of the heaps, the situation hasn't changed much from Windows 3.x days. Each executable file or DLL has its own heap. A program with three DLLs will end up having four separate heaps (one for the EXE, and one for each of the DLLs). An allocation made in a given DLL will come from that DLL's heap. Contrast this to the Win32 HeapAlloc function, which — no matter where it comes from — allocates memory from the application's heap (assuming that you always pass in the default process heap handle).

Rather than using the high-level operating system functions such as HeapAlloc, the heaps provided by the C compiler RTLs use their own data structures and memory management code. This can make it difficult to mix and match HeapAlloc'ed and malloc'ed memory in the same program (as a fellow programmer at Nu-Mega found out the hard way).

By digging deep enough into some C/C++ RTL code, we can see how malloc maps to the underlying OS functions. I did the hard work of burrowing down through all the levels of the Borland C++ 4.5 RTL so that you don't have to. A call stack showing how malloc is implemented on top of Windows 95 functions looks like this:

```
malloc (HEAP.C)
    _getmem (GETMEM.C)
        _virt_reserve (VIRTMEM.C)
            VirtualAlloc( NULL, size, MEM_RESERVE, PAGE_NOACCESS )
```

Aha! The C runtime library allocates big blocks of memory from the OS using VirtualAlloc, which is essentially the same thing HeapAlloc does. The pages in the allocated area are initially reserved (decommitted), and must be committed with _virt_commit before they can be used. (_virt_commit is just a wrapper around VirtualCommit.) Does this method of committing pages as they are accessed sound familiar? It should. This is the same way that Windows 95 commits memory to its heaps. Go back and reread the section on hpCarve and hpCommit if you need a refresher.

The runtime libraries aren't going to call VirtualAlloc for each call to malloc. They need to set up and maintain internal data structures to keep track of what blocks are allocated or not, as well as keep a free list for fast allocations. What do the heap blocks look like? This comment from HEAP.C is illuminating:

```
/*----------------------------------------------------------------------
 * Knuth's "boundary tag" algorithm is used to manage the heap.
 * Each block in the heap has tag words before and after it, which
 * contain the size of the block:
 *  SIZE
 *  block ...
 *  SIZE
 * The size is stored as a long word, and includes the 8 bytes of
 * overhead that the boundary tags consume.  Blocks are allocated
 * on LONG word boundaries, so the size is always even.  When the
 * block is allocated, bit 0 of the size is set to 1.  When a block is
 * freed, it is merged with adjacent free blocks, and bit 0 of the
 * size is set to 0.
 *
 * When a block is on the free list, the first two LONG words of the block
 * contain double links.  These links are not used when the block is
 * allocated, but space needs to be reserved for them.  Thus, the minimum
 * block size (not counting the tags) is 8 bytes.
```

Hmm . . . the retail build of Windows 95 manages heap blocks in a similar (but not identical) manner. However, the overhead of a HeapAlloc block is only 4 bytes (for the size), but the Borland C++ runtime library uses 8 bytes per block. Note also the similarities in how Borland C++ and the HeapAlloc function use memory in a free block to point to another free block.

A potential gotcha when using the heaps provided by a runtime library is their lifetime. When a DLL unloads from memory and receives the DLL_PROCESS_DETACH notification, the runtime library calls VirtualFree to release the heap's memory. If other DLLs have pointers into this memory block, the pointers will suddenly become invalid. If another DLLs unloads later on, and uses one of these pointers during its DLL_PROCESS_DETACH processing, you'll have program crashes that are difficult to debug. Take it from somebody who learned this painfully.

So, to answer my original question, malloc is essentially a compiler implemented version of the Windows 95 HeapAlloc function, with at least two key differences. First, each EXE and DLL has its own heap provided by the runtime library, whereas all HeapAlloc allocations come from the default process heap set up by the system. Second, the lifetime of the runtime library heaps is shorter than that of the default process heap. In certain sequence-related operations, there can be problems with using the runtime library heaps. This is not to say that you should avoid new or malloc, however. Just be aware of what they are and the potential tradeoffs.

SUMMARY

Whew! This chapter (although by far the longest in the book) has barely touched on all the various aspects of Windows 95 memory management. We've examined memory paging by the CPU, separate address spaces for each process, and the memory regions that Windows 95 shares among all processes. At the Win32 API level, we've seen how the VirtualXXX functions manage pages at the page level, and the HeapXXX functions provide memory management at a much finer level of granularity. The holdover heap functions ported from the Win16 API (that is, the GlobalXXX and LocalXXX functions) are really just a thin layer over the HeapXXX functions. In the next chapter we'll see how the ring 3 KERNEL32.DLL communicates with the ring 0 virtual memory manager to obtain the basic building block services that the heap functions are built atop.

VWINKERNEL32386

6

*O*ne day, several coworkers and I were hanging out in an office, ruminating about the core architecture of Windows 95. As is often the case, the topic at hand turned to how various components of Windows 95 have intimate knowledge of other components. (This is usually considered a Bad Thing; something to be avoided if possible.) This particular day, one of my colleagues wondered, "Why does Microsoft bother having separate 16- and 32-bit kernels, as well a kernel-like VXD? Why don't they just ram them all together into one file and be done with it?"

In this chapter, I examine that issue. In fact, the title of this chapter (VWINKERNEL32386) is a contraction of the components just mentioned: VWIN32.VXD, KERNEL32.DLL, and KRNL386.EXE. Warning: This chapter contains some pretty advanced stuff. It's not essential to understand this chapter to continue on with the rest of the book.

Windows application programmers will immediately recognize KRNL386.EXE as the 16-bit KERNEL, and KERNEL32.DLL as its 32-bit equivalent. These DLLs export the core set of functions that every Win16 or Win32 application uses (for instance, LoadLibrary, _lread, and so on). (Most of) the functions in these DLLs are documented in the standard system header files provided with the SDK or your compiler. For 16-bit programs, the WINDOWS.H file prototypes the functions in KRNL386.EXE. Under Win32, WINBASE.H and WINCON.H describe most of the functions in KERNEL32.DLL.

Unfortunately, the third kernel listed above (VWIN32.VXD) is barely mentioned in any Microsoft documentation or header files. In fact, to my knowledge, the only acknowledgment that VWIN32.VXD exists is the VWIN32.H file from the Windows 95 DDK. Calling VWIN32.H "documentation" is a stretch, especially when you learn that VWIN32.VXD is one of the top two most important VxDs (along with the Virtual Machine Manager, or VMM). VWIN32.VXD provides key operating system primitives at ring 0 — primatives that are used by both the 16-bit KRNL386 and the 32-bit KERNEL32. As I discovered repeatedly throughout the research for this book, any serious attempt to examine KRNL386 or KERNEL32 quickly drags you into the realm of VWIN32.VXD.

Seeing as how Microsoft's documentation on VWIN32.VXD is so deficient, I tried to remedy that situation in this chapter. First, I describe VWIN32.VXD and its interfaces. Then I show how all three kernel components are interrelated and have knowledge of one another. Spelling this out:

- KRNL386.EXE knows about and calls into VWIN32.VXD.

- KRNL386.EXE knows about and calls into KERNEL32.DLL.

- KERNEL32.DLL knows about and calls into KRNL386.EXE.

- KERNEL32.DLL knows about and calls into VWIN32.VXD.

- VWIN32.VXD knows about and exchanges information with KERNEL32.DLL.

- VWIN32.VXD knows about and exchanges information with KRNL386.EXE.

Of particular interest in all these permutations is the one where KERNEL32 calls into KRNL386.EXE. Microsoft's reviewer's guide swears that this doesn't happen, yet *Unauthorized Windows 95* proved Microsoft's claims to be false. In this chapter, I provide a comprehensive listing of exactly which functions KERNEL32 calls down to KRNL386.EXE for.

Another subject *Unauthorized Windows 95* touched on is Win32 VxD services. These services provide an easy way for Win32 programs to call into VxDs using a standard C-style calling convention. Win32 VxD services are a major part of the Windows 95 architecture. As one example of this, every file I/O call is eventually translated into a Win32 VxD service call.

(Strange as it may seem, the particular Win32 VxD service ultimately calls the VMM.VXD Exec_PM_Int with an interrupt number of 21h. Sound familiar? DOS just will *not* die, will it?)

Unfortunately, Microsoft chose not to formally document Win32 VxD services. Since *Unauthorized Windows 95* was able to devote only a couple of pages to these crucial Win32 VxD services, I discuss them in more depth in this chapter. Often, the best way to learn and explore undocumented interfaces is to write tools. Thus, this chapter includes a spy program (W32SVSPY) to monitor calls to Win32 VxD services. I had to cross quite a few hurdles — some of them intentionally thrown up by Microsoft — to make W32SVSPY work properly. Toward the end of the chapter I describe how W32SVSPY works its magic. The techniques involved might prove handy in your own system-level programming.

A Crash Course in VxDs

Since I'm going to be talking extensively about VWIN32.VXD in the pages to come, it would be helpful to be at least passingly familiar with the basics of VxDs. For the benefit of those readers who aren't VxD-heads (and I'm certainly not one), a quick overview of VxDs is in order. If you've written VxDs and know them cold, you can skip over this section.

As its name implies, a VxD *can* be a Virtual Device Driver. That is, it can be used to virtualize a particular hardware device among multiple programs that use it. However, nothing says that a VxD has to be associated with an actual device. A VxD is really nothing more than a DLL that runs at the highest privilege level of the processor (ring 0). Since VxDs run at ring 0, there's essentially nothing they can't do. However, in exchange for all their power, VxDs are typically difficult to write, and can't be called as easily as regular ring 3 DLLs.

I'm not going to attempt to describe how to write VxDs, or go into all the various nifty tricks and techniques that are available to VxD writers. There are books like *Unauthorized Windows 95* and Dave Thielen's *Writing Windows Device Drivers* that cover VxDs in far more depth than I will here. My goal is to explain just enough about VxDs so that I can move on to describe VWIN32.VXD.

When loaded into memory, VxDs are uniquely identified by their 16-bit device number. VxD device ID 1 is VMM.VXD, whereas the Virtual Keyboard Device (VKD) uses a device ID of 0Dh. The ID for VWIN32.VXD (the focus of much of this chapter) is 2Ah. You can get a fairly complete list of the standard predefined VxDs and their IDs by looking for the *xxx*_DEVICE_ID definitions in the VMM.INC or VMM.H files in the Windows 95 DDK. Note that VxD IDs below 512 are reserved for Microsoft's use. Other companies that write VxDs are supposed to request VxD IDs from Microsoft.

Calling VxD functions from other VxDs

Just as ring 3 system DLLs have a standard method of exporting functions for use by EXEs and other DLLs, there are provisions for allowing certain functions in a VxD to be called by other VxDs. When the VxD is created, all the functions that are externally callable are listed in an array. Each of these functions is called a *service*. When one VxD calls into another VxD, it doesn't use the name of the service. Rather, it uses the index number of the function within the array. For instance, consider the following snippet from VMM.INC:

```
Begin_Service_Table VMM, VMM
VMM_Service   Get_VMM_Version, LOCAL
VMM_Service   Get_Cur_VM_Handle
VMM_Service   Test_Cur_VM_Handle
VMM_Service   Get_Sys_VM_Handle
```

A VxD that calls the Get_VMM_Version function will be calling VMM service 0. A call to Get_Cur_VM_Handle is really a call to VMM service 1. The Test_Cur_VM_Handle function is VMM service 2, and so forth.

The actual mechanics of a call from one VxD to the service of another are quite interesting. Unlike ring 3 system DLLs, the VxD loader doesn't patch up CALL instructions in the originating VxD's code to contain the address of the destination service function. In fact, when a VxD is built, there's no CALL instruction put into the code at all! In place of a CALL instruction, a call to a VxD service function looks like this:

```
INT 20h
DD  device_and_service_number   ;; A different value for each VxD service
```

The contents of the DWORD that follow the INT 20h aren't just randomly chosen values. Rather, the high WORD contains the device number (which I described earlier), and the low WORD contains the service number within the device. Returning to our earlier example, a call to the Test_Cur_VM_Handle (VMM service 2) would be encoded like this:

```
    INT 20h
    DD  00010002h   ;; 0001=VMM device ID, 0002=service # for
Test_Cur_VM_Handle
```

To give another example, the GetSystemTime service is the third service in VWIN32.VXD. Therefore, when the VxD is built, its encoding would be:

```
    INT 20h
    DD  002A0002h   ;; 002A=VWIN32 device ID, 0002=service # for
                    ;; GetSystemTime (service numbers start at 0)
```

When the ring 0 INT 20h handler is invoked, it examines the DWORD following the interrupt instruction, and uses the device ID and service number to look up the desired target address. If this sounds slow, never fear. After a given INT 20h in the code has been invoked once, the INT 20h handler patches the code to be an actual CALL instruction. This works out nicely, since an INT 20 followed by a DWORD takes up 6 bytes, which is exactly what a near 32-bit indirect call takes up (that is, call DWORD PTR [*xxxxxxxx*]). One way to view this is that the VxD loader doesn't patch up all calls to imported functions at VxD load time. Rather, it fixes up only the code locations that are actually used.

A twist to this system of dynamically fixing up VxD code via INT 20h's occurs when the low WORD of the service number has its high bit (0x8000) set. When this is the case, the code is patched to a JMP instruction, rather than to a CALL. For example, the following would be a JMP to the Test_Cur_VM_Handle function, rather than a CALL:

```
    INT 20h
    DD  00018002h
```

Calling VxD functions from Win16 (protected mode) code

If only VxDs were allowed to call other VxDs, Windows would be a pretty boring place. Since VxDs can go anywhere and do anything it's only natural that there should be a way for regular ring 3 application code to call VxDs.

This ability to get up into ring 0 code from ring 3 application code allows applications to do things that they ordinarily wouldn't be able to do on their own. The popular thinking these days is that whenever you come to a brick wall where something can't be done in normal application code, you just write a VxD and call it from the application.

Some people (myself included) would argue that this strategy should be used sparingly. Anybody can write a VxD that's unrestricted from doing horrible things to the system (either intentionally or unintentionally). Personally, I think that if you can avoid writing a VxD, you should. The less all-powerful, unrestricted code in the system, the better. I dread the day when my hard drive is littered with vanity VxDs because inexperienced programmers figured a VxD was the only way to accomplish something. This book covers quite a bit of ground and creates more than its share of intentional mayhem without ever using a VxD.

Putting my personal opinion aside, calling a VxD from a DOS or Win16 program is somewhat of a pain, but not difficult. A VxD can export a set of functions that are callable from V86 (real) mode, ring 3 protected mode (Win16 code), or both. The VxD has separate entry points for calls made from V86 mode programs versus ring 3 protected mode, although both entry points can be set to the same address if desired.

To call a VxD from V86 or 16-bit protected mode, the application first acquires an address that it can make a far CALL to. This address is obtained by calling INT 2Fh, with 1684h in the AX register. To identify which VxD an entry point is being requested for, the BX register is set to the 16-bit VxD ID that I mentioned earlier. Upon return from the INT instruction, the ES:DI registers contain a 16:16 far pointer that can be called to transfer control to the VxD running at ring 0.

Let's look at a code snippet from KRNL386 that shows how KRNL386 gets the entry point for VWIN32.VXD (and that queries the version of VWIN32.VXD while it's at it):

```
XOR    DI,DI          ; Zero out ES:DI in case the operation fails.
MOV    ES,DI
MOV    AX,1684        ; INT 2Fh, AX = 1684h -> Get Device Entry Point
MOV    BX,002A        ; 002Ah = Device ID for VWIN32.VXD
INT    2F
MOV    AX,ES          ; ES:DI should now contain the entry point.
OR     AX,AX          ; Is the segment part of the return address 0?
JE     failure        ; Yes? Go to the failure case code.

MOV    AH,00          ; VWIN32 service 0 = VWIN32_Get_Version
```

```
PUSH   DS                          ; Save away the current DS on the stack.
MOV    DS,WORD PTR CS:[0002]       ; Load DS with KRNL386's DGROUP selector.

MOV    WORD PTR [lpfnVWIN32],DI    ; Save away the entry point (in ES:DI).
MOV    WORD PTR [lpfnVWIN32+2],ES
CALL   FAR [lpfnVWIN32]            ; Call the entry point with AH = 0.
```

Those of you familiar with protected mode on Intel architecture CPUs may be scratching your head, wondering how this all works. Ring 3 code cannot just call ring 0 code; there are protection mechanisms that prevent this. (A full discussion of ring levels and protection is beyond the scope of this chapter.) Ring 3 code that tries to call (that is, load) a selector with a ring 0 privilege level will GP fault unless special arrangements are made. The Intel architecture supports a rarely used mechanism called *call gates;* call gates allow ring 3 code to call into ring 0 code in a very controlled manner. However, there's nothing so elegant at work here.

If you were to pop into a system debugger like SoftIce/W or WDEB386 and disassemble at the address returned by the INT 2Fh, AX=1684h call shown in the previous code snippet, you'd see something like this:

```
:u 3B:03d0
003B:000003D0   INT     30 ; #0028:C025DB52   VWIN32(04)+0742
003B:000003D2   INT     30 ; #0028:C0002BC9   VMM(01)+1BC9
003B:000003D4   INT     30 ; #0028:C022F713   VMM(0D)+0713
```

Hmm . . .That's strange. The entry point returned by the INT 2Fh call points at an INT 30h instruction. What's going on here? Windows is using an INT 30h to force the CPU from ring 3 up to ring 0. Any interrupt or exception implicitly causes the CPU to transfer control to the appropriate ring 0 handler address stored in the Interrupt Descriptor Table (IDT). The Windows 95 INT 30 handler uses the CS:IP of the invoked INT 30h instruction to look up a ring 0 address that the handler should transfer control to. In this listing, the address following the ; (the semicolon) is the address that will handle each particular INT 30h when invoked. (SoftIce/W knows how to find and decode the dispatch table used by the INT 30h handler, so it's able to show the handler addresses.) It's not surprising that the INT 30h handler address for the VWIN32.VXD entry point lies within VWIN32.VXD itself. If we go a step farther and unassemble at the ring 0 address assigned to VWIN32 entry point INT 30h, we'll come to the following:

```
:u 28:c025db52

0028:C025DB52   MOVZX   EAX,BYTE PTR [EBP+1D]   ; Get AH value at INT 30h.

0028:C025DB56   CMP     EAX,+15                 ; There are 16 VWIN32 PM
0028:C025DB59   JA      C025DB62                ; services. Is it within
                                                ; range? If not, go to
                                                ; the error-reporting code.

0028:C025DB5B   JMP     [C03229A4+4*EAX]        ; Call through the service
                                                ; JMP table to the appropriate
                                                ; service entry point.

0028:C025DB62   PUSH    C03229FC    ; string ptr -> "VWIN32_PMAPI_Proc: "
                                    ; "invalid function number\r\n"

0028:C025DB67   INT     20 VXDCall _Debug_Out_Service   ; Emit error diagnostic.
```

The first instruction needs some explanation. When a VxD V86/PM API routine is called, the application doesn't push arguments on the stack. The primary reason for this is that the ring 0 VxD code uses a different stack than the ring 3 application stack. (When the CPU switches between protection levels, it also switches the stack registers to a stack specifically designated for use by code at the new ring level.)

Since the ring 3 code can't push parameters to the VxD function, the convention is that parameters to VxD functions are put into registers prior to invoking the INT 30h. When the INT 30h handler calls the appropriate ring 0 handler, it passes a pointer to a structure containing the ring 3 register values at the time of the INT 30h. This pointer is a flat, 32-bit pointer, and is kept in the EBP register. The structure that EBP points to is called the Client Register Structure (see Client_Reg_Struc in VMM.INC). VxDs that provide APIs callable by V86 or 16-bit ring 3 protected mode programs know that they can read and write the ring 3 register values through the client register structure pointer in EBP.

In the first instruction (in the code snippet you just saw), the handler is loading EAX with the value that was in the AH register at the time of the INT 30h. The convention used for calling VxD functions from V86 or ring 3 16-bit protected mode is that the function number is put into the AH register. If the function ID is within range, the handler code uses a JMP table to transfer control to the appropriate function entry point in VWIN32.VXD. If the function ID is out of range, the handler prints an error message.

CALLING VxD FUNCTIONS FROM WIN32 CODE

The two interfaces to VxDs that I've just described date back to Windows 3.0. In Windows 95 there weren't any fundamental changes to these two interfaces. However, Windows 95 does add yet another interface for calling VxDs. Since Windows 95 supports running Win32 applications in addition to running DOS and Win16 applications, it's no surprise that Microsoft has provided a way for Win32 code to call into VxDs. This brings the total number of VxD interfaces up to four (ring 0 VxD services, calls from V86 mode programs, calls from ring 3 16-bit protected mode code, and the new interface, which I'll be describing next).

Because this new method of interfacing to VxDs is available only to ring 3 Win32 code, functions in this new interface are called Win32 VxD services. The term Win32 VxD service should not be confused with regular VxD services (which are VxD functions that can be called by other VxDs). Nor should Win32 VxD services be confused with the Win32 Services that you'd find in Windows NT. Windows NT Services are more like daemon processes, and are completely unrelated to Win32 VxD services.

Alas, for reasons that make no sense (at least not to me), Microsoft has chosen to hide Win32 VxD service interface. This may be to discourage people from writing code that's not portable to Windows NT, since Windows NT doesn't support VxDs. Instead, Microsoft wants you to use the DeviceIoControl Win32 API, which is semi-portable between Windows NT and Windows 95. The problem is, the DeviceIoControl interface is clunkier and slower than using straight Win32 VxD Services. In fact, in Windows 95, DeviceIoControl eventually ends up calling a Win32 VxD service anyhow!

Since Windows 95 has a much higher content of code written in C than earlier versions of Windows, it's only natural that the Win32 VxD service interface should be C-callable. That is, the Win32 VxD service functions can easily be invoked by ring 3 code written in C. The parameters to Win32 VxD services are passed on the stack, just like a call to a normal function. This is a marked improvement over the other VxD interfaces, which are normally invoked using assembly language, since the parameters need to be placed into registers.

Viewing VxD Interfaces in SoftIce/W

SoftIce/W for Windows 95 knows about all the various VxD interfaces that I've been describing in this section, including the new Win32 VxD services. You can see this by using the VxD command in conjunction with a specific VxD name. For example, the command "VXD REBOOT" produces the following output:

```
:VXD REBOOT
VxD Name  Address   Length  Seg   ID    DDB         Control   PM  V86  VxD  Win32
REBOOT    C00910CC  0002F0  0001  0009  C0091334    C00910CC  Y   N    4    2
REBOOT    C0201F94  0002E9  0002
REBOOT    C037E9A0  00010C  0003
REBOOT    C02269D4  0000EE  0004
REBOOT    C0233B44  00009C  0005
REBOOT    C02373BC  00004B  0006
Total Memory:    3K
Init Order=24000000  Reference Data=0  Version 4.00
PM API=C02269D4 (3B:3EC)  V86 API=0 (0:0)
4 VxD Services
  0000  C00912D5
  0001  C00912DA
  0002  C00912E2
  0003  C009123B
2 Win32 Services ────────
  0000  C0226A04  Parms=02
  0001  C0226A19  Parms=02
```

The first couple of lines give us a wealth of information. We know (from the "Y" under the "PM") that the REBOOT device provides an interface for calling it from ring 3 16-bit protected mode programs. We also know (from the "N" under "V86") that the REBOOT device doesn't provide an interface for calling it from V86 mode code. Continuing on, we see that the REBOOT device has four regular VxD services (callable by other VxDs), and two Win32 VxD services.

Moving down to the end of the report, notice the last three lines, which concern themselves with the Win32 VxD services provided by the REBOOT device. There are two of these services, and their details are found on the last two lines. Both lines contain the entry point address for the service, as well as the number of DWORD parameters that the service expects. From this information (or by studying the correct parts of VMM.INC), you can deduce that each Win32 VxD service has an 8-byte (2 DWORDs) structure associated with it:

```
DWORD  pfnService;   // The address of the service function.
DWORD  cParams;      // The number of DWORD parameters.
```

Continued

> *Continued from previous page*
>
> I call this structure a *service table entry*. When a VxD starts up, it has to register its Win32 VxD services with the system. It does this by calling the _Register_Win32_Services function in VMM.VXD. One of the parameters to the _Register_Win32_Services function is a pointer to the Win32 VxD service table for the VxD. This pointer is stored in the VxD's Device Descriptor Block (DDB), which is where SoftIce/W is getting all the information shown in the previous output.

Calling a Win32 VxD service is different from calling any of the other available VxDs interfaces. Instead of invoking an interrupt or calling through a function pointer, a call to a Win32 VxD service begins by calling an undocumented function in KERNEL32 named VxDCall. Prior to calling the VxDCall function, the calling code pushes any arguments to the Win32 VxD service on the stack. The final value pushed on the stack prior to the VxDCall invocation is a DWORD similar in form to a regular VxD service ID. That is, the high WORD specifies which VxD is to be used, and the low WORD contains a zero-based function index. In this case, the function index is an index into the Win32 VxD service table, rather than into the regular ring 0 VxD service table.

An example makes this clearer. The following code invokes the VWIN32_sleep function in VWIN32.VXD. VWIN32_sleep is the tenth Win32 VxD service provided by VWIN32.VXD, so its function number is 9 (Win32 VxD service functions are numbered starting from 0).

```
PUSH    DWORD PTR [EBP+08]   // Push a parameter.
PUSH    002A0009             // 002A = VWIN32, 0009 = VWIN32_sleep
CALL    VxDCall
```

The VxDCall function is a stdcall function (meaning parameters are passed right to left, and the callee cleans the stack). The previous code written in C would look like this:

```
VxDCall( 0x002A0009, parameter );
```

If you dump out the exports from KERNEL32.DLL, you'll find that the first eight exported entry points (export ordinals 1 through 9) all refer to the same address. This address is the VxDCall function. Why eight separate entry points for the same function? To make a long story short: Internally, these entry points are called VxDCall@0, VxDCall@4, VxDCall@8 and so on through VxDCall@28. The Microsoft C compiler "mangles" the names of stdcall functions (such as VxDCall) to include an @ (an asterisk), followed by the number of parameter bytes that the function uses. Since different Win32 VxD services take different number of arguments, one call to the VxDCall function may end up being translated to VxDCall@4 by the compiler, while another becomes VxDCall@16. By providing multiple entry points with slightly varying names, the linker is able to resolve all the calls to the VxDCall function, regardless of how many parameters a particular VxDCall call uses. For the purposes of this chapter, I'm going to refer to all of these entry points collectively as the *VxDCall function*. (If you've read *Unauthorized Windows 95*, note that in that book the VxDCall function is referred to as VxDCall0).

Summing up what we've learned to date, Win32 code that calls a Win32 VxD service first pushes any parameters on the stack and then pushes the DWORD service ID. This DWORD identifies both the VxD to be called and the Win32 VxD service function within that VxD. Finally, the code calls the VxDCall function in KERNEL32.DLL. When the Win32 VxD service returns, execution resumes at the instruction immediately following the call to VxDCall, with all the parameters removed off the stack.

Okay, that's how calling Win32 VxD services looks like from the outside. Let's jump into the details of how Win32 VxD services are actually implemented. We'll start by looking at the code for the VxDCall function:

```
VxDCall:

MOV     EAX,DWORD PTR [ESP+04]    ; Get service code (e.g., 0x002A0010) into EAX.

POP     DWORD PTR [ESP]           ; Move the return address up on stack so
                                  ; that the call below returns directly to
                                  ; the caller.

CALL    FWORD PTR CS:[BFFC9004]   ; 16:32 CALL to INT 30 instruction that
                                  ; transfers control to ring 0.
```

The first two instructions have the net effect of removing the DWORD VxD service ID off the stack and putting it into EAX. The return EIP pushed by the 32-bit near call to the VxDCall function is then slid up on the stack to occupy the place formerly held by the Win32 VxD service ID. The third instruction is a 32-bit far call to an INT 30h instruction. Hey! We've seen

INT 30hs before! They're the way that V86 mode and 16-bit protected mode programs call VxDs. However, this isn't a normal INT 30h instruction:

```
u 3B:000003DE:    // The 16:32 pointer found at BFFC9004

003B:000003DE    INT    30 ; #0028:C02301E4  VMM(0D)+11E4
```

This INT 30h used by the VxDCall function to transfer control to ring 0 jumps somewhere inside VMM.VXD. Let's look at some pseudocode for what we find at that address in VMM.VXD:

```
//---------------------------------------
// Entry point for all Win32 VxD Services (in VMM.VXD).
//---------------------------------------
// Parameters:
//     Client_Reg_Struct   * pClientRegs
// Locals:
//     PVOID   pRing3StackFrame // ESP at time of INT 30 call that got us here.
//     DWORD   service_DWORD;
//     WORD    vxd_id;          // HIWORD of the service_DWORD.
//     WORD    service_index;   // LOWORD of the service_DWORD.
//     DWORD   cParams;         // # of parameters for this service.
//     PROC    pfnService;      // The address of the service entry point.

    DS = pClientRegs->Client_SS;

    pRing3StackFrame = pClientRegs->Client_ESP;

    // pRing3StackFrame now points to following on the ring 3 stack:
    //
    // Args pushed for VxDCall()       <- pRing3StackFrame + C
    // Return Address for VxDCall()    <- pRing3StackFrame + 8
    // CALL FWORD PTR CS value         <- pRing3StackFrame + 4
    // CALL FWORD PTR EIP value        <- pRing3StackFrame + 0

    access_rights = LAR pClientRegs->Client_SS;

    if ( !(access_rights & BIG_BIT) )   // If "big" bit not set, use just
    {                                   // the low WORD of pRing3StackFrame.
        pRing3StackFrame = LOWORD(pRing3StackFrame);
    }
```

```
// Fill in the client registers with the CS:EIP that ring 3 execution
// should resume at. The CS value on the ring 3 stack comes from the
// CALL FWORD PTR [xxxxxxxx] to the INT 30h. The EIP is the return
// address from the call to VxDCall0. (Yes, this is goofy.)

pClientRegs->Client_EIP = pRing3StackFrame->EIP;
pClientRegs->Client_CS - pRing3StackFrame->CS;

// Advance pRing3StackFrame to the location in the ring 3 stack where
// the VxDCall parameters are located.
pRing3StackFrame += 0xC;

// Get the service DWORD param to VxDCall (e.g., 0x002A0014).
service_DWORD = pClientRegs->Client_EAX;

vxd_id = service_DWORD >> 0x10; // Which VxD is it? (Look in the high word.)

if ( vxd_id < 0x40 )    // 0x40 is the last of the "standard" VxDs.
{
    // Does this particular VxD even have a Win32 VxD service table?
    if ( ppServiceTable[ vxd_id ] == 0 )
      goto error;

    // If we get here, this VxD supports Win32 VxD services. Is the
    // service index within the range of services provided?
    service_index = LOWORD( service_DWORD );

    if ( ppServiceTable[ vxd_id ].cServices <= service_index )
      goto error;

    service_index++;    // Bias the index up by 1, since the first entry
                        // in a service table holds the # of services.

    // Index into the Win32 service table and grab out the number of
    // DWORD params for this service, as well as the entry point address
    // of this service.

    cParams = ppServiceTable[ vxd_id ].cParams;
    pfnService = ppServiceTable[ vxd_id ].pfnService;

    // Now we start some stack contortions. The parameters pushed on the
    // ring 3 stack prior to the VxDCall now need to be copied to the
    // ring 0 stack.

    POP     EAX    // Remove return address from stack and save it
                   // away in EAX. (This is an address in VMM.)

    ESP -= cParam * 4;    // Make space on the stack for the arguments.
```

```
    EDI = ESP;                // Point destination register to the space
                              // we made on the stack for the arguments.


    PUSH    EBX     // Push current VM Handle.
    PUSH    EBP     // Push pointer to client regs struct.
    PUSh    EAX     // Push return address (saved away earlier).

    // If this service takes 1 or more parameters, copy them to the
    // ring 0 stack location we just made.

    if ( cParams )
        REP MOVSD   // ECX = cParams, ESI = pRing3StackFrame, EDI=

    // At this point, the stack looks like this:
    //
    // Args copied by REP MOVSD            <- ESP+0Ch
    // Current VM handle                   <- ESP+08h
    // Client reg struct pointer           <- ESP+04h
    // Return address from this PM API call <- ESP+00h

    DS = SS     // Ain't the flat model great?

    // Set the ring 3 ESP upon return to point just past the parameters
    // pushed on the stack by the call to VxDCall().

    pClientRegs->Client_ESP = pRing3StackFrame + (cParams * 4)

    goto    pfnService // Jump to the service entry point.
}
```

The VxDCall handler in VMM.VXD is complicated (to put it nicely). However, if you study it long enough, the code decomposes into a small number of specific tasks:

1. Read in important register values from the client register structure pointed to by EBP. These values include the ring 3 EAX (which contains the service ID), and the ring 3 ESP (which points to the ring 3 stack where the parameters were pushed).

2. Modify the CS and EIP register values in the client register structure so that when the ring 0 code returns, control continues at the instruction after the call to the KERNEL32 VxDCall function. Likewise, the code changes the ring 3 ESP register value to effectively pop the parameters that were pushed prior to the call.

3. Take the Win32 VxD Service ID DWORD and break it down into its components (the 16-bit VxD ID and the 16-bit service ID within the VXD). The code verifies whether the VxD ID is one of the standard system VxDs, and whether the designated VxD actually provides Win32 VxD services. If so, the code continues and checks to make sure the 16-bit service ID is within the range of function IDs that the VxD provides.

4. Copy the parameters pushed on the ring 3 stack over to the ring 0 stack.

5. Look up the entry point of the specified Win32 VxD service and JMP to it. Since the function may need access to the current VM handle or the client register structure values, the code first pushes these values before doing the JMP.

When the Win32 VxD service function finishes and returns, control transfers back into VMM.VXD. VMM.VXD handles the work of returning the CPU back to ring 3 with the registers set to the values contained in the client register structure.

WHERE CAN I FIND WIN32 VXD SERVICES?

As I mentioned earlier, Microsoft hasn't formally documented Win32 VxD services, so the DDK isn't forthcoming with a list of VxDs that provide Win32 VxD services. Based on my browsing around with the SoftIce/W VXD command, I've determined that the following VxDs export Win32 VxD services (although there may be others):

VxD	ID	Services	Description
VMM	0001h	41	Virtual Machine Manager
REBOOT	0009h	2	Reboot device
VNETBIOS	0014h	2	Virtual NetBios device
VWIN32	002Ah	79	Virtual Win32 "device"
VCOMM	002Bh	27	Virtual COMM device
VCOND	0038h	53	Virtual Console device

As I've shown elsewhere throughout this book, KERNEL32.DLL is a heavy user of the VWIN32, VMM and VCOND, and VCOMM devices. In some cases, exported KERNEL32 functions are just wrappers around a Win32 VxD service. This is even more the case in ADVAPI32.DLL. The

Win32 VxD services provided by VMM.VXD include registry functions that parallel the Win32 API registry functions. The exported registry functions in ADVAPI32.DLL are very thin layers wrappers around calls to the VMM Win32 VxD services.

WIN32 VXD SERVICES PROVIDED BY VMM

The focus of this chapter is Win32 VxD services and VWIN32.VXD. However, I'd be remiss if I didn't at least list the VxD services IDs for the Win32 VxD services exported by VMM.VXD:

00010000h	PageReserve	00010014h	RegDeleteKey
00010001h	PageCommit	00010015h	RegSetValue
00010002h	PageDecommit	00010016h	RegDeleteValue
00010003h	PagerRegister	00010017h	RegQueryValue
00010004h	PagerQuery	00010018h	RegEnumKey
00010005h	HeapAllocate	00010019h	RegEnumValue
00010006h	ContextCreate	0001001Ah	RegQueryValueEx
00010007h	ContextDestroy	0001001Bh	RegSetValueEx
00010008h	PageAttach	0001001Ch	RegFlushKey
00010009h	PageFlush	0001001Eh	GetDemandPageInfo
0001000Ah	PageFree	0001001Fh	BlockOnID
0001000Bh	ContextSwitch	00010020h	SignalID
0001000Ch	HeapReAllocate	00010021h	RegLoadKey
0001000Dh	PageModifyPermissions	00010022h	RegUnLoadKey
0001000Eh	PageQuery	00010023h	RegSaveKey
0001000Fh	GetCurrentContext	00010024h	RegRemapPreDefKey
00010010h	HeapFree	00010025h	PageChangePager
00010011h	RegOpenKey	00010026h	RegQueryMultipleValues
00010012h	RegCreateKey	00010027h	RegReplaceKey
00010013h	RegCloseKey		

I haven't provided information on the parameters to each of these functions for the simple reason that I don't know them myself. For the purposes of doing research for this book, simply knowing the names of the VMM Win32 VxD services was usually sufficient. No doubt, as time goes by, these parameters to these services will become known. However, the parameters for the registry-related services can be inferred by examining the documentation for the Win32 function corresponding with the service.

In many other cases, the Win32 VxD service corresponds exactly with a regular ring 0 VxD service that's described in the documentation for VMM.VXD. For example, the Win32 VxD service listed above with the name _PagerQuery corresponds exactly to the _PagerQuery service described in VMM.HLP. Connect the dots yourself.

The Win32 VxD services provided by VMM.VXD can be broken down into the following categories:

Category	Win32VxD services
Page-based memory management	_GetDemandPageInfo, _PageAttach, _PageCommit, _PageDecommit, _PageFlush, _PageFree, _PageModifyPermissions, _PageQuery, _PageReserve
Virtual memory paging support	_PageChangePager, _PagerRegister, _PagerQuery
Ring 0 heap management	_HeapAllocate, _HeapFree, _HeapReAllocate
Memory context management	_ContextCreate, _ContextDestroy, _ContextSwitch, _GetCurrentContext
Registry functions	_RegCloseKey, _RegCreateKey, _RegDeleteKey, _RegDeleteValue, _RegEnumKey, _RegEnumValue, _RegFlushKey, _RegLoadKey, _RegOpenKey, _RegQueryMultipleValues, _RegQueryValue, _RegQueryValueEx, _RegRemapPreDefKey, _RegReplaceKey, _RegSaveKey, _RegSetValue, _RegSetValueEx, _RegUnLoadKey
Synchronization	_BlockOnID, _SignalID

As you saw in Chapters 3 and 5, KERNEL32 definitely uses the page-based memory- and context-management services. Other areas of KERNEL32.DLL that aren't described in this book use the other categories of services. The registry services are an exception, however. They're invoked by ADVAPI32.DLL (through the VxDCall function in KERNEL32.DLL).

CALLING WIN32 VXD SERVICES ON YOUR OWN

To my knowledge, the only Microsoft code that calls Win32 VxD services is within the Windows 95 system DLLs. However, there's no reason that regular application programs can't call Win32 VxD services too. To prove this, I wrote the WIN95MEM program shown in Figure 6-1 (the complete sources are on the disk accompanying this book).

```c
//=================================================================
// WIN95MEM - Matt Pietrek 1995
// FILE: WIN95MEM.C
// Demonstrates calling a Win32 VxD service from application code
//=================================================================
#include <windows.h>
#include "win95mem.h"
#include "d:\chicddk\inc32\vmm.h"

DWORD WINAPI VxDCall2( DWORD service_number, DWORD, DWORD );

void Handle_WM_TIMER(HWND hWndDlg, WPARAM wParam, LPARAM lParam)
{
    struct DemandInfoStruc dis;
    char szBuffer[256];

    // Demonstrate calling a Win32 VxD service (in this case, the
    // _GetDemandPageInfo service).
    VxDCall2( 0x0001001E, (DWORD)&dis, 0 );

    wsprintf(szBuffer, "Comm: %uK", dis.DICommit_Count * 4);
    SetDlgItemText( hWndDlg, IDC_TEXT_commited, szBuffer );

    wsprintf(szBuffer, "Phys: %uK", dis.DIPhys_Count * 4);
    SetDlgItemText( hWndDlg, IDC_TEXT_physical, szBuffer );

    wsprintf(szBuffer, "%u%%",
                (dis.DICommit_Count * 100) / dis.DIPhys_Count);
    SetDlgItemText( hWndDlg, IDC_TEXT_percentage, szBuffer );
}

BOOL CALLBACK Win95MemDlgProc(HWND hWndDlg, UINT msg,
                              WPARAM wParam, LPARAM lParam)
{
```

```
switch ( msg )
{
    case WM_INITDIALOG:
        SetTimer( hWndDlg, 0, 1000, 0 ); return TRUE;
    case WM_TIMER:
        Handle_WM_TIMER(hWndDlg, wParam, lParam); return TRUE;
    case WM_CLOSE:
        KillTimer(hWndDlg, 0);
        EndDialog(hWndDlg, 0);
        return FALSE;
}

    return FALSE;
}
```

Figure 6-1
The Win95Mem program.

WIN95MEM uses the _GetDemandPageInfo Win32 VxD service provided by VMM.VXD. This service is just a wrapper around a call to the regular ring 0 VxD service of the same name. As I mentioned in Chapter 5, the Win32 GlobalMemoryStatus function uses this Win32 VxD service and simply returns selected chunks of information returned by the _GetDemandPageInfo service. Why use GlobalMemoryStatus and get a filtered view of the system information, when you can go straight to same source it uses?

The _GetDemandPageInfo service expects a parameter that's a pointer to a DemandInfoStruc structure. The service fills in this structure, which has the following fields:

DWORD	DILin_Total_Count
DWORD	DIPhys_Count
DWORD	DIFree_Count
DWORD	DIUnlock_Count
DWORD	DILinear_Base_Addr
DWORD	DILin_Total_Free
DWORD	DIPage_Faults
DWORD	DIPage_Ins
DWORD	DIPage_Outs

DWORD	DIPage_Discards
DWORD	DIInstance_Faults
DWORD	DIPagingFileMax
DWORD	DIPagingFileInUse
DWORD	DICommit_Count
DWORD	DIReserved

I'm not going to describe all the fields listed here. If you're interested, see the description of _GetDemandPageInfo in the VMM documentation from the Windows 95 DDK. For the purposes of the WIN95MEM program, we're interested in two fields, DICommit_Count and DIPhys_Count. DICommit_Count is the total number of pages that have been allocated (or committed) from the VMM memory manager. Note that a committed page isn't necessarily mapped to actual RAM. Rather, it's more like a reservation for a page to be used at some future date. The DIPhys_Count field contains the number of pages of RAM under the control of the virtual memory manager. This memory is all the memory that was available when the protected-mode portion of Windows 95 started out. It doesn't count any memory allocated via DPMI by TSRs and device drivers during the DOS load phase of Windows 95.

Since Windows 95 supports virtual memory, it's common for the amount of committed memory to exceed the amount of physical memory under the control of the Windows 95 virtual memory manager. The WIN95MEM program shows both the committed and physical memory (in kilobytes) in a dialog box. These two figures (along with their ratio expressed as a percentage) are updated once a second. Figure 6-2 shows the WIN95MEM program in action. (Yes, the user interface isn't spectacular, but it's a throwaway program, right?)

Figure 6-2
The running WIN95MEM program shows how to call VxDCALL from an application program.

The important part of the WIN95MEM code is the call to the VxDCall function. Since VxDCall is an undocumented function, the WIN95MEM.C file prototypes a function called VxDCall2 (the 2 means two parameters). Because there are actually three parameters when you add in the Win32 VxD service ID DWORD (0x0001001E), the compiler creates a reference to an external function called VxDCall2@12. (There's an @12 at the end because the function is prototyped as a stdcall [WINAPI] function). The K32LIB.LIB file that I created to let me call undocumented KERNEL32 functions exports a function called VxDCall2@12, so the linker is able to resolve everything nicely. Appendix A describes the K32LIB.LIB file.

The actual call to the VxDCall function is almost anticlimactic:

```
VxDCall2( 0x0001001E, (DWORD)&dis, 0 );
```

The first parameter is the DWORD service ID (the combination of the VMM device ID and the _GetDemandPageInfo function ID). The second parameter is a pointer to a DemandInfoStruc declared locally on the stack. The meaning of the final parameter is unknown. I passed 0 since GlobalMemoryStatus passes 0 when it calls this service. That's all there is to it!

Examining VWIN32.VXD

Now that we've gone through our whirlwind tour of VxD interfaces, I'm going to narrow the chapter's focus and describe VWIN32.VXD. This VxD is new in Windows 95 (meaning it wasn't in Windows 3.1 and earlier). The 16-bit VxD ID for VWIN32.VXD is 0x002A (in case you missed it the dozen times I've mentioned it already). The distinction between what VWIN32.VXD does and what VMM.VXD does isn't clear (at least not outside the hallowed halls of Microsoft). However, one generalization that can be made about VWIN32.VXD is that it contains the Win32 VxD services that affect process and thread scheduling and synchronization. I think of VMM.VXD and VWIN32.VXD as a team that does the ring 0 work needed to keep Windows 95 up and running.

VWIN32.VXD doesn't export a V86 mode API. It does however, provide ring 0 VxD services, 16-bit protected mode services, and Win32 VxD services. Of all the VxDs in Windows 95, VWIN32 has (by far) the greatest number of Win32 VxD services. If VWIN32.VXD didn't provide so many Win32 VxD services, and if these services weren't so crucial to KERNEL32's operation, I wouldn't have bothered to write the preceding sections on Win32 VxD services. So, with that said, let's jump into the nitty-gritty of VWIN32.VXD!

The VWIN32.VXD ring 0 VxD service API

The first interface to VWIN32.VXD we'll look at is the services that it provides to other VxDs. Luckily, Microsoft left a list of these services in the VWIN32.H and VWIN32.INC files from the Windows 95 DDK. For the benefit of readers who don't live their life parked in front of a keyboard like I do, I've provided a copy of the list in Figure 6-3. Luckily, the SoftIce/W VxD command knows about these services, so it's easy to get a list of the service names, along with their function IDs.

```
:vxd vwin32

VxD Name  Address   Length  Seg   ID    DDB       Control   PM  V86  VxD  Win32
VWIN32    C0075654  0026FC  0001  002A  C0076DE0  C0075654  Y   N    29   79

... some output omitted for brevity

29 VxD Services
  0000  C00756BF  VWIN32_Get_Version
  0001  C0075776  VWIN32_DIOCCompletionRoutine
  0002  C007678F  _VWIN32_QueueUserApc
  0003  C0261002  _VWIN32_Get_Thread_Context
  0004  C0261293  _VWIN32_Set_Thread_Context
  0005  C025E4F8  _VWIN32_CopyMem
  0006  C025E568  _VWIN32_Npx_Exception
  0007  C0262D16  _VWIN32_Emulate_Npx
  0008  C0076AA8  _VWIN32_CheckDelayedNpxTrap
  0009  C0260971  VWIN32_EnterCrstR0
  000A  C0260A9C  VWIN32_LeaveCrstR0
  000B  C025EC78  _VWIN32_FaultPopup
  000C  C007662B  VWIN32_GetContextHandle
  000D  C007575F  VWIN32_GetCurrentProcessHandle
  000E  C02620B6  _VWIN32_SetWin32Event
  000F  C02620F7  _VWIN32_PulseWin32Event
  0010  C026213F  _VWIN32_ResetWin32Event
  0011  C0262229  _VWIN32_WaitSingleObject
  0012  C0262175  _VWIN32_WaitMultipleObjects
  0013  C0260D2C  _VWIN32_CreateRing0Thread
  0014  C0076A78  _VWIN32_CloseVxDHandle
  0015  C0078D51  VWIN32_ActiveTimeBiasSet
  0016  C00756D4  VWIN32_GetCurrentDirectory
  0017  C0075802  VWIN32_BlueScreenPopup
  0018  C025E972  VWIN32_TerminateApp
  0019  C007683F  _VWIN32_QueueKernelAPC
  001A  C025EB9D  VWIN32_SysErrorBox
  001B  C00757C0  _VWIN32_IsClientWin32
  001C  C007572E  VWIN32_IFSRIPWhenLev2Taken
```

▌ Figure 6-3
VWIN32 Ring 0 VxD services.

In this output, the left column is the service ID within VWIN32.VXD. The middle column is the address of the service function. The right column is the name of the service, as given in VWIN32.INC.

The list of ring 0 VWIN32 services is a mixed bag. However, there's a strong representation among functions in the thread synchronization category. There's also a smattering of functions that imply that VWIN32.VXD has specific knowledge of processes (the VWIN32_GetCurrentProcessHandle, VWIN32_GetCurrentDirectory, and VWIN32_TerminateApp services). This is interesting primarily because VMM.VXD is only aware of threads, and doesn't provide process-management-related functionality. VMM.VXD leaves the process management to VWIN32.VXD.

The VWIN32.VXD 16-bit protected mode API

Microsoft doesn't document the functions in VWIN32.VXD's 16-bit protected mode API in the shipping Windows 95 DDK. However, a list of these functions originally appeared in my August 1993 *Microsoft Systems Journal* article, "Stepping Up to 32 Bits: Chicago's Process, Thread, and Memory Management." At the time this article was written, these functions were included in VWIN32.INC. Therefore, since the cat's already out of the bag, I've listed the functions here.

VWIN32_GET_VER	AH = 0
VWIN32_THREAD_SWITCH	AH = 1
VWIN32_DPMI_FAULT	AH = 2
VWIN32_MMGR_FUNCTIONS	AH = 3
subfunctions:	
VWIN32_MMGR_RESERVE	AH = 3, AL = 0
VWIN32_MMGR_COMMIT	AH = 3, AL = 1
VWIN32_MMGR_DECOMMIT	AH = 3, AL = 2
VWIN32_MMGR_PAGEFREE	AH = 3, AL = 3
VWIN32_EVENT_CREATE	AH = 4
VWIN32_EVENT_DESTROY	AH = 5
VWIN32_EVENT_WAIT	AH = 6
VWIN32_EVENT_SET	AH = 7
VWIN32_PDB_INFO	AH = 8

VWIN32_THREAD_BOOST_PRI	AH = 9
VWIN32_WAIT_CRST	AH = 10
VWIN32_WAKE_CRST	AH = 11
VWIN32_SET_FAULT_INFO	AH = 12
VWIN32_EXIT_TIME	AH = 13
VWIN32_BOOST_THREAD_GROUP	AH = 14
VWIN32_BOOST_THREAD_STATIC	AH = 15
VWIN32_WAKE_IDLE_SYS	AH = 16
VWIN32_MAKE_IDLE_SYS	AH = 17
VWIN32_DELIVER_PENDING_KERNEL_APCS	AH = 18

So, what might be calling these particular functions? None other than
KRNL386 itself. These functions are how the ring 3 16-bit side of Windows
95 interfaces with the ring 0 VWIN32 component. Most of the functions in
this API fall into broad categories: thread scheduling, thread synchronization,
memory management, and fault handling.

One function in the previous list that bears special mention is the
VWIN32_MAKE_IDLE_SYS function. This function is invoked from the
ring 3 Win16 scheduler in KRNL386.EXE when there are no tasks to be
scheduled. (See the Reschedule function, if you have my book *Windows
Internals*.) When the 16-bit KRNL386 scheduler falls into its idle loop,
KRNL386 calls the VWIN32_MAKE_IDLE_SYS function. Control doesn't
return to KRNL386 until some activity in a 16-bit application occurs.

Incidentally, the VWIN32_EXIT_TIME function in the previous table
falls into the category of fault handling. If you read *Undocumented
Windows*, you may remember a function called Bunny_351. In Windows
3.1 and Windows 95, Bunny_351 is called when Windows shuts down. It's
sole purpose is to change the default unhandled exception handler's address.
In Windows 95, Bunny_351 is now just a wrapper around a call to the
VWIN32_EXIT_TIME function in VWIN32.VXD.

The VWIN32.VXD Win32 VxD service API

In the two previous APIs for VWIN32.VXD, we were lucky: Microsoft has
documented their service names and IDs. Unfortunately, we're not so lucky
with the Win32 VxD service interface. Over time, though, I've managed to

construct a list of known service entry points for this interface. I'll say up front that the list, shown in the following table, isn't complete and that some of the function names are guesses, based on observations of the KERNEL32 and VWIN32 code.

Service ID	Purpose
0x002A0000	GetVersion
0x002A0001	Stuff VWIN32 code pointers into caller-supplied buffer
0x002A0002	GetSystemTime
0x002A0003	Stuff code pointers from KERNEL32 into VWIN32's Data area
0x002A0004	Block on some semaphore
0x002A0005	Calls Signal_Semaphore_No_Switch on some semaphore
0x002A0006	Calls VMM Create_Semaphore, and stuffs into global var
0x002A0007	Calls VMM Destroy_Semaphore on semaphore created by 0x002A0006
0x002A0008	VWIN32_CreateThread (including allocating TDBX)
0x002A0009	VWIN32_sleep
0x002A000A	WakeThread
0x002A000B	TerminateThread
0x002A000C	Some sort of initialization function
0x002A000D	_VWIN32_QueueUserApc
0x002A000E	VWIN32_Initialize
0x002A000F	_VWIN32_QueueKernelApc
0x002A0010	VWIN32_Int21Dispatch
0x002A0011	Calls IFSMgr_Win32DupHandle
0x002A0012	VWIN32_BlockThreadSetBit
0x002A0013	Adjust_Thread_Exec_Priority
0x002A0014	_VWIN32_Get_Thread_Context
0x002A0015	_VWIN32_Set_Thread_Context
0x002A0016	Read process memory (used by ReadProcessMemory)
0x002A0017	Write process memory (used by WriteProcessMemory)
0x002A0018	Calls VMCPD_Get_CR0_State
0x002A0019	Calls VMCPD_Set_CR0_State
0x002A001A	SuspendThread
0x002A001B	ResumeThread
0x002A001C	??? (unknown)
0x002A001D	WaitCrst
0x002A001E	WakeCrst
0x002A001F	Something to do with loading/unloading VxDs
0x002A0020	VMCPD_Get_Version
0x002A0021	Set_Thread_Win32_Pri
0x002A0022	Calls Boost_With_Decay
0x002A0023	Calls Set_Inversion_Pri
0x002A0024	Calls Release_Inversion_Pri_ID
0x002A0025	Calls Release_Inversion_Pri
0x002A0026	Calls Attach_Thread_To_Group
0x002A0027	Calls Set_Thread_Static_Boost
0x002A0028	Calls Set_Group_Static_Boost
0x002A0029	VWIN32_Int31Dispatch

Service ID	Purpose
0x002A002A	VWIN32_Int41Dispatch
0x002A002B	VWIN32_BlockForTermination
0x002A002C	TerminationHandler2
0x002A002D	??? (unknown)
0x002A002E	dwBlockSingleWnod (WaitForSingleObject)
0x002A002F	dwBlockMultipleWnod (WaitForMultipleObjects)
0x002A0030	VWIN32_SetEvent
0x002A0031	Something to do with delivering APCs
0x002A0032	??? (unknown)
0x002A0033	InitUserAPCList
0x002A0034	??? (unknown)
0x002A0035	Calls VMM Signal_Semaphore_No_Switch
0x002A0036	Calls System_Control(KERNEL32_INITIALIZED)
0x002A0037	VWIN32_CommonFaultPopup
0x002A0038	VWIN32_ForceCrsts
0x002A0039	??? (unknown)
0x002A003A	VWIN32_FreezeAllThreads
0x002A003B	VWIN32_UnFreezeAllThreads
0x002A003C	Calls IFSMgr_Ring0_FileIO
0x002A003D	Calls Get_Initial_Thread_Handle, Attach_Thread_To_Group, and Boost_Thread_With_VM
0x002A003E	VWIN32_ActiveTimeBiasSet
0x002A003F	ModifyPagePermission (used by VirtualQueryEx)
0x002A0040	Used by VirtualQueryEx
0x002A0041	ForceLeaveCrst
0x002A0042	ForceEnterCrst
0x002A0043	Calls VMCPD_Set_Thread_Excpt_Type
0x002A0044	VTD_Get_Real_Time
0x002A0045	Calls System_Control(SET_DEVICE_FOCUS)
0x002A0046	Calls VWIN32_UnFreezeThread
0x002A0047	Calls VMM_Replace_Global_Environment
0x002A0048	Calls System_Control(KERNEL32_SHUTDOWN)
0x002A0049	??? (unknown)
0x002A004A	VW32_AddSysCrst
0x002A004B	VW32_SetTimeOut
0x002A004C	VW32_Cancel_Time_Out
0x002A004D	??? (unknown)
0x002A004E	Something to do with setting and reflecting hotkeys

Notes:

Crst means Critical Section.

APC means Asynchronous Procedure Call.

VMCPD is the Virtual Math Coprocessor Device.

IFSMgr is the Installable File System Manager.

System_Control is the VMM.VXD ring 0 service that broadcasts system control messages to VxDs.

As you can tell from looking at this table, VWIN32 provides numerous Win32 VxD services — so many, in fact, that I could probably write an entire book on them. Another book, though; not this one. In this book, I'd like to focus on just three of the services listed in the previous table:

0x002A0010 — VWIN32_Int21Dispatch (the DOS interrupt)

0x002A0029 — VWIN32_Int31Dispatch (the DPMI interrupt)

0x002A002A — VWIN32_Int41Dispatch (the debugger notification
interrupt)

Microsoft has stated that Win32 isn't able to invoke interrupts like Win16 code can. However, this doesn't mean that the need to use interrupts has gone away. When Win32 code needs to invoke INT 21h, 31h, or 41h, Win32 VxD services in VWIN32.VXD are available to do precisely what's needed. KERNEL32.DLL uses these interrupt dispatching functions all over the place. Let's look at code for the VWIN32_Int31Dispatch service function in VWIN32.VXD to see how it works:

Pseudocode for VWIN32_Int31Dispatch

```
// Parameters:
//      Client_Reg_Struct   * pClientRegs
//      DWORD    ring3_EAX
//      DWORD    ring3_ECX

    _Debug_Flags_Service( DFS_TEST_BLOCK );

    EAX = pClientRegs->Client_EAX = ring3_EAX
    ECX = pClientRegs->Client_EAX = ring3_ECX

    Exec_PM_Int( EAX = 0x31 );

    if ( carry set )
        _Debug_Out_Service( "VW32_Int31Dispatch: Exec_PM_Int Failed!\r\n" );
```

There's not much to these interrupt dispatching services in VWIN32. The Win32 VxD services for dispatching interrupts are just wrappers around calls to the ring 0 Exec_PM_Int service. Much of the hype around Windows 95 centers on the notion that DOS is supposedly gone. Since almost all of what used to be called DOS functionality is now in VxDs, these interrupt dispatching Win32 VxD services shouldn't be used that much, right? Well, examine the pseudocode for the KERNEL32.DLL FindClose function below and decide for yourself.

Pseudocode for FindClose

```
// Parameters:
//  HANDLE  hFile;

    x_LogSomeKernelFunction( function number for FindClose );

    if ( hFile == HFILE_ERROR )
        goto error;        // Calls SetLastError(ERROR_INVALID_HANDLE), then
                           // returns FALSE to caller.

    EAX = 71A1h            // 71A1h == Long Filename FindClose code
    EBX = hFile;
    INT_21H_DISPATCH();

    if ( carry flag set )
        goto error;        // Calls SetLastError(ERROR_INVALID_HANDLE), then
                           // returns FALSE to caller.
    return TRUE;
```

Pseudocode for INT_21h_DISPATCH

```
    return VxDCall( 0x002A0010, EAX, ECX );
```

Truth be told, KERNEL32 makes dozens of calls to the VWIN32_Int21Dispatch service. A search through KERNEL32.DLL reveals that KERNEL32.DLL makes the following INT 21h (DOS) calls:

DOS Subfunction	Purpose
0E00	Set default drive
1900	Get current drive
2A00	Get system date
2B00	Set system date
2C00	Get system time
2D00	Set system time
3600	Get disk free space
3D00	Open existing file — read only
3D02	Open existing file — read/write
3E00	Close file
3F00	Read file
4000	Write file
4200	Set current file position — relative to start of file
4201	Set current file position — relative to current position

DOS Subfunction	Purpose
4202	Set current file position — relative to end of file
4400	IOCTL — get device information
4401	IOCTL — set device information
4408	IOCTL — check if block device removable
4409	IOCTL — check if block device remote
440D	IOCTL — generic block device request
4B00	Exec program
4D00	Get return code
5000	Set current PSP
5700	Get file date/time
5701	Set file date/time
5704	Set extended file attributes
5705	??? (unknown)
5706	??? (unknown)
5707	??? (unknown)
5900	Get extended error info
5C00	Lock file region
5C01	Unlock file region
5E00	Network functions
5F32	??? (unknown)
5F33	??? (unknown)
5F34	??? (unknown)
5F35	??? (unknown)
5F36	??? (unknown)
5F37	??? (unknown)
5F38	??? (unknown)
5F3B	??? (unknown)
5F3C	??? (unknown)
5F4D	??? (unknown)
5F4F	??? (unknown)
5F52	??? (unknown)
6800	Commit file
7139	LFN create directory
713A	LFN remove directory
713B	LFN change directory
7141	LFN delete file
7143	LFN get/set file attributes
7147	LFN get current directory
714E	LFN find first file
714F	LFN find next file
7156	LFN rename file
7160	LFN get canonical filename

DOS Subfunction	Purpose
716C	LFN Extended open/create
71A0	LFN Get Volume Information
71A1	LFN Find Close
71A3	??? (unknown)
71A4	??? (unknown)
71A5	??? (unknown)
71A6	LFN Get File Info By Handle
71A7	LFN File Time To DOS Time
B400	??? (unknown)
EA00	??? (unknown)

Wow! There are a lot of INT 21h calls being made by KERNEL32.DLL. It looks like the memories of INT 21h continue to haunt us, even after DOS was supposedly killed off by Windows 95. The only thing that's changed is that the INT 21hs are being called by KERNEL32.DLL now, rather than directly from your own code.

Why would Microsoft go through all the hassle of performing these INT 21h's? Couldn't they just directly call the low-level operating-system functions directly and bypass this 15-year-old INT 21h interface? The answer is that yes, they could. However, device drivers and VxDs that hook INT 21h calls would break if Microsoft were to do this. These drivers and VxDs wouldn't see the basic operating system actions that they're expecting to be able to watch. Once again, Microsoft is in the position of putting in less than pretty code to retain backward compatibility with old applications and device drivers.

Returning now to our earlier discussion of VWIN32.VXD's dispatching of certain interrupts, you're probably familiar with INT 21h (DOS) and INT 31h (the DPMI interrupt). However, INT 41h may not ring any bells. INT 41h is the interrupt used by the operating system KERNEL to tell system-level debuggers (WDEB386, SoftIce/W) of important events in the system. For example, KERNEL32.DLL invokes the following INT 41h subfunctions (which are listed in DEBUGSYS.INC from the DDK):

```
DS_LoadSeg_32   equ  0150h ; Define a 32-bit segment for Windows 32.
DS_FreeSeg_32   equ  0152h ; Notify the debugger that a segment has been freed.
DS_Printf       equ  0073h ; Formatted output standard "C" printf syntax.
DS_Out_Str      equ  0002h ; Function to display a NUL terminated string.
DS_IntRings     equ  0020h ; Tell debugger which INT 1's & 3's to grab.
DS_CheckFault   equ  007Fh ; Checks if the debugger wants control on the fault.
DS_CondBP       equ  F001h ; Conditional breakpoint.
```

THE **VWIN32 TDBX**

In Chapter 3, I described the process databases and thread databases that KERNEL32 maintains. Seeing as how VWIN32 is so intimately involved with the mechanics of threads and processes, it's not surprising that VWIN32 also has its own data structure for keeping track of processes and threads. This data structure is called a TDBX, and was referenced briefly in Chapter 3.

There's one TDBX data structure for each thread in the system. As some of you VxD hackers have no doubt guessed by now, pointers to TDBXs are kept in a thread local storage (TLS) slot in the thread control block (THCB). Thread control blocks are the basic data structure that the VMM thread manager uses to keep track of all the threads it has created. Other VxDs can request slots within the THCB for their own per-thread storage. They do this via the VMM _AllocateThreadDataSlot function, which returns an offset inside the THCB where a pointer to the per-thread data can be kept. The VWIN32 TDBX structure is allocated in response to KERNEL32 calling Win32 VxD Service 0x002A0008 (VWIN32_CreateThread). The pointer to the TDBX structure is kept in the DWORD slot that's reserved for it in each VMM thread control block.

Without further ado, let's look at the contents of a VWIN32 TDBX structure. Unlike most of the other structures described in this book, the meaning of many of the TDBX fields can only be guessed at, based on the name.

00h   DWORD   ptdb
A pointer to the ring 3 PROCESS_DATABASE structure associated with this thread. The format of this structure is given in "The Windows 95 Process Database" section in Chapter 3.

04h   DWORD   ppdb
A pointer to the ring 3 THREAD_DATABASE structure associated with this thread. The format of this structure is given in Chapter 3.

08h   DWORD   ContextHandle
A pointer to the memory context structure for this thread's process. Memory contexts are described in Chapter 5.

0Ch   DWORD   un1
Unknown.

10h   DWORD   TimeOutHandle
Unknown.

14h   *DWORD*   *WakeParam*
Unknown.

18h   *DWORD*   *BlockHandle*
Unknown.

1Ch   *DWORD*   *BlockState*
Unknown.

20h   *DWORD*   *SuspendCount*
The number of times that the Win32 SuspendThread function has been
called for this particular thread.

24h   *DWORD*   *SuspendHandle*
Unknown.

28h   *DWORD*   *MustCompleteCount*
When this value is nonzero, this thread can't be interrupted. The
EnterMustComplete and LeaveMustComplete functions mentioned in
Chapters 3 and 5 increment and decrement this value.

2Ch   *DWORD*   *WaitExFlags*
Flags for this thread. The following values are known:

0x00000001	WAITEXBIT
0x00000002	WAITACKBIT
0x00000004	SUSPEND_APC_PENDING
0x00000008	SUSPEND_TERMINATED
0x00000010	BLOCKED_FOR_TERMINATION
0x00000020	EMULATE_NPX
0x00000040	WIN32_NPX
0x00000080	EXTENDED_HANDLES
0x00000100	FROZEN
0x00000200	DONT_FREEZE
0x00000400	DONT_UNFREEZE
0x00000800	DONT_TRACE
0x00001000	STOP_TRACING
0x00002000	WAITING_FOR_CRST_SAFE
0x00004000	CRST_SAFE
0x00040000	BLOCK_TERMINATE_APC

30h *DWORD* *SyncWaitCount*
Unknown.

34h *DWORD* *QueuedSyncFuncs*
Unknown.

38h *DWORD* *UserAPCList*
(APC means Asynchronous Procedure Call.)

3Ch *DWORD* *KernAPCList*
(APC means Asynchronous Procedure Call.)

40h *DWORD* *pPMPSPSelector*
A pointer to the protected mode PSP selector.

44h *DWORD* *BlockedOnID*
Unknown.

48h *DWORD* *un2[7]*
Unknown.

64h *DWORD* *TraceRefData*
Unknown.

68h *DWORD* *TraceCallBack*
Unknown.

6Ch *DWORD* *TraceEventHandle*
Unknown.

70h *WORD* *TraceOutLastCS*
Unknown.

72h *WORD* *K16TDB*
The Win16 Task Database (TDB) selector associated with this thread's process.

74h *WORD* *K16PDB*
The Win16 Program Segment Prefix (PSP) selector associated with this thread's process.

76h *WORD* *DosPDBSeg*
The real mode segment value of the PSP associated with this thread's process.

78h *WORD* *ExceptionCount*
Unknown.

The first two fields of the TDBX are the most interesting. They provide the ring 0 VWIN32.VXD with pointers to the process and thread data structures that the ring 3 KERNEL32.DLL uses. (As you may recall from Chapter 3, KERNEL32 keeps a pointer to the TDBX for each thread in the ring 3 THREAD_DATABASE structure. Putting two and two together, you can see that the KERNEL32.DLL THREAD_DATABASE and the VWIN32.VXD TDBX structure circularly reference each other.)

A few other TDBX fields also bear closer examination. At offset 8 is a pointer to the memory context for the thread (actually, for the thread's owner process). Also, as we saw in Chapters 3 and 5, the MustCompleteCount field is crucial to the lowest level of thread synchronization, when a thread absolutely shouldn't be interrupted.

Near its end, the TDBX structure contains a selector to the Win16 Task Database that every process gets (be it 16- or 32-bit). The last two fields are protected and real mode pointers to the Program Segment Prefix for the thread's owning process. Obviously, the ring 0 VWIN32.VXD needs to know about DOS data structures as well as Win16 KRNL386 data structures. The main point is that all three Windows 95 kernel components (the 16-bit KRNL386.EXE, the ring 3 KERNEL32.DLL, and the ring 0 VWIN32.VXD) all have knowledge of one another. We'll look at these interrelationships next.

HOW THE THREE WINDOWS 95 KERNELS COMMUNICATE

After taking you on a long and winding tour through VWIN32.VXD, I've finally laid sufficient groundwork to show how all three of the Windows 95 kernels communicate with each other. The extent of the communication and interactions between the three Windows 95 kernel components is surprising, at least to me. Why is this? In my (admittedly unrealistic) view of things, I think of an operating system kernel as an independent entity, not reliant on anything else. It's the foundation upon which everything else is built, so it shouldn't depend on outside components. Put another way, I'd like to think that a kernel can be treated as a black box. Understanding the workings of the black box shouldn't require knowing anything about components outside the box. However, as I've shown throughout this book, these three kernel black boxes aren't really so black. What I'll do next is show how each kernel has explicit knowledge of and interactions with the other kernels.

VWIN32 knowledge of KRNL386

The first indication that VWIN32.VXD knows about KRNL386 and its data comes near the end of the TDBX structure, where you'll find the Win16 Task Database (TDB) selector for the process that the TDBX is associated with. However, a much more dramatic example of VWIN32's knowledge of KRNL386 comes from the pseudocode for a routine in VWIN32.VXD that I call ThreadSwitchCallback.

ThreadSwitchCallback is called by VMM.VXD whenever the thread scheduler switches to a new thread. The ThreadSwitchCallback function is where the pre-emptive multithreading Win32 meets the non-preemptive view of the Win16 KRNL386.EXE. It's also where the multitasking Win32 joins up with the single tasking MS-DOS. Make no mistake about it, ThreadSwitchCallback plays a starring role in making Windows 95 appear as a full-blown multitasking system to some parts of Windows 95, and like DOS/Windows 3.1 to other parts.

Pseudocode for ThreadSwitchCallback

```
// Parameters:
//   THCB    *pCurrentTHCB, *pOldTHCB;    // Pointer to Thread Control Blocks.
// Locals:
//   PTDBX   pNewTDBX, pOldTDBX;          // Pointers to TDBX structures.

    // On entry, EAX is the old THCB and EDI is the current THCB
    // (THCB = thread control block).

    pNewTDBX = pCurrentTHCB->TDBX_pointer;
    if ( !pNewTDBX )
        return;

    pOldTDBX = pOldTHCB->TDBX_pointer;
    if ( !pOldTDBX )
        return;

    // Make sure the parameter that points to the old thread database
    // matches what VWIN32.VXD has saved away in a global variable. (cur_ptdb)
    if ( pOldTDBX->ptdb != cur_ptdb )
        _Debug_Out_Service( "VWin32: invalid current Win32 thread\r\n" );

    cur_ptdb = pNewTDBX->ptdb;   // Update VWIN32 current thread global var.
    cur_ppdb = pNewTDBX->ppdb;   // Update VWIN32 current process global var.
    CurTDBX = pNewTDBX;          // Update VWIN32 current TDBX global var.
```

```
// This line bashes the CurTDB global variable in KRNL386.EXE.
*pWin16CurTDB = pNewTDBX->K16TDB;

// If the new thread differs from the old thread, update the PSP
// segment down in DOS, and save away the old PSP segment.
if ( prevTDBX != pNewTDBX )
{
    // Save away the current PSP segment for the previous thread.
    prevTDBX->DosPDBSeg
            = Get_Set_Real_DOS_PSP( ECX=0, EBX = Get_Sys_VM_Handle() );

    // Set the current PSP segment for the new thread. This should
    // bash a variable down in DOS.
    Get_Set_Real_DOS_PSP( AX = pNewTDBX->DosPDBSeg, ECX=1,
                            EBX = Get_Sys_VM_Handle() );

    prevTDBX = pNewTDBX;        // prevTDBX is a VWIN32 global variable.
}

// Switch the memory address context.
if ( pNewTDBX->ContextHandle )
{
    CurContext = pNewTDBX->ContextHandle;    // Update VWIN32 global var.

    _ContextSwitch( pNewTDBX->ContextHandle );
}
```

After doing some preliminary sanity checking, ThreadSwitchCallback updates the global variable pointers that VWIN32 keeps to the current ring 3 process and thread databases. At the same time, it updates the global variable that VWIN32 uses to point at the current TDBX structure. Next, ThreadSwitchCallback does something that stunned me when I first saw it happen in SoftIce/W. Seemingly out of nowhere, the ring 0 VWIN32.VXD smashes the CurTDB global variable in KRNL386.EXE.

Up until Windows 95 came along, CurTDB was sacred. The only way that CurTDB could change was for Windows to call the core scheduling routine in Windows 3.*x* (that is, the Reschedule function). The nice orderly world of cooperative multitasking in Windows 3.*x* collided head-on with pre-emptive multitasking in Windows 95, and pre-emptive multitasking won. It's a sick, sick world when something as fundamental as the current task global variable in KRNL386 can be bashed by another component that few programmers are even aware of. (Of course, you know about VWIN32 since you're reading this chapter, but my point is still valid.)

The remaining chores of ThreadSwitchCallback are housecleaning related to multitasking. The PSP segment of the outgoing thread is saved away in its TDBX structure. Next, the code takes the incoming thread's PSP segment and uses it to set the current PSP segment in the system VM. This PSP switching isn't new to Windows 95. Windows 3.1 did something similar to this, albeit in ring 3 KRNL386 code. The last thing ThreadSwitch-Callback does is to switch the current memory context to that of the incoming thread. As Chapter 5 describes, the switching of memory contexts is what allows each process to have its own private address space. In Windows 95, the process private address space is above 4MB and 2GB in the linear address range.

VWIN32 knowledge of KERNEL32.DLL

The primary indication that VWIN32 knows about KERNEL32 is the presence of pointers to the THREAD_DATABASE and PROCESS_DATABASE in the TDBX structures used by VWIN32. VWIN32 also keeps global variables with pointers to the current process and thread structures as maintained by KERNEL32.DLL. Beyond processes and threads, VWIN32.VXD obtains a list of pointers to routines in KERNEL32.DLL during KERNEL32's startup phase. KERNEL32.DLL willingly serves up this information by passing the function addresses as parameters to Win32 VxD service 0x002A0003.

KERNEL32.DLL knowledge of VWIN32

By far, the biggest proof that KERNEL32 knows about VWIN32 is the fact that KERNEL32 calls the Win32 VxD services provided by VWIN32. This has been shown throughout this book, especially in preceding sections of this chapter. There's not much more to be said here on this particular topic.

Beyond Win32 VxD services, additional cooperation between KERNEL32 and VWIN32.VXD occurs when VWIN32.VXD hands over a list of function addresses within VWIN32.VXD during a particular Win32 VxD service call. The call in question is Win32 VxD service 0x002A0001, which is called by the FInitPager function in KERNEL32.DLL. Presumably, KERNEL32.DLL will call back these VWIN32.VXD addresses during page fault handling. As shown in *Unauthorized Windows 95*, the VMM page fault handler calls (at ring 0!) into KERNEL32.DLL's code. It's not a stretch, therefore, to believe that VWIN32 would be passing the addresses of its routines to KERNEL32.DLL during KERNEL32.DLL's paging initialization.

KERNEL32.DLL knowledge of KRNL386.EXE (or, What Microsoft isn't telling you)

According to Microsoft's Windows 95 technical marketing material, the 32-bit KERNEL32 doesn't rely on KRNL386 for any of its functionality. (Contrast this to the USER and GDI components, where Microsoft willingly admits that 32-bit component's code thunks down to the Win16 component.) *Unauthorized Windows 95* completely shredded Microsoft's claim that KERNEL32.DLL doesn't call the 16-bit KRNL386.EXE. However, the extent to which KERNEL32 calls KRNL386 hasn't been known until now.

I won't attempt to duplicate that book's excellent explanation of the thunking between KERNEL32 and KRNL386.EXE in Windows 95. However, I can offer something new — a list of functions in KRNL386.EXE called by KERNEL32.DLL. If this isn't interesting, I don't know what is. This list is especially relevant in light of Microsoft's claims that calling any KERNEL32 function can't result in the calling thread waiting to acquire the Win16Mutex. As you can see in the following table, there is a nontrivial set of KERNEL32 functions that will in fact block on the Win16Mutex.

Lest you think that these functions can't cause problems, consider the profile functions (for example, GetPrivateProfileSection). Typically, they'll access your hard disk and return quickly. However, what if the file they're looking for is on a CD-ROM drive, and there's no disk in the drive? The CD-ROM driver may take many seconds to time out, and during this whole time, the Win16Mutex is owned by the calling task. (This exact scenario really happened to me during the Windows 95 beta.)

A word of explanation on the following table is in order. The names in the left column are the names that KERNEL32 uses internally. If a special KERNEL32 internal flag is set, KERNEL32 emits these strings to the debug terminal. Some of these functions turn out to be regular, exported KERNEL32 functions. Other functions in the left column are undocumented, or variations on exported KERNEL32 functions. It's doubtful that normal applications will call them. For example, LoadLibrary16 calls the 16-bit LoadLibrary in KRNL386. LoadLibrary16 is exported from KERNEL32.DLL with an export ordinal of 35, but it *is not* the same as the regular KERNEL32.DLL LoadLibrary function. Likewise, the WritePrivateProfileSection32A function is not the same as the regular KERNEL32 WritePrivateProfileSectionA function. The names have to match *exactly*.

The smattering of function names in the right column of the following table are the set of functions that the KERNEL32 to KRNL386 thunk calls directly. If a function name isn't provided in this column, the thunk doesn't call the exported function directly. More often than not, the thunk called the internal version of the function in KRNL386, rather than the exported, wrapper function.

KERNEL32.DLL Internal Name	KRNL386.EXE Exported Name
TerminateZombie	
DiagOutput16	DiagOutput
DispatchRITInput	
GetFastQueue	KERNEL.625
SetVolumeLabel16	
PK16FNF	
CommConfigThk	
InitAtomTable	
GetAtomNameA	
DeleteAtom	
FindAtomA	
AddAtomA	
GlobalLock16	GlobalLock
IsDriveCDRom	
ExecConsoleAgent	
ThkOpenFile	OpenFile
GetErrorMode	
SetErrorMode16	
GetSystemDirectoryA	GetSystemDirectory
GetWindowsDirectoryA	GetWindowsDirectory
GlobalGetAtomNameA	
GlobalDeleteAtom	
GlobalFindAtomA	
GlobalAddAtomA	
GetPrivateProfileSectionNames32A	GetPrivateProfileSectionNames
WritePrivateProfileStruct32A	WritePrivateProfileStruct
GetPrivateProfileStruct32A	GetPrivateProfileStruct
WriteProfileSectionA	WriteProfileSection
GetProfileSectionA	GetProfileSection
WritePrivateProfileSection32A	WritePrivateProfileSection
GetPrivateProfileSection32A	GetPrivateProfileSection
WritePrivateProfileString32A	WritePrivateProfileString
GetPrivateProfileString32A	

KERNEL32.DLL *Internal Name*	KRNL386.EXE *Exported Name*
WriteProfileStringA	WriteProfileString
GetProfileStringA	
GlobalHandle16	GlobalHandle
GlobalSize16	GlobalSize
GlobalFlags16	GlobalFlags
GlobalUnlock16	GlobalUnlock
GlobalFree16	GlobalFree
GlobalReAlloc16	GlobalRealloc
GlobalAlloc16	GlobalAlloc
WinExecEnv	
PrivateGetModuleFileName	GetModuleFileName
GetProductName	GetProductName
GetWinFlags	GetWinFlags
GetModuleName16	
GetTaskName16	
SetTaskName16	
ThkDeleteTask	
ThkCreateTask	
ThkInitWin32Task	
FreeSelector16	
ThunkInitLSWorker16	
GetProcAddress16	
FreeLibrary16	FreeLibrary
LoadLibrary16	LoadLibrary
GlobalUnWire16	GlobalUnwire
GlobalWire16	GlobalWire
GlobalUnfix16	GlobalUnfix
GlobalFix16	GlobalFix
GlobalNukeGroup	
CheckHGHeap	
SegCommonThunkDetach32	
SegCommonThunkAttach32	
GrowMBABlock	
FakeThunkTheTemplateHandle	
TCD_UnregisterPDB32	
TCD_Enum	
WOWGlobalLockSize16	
WOWGlobalUnlockFree16	
WOWGlobalAllocLock16	
WOWGlobalUnlock16	GlobalUnlock
WOWGlobalLock16	GlobalLock

KERNEL32.DLL Internal Name	KRNL386.EXE Exported Name
WOWGlobalFree16	GlobalFree
WOWGlobalAlloc16	
WOWDirectedYield16	DirectedYield
WOWYield16	Yield
Yield16	
FreeLibrary16ByName	
SSChk	
UTThunkLSHelper	
UTUnregisterInt	
UTRegisterInt	
UTProcessExit	
FreeCB	

I've noticed that many Windows 95 programmers are anxious to know which KERNEL32 functions can block on the Win16Mutex during the journey down to KRNL386. Microsoft's claims that none of them block is utterly bogus. By studying the list in the next table, you can easily consolidate the functions into a few categories of KERNEL32 functions that can in fact block while waiting for the Win16Mutex.

Function Category	Function Names
Atom functions	AddAtomA, DeleteAtom, FindAtomA, GetAtomNameA, GlobalAddAtomA, GlobalDeleteAtom, GlobalFindAtomA, GlobalGetAtomNameA, InitAtomTable
Directory functions	GetSystemDirectoryA, GetWindowsDirectoryA
Selected WIN.INI file functions	GetProfileSectionA, GetProfileStringA, WriteProfileSectionA, WriteProfileStringA,

KERNEL32 also knows about specific global variables in KRNL386.EXE. We saw earlier how VWIN32.VXD parties with a KRNL386.EXE global variable (for example, CurTDB). In the case of KERNEL32, the most glaring example of its use of KRNL386 global variables is the Win16Mutex. The Win16Mutex is actually just a CRITICAL_SECTION structure that's kept in KRNL386.EXE's DGROUP segment. How does KERNEL32 get hold of the address of the Win16Mutex? KRNL386.EXE passes it to KERNEL32.DLL as part of an initialization call that KRNL386 makes after loading KERNEL32.DLL.

KRNL386 knowledge of KERNEL32.DLL

Just as KERNEL32 has a laundry list of functions that it calls in KRNL386.EXE, the exact opposite is also true. The following table lists the functions that KRNL386 calls up to KERNEL32.DLL for.

Function Category	Function Names
Process management functions	CreateProcessFromWinExec, IFatalAppExit, NukeProcess, RegisterServiceProcess, ThunkExitProcess, ThunkMapProcessHandle, ThunkCreateProcessWin16, WinExecWait
Thread management functions	IsThreadId, ThunkCreateThread16, ThunkTerminateThread,
Module management functions	GetModuleHandle32, GetNEPEBuddyFromFileName32, LoadLibraryEx32W, ThunkFreeLibrary32 (free a Win32 DLL), ThunkGetHModK16FromHModK32 (get the Win16 HMODULE from a Win32 HMODULE), ThunkGetModuleFileName, ThunkLoadLibrary32 (load a Win32 DLL),
Directory management functions	GetCurrentDirectory (stored in the KERNEL32 process database for each process), SetCurrentDirectory32, ThunkGetCurrentDirectory
File I/O functions	FindClose, FindFirstFile, FindNextFile (16-bit versions of the Win32 FindXXX functions), FileTimeToDosDateTime, OpenFileEx16And32, ThunkCloseDOSHandles, ThunkCloseW32Handle,
32-bit heap functions	LocalAlloc32NG, ThunkLocal32Alloc, ThunkLocal32Free, ThunkLocal32Init, ThunkLocal32ReAlloc, ThunkLocal32SizeThkHlp, ThunkLocal32Translate, ThunkLocal32ValidHandle
Synchronization functions	ThunkCreateW32Event, ThunkResetW32Event, ThunkSetW32Event, WaitForMultipleObjects, WaitForSingleObject
Fault handling functions	CreateFaultThread, FaultRestore, FaultSave,
WINOLDAP support functions	WOAAbort, WOACreateConsole, WOADestroyConsole, WOAFullScreen, WOAGimmeTitle, WOASpawnConApp, WOATerminateProcesses
Cleanup functions	FreeInitResources32, HGCleanupDepartingHTask, NotifyDetachFromWin16, ThunkDeallocOrphanedCrsts
Miscellaneous functions	CallProc32WFixHelper, CallProc32WHelper, FlatCommonThunkConnect16, FullLoRes, GetProcessDword, GetVersionEx, InitK32AfterSysDllsLoaded, ISetErrorModeEx, InvalidateNLSCache, LateBindWin32ThunkPartner, SetProcessDword, SmashEnvironment, ThunkConvertToGlobalHandle, ThunkGetProcAddress32, ThunkTheTemplateHandle, VirtualFree

If you're wondering where the names in the previous table come from, they're embedded in KERNEL32.DLL. As I was studying my listings for KERNEL32.DLL, I noticed a consistent pattern in the code for the functions that KRNL386 thunks up to. Part of that pattern included a pointer to the function name. It was a simple matter to write an editor macro to find all the locations in KERNEL32.DLL with this code pattern and copy the function name strings out to a file.

KRNL386 knowledge of VWIN32

KRNL386.EXE's knowledge of VWIN32.VXD is embodied by its calls to the VWIN32 PM API services. These are the services that I described in the previous section titled "The VWIN32.VXD 16-bit protected mode API."

THE WIN32 VXD SERVICE SPY (W32SVSPY)

This chapter wouldn't be complete without a program that lets you explore the areas I've been describing. I wrote the W32SVSPY program for monitoring Win32 VxD Service calls. In some ways, it's like the API spy program from Chapter 10 — just not as complete. However, there were a couple of technical hurdles in writing W32SVSPY that I think I solved in interesting, nonobvious ways. Therefore, I'll take a little bit of time to show some tricks to be learned from W32SVSPY.

The complete sources are on the disk that accompanies this book. I'm not going to describe all the inner workings of W32SVSPY because they're fairly complicated, and probably not of interest to a great number of people. The output from W32SVSPY, on the other hand, should be of interest to the general spelunking population.

Figure 6-4 shows the initial screen of W32SVSPY. The large listbox that dominates its window holds the output from a spying session. To start watching Win32 VxD service calls, click the Start button. Logging will commence immediately, and continue until you click the Stop button, or until W32SVSPY's buffer fills up. (I arbitrarily chose 16K as the number of calls that can be saved. You can change this by recompiling the W32SVSPY source.) The Save. . . button lets you save the results of a spying session out to a text file.

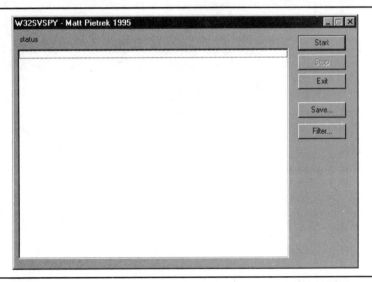

Figure 6-4
The initial W32SVSPY screen

The Filter. . . button brings up the dialog shown in Figure 6-5. This dialog lets you filter out arbitrary Win32 VxD services from the session results — as you'll see later, there can be quite a bit of noise in the Win32 VxD services, and it can be useful to filter them out. The Filter dialog has two listboxes. Selecting a VxD in the left listbox updates the right listbox with the known Win32 VxD services in that VxD. Services that have + (a plus sign) in front of them are enabled (will be shown). By double-clicking on a service line in the right list-box, you can toggle its state between enabled (+) and disabled (–). The default is to have all services enabled. As provided, W32SVSPY knows only about the VMM and VWIN32 services. It will log all Win32 VxD service calls, but can only provide names for the Win32 VxD services that it knows about. If you want to add in knowledge of additional Win32 VxD services in other VxDs, the W32SRVDB.C file is where the additions would go.

Any filtering you perform in this dialog is preserved across invocations of W32SVSPY by saving the filtered service IDs (in binary form) out to a .FLT file. If you want to turn off filtering (that is, if you want to see every-thing) delete the .FLT file before starting up W32SVSPY. Alternatively, go back into the Filter... dialog and reenable all the functions.

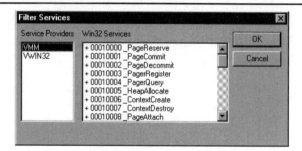

Figure 6-5
The W32SVSPY filter dialog.

The format of each line of W32SVSPY's output is as follows:

```
<CurrentTaskName>  <Service Name>(<parameter 1 value>)
```

For example, take the following line:

```
Explorer VWIN32_SetEvent(8154A230)
```

In this example, the current process (that is, the one making the call) is the
Explorer. The service being called is VWIN32_SetEvent. The value of the
first parameter (in parentheses) is 8154A230h. W32SVSPY doesn't show
the value of all the parameters to each Win32 VxD services because it
would greatly complicate the logging process. If you want this feature, you
can add it as an exercise.

If the Win32 VxD service call is VWIN32_Int21Dispatch, W32SVSPY
decodes the first parameter value to a string describing the DOS function
being invoked. In this case, the DOS function name string will appear after
the service name (VWIN32_Int21Dispatch), but before the first parameter
value; for example:

```
Calc    VWIN32_Int21Dispatch LFN File Time To DOS Time(000071A7)
```

Occasionally, you may see a line like this:

```
FFFF56F3 VWIN32_Int41Dispatch(00000150)
```

In this case, the first thing on the line is a process ID. This is because
W32SVSPY couldn't extract the process name from the Win16 Task
Database (TDB) that Windows 95 creates for each process. This usually
happens only during application startup, before KERNEL32.DLL has

bashed the correct process name into the task database. It's usually not hard to figure out which process these IDs refer to — just search through the entries until they stop. The next task in the list of service calls whose name hasn't appeared previously is likely to be the process you're looking for.

A sample W32SVSPY session

To show off what W32SVSPY can do, let's watch the Win32 VxD services that occur when starting an application from a shortcut on the desktop. For the application to start up, choose CALC.EXE and make a shortcut to it on the desktop. Then start up W32SVSPY and click the Start button. Immediately afterward, double-click on the CALC shortcut. Finally, click the Stop button in W32SVSPY. The results of the run will appear in the main W32SVSPY listbox, which is shown in Figure 6-6. At this point, you can browse through the services in the listbox, or you can save the results to a file with the Save... listbox.

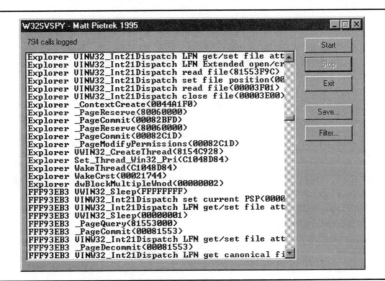

■ Figure 6-6
Running CALC under W32SVSPY.

I've taken the output from a run performed exactly as I've described above and condensed it to eliminate a lot of noise and repeated sequences. I've also annotated it a bit. Figure 6-7 shows the result:

```
... Many preliminary calls to DOS and the registry by the Explorer omitted

// Create the memory context for the new process.
Explorer _ContextCreate(004463D8)

Explorer _PageReserve(80060000)
Explorer _PageCommit(000828B4)
Explorer _PageReserve(80060000)
Explorer _PageCommit(000828D4)
Explorer _PageModifyPermissions(000828D4)

// Create the initial thread for the new process.
Explorer VWIN32_CreateThread(8154915C)

// Set the priority of the initial thread of the new process.
Explorer Set_Thread_Win32_Pri(C10464D8)

// Wake up the initial thread of the new process. This should cause
// the new memory context to be switched to.
Explorer WakeThread(C10464D8)

Explorer WakeCrst(&Win16Mutex)
Explorer dwBlockMultipleWnod(00000002)

// The first act of the new process (take a nap!).
FFFF56F3 VWIN32_Sleep(FFFFFFFF)

// Do file I/O (presumably with the EXE file of the process).
FFFF56F3 VINW32_Int21Dispatch set current PSP(000050F7)
FFFF56F3 VINW32_Int21Dispatch LFN get/set file attributes(00007143)
FFFF56F3 VWIN32_Sleep(00000001)
FFFF56F3 VINW32_Int21Dispatch LFN get/set file attributes(00007143)
FFFF56F3 VINW32_Int21Dispatch LFN get canonical filename(00007160)
FFFF56F3 VINW32_Int21Dispatch set current PSP(000050B7)
FFFF56F3 VINW32_Int21Dispatch LFN Extended open/create(0000716C)
FFFF56F3 VINW32_Int21Dispatch read file(828D3F60)
FFFF56F3 VINW32_Int21Dispatch set file position(00004200)
FFFF56F3 VINW32_Int21Dispatch read file(00003F01)
FFFF56F3 VINW32_Int21Dispatch set file position(00004200)
FFFF56F3 VINW32_Int21Dispatch read file(00003F01)
FFFF56F3 VINW32_Int21Dispatch LFN get canonical filename(00007160)

// Reserve and commit the memory to be used by the process.
FFFF56F3 _PageReserve(00000400)
FFFF56F3 _PageCommit(00000400)        < - repeat similar calls 11 times
FFFF56F3 _PageReserve(80000400)
FFFF56F3 _PageCommit(00000420)
```

```
FFFF56F3 _PageReserve(80000400)
FFFF56F3 _PageCommit(00000440)
FFFF56F3 _PageFree(00440000)
FFFF56F3 _PageFree(00420000)

FFFF56F3 VINW32_Int21Dispatch set current PSP(0000502B)

// Tell the system debugger (WINICE) about the EXE's 6 sections.
FFFF56F3 VWIN32_Int41Dispatch(00000150)    < - repeat this sequence 6 times

FFFF56F3 _RegQueryValueEx(C1126A54)

// Reserve and commit the memory range where SHELL32.DLL is mapped in.
// Since some other process has already loaded SHELL32.DLL, certain
// SHELL32.DLL pages can be shared with this process. Share the pages
// by calling PageAttach.
FFFF56F3 _PageReserve(0007FE10)
FFFF56F3 _PageCommit(0007FE10)
FFFF56F3 _PageAttach(0007FE11)
FFFF56F3 _PageAttach(0007FE70)
FFFF56F3 _PageAttach(0007FE71)
FFFF56F3 _PageAttach(0007FE74)
FFFF56F3 _PageCommit(0007FE76)
FFFF56F3 _PageCommit(0007FE77)
FFFF56F3 _PageAttach(0007FE78)
FFFF56F3 _PageAttach(0007FEC8)

// Tell the system debugger (WINICE) about all the DLL sections.
FFFF56F3 VWIN32_Int41Dispatch(00000150)    < - repeat this sequence 33 times

// Checks if the debugger wants control during a fault.
FFFF56F3 VWIN32_Int41Dispatch(0000007F)

FFFF56F3 _VWIN32_Get_Thread_Context(00000000)
FFFF56F3 _VWIN32_Set_Thread_Context(00000000)
... Omitted rest of output
```

Figure 6-7
Condensed VV32SVSPY output from starting CALC.EXE.

From studying the output in Figure 6-7, you can see the birth of a new process. It's important to note that the process name shown on the left of the events is merely the current process. Most of the calls to the Win32 VxD services are being made from inside KERNEL32.DLL, acting on behalf of the current process (Explorer in our example here).

The output starts with the Explorer process (executing inside KER-NEL32.DLL) creating a new memory context. However, a memory context does not a process make. There's more work to be done. A few lines later in the output, note the creation of an initial thread for the new process, as well as the setting of the thread's priority. The next act of KERNEL32 is to call WakeThread on the new thread, which causes the new thread to become the currently executing thread a couple of lines later. (This is the first line where the process name is given as FFFF56F3.)

Once the new thread wakes up, it starts performing file I/O. This is presumably where the new process is examining its EXE file and loading it into memory. Naturally, loading the EXE into memory requires that the process use the page-based memory management Win32 VxD services to reserve and commit memory within the process's context. An interesting effect that shows up during this phase is that the system realizes it can share certain memory pages with a DLL that's already loaded in the private address space of another process. In this case, the DLL is SHELL32.DLL. When the system realizes that certain pages can be shared (primarily code pages), it uses the VMM _PageAttach service to start sharing the pages with the other process (or processes).

Technical challenges in writing W32SVSPY

When I first conceived of writing W32SVSPY, the first problem that sprang to mind was that the KERNEL32 VxDCall function is called in the memory context of all applications in the system. As I described earlier, Win32 VxD services are invoked via calls to the VxDCall function. I therefore had to put the code that actually handled the redirected service calls someplace in memory that's accessible to all processes (in other words, I had to put the code in shared memory).

Another problem with having Win32 VxD service calls being invoked in all memory contexts is that I couldn't use file I/O operations to just log the calls as they occurred. The reason I couldn't do this is because file handles are valid only in the context in which they were opened. Opening and closing a file handle each time a Win32 VxD service was invoked was also not an option. KERNEL32 uses Win32 VxD services for file I/O, so this would clearly cause a reentrancy issue. (Not to mention that opening and closing file handles for each call would make performance grind to a halt.) Again, the answer was to use shared memory accessible to all processes. W32SVSPY saves away information about each Win32 VxD service call into a memory buffer, and retrieves the information from the buffer for display when it's safe.

A third problem I encountered when writing W32SVSPY was intercepting the Win32 VxD services. Earlier, I showed that the VxDCall function looks like this:

```
VxDCall:
MOV     EAX,DWORD PTR [ESP+04]
POP     DWORD PTR [ESP]
CALL    FWORD PTR CS:[BFFC8004]
```

Intercepting the calls to Win32 VxD services should be as simple as plugging the address at BFFC8004 with an address in my code and in my interception routine, chaining on to the original address. In fact, this isn't hard at all. What's tough is finding the address of the VxDCall function. I needed to find the address of VxDCall so that I could reach in and grab the offset where the pointer to the INT 30h instruction is located.

Why couldn't I just call GetProcAddress on VxDCall? This function is undocumented, and isn't exported by name. I couldn't use GetProcAddress with VxDCall's ordinal value, either. Chapter 3 shows how the GetProcAddress specifically prevents applications from looking up KERNEL32.DLL functions by ordinal. Why did Microsoft do this? No doubt to prevent applications like W32SVSPY from being written. As you know by now, Microsoft's preventative efforts failed and W32SVSPY was able to circumvent the crude anti-hacking kludge.

Putting W32SVSPY into shared memory

The first part of getting W32SVSPY up and running was to get its code into memory shared by all processes. In Chapter 3, I showed that the way to do this is to put the code into DLLs. Therefore, W32SVSPY has a DLL component (W32SPDLL.DLL) in addition to its EXE. However, simply putting my spy code into a DLL isn't enough. The DLL needs to be loaded at a location where memory is shared across all processes. In Windows 95, that means in the memory range between 2GB and 3GB. This is where the system DLLs like KERNEL32.DLL and USER32.DLL can be found. We need to somehow make Windows 95 load W32SPDLL.DLL into this shared memory region.

Now, your first tendency might be to tell the linker to base W32SPDLL.DLL at an address between 2GB and 3GB. Although you can get the linker to base a DLL at whatever address you want, this isn't enough. My first attempt at basing W32SPDLL.DLL at an address above 2GB and then loading it failed. Oh, the DLL loaded all right. The problem was, the operating system relocated the DLL so that it was in the application's private address area. Clearly, the Windows 95 loader didn't want my DLL in the shared region supposedly reserved for system DLLs and shared memory.

After studying Microsoft-supplied DLLs that the loader will load above 2GB, a common pattern struck me. Every DLL that the Windows 95 loader successfully loaded into shared memory above 2GB had all its writeable data sections marked as shared. In retrospect, this seems obvious, since if the loader were to load the DLL into the shared memory region above 2GB, Windows 95 certainly can't be providing per-process data in the data sections. It was the per-process data sections of the DLL that were causing the problem.

By doing the following two things, I was finally able to get W32SPDLL.DLL loaded above 2GB:

- Have the linker base the DLL at an address above 2GB. I picked the address of where KERNEL32.DLL loads, since I know that the Windows 95 loader will relocate DLLs that have overlapping base addresses.

- Make the .data, .bss, and .idata sections of the DLL shared. I did this in the W32SVSPY makefile by using the /section: switch to the linker.

Both of these requirements are implemented by the following lines in the linker response file:

```
-BASE:0xBFF70000
/section:.data,RWS
/section:.idata,RWS
/section:.bss,RWS
```

(Note that RWS means readable, writeable, shared.)

Finding the address of VxDCall

Earlier, I mentioned that the Windows 95 KERNEL32.DLL goes to great lengths to prevent applications from getting the address of undocumented KERNEL32 functions like VxDCall. GetProcAddress simply won't work for these functions. However, if you can implicitly link to a function, you can easily find the function's address. In C or C++, you can just use the function's name without the ()'s. Now, there *has* to be a way to implicitly link to these undocumented functions. Otherwise, why would Microsoft have bothered to export them?

In Appendix A, I show how I built an import library for the 100 or so undocumented functions exported by KERNEL32. This import library is set up so that when you import a function in the library, you're importing it by the function's ordinal value. In W32SPDLL.C, I had to prototype the desired function:

```
_ _declspec(dllimport) int WINAPI VxDCall0(void);
```

Then, I had to take its address by using the function name without parens:

```
pfnVxDCall0 = VxDCall0;
```

Once I know the address of VxDCall0 within KERNEL32.DLL, it's a simple matter to reach into the function's code and pull out the address where the 16:32 pointer to the INT 30h instruction is kept:

```
ppfnOriginalVxDCall = (PBYTE)*(PDWORD)((DWORD)pfnVxDCall0 + 0xA);
```

This line may look unintelligible, but it's really not so bad. It's just grabbing the DWORD that's 0xA bytes into the code for the VxDCall function, and then typecasting that DWORD to be a pointer.

Yes, it's rather disgusting to be relying on a fixed offset within the VxDCall functions to find the pointer I'm after. But when you're writing low-level system-hacking tools like W32SVSPY, it's the nature of the business. Microsoft could easily break W32SVSPY by rearranging the code for VxDCall so that the pointer I'm after isn't 0xA bytes into the code. But then, they really have no reason to muck with the VxDCall, other than perhaps to be malicious and break W32SVSPY. It will be interesting to see what happens in future revisions of Windows 95.

SUMMARY

In this chapter, I've thrown a lot of undocumented functions and fairly technical material at you. It's not necessary to remember or retain all this information in one reading for the chapter to be of value. The important point I've tried to convey is that Windows 95 has three separate pieces that could be called kernels (KRNL386.EXE, KERNEL32.DLL, and VWIN32.VXD). Each of these kernels has detailed knowledge and extensive interaction with the other two kernels.

Understanding any one of these components without knowing about and understanding the other components is a difficult feat. You may find yourself coming back and rereading this chapter from time to time to pick up on some subtle point you missed the first time. I hope I've shown you the scope of the interactions between the three kernel components of Windows 95, and enabled you to do more exploring on your own. I know I have quite a bit more spelunking ahead of me, too!

Win16 Modules and Tasks

*I*t may seem a little odd to include a chapter on the core 16-bit KERNEL data structures in a book that focuses on the 32-bit architecture of Windows 95. However, as you'll soon see, these data structures play an integral role in the overall architecture of Windows 95, both for 16- and 32-bit applications.

In this chapter, we'll be taking a tour of the 16-bit modules and tasks that KRNL386 maintains. If you're familiar with modules and tasks from Windows 3.1, at first glance they'll appear unchanged in Windows 95. Why bother with these old 16-bit concepts when there's new and exciting Win32 components to explore? If you dig a little deeper, you'll see that the 16-bit KRNL386.EXE, the 32-bit KERNEL32.DLL, and the VWIN32 VxD all know about each other, and are intertwined in their operations. Therefore, an examination of 16-bit modules and tasks is an important part of learning about the Windows 95 architecture.

We'll start out by looking at modules, which are the mechanism by which the 16-bit side of Windows 95 tracks all the EXEs and DLLs that are loaded in the system. Strange as it may seem, Windows 95 creates 16-bit modules not only for 16-bit EXEs and DLLs, but also for 32-bit EXEs and DLLs. Following a description of the specifics of 16-bit modules, I'll show some pseudocode for some useful 16-bit KRNL386 functions that demonstrate the use of modules in action.

Next, I'll turn to the subject of 16-bit tasks and the data structures that KRNL386 uses to maintain them. (Tasks are created from modules, so it's only natural to describe modules first, then tasks.) As if the fact that Windows 95 creates 16-bit modules for 32-bit EXEs and DLLs wasn't enough, you might be surprised to learn that Windows 95 maintains a 16-bit task for each Win32 process. After describing the layout and characteristics of tasks, I provide pseudocode for some KRNL386 functions that manipulate and use task information.

In "The SHOW16 Program" section at the end of the chapter, I've included a discussion about the 16-bit SHOW16.EXE program I wrote that allows you to easily browse through the 16-bit modules and tasks in your system. While I could have used TOOLHELP to obtain much of the information for SHOW16, I chose to get the data fresh from the modules and tasks themselves. Doing it this way proves that modules and tasks aren't some magical thing that only the coders at Microsoft are allowed to touch. The results of a little browsing with SHOW16 may surprise you!

Before plunging into the details of modules and tasks, a minor point needs to be explained. Throughout this chapter, I often refer to global memory handles and CPU selectors as if they were the same thing. In Windows 3.1 and Windows 95, a 16-bit FIXED global heap handle is a ring 3 selector value. A MOVEABLE handle can easily be converted to a selector by turning on the bottommost bit of the handle value. This is essentially all that GlobalLock does. I'm mentioning this up front so that I don't have to bog down the rest of the text with minor distinctions between selectors and global memory handles. For the purposes of the discussion in this chapter, they can be considered the same thing.

WHY HAVE 16-BIT REPRESENTATIONS OF 32-BIT MODULES AND PROCESSES?

You may be wondering why Microsoft bothered to go through the hassle of representing 32-bit programs and DLLs in their old 16-bit equivalent. The answer is simple. Unlike Windows NT, Windows 95 doesn't wall off 16-bit applications in their own virtual machine(s), separate from the 32-bit side of the world. Instead, 16- and 32-bit programs coexist within the same virtual machine, and even share address spaces to some extent (see Chapter 5 for details on this). In addition, large portions of the code used by *all* Windows 95 applications resides in 16-bit DLLs (for example, USER, GDI, COMMDLG, and, yes, even KRNL386).

16-BIT MODULES

In the 16-bit world of Windows 95, *modules* are the data structures used by KRNL386 to represent the code, data, and resources of anEXE or .DLL file that's loaded in memory. Included in the category of DLLs are files with different extensions, such as .DRV and .FON. Every module is associated with a disk file somewhere on the system.

In this section, I describe the 16-bit Windows 95 modules that are derived from the 16-bit modules of Windows 3.1. Every loaded EXE or DLL in the system, regardless of whether it's 16- or 32-bit based, has a 16-bit module. However, it's important to be aware that 32-bit EXEs and DLLs are also simultaneously represented as 32-bit modules in 32-bit land by KERNEL32.DLL. In general, the 16-bit representation of a module is used by the 16-bit system DLLs (for example, KRNL386 and USER), while the 32-bit representation is used by the 32-bit system DLLs (for example, KERNEL32). For more information on 32-bit modules, see Chapter 3.

All of a 16-bit module's data is kept in a segment allocated from the 16-bit global heap via a call to GlobalAlloc. This segment with module information is known as a *module database*. The handle of the global heap block containing a module database is known as a *module handle* or, more familiarly, as an *HMODULE*. This is the handle that functions such as GetModuleHandle refer to.

In Windows 3.1, all modules were created inside the LoadModule routine. Calling the LoadLibrary or WinExec API functions ultimately ended up in a call to LoadModule. In Windows 95, modules for 16-bit EXEs and DLLs are still created within the LoadModule function in KRNL386, while the 16-bit modules that represent 32-bit EXEs and DLLs are created by KERNEL32.DLL. The selectors used for 32-bit–based NE modules aren't in the global heap's list of handles, so finding these HMODULEs can be tricky (as we'll see later).

The format of a 16-bit module database is based on the 16-bit executable format used by Windows and OS/2 1.*x* since their inception. This file format is known as *the New Executable (NE) format*. In the remainder of this chapter, I refer to 16-bit modules in Windows 95 as *NE modules* to distinguish them from 32-bit modules (which are based on the Portable Executable format, and known as *PE modules*). I won't be describing the format of NE files in this chapter since they're covered more than adequately in the Microsoft documentation and elsewhere. In the following section I go over the format of the module database that's created from reading in an NE file. If you compare the NE file format with the NE module database, you'll see that although they're similar, they have several important differences.

Near the beginning of each NE file is a 0x40-byte data structure known as the *NE header*. The structure has this name because its first WORD contains the value 0x454E, which, when viewed in ASCII characters, is NE (short for New Executable). Early on in the LoadModule code, KRNL386 reads the NE header from the executable file into the beginning of the module database that it's constructing. Many of the fields in the NE file are therefore identical to the corresponding offsets in the NE module in memory. However, KRNL386 recycles some of the fields that are meaningful only for the NE header on disk, and uses them for other purposes.

Following the 0x40 byte NE header in the module database is the *segment table*. The segment table is an array of structures that contain vital information (size, code or data, and so on) for each of the module's code and data segments. Following the segment table is the *resource table*, which contains information about all the resources that can be found in the corresponding NE file, although not the actual resources themselves. Rather, the resource table is a sort of table of contents that tells KRNL386 where it can look in the NE file for the actual resource data.

Following the segment and resource information, you'll find information about the module's imports and exports. Calling functions in another EXE or DLL is known as *importing the functions*. For example, USER.EXE calls functions in KRNL386.EXE, so USER.EXE imports KRNL386 and its functions. Not surprisingly, the opposite of importing a function is *exporting a function*. Exporting a function means that you're making the function available to be called by other EXEs or DLLs. In the example I just mentioned, KRNL386 exports its functions and USER.EXE imports them.

At the bits and bytes level, exporting a function means that you're putting its address in a table known as an *entry table*. When you load an NE file that imports functions from another module, the Windows loader (that is, the LoadModule function) uses the entry table to look up the addresses of the exported functions in the target module. How does the loader know which slot in the entry table to use? When you export a function, the linker assigns it an ordinal value that can be thought of as an index into the module's entry table. Other EXEs or DLLs that link to the first module will typically carry around the ordinal entry table values of the functions they import.

It's also possible to import a function by its name rather than by its entry table ordinal. This is where the resident and nonresident names tables come into play. These two tables associate a function name with the address of a function exported by the module. A module database segment contains the entire resident names table within itself, but only provides a file offset to the nonresident names table (hence the resident versus nonresident distinction).

Under Windows 3.*x*, KRNL386 maintains the module databases in a linked list. As new modules are created by LoadModule, they are added to the end of the list. At the head of the list is KRNL386, which is the first module brought into the system. You can easily walk the module list yourself (as my SHOW16 program does), or you can let the TOOLHELP ModuleFirst and ModuleNext functions do the walking. (Internally, TOOLHELP does the same thing as SHOW16 does, but it's officially sanctioned by Microsoft, whereas walking system data structures yourself isn't.)

Under Windows 95, KRNL386 maintains the NE modules for 16-bit EXEs and DLLs in the same manner. However, the 16-bit module databases that represent 32-bit PE files are not added to the list. Instead, they just hang out in the global heap, disassociated from the 16-bit module list and from each other. With 16-bit code, I'm not aware of any elegant way to enumerate through the 32-bit NE modules. However, a brute force approach does work, as SHOW16 demonstrates.

Before diving into its actual format, let's do a quick high-level review of the components of the 16-bit module database: As Figure 7-1 shows, the 0x40-byte NE header is at the beginning of the module database. This is followed by the segment table and the resource table. Bringing up the rear are the tables with information about imported modules (the imported names table and the module reference table) and exported functions (the entry table and the resident names table).

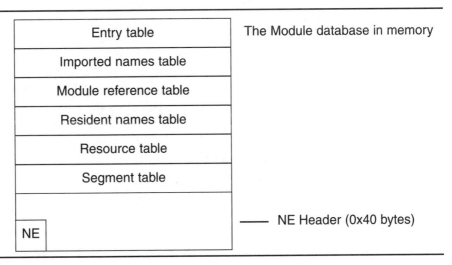

Figure 7-1
The various components of the 16-bit module database.

THE NE HEADER

If you're just interested in a quick review of the fields in a module database, refer to the HMODULE.H header file from the SHOW16 sample program (it's on the disk that comes with this book). Here, I'm going to go over the fields of the 0x40 byte NE header in detail. The first line of each field description gives its offset in the module database, its type (for example, WORD or DWORD), and a short description.

00h   WORD   *Signature*

This WORD always contains the value 0x454E, which when represented as ASCII characters is NE (for New Executable). Putting a signature WORD at or near the beginning of executable files is a tradition of Microsoft and IBM operating systems. Other signatures used in executable files are PE (for the Win32 Portable Executable format), LE (Linear Executables, used for Windows 3.*x* and Windows 95 VxDs), and LX (also meaning Linear Executable, but used by 32-bit OS/2 2.*x* programs).

02h   WORD   *module usage (reference) count*

This WORD represents the number of other modules that are using this module. For example, if a DLL is being used by three programs, this field will contain the value 3. If you load a DLL via LoadLibrary, this field in the DLL's module database will be 1. Each subsequent call to LoadLibrary or LoadModule for the DLL will increment this value by one, and each call to FreeLibrary will decrement the value by one. The rules for determining the value of this field are not always so clear, however. For example, if a program uses two DLLs (let's say *A* and *B*) that both use a third DLL (*C*), module *C*'s reference count will be 1, not 2. My May 1994 *Microsoft Systems Journal* Q&A column (available on the MSDN CD-ROM) describes IncExeUsage and DecExeUsage, which are the KRNL386 internal functions responsible for incrementing and decrementing the module reference count, including those tough situations with circularly referencing DLLs.
In NE modules created for PE files, the module reference count is set to 1 initially, and never seems to vary.

When the module reference count drops to 0, KRNL386 frees up the module's segments and resources, calls the WEP routine if the module is a DLL module (and if a WEP routine is present), and, finally, GlobalFree's the module database segment.

04h   WORD   *near pointer to entry table*

This field is a near pointer (relative to the HMODULE segment) to the module's entry table. The entry table is a list of functions that the module exports for use by other modules. Each module table entry contains the function's address, its import ordinal value, and some flags. See "The Entry Table" section for more details about the entry table. NE modules for Win32 executables don't contain an entry table, because the entry table assumes 16-bit far addresses, which PE modules don't support.

06h   HMODULE   *next module database*

This WORD-sized field holds the HMODULE of the next module in the linked list of NE modules. The KERNEL module (KRNL386.EXE) is always at the head of the list. There are two ways to obtain KERNEL's HMODULE: You can either call GetModuleHandle(KERNEL), or you can call GetModuleHandle for any other module, and KERNEL's HMODULE will be in the DX register upon the function's return. As new modules are loaded, they're appended at the end of the list. The last module in the list has a 0 in this field. NE modules for Win32 files aren't kept in the linked list of modules. Instead, they all have the value 0 in this location.

08h   WORD   *near pointer to DGROUP segment entry*

This field is a near pointer (relative to the HMODULE segment) to the segment table entry for the module's DGROUP segment. The segment table format is described in a later section, called (not surprisingly) "The Segment Table." The DGROUP segment is the data segment that all the module's regular data goes into by default. The DGROUP segment usually also contains a local heap and, in EXE modules, the program's stack. For 16-bit modules created for Win32 EXEs and DLLs, this field contains 0.

**0Ah   WORD   *near pointer to modified OFSTRUCT with*
                                          *file name***

This field is a near pointer (relative to the HMODULE segment) to a data structure that's very similar to the OFSTRUCT given in the Win16 WINDOWS.H file. In the Windows 95 DDK, the 16-bit WINDOWS.H file calls this structure an OFSTRUCTEX.

```
typedef struct tagOFSTRUCTEX
{
    WORD cBytes;            // The length of the struct, in bytes.
    BYTE fFixedDisk;        // TRUE if nonremoveable media.
    UINT nErrCode;          // DOS error code if OpenFile failed.
    DWORD fileDateTime;     // Date/Time of file in MS-DOS format.
    char szPathName[260];   // The path to the file.
} OFSTRUCTEX;
```

The primary difference between this structure and a regular OFSTRUCT is that the cBytes field is a WORD, rather than a BYTE. Why's this? Because Windows 95 supports long filenames (up to 260 characters). Therefore, a single BYTE in the structure couldn't contain the entire length of the structure. In addition, the end of the structure (which contains the path name), is 260bytes rather than the 128 bytes of an OFSTRUCT.

0Ch   WORD module   flags

This WORD contains bitfield flags that hold information about the module in memory. The meaning of many of these flags is different from the flags used in the NE file on the accompanying disk. The known flags for Windows 95 NE modules are

Flag Name and Bit Value	Description
MODFLAGS_DLL 0x8000	For true 16-bit NE modules, this flag indicates that the module is a DLL, rather than an EXE. This bit appears to always be set in the NE module databases created to represent Win32 modules.
MODFLAGS_CALL_WEP 0x4000	This flag, which is valid only for DLL modules, indicates that the DLL's WEP routine should be called when the DLL is unloaded. This flag is almost always set, except for task modules and Win32 modules.
MODFLAGS_SELF_LOADING 0x0800	This flag indicates that the module uses the self-loading mechanism. In this scheme, the module provides its own segment loader that LoadModule calls to bring the module's segments into memory. Microsoft strongly discourages the use of self-loading programs, and barely documents their use. However, in the past, several of Microsoft's applications (such as early versions of Word for Windows and Microsoft Fortran) used the self-loading feature. Optlink 5.x from SLR systems (now owned by Symantec) can produce EXEs that use self-loading to shrink executable file size. When the OPTLINK linker writes the segment data to the NE file, it compresses the information. When the module is loaded into memory, the bound-in self-loading code uncompresses the segment data as it brings the segment into memory.
MODFLAGS_APPTYPE a 0x0300 (0x0200 | 0x0100)	These two bits are a holdover from the days of OS/2 1.x, in which program's user interface could be one of three possible types. The bit value 0x0300 means that the program uses the operating system's GUI windowing API. The bit value 0x0200 means that the application is a console (text mode) application, but limits its screen output to the text mode output functions that can be virtualized to display in a GUI window. (An example of this would be running an MS-DOS prompt in a windowed session). The bit value 0x0100 means that the application directly manipulates the video buffer, so it must be run in full screen mode.

Flag Name and Bit Value	Description
	Regular Windows NE modules always have the value 0x0300 for these flags, meaning they use the GUI API. In Windows 95, the NE modules for Win32 files don't bother to set any of the bits, meaning the field's value is 0, which is undefined according to the NE specification.
MODFLAGS_IMPLICIT_LOAD 0x0040	This flag means that the module is in memory because another module has an implicit link to it. Task modules won't have this flag, nor will DLLs that are loaded via LoadLibrary. However, if a DLL loaded via LoadLibrary implicitly loads other DLLs, this flag will be set in the module database of those DLLs.
MODFLAGS_WIN32 0x0010	This new Windows 95 flag indicates that this NE module represents a Win32 PE file.
MODFLAGS_AUTODATA 0x0002	This flag tells the Win16 loader that each module should get a separate DGROUP instance for each user of the module. This flag is for EXE modules, in which each running instance of a program needs its own DGROUP segment.
MODFLAGS_SINGLEDATA 0x0001	This module indicates that a single DGROUP should be used for all users of the module. This flag is set only in DLL modules, since 16-bit DLLs always use the same DGROUP segment no matter which task is calling them.
	If neither the MODFLAGS_AUTODATA or MODFLAGS_SINGLEDATA flags are set, then the module doesn't have a DGROUP segment or a local heap. Interestingly, the SYSTEM module (loaded directly after KERNEL) falls into this category.
	NE modules for Win32 files always contain the value 0x8010 for the flags field in the module database. This translates to MODFLAGS_DLL and MODFLAGS_WIN32.

0Eh   WORD segment   *index of DGROUP segment*

This field contains the 1-based index in the segment table of the module's DGROUP segment. This field is somewhat redundant because the near pointer at offset 08h in the module database provides the same information (albeit in a different form). In Win32 NE modules, this field is always 0.

10h   WORD   *initial local heap size*

This WORD is the initial amount of memory in the module's DGOUP that the Windows loader should reserve for the local heap. If necessary, the local heap can be grown later. If the heap is grown, this field is not updated. (It wouldn't make sense to update it, since this heap size will need to be used if another instance of a program starts up.) Many of the standard 16-bit system

DLLs have 0 for their initial heap size. Interestingly, in Windows 95, a couple of the system DLLs had their initial heap size shrunk down compared to the same DLL in Windows 3.1. This was probably part of the effort to reduce Windows 95's memory footprint as much as possible. In Win32 NE modules, this field is always 0.

12h   WORD   stack size

This WORD contains the size of the stack that the loader should reserve space for in the module's DGROUP segment. The stack size has meaning only for EXE modules, since the code in DLLs runs on the stack of the calling application. The minimum stack size for 16-bit applications in Windows 3.*x* and Windows 95 is 5K. If this field is less than 5K in the EXE file, the loader increases it to 5K when it creates the NE module. In Win32 NE modules, this field is always 0.

14h   FARPROC   entry point of module

This member of the module table structure contains the module's entry point. For EXE modules, the entry point is where program execution begins. In EXEs compiled as C or C++ programs, the entry point is where the compiler's runtime library startup code starts. The C/C++ startup code eventually calls the WinMain procedure. In DLL modules, the entry point is the start of the runtime library code that eventually calls the LibMain procedure. An EXE module must have a nonzero entry point, whereas DLL modules (such as fonts) can have a NULL entry point, in which case the loader doesn't try to call anything.

The address stored in this field is a logical address. A logical address is a 16:16 address, but the segment portion isn't a real selector value. Rather, the segment is an index into the segment table that follows the NE header. Thus, if the module's entry point was 0x017C bytes into the third segment in the module, the entry point is 0003:017C. When it comes time for the loader to call the module's entry point, it needs to figure out the actual selector assigned to the segment. The loader uses the logical segment value as an index into the array of segment entries that follow the NE header.

In NE modules for Win32 files, the entry point is always 0. This makes sense, since 32-bit code uses 32-bit offsets, rather than 16:16 far pointers.

18h   DWORD   initial stack pointer value

This field contains the initial value that an EXE module's SS:SP should contain when the entry point is called. Like the preceding field, this address is a logical address, rather than an actual selector:offset. The logical segment portion of this address should always be identical to the DGROUP segment index given in the WORD at offset 0Eh. For DLL modules and all Win32 NE modules, this field always contains 0.

1Ch   WORD   number of segments in module

This WORD holds the number of segments (code or data) that the module contains. Following the NE header in the module table is an array of 10-byte segment table entries. The number of entries in the array is given by the value of this field. It's possible for a module to have 0 segments; a perfect example of this is a font module. Font modules typically contain only resources, and no segments. This field is always 0 for PE-file–based NE modules.

1Eh   WORD   number of imported modules

This field contains the number of modules that this module implicitly links to. For example, if an EXE calls functions in KERNEL, USER, and GDI, this field will have a value of 3. This field is used in conjunction with the module reference table (see field 28h). The number of entries in the module reference table corresponds to the value of this field. (In the example I just mentioned, there would be three entries, to correspond with the field value of 3.) Win32 NE modules always contain 0 in this field.

20h   WORD   size of nonresident names table

This field contains the size of the nonresident names table in the NE file. The nonresident names table (and the resident names table referred to by field 26h) associate an exported symbol (usually a function name) with the exported ordinal value. To access the nonresident names table, KERNEL needs to seek to the table's starting offset in the NE file (see field 2Ch), and read in the number of bytes given by this field. (See "The Resident and Nonresident Names Table" section for more details.) In Win32 NE files, this field is always 0.

22h   WORD   near pointer to segment table

This field is a near pointer (relative to the HMODULE segment) to the module's segment table. The segment table is an array of 10 byte structures, one for each code and data segment managed by the module. (See the following section for more details.) Since the segment table always immediately follows the 0x40 byte NE header, this field always contains the value 0x40 for normal NE modules. For Win32 NE modules, this field always holds 0x4C — but this is meaningless, since Win32 files don't have 16-bit segments or a segment table.

24h   WORD   near pointer to the resource table

This field is a near pointer (relative to the HMODULE segment) to the module's resource table. The resource table is a sort of "table of contents" to the actual resource data, which is stored elsewhere in the executable file. (The format of the resource table is described in "The Resource Table" section.) Interestingly, this field is actively used by both 16- and 32-bit NE modules. This suggest that the 16-bit code that uses resources is used to deal with resources in both 16-bit NE files and 32-bit PE files.

26h   WORD   near pointer to resident names table

This field is a near pointer (relative to the HMODULE segment) to the module's resident names table. The resident names table is used to associate a function name exported from the module with its exported ordinal value. The resident names table shares the same format with the nonresident names table. The key distinction is that the resident names table is always in memory (within the HMODULE segment), while the nonresident names table is loaded from disk whenever needed. The format of the two names tables is described in "The Resident and Nonresident Names Table" section.

All NE modules have a resident names section, regardless of whether they're created from an NE file or a PE file. The reason for this is that every module must have a name (for example, KERNEL, USER, TOOLHELP, and so on). The module's name is always the first entry in the resident names table. Therefore, when KERNEL32 builds its minimal NE module database, it always includes a resident names table with one entry — the module name itself.

28h   WORD   near pointer to the module reference table

This field is a near pointer (relative to the HMODULE segment) to the module reference table. The module reference table is a list of all modules that are used by (that is, imported by) this module. The list is nothing more than an array of HMODULEs. In the executable's relocation information, you'll find that the relocation information for each imported function contains an index into this module table. For example, a program calls SetPixel in GDI.EXE. SetPixel's export ordinal from GDI.EXE is 31. In the program's module reference table, GDI is the fourth module. Therefore, the relocation information for this call to SetPixel will contain both the value 4 (the module reference table index for GDI's HMODULE), and the value 31 (the export ordinal of SetPixel within GDI).

2Ah   WORD   *near pointer to the imported names table*

This field is a near pointer (relative to the HMODULE segment) to the module's imported names table. The imported names table is a series of PASCAL-style strings that are the module names of all the DLLs imported by this module. The imported names table can also contain the names of functions that are imported by name, rather than by ordinal value (this is rarely done, however). When creating the module database, KRNL386 uses the module names in this table to look up or load the other modules that this module references (imports). As KRNL386 finds or loads each imported module, it stores the loaded module's HMODULE into the module reference table (field 28h). Once a module has been created, Windows doesn't have any real use for the imported names table. In Win32 NE modules, this field is a nonzero value. The value is meaningless, however, because there is no imported names table in these module databases.

2Ch   DWORD   *file offset of the nonresident names table*

This field contains the file offset (in bytes) of the nonresident names table in the NE file. This value is used in conjunction with field 20h to load the table into memory when necessary. In Win32 NE modules, this field is always 0. See field 20h and the entry table description later in the chapter for more information.

30h   DWORD   *number of moveable entries in the entry table*

This field is effectively obsolete with the demise of real mode Windows. It contains the number of entries in the entry table that have addresses that could change because of real mode segment movement. In protected mode windows, selectors and descriptors hide the movement of segments within memory, so moveable entries are no longer necessary. Moveable versus fixed entries in the entry table are described later in "The Entry Table" section.

32h   WORD   *alignment shift*

In an NE module, the file offsets to the raw segment data and resources aren't stored as DWORD offsets (which is how you might expect them to be stored). Instead, the locations of segments and resources in the NE file are stored in terms of "sector" values. A sector in NE module parlance isn't a disk sector. Rather, the size of a sector is always a power of 2 (2, 4, 8, 16, 32, and so forth). To determine the sector size for a given NE module, you raise the value 2 to the power given by the value of this field. Put another way, you can take the number 1, and shift it left by the number given in this field.

A typical value of this field for NE modules is 9. (1 << 9) == 2 ^ 9 == 512, meaning the sector size is 512 bytes. If a segment started at offset 1536 in the file, its location would be given as sector 3. Another common value for this field is 4. (1 << 4) == 16 bytes. You can configure the sector sized for an NE file when you link the file. For NE modules created for PE files, the alignment size is always 1.

In general, it's a good idea to use the smallest alignment size that will allow your file to be linked. If you use a larger alignment than necessary, you'll almost always waste space in the file, since the linker must add extra padding to make sure each segment and resource starts at a file offset that's a multiple of the sector size. Segment and resource sector offsets are stored in WORDs, so the maximum possible file size when using 16-bit sectors is 1MB (65535 times 16 bytes/sector == 1MB). If you're using 512 byte alignment (the default for most linkers), the maximum file size is 32MB.

34h *WORD*   *unknown*

In Windows 3.1, this field appeared to contain the value 2 if the module contained TrueType fonts. In Windows 95, this field appears to be unused and is always 0.

36h *BYTE*   *intended operating system*

This WORD contains a value representing which operating system this module is intended to be used with. The known values are the following:

0   Unknown (although Window 1.0 files used this value)

1   OS/2

2   Windows

3   European DOS 4 (a multitasking version of DOS not released in the U.S.).

4   Windows/386 (existed only during the time of Windows 2.*x*)

In general, unless you work with 16-bit OS/2, you'll rarely encounter any value other than 2 in NE files. In Win32 NE modules, this field is always 0.

37h *BYTE*   *other module flags*

This BYTE contains some additional flags that were added to the module database format after Windows 1.*x*. (Otherwise, they probably would have appeared in the flags in the WORD at offset 0Ch, or the 0Ch field would have been expanded to a DWORD.)

In Windows 3.*x*, the bit values 0x02 and 0x04 were used to indicate modules written for Windows 2.*x* that were checked out as being okay to run under Windows 3.*x*. Since Windows 95 doesn't support running any 2.*x* or earlier applications, these flags are effectively obsolete.

The flag value 0x08 indicates that the NE file has a gangload (a.k.a. fast-load) area. The gangload area is a collection of segments and resources that have been clustered together in one section of the file. The windows loader can bring these segments into memory with a single read, rather than doing individual seeks and reads of each segment or resource. The goal is to save time during the initial load of the module.

In Windows 95, a new bit flag (0x10) has appeared in some 16-bit modules. It appears that if this flag is set, KRNL386 doesn't bother to look for and call the DLLENTRYPOINT function in 16-bit DLLs. Win32 NE modules always have 0 in this field. The new DLLENTRYPOINT functionality for Win16 DLL under Windows 95 is described in Microsoft's documentation for the thunk compiler (THUNK.EXE).

38h   WORD   *near pointer to imported names table*
This field always appears to point at the resident names table, and is always identical to the value in field 2Ah.

3Ah   WORD   *near pointer to imported names table*
This field always appears to point at the resident names table, and is always identical to the values in fields 2Ah and 38h. The one exception to this rule is for the first module, KERNEL. This exception may be nothing more than a harmless oversight, since KRNL386 is loaded by a section of code separate from the regular Windows loader in Windows 3.1, and this loader behavior remains in Windows 95.

3Ch   WORD   *unknown*
The meaning of this value is unclear. However, it always seems to be a multiple of 0x10. With an occasional exception, its value rises in each subsequent module in the list of 16-bit NE modules. Win32 NE modules always have 0 in this field.

3Eh   WORD   *expected Windows version*
This WORD contains the minimum version of Windows required for use with this module. Common values are for Windows 3.0 (0x0300), Windows 3.1 (0x0310), Windows 95 (0x0400), and Windows "NT 3.5" (Windows NT 3.5 == 0x0350). The HIBYTE of this word is the Windows

major version number, and the LOBYTE is the minor version, in decimal. The correct printf string for displaying the version number is

%u.%02u

as demonstrated in the SHOW16 program on the accompanying disk.

New module database fields in Windows 95

The next three fields are new in Windows 95, and they exist only in PE-file–based NE modules (that is, the 0x0010 bit is set in the flags field of the NE header). If the module database was created from an NE file, these fields don't exist; in their place is the first entry of the segment table.

40h   DWORD base   address of associated PE file
This DWORD is a relative virtual address (a flat 32-bit pointer) to the location in memory where the 32-bit side of Windows 95 loaded the PE file. This value is the same as the HMODULE of the 32-bit PE file as seen from a 32-bit program.

44h   DWORD   base address of associated PE file
This field appears to always be identical to the preceding DWORD (40h).

48h   DWORD   base address of resource section in
*   memory mapped PE file*
This DWORD contains the 32-bit linear address of the resource section (.rsrc) in the PE file that's associated with this 16-bit HMODULE. As you'll see later in "The Resource Table" section, the 16-bit components of Windows 95 have knowledge of resources in 32-bit PE files.

THE SEGMENT TABLE

Immediately following the 0x40 byte NE header in the module database is the segment table (although NE modules for Win32 files don't have a segment table). The segment table is an array of data structures, with each structure describing the characteristics of one code or data segment. The first eight bytes of each structure correspond identically to the segment table structure for NE files. The extra WORD in the in-memory representation is for holding the selector that the 16-bit Windows loader has assigned to that segment. This is an important point: KRNL386 is always able to associate a segment in the NE file with the selector used to access the segment once the segment is loaded in memory, and vice versa.

The format of each segment table entry is as follows:

00h   *WORD*   *sector offset in NE file*

This WORD holds the location in the NE file where the raw data for the segment can be found. Rather than a file offset in bytes, the offset is given in units of sectors. The size of a sector varies from file to file, and is calculated by the align shift value at offset 32h in the NE header. Typical values for a sector size are 16 bytes and 512 bytes. If the value of this field is 0, this is a segment for uninitialized data, and there's no raw data for that segment kept in the NE file.

02h   *WORD*   *segment length in file*

This WORD holds the size of the segment's data in the NE file. Note that this isn't necessarily the size of the memory block that KRNL386 should allocate to load the segment into. For the size of segment in memory, see field 06h. Why would the two segment sizes differ? The most common reason would be for data segments where you put uninitialized data (BSS) at the end of the segment. For example, let's say you had 3K of actual data, but also needed a 4K block of uninitialized data (for an array, say). In the segment table entry for this segment, you'd have the value 3K in this field, and 7K in the allocation size field (06h).

04h   *WORD*   *flags*

This WORD contains flags with information about the segment. The meaning of the flags listed in the following table match the flags as given in the NE file specification. However, if you examine the flags in an in-memory module database, you'll find that KRNL386 has turned on some additional bits not in the NE file specification. The known flags are the following:

Flag and Bit Value	Description
DATA 0x0001	The segment is a data segment. If this flag is not set, the segment is a code segment.
ITERATED 0x0008	The segment contains iterated (run length encoded) data.
MOVEABLE 0x0010	The segment is moveable in linear memory. If this flag is not set, the segment is FIXED. The Windows loader will turn off this bit in an EXE file module, because EXE files rarely need fixed memory.

Flag and Bit Value	Description
PRELOAD 0x0040	The segment should be loaded when the module is loaded, rather than being loaded when first accessed.
RELOC 0x0100	The segment contains relocation information immediately following the raw segment data in memory.
DISCARDABLE 0x1000	The segment is discardable. If memory becomes in short supply, KRNL386 can mark the segment's descriptor as not-present, and reassign the RAM to something else.
32BIT 0x2000	The segment is a 32-bit code segment. When the loader allocates the selector for this segment, it sets the "big" bit in the descriptor so this segment will be interpreted as 32-bit code.

06h   *WORD*   *allocation size*

This is the size of the memory block that KRNL386 should allocate when loading the segment into memory. This size may be larger than the amount of raw data for the segment in the NE file. See field 02h for more information.

08h   *WORD*   *global memory handle*

This is the global heap memory handle for the memory block that KRNL386 has allocated to hold the segment's data in memory. If the handle ends with a 06h or 0Eh (for example, 0476h or 047Eh), the segment is a moveable segment. Otherwise, the handle ends in a 07h or 0Fh, in which case it's a FIXED segment.

The order of entries in the segment table is significant because it provides the foundation for logical addresses. When programs such as linkers and debuggers need to work with addresses in the module's segments, they do so in terms of logical addresses, rather than with actual selectors and offsets. They can't use actual selector values, since the selectors that Windows uses to hold a module's segments will vary from load to load. Therefore, instead of using selector values, a logical address uses a 1-based index into the segment table to describe which segment it's referring to. The first segment in the segment table array is logical segment 1, the second segment in the array is logical segment 2, and so on. If you look at the addresses of functions in a linker-produced .MAP file, you'll be able to see logical addresses in action:

0001:5F46	_free
0001:5F5C	__GetSubAllocClientData
0002:0030	_errno
0002:0032	__protected

At most, a module can have 253 segments. This is because the entry table (described later in its own section) stores the addresses of the exported functions as logical addresses, and uses only one byte to store the logical segment number. Logical segments 0, 0FEh, and 0FFh have special meanings to the Windows loader, so the maximum number of segments in an NE module is 253 rather than 256.

THE RESOURCE TABLE

In addition to segment information, each module database also contains the locations and attributes of all the resources (icons, bitmaps, and so on) that are bound into the executable. Contrary to some programmer's belief, resources don't count as segments in the module's segment table, and you can certainly have more than 255 resources.

Usually, the resource table immediately follows the segment table in the module database. Unlike the segment table, the resource table isn't an array. Instead, it's a somewhat free-form format, and you must do a fair amount of on-the-fly calculations to find a given resource. The format of resources in the module database closely mirrors the resource table in the associated NE file.

The first WORD in the resource table is the alignment shift count (sector size) that is used for calculating the offsets of resources in the associated NE file. This sector size is identical in meaning to the main NE sector size described for field 32h in the previous section on NE headers. The sector size in this WORD should match field 32h in that same section. If it doesn't, something is wrong with the NE file.

Following the first WORD is a series of variable-length sections. Each section holds the information about one particular type of resource. For instance, USER.EXE has sections for cursors, icons, bitmaps, menus, dialogs, string tables, and version information. Within each section is an array of data structures, one data structure for each particular resource instance. For example, if you have an NE file with five icons, you'll have an icon section that includes five structures.

Each of these sections immediately follows the preceding resource in memory. Therefore, to find a particular instance of a resource, you need to figure out how large each section is, based on how many instances of its particular resource it contains. The SHOW16 program on the accompanying disk shows an example of traversing the resource table if this is confusing. Each resource type section (icons, bitmaps, and so forth) starts with the following structure (see HMODULE.H for a C-style structure definition):

00h   WORD   *resource ID*

This is the ID value of the resource. If the high bit 0x8000) is set, it's a predefined resource. Masking off the high bit, the type of resource is given by the following values:

1 — Cursor

2 — Bitmap

3 — Icon

4 — Menu

5 — Dialog

6 — String table

7 — Font directory

8 — Font

9 — Accelerator

10 — RC data (user-defined data)

11 — Error table

12 — Group cursor

13 — Unknown

14 — Group icon

15 — Name table (went away in Windows 3.1)

16 — Version info

See the NE file format specification for a complete description of the various resource types.

If the high bit of the resource ID isn't set, the resource is a user-defined named resource. In this case, the ID value is an offset (relative to the start of the resource table in the NE module) to the resource type name. This name is a Pascal-style (length-prefixed) string.

02h   WORD   *number of resources of this type*

This WORD contains the number of instances of this particular type of resource. This field is essential to determining how long this resource type section is, since the data for the individual resources immediately follows this structure.

04h   DWORD   *resource handler function*

This field contains the handler function for these resources. The handler function is apparently responsible for locking the resource into memory when required. Since low-level resource manipulation is something Microsoft doesn't expect mere mortals to be able to handle, the documentation on resource handler functions is (as usual) very sparse. See the SDK documentation for SetResourceHandler and LoadProc for what little information Microsoft provides.

The resource handler function for a particular resource type can be changed on a per-module basis with the SetResourceHandler function. What? This function's documentation says it requires an HINSTANCE, and all you've got is an HMODULE? Just pass it the HMODULE. This is yet another example of how Microsoft has managed to get the meanings of 16-bit HINSTANCEs and HMODULEs confused. More on this later in the chapter.

Immediately following each resource type header is an array of structures. For each instance of that resource type, there is one structure; each structure is 12 bytes in length. The number of elements in the array is given by the WORD at offset 02h in the resource type header. Each array element has the following format (see HMODULE.H for a C-style structure definition):

00h   WORD   *offset in NE file*

For NE file-based modules, this field is the offset of this particular resource instance in the NE file. The units are in sectors, not bytes (see the description of offset 32h for the details on NE file sectors). For PE file-based modules, this field is an offset (relative to the start of the overall resource section) to a DWORD. The value in this DWORD is the offset (relative to the .rsrc section) of a PE file IMAGE_RESOURCE_DATA_ENTRY structure. In the IMAGE_RESOURCE_DATA_ENTRY you'll find the location and size of the raw resource data in the PE image. See Chapter 8 for details on the PE file format. If this information is going to be of any use to the 16-bit components of Windows 95, they have to know where the PE file's .rsrc section is located in memory. How can they determine the base address of the .rsrc section? Simple. See field 48h in the NE module header of a PE file-based NE module.

02h   WORD   length

For NE file-based modules, this WORD is the length of the resource in units of the sector size. For PE file-based modules, this field is the actual size of the resource data, in bytes. This field identically matches the IMAGE_RESOURCE_DATA_ENTRY.Size value given in the PE file's .rsrc section.

04h   WORD   flags

Contains flags relating to this particular resource. In general, these flags are identical to the segment flags (see field 04h in "The Segment Table" section earlier in this chapter). However, it appears that KRNL386 is turning on some additional bits whose meaning is unknown. The known flags are these:

Flag Name and Bit Value	Description
LOADED 0x0004	The resource is currently loaded in memory.
MOVEABLE 0x0010	The segment is moveable in linear memory. If this flag is not set, the segment is FIXED.
READONLY 0x0020	The resource shouldn't be modified in memory.
PRELOAD 0x0040	The segment should be loaded when the module is loaded, rather than being loaded when first accessed.
DISCARDABLE 0x1000	The segment is discardable. If memory becomes in short supply, KRNL386 can mark the segment's descriptor as not-present, and reassign the RAM to something else.

06h   WORD   ID

This WORD is the ID of the resource as given by the resource compiler. If the high bit (0x8000) is set, this resource is referred to by its integer ID value. Otherwise, it's a named resource. In this case, the ID is an offset (relative to the start of the overall resource table) to the resource's name. The name is in Pascal-style (length-prefixed) form. A typical example of a named resource is a dialog box. For example, from an .RC file

```
Show16Dlg DIALOG 8, 18, 360, 280
```

The ID for this dialog will be of the offset of the Pascal-style string Show16Dlg, relative to the start of the resource table.

08h   **WORD**   *handle*
If the resource has been loaded into memory, this is the global heap handle that points at the resource's data. If the resource hasn't been loaded, this field is 0. This field correlates with the LOADED flag in the resource flags (field 04h). If the LOADED flag isn't set, this field is 0.

0Ah   **WORD**   *usage*
This WORD holds the usage count of the resource. This field can be incremented by calling LockResource, and decremented by calling FreeResource.

THE ENTRY TABLE

The entry table of an NE module is the method by which modules export functions for use by other modules. In the days of real mode windows, the entry table also served as a central thunking location for all far functions in MOVEABLE segments. Here, I'm going to ignore that aspect of the entry table, and just pretend that its sole use is to export functions.

Unlike the segment and resource tables, an entry table in a module database bears only a passing resemblance to its NE file equivalent. While the entry table in the NE file is optimized to save space, the in-memory entry table is optimized for quick scanning. Like the resource table, at the outermost level, the entry table is composed of variable-length chunks that require on-the-fly calculation in order for you to traverse it.

Because the export ordinal values of a module's functions don't have to be contiguous and start at the number 1, the entry table is composed of a series of "bundles" that describe a range of contiguous exported ordinals. Looking up a particular function in the entry table is a matter of scanning through the bundles until you find the bundle containing the desired export ordinal. Each bundle of contiguous entries starts with a header of the following layout:

00h   WORD   first export ordinal value in this bundle – 1

This WORD contains a value one less than the export ordinal of the first entry in this bundle. For instance, if this bundle of entries was for export ordinals 3 through 14, this WORD would contain the value 2.

02h   WORD   last export ordinal value in this bundle

This field contains the value of the last export ordinal described within this bundle. For example, if this bundle of entries was for export ordinals 3 through 14, this field would contain the value 14. By subtracting the WORD at offset 0h from the value of this field, you can calculate how many elements are in the array of function entry-point data structures that follow. Returning to the previous example, this bundle describes (14 – 2 == 12) entry points (entry ordinals 3 through 14, inclusive).

Immediately following the bundle header is an array of data structures, one structure for each exported function. Each exported function is described by the information in its corresponding structure. The structures have the following layout:

00h   BYTE   segment type

If this value is 0FFh, this segment is MOVEABLE, and requires a special thunk if the program is to run in real mode. In protected mode, a thunk isn't necessary because the selector values of code segments don't change if the segment's data moves in the linear address space.

If this field is 0FEh, this entry is a special entry. Entries of this type don't have an actual far address. Rather, the offset field is used as a sort of global variable in the code that links to this entry. The only known examples of this type of entry are the exported values from KRNL386: __AHSHIFT, __0000H, and so on. See Chapter 5 of *Undocumented Windows* for a complete list and description of these special entries. If this field is not 0FFh or 0FEh, then it contains the logical segment number of the exported function's address. In this case, it should be identical to the BYTE at offset 02h in the structure.

01h   BYTE   flags

Flags for this entry point. The following flags are known:

Flag	Description
0x01	The function is exported. Except in programs that need to run in real mode, this flag should always be set. If it's not set, it's a function that needs a real mode thunk, but that shouldn't be exported for use by other modules.

Flag	Description
0x02	The function uses a common data segment for all callers. This should happen only in DLL modules. By default, this flag is off for EXE modules, and on for DLL modules. However, you can force this flag off for a DLL exported function with the NODATA statement on the appropriate EXPORTS line in the .DEF file.

02h   *BYTE*   *logical segment number*

This BYTE holds the logical segment number portion of the exported function's address. This segment number can be used as an index into the NE module's segment table to determine the actual selector value for the segment.

03h   *WORD*   *offset*

This WORD is the starting offset of the exported function within the segment given by the preceding field (02h).

To look up the address of a given exported function (like KRNL386 does), you scan through the bundle headers, looking for the bundle that contains the exported entry. When you find it, you can then determine the array index of the exported function, relative to the first array entry in the bundle. For example, using our usual example of a bundle encompassing entries 3 through 14, the address of exported function 7 would be found in the fifth array element in the bundle.

In all this description of the entry table, nowhere has the subject of function names come into play. However, the GetProcAddress function allows you to look up the address of an exported function in another module by specifying the function's name. Therefore, there must be some way to associate a function name with its export ordinal, which brings us to the subject of . . .

THE RESIDENT AND NONRESIDENT NAMES TABLES

The resident and nonresident names tables are the means by which NE modules bind a function name to an export ordinal. Both of these tables share the identical format. Each entry in the table has the following layout:

Offset	Description
01 BYTE	Length of exported name to follow.
?? char	The name of the exported symbol (function). Not null terminated.
?? WORD	The exported ordinal value of this symbol.

For example, the SetPixel function in GDI has an export ordinal of 31. Somewhere in GDI's nonresident names table exists the following data (8 is the string length of SetPixel, and 31 is the export ordinal):

```
8, 'S', 'E', 'T', 'P', 'I', 'X', 'E', 'L', 31
```

The first entry of both the resident and nonresident names table has a special meaning. The first entry also has an export ordinal of 0 in both cases. In the resident names table, the first entry is the module name (for example, KERNEL, GDI, TOOLHELP, and so on). This string is exactly the same string given on the NAME or LIBRARY line in the .DEF file used to create the NE file.

In the nonresident names table, the first is the description field. This string is a short description of what the module is supposed to do. The linker determines the contents of this string by copying whatever's on the DESCRIPTION line of the .DEF file used to link the NE file. If no DESCRIPTION line is given, the linker defaults to using the name of the EXE or DLL. Typical description strings from Windows 95's KRNL386, USER, and GDI modules are as follows:

```
KRNL386: 'Microsoft Windows Kernel Interface Version 4.00'
USER:    'Microsoft Windows User Interface'
GDI:     'Microsoft Windows Graphics Device Interface'
```

Why are there two names tables? The only reason for having two tables is to save space. Most programs and DLLs import functions by ordinal values rather than by their names. Therefore, in the DLLs that are exporting functions, it doesn't make sense to have a whole bunch of names sitting around in the module database in memory when they're not needed. These names should be put in the nonresident names table, which is loaded from disk only when needed (such as during a GetProcAddress call). Names that you need to be able to look up quickly, or that you'll need in situations where you don't want to do disk I/O, should be put in the resident names table.

You can use the .DEF file to control which name table an exported function goes into. If you export a function and explicitly give it an ordinal value in the .DEF file, it will end up in the nonresident names table. However, if you don't specify an export ordinal value for the function in the .DEF file, the linker will put the function name in the resident names table. Alternatively, you can add the RESIDENTNAME to the exported function's line, and the linker will always put the name in the resident names table. In general, if you have a DLL with many exported functions, you should dump out the file with a program like TDUMP or EXEHDR and then see which table your exported functions names are in. Unless you have a good reason for wanting the functions in the resident names table, you should do whatever's necessary to ensure that the nonresident names table is used. That way, you won't chew up potentially precious memory with the names of all your DLL's functions.

HMODULEs versus HINSTANCEs

One of the most confusing things in Win16 programming is differentiating between a module handle (an HMODULE) and an instance handle (an HINSTANCE). As I just showed, an HMODULE represents a loaded EXE or DLL in memory. And, as I describe in the next section, an HINSTANCE is simply the global heap handle of the default data segment for a running task or a DLL. Conceptually, an HMODULE and an HINSTANCE are quite different. An HMODULE can lead you to a wealth of information about a loaded executable (such as where its resources are located). An HINSTANCE, on the other hand, doesn't give you anything of value other than the data in the segment.

The confusion between HMODULEs and HINSTANCEs arises because many of the Win16 API functions specify an HINSTANCE parameter in cases where the function actually needs an HMODULE. For example, take the DialogBox function. Its first parameter is an HINSTANCE. However, consider for a moment what's needed to create a dialog box. Specifically, the DialogBox function needs to know where the dialog resource that describes the dialog can be found. Resources are kept in EXEs or DLLs, so it would make sense that DialogBox would want the HMODULE of the NE file that contains the dialog resource. Passing an HINSTANCE to DialogBox doesn't really make any sense, since the global heap handle of a data segment (an HINSTANCE) won't help the function find the dialog resource. However, as you probably know, you can pass an HINSTANCE to the DialogBox function and have the function succeed. Therefore, something must be going on under the surface.

The undocumented GetExePtr function provides a key to understanding how DialogBox (and other API functions) can function with an HINSTANCE value:

```
HMODULE GetExePtr( HANDLE );
```

GetExePtr is a magical function that does just about everything in its power to return the HMODULE associated with the handle that was passed in. If you pass in an HINSTANCE handle, GetExePtr scans through all the DLLs and all the tasks, looking for one with an HINSTANCE that matches what was passed to GetExePtr. If a match is found, GetExePtr returns the HMODULE associated with that DLL or EXE. Passing an HMODULE to GetExePtr causes GetExePtr to immediately return the same HMODULE back to you. If you were to step into the DialogBox function, you'd see that the code calls GetExePtr, and subsequently uses the returned HMODULE to locate the dialog resource. Thus, it turns out that you can pass either a valid HMODULE or HINSTANCE to DialogBox and expect it to work. The same is true for many other API functions that are documented as expecting an HINSTANCE parameter.

Knowing what the HINSTANCE/HMODULE parameter is used for, you can answer many of those often-asked questions like "I want to pop up a dialog in my EXE, but the dialog resource is in my DLL. Which HIN-STANCE should I pass to DialogBox?" The answer is, of course, to pass the HINSTANCE or HMODULE or whichever NE file contains the resource. If the Microsoft documentation was clearer about exactly what the parameters to API functions are used for, things wouldn't be so confusing.

You may be wondering why numerous Windows API functions are documented as accepting an HINSTANCE when internally they're going to immediately turn the HINSTANCE into an HMODULE. The best reason that I'm aware of is that HINSTANCEs are much easier to come by in your program than are HMODULEs. Normally, a program or DLL doesn't know its HMODULE, and must look it up by calling GetModuleHandle. In contrast, both EXEs and DLLs are passed their HINSTANCE when they start up. You can also easily retrieve the HINSTANCE of the main program by retrieving the value of the SS register. This is true even when executing in DLL code. When an EXE starts up, its SS register is set to the same value as the DS register. Although the DS register will change when going between EXE code and DLL code, the SS register retains the same value — that is, the value of the EXE's DS register.

In Win32 programs (with the exception of Win32s), this blurring of the meaning of an HINSTANCE versus an HMODULE becomes complete. In Win32, the HMODULE and the HINSTANCE are the same thing; specifically, the HMODULE and HINSTANCE are both the base address in memory where the EXE or DLL was loaded.

MODULE-RELATED FUNCTIONS

Now that we've looked at the 16-bit module database, let's look at some functions that access or manipulate the information in a module database. For this chapter, I've chosen a reasonable set of functions that I've provided pseudocode for. There are other functions (like LoadModule) that I've chosen not to cover because they're extraordinarily complex, and I wanted to finish this book before the turn of the century.

The GetModuleHandle function

When you're examining module-database–related functions, GetModuleHandle is a good function to look at first. That's because it demonstrates some of the most important module concepts but doesn't require huge amounts of pseudocode to do so. GetModuleHandle is documented as accepting the name of a module in memory, and returning the global heap handle of the module's database segment (that is, its HMODULE). However, the documentation is unclear on exactly what the module name means. Does it mean the actual module name (the first entry in the module's resident names table), or does it mean the name of the module's filename? Also, as you'll see in the pseudocode that follows, the documentation leaves out some other goodies in GetModuleHandle's behavior.

The GetModuleHandle code starts out with the parameter-validation layer code. The code tests the single parameter to ensure that it's a valid string pointer. If not, the debug version RIPs with a code of 0x700A (ERR_BAD_STRING_PTR), and the function returns to the caller. If the string parameter test succeeds, the code jumps to the IGetModuleHandle code (leaving the string parameter on the stack).

The first section of IGetModuleHandle is a bit surprising. It tests for a 0 value in the HIWORD of the module name to look for. If a 0 is found, the code skips all the normal code that would execute. Instead, IGetModuleHandle passes the string parameter's offset to GetExePtr, and returns whatever GetExtPtr finds (GetExePtr, which is discussed in the following section, returns the HMODULE associated with a given global handle). The ability to pass 0 as the HIWORD of the GetModuleHandle's string parameter is undocumented. You can pass almost any global handle associated with a module (such as its HINSTANCE) to GetModuleHandle, and get back the corresponding HMODULE. Just remember to pass 0 in the HIWORD of the string argument to GetModuleHandle, and your handle as the LOWORD. This handle can be an HINSTANCE, a code or data segment from the module, or any other handle that the GetExePtr function knows how to deal with.

The main body of IGetModuleHandle is for searching through the module list, looking for a module database with the same name as the string parameter to GetModuleHandle. It checks three different possibilities, in the following order:

- *Possibility 1:* GetModuleHandle was passed a module name that exactly matches the first entry in the resident names table of some module. The function that iterates through each of the system's module databases comparing names is FindExeInfo. Pseudocode for FindExeInfo follows the IGetModuleHandle pseudocode and is simple enough to follow without additional annotation.

- *Possibility 2:* GetModuleHandle was passed a module name that matches the first entry in the resident names table of some module, but the two strings differ in case. Checking for this situation is exactly like testing for the first possibility, but IGetModuleHandle first uppercases the string parameter before invoking FindExeInfo.

- *Possibility 3:* The code was passed a filename. There are two subcases here: a base filename alone (for example, KRNL386.EXE), or a complete pathname (for example, C:\WINDOWS\SYSTEM\KRNL386.EXE). IGetModuleHandle takes care of both cases by extracting just the base filename portion (for example, KRNL386.EXE) before calling FindExeFile. FindExeFile is very similar to FindExeInfo, but it compares the module's filenames to the input string rather than to the module name.

The last section of IGetModuleHandle hides two more undocumented secrets. In Windows 3.1, there was a DLL called TIMER.DRV; this DLL went away in Windows 95. Presumably some applications were testing for its presence by calling GetModuleHandle(TIMER). It appears that Microsoft tried to keep these applications functioning by having IGetModuleHandle check for the string TIMER and returning the value 1 if the string was found. Of course, an application that tries to use this module handle won't have much luck — but whatever works, right? The second undocumented behavior of IGetModuleHandle was mentioned earlier. Any call to GetModuleHandle that makes it past the parameter validation code will return the head of the module list (KERNEL) in the DX register.

As a final note on GetModuleHandle, don't bother using it to try to find the 16-bit module databases for Win32 modules. These modules aren't inserted in the list of HMODULEs. The SHOW16 program later in this chapter shows a brute-force method to find these HMODULEs.

Pseudocode for GetModuleHandle

```
// Parameters:
//      LPSTR    lpszModName

    Verify that lpszModName is either a valid string pointer, or has
    a 0 in its HIWORD(). If not, RIP in the debug KERNEL with a code
    of 700A (ERR_BAD_STRING_PTR).
    goto IGetModuleHandle
```

Pseudocode for IGetModuleHandle

```
// Parameters:
//      LPSTR    lpszModName
// Locals:
//      char     szBuffer[130];
//      WORD     len;
//      LPSTR    lpszBaseFilename;

    if ( HIWORD(lpszModName) == 0 )
        goto global_handle_in_LOWORD;

    // First let's assume that the user passed in a real module name (such as what
    // you'd put in the NAME or LIBRARY line in a .DEF file).
```

```
// Copy the string into a local buffer, but make the first byte
// be the length of the copied string (that is, make it a PASCAL string).
// 0 as the last parameter means copy the source exactly.
// Returns the length of the copied string.
len = CopyName( lpszModName, szBuffer, 0 );

// Scan through the list of modules in the system, looking for
// one with a module name that exactly matches the string passed
// to FarFindExeInfo. If a match is found, return the HMODULE in AX.
// The len parameter lets the function quickly eliminate modules with
// names of different lengths than the input module.
// This particular call is looking for the module name exactly as it
// was passed to GetModuleHandle.
AX = FarFindExeInfo( szBuffer+1, len );
if ( AX )
    goto return_AX;

// Do like the first CopyName call above, but this time the last
// parameter is -1, meaning uppercase the destination string.
len = CopyName( lpszModName, szBuffer, -1 );

// Do like the previous call to FarFindExeInfo, but this time we're
// searching for the uppercased version of the module name passed
// to GetModuleHandle.
AX = FarFindExeInfo( szBuffer+1, len );
if ( AX )
    goto return_AX;

// If we get here, we didn't find a real module name, so let's try
// looking for modules that have a filename matching what was
// passed to GetModuleHandle.

// NResGetPureName scans backward from the end of the string param
// until it finds a :, a \\, a /, or the start of the string. It
// returns a pointer to the next character. Essentially, this
// function returns a pointer to the base filename portion of a
// complete path. This allows you to pass names like
// C::\\WINDOWS\\SYSTEM\\KRNL386.EXE to GetModuleFileName

lpszBaseFilename = NResGetPureName( &szBuffer+1 );

// This function is essentially like FarFindExeInfo (above), but
// instead of comparing module names in the resident names table,
// it compares the base filenames.
AX = FindExeFile( lpszBaseFilename );
if ( AX )
    goto return_AX;
```

```
    // If we get here, we didn't find a matching real module name or a
    // matching filename. Do one last check to see if the string passed
    // to GetModuleFileName was TIMER. In Windows 3.1, there was a
    // TIMER.DRV, but that DLL doesn't exist in Windows 95. Perhaps this
    // special-case code is to keep applications that look for the TIMER
    // module from failing.
    if ( 0 == strcmp(szBuffer+1, "TIMER") )
    {
        AX = 1;
        goto return_AX;
    }

global_handle_in_LOWORD:
    AX = GetExePtr( LOWORD(lpszModName) );

return_AX:          // Return whatever value is in the AX register.

    DX = hExeHead;  // Also return the head of module list in DX.
                    // Seems to always be KERNEL (KRNL386.EXE).
```

Pseudocode for FindExeInfo (Called by FarFindExeInfo, with same params)

```
// Parameters:
//      LPSTR    lpszSearchName;
//      WORD     len;
// Locals:
//      LPMODULE lpModule;
//      LPBYTE   lpResNames;

    if ( !hExeHead  )
        return 0;

lpModule=MAKELP(hExeHead,0);
    while ( lpModule ) // Iterate through the list of modules.
    {
        // Get a pointer to the current module's name (the first entry in
        // the resident names table). The module name is prefixed by
        // a length byte.
        lpResNames = MAKELP(SELECTOROF(lpModule), lpModule->ne_resNamesTab);

        // If the length of the current module's name is the same as the
        // module name we're searching for, compare the two strings.  If
        // they match, we found the right module, so return its global
        // memory handle (its HMODULE). If the two strings differ in
        // length, don't bother to compare the strings.
        if ( *lpResNames == len )
```

```
    {
        if ( 0 == strcmp(lpResNames+1, lpszSearchName) )
            return SELECTOROF(lpModule);
    }

    // A match was not found. Try the next module in the module list.
    lpModule = MAKELP( lpModule->ne_npNextExe, 0 );
}
return 0;
```

The GetExePtr function

GetExePtr is arguably the most useful undocumented 16-bit function in
Windows 95. Its interface is simple and unlikely to change, so it's a mystery
why Microsoft has chosen to hide this wonderful function. Examining
GetExePtr is a great way to see the interconnectedness of modules, tasks,
instances, and global memory handles. Essentially, looking at GetExePtr is
tantamount to taking a mini-tour of the 16-bit KERNEL data structures!

GetExePtr's job is to take an input global heap handle and somehow find
the HMODULE associated with that handle. Typically, GetExePtr is used
internally by KRNL386 to convert HINSTANCEs to HMODULEs. If you
look at almost any Windows function that takes an HINSTANCE parameter, that function internally calls GetExePtr to get an HMODULE. However,
GetExePtr isn't limited to instance handles. The input handle can be almost
any type of global memory handle. Besides HINSTANCEs, GetExePtr also
accepts HTASK parameters and returns the HMODULE that the task was
created from. Likewise, you can pass a code or data selector belonging to an
in-memory module, and GetExePtr returns the owning HMODULE. You can
even pass in a handle allocated by GlobalAlloc. GetExePtr will return the
HMODULE associated with the task that owns the allocated block. In short,
GetExePtr is a do-it-all function that doesn't give up easily.

Although I haven't formally described tasks and task databases (TDBs),
they are prominently featured in the GetExePtr code. Tasks aren't described
until the next major section in the chapter, so I'll have to jump the gun a little bit and show tasks in the GetExePtr pseudocode.

The GetExePtr code begins by converting the input handle to a selector.
Basically this means ensuring that the bottom bit of the handle is turned on.
Next, GetExePtr checks for the best possible scenario: that it was passed an
HMODULE. This test consists of looking for the NE signature in the segment's

first WORD. If the test succeeds, GetExePtr's work is done, and it simply returns the HMODULE. If the input handle wasn't an HMODULE, GetExePtr has some searching to do. The first thing it checks is to see if the input parameter is the HINSTANCE of a running task. The code checks this by running through the task list, looking for a task with an HINSTANCE that matches the input parameter. If GetExePtr finds a matching HINSTANCE, it returns the HMODULE that was used to create the task with the matching HINSTANCE.

If the input handle was neither an HMODULE nor a task's HINSTANCE, GetExePtr passes the input handle to a helper function that does a more exhaustive job of searching through system data structures. In the pseudocode, I've called this function GetExePtrHelper. GetExePtrHelper first verifies that the input handle is a valid ring 3 selector with the CPU's LAR instruction. If it's not a valid selector, GetExePtrHelper returns 0.

Assuming that a valid handle parameter was passed, GetExePtrHelper's next course of action is to find the owner of the input handle. The owners of most global heap blocks are typically either HMODULEs or PDB segments (PDB segments are similar to DOS PSPs). A good example of a block owned by an HMODULE is a code segment in an EXE or DLL file. Memory blocks allocated via GlobalAlloc without the GMEM_SHARE flag are owned by the PDB of the current task at the time of the allocation. After retrieving the owner of the input handle, GetExePtrHelper tests the handle to see if it's an HMODULE. If so, GetExePtrHelper is done, and returns the owning HMODULE.

If the owner wasn't an HMODULE, GetExePtrHelper next determines if the input handle was an HTASK by looking for the TD signature in the task database (described later in "The Task Database [TDB]" section). If the input handle isn't an HTASK, then the input handle's owner might be the PDB segment of an active task. To check this possibility, GetExePtrHelper scans through the task list, retrieves the PDB selector of each task, and compares it to the input handle. If a match is found, GetExePtrHelper returns the HMODULE associated with the task that it found the matching PDB segment in.

One way or another, GetExePtrHelper returns control to GetExePtr. If GetExePtrHelper found an HMODULE, GetExePtr returns that HMODULE to its caller. Otherwise, GetExePtrHelper returns 0, so GetExePtr knows that it was passed a bogus input handle. In the debug version of KRNL386, the code will RIP with the message

```
wn K16 GetExePtr(#ax) invalid parameter
```

in which #ax is replaced by the value passed to GetExePtr.

GetExePtr's implementation has changed somewhat from Windows 3.1. In Windows 3.1, GetExePtr would choke if you passed in an HTASK parameter, even though that seems like a perfectly reasonable thing to do, given the great lengths GetExePtr goes to find an HMODULE. In Windows 95, GetExePtr works fine if you pass in an HTASK. This change may in part be due to my complaining about the implementation of the Windows 3.1 version in *Windows Internals*.

Pseudocode for GetExePtr

```
// Parameters:
//      HANDLE handle;
// Locals:
//      LPMODULE lpModule;
//      LPTDB lpTDB;    // Far pointer to Task Database.
//      WORD temp;

    if ( !(handle & 1) )    // If a MOVEABLE handle (bit 0 off), convert
    {                       // to a selector.
        handle = MYLOCK( handle );  // MYLOCK is similar to GlobalLock.
        if ( !handle )
            goto invalid_param;
    }

    // Try the obvious first: Were we passed an HMODULE?
    lpModule = MAKELP( handle, 0 );
    if ( lpModule->ne_signature == 'NE' )
    {
        AX = handle;
        goto return_AX;
    }

    // Okay. It's not a module. Perhaps it's the HINSTANCE of a task.
    // Or perhaps it's an HTASK. Walk through the list of tasks, checking
    // for this.

    lpTDB = MAKELP( HeadTDB, 0 );

    while ( lpTDB ) // While not at the end of the task list...
    {
        // Does this TDB match the handle passed in?
        if ( SELECTOROF(lpTDB) == handle )
            goto call_GetExePtrHelper   // Why not just return the HMODULE
                                        // here, rather than calling
                                        // GetExePtrHelper???
```

```
        // Does the HINSTANCE of this task match the handle passed in?
        if ( handle == lpTDB->TDB_HInstance )
        {
            AX = lpTDB->TDB_HMODULE;    // Yes! Return the HMODULE stored
            goto return_AX;             // in this task's TDB.
        }
        else
            lpTDB = MAKELP( lpTDB->TDB_next, 0 );   // Go on to next task.
    }

call_GetExePtrHelper:

    // Bring out the big guns by checking the PDBs in the task list in addition
to looking for the owning HMODULE in the Burgermaster arenas.
    // GetExePtrHelper returns an HMODULE, or 0.
    temp = GetExePtrHelper( handle );
    if ( temp )
        return temp;

    // Hmmm.... We still didn't find anything. Complain in the debug KERNEL.

    AX = handle
    _KRDEBUGTEST( "wn K16 GetExePtr(#ax) invalid parameter" );

    _AX = 0;    // Return 0 to the caller.

return_AX:
    CX = AX     // Return value both in AX and CX (good for JCXZ tests).
```

Pseudocode for GetExePtrHelper

```
// Parameters:
//     WORD    handle;
// Locals:
//     LPMODULE lpModule;
//     LPTDB lpTDB;
//     WORD owner;

    LAR handle  // LAR instruction -> Load Access Rights (of selector).

    if ( LAR instruction returns failure code ) // Not a valid selector?
        return 0;

    if ( present bit not set in access rights )
    {
        owner = low 16-bits of handle's limit in the LDT
```

```
            // In a not-present segment under Windows, the low 16 bits of
            // the offset in the segment's descriptor hold the HMODULE
            // that owns that segment (if it's code/data segment belonging
            // to the module).
        }
        else
        {
            owner = GetOwner( handle );  // Retrieve the owner out of the
            if ( !owner )                // appropriate arena in the
                return 0;                // Burgermaster segment.
        }

        // See if the owner of the block is an HMODULE. If so, return it.
        lpModule = MAKELP( owner, 0 );
        if ( lpModule->ne_signature == 'NE' )
            return SELECTOROF( lpModule );

        // The owner wasn't an HMODULE. Is the handle parameter an HTASK?
        // If so, return it.
        LSL handle  // Get size of handle's segment.
        if ( size of segment > 0xFB )
        {
            lpTDB = MAKELP( handle, 0 );

            if ( lpTDB->TDB_sig == 'TD' )
                return lpTDB->TDB_HMODULE;
        }

        // Global memory blocks allocated without GMEM_SHARE are owned by
        // the PDB of the task that allocated the memory. Walk the list
        // of tasks looking for a task whose PDB matches the handle's owner.
        // If a match is found, return the HMODULE associated with that task.

        if ( HeadTDB == 0 ) // If no tasks, there is nothing more we can do to
            return 0;       // try to find additional modules.

        lpTDB = MAKELP( HeadTDB, 0 )

        while ( lpTDB )
        {
            if ( owner == lpTDB->TDB_PSP )
                return lpTDB->TDB_HMODULE;

            lpTDB = MAKELP( lpTDB->TDB_next, 0 );
        }
        return 0;
```

The GetProcAddress function

I've included GetProcAddress in this list of 16-bit module-related functions for several reasons. First, this function provides a very good example of how the module's entry table and its resident/nonresident names tables are connected. Second, an examination of GetProcAddress will help you understand how the Windows loader resolves fixups to other modules. And third, you can use GetProcAddress to peer inside the Windows dynamic linking mechanism, which is one of Window's most powerful features.

GetProcAddress (like many other Windows API functions) starts out with a short block of code that validates the input parameters. In the case of GetProcAddress, the validation code ensures that you've passed some sort of valid selector (or 0 or –1) for the HINSTANCE parameter. For the second parameter (the name of the function to find), the validation code tests if you passed a valid LPSTR or a MAKEINTATOM type string: 0 in the HIWORD, and a nonzero value in the LOWORD. GetProcAddress uses the latter case to mean that you know the export ordinal of the function you're looking for, and have put the ordinal in the low WORD of the LPSTR parameter. If either of these two parameter tests fail, GetProcAddress returns immediately to the caller. The exception is if you're running the debug KRNL386, in which case you'll RIP with either error code 0x6002 or 0x700A. If both parameters are okay, GetProcAddress jumps to the IGetProcAddress code, where the real meat of the code resides.

The first thing IGetProcAddress does is to use the trusty GetExePtr function to convert what you passed as the HINSTANCE parameter to an HMODULE. As I described earlier, GetExePtr will convert just about any handle to an HMODULE, so you're not really limited to passing an HINSTANCE to GetProcAddress. Any global handle that GetExePtr can associate with a module database will do. Once IGetProcAddress has the HMODULE that it will be looking for the function in, it checks to make sure that the HMODULE belongs to a DLL; if it's not a DLL, IGetProcAddress fails the call. If you're running the debug KRNL386 when this happens, you'll get a message that says:

```
Can not GetProcAddress a task.
```

Why is this? The Windows coders put in this check to prevent programs from calling GetProcAddress for functions in EXE files. Code in EXE files expects to be called only in the EXE program's task context, and with the stack register (SS) set to the program's DGROUP. By making it difficult to get the address of an exported function in an EXE file, KRNL386 prevents problems caused by programmers who call functions in EXE files while executing in the wrong task context and on the wrong stack. The one exception to this rule is if you pass 0 as the HINSTANCE parameter to GetProcAddress. In this scenario, IGetProcAddress uses the HMODULE that your task was created from. Put another way, you can use GetProcAddress on your own EXE and with DLLs, but not with other EXEs.

Once IGetProcAddress knows which HMODULE it will be searching in, the next step is to figure out the entry table ordinal of the desired function. If you passed in an LPSTR parameter with 0 as the high WORD, the export ordinal is in the low WORD, so IGetProcAddress can jump immediately to the code that looks up the export ordinal in the module's entry table. More often than not, however, GetProcAddress is passed an ASCII string. Therefore, IGetProcAddress must convert that string into the appropriate export ordinal in the target module.

Converting the LPSTR parameter into an export ordinal is the job of the FarFindOrdinal function. I haven't provided pseudocode for FarFindOrdinal because it's not that difficult to visualize what it does. FarFindOrdinal calls FindOrdinal, which simply scans through the resident and nonresident names table, comparing each string to the GetProcAddress input string. When a match is found, the export ordinal is the WORD that immediately follows the matching string in the resident or nonresident names table. Another undocumented use of GetProcAddress that's taken care of by FindOrdinal is converting strings like #97 to ordinal values. In this case, FindOrdinal just strips off the # and converts the string into its binary value (which is 97).

The ability to pass ordinal values as #-prefixed strings means that there are three different ways of achieving the same result with GetProcAddress. For example, let's say you wanted to find the address of GetMessage (export ordinal 108 from USER.EXE). Any of the following three lines would work:

```
GetProcAddress( GetModuleHandle("USER"), "GetMessage" );
GetProcAddress( GetModuleHandle("USER"), MAKELONG(108, 0) );
GetProcAddress( GetModuleHandle("USER"), "#108" );
```

One way or another, IGetProcAddress gets hold of an HMODULE and an export ordinal of a function within that HMODULE. It then scans through the entry table of the module, looking for the entry that belongs to the specified export ordinal. The export entry will then contain the information necessary to calculate the address of the desired function in memory. This job of scanning the entry table and retrieving the function address is the job of the FarEntProcAddress function, which is just a wrapper around the EntProcAddress function.

Immediately after the IGetProcAddress pseudocode that follows, you'll find pseudocode for EntProcAddress. EntProcAddress scans through the list of entry table bundles that I described earlier in "The Entry Table" section. To quickly refresh your memory, an entry table bundle is a collection of entry table records for exported functions with contiguous export ordinals. At each bundle, EntProcAddress checks to see if the export ordinal it's searching for is contained within the bundle's array of records. When EntProcAddress finds the correct bundle, it makes a pointer to the appropriate entry table record within the bundle. This particular record can now be used to calculate the actual address of the exported function in memory.

If you flip back to "The Entry Table" section and look at the format of an entry table record, you'll see that each entry contains the offset of the function within its segment, but not an actual selector value. Instead, an entry table record contains a logical segment number. Therefore, EntProcAddress needs to convert this logical segment number to the selector assigned to that segment in memory by the Windows loader.

How can EntProcAddress convert the logical segment number to a selector? Simple. Each module database contains a segment table array (described earlier in "The Segment Table" section). The logical segment index from the entry table record is used as an index into the array of segment table entries. The selector value for the function that we're looking for can easily be plucked from the last WORD of the appropriate segment table entry. All that remains is for EntProcAddress to combine the selector value with the function's offset to make a far pointer. EntProcAddress returns this far pointer to FarEntProcAddress, which in turn returns the far address to IGetProcAddress, which finally returns the address of the function to the caller of GetProcAddress.

Pseudocode for GetProcAddress

```
// Parameters:
//      HINSTANCE   hinst;
//      LPSTR       lpszProcName

    Validate the hinst parameter. The following rules apply:
        - If hinst is 0, it's okay.
        - If LDT bit (bit 2) is not set in selector, it's bad.
```

- If hinst is -1, it's okay.
- If LAR hints fails, it's bad.

If any of these tests fail, RIP in the debug KERNEL with code 6022
(ERR_BAD_GLOBAL_HANDLE).

Validate the lpszProcName parameter. The following rules apply:
- If lpszProcName is NULL, it's bad.
- If HIWORD(lpszProcName) is 0, it's okay (unless LOWORD is also 0).
- If lpszProcName is an invalid pointer, it's bad.
- If lpszProcName is > 0x100 bytes long, it's bad.

If any of these tests fail, RIP in the debug KERNEL with code 700A
(ERR_BAD_STRING_PTR).
goto IGetProcAddress

IGetProcAddress proc

```
// Parameters:
//      HINSTANCE    hinst;
//      LPSTR        lpszProcName
// Locals:
//      char         szBuffer[130];
//      WORD         hModule;
//      WORD         exportOrdinal;
//      LPMODULE     lpModule;

    if ( hinst )
    {
        hModule = GetExePtr(hinst)
        if ( !hModule )
            return 0;

        lpModule = MAKELP(hModule, 0);
        if ( lpModule->ne_flags & MODFLAGS_DLL )
            goto have_HMODULE;

        FarKernelError( "Can not GetProcAddress a task." );
        return 0;
    }
    else    // hinst parameter was 0.
    {
        hModule = CurTDB->TDB_HMODULE;
    }

have_HMODULE:
```

```
        if ( HIWORD(lpszProcName) == 0 )
        {
            exportOrdinal = LOWORD( lpszProcName );
            goto have_export_ordinal;
        }

        CopyName( lpszProcName, szBuffer, 0 );

        exportOrdinal = FarFindOrdinal( hModule, szBuffer, -1, 0 );
        if ( exportOrdinal )
            goto have_export_ordinal;

        CopyName( lpszProcName, szBuffer, 0 );

        exportOrdinal = FarFindOrdinal( hModule, szBuffer, -1, 0 );
        if ( !exportOrdinal )
            return 0;

        // RIP in the debug KERNEL with code 0x5000.
        _KRDEBUGTEST("wn K16 GetProcAddress(@ES:BX) case-sensitive new for Win4");

have_export_ordinal:

        return FarEntProcAddress( hModule, exportOrdinal );
```

Pseudocode for EntProcAddress proc

```
// Parameters:
//      HMODULE      hModule
//      WORD         exportOrdinal
//      WORD         fComplain
// Locals:
//      LPENTRY_BUNDLE_HEADER lpBundle;    // See HMODULE.H.
//      LPENTRY lpEntry;                   // See HMODULE.H.
//      LPMODULE lpModule;
//      LPSEGMENT_RECORD    lpSeg;

    lpModule = MAKELP( hModule, 0 );    // Make pointer to module database.

    // Check for invalid export ordinals.
    if ( (exportOrdinal == 0) || (exportOrdinal == 0x8000) )
        goto invalid_ordinal;

    exportOrdinal--;    // Ordinals in entry table are zero-based, so adjust.
```

```
        // Make a pointer to the module's entry table.
        lpBundle = MAKELP( hModule, lpModule->ne_npEntryTable );

        // Walk through the list of bundles. Look for the bundle whose  starting
        // and ending ordinals encompass the exportedOrdinal that was passed.
        while ( lpBundle->firstEntry < exportOrdinal )
        {
            if ( lpBundle->lastEntry > exportOrdinal )
            {
                // Each bundle is immediately followed by an array of ENTRY
                // structures.
                lpEntry = address of the appropriate slot in the array
                            of ENTRY structures following the bundle header.

                goto have_entry_pointer;
            }

            // Go on to the next bundle.
            lpBundle = MAKELP( hModule, lpBundle->nextBundle );
        }

invalid_ordinal:

    // Something went wrong...
    if ( !fComplain )
    {
        // RIP in the debug KERNEL with code 0x5004.
        BX = exportOrdinal
        _KRDEBUGTEST("wn K16 Invalid ordinal reference (##BX) to %ES1");
    }

    return 0;

have_entry_pointer:
    // At this point, we've found the correct entry in the entry table.
    // Now we have to decode the entry information to an address that we
    // can pass back to the caller.

    // If this entry is from segment 0xFE, it's one of the special
    // entries (for example, __F000H). Return the entry's offset.
    if ( lpEntry->segType == 0xFE )
        return MAKELP( 0xFFFF, lpEntry->offset );

    // There are two types of entries: MOVEABLE or FIXED.
    // FIXED entries have segment numbers between 1 and 253.
    // MOVEABLE entries are indicated by a segment number of
    // 0xFF. Take special action if it's a FIXED entry.
```

```
        if ( lpEntry->segType != 0xFF )
        {
            // The entry is in a FIXED segment. Make sure that segment is
            // loaded in memory.
            if ( !LoadSegment(hModule, lpEntry->segNumber, -1, -1) )
                goto invalid_ordinal;
        }

        // Point at the appropriate segment structure in the segment table.
        // We need to do this in order to look up the handle/selector assigned
        // to the segment by the Windows loader.
        lpSeg = lpModule->ne_segtab[lpEntry->segNumber-1];
        if ( lpSeg->handle == 0 )   // Make sure there's a handle for this segment.
            return 0;

        // Combine the segment and the offset to create the entry point address.
        return MAKELP( lpSeg->handle & 1, lpEntry->offset );
```

16-BIT TASKS

If Windows modules are envisioned as representing the components of a lifeless body, then tasks can be thought of as the sparks that bring that body to life. Before I describe how tasks manage that feat, however, I need to mention a couple of issues about terminology. Tasks are sometimes referred to as programs, but in 16-bit Windows the correct term is *tasks*, not programs. On the Win32 side of things, the term *process* replaces the word task, even though conceptually 16-bit tasks and 32-bit processes mean the same thing. In this section, we're going to look at tasks in the 16-bit side of Windows 95.

Tasks represent two things in Windows 95. First, a task represents execution of code. In Windows 3.*x* and earlier, tasks were the fundamental unit of scheduling. At any given time, only one task is executing. The second thing a task represents is ownership. Each task owns its own set of file handles, the windows it creates, the memory it allocates, and so forth. I'll come back to both of these points later in this section.

Every time Windows 95 starts a program, KRNL386 creates a new task. If you start up two copies of CALC.EXE, Windows 95 adds two tasks to KRNL386's list of tasks. Even for Win32 processes, Windows 95 creates a 16-bit task representation. This may be to keep the 16-bit components happy by representing the existence of the Win32 process in a form that the old 16-bit code recognizes.

The primary indicator of a task's existence is a data structure known as a Task Database (or TDB for short). The task database contains information specific to one particular instance of a program. The individual TDB fields are described in the next section; this section focuses on more general, task-related TDB concepts.

The TDB is a collection of fields in a segment allocated from the 16-bit global heap. The global heap handle for this segment is known as an HTASK. Knowing that an HTASK is just a selector, you can directly read the fields in the TDB. In this way, a task database and its HTASK is similar to the module database and its HMODULE. GetCurrentTask returns an HTASK, and you pass HTASKs to functions like PostAppMessage and EnumTaskWindows.

In some ways, a Windows task is similar to a DOS program. In DOS, each running program has its own Program Segment Prefix (PSP) area, which contains a file handle table and additional information, such as the program's command line. Since Windows was originally an extension to DOS, a Windows task has always carried around a DOS PSP in its HTASK segment. In versions of Windows prior to Windows 95, Windows actually used the PSP area in the task's TDB when performing real mode DOS operations like file I/O. In Windows parlance, the PSP area in a TDB is called a PDB (for "Process Database"); this should not be confused with a Win32 process database. Thus, the Windows function that returns the PSP of the current task is called GetCurrentPDB, rather than GetCurrentPSP. Rest assured, a PSP and a PDB mean the same thing in Windows. The point here is that a Windows TDB contains a mixture of old real mode DOS things, and newer things that are only meaningful in the 16-bit protected mode environment. Adding to the mixture, in Windows 95, a TDB contains a pointer to a Win32 Thread database, so a Windows 95 Task Database is really a compendium of DOS, Win16 and Win32 information.

Just as a body is necessary to maintain life (theological arguments notwithstanding), a task cannot exist without a module. Every task is associated with a MODULE, but the converse is not true. When you start a program for the first time, Windows 95 creates a 16-bit module database and then creates a task database for the new task. If you then start up a new copy of the program (while leaving the original instance running), Windows 95 creates another task database, but doesn't make a new module database. Instead, both tasks are associated with the same module database (HMODULE). Modules represent items such as code and resources that are common between multiple running copies of a program. Tasks represent information that will differ between multiple copies of a program. Examples of this are stack segments and the current working directory.

Forgetting about 32-bit processes and threading issues for the moment, at any given time Windows 95 is executing one and only one task. All threads other than the currently executing tasks are blocked, and will not run until the running task voluntarily gives up control of the CPU. This is known as *cooperative multitasking*. Each task runs for as long as it needs to, and then gives up control of the CPU so that another task can run.

How does a task give up control, (or *yield*, in Windows terminology)? Usually, tasks yield control by using functions such as GetMessage, PeekMessage, SendMessage, and WaitMessage. If these functions determine that there's no need for the task to continue running (for example, if there are no messages waiting to be processed), they'll call into the 16-bit scheduler. If the 16-bit scheduler sees that another task has something to do, it suspends the first task and switches to the task with something to do. Most of the time, the need to yield is hidden from the programmer, because functions like GetMessage transparently handle the cooperative multitasking.

Windows 95 keeps track of the task list in a manner similar to the 16-bit module database list. A WORD field in each TDB contains the selector of the next task in the list. The linked list of tasks isn't static like the module list described earlier. Instead, the ordering of tasks changes constantly to facilitate 16-bit scheduling. Interestingly, the TDBs created to represent Win32 processes in 16-bit land don't appear to have their order shifted by the actions of the 16-bit scheduler. Instead, it looks as if the TDBs created for Win32 processes are planted at the head of the list, and don't move until the task/process exits. See the description of offset 8 in "The Task Database (TDB)" section later on for more details.

The Microsoft-approved method of walking the task list is to use the TOOLHELP TaskFirst and TaskNext functions. If you want to walk the list directly (like the SHOW16 program does), you can find the head of the list of tasks in the DX register after GetCurrentTask is called. Alternatively, you can find the first TDB in the list by reading the WORD 0xE bytes past the THHOOK symbol exported by KRNL386. (That is, call GetProcAddress for THHOOK, add 0xE to the offset portion of the returned address, and then read in the WORD at that location). The memory around THHOOK contains several other useful KRNL386 global variables:

THHOOK+0   *hGlobalHeap*

This is the handle (selector –1) to the Burgermaster data structure that maintains the information about the 16-bit global heap. See Chapter 2 of *Windows Internals* for more information on this. This value is also returned in the AX register after calling the undocumented KRNL386 GlobalMasterHandle function.

THHOOK+2   *pGlobalHeap*

This is the selector that points to the Burgermaster segment, and is essentially the same thing that's returned by the hGlobalHeap field. This value is in the DX register after calling GlobalMasterHandle.

THHOOK+4   *hExeHead*

This WORD holds the HMODULE of the first module in the list of 16-bit modules. The first module is always KERNEL (KRNL386.EXE). This value can also be found in the DX register after a successful call to GetModuleHandle. See the description of offset 06h in the module database (in "The NE Header" section earlier in the chapter) for additional information.

THHOOK+8   *topPDB*

The selector of KRNL386.EXE's PSP (a.k.a. PDB) segment. This is the PSP that KRNL386 was loaded from as a real mode DOS executable. This value is returned by GetCurrentPDB in the DX register.

THHOOK+0Ah   *headPDB*

The PDB/PSP selector of the first PDB in the list of PDBs.

THOOK+0Eh   *HeadTDB*

The first TDB in the list of TDBs. This value is returned by GetCurrentTask in the DX register.

THHOOK+10h   *CurTDB*

The TDB selector of the currently executing task. This is almost always the last task in the list. This value is returned by GetCurrentTask in the AX register.

THHOOK+12h   *LoadTDB*

This field is set to 0, except when a new task is in the process of being created. In this case, it contains the value of the TDB selector that the new task will use.

THHOOK+16   *SelTableLen*

This WORD is the length of the selector table (an array of DWORDs) in the Burgermaster segment. See Chapter 2 of *Windows Internals* for details.

THHOOK+18   *SelTableStart*

This DWORD is the starting offset of the selector table (an array of
DWORDs) in the Burgermaster segment. See Chapter 2 of *Windows
Internals* for details.

Unlike module databases, Windows 95 is good about keeping all the
task databases — whether they're for 16- or 32-bit applications — in the
task list. You can therefore use the 16-bit TOOLHELP.DLL's TaskFirst and
TaskNext functions to walk the list of all running programs, regardless of
whether they're 16- or 32-bit–based. Also, unlike 16-bit modules, all tasks
have a corresponding representation in the 32-bit side of Windows 95.
Specifically, each Windows 95 task database contains a 32-bit flat pointer to
a Win32 thread database. This is true even for 16-bit programs. To summarize: Every program (whether it's a 16-bit NE program or a 32-bit PE program) has both a 16-bit task database and a 32-bit thread database (as well
as a corresponding 32-bit process).

SOME COMMON MISCONCEPTIONS ABOUT TASKS

Tasks can sometimes be difficult to understand, so it's not surprising that
programmers often have misconceptions about them. This section describes
and clarifies a couple of misconceptions I encounter frequently.

One of the most common misconceptions about tasks is that every task
has a window. Although a window on the screen is the most visible indicator of a task's existence, tasks and windows are completely unrelated and
shouldn't be confused with one another. A task represents execution, and
nothing else. The decision about whether or not the task displays a window
is completely up to you. It's certainly easy to create a task that never creates
a window, yet does useful work. This is an important point to remember
when you look at the "task list" in Windows 95. That list shows the top-
level windows, and is completely different from the true task list maintained
by KRNL386. If you run the SHOW16 program on the disk that accompanies this book, it's likely that you'll see tasks that don't show up in the
Explorer window list.

Another common misconception some programmers have is thinking
that DLLs have task-like qualities. These programmers say things such as,
"I want my DLL to create a window that will be used for all the client
programs of the DLL." Another example: "My DLL will open a file handle
that will be used by several different programs that use the DLL." These

statements indicate that the programmers have the mistaken idea that the DLL owns the window or the file handle. As I mentioned earlier, tasks — not DLLs — own file handles and windows. A DLL is nothing more than additional code that a task uses. The fact that the DLL's code is in a file separate from the EXE's is irrelevant when it comes to ownership of system resources.

A DLL that creates a window or opens a file handle is doing so on behalf of the task that has called into the DLL. The DLL itself has no power to own these things. Therefore if you call CreateWindow from within a DLL, it's the currently executing task that owns the window, not the DLL. If the task goes away, so will the window, even if the DLL remains in memory. Likewise, if a DLL opens a file handle, that handle belongs to the current task. If another task calls into the DLL and the DLL attempts to use the file handle opened for the first task, an error will result — or worse, the wrong file will be used. Why? Because the file handle is only valid when the first task (the task that opened the file) is executing.

THE TASK DATABASE (TDB)

The preceding sections have used broad strokes to describe some task-related issues that were rather general in scope. In this section, however, I provide the gritty details about the contents of the task database (TDB). Each field in a Windows TDB is listed and described here; if you'd prefer to see just a quick overview of the TDB's fields, refer to the TDB.H header file in the SHOW16 code on the accompanying disk. As in previous sections of this chapter, the three items in the first line of each field description are the field's offset in the module database, the field's type (for example, WORD or DWORD), and a short description.

00h   *WORD*   *next TDB*
This WORD is the HTASK of the next task in the list of Win16 tasks. The head of the list is given by the HeadTDB KRNL386 global variable (returned in the DX register after calling GetCurrentTask). The end of the list is indicated by a 0 in this field.

02h   *DWORD*   *task SS:SP*
This DWORD is the SS:SP of the task when the task is parked inside the 16-bit scheduler. At fixed offsets from this address you can find the register values that will be restored to the CPU register when this task is scheduled.

In fact, the TOOLHELP TaskSwitch and TaskSetCSIP rely on this to perform their magic. This field is meaningless in the TDB of the currently executing task, since the task is not blocked inside the 16-bit scheduler.

06h   WORD   *number of events*
This WORD holds the number of events waiting for the task to process. Usually, the topic of events doesn't come up in the course of Windows programming. When an event does come up, it usually represents a waiting window message for the task to handle. For example, if you post a message to an application, the message is written to the task's message queue, and the task's event count field is incremented. However, events are not synonymous with window messages, and a task can have waiting events without a corresponding waiting window message. Events are the measure by which the 16-bit task scheduler decides if a task should be awakened to start executing. The scheduler only restarts tasks that have a nonzero event count.

08h   BYTE   *priority*
This BYTE holds the relative scheduling priority of the task. However, this field doesn't appear to be used by any Windows applications, and the applications all end up running at the same relative priority. In theory, the value of this field can range between −32 and 15, and is set with the undocumented SetPriority function in KRNL386. KRNL386 keeps the task in priority-sorted order, with lower values coming first in the list. Because of the Win16 scheduler algorithm, tasks with a lower priority value are the first to be checked for waiting events. However, adjusting your task's priority typically won't buy you anything, since the scheduler will only schedule a task that has an event waiting for it. You can give your task a priority value of −32, but if it doesn't have any waiting events, it still won't be scheduled.

09h   BYTE
This field is apparently unused.

0Ah, 0Eh, 10h, 12h   *WORD   unused fields*
These fields in the TDB may have been used for thread information by OS/2 1.*x* programs back in the days when OS/2 1.*x* and Windows shared a lot of code. In Windows 3.*x* and Windows 95, these fields appear to be unused, and are always set to 0.

0Ch   WORD   *this TDB*
This WORD holds the TDB of this TDB (that is, it references itself).

14h   *WORD*   *floating-point control word*

In Windows 3.*x*, this WORD held the floating-point control word of the task when the task was switched away from. The floating-point control word contains state flags for the 80x87 math coprocessor, and is saved and restored with the FLDCW and FSTCW CPU instructions. In Windows 95, this field appears to be unused. This may be because Windows 95 task switches also involve Win32 thread switches, and the floating-point control word may be saved and restored at the ring 0 thread switching level.

16h   *WORD*   *task flags*

This WORD holds the following bitfield flags:

Flag Name and Bit Value	Description
TDBF_WIN32 0x0010h	If set, this task is a Win32 program. This bit is also set in the TDBs created for Win32 applications running under Win32s.
TDBF_NEWTASK 0x0008	This flag is set when a Win16 task is created. It's cleared the first time the task goes through the 16-bit scheduler (the Reschedule function).
TDBF_WINOLDAP 0x0001h	This task is WINOA386.MOD (module name: WINOLDAP). The WINOLDAP task is used for running DOS programs in their own virtual machine under Windows 95. WINOLDAP acts as a sort of wrapper around the DOS program. In the task list, you'll see the name WINOLDAP, rather than the name of the DOS program.

18h   *WORD*   *error mode*

This WORD contains a set of bitfields that customize Windows 95's response to certain errors that occur in the task. These flags can be set with the SetErrorMode API functions. The documented flags are the following:

Flag Name and Bit Value	Description
SEM_FAILCRITICALERRORS 0x0001	Silently return failure from DOS function calls that have encountered a critical error (indicated by the "Abort, Retry, Ignore?" error message). If this flag is not set, Windows 95 pops up a dialog box asking for directions on how to proceed.

Flag Name and Bit Value	Description
SEM_NOGPFAULTERRORBOX 0x0002	When a GP fault occurs, do not display the normal GP fault dialog box. In Windows 3.x, this flag was primarily used by debuggers that wanted to terminate the application being debugged. The debugger sets this flag in the debuggee, and then modifies the debuggee so that when it resumes execution, it GP faults and Windows terminates the application (without showing a GP fault dialog). Also refer to the TOOLHELP TerminateApp documentation, because TerminateApp can optionally set this flag.
SEM_NOOPENFILEERRORBOX 0x8000	Do not display the dialog box when a file cannot be found. This flag is most often set when you want failing calls to LoadLibrary to fail silently instead of by displaying the File Not Found dialog.

1Ah   WORD   expected windows version

This WORD holds the minimum version of Windows required to run this program. This field is a copy of the expected Windows version at offset 0x3E in the module database of the executable that this task was created from. See the 06h entry in "The NE Header" section for more information.

1Ch   WORD   HINSTANCE of this task

This WORD holds the HINSTANCE of this task. The HINSTANCE is nothing more than the global heap handle of the task's default data segment (a.k.a., the DGROUP segment). This HINSTANCE value is passed as the first parameter to the WinMain function. The HINSTANCE/DGROUP segment is also the same as the task's stack segment. Each copy of a task has its own HINSTANCE value, and HINSTANCEs are often used to distinguish between running programs (although TDBs are equally good for this job). For Win32 tasks, the HINSTANCE value in the TDB is the same as the HMODULE field (offset 1Eh, described next).

1Eh   WORD   module handle of this task

This WORD holds the HMODULE of the loaded EXE file that this task was created from. This handle can be passed to GetModuleFileName to retrieve the name of the EXE file associated with this task.

20h   WORD   message queue

This field contains the selector of the task's message queue. The message queue is where messages that are posted to a task's windows reside. Unlike earlier versions of Windows, in Windows 95 there's no fixed limit on the number of messages that can be held in each queue. Chapter 4 describes this in more detail.

22h   WORD   parent TDB

This WORD is the TDB selector of the task that WinExec'ed this task. For instance, if you're debugging a program, that task's parent will be the debugger task's TDB. Typically, the parents of applications are EXPLORER.EXE if you launched the program from the Explorer, or MSGSRV32.EXE if you started the program from the DOS command line. For Win32 applications, the parent TDB is always 0.

24h   WORD   application signal action

In Windows 3.1, the value of this WORD affected what the task's application signal procedure did, although the exact meaning was unknown. In Windows 95, the application signal procedure address (offset 26h) appears to be unused.

26h   DWORD   Windows 3.1 application signal procedure

In Windows 3.x, this field held the pointer to the application's signal procedure. The application signal procedure was a means by which a program could get called back when Ctrl-Break was pressed. The signal procedure was set by calling the undocumented SetSigHandler function. In Windows 95, SetSigHandler is no more, and this field appears to always be 0.

2Ah   DWORD   USER signal procedure

This field holds a pointer to the USER signal procedure. The USER signal procedure is called when a DLL is loaded or unloaded. This gives USER the opportunity to clean up any system resources that were left around. During the unload callback, USER also calls the GDI SignalProc function, giving GDI a chance to clean up (or mark for future cleanup) any unfreed GDI resources.

You can change the signal handler in the TDB by calling the undocumented SetTaskSignalProc (KERNEL.38). The function is prototyped as follows:

```
FARPROC SetTaskSignalProc( HTASK hTask, FARPROC lpfnNewSignalProc );
```

The return value is the old signal procedure address.

The USER signal procedure callback function is as follows:

```
void FAR PASCAL UserSignalProc(
                    HMODULE hModule,    // Module under consideration.
                    WORD actionCode,    // See actionCode values, below.
                    WORD unknown,
                    HISNTANCE hInstance,
                    WORD hQueue);

    actionCode values:
    0x0040  DLL Load
    0x0080  DLL Unload
    0x0100  ??? (task exit?)
```

In Windows 3.1, TOOLHELP.DLL replaced the USER signal proc with its own handler. In TOOLHELP's handler, TOOLHELP unhooked any installed interrupt or notification handlers for the task that was exiting. In Windows 95, TOOLHELP no longer fudges with the signal procedure. Instead, TOOLHELP uses the new DLLENTRYPOINT mechanism described in the Windows 95 thunk compiler documentation.

2Ch   DWORD   GlobalNotify callback
This DWORD hold a pointer to the task's GlobalNotify callback procedure. KRNL386 calls this procedure when it's about to discard a DISCARDABLE global heap block. The callback function can allow KRNL386 to discard the block, or prevent it from discarding the block, based on the value that the callback function returns. This field is initialized to 0 (no callback) when a new task is created.

30   DWORD [7]   task interrupt handlers (INTs 0, 2, 4, 6, 7, 3Eh, 75h)
For most interrupts, Windows 95 has a global handler that's used for all tasks. However, Windows 95 allows tasks to install their own handlers for certain interrupt handlers (via an INT 21h, function 25h). When one of these interrupts occurs, Windows 95 looks up the interrupt handler in the TDB of the current task and calls that function. In the TDB is an array of seven DWORDs, with each DWORD holding the interrupt handler for a specific interrupt number. The interrupts that are handled on a per-task basis are these:

0   —   Divide by Zero

2   —   NMI

4   —   INTO

6   —   Invalid Opcode

7   —   Coprocessor Not Available

3Eh —   80x87 emulator

75h —   80x87 error

Default handler procedures are provided in the TDB of each task as it's created. A good example of a task that changes the interrupt vectors is CALC.EXE. The SHOW16 program on the accompanying disk is a good way to see which interrupt handlers a task has installed.

4Eh   DWORD   compatibility flags

This field, which was introduced in Windows 3.1, tells Windows to retain the behavior of previous versions of Windows for programs that rely on behavior that was changed in Windows 3.1. When Windows sees that it's running one of these tasks, it checks these flags, and adjusts what it does accordingly. If you look in the [Compatibility] section of the WIN.INI file, you'll see the module name of the programs that need these compatibility hacks. Somewhat surprisingly, many of the applications listed are Microsoft programs. Chapter 5 of *Undocumented Windows* contains a list of the bit-fields and their meanings in Windows 3.1. It appears that additional flags have been added in Windows 95. You can retrieve the compatibility flags of a particular task with the undocumented GetAppCompatFlags function:

```
DWORD FAR PASCAL GetAppCompatFlags(HTASK hTask);
```

52h   WORD   TIB selector

This is the value of the FS register used by the Win32 threading code to access the TIB (thread information block) structure. All tasks (even 16-bit tasks) have Win32 processes and threads maintained for them. A copy of the pointers and selectors used to access the task's Win32 thread information is kept in each task's TDB segment.

The thread information block contains per-thread information, including the following fields:

```
00h DWORD   pvExcept        // Head of exception record list.
04h DWORD   pvStackUserTop  // Top of thread's stack.
08h DWORD   pvStackUserBase // Base of thread's stack.
2Ch DWORD   pvTLSArray      // Pointer to Thread Local Storage array.
```

The TIB structure starts 0x10 bytes inside the thread database. The flat 32-bit address of the thread database is given in the next field of the TDB (offset 54h). See Chapter 3 for more detailed information on the TIB.

54h   DWORD   *linear address of the task's*
                                    THREAD_DATABASE

This DWORD holds the flat 32-bit linear address of the ring 3 thread database associated with this task. The thread database encompasses the Thread Information Block (see field 52h), and starts 0x10 bytes before the Thread Information Block. See Chapter 3 for more detail on the THREAD_DATABASE.

58h   WORD DGROUP   *handle of task*

For 16-bit–based tasks, this WORD is the global heap handle of the DGROUP segment. Based on error messages in the debug version of KRNL386, this field may be used during 16-/32-bit thunking to obtain the handle of the task's atom table segment (that is, its DGROUP). For Win32-based tasks, this field is always 0.

5Ah   BYTE[6]   *unused*

These six bytes don't appear to be used in Windows 95.

60h   WORD   *PDB of task*

This WORD is the selector of the task's PDB (a.k.a. PSP) segment. The PDB/PSP contains the task's file handle table, its command line, and other assorted fields that are documented in numerous DOS programming books. In Win16 tasks, the PDB for each task is stored at the tail end of the memory accessible by the HTASK selector. Specifically, the base address of the PDB selector is always 0x210 bytes greater than the base address of the HTASK selector. For Win32 tasks, the PDB is always at a linear address below 1MB, while the TDB segment is usually up above 2GB.

The GetCurrentPDB function returns the value of this field for the current TDB.

62h   DWORD   DOS Disk Transfer Area

This DWORD points to the MS-DOS Disk Transfer Area (DTA). Refer to DOS programming books for details on the DTA. For Win16 tasks, the initial value of the DTA is 80h bytes into the PDB segment (that is, the selector portion of this field matches the WORD at offset 60h). All Win32 tasks share a common DTA value.

66h   BYTE   current drive

This BYTE contains the drive portion of the task's current directory. This value is biased by 0x80, so you have to subtract 0x80 to get the drive number. (0x80 = drive *A*, 0x81 = drive *B*, and so forth). In Windows 3.*x*, the directory portion of the current directory was stored immediately following this field, but in Windows 95 the path has moved to offset 0x100. See 0x100 for more information.

67h   char[65]   unused

In Windows 3.*x*, this array of characters held the path portion of the task's current directory. In Windows 3.*x*, the maximum directory size was limited to 65 characters. With the advent of long filenames in Windows 95, this size became too small to hold the maximum possible path; the current directory is now stored at offset 0x100 in the TDB.

A8h   WORD   initial task validity check

Under Windows 3.*x*, this WORD is set to the initial value that AX will contain when the task starts up. However, there doesn't appear to be any startup code that tests this value, so it is essentially an unused field.

AAh   WORD   next task to schedule (DirectedYield)

If nonzero, this WORD holds the HTASK value that the Win16 scheduler should wake up when the scheduler is called. This value is always 0, except when you call DirectedYield to specify a particular task to run next. DirectedYield stores the HTASK parameter into this field, and then calls the Win16 scheduler (Reschedule). Near the beginning of the Reschedule function, it checks the value of this field and, if nonzero, bypasses its regular search for the next task to schedule. Reschedule zeroes out this field, so the field is rarely seen with a nonzero value.

ACh   DWORD   selector:offset to list of DLLs to initialize

At application startup, this DWORD holds a pointer to a 0-terminated array of DLL module handles. All of these DLLs are being loaded into memory for the first time, so they each need to have their LibMain entry point called. If an implicitly referenced DLL was already in memory when this task started, its HMODULE is not in this list. The InitTask function iterates through this array of HMODULEs, calling their LibMain entry points. Afterward, InitTask frees the memory containing the HMODULE list and sets this DWORD to 0. Note: The far pointer in this field has its selector and offset fields reversed from a normal far pointer. In this field, the selector is in the low WORD and the offset in the high WORD.

B0h   WORD   *code segment alias for this TDB*
Windows 95 initially creates MakeProcInstance thunks in the TDB itself (see field BAh). Since the CPU cannot execute code using a data selector (and the TDB is a data selector), KRNL386 creates an alias selector that's a code selector and stores it in this field. The alias selector is identical in base address and length to the TDB selector; the only difference is that the alias is set up as a code selector rather than as a data selector. The address of the first seven MakeProcInstance thunks you create will have a selector portion that's the same as this field.

B2h   WORD   *selector of segment with additional thunks*
If more than seven MakeProcInstance thunks are created, KRNL386 allocates another code segment to hold another seven thunks. This segment has the same format as field B0h through F1h (inclusive) of the TDB. If even more thunks are needed, additional segments are allocated; the segments are put at the end of the linked list, with this field acting as the "next" pointer for each node in the list.

B4h   WORD   *PT signature (5450h)*
This field contains the value 5450h, which when expressed in ASCII characters is PT. The term "PT" is presumably short for something like Procedure Thunks or ProcInstanc Thunk.

B6h   WORD   *unused*
This WORD does not appear to be used and is set to 0.

B8h   WORD   *offset of next available thunk slot + 6*
By subtracting 6 from the value of this field, you'll obtain the offset in the TDB where the next MakeProcInstance thunk will be created. As each thunk is created, this value goes up by 8.

BAh   [38h]   *MakeProcInstance thunk area*

This region holds up to seven MakeProcInstance thunks. Each thunk is 8 bytes long and is of the following form:

```
MOV AX, hInstance        ; hInstance == parameter 2 to MakeProcInstance
JMP FAR PTR lpfnProc     ; lpfnProc == parameter 1 to MakeProcInstance
```

F2h   char[8]   *module name for task*

This field holds the module name of the task. This name is simply copied from the module database (HMODULE) that this task was created with. If the module name is a full 8 characters, there is no NULL terminator.

FAh   TD   *signature*

This WORD contains 0x4454, which when expressed as ASCII characters is TD (short for Task Database). The IsTask functions and other KRNL386 routines use this signature to guarantee that they're working with a valid task database.

FCh   DWORD   *unused*

This DWORD does not appear to be used, and is set to 0.

100h   char[110h]   *current directory of task*

Since Windows 95 supports long filenames, the current working directory of the task no longer fits in the space at offset 67h. Therefore, the current directory (minus the drive portion) is stored in this character array.

210h   char[110h]   *PDB/PSP of task (Win16 tasks only)*

For Win16-based tasks, this region holds the PDB/PSP of the task. This region is also pointed at by the selector at offset 60h in the TDB. It's somewhat strange that this field is 110h bytes in size, since prior to Windows 95/DOS 7, the PSP has always been only 100h bytes long.

TASK-RELATED FUNCTIONS

Now that we've seen what a Windows 95 16-bit TDB looks like, let's look at some functions that access and manipulate the TDB structure. The functions I've chosen are mostly simple functions, primarily because a function like the core Windows scheduler (the Reschedule function) could easily take a chapter all by itself.

The GetCurrentTask() function

GetCurrentTask is the most basic of the task-related functions. The documented return value of this function is placed in the AX register, and the head of the task list is put in the DX register. Both the current task and the head task list are kept in KRNL386 global variables. Since KRNL386's data segment is FIXED and pagelocked, the two variables that the function retrieves will always be physically present in memory. Therefore, GetCurrentTask is completely safe to call from within an interrupt handler. This directly contradicts Microsoft's stern warnings that the only safe function to call from within an interrupt handler is PostMessage. Who are you going to believe? Look at the evidence and decide for yourself.

Since GetCurrentTask is such a simple function, it's clearer to present the few assembler instructions it uses than to show the function in C pseudocode.

Code for GetCurrentTask

```
    PUSH    DS                        ; Save caller's DS.
    MOV     DS,WORD PTR CS:[MYCSDS]    ; MyCSDS is a global var kept in the
                                      ; code segment that holds the selector
                                      ; of KRNL386's data segment (segment 4).
    MOV     AX,[CurTDB]               ; Load documented return value into AX.
    MOV     DX,WORD PTR [HeadTDB]     ; Undocumented head of task list.

    POP     DS                        ; Restore caller's DS.
    RETF
```

The IsTask() function

IsTask is a handy function you can use to verify that you've got a valid task handle. It's not entirely rigorous, as the only test is to see if there's a WORD with the value 0x4454 (TD) at offset 0xFA in the passed-in segment. (In fact, you can easily construct a segment that passes this test but is not a valid HTASK segment.)

One interesting thing to note in IsTask is that there don't appear to be any tests to make sure the handle is in fact a valid global memory handle. You might think that passing in a bogus selector value would therefore cause a GP fault, causing Windows to terminate your application. As it turns out, a GP fault does occur in this situation but KRNL386 is prepared for this possibility.

To handle code sequences where GP faults are a possibility, KRNL386 has a table of address ranges where a GP fault might occur. Associated with each address range is a safe recovery address. If the KRNL386 GP fault handler sees a GP fault occur in one of these ranges, it transfers control to the recovery address. In the case of IsTask, the recovery address simply puts 0 (that is, FALSE) in the AX register and returns to the code that called IsTask. If this mechanism sounds suspiciously like Win32-structured exception handling, it essentially is, although there are some important differences. For more information on KRNL386's version of structured exception handling, see the entries for __GP and HasGPHandler in *Undocumented Windows*.

Pseudocode for GetCurrentTask

```
// Parameters:
//      HTASK hTask
// Locals:
//      TDB far * lpTDB      // Pointer to TDB structure.

    if ( hTask == 0 )
        return FALSE;

    lpTDB = MAKELP( hTask, 0 );

    BX = *(LPWORD)MAKELP( hTask, 0x202 );    // ??? Offset 0x202 in the TDB
                                             // is near the end of the current
                                             // directory area.

    if ( lpTDB->TDB_sig == 0x4454 )          // Look for the TD signature.
        return TRUE;                         // (0x4454)
    else
        return FALSE;
```

The GetTaskQueue() function

GetTaskQueue is an undocumented function that returns the message queue handle associated with the HTASK parameter passed in. If the HTASK parameter is 0, GetTaskQueue returns the queue handle for the current task. Chapter 4 describes the message queue in more detail.

GetTaskQueue is a useful function for determining if a task is able to receive window messages yet (a message queue is necessary to receive posted or sent messages). The application's message queue isn't created until the application calls the InitApp function in its startup code. The call to InitApp doesn't occur until after the LibMain's of implicitly loaded DLLs are called, so a significant portion of a task's life can be spent without a message queue. Windows-hosted debuggers in particular need to know if the task they're debugging has a message queue; this information makes a difference in how they handle the debuggee process and its window messages when the debuggee is stopped.

The GetTaskQueue function doesn't do rigorous checking of its input parameters. If you pass a nonzero value that's not a valid selector, you'll receive a GP fault inside KRNL386.

Pseudocode for GetTaskQueue

```
// Parameters:
//      HTASK hTask
// Locals:
//      TDB far * lpTDB      // Pointer to TDB structure.

    lpTDB = GetATaskSomehow( hTask );   // See following pseudocode.

    if ( lpTDB->TDB_Queue )
        return lpTDB->TDB_Queue;    // Return message queue.
    else
        return -1;                  // Windows 3.1 didn't do this, and
                                    // returned whatever was in the TDB.
```

Pseudocode for GetATaskSomehow

```
// Parameters:
//   HTASK   hTask

    if ( hTask )        // If any nonzero hTask passed in, return it;
        return hTask;   // otherwise, return the current task.
    else
        return CurTDB;
```

The MakeProcInstance() function

Although much of the need for MakeProcInstance has gone away with newer compilers, this function is usually required in cases where you want callback functions in your EXE's code rather than in a DLL. For example, you might want to use TOOLHELP NotifyRegister or InterruptRegister callbacks in your EXE's code. If you use the _ _loadds function modifier, you'll end up limiting the program to a single instance. MakeProcInstance thunks come to the rescue in such situations.

The job of the MakeProcInstance thunk is simple: Jump to a specified address after setting the AX register to the DS register value that the function should use. It's expected that the function's prologue code will take the AX register value and put it into DS.

MakeProcInstance has parameter validation layer code that first makes sure that a valid target address and HINSTANCE were passed. The pseudocode for ValidateHInstance and ValidateCodePtr (shown later in this section) lists the parameters that MakeProcInstance considers to be valid: HANDLE for ValidateHInstance and FARPROC for ValidateCodePtr. If either of these parameters is invalid, MakeProcInstance returns without creating a thunk. If you're running the debug version of KRNL386, MakeProcInstance RIPs with an appropriate error code, telling you of your bad programming.

After validating the parameters, MakeProcInstance jumps to the IMakeProcInstance code, which is where the thunk is actually created. IMakeProcInstance starts out by doing some additional tests of its own before committing to making a thunk. If the HINSTANCE parameter isn't the same as the DS register in the calling code, you'll get a message to the effect of "MakeProcInstance only for current instance." This means that you can't make a thunk for an EXE module other than your own. (That is, unless you get sneaky and change your DS to the right value before calling MakeProcInstance.)

Another important check MakeProcInstance makes is to see if you're requesting a thunk for a function in a DLL. DLLs don't need MakeProcInstance thunks, since they can use the exported function prologue code that uses a hard-coded DS value. For example:

```
MOV AX,17C7h
MOV DS,AX
```

If you do pass the address of a routine in a DLL, MakeProcInstance silently returns to you the address you passed in, unmodified.

The next major portion of IMakeProcInstance is to determine where it will create the new thunk. If you've created less than seven thunks so far, the thunk will come from a region within the TDB segment of the current task. Otherwise, IMakeProcInstance looks in the additional segments that it creates for storing additional thunks. If there's no open slot in these segments, IMakeProcInstance allocates another segment (with GlobalAlloc), initializes the segment, and adds it to the linked list of thunk segments.

Once IMakeProcInstance knows where the new thunk will be created, the actual creation is amazingly simple. A MakeProcInstance stub looks like this:

```
MOV AX, hInstance
JMP FAR PTR lpfnProc
```

Creating the thunk is just a matter of creating the completed instructions. Bytes 0 and 3 are filled with constant values (the opcodes 0xB8 and 0xEA). The WORD at offset 1 is set to the value of the hinstance parameter to MakeProcInstance, and the DWORD at offset 4 is set to the lpProc parameter value.

Pseudocode for MakeProcInstance

```
// Parameters:
//      FARPROC     lpProc
//      HINSTANCE   hinst

    ValidateCodePtr( lpfnProc );    // If either of these functions fail,
    ValidateHInstance( hinst );     // the function returns without JMP'ing
    goto IMakeProcInstance          // to IMakeProcInstance.
```

Pseudocode for ValidateHInstance()

```
// Parameters (in AX):
//      HANDLE handle

    if ( handle == 0 )
        return;

    // Make sure the LDT bit is on. Win16 code only deals with LDT
    // selectors, and not with GDT selectors.
    if ( (handle & 0x0004) == 0 )
        RIP in the debug KERNEL (code 6022 - ERR_BAD_GLOBAL_HANDLE)

    if ( handle == -1 ) // Apparently -1 is allowed.
        return;
```

```
        LAR handle                    // Get access rights WORD.
        if ( LAR instruction fails )
            RIP in the debug KERNEL (code 6022 - ERR_BAD_GLOBAL_HANDLE)

    return
```

Pseudocode for *ValidateCodePtr()*

```
// Parameters ( in CX:AX ):
//      FARPROC lpfn;
// Locals:
//      WORD    opcode

    LAR SELECTOROF( lpfn )                    // Get access rights WORD.
    if ( LAR instruction fails )
        RIP in the debug KERNEL (code 7088)

    if ( Code bit (0x0008) not set in access rights )
        RIP in the debug KERNEL (code 7088)

    AL = *(LPBYTE)lpfn  // Test to see if the memory can be read. If it
                        // GP faults, the KERNEL __GP handler will catch it.

    opcode = *(LPWORD)(lpfn+2); // Grab the opcode bytes 2 bytes into the PROC.

    // Verify that the code pointer passed to us has an export prologue
    // in it. 0x581E == PUSH DS / POP AX,  0xD88C == MOV AX,DS.
    if ( (opcode != 0x581E) && (opcode != 0xD88C) )
        RIP in the debug KERNEL (code 7088);

    return;
```

Pseudocode for *IMakeProcInstance()*

```
typedef struct
{
    BYTE    mov_ax_opcode
    WORD    hinstValue;
    BYTE    jmp_far_opcode;
    DWORD   lpfn;
} MAKEPROCINSTANCE_THUNK;
// Parameters:
```

```
//      FARPROC     lpProc
//      HINSTANCE   hinst
// Locals:
//      LPMODULE    lpModule;
//      MAKEPROCINSTANCE_THUNK far * lpThunk;
//      WORD newThunkSegment;        // If additional thunk slots are needed.

    if ( hInstance )
    {
        if ( HIWORD(GlobalHandle(hinst)) != Calling application's DS. )
            _KRDebugTest("fatl K16 %dx2 MakeProcInstance only for"
                        " current instance.");
    }

    // Get the owner of the hinst segment, which should be an HMODULE,
    // and make a far pointer out of it.
    lpModule = MAKELP( FarGetOwner(hinst), 0 );

    // Check if the owning segment is a valid HMODULE by looking for
    // the NE signature. If HMODULE isn't valid, something is seriously wrong,
    // so pop into a debugger with an INT 3.
    if ( 'NE' != lpModule->ne_signature )
        INT 3

    // If the owning module is a DLL, just return the FARPROC passed in.
    // MakeProcInstance thunks aren't necessary for DLLs.
    if ( lpModule->ne_flags & MODFLAGS_DLL )
        return lpProc;

    if ( spaces left in TDB for thunk )
    {
        lpThunk = MAKELP( TDB, TDB->TDB_next_MPI_thunk );
        goto InsertThunk
    }

    if ( space in the add-on thunk segment (offset B2h in TDB) )
    {
        lpThunk = MAKELP( segment & offset of next free slot in
                         add-on segment );
        goto InsertThunk
    }

    // Allocate memory for a new thunk segment (0x40 bytes in size).
    newThunkSegment = GlobalAlloc( GMEM_ZEROINIT, 0x40 );
    if ( newThunkSegment == 0 )
        goto ReturnFailure;
```

Use AllocSelector and PrestoChangoSelector to make a new code segment alias for the thunk segment.

```
if ( AllocSelector fails )
    goto ReturnFailure;
```

Initialize fields of new thunk segment to be the same format as offsets B0H through F1h of the Task Database. Link this new segment into the linked list of thunk segments. The head of this list is the WORD at offset 0xB2 in the current TDB.

```
lpThunk = first slot in newly created thunk segment

goto InsertThunk;
```

ReturnFailure:

```
_KRDEBUGTEST( "err K16 MakeProcInstance failed. Did you check return"
             " values?" );
return 0;
```

InsertThunk:

Update the nextThunk field to point at the next available slot in whatever segment we're putting the new thunk into.

```
lpThunk->mov_ax_opcode = 0xB8;
lpThunk->hinstValue = hinst;
lpThunk->jmp_far_opcode = 0xEA;
lpThunk->lpfn = lpProc;

// Return a far pointer that's a callable code address.
return MAKELP( code alias selector, OFFSETOF(lpThunk) );
```

The TaskFindHandle() function

I chose to include the TOOLHELP TaskFindHandle function in this chapter since many programmers are under the impression that the TOOLHELP functions are somehow magic. As you can see in the pseudocode, TaskFindHandle is merely a convenient way to access selected fields in a task database. A downside to TaskFindHandle is that you'll get a whole collection of information, even if you only need to know one particular value. If you have time-critical code that's called many times a second, you might want to forego TaskFindHandle and read the information out of the Task Database directly. Some might argue that you sacrifice portability, but at this stage in the game, the fields in the TDB that TaskFindHandle collects aren't going to change; too many applications would break.

Like almost all the TOOLHELP functions, TaskFindHandle first checks to make sure that you've passed reasonable parameters. This means that you've passed a valid pointer to a TASKENTRY structure, and that the first field (dwSize) is initialized to the size of a TASKENTRY structure. After these tests, TaskFindHandle calls an internal routine that does the real work of copying the information out of the TDB and into the TASKENTRY struct. I've called this function CopyTaskInformation in the pseudocode.

The only test that CopyTaskInformation makes to ensure you've passed a valid HTASK is to look for the TD signature WORD at offset 0xFA in the TDB. You could easily construct a dummy segment that passes this very lax test. In its defense, the IsTask API function isn't any more stringent. Assuming that the TD signature test succeeds, the majority of CopyTaskInformation consists of copying fields in the TDB segment into the TASKENTRY structure. At the very end of the routine, the code makes a brief excursion into the task's stack segment in order to copy the stack's top, bottom, and minimum values into the TASKENTRY structure.

The code for CopyTaskInformation has two changes from the Windows 3.1 version of TOOLHELP; both changes are related to 32-bit tasks. The first change was made because the pseudo tasks created for Win32 processes don't have an HINSTANCE segment. For these tasks, TOOLHELP fills in the TASKENTRY.hInst field with the task's TDB segment. The second change involves the stack boundary fields (wStackTop, and so on). The TDBs of Win32 processes have 0 in the fields where the SS:SP would normally go. Therefore, CopyTaskInformation doesn't bother to fill in the wStackTop, wStackMinimum, and wStackBottom fields for Win32 tasks.

Pseudocode for TaskFindHandle

```
// Parameters:
//    TASKENTRY far * lpTask
//    HTASK          hTask

        // Verify that TOOLHELP has been initialized, that a nonzero LPTASKENTRY
        // has been passed, and that the dwSize field of the TASKENTRY struct
```

```
                 // has been filled in.
                 if (   (ToolhelpInitialized == FALSE)
                     || ( lpTask == NULL )
                     || (lpTask->dwSize != sizeof(TASKENTRY)) )
                 {
                     return FALSE;
                 }

                 // Internal function that fills in the TASKENTRY struct.
                 CopyTaskInformation( lpTask, hTask );
```

Pseudocode for CopyTaskInformation

```
      // Parameters:
      //   TASKENTRY far * lpTask
      //   HTASK          hTask
      // Locals:
      //   LPTDB          lpTDB;

          hTask |= 1;      // If a MOVEABLE handle was passed, convert to a selector.

          Make sure the segment referenced by the hTask segment is at least
          0x204 bytes long. If not, return FALSE.

          lpTDB = MAKELP( hTask, 0 );      // Make a pointer to the TDB segment.

          if ( lpTDB->tdb_sig != 0x4454 )      // Verify TD signature is present.
             return FALSE;

          // Start filling in fields in the TASKENTRY struct, copying the data
          // from the TDB segment.

          lpTask->hNext = lpTDB->TDB_next;          // Next task.
          lpTask->hTask = hTask;                    // Current task.
          lpTask->hTaskParent = lpTDB->TDB_Parent;  // Parent task.

          lpTask->wSS = lpTDB->TDB_taskSS;          // Task's SS:SP.
          lpTask->wSP = lpTDB->TDB_taskSP;

          lpTask->wcEvents = lpTDB->TDB_nEvents;     // Number of waiting events.
          lpTask->hQueue = lpTDB->TDB_Queue;         // Message queue handle.

          lpTask->wPSPOffset = lpTDB->TDB_PSP;       // PSP/PDB of task.

          if ( lpTDB->TDB_flags & TDB_FLAGS_WIN32 )
              lpTask->hInst = hTask;  // Win32 programs don't have real HINST's.
```

```
        else
            lpTask->hInst = lpTDB->TDB_HInstance;    // HINSTANCE of task.

        lpTask->hModule = lpTDB->TDB_HMODULE;         // HMODULE of task.

        // Copy the module name from the TDB over into the TASKENTRY struct.
        memcpy( &lpTask->szModule, lpTDB->TDB_ModName, 8 )
        lpTask->szModule[8] = 0;    // Null-terminate the string.

        // If it's a Win32 program, don't bother to try and retrieve the
        // stack bounds values listed below. Just return TRUE.
        if ( lpTDB->TDB_flags & TDB_FLAGS_WIN32 )
            return TRUE;

        if ( VERR lpTDB->wSS fails )    // Make sure the task's stack segment
            return TRUE;                // is accessible.

        // Copy the stack boundary fields:
        lpTtask->wStackTop = WORD at offset 0x0A in lpTask->wSS segment;
        lpTtask->wStackMinimum = WORD at offset 0x0C in lpTask->wSS segment;
        lpTtask->wStackBottom = WORD at offset 0x0E in lpTask->wSS segment;

        return TRUE;
```

THE **SHOW16** PROGRAM

I wrote the SHOW16 program to illustrate the concepts I've described in this chapter. (The source code for SHOW16 is on the accompanying disk.) This program shows the task list, the module list, and details about the currently selected task or module. In addition, you can double-click certain lines in the details window to access even more in-depth information about that particular line.

SHOW16 is a Windows 95–specific application, and is almost guaranteed to not work properly on other Win16 environments such as Windows 3.1, NT, or OS/2 2.x. The goal of SHOW16 is to show as much as possible about Windows 95 tasks and modules, not to be portable.

When you first start up SHOW16, it looks something like the screenshot in Figure 7-2. The listbox on the left shows either the task list (the default when starting up) or the module list. Clicking on the two radio buttons in the top left of this listbox toggles between the two lists. Each time you click on a radio button, the appropriate list is updated from scratch, so this is a handy way to force a refresh of either list.

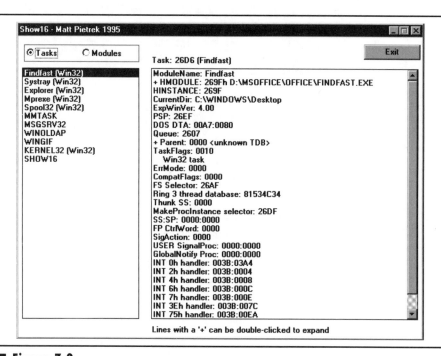

Figure 7-2

The opening screen of the SHOW16 program contains two listboxes that provide information about the currently selected task or module. The listbox on the left lets you view either the task list or the module list, and the listbox on the right shows details about items in those lists.

The listbox on the right (the details window) shows details on whatever item is selected in the left listbox. These details are made up of information extracted from the Task Database or Module Database directly, rather than from TOOLHELP functions. Items in the details window preceded by a + (plus) symbol can be double-clicked to change the details window. If the line is a TDB or HMODULE line, the details window changes to show the details for the TDB or HMODULE you double-clicked. Otherwise, the details window changes to a more detailed report on the specific line you double-clicked.

The task view in Figure 7-2 has several items of note. In the task list in the left listbox, task names that are followed by (Win32) are 32-bit processes. In the right listbox, the second line down shows the HMODULE associated with the task, and has a + at the beginning. The HMODULE value has been passed to GetModuleFileName to retrieve the path of the associated EXE or DLL, which is also displayed. If you double-click this line, the details window will change to the module database details view for this HMODULE. (The module database detail view is described a bit later in this section.) The other line that you can double-click in the task details window is the parent task. This changes the details view to the details view of the parent task.

The task details window shows all the fields in a task database that might be of even remote interest. Fields in the TDB that don't provide any useful information are not shown. In addition, fields that are described as unused in the earlier TDB description receive special treatment. At the end of the code that displays the task details is a series of assert statements. Each of the assert lines checks to make sure that an unused field is set to 0. If any of these asserts fails, it indicates that the field is probably used for something that I haven't uncovered.

Figure 7-3 shows the other major display given by SHOW16. This is the module list, which is obtained by selecting the Modules radio button. The first set of modules in the left listbox are regular module databases from 16-bit EXEs and DLLs. These modules are found by walking the module database list using the linked list fields described earlier. At the end of the list of modules are the pseudo module databases created for Win32 EXEs and DLLs (you may have to scroll down to see them). These modules all have (Win32) appended to the end of the module name. Since these modules aren't in the regular module database list, SHOW16 takes a brute force approach to finding them. At the end of the UpdateModuleList function in SHOW16.C, the code examines every possible ring 3 LDT selector, looking for segments that are module databases. For each module database it finds, the code looks for the MODFLAGS_WIN32 flag at offset 0xC in the module database; if this flag is set, the code adds the module to the end of the window's list.

Figure 7-3 shows the module details window, which has many interesting things to click on. For starters, look at the "imported modules" line. Each of the indented lines below it is a DLL that the module implicitly links to. Double-clicking on one of these indented lines causes the module details window to show details about the selected module. There are also numerous more specialized details views available at the top of this view. Specifically, you can switch to a details view of the following module-database items:

- Segment table
- Entry table
- Resources
- Resident names
- Nonresident names

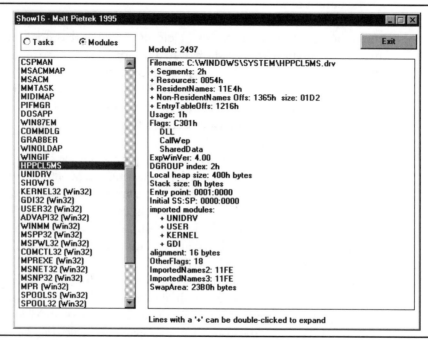

Figure 7-3
The module list in the left listbox shows the regular module databases and the pseudo module databases. The right listbox shows the details of the currently highlighted module.

A typical segment table is shown in Figure 7-4. For each segment in the module's segment table, the details view shows the segment's ordinal number (the segment portion of a logical address), global heap handle, type (either code or data), and size. An ambitious programmer could modify the SHOW16 source to bring up a hex dump window when one of these lines is double-clicked. Incidentally, font modules don't have segment tables, so double-clicking on the segments, entry table, resident names, or nonresident names table lines won't change the details view.

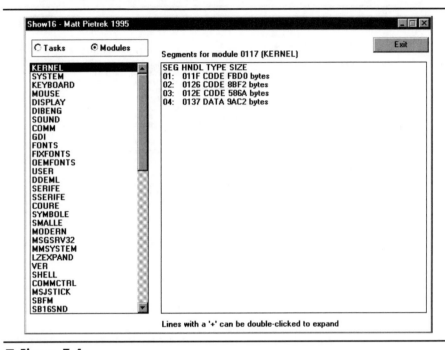

Figure 7-4

The details window for this segment window table shows each segment's ordinal number, global heap handle, type, and size.

Figure 7-5 shows a resource view details window. As you can see, the information in this window is presented in a format similar to the layout of the resource table in the module database. Each section starts out with the type of the resources that will follow (for example, Version Info, Icon, and so on). Immediately following the resource-type line is a series of indented lines, each representing one resource instance (that is, one bitmap, one cursor, and so on). Each of the indented lines provides the following information about that resource: the offset of the resource in the file (in sectors for Win16 modules), the size of the resource (in sectors), the ASCII name or ID of the resource, and the resource's global heap handle (if loaded in memory). An expanded version of SHOW16 would let you double-click on each of these lines and see the resource graphically.

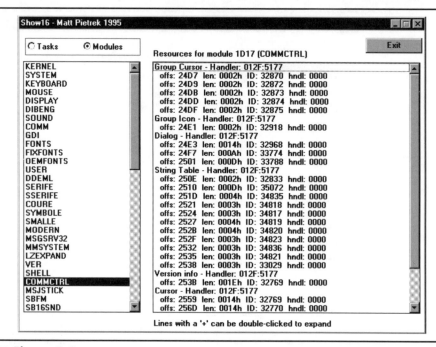

Figure 7-5

The resource view details window presents information in a format similar to the layout of a resource table in the module database.

Figure 7-6 shows a resident names details view. This view shares the same format as the nonresident names detail view. In the SHOW16 code, the main difference between the two views is that nonresident names have to be read in from the disk file, whereas resident names can be processed straight out of the module database. Each line in the resident/nonresident names detail view starts with an export ordinal and is followed by the name of the exported function or variable. The first line in the resident names view has an export ordinal of 0 and is the module name (for example, USER). The first line in the nonresident names view has an export ordinal of 0 and is the module description (for example, Microsoft Windows User Interface).

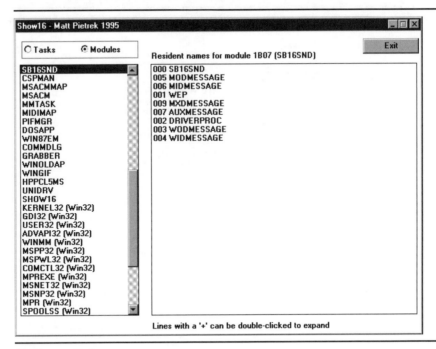

Figure 7-6

The resident names detail view, showing exported functions and their ordinal value. It has the same format as the nonresident names detail view.

Figure 7-7 shows the last details view, which is the entry table. Each line represents one slot in the module's entry table, and starts with the export ordinal and logical address for the entry. The remainder of the line contains the flags for the entry. Every entry is either MOVEABLE or FIXED, and usually is EXPORTED. It would have been really nice to display the function name of the entry. However, this would have required a significant amount of time to do, since most of a module's names are usually found in the nonresident names table, which requires a disk read to get at. In addition, there's no way to quickly find the name for a given export ordinal in a resident/nonresident names tables. The overhead of displaying the entry names wouldn't be bad for a small DLL, but for something like USER (which has several hundred entries), you could tie up the system for quite a while.

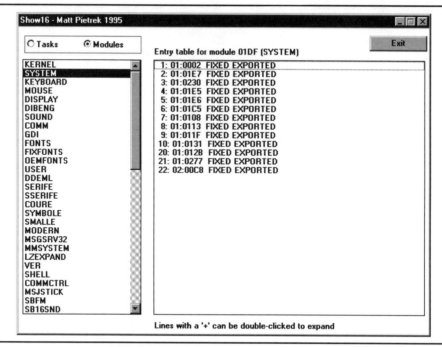

Figure 7-7
The entry table view shows the export ordinal, the logical address, and the flags for the entry.

SUMMARY

Although Windows 95 is marketed as a 32-bit operating system, there are still many parts of it that rely on 16-bit code. In addition, until most application development becomes 32-bit based, Windows 95 will primarily be used to run 16-bit programs. Therefore, it's useful to have an understanding of how the 16-bit components of Windows 95 work. In this chapter, we've looked at two of the key 16-bit data structures (the module and task databases). I've shown in some places how these 16-bit data structures run parallel to their 32-bit equivalents (which I discussed in Chapter 3). Although I haven't covered all aspects of Windows 95's support for 16-bit modules and tasks, the information I've presented in this chapter should be sufficient for all but the most hard-core spelunker.

THE PORTABLE EXECUTABLE AND COFF OBJ FORMATS

*T*he format of an operating system's executable file is in many ways a mirror of the operating system's built-in assumptions and behaviors. Although studying the ins and outs of an executable file format isn't something that usually appears high on most programmers' list of things to do, a great deal of useful knowledge about the operating system can be gleaned from doing this. Dynamic linking, loader behavior, and memory management are just three examples of operating system specifics that can be inferred by studying the executable format.

In this chapter, I'll provide a real-world tour of the Portable Executable (PE) file format that Microsoft has designed for use by all its Win32 operating systems (Windows NT, Windows 95, and Win32s).

You may be wondering why I cover the PE format in this book, since there are several descriptions of the format on the Microsoft Developer Network CD-ROM. The primary reason I describe PE format executables here is because the structures used in PE files are also key data structures within Windows 95 itself. For example, Windows 95 maps the header section of a PE file into memory and uses it to represent a loaded module. To understand how the Windows 95 kernel works, you need to understand the PE format: It's that simple.

Another reason I discuss PE files in this book is that, like almost all specifications from Microsoft, Microsoft's PE documentation assumes that you live and breathe this executable file format. Calling the Microsoft documentation terse would be an understatement. My goal in this chapter is to flesh out that documentation and correlate it to things you experience every day. Along the way I've shown a variety of ways in which the PE format affects the operating system implementation and vice versa.

The PE format plays a key role in all of Microsoft's operating systems for the foreseeable future, including Cairo. Even if you're programming for Windows 3.1 using Visual C++, you're still using PE files (the 32-bit DOS extended components of Visual C++ use this format). If you're going to do almost any sort of low-level system programming in Windows 95, a working knowledge of PE files is essential.

In discussing the PE format, I won't be laboriously going over endless hex dumps and explaining the significance of individual bits for pages on end. Instead, I'll present the concepts embedded in the PE file format and relate them to things you encounter everyday as part of your Win32 programming. For example, the notion of thread local variables (à la "declspec(thread)) drove me crazy until I saw how it was implemented with elegant simplicity in the executable file. Since many Win32 programmers are coming from a Win16 background, I'll correlate the constructs of the PE file format back to their 16-bit file-format equivalents.

At the same time that Microsoft introduced a different executable format, it also introduced new object module and library formats that its compilers and assemblers produce. (The new LIB file format is essentially just a bunch of OBJ files strung together along with an index, so when I refer to OBJ files from here on out, I'm referring to both COFF OBJ and LIB files.) These new OBJ and LIB file formats share many concepts with the PE format. Until recently, there was no publicly available information on Microsoft's OBJ and LIB files — and even at the time of this writing, information is scant. Therefore, it's worthwhile to cover the OBJ and LIB file formats as well.

It's common knowledge that Windows NT (the first of the Win32 operating systems) has a VAX VMS and UNIX heritage. Many of the key NT developers designed and coded for those platforms before coming to Microsoft. When it came time to design NT, it was only natural that they tried to minimize their bootstrap time by using previously written and tested tools. The executable and object module format that these tools produced and worked with is called COFF (Common Object File Format).

The relatively old (in computer years) nature of COFF can be seen in the fact that certain fields in the files are specified in octal format. The COFF format by itself was a good starting point, but needed to be extended to meet all the needs of a modern operating system such as Windows NT or Windows 95. The result of this updating is the PE (remember, this stands for Portable Executable) format. It's called *portable* because all the implementations of NT on various platforms (Intel 386, MIPS, Alpha, Power PC, and so on) use the same executable format. Sure, there are differences in things such as the binary encodings of CPU instructions. You can't run a MIPS compiled PE executable on an Intel system. However, the important thing is that the operating system loader and programming tools don't have to be completely rewritten for each new CPU that arrives on the scene.

The strength of Microsoft's commitment to get Windows NT up and running quickly is evidenced by the fact that it abandoned existing Microsoft 32-bit tools and file formats. Virtual device drivers written for Windows 3.*x* were using a different 32-bit file layout (the LE format) long before NT appeared on the scene. In a testimonial to the "if it ain't broke, don't fix it" nature of Windows, Windows 95 uses both the PE format and the LE format. This allowed Microsoft to use existing Windows 3.*x* code in a big way.

Although it's reasonable to expect a completely new operating system (Windows NT, that is) to have a completely different executable format, it's a different story when it comes to object module (.OBJ and LIB) formats. Before Visual C++ 32-bit edition 1.0, all Microsoft compilers used the Intel OMF (Object Module Format) specification. The Microsoft compilers for Win32 implementations produce COFF format OBJ files. Some Microsoft competitors such as Borland have chosen to forego the COFF format OBJs and stick with the Intel OMF format. The result of this is that companies producing OBJs or LIBs for use with multiple compilers will need to go back to distributing separate versions of their products for different compilers (if they weren't already).

Those of you who like to read conspiracy into Microsoft's actions might see the decision to change OBJ formats as evidence of Microsoft trying to hinder its competitors. To claim true Microsoft "compatibility" down to the OBJ level, other vendors will need to convert all their 32-bit tools over to the COFF OBJ and LIB formats. In short, the OBJ and LIB file format can be viewed as yet another example of Microsoft abandoning existing standards in favor of something that suits it better.

The PE format is documented (in the loosest sense of the word) in the WINNT.H header file, along with certain structure definitions for COFF format OBJs. (I'll be using the field names from WINNT.H later in the chapter.) About midway through WINNT.H is a section titled "Image Format." This section of the file starts out with small tidbits from the old familiar DOS MZ format and NE format headers before moving into the newer PE information. WINNT.H provides definitions of the raw data structures used by PE files, but contains only the barest hint of useful comments to explain what the structures and flags mean. The author of the header file for the PE format (a certain Michael J. O'Leary) is certainly a believer in long, descriptive names, along with deeply nested structures and macros. When coding with WINNT.H, it's not uncommon to have expressions like this:

```
pNTHeader->OptionalHeader.DataDirectory[IMAGE_DIRECTORY_ENTRY_DEBUG].VirtualAddress;
```

Besides just reading about what PE files are composed of, you'll also want to dump out some PE files to see for yourself the concepts presented here. If you use Microsoft tools for Win32 development, the DUMPBIN program from Visual C++ and the Win32 SDK can dissect and output PE files and COFF OBJ/LIB files in human-readable form. DUMPBIN even has a nifty option to disassemble the code sections in the file it's taking apart. In light of Microsoft's claims that you're not allowed to disassemble its products, it's pretty interesting that it would provide a tool that makes it so easy to disassemble its programs and DLLs. If the ability to disassemble EXEs and OBJs wasn't useful, why would Microsoft have bothered to add this feature to DUMPBIN? It sure sounds like another case of "Do as we say, not as we do."

Borland users can use TDUMP to view PE files, but TDUMP doesn't understand the COFF style OBJ files. This isn't a huge issue since the Borland compiler doesn't produce COFF format OBJs in the first place. Throwing my own hat into the ring, I've written a PE and COFF OBJ/LIB file dumping program (PEDUMP) that I think provides more understandable output than DUMPBIN. Although it doesn't have a disassembler, it is otherwise functionally equivalent to DUMPBIN, and adds a few new features to make it worth considering. The source code for PEDUMP is on the disk included with this book, so I won't list it here in its entirety. Instead, I'll provide sample output from PEDUMP to illustrate the concepts as I describe them.

THE PEDUMP PROGRAM

The PEDUMP program is a command-line utility for dumping PE files and COFF OBJ/LIB format files. It uses the Win32 console capabilities to eliminate the need for extensive user-interface work. The syntax for PEDUMP is as follows:

```
PEDUMP [switches] filename
```

The switches can be seen by running PEDUMP with no arguments. PEDUMP uses the following switches:

```
/A      include everything in dump (essentially, enable all the switches)
/H      include a hex dump of each section at the end of the dump
/I      include Import Address Table thunk addresses
/L      include line number information (both PE and COFF OBJ files)
/R      show base relocations (PE files only)
/S      show symbol table (both PE and COFF OBJ files)
```

By default, none of the switches are enabled. That way, most of the information you need will be available, but you won't create a huge amount of output.

PEDUMP sends its output to the standard output file (for example, the screen), so its output can be redirected to a file with an > (greater-than sign) on the command line.

The sources for PEDUMP are included with it. PEDUMP was built with the Microsoft Visual C++ 2.0 compiler, although I have also compiled it with Borland C++ 4.*x* throughout its development.

BASIC WIN32 AND PE CONCEPTS

Before jumping into a discussion of the layout of a PE file, I need to go over a few fundamental ideas that permeate its design. For this discussion, I'll use the term *module* to mean the code, data, and resources of an executable file or DLL that has been loaded into memory. Besides code and data that your program uses directly, a module is also composed of the supporting data used by Windows to determine where the code and data is located in memory. In Win16, the supporting data structures are in the module database (the segment referred to by an HMODULE). In Win32, this information is kept in the PE header (the IMAGE_NT_HEADERS structure), which I'll explain in detail shortly.

The most important thing to know about PE files is that the executable file on disk is very similar to what the module will look like after Windows has loaded it. That's because the Windows loader doesn't need to work extremely hard to create a process from the disk file. Rather, the loader can take it easy and use Win32 memory mapped files to load the appropriate pieces of the PE file into a program's address space. To use a construction analogy, a PE file is like a prefabricated house: There are relatively few pieces, and each piece can be snapped into place with just a small amount of work. And, just as it's fairly easy to hook up the electricity and water connections in a prefab house, it's also a simple matter to wire a PE file up to the rest of the world (that is, connect it to its DLLs, and so on).

This same ease of loading applies to DLLs as well. Once an EXE or .DLL module has been loaded, Windows can effectively treat it like any other memory mapped file. This is in marked contrast to the situation in 16-bit Windows. The 16-bit NE file loader reads in portions of the file and creates separate data structures to represent the module in memory. When a code or data segment needs to be loaded, the loader has to allocate a new segment from the global heap, find where the raw data is stored in the executable file, seek to that location, read in the raw data, and apply any applicable fixups. In addition, each 16-bit module is responsible for remembering all the selectors it's currently using, whether the segment has been discarded, and so on.

For Win32, however, all the memory used by the module for code, data, resources, import tables, export tables, and other things is in one contiguous range of linear address space. All you need to know in this situation is the address where the loader mapped the executable file into memory. You can then easily find all the various pieces of the module by following pointers stored as part of the image.

Another idea you should be acquainted with before we start is the Relative Virtual Address, or RVA. Many fields in PE files are specified in terms of RVAs. An RVA is simply the offset of some item, relative to where the file is memory mapped to. For example, let's say the Windows loader mapped a PE file into memory starting at address 0x400000 in the virtual address space. If a certain table in the image starts at address 0x401464, the table's RVA is 0x1464:

(virtual address 0x401464) − (base address 0x400000) = RVA 0x1464

To convert an RVA into a usable pointer to memory, simply add the RVA to the base address where the module was loaded into. The term *base address* is another important concept to remember. A base address describes the starting address of a memory mapped EXE or DLL. For convenience, Windows NT and Windows 95 use the base address of a module as the module's instance handle (HINSTANCE). In Win32, calling the base address of a module an HINSTANCE is somewhat confusing, because the term *instance handle* comes from 16-bit Windows. Each copy of an application in Win16 gets its own separate data segment (and an associated global handle) that distinguishes it from other copies of the application; hence the term, instance handle.

In Win32, applications don't need to be distinguished from one another because they don't share the same address space. Still, the term HINSTANCE persists to keep at least the appearance of continuity between Win16 and Win32. What's important for Win32 is that you can call GetModuleHandle() for any DLL that your process uses, and get a pointer that you can use to access the module's components. By components, I mean its imported and exported functions, its relocations, its code and data sections, and so on.

Another concept to be familiar with when investigating PE files and COFF OBJs is the *section*. A section in a PE file or COFF OBJ file is roughly equivalent to a segment or the resources in a 16-bit NE file. Sections contain either code or data. Some sections contain code or data that your program declared and uses directly, while other data sections are created for you by the linker and librarian, and contain information vital to the operating system. In some of Microsoft's descriptions of the PE format, sections are also referred to as *objects*. This term has so many possibly conflicting meanings, however, that I'll stick to calling the code and data areas *sections*. I'll discuss sections more thoroughly in the "Commonly Encountered Sections" part of this chapter; for now, it's just important for you to know what a section *is*.

Before jumping into the details of the PE file, examine Figure 8-1, which shows the overall layout of a PE file. I'll be explaining the pieces individually, but it's helpful to see them all together in one place.

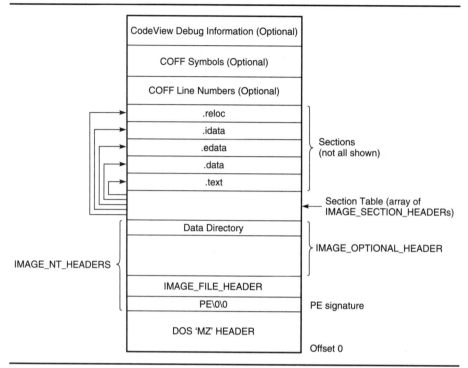

Figure 8-1
The overall layout of a PE file.

THE PE HEADER

The first stop on our tour of the PE format is the PE header. Like all other
Microsoft executable file formats, the PE file has a collection of fields at a
known (or easy-to-find) location that define what the rest of the file looks
like. The PE header contains vital pieces of information such as the location
and size of the code and data areas, what operating system the file is
intended to be used with, and the initial stack size.

As with other executable formats from Microsoft, the PE header isn't at
the very beginning of the file. Instead, the first few hundred bytes of the typical
PE file are taken up by the *DOS stub*. This stub is a minimal DOS program
that prints out something to the effect of "This program cannot be run in DOS
mode." The intent is that if you run a Win32 program in an environment that
doesn't support Win32, you'll get an informative (and frustrating) error message. When the Win32 loader memory maps a PE file, the first byte of the file
mapping corresponds to the first byte of the DOS stub. That's right. With every
Win32 program you start up, you get a complimentary DOS program loaded
for free! (In Win16, the DOS stub isn't loaded into memory.)

As in other Microsoft executable formats, you find the real header by looking up its starting offset, which is stored in the DOS header. The WINNT.H file includes a structure definition for the DOS stub header that makes it very easy to look up where the PE header starts. The e_lfanew field is a relative offset (or RVA, if you prefer) to the actual PE header. To get a pointer to the PE header in memory, just add the field's value to the image base:

```
// Ignoring typecasts and pointer conversion issues for clarity...
pNTHeader = dosHeader + dosHeader->e_lfanew;
```

Once you have a pointer to the main PE header, the real fun begins. The main PE header is a structure of type IMAGE_NT_HEADERS, defined in WINNT.H. The IMAGE_NT_HEADERS structure in memory is what Windows 95 uses as its in-memory module database. Each loaded EXE or DLL in Windows 95 is represented by an IMAGE_NT_HEADERS structure. This structure is composed of a DWORD and two substructures, and is laid out as follows:

```
DWORD Signature;
IMAGE_FILE_HEADER FileHeader;
IMAGE_OPTIONAL_HEADER OptionalHeader;
```

The Signature field viewed as ASCII text is PE\0\0 (PE followed by two 0 bytes). If the e_lfanew field in the DOS header pointed to an NE signature at this location instead of a PE signature, you'd be working with a Win16 NE file. Likewise, an LE in the signature field would indicate a Virtual Device Driver (VxD) file. An LX here would be the mark of a file for Windows 95's arch rival, OS/2.

Following the PE signature DWORD in the PE header is a structure of type IMAGE_FILE_HEADER. The fields of this structure contain only the most basic information about the file. The structure appears to be unmodified from its original COFF implementations. Besides being part of the PE header, it also appears at the very beginning of the COFF OBJs produced by the Microsoft Win32 compilers. The fields of the IMAGE_FILE_HEADER follow.

WORD   *Machine*
The CPU that this file is intended for. The following CPU IDs are defined:

Intel I386	0x14C
Intel i860	0x14D
MIPS R3000	0x162

MIPS R4000	0x166
DEC Alpha AXP	0x184
Power PC	0x1F0 (little endian)
Motorola 68000	0x268
PA RISC	0x290 (Precision Architecture)

WORD   NumberOfSections
The number of sections in the EXE or OBJ.

DWORD   TimeDateStamp
The time that the linker (or compiler for an OBJ file) produced this file. This field holds the number of seconds since December 31, 1969, at 4:00 P.M.

DWORD   PointerToSymbolTable
The file offset of the COFF symbol table. This field is used only in OBJ files and PE files with COFF debug information. PE files support multiple debug formats, so debuggers should refer to the IMAGE_DIRECTORY_ENTRY_DEBUG entry in the data directory (defined later).

DWORD   NumberOfSymbols
The number of symbols in the COFF symbol table. See the preceding field.

WORD   SizeOfOptionalHeader
The size of an optional header that can follow this structure. In executables, it is the size of the IMAGE_OPTIONAL_HEADER structure that follows this structure. In OBJs, Microsoft says this field is supposed to always be 0. However, in dumping out the KERNEL32.LIB import library, there's an OBJ in there with a nonzero value in this field, so take their advice with a grain of salt.

WORD   Characteristics
Flags with information about the file. Some important fields are described here (other fields are defined in WINNT.H):

0x0001	There are no relocations in this file.
0x0002	File is an executable image (that is, not a OBJ or LIB).
0x2000	File is a dynamic link library, not a program.

The third component of the PE header is a structure of type IMAGE_ OPTIONAL_HEADER. For PE files, this portion certainly isn't optional. The COFF format allows individual implementations to define a structure of additional information beyond the standard IMAGE_FILE_HEADER. The fields in the IMAGE_OPTIONAL_HEADER are what the PE designers felt was critical information beyond the basic information in the IMAGE_FILE_HEADER.

All the fields of the IMAGE_OPTIONAL_HEADERS aren't necessarily critical for you to know. The more important ones are the ImageBase and the Subsystem fields. If you want, you can skim over or skip the following description of the fields.

WORD   Magic

A signature WORD that identifies the state of the image file. The following values are defined:

0x0107   A ROM image.

0x010B   A normal executable image. (Most files contain this value.)

BYTE   MajorLinkerVersion
BYTE   MinorLinkerVersion

The version of the linker that produced this file. The numbers should be displayed as decimal values, rather than as hex. A typical linker version is 2.23.

DWORD   SizeOfCode

The combined and rounded-up size of all the code sections. Usually, most files have only one code section, so this field typically matches the size of the .text section.

DWORD   SizeOfInitializedData

This is supposedly the total size of all the sections that are composed of initialized data (not including code segments.) However, it doesn't seem to be consistent with the size of the initialized data sections in the file.

DWORD   SizeOfUninitializedData

The size of the sections that the loader commits space for in the virtual address space, but that don't take up any space in the disk file. These sections don't need to have specific values at program startup, hence the term *uninitialized data*. Uninitialized data usually goes into a section called .bss.

DWORD   *AddressOfEntryPoint*

The address where the image begins execution. This is an RVA, and usually can be found in the .text section. This field is valid for both EXEs and DLLs.

DWORD   *BaseOfCode*

The RVA where the file's code sections begin. The code sections typically come before the data sections, and after the PE header in memory. This RVA is usually 0x1000 in Microsoft Link produced EXEs. Borland's TLINK32 typically has a value of 0x10000 in this field because it defaults to aligning objects on 64K boundaries, rather than 4K like the Microsoft linker.

DWORD   *BaseOfData*

The RVA where the file's data sections begin. The data sections typically come last in memory, after the PE header and the code sections.

DWORD   *ImageBase*

When the linker creates an executable, it assumes that the file will be memory mapped to a specific location in memory. That address is stored in this field. Assuming a load address allows linker optimizations to take place. If the file really is memory mapped to that address by the loader, the code doesn't need any patching before it can be run. I'll talk more about this in the discussion of the base relocations. In NT 3.1 executables, the default image base was 0x10000. For DLLs, the default was 0x400000. In Windows 95, the address 0x10000 can't be used to load 32-bit EXEs because it lies within a linear address region that's shared by all processes. Therefore, in Windows NT 3.5, Microsoft changed the default base address for Win32 Executables to 0x400000. Older programs that were linked assuming a base address of 0x10000 will take longer to load under Windows 95 because the loader needs to apply the base relocations. I'll describe base relocations in detail later.

DWORD   *SectionAlignment*

When mapped into memory, each section is guaranteed to start at a virtual address that's a multiple of this value. For paging reasons, the minimum section alignment is 0x1000, which is what the Microsoft linker uses by default. Borland C++'s TLINK defaults to 0x10000 (64KB).

DWORD   *FileAlignment*

In the PE file, the raw data that comprises each section is guaranteed to start at a multiple of this value. The default value is 0x200 bytes, probably to ensure that sections always start at the beginning of a disk sector (which are also 0x200 bytes in length). This field is equivalent to the segment/resource alignment size in NE files. Unlike NE files, PE files typically don't have hundreds of sections, so the space wasted by aligning the file sections is usually very small.

WORD *MajorOperatingSystemVersion*
WORD *MinorOperatingSystemVersion*
The minimum version of the operating system required to use this executable.
This field is somewhat ambiguous since the subsystem fields (a few fields later)
appear to serve a similar purpose. In most Win32 files to date, this field contains
version 1.0.

WORD *MajorImageVersion*
WORD *MinorImageVersion*
A user-definable field. This field allows you to have different versions of an EXE
or a DLL. You set these fields with the linker /VERSION switch, for example:

   LINK /VERSION:2.0 myobj.obj

WORD *MajorSubsystemVersion*
WORD *MinorSubsystemVersion*
Contains the minimum subsystem version required to run the executable. A
typical value for this field is 4.0 (meaning Windows 4.0, a.k.a. Windows 95).

DWORD *Reserved1*
Seems to always be 0.

DWORD *SizeOfImage*
This appears to be the total size of the portions of the image that the loader
has to worry about. It is the size of the region starting at the image base, up
through the end of the last section. The end of the last section is rounded up
to the nearest multiple of the section alignment.

DWORD *SizeOfHeaders*
The size of the PE header and the section (object) table. The raw data for
the sections starts immediately after all the header components.

DWORD *CheckSum*
Supposedly a CRC checksum of the file. As with other Microsoft executable
formats, this field is usually ignored and set to 0. However, all driver DLLs,
DLLs loaded at boot time, and server DLLs must have a valid checksum.
The checksum algorithm can be found in IMAGEHLP.DLL. The sources for
IMAGEHLP.DLL are distributed in the WIN32 SDK.

WORD   Subsystem

The type of subsystem that this executable uses for its user interface. WINNT.H defines the following values:

NATIVE = 1	Doesn't require a subsystem (for example, a device driver)
WINDOWS_GUI = 2	Runs in the Windows GUI subsystem
WINDOWS_CUI = 3	Runs in the Windows character subsystem (a console application)
OS2_CUI = 5	Runs in the OS/2 character subsystem (OS/2 1.*x* applications only)
POSIX_CUI = 7	Runs in the Posix character subsystem

WORD   DllCharacteristics (marked as obsolete in NT 3.5)

A set of flags indicating which circumstances a DLL's initialization function (for example, DllMain()) will be called for. This value appears to always be set to 0, yet the operating system still calls the DLL initialization function for all four events.

The following values are defined:

1 — Call when DLL is first loaded into a process's address space.

2 — Call when a thread terminates.

4 — Call when a thread starts up.

8 — Call when DLL exits.

DWORD   SizeOfStackReserve

The amount of virtual memory to reserve for the initial thread's stack. Not all of this memory is committed, however (see the next field). This field defaults to 0x100000 (1MB). If you specify 0 as the stack size to CreateThread(), the resulting thread will also have a stack of this same size.

DWORD   SizeOfStackCommit

The amount of memory that's initially committed for the initial thread's stack. This field defaults to 0x1000 bytes (1 page) in Microsoft Linkers, while TLINK32 sets it to 0x2000 bytes (2 pages).

DWORD   SizeOfHeapReserve

The amount of virtual memory to reserve for the initial process heap. This heap's handle can be obtained by calling GetProcessHeap(). Not all of this memory is committed (see the next field).

DWORD   SizeOfHeapCommit

The amount of memory initially committed in the process heap. The linker defaults to putting 0x1000 bytes in this field.

DWORD   LoaderFlags (marked as obsolete in NT 3.5)

From WINNT.H, these appear to be fields related to debugging support. I've never seen an executable with either of these bits enabled, nor is it clear how to get the linker to set them. The following values are defined:

1 — Invoke a breakpoint instruction before starting the process?

2 — Invoke a debugger on the process after it's been loaded?

DWORD   NumberOfRvaAndSizes

The number of entries in the DataDirectory array (see the following field description). This value is always set to 16 by the current tools.

IMAGE_DATA_DIRECTORY DataDirectory[IMAGE_NUMBEROF_DIRECTORY_ENTRIES]

An array of IMAGE_DATA_DIRECTORY structures. The initial array elements contain the starting RVA and sizes of important portions of the executable file. Some elements at the end of the array are currently unused. The first element of the array is always the address and size of the exported function table (if present). The second array entry is the address and size of the imported function table, and so on. For a complete list of defined array entries, see the IMAGE_DIRECTORY_ENTRY_xxx #define's in WINNT.H.

The intent of this array is to allow the loader to quickly find a particular section of the image (for example, the imported function table), without needing to iterate through each of the image's sections, comparing names as it goes along.

Most array entries describe an entire section's data. However, the IMAGE_DIRECTORY_ENTRY_DEBUG element encompasses only a small portion of the bytes in the .rdata section. There's more information on this in "The .rdata section" portion of this chapter.

THE SECTION TABLE

Between the PE header and the raw data for the image's sections lies the section table. The section table contains information about each section in the image. The sections in the image are sorted by their starting address rather than alphabetically.

At this point, it would be worthwhile to clarify what a section is. In an NE file, your program's code and data are stored in distinct *segments* in the file. Part of an NE header is an array of structures, one for each segment your program uses. Each structure in the array contains information about one segment. The stored information includes the segment's type (code or data), its size, and its location elsewhere in the file. In a PE file, the section table is analogous to the segment table in the NE file.

Unlike an NE file segment table though, a PE section table doesn't store a selector value for each code or data chunk. Instead, each section table entry stores an address where the file's raw data has been mapped into memory. Although sections are analogous to 32-bit segments, they really aren't individual segments. Instead, a section simply corresponds to a memory range in a process's virtual address space.

Another way in which PE files diverge from NE files is how they manage the supporting data that your program doesn't use, but that the operating system does. Two examples are the list of DLLs that the executable uses and the location of the fixup table. In an NE file, resources aren't considered to be segments. Even though they have selectors assigned to them, information about resources isn't stored in the NE header's segment table. Instead, resources are relegated to a separate table toward the end of the NE header. Information about imported and exported functions also doesn't warrant its own segment, but is instead crammed into the confines of the NE header.

The story with PE files is different. Anything that might be considered vital code or data is stored in a full-fledged section. Thus, information about imported functions is stored in its own section, as is the table of functions that the module exports. The same is true for the relocation data. Any code or data that might be needed by either the program or the operating system gets its own section.

I'll discuss specific sections in just a bit, but first I need to describe the data that the operating system manages the sections with. Immediately following the PE header in memory is an array of IMAGE_SECTION_HEADERs. The number of elements in this array is given in the PE header (the IMAGE_NT_ HEADER.FileHeader.NumberOfSections field). The PEDUMP program outputs the section table and all of the section's fields and attributes. Figure 8-2 shows the PEDUMP output of a section table for a typical EXE file. Figure 8-3 shows the output of a section table in an OBJ file.

```
01 .text   VirtSize: 00005AFA VirtAddr:  00001000
   raw data offs:   00000400  raw data size: 00005C00
   relocation offs: 00000000  relocations:   00000000
   line # offs:     00009220  line #'s:      0000020C
   characteristics: 60000020
     CODE  MEM_EXECUTE  MEM_READ

02 .bss     VirtSize: 00001438  VirtAddr:  00007000
   raw data offs:   00000000  raw data size: 00001600
   relocation offs: 00000000  relocations:   00000000
   line # offs:     00000000  line #'s:      00000000
   characteristics: C0000080
     UNINITIALIZED_DATA  MEM_READ  MEM_WRITE

03 .rdata   VirtSize: 0000015C  VirtAddr:  00009000
   raw data offs:   00006000  raw data size: 00000200
   relocation offs: 00000000  relocations:   00000000
   line # offs:     00000000  line #'s:      00000000
   characteristics: 40000040
     INITIALIZED_DATA  MEM_READ

04 .data    VirtSize: 0000239C  VirtAddr:  0000A000
   raw data offs:   00006200  raw data size: 00002400
   relocation offs: 00000000  relocations:   00000000
   line # offs:     00000000  line #'s:      00000000
   characteristics: C0000040
     INITIALIZED_DATA  MEM_READ  MEM_WRITE

05 .idata   VirtSize: 0000033E  VirtAddr:  0000D000
   raw data offs:   00008600  raw data size: 00000400
   relocation offs: 00000000  relocations:   00000000
   line # offs:     00000000  line #'s:      00000000
   characteristics: C0000040
     INITIALIZED_DATA  MEM_READ  MEM_WRITE

06 .reloc   VirtSize: 000006CE  VirtAddr:  0000E000
   raw data offs:   00008A00  raw data size: 00000800
   relocation offs: 00000000  relocations:   00000000
   line # offs:     00000000  line #'s:      00000000
   characteristics: 42000040

     INITIALIZED_DATA  MEM_DISCARDABLE  MEM_READ
```

Figure 8-2
A typical section table from an EXE file.

```
01 .drectve  PhysAddr: 00000000  VirtAddr:  00000000
   raw data offs:    000000DC  raw data size: 00000026
   relocation offs: 00000000  relocations:   00000000
   line # offs:      00000000  line #'s:      00000000
   characteristics: 00100A00
     LNK_INFO  LNK_REMOVE

02 .debug$S  PhysAddr: 00000026  VirtAddr:  00000000
   raw data offs:    00000102  raw data size: 000016D0
   relocation offs: 000017D2  relocations:   00000032
   line # offs:      00000000  line #'s:      00000000
   characteristics: 42100048
     INITIALIZED_DATA  MEM_DISCARDABLE  MEM_READ

03 .data     PhysAddr: 000016F6  VirtAddr:  00000000
   raw data offs:    000019C6  raw data size: 00000D87
   relocation offs: 0000274D  relocations:   00000045
   line # offs:      00000000  line #'s:      00000000
   characteristics: C0400040
     INITIALIZED_DATA  MEM_READ  MEM_WRITE

04 .text     PhysAddr: 0000247D  VirtAddr:  00000000
   raw data offs:    000029FF  raw data size: 000010DA
   relocation offs: 00003AD9  relocations:   000000E9
   line # offs:      000043F3  line #'s:      000000D9
   characteristics: 60500020
     CODE  MEM_EXECUTE  MEM_READ

05 .debug$T  PhysAddr: 00003557  VirtAddr:  00000000
   raw data offs:    00004909  raw data size: 00000030
   relocation offs: 00000000  relocations:   00000000
   line # offs:      00000000  line #'s:      00000000
   characteristics: 42100048

     INITIALIZED_DATA  MEM_DISCARDABLE  MEM_READ
```

Figure 8-3
A typical section table from an OBJ file.

Each IMAGE_SECTION_HEADER is a complete database of information about one section in the EXE or OBJ file, and has the following format:

BYTE   *Name[IMAGE_SIZEOF_SHORT_NAME]*
This is an 8-byte ANSI name (not Unicode) that names the section. Most section names start with a . (a period; for example, .text), but this is *not* a

requirement, in spite of what some PE documentation would have you believe. You can name your own sections with either the segment directive in assembly language, or with #pragma data_seg and #pragma code_seg in the Microsoft C/C++ compiler. (Borland C++ users should use #pragma codeseg.) It's important to note that if the section name takes up the full 8 bytes, there is no NULL terminator byte. (TDUMP from Borland C++ 4.0*x* overlooked this fact, and would spew forth garbage on certain PE EXEs.) If you're a printf() devotee, you can use "%.8s" to avoid having to copy the name string to another buffer to null terminate it.

union {
DWORD   PhysicalAddress
DWORD   VirtualSize
} Misc;

This field has different meanings, depending on whether it occurs in an EXE or an OBJ. In an EXE, it holds the virtual size of the code or data section. This is the size before rounding up to the nearest file-alignment multiple. The SizeOfRawData field later on in the structure holds this rounded-up value. Interestingly, Borland's TLINK32 reverses the meaning of this field and the SizeOfRawData field, and appears to be the correct linker. For OBJ files, this field indicates the physical address of the section. The first section starts at address 0. To find the physical address of the next section, add the SizeOfRawData value to the physical address of the current section.

DWORD   VirtualAddress

In EXEs, this field holds the RVA for where the loader should map the section to. To calculate the real starting address of a given section in memory, add the base address of the image to the section's VirtualAddress stored in this field. With Microsoft tools, the first section defaults to an RVA of 0x1000. In OBJs, this field is meaningless and is set to 0.

DWORD   SizeOfRawData

In EXEs, this field contains the size of the section after it's been rounded up to the file-alignment size. For example, assume a file-alignment size of 0x200. If the VirtualSize field says that the section is 0x35A bytes in length, this field will say that the section is 0x400 bytes long. In OBJs, this field contains the exact size of the section emitted by the compiler or assembler. In other words, for OBJs, it's equivalent to the VirtualSize field in EXEs.

DWORD   *PointerToRawData*

This is the file-based offset to where the raw data for the section can be found. If you memory map a PE or COFF file yourself (rather than letting the operating system load it), this field is more important than the VirtualAddress field. That's because in this situation you'll have a completely linear mapping of the entire file, so you'll find the data for the sections at this offset rather than at the RVA specified in the VirtualAddress field.

DWORD   *PointerToRelocations*

In OBJs, this is the file-based offset to the relocation information for this section. The relocation information for each OBJ section immediately follows the raw data for that section. In EXEs, this field (and the subsequent field) are meaningless, and are set to 0. When the linker creates the EXE, it resolves most of the fixups, leaving only base address relocations and imported functions to be resolved at load time. The information about base relocations and imported functions is kept in the base relocation and imported functions sections, so there's no need for an EXE to have per-section relocation data following the raw section data.

DWORD   *PointerToLinenumbers*

The file-based offset of the line number table. A line number table correlates source-file line numbers to the addresses where the code generated for a given line can be found. In modern debug formats like the CodeView format, line number information is stored as part of the debug information. In the COFF debug format, however, the line number information is conceptually distinct from the symbolic name/type information. Usually, only code sections (for example, .text or CODE) have line numbers. In EXE files, the line numbers are collected toward the end of the file, after the raw data for the sections. In OBJ files, the line number table for a section comes after the raw section data and the relocation table for that section. I'll discuss the format of line number tables in "The COFF Debug Information" section later in the chapter.

WORD   *NumberOfRelocations*

The number of relocations in the relocation table for this section (the PointerToRelocations field listed previously). This field appears to be used only in OBJ files.

WORD   *NumberOfLinenumbers*

The number of line numbers in the line number table for this section (the PointerToLinenumbers field listed previously).

DWORD   Characteristics

What most programmers call *flags*, the COFF/PE format refers to as *characteristics*. This field is a set of flags that indicate the section's attributes (code/data, readable, writeable, and so on). For a complete list of all possible section attributes, see the IMAGE_SCN_XXX_XXX #defines in WINNT.H. Some of the more important flags are listed in Table 8-1:

Table 8-1

COFF section flags

Flag	Usage
0x00000020	This section contains code. It is usually set in conjunction with the executable flag (0x80000000).
0x00000040	This section contains initialized data. Almost all sections except executable and the .bss section have this flag set.
0x00000080	This section contains uninitialized data (for example, the .bss section).
0x00000200	This section contains comments or some other type of information. A typical use of this section is the .drectve section emitted by the compiler, which contains commands for the linker.
0x00000800	This section's contents shouldn't be put in the final EXE file. This section is used by the compiler/assembler to pass information to the linker.
0x02000000	This section can be discarded, since it's not needed by the process once it's been loaded. The most common discardable section is the base relocations section (.reloc).
0x10000000	This section is shareable. When used with a DLL, the data in this section is shared among all processes using the DLL. The default is for data sections to be nonshared, meaning that each process using a DLL gets its own separate copy of this section's data.
	In more technical terms, a shared section tells the memory manager to set the page mappings for this section so that all processes using the DLL refer to the same physical page in memory. To make a section shareable, use the SHARED attribute at link time. For example: LINK /SECTION:MYDATA,RWS ... tells the linker that the section called MYDATA should be readable, writeable, and shared. By default, Borland C++ DLL data segments have the shared attribute.
0x20000000	This section is executable. This flag is usually set whenever the Contains Code flag (0x00000020) is set.
0x40000000	This section is readable. This flag is almost always set for sections in EXE files.
0x80000000	The section is writeable. If this flag isn't set in an EXE's section, the loader should mark the memory mapped pages as read-only or execute-only. Typical sections with this attribute are .data and .bss.

It's interesting to note what's missing from the information stored for each section. First, notice there's no indication of any PRELOAD attributes. The NE file format lets you specify a PRELOAD attribute for segments that should be loaded immediately at module load time. The OS/2 2.0 LX format has something similar, allowing you to specify that up to 8 pages should be preloaded. The PE format, on the other hand, has nothing like this. Based on this, we have to assume that Microsoft is confident in the performance of the demand-paged loading of their Win32 implementations.

Also missing from the PE format is an intermediate page lookup table. The equivalent of an IMAGE_SECTION_HEADER in the OS/2 LX format doesn't point directly to where the code or data for a section can be found in the file. Instead, an OS/2 LX file contains a page lookup table that specifies attributes and the location in the file of specific ranges of pages within a section. The PE format dispenses with all that and guarantees that a section's data will be stored contiguously in the file. Of the two formats, the LX method may allow more flexibility, but the PE style is significantly simpler and easier to work with. Having written file dumpers and disassemblers for both formats, I can personally vouch for this!

Another welcome change in the PE format from the older NE format is that the locations of items are stored as simple DWORD offsets. In the NE format, the location of almost everything was stored as a sector value. To find the real file offset, you need to first look up the alignment unit size in the NE header, and convert it to a sector size (typically, 16 or 512 bytes). You then need to multiply the sector size by the specified sector offset to get an actual file offset. If by chance something isn't stored as a sector offset in an NE file, it's probably stored as an offset relative to the NE header. Since the NE header isn't at the beginning of the file, you need to drag around the file offset of the NE header in your code. In contrast, PE files specify the location of various items by using simple offsets relative to where the file was memory mapped to. All in all, the PE format is much easier to work with than the NE, LX, or LE formats (assuming you can use memory mapped files).

COMMONLY ENCOUNTERED SECTIONS

Now that you've got an overall picture of what sections are and how they're located, you can learn more about the common sections you'll find in EXE and OBJ files. Although this list of sections is by no means complete, it does include the sections you encounter every day (even if you're not aware of it). The sections are presented in order of their importance and by how frequently they're likely to be encountered.

The .text section

The .text section is where all general-purpose code emitted by the compiler or assembler ends up. Since PE files run in 32-bit mode and aren't restricted to 16-bit segments, there's no reason to break up the code from separate source files into separate sections. Instead, the linker concatenates all the .text sections from the various OBJs into one big .text section in the EXE. If you use Borland C++ the compiler emits its code to a segment named CODE. Thus, PE files produced with Borland C++ have a section named CODE, rather than a .text section. See the section of this chapter called "The Borland CODE and .icode sections" for details.

I was surprised to find out that there was additional code in the .text section beyond what I created with the compiler or used from the runtime libraries. In a PE file, when you call a function in another module (for example, GetMessage() in USER32.DLL), the CALL instruction emitted by the compiler doesn't transfer control directly to the function in the DLL. Instead, the call instruction transfers control to a JMP DWORD PTR [XXXXXXXX] instruction that's also in the .text section. The JMP instruction jumps to an address stored in a DWORD in the .idata section. This .idata section DWORD contains the real address of the operating system function entry point, as shown in Figure 8-4.

After contemplating this for awhile, I came to understand why calls to DLLs are implemented this way. By funneling all calls to a given DLL function through one location, there's no longer any need for the loader to patch every instruction that calls a DLL. All the PE loader has to do is put the correct address of the target function into the DWORD in the .idata section. No CALL instructions need to be patched. This is markedly different from NE files, where each segment contains a list of fixups that need to be applied to the segment. If the segment calls a given DLL function 20 times, the loader must copy the function's address into that segment 20 times. The downside to the PE method is that you can't initialize a variable with the true address of a DLL function. For example, you'd think that something like:

```
FARPROC pfnGetMessage = GetMessage;
```

would put the address of GetMessage into the variable pfnGetMessage. In Win16, this works, but in Win32 it doesn't. In Win32, the variable pfnGetMessage ends up holding the address of the JMP DWORD PTR [XXXXXXXX] thunk in the .text section that I mentioned earlier. If you wanted to call through the function pointer, things would work as you'd expect. If you want to read the bytes at the beginning of GetMessage(), however, you're out of luck (unless you do additional work to follow the .idata "pointer" yourself). I'll come back to this topic later, in the "PE File Imports" section.

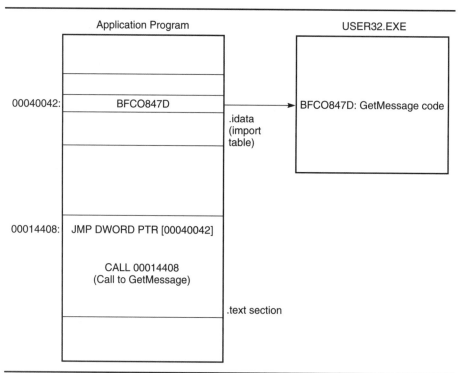

■ **Figure 8-4**
A PE file calling imported functions.

After I wrote the original version of this chapter, Visual C++ 2.0 was released; this version introduced a new twist to calling imported functions. If you look in the system header files from Visual C++ 2.0 (for example, WINBASE.H), you'll see a difference from the Visual C++ 1.0 headers. In Visual C++ 2.0, the operating system function prototypes in the system DLLs include a __declspec(dllimport) as part of their definition. The __declspec(dllimport) turns out to have quite a useful effect when calling imported functions. When you call an imported function prototyped with __declspec(dllimport), the compiler doesn't generate a call to a JMP DWORD PTR [XXXXXXXX] instruction elsewhere in the module. Instead, the compiler generates the function call as CALL DWORD PTR [XXXXXXXX].

The [XXXXXXXX] address is in the .idata section. It's the same address that would have been used had the old JMP DWORD PTR [XXXXXXXX] form been used. To my knowledge, up to and including version 4.5, Borland C++ doesn't have this feature.

The Borland CODE and .icode sections

The Borland C++ compiler and linker don't work with COFF format OBJs. Instead, Borland has chosen to stick with the 32-bit version of Intel OMF format. Although Borland could have had the compiler emit segments with a name of .text, it chose a default segment name of CODE. To determine a section name in the PE file, the Borland linker (TLINK32.EXE) takes the segment name from the OBJ file and truncates it to 8 characters (if necessary). Because of this, PE files with Borland C++ will have a CODE section, not a .text section.

The difference in the section names is a small matter, But there's a more important difference in how Borland PE files link to other modules. As I mentioned previously in the .text description, all calls to OBJs go through a JMP DWORD PTR [XXXXXXXX] thunk. Under the Microsoft system, this thunk comes to the EXE from the .text section of an import library. The library manager creates the import library (and the thunk) when you link the external DLL. As a result, the linker doesn't have to "know" to generate these thunks itself. The import library is really just some more code and data to link into the PE file.

The Borland system of dealing with imported functions is different, and is simply an extension of the way things were done for 16-bit NE files. The import libraries that the Borland linker uses are really just a list of function names and the DLL they're in. TLINK32 is therefore responsible for determining which fixups are to external DLLs, and for generating an appropriate JMP DWORD PTR [XXXXXXXX] thunk for it. In Borland C++ 4.0, TLINK32 stored the thunks it creates in a section named .icode. In Borland C++ 4.02, TLINK32 was changed to incorporate all the JMP DWORD PTR [XXXXXXXX] thunks into the CODE section.

The .data section

Just as .text is the default section for code, the .data section is where your initialized data goes. Initialized data consists of global and static variables that are initialized at compile time. It also includes string literals (for example, the string "Hello World" in a C/C++ program). The linker combines all the .data sections from the OBJ and LIB files into one .data section in the EXE. Local variables are located on a thread's stack and take no room in the .data or .bss sections.

The DATA section

Borland C++ uses the name DATA for its default data section. This is equivalent to the .data section for Microsoft's compiler (see the previous section, "The .data section").

The .bss section

The .bss section is where any uninitialized static and global variables are stored. The linker combines all the .bss sections in the OBJ and LIB files into one .bss section in the EXE. In the section table, the RawDataOffset field for the .bss section is set to 0, indicating that this section doesn't take up any space in the file. TLINK32 doesn't emit a .bss section. Instead, it extends the virtual size of the DATA section to account for uninitialized data.

The .CRT section

The .CRT section is another initialized data section used by the Microsoft C/C++ runtime libraries (hence the name .CRT). The data in this section is used for things such as calling the constructors of static C++ classes before main or WinMain is invoked.

The .rsrc section

The .rsrc section contains the resources for the module. In the early days of NT, the .RES file output of the 16-bit RC.EXE wasn't in a format that the Microsoft linker could understand. The CVTRES program converted these .RES files into a COFF format OBJ, placing the resource data into a .rsrc section within the OBJ. The linker could then treat the resource OBJ as just another OBJ to link in, which meant the linker didn't have to "know" anything special about resources. More recent linkers from Microsoft appear to be able to process the .RES files directly. I'll cover the format of the resource section in the "PE File Resources" section later in this chapter.

The .idata section

The .idata section contains information about functions (and data) that the module imports from other DLLs. This section is equivalent to an NE file's module reference table. A key difference is that each function that a PE file imports is specifically listed in this section. To find the equivalent information in an NE file, you'd have to go digging through the relocations at the end of the raw data for each of the segments. I'll cover the format of the imports table in detail in the "PE File Imports" section later in this chapter.

The .edata section

The .edata section is a list of the functions and data that the PE file exports for use by other modules. Its NE file equivalent is the combination of the entry table, the resident names table, and the nonresident names table. Unlike in Win16, there's seldom a reason to export anything from an EXE file, so you usually see only .edata sections in DLLs. The exception to this is EXEs produced by Borland C++, which always appear to export a function (__GetExceptDLLinfo) for internal use by the runtime library.

The format of the exports table is discussed in the "PE File Exports" section later in this chapter. When using Microsoft tools, the data in the .edata section comes to the PE file via the .EXP file. Put another way, the linker doesn't generate this information on its own. Instead, it relies on the library manager (LIB32) to scan the OBJ files and create the .EXP file that the linker adds to its list of modules to link. Yes, that's right! Those pesky .EXP files are really just OBJ files with a different extension. You can see the functions exported via an .EXP by using the PEDUMP program (presented later in this chapter) with the /S (show symbol table) option.

The .reloc section

The .reloc section holds a table of *base relocations*. A base relocation is an adjustment to an instruction or initialized variable value; an EXE or a DLL needs this adjustment if the loader couldn't load the file at the address where the linker assumed it would be. If the loader can load the image at the linker's preferred base address, the loader ignores the relocation information in this section.

If you want to take a chance and hope that the loader can always load the image at the assumed base address, you can use the /FIXED option to tell the linker to strip this information. Although this might save space in the executable file, it might also cause the executable to not work on other Win32 platforms. For example, let's say you built an EXE for NT and based the EXE at 0x10000. If you told the linker to strip the relocations, the EXE wouldn't run under Windows 95, where the address 0x10000 isn't available (the minimum load address in Windows 95 is 0x400000; that is, 4MB).

It's important to note that the JMP and CALL instructions generated by a compiler use offsets relative to the instructions, rather than actual offsets in the 32-bit flat segment. If the image needs to be loaded somewhere other than the location the linker assumed was a base address, these instructions don't need to change, since they use relative addressing. As a result, there are not as many relocations as you might think. Relocations are usually needed only for instructions that use a 32-bit offset to some data. For example, let's say you had the following global variable declarations:

```
int i;
int *ptr = &i;
```

If the linker assumed an image base of 0x10000, the address of the variable *i* will end up containing something like 0x12004. At the memory used to hold the pointer ptr, the linker will have written out 0x12004, since that's the address of the variable *i*. If the loader (for whatever reason) decided to load the file at a base address of 0x70000, the address of *i* would then be 0x72004. However, the pre-initialized value of the ptr variable would then be incorrect because *i* is now 0x60000 bytes higher in memory.

This is where the relocation information comes into play. The .reloc section is a list of places in the image where the difference between the linker-assumed load address and the actual load address needs to be taken into account. I'll talk more about relocations in the "PE File Base Relocations" section.

The .tls section

When you use the compiler directive "_ _declspec(thread)", the data that you define doesn't go into either the .data or .bss sections. Rather, a copy of it ends up in the .tls section. The .tls section derives its name from the term *thread local storage,* and is related to the TlsAlloc() family of functions.

To briefly summarize thread local storage, think of it as a way to have global variables on a per-thread basis. That is, each thread can have its set of static data values, yet the code that uses the data does so without regard to which thread is executing. Consider a program that has several threads working on the same task, and thereby executing through the same code. If you declared a thread local storage variable, for instance:

```
__declspec (thread) int i = 0;        // This is a global variable declaration.
```

each thread would transparently have its own copy of the variable *i*.

It's also possible to explicitly ask for and use thread local storage at run-time by using the TlsAlloc, TlsSetValue, and TlsGetValue functions. (Chapter 3 describes the TlsXXX functions in detail.) In most cases, it's much easier to declare your data in your program with __ declspec (thread) than it is to allocate memory on a per-thread basis and store a pointer to the memory in a TlsAlloc()'ed slot.

There's one unfortunate note that must be added about the .tls section and __ declspec(thread) variables. In NT and Windows 95, this thread local storage mechanism won't work in a DLL if the DLL is loaded dynamically by LoadLibrary(). In an EXE or an implicitly loaded DLL, everything works fine. If you can't implicitly link to the DLL, but need per-thread data, you'll have to fall back to using TlsAlloc() and TlsGetValue() with dynamically allocated memory. It's important to note that the actual per-thread memory blocks aren't stored in the .tls section at runtime. That is, when switching threads, the memory manager doesn't change the physical memory page that's mapped to the module's .tls section. Instead, the .tls section is merely the data used to initialize the actual per-thread data blocks. The initialization of per-thread data areas is a cooperative effort between the operating system and the compiler runtime libraries. This requires additional data — the TLS directory — that's stored in the .rdata section.

The .rdata section

The .rdata section is used for at least four things. First, in EXEs produced by Microsoft Link, the .rdata section holds the debug directory (there is no debug directory in OBJ files). In TLINK32 EXEs, the debug directory is in a section named .debug. The debug directory is an array of IMAGE_DEBUG_DIREC-TORY structures. These structures hold information about the type, size, and location of the various types of debug information stored in the file. Three main types of debug information can appear: CodeView, COFF, and FPO. Figure 8-5 shows the PEDUMP output for a typical debug directory.

Type	Size	Address	FilePtr	Charactr	TimeData	Version
COFF	000065C5	00000000	00009200	00000000	2CF8CF3D	0.00
(unknown)	00000114	00000000	0000F7C8	00000000	2CF8CF3D	0.00
FPO	000004B0	00000000	0000F8DC	00000000	2CF8CF3D	0.00
CODEVIEW	0000B0B4	00000000	0000FD8C	00000000	2CF8CF3D	0.00

Figure 8-5
A typical debug directory.

The debug directory isn't necessarily found at the beginning of the .rdata section. Instead, to find the start of the debug directory, you have to use the RVA found in the seventh entry (IMAGE_DIRECTORY_ENTRY_DEBUG) of the data directory. (The data directory is at the end of the PE header portion of the file.) To determine the number of entries in a Microsoft Link debug directory, divide the size of the debug directory (found in the size field of the data directory entry) by the size of an IMAGE_DEBUG_DIRECTORY structure. In contrast, TLINK32 emits an actual count of the debug directories in the size field, not the total length in bytes. The PEDUMP sample program handles either situation.

The second useful portion of an .rdata section is the description string. If you specified a DESCRIPTION entry in your program's .DEF file, the specified description string appears in the .rdata section. In the NE format, the description string is always the first entry of the nonresident names table. The description string is intended to hold a useful text string describing the file. Unfortunately, I haven't discovered an easy way to find it. I've seen PE files that had the description string before the debug directory, and other files that had it after the debug directory. I'm not aware of any consistent method of finding the description string (or even to determine if it's present at all).

A third use of the .rdata section is for GUIDs used in OLE programming. The UUID.LIB import library contains a collection of 16-byte GUIDs that are used for things such as interface IDs. These GUIDs end up in the EXE or DLL's .rdata section.

The final use of the .rdata section that I'm aware of is as a place to put the TLS (Thread Local Storage) directory. The TLS directory is a special data structure used by the compiler runtime library to transparently provide thread local storage for variables declared in program code. The format of the TLS directory is found on the MSDN (Microsoft Developer Network) CD-ROM under Specs: Portable Executable and Common Object File Format. Of primary interest in the TLS directory are pointers to the start and end of a copy of the data to be used to initialize each thread local storage block. An RVA for the TLS directory can be found in the IMAGE_DIRECTORY_ENTRY_TLS entry in the PE header's data directory. The actual data to be used for TLS block initialization is found in the .tls section (described earlier).

The .debug$S and .debug$T sections

The .debug$S and .debug$T sections appear only in COFF OBJs, and contain the CodeView symbol and type information. The section names are derived from the segment names used for this purpose by previous Microsoft compilers ($$SYMBOLS and $$TYPES). The sole purpose of the .debug$T section is to hold the pathname to the .PDB file that holds the CodeView type information for all the OBJs in the project. The linker uses the .PDB file to create certain portions of the CodeView information for the generated EXE file.

The .drective section

This section appears only in OBJ files. It contains textual representations of commands for the linker. For example, in any OBJ I compile with the Microsoft Visual C++ compiler, the following strings appear in the .drectve section:

```
-defaultlib:LIBC -defaultlib:OLDNAMES.
```

When you use _ _ declspec(export) in your code, the compiler simply emits the command-line equivalent into the .drectve section (for instance, export:MyFunction).

Sections containing $ (OBJs/LIBs only)

In OBJ files, sections with names containing $ (for example, .idata$2) are treated specially by the linker. The linker combines all sections that have the same name up to the $ character. The name of the finished section is everything up to the $ character. Thus, if the linker encountered two sections, .idata$2 and .idata$6, it would combine them into a section called .idata.

The ordering of sections to be combined is governed by the characters after the $. The linker sorts in lexical order, so .idata$2 will come before .idata$6. .data$A will likewise come before .data$B.

So what is this $ convention used for? The most prevalent use is by import libraries, which use .idata$x sections to hold various portions of a final .idata (import) section. This is rather interesting. The linker itself doesn't have to generate the .idata section from scratch. Rather, the final .idata section is built primarily from sections in OBJ and LIB files that the linker treats just like any other section to be linked in.

Miscellaneous sections

In playing around with PEDUMP, I've encountered other sections from time to time. For instance, the Windows 95 GDI32.DLL contains a data section named _GPFIX, which presumably has something to do with GP fault handling.

The points to be drawn from this are twofold. First, don't feel constrained to use only the standard sections provided by the compiler or assembler. If you need a separate section, don't hesitate to use one. In the Microsoft C/C++ compiler, use the #pragma code_seg and #pragma data_seg. Borland users can use #pragma codeseg and #pragma dataseg. In assembly language, just create a 32-bit segment with a name that is different from the standard sections. TLINK32 combines code segments of the same class, so you'll need to either give each of your code segments a unique class name or turn off code segment packing. The other thing to take away from this discussion is that unusual section names can often give a deeper insight into the purpose and implementation of a particular PE file.

PE File Imports

Earlier, I described how function calls to outside DLLs don't call the DLL directlyl. Instead, the CALL instruction goes to a JMP DWORD PTR [XXXXXXXX] instruction somewhere in the executable's .text section (or .icode section if you're using Borland C++ 4.0). Alternatively, if _ _ declspec(dllimport) was used in Visual C++, the function call becomes a "CALL DWORD PTR [XXXXXXXX]". In either case, the address that the JMP or CALL instruction looks up is stored in the .idata section. The JMP or CALL instruction transfers control to that address, which is the intended target address. If you're still unclear on this, refer back to Figure 8-4.

Before it's loaded into memory, the information stored in a PE file's .idata section contains the information necessary for the loader to determine the addresses of the target functions and patch them into the executable image. After the .idata section has been loaded, it contains pointers to the functions that the EXE/DLL imports. Note that all the arrays and structures I'm discussing in this section are contained in the .idata section.

The .idata section (or *import table,* as I prefer to call it) begins with an array of IMAGE_IMPORT_DESCRIPTOR's. There is one IMAGE_IMPORT_DESCRIPTOR for each DLL that the PE file implicitly links to. No count is kept to indicate the number of structures in this array. Instead, the last element of the array is indicated by a final IMAGE_IMPORT_DESCRIPTOR that has fields filled with NULLs. The format of an IMAGE_IMPORT_DESCRIPTOR is as follows:

DWORD   Characteristics/OriginalFirstThunk

This field is an offset (an RVA) to an array of DWORDs. Each of these DWORDs is actually an IMAGE_THUNK_DATA union. Each IMAGE_THUNK_DATA DWORD corresponds to one function imported by this EXE/DLL. I'll describe the format of an IMAGE_THUNK_DATA DWORD a bit later in this section. If you run the BIND utility, this array of DWORDS is left alone, whereas the FirstThunk DWORD array (described momentarily) is modified.

DWORD   TimeDateStamp

The time/date stamp indicating when the file was built. This field normally contains 0. However, the Microsoft BIND utility updates this field with the time/date stamp of the DLL that this IMAGE_IMPORT_DESCRIPTOR refers to.

DWORD   ForwarderChain

This field relates to forwarding, which involves one DLL forwarding references to one of its functions to another DLL. For example, in Windows NT, KERNEL32.DLL forwards some of its exported functions to NTDLL.DLL. An application may think it's calling a function in KERNEL32.DLL, but it actually ends up calling into NTDLL.DLL. This field contains an index into the FirstThunk array (described momentarily). The function indexed by this field will be forwarded to another DLL. Unfortunately, the format of how a function is forwarded is just barely described in the Microsoft documentation. For more information on forwarding, see the "Export forwarding" section presented later in this chapter.

DWORD   Name

This is an RVA to a null-terminated ASCII string containing the imported DLL's name (for example, KERNEL32.DLL or USER32.DLL).

PIMAGE_THUNK_DATA FirstThunk;

This field is an offset (an RVA) to an array of IMAGE_THUNK_DATA DWORDs. In most cases, the DWORD is interpreted as a pointer to an IMAGE_IMPORT_BY_NAME structure. However, it's also possible to import a function by ordinal value.

The important parts of an IMAGE_IMPORT_DESCRIPTOR are the imported DLL name and the two arrays of IMAGE_THUNK_DATA DWORDs. Each IMAGE_THUNK_DATA DWORD corresponds to one imported function. In the EXE file, the two arrays (pointed to by the Characteristics and FirstThunk fields) run parallel to each other, and are terminated by a NULL pointer entry at the end of each array.

Why are there two parallel arrays of pointers to the IMAGE_THUNK_DATA structures? The first array (the one pointed to by the Characteristics field) is left alone and is never modified. It's sometimes called the *hint-name table*. The second array (pointed to by the FirstThunk field in the IMAGE_IMPORT_DESCRIPTOR) is overwritten by the PE loader. The loader iterates through each IMAGE_THUNK_DATA and finds the address of the function that it refers to. The loader then overwrites the IMAGE_THUNK_DATA DWORD with the address of the imported function.

Earlier, I mentioned that CALLs to DLL functions go through a "JMP DWORD PTR [XXXXXXXX]" thunk. The [XXXXXXXX] portion of the thunk refers to one of the entries in the FirstThunk array. Since the array of IMAGE_THUNK_DATAs that's overwritten by the loader eventually holds the addresses of all the imported functions, it's called the "Import Address Table." Figure 8-6 shows these two arrays.

For you Borland users, there's a slight twist to this description. A PE file produced by TLINK32 is missing one of the arrays. In such an executable, the Characteristics field in the IMAGE_IMPORT_DESCRIPTOR (a.k.a. the hint-name array) is 0 (apparently the Win32 loaders don't need this array). Therefore, only the array pointed to by the FirstThunk field (the Import Address Table) is guaranteed to exist in all PE files.

The story would end here, except that I ran into an interesting problem when writing PEDUMP. In the never-ending search for optimizations, Microsoft "optimized" the IMAGE_THUNK_DATA arrays in the Windows NT system DLLs (for example, KERNEL32.DLL). In this optimization, the IMAGE_THUNK_DATAs don't contain the information to find the imported function.

Instead, the IMAGE_THUNK_DATA DWORDs already contain the addresses of the imported function. In other words, the loader doesn't need to look up function addresses and overwrite the thunk array with the imported function's addresses. The array already contains the imported function's addresses even before it was loaded. (The BIND utility program from the Win32 SDK performs this optimization.) Unfortunately, this causes a problem for PE dumping programs that are expecting the array to contain RVAs to IMAGE_THUNK_DATAs. You might be thinking, "But Matt, why don't you just use the hint-name table array?" That would be an ideal solution, except that the hint-name table array doesn't exist in Borland files. The PEDUMP program handles both of these situations, but the code is understandably messy.

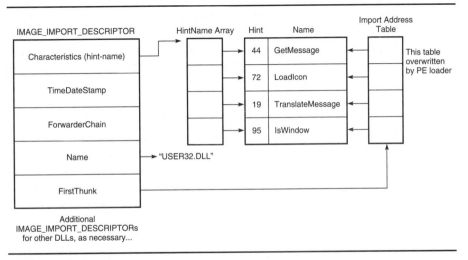

Figure 8-6
How a PE file imports functions.

Since the import address table is usually in a writeable section, it's relatively easy to intercept calls that an EXE or a DLL makes to another DLL. You simply patch the appropriate import address table entry to point to the desired interception function. There's no need to modify any code in either the caller or callee images. This capability can be very useful. In fact, in Chapter 10, I build a Win32 API spy program that relies heavily on this trick.

It's interesting to note that in Microsoft-produced PE files, the import table isn't wholly synthesized by the linker. Instead, all the pieces necessary to call a function in another DLL reside in an import library. When you link a DLL, the library manager (LIB.EXE) scans the OBJ files being linked and creates an import library. This import library is different from the import libraries used by 16-bit NE file linkers. The import library that the 32-bit LIB produces has a .text section and several .idata$ sections. The .text section in the import library contains the JMP DWORD PTR [XXXXXXXX] thunk that I mentioned earlier. That thunk has a name stored for it in the OBJ's symbol table. The name of the symbol is identical to the name of the function being exported by the DLL (for example, _DispatchMessage@4).

One of the .idata$ sections in the import library contains the DWORD that the thunk dereferences through. Another of the .idata$ sections has a space for the "hint ordinal" followed by the imported function's name. These two fields make up an IMAGE_IMPORT_BY_NAME structure. When you later link a PE file that uses the import library, the import library's sections are added to the list of sections from your OBJs that the linker needs to process. Since the thunk in the import library has the same name as the function being imported, the linker thinks the thunk is really the imported function, and fixes up calls to the imported function to point at the thunk. The thunk in the import library is essentially seen as the imported function.

Besides providing the code portion of an imported function thunk, the import library provides the pieces of the PE file's .idata section (or import table). These pieces come from the various .idata$ sections that librarian put into the import library. In short, the linker doesn't really know the differences between imported functions and functions that appear in a different OBJ file. The linker just follows its preset rules for building and combining sections, and everything falls into place naturally.

The IMAGE_THUNK_DATA DWORD

As I mentioned earlier, each IMAGE_THUNK_DATA DWORD corresponds to an imported function. The interpretation of the DWORD varies depending on whether the file has been loaded into memory yet and whether the function was imported by name or by ordinal (importing by name is much more common).

When a function is imported by its ordinal value (the rare case), the high bit (0x80000000) is set in the EXE file's IMAGE_THUNK_DATA DWORD. For example, consider an IMAGE_THUNK_DATA with the value 0x80000112 in the GDI32.DLL array. This IMAGE_THUNK_DATA is importing the 112'th exported function from GDI32.DLL. The problem with importing by ordinal is that Microsoft didn't bother to keep the export ordinals of the Win32 API functions consistent between Windows NT, Windows 95, and Win32s.

If a function is imported by name, its IMAGE_THUNK_DATA DWORD contains an RVA for an IMAGE_IMPORT_BY_NAME structure. An IMAGE_IMPORT_BY_NAME structure is very simple, and looks like this:

WORD   Hint
The best guess as to what the export ordinal for the imported function is. Unlike with NE files, this value doesn't have to be correct. Instead, the loader uses it as a suggested starting value for its binary search for the exported function.

BYTE[?]
An ASCIIZ string with the name of the imported function. The final interpretation of the IMAGE_THUNK_DATA DWORD is after the PE file has been loaded by the Win32 loader. The Win32 loader uses the initial information in the IMAGE_THUNK_DATA DWORD to look up the address of the imported function (either by name or by ordinal). The loader then overwrites the IMAGE_THUNK_DATA DWORD with the address of the imported function.

Putting IMAGE_IMPORT_DESCRIPTORs and IMAGE_THUNK_DATAs together

Now that you've seen both the IMAGE_IMPORT_DESCRIPTOR and IMAGE_THUNK_DATA structures, it's easy to construct a report on all the imported functions that an EXE or a DLL uses. Simply iterate through the array of IMAGE_IMPORT_DESCRIPTORs (each of which corresponds to one imported DLL). For each IMAGE_IMPORT_DESCRIPTOR, locate the array of IMAGE_THUNK_DATA DWORDs and interpret them appropriately. Figure 8-7 shows the PEDUMP output for this operation. (Functions with no name are imported by ordinal.)

```
Imports Table:
USER32.dll
Hint/Name Table: 0001F50C
TimeDateStamp:   2EB9CE9B
ForwarderChain:  FFFFFFFF
First thunk RVA: 0001FC24
Ordn  Name
 268  GetScrollInfo
```

```
  133   DispatchMessageA
  333   IsRectEmpty
  431   SendMessageCallbackA
  255   GetMessagePos
   //   Rest of table omitted...


GDI32.dll
Hint/Name Table: 0001F178
TimeDateStamp:    2EB9CE9B
ForwarderChain:   FFFFFFFF
First thunk RVA: 0001F890
Ordn  Name
   31   CreateCompatibleDC
  309   SetTextColor
  276   SetBkColor
   99   ExtTextOutA
    9   BitBlt
   //   Rest of table omitted...


MPR.dll
Hint/Name Table: 0001F2F0
TimeDateStamp:    2EAF4824
ForwarderChain:   FFFFFFFF
First thunk RVA: 0001FA08
Ordn  Name
   26
   35
   34
   33
   55
   //   Rest of table omitted...


KERNEL32.dll
Hint/Name Table: 0001F1CC
TimeDateStamp:    2EB9DA61
ForwarderChain:   FFFFFFFF
First thunk RVA: 0001F8E4
Ordn  Name
  636   SetEvent
  348   GetTimeFormatA
  375   GlobalGetAtomNameA
  301   GetProcAddress
  572   RtlZeroMemory
   //   Rest of table omitted...


COMCTL32.dll
Hint/Name Table: 0001F0DC
TimeDateStamp:    2EAD4AE5
```

```
ForwarderChain:  FFFFFFFF
First thunk RVA: 0001F7F4
Ordn  Name
 152
  21  ImageList_Draw
 354
 352
  28  ImageList_GetIconSize
  //  Rest of table omitted...

ADVAPI32.dll
Hint/Name Table: 0001F0A0
TimeDateStamp:   2EA8A148
ForwarderChain:  FFFFFFFF
First thunk RVA: 0001F7B8
Ordn  Name
 149  RegQueryValueA
 119  RegCloseKey
 142  RegOpenKeyExA
 131  RegEnumKeyExA
 126  RegDeleteKeyA
  //  Rest of table omitted...
```

Figure 8-7
A typical import table from an EXE file (EXPLORER.EXE).

PE FILE EXPORTS

The opposite of importing a function is exporting a function for use by
EXEs or other DLLs. A PE file stores information about its exported functions in the .edata section. Generally, Microsoft LINK-produced PE EXE
files don't export anything, so they don't have an .edata section. TLINK32
EXEs, on the other hand, usually export one symbol, so they do have an
.edata section. Most DLLs export functions and have an .edata section. The
primary components of an .edata section (a.k.a. the export table) are tables
of function names, entry point addresses, and export ordinal values. In an
NE file, the equivalents of an export table are the entry table, the resident
names table, and the nonresident names table. In the NE file, these tables
are stored as part of the NE header rather than in segments or resources.

At the beginning of an .edata section is an IMAGE_EXPORT_DIRECTORY structure. This structure is immediately followed by the data pointed to by fields in the IMAGE_EXPORT_DIRECTORY structure. An IMAGE_EXPORT_DIRECTORY looks like this:

DWORD   Characteristics
This field appears to be unused and is always set to 0.

DWORD   TimeDateStamp
The time/date stamp indicating when this file was created.

WORD   MajorVersion
WORD   MinorVersion
These fields appear to be unused and are set to 0.

DWORD   Name
The RVA of an ASCIIZ string with the name of this DLL (for example, MYDLL.DLL).

DWORD   Base
The starting export ordinal number for functions exported by this module. For example, if the file exported functions with ordinal values of 10, 11, and 12, this field would contain 10.

DWORD   NumberOfFunctions
The number of elements in the AddressOfFunctions array. This value is also the number of functions exported by this module. Usually this value is the same as the NumberOfNames field (see the next description), but they can be different.

DWORD   NumberOfNames
The number of elements in the AddressOfNames array. This value contains the number of functions exported by name, which usually (but not always) matches the total number of exported functions.

*PDWORD   *AddressOfFunctions*
This field is an RVA and points to an array of function addresses. The function addresses are the entry-point RVAs for each exported function in this module.

*PDWORD   *AddressOfNames*
This field is an RVA and points to an array of string pointers. The strings contain the names of the functions exported by name from this module.

*PWORD   *AddressOfNameOrdinals*

This field is an RVA, and points to an array of WORDs. The WORDs are essentially the export ordinals of all the functions exported by name from this module. However, don't forget to add the starting ordinal number specified in the Base field (described a few fields back).

The layout of the export table is somewhat odd. As I mentioned earlier, the requirements for exporting a function are an address and an export ordinal. Optionally, if you export the function by name, there will be a function name. You'd think that the designers of the PE format would have put all three of these items into a structure and then have an array of these structures. Instead, you have to look up the various pieces in three separate arrays.

The most important of the arrays pointed to by the IMAGE_EXPORT_ DIRECTORY is the array pointed to by the AddressOfFunctions field. This is an array of DWORDs, each DWORD containing the address (RVA) of an imported function. The export ordinal for each exported function corresponds to its position in the array. For instance (assuming ordinals start at 1), the address of the function with export ordinal 1 would have its address in the first element of the array. The function with export ordinal 2 would have its address in the second element of the array, and so on.

There are two important things to remember about the AddressOf-Functions array. First, the export ordinal needs to be biased by the value in the Base field of the IMAGE_EXPORT_DIRECTORY. If the Base field contains the value 10, then the first DWORD in the AddressOfFunctions array corresponds to export ordinal 10, the second entry to export ordinal 11, and so forth. The other thing to remember is that the export ordinals can have gaps. Let's say that you explicitly export two functions in a DLL, with ordinal values 1 and 3. Even though you exported only two functions, the AddressOfFunctions array has to contain three elements. Any entries in the array that don't correspond to an exported function contain the value 0.

When the Win32 loader fixes up a call to a function that's imported by ordinal, it has very little work to do. The loader simply uses the function's ordinal value as an index into the target module's AddressOfFunctions array. Of course, the loader also has to take into account that the lowest export ordinal may not be 1, and must adjust its indexing appropriately.

More often than not, Win32 EXEs and DLLs import functions by name rather than by ordinal. This is where the other two arrays pointed to in the IMAGE_EXPORT_DIRECTORY structure come into play. The AddressOfNames and AddressOfNameOrdinals arrays exist to allow the loader to quickly find the export ordinal corresponding to a given function name. The AddressOfNames and AddressOfNameOrdinals arrays both contain the same number of elements (given by the NumberOfNames field of the IMAGE_EXPORT_DIRECTORY). The AddressOfNames array is an array of pointers to function names, and the AddressOfNameOrdinals array is an array of indexes into the AddressOfFunctions array.

Let's see how the Win32 loader would fix up a call to a function that's imported by name. First, the loader would search the strings pointed to in the AddressOfNames array. Let's say it finds the string it's looking for in the third element. Next, the loader would use the index it found to look up the corresponding element in the AddressOfNameOrdinals array (in this case, the third element). This array is just a collection of WORDs, with each WORD acting as an index into the AddressOfFunctions array. The final step is to take the value in the AddressOfNameOrdinals array and use it as an index into the AddressOfFunctions array.

In C code, finding a function address that's imported by name would look something like this:

```
WORD nameIndex = FindIndexOfString( AddressOfNames, "GetMessageA" );
WORD functionIndex = AddressOfNameOrdinals[ nameIndex ];
DWORD functionAddress = AddressOfFunctions[ functionIndex - OrdinalBase ];
```

Figure 8-8 shows the format of the export section and its three arrays.

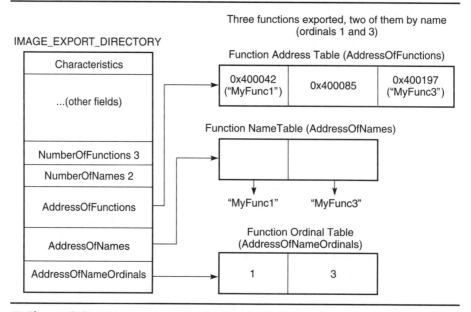

Figure 8-8
A typical exports table from an EXE file.

Figure 8-9 shows the PEDUMP output for the KERNEL32.DLL export section.

```
Name:            KERNEL32.dll
Characteristics: 00000000
TimeDateStamp:   2C4857D3
Version:         0.00
Ordinal base:    00000001
# of functions:  0000021F
# of Names:      0000021F

Entry Pt  Ordn  Name
00005090     1  AddAtomA
00005100     2  AddAtomW
00025540     3  AddConsoleAliasA
00025500     4  AddConsoleAliasW
00026AC0     5  AllocConsole
00001000     6  BackupRead
00001E90     7  BackupSeek
00002100     8  BackupWrite
0002520C     9  BaseAttachCompleteThunk
00024C50    10  BasepDebugDump
// Rest of table omitted...
```

Figure 8-9
The PEDUMP output for the KERNEL32.DLL export section.

Incidentally, if you dump out the exports from the system DLLs (for example, KERNEL32.DLL and USER32.DLL), you'll see that in many cases two functions differ only by one character at the end of the name, for instance, CreateWindowExA and CreateWindowExW. This is how Unicode support is implemented "transparently." The functions that end with *A* are the ASCII (or ANSI) compatible functions; those ending in *W* are the Unicode version of the function. In your code, you don't explicitly specify which function to call. Instead, the appropriate function is selected in WINDOWS.H with preprocessor #ifdefs. The following excerpt from the NT WINDOWS.H is an example of how this works:

```
#ifdef UNICODE
#define DefWindowProc   DefWindowProcW
#else
#define DefWindowProc   DefWindowProcA
#endif // !UNICODE
```

Export forwarding

Sometimes it can be useful for a DLL to export a function, but to have the actual code exist in another DLL. In this scenario, a DLL can forward a function to another DLL. When the Win32 loader encounters a call to a forwarded function, it resolves the fixup to the function to point at the function in the DLL containing the actual code.

An example will make this clearer. Consider the following excerpted PEDUMP output for the Windows NT 3.5 KERNEL32.DLL:

```
00043FC3   335   HeapAlloc (forwarder -> NTDLL.RtlAllocateHeap)
00044005   339   HeapFree (forwarder -> NTDLL.RtlFreeHeap)
0004402C   341   HeapReAlloc (forwarder -> NTDLL.RtlReAllocateHeap)
0004404D   342   HeapSize (forwarder -> NTDLL.RtlSizeHeap)
0004466F   442   RtlFillMemory (forwarder -> NTDLL.RtlFillMemory)
00044691   443   RtlMoveMemory (forwarder -> NTDLL.RtlMoveMemory)
000446AF   444   RtlUnwind (forwarder -> NTDLL.RtlUnwind)
000446CD   445   RtlZeroMemory (forwarder -> NTDLL.RtlZeroMemory)
```

Each function in this output is forwarded to a function in NTDLL. Thus, a program that calls HeapAlloc is really calling the RtlAllocateHeap function in NTDLL.DLL. Likewise, a call to HeapFree is really a call to NTDLL's RtlHeapFree function.

So how do you tell if a function is forwarded? The only indication that a function is forwarded is that the function's address falls within the export table (the .edata section). If this is the case, the so-called function address is really an RVA to a string containing the forwarded DLL and function name. For example, in the previous output, HeapAlloc's RVA is 0x43FC3. Offset 0x43FC3 in KERNEL32.DLL is inside the .edata section. At offset 0x43FC3 in KERNEL32.DLL is the string NTDLL.RtlAllocateHeap. The DumpExportsSection function in the PEDUMP program shows how forwarded functions can be identified.

Although export forwarding looks like a really nifty feature, Microsoft doesn't describe how you can use forwarding in your own DLLs. Also, to date, I've seen forwarding used by only one DLL (the aforementioned Windows NT KERNEL32.DLL). Even though I haven't seen any DLLs with forwarders in Windows 95, the Windows 95 loader does support this functionality, as I showed in Chapter 3.

PE FILE RESOURCES

Compared to their NE file equivalents, finding resources in a PE file is more complicated. The formats of the individual resources (for example, a menu) haven't changed significantly from their NE siblings, but you need to traverse a complex hierarchy to find them.

Navigating the resource directory hierarchy is like navigating on a hard disk. There's a master directory (the root directory) which has sub-directories. The subdirectories have subdirectories of their own. In those subdirectories you can find files. The files are analogous to the raw resource data containing things such as dialog templates. In the PE file, both the root directory and all its subdirectories are structures of type IMAGE_RESOURCE_ DIRECTORY. The IMAGE_RESOURCE_DIRECTORY structure has the following format:

DWORD   Characteristics
Theoretically, this field could hold flags for the resource, but it appears to always be 0.

DWORD   TimeDateStamp
The time/date stamp describing the creation time of the resource.

WORD   MajorVersion
WORD   MinorVersion
Theoretically, these fields would hold a version number for the resource. These field appear to always be set to 0.

WORD   NumberOfNamedEntries
The number of array elements (described later) that use names, and that follow this structure. See the description for the DirectoryEntries field for more information.

WORD   NumberOfIdEntries
The number of array elements that use integer IDs, and that follow this structure and any named entries. See the following description for the DirectoryEntries field for more information.

IMAGE_RESOURCE_DIRECTORY_ENTRY   DirectoryEntries[]
This field isn't formally part of the IMAGE_RESOURCE_DIRECTORY structure. Rather, it's an array of IMAGE_RESOURCE_DIRECTORY_ ENTRY structures that immediately follow it. The number of elements in the

array is the sum of the NumberOfNamedEntries and NumberOfIdEntries fields. The directory entry elements that have name identifiers (rather than integer IDs) come first in the array.

A directory entry can either point to a subdirectory (that is, to another IMAGE_RESOURCE_DIRECTORY) or to an IMAGE_RESOURCE_DATA_ENTRY, which describes where the resource's raw data can be found in the file. Generally, there are at least three directory levels before you get to the IMAGE_RESOURCE_DATA_ENTRY for a given resource. The top-level directory (of which there's only one) is always found at the beginning of the resource section (.rsrc). The subdirectories of the top-level directory correspond to the various types of resources found in the file. For example, if a PE file includes dialogs, string tables, and menus, these three subdirectories would be a dialog directory, a string table directory, and a menu directory. Each of these "type" subdirectories will in turn have "ID" subdirectories. There will be one ID subdirectory for each instance of a given resource type. In the above example, if there are four dialog boxes, the dialog directory will have four ID subdirectories. Each ID subdirectory will have either a string name (for example, MyDialog) or the integer ID used to identify the resource in the .RC file. Figure 8-10 shows the resource directory hierarchy in a more understandable visual form.

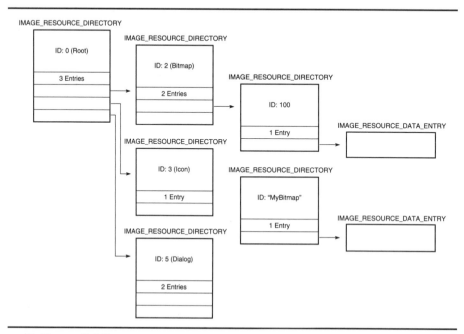

Figure 8-10

A typical PE file resource hierarchy.

Figure 8-11 shows the PEDUMP output for the resources in the Windows NT 3.5 CLOCK.EXE. Looking at the second level of indentation, you can see there are icons, menus, dialogs, stringtables, group icons, and version resources. On the third level, there are two icons (with IDs 1 and 2), two menus (with names CLOCK and GENERICMENU), two dialogs (one named ABOUTBOX, and the other with integer ID 0x64), and so forth. And at the fourth level of indentation, the data for icon 1 is at RVA 0x9754 and is 0x130 bytes long. Likewise, the data for the CLOCK menu is at offset 0x952C and takes up 0xEA bytes.

```
Resources
ResDir (0) Named:00 ID:06 TimeDate:2E601E3C Vers:0.00 Char:0
    ResDir (ICON) Named:00 ID:02 TimeDate:2E601E3C Vers:0.00 Char:0
        ResDir (1) Named:00 ID:01 TimeDate:2E601E3C Vers:0.00 Char:0
            ID: 00000409  DataEntryOffs: 000001E0
            Offset: 09754  Size: 00130  CodePage: 0
        ResDir (2) Named:00 ID:01 TimeDate:2E601E3C Vers:0.00 Char:0
            ID: 00000409  DataEntryOffs: 000001F0
            Offset: 09884  Size: 002E8  CodePage: 0
    ResDir (MENU) Named:02 ID:00 TimeDate:2E601E3C Vers:0.00 Char:0
        ResDir (CLOCK) Named:00 ID:01 TimeDate:2E601E3C Vers:0.00 Char:0
            ID: 00000409  DataEntryOffs: 00000200
            Offset: 0952C  Size: 000EA  CodePage: 0
        ResDir (GENERICMENU) Named:00 ID:01 TimeDate:2E601E3C Vers:0.00 Char:0
            ID: 00000409  DataEntryOffs: 00000210
            Offset: 09618  Size: 0003A  CodePage: 0
    ResDir (DIALOG) Named:01 ID:01 TimeDate:2E601E3C Vers:0.00 Char:0
        ResDir (ABOUTBOX) Named:00 ID:01 TimeDate:2E601E3C Vers:0.00 Char:0
            ID: 00000409  DataEntryOffs: 00000220
            Offset: 09654  Size: 000FE  CodePage: 0
        ResDir (64) Named:00 ID:01 TimeDate:2E601E3C Vers:0.00 Char:0
            ID: 00000409  DataEntryOffs: 00000230
            Offset: 092C0  Size: 0026A  CodePage: 0
    ResDir (STRING) Named:00 ID:02 TimeDate:2E601E3C Vers:0.00 Char:0
        ResDir (1) Named:00 ID:01 TimeDate:2E601E3C Vers:0.00 Char:0
            ID: 00000409  DataEntryOffs: 00000240
            Offset: 09EA8  Size: 000F2  CodePage: 0
        ResDir (2) Named:00 ID:01 TimeDate:2E601E3C Vers:0.00 Char:0
            ID: 00000409  DataEntryOffs: 00000250
            Offset: 09F9C  Size: 00046  CodePage: 0
    ResDir (GROUP_ICON) Named:01 ID:00 TimeDate:2E601E3C Vers:0.00 Char:0
        ResDir (CCKK) Named:00 ID:01 TimeDate:2E601E3C Vers:0.00 Char:0
            ID: 00000409  DataEntryOffs: 00000260
            Offset: 09B6C  Size: 00022  CodePage: 0
    ResDir (VERSION) Named:00 ID:01 TimeDate:2E601E3C Vers:0.00 Char:0
        ResDir (1) Named:00 ID:01 TimeDate:2E601E3C Vers:0.00 Char:0
            ID: 00000409  DataEntryOffs: 00000270
            Offset: 09B90  Size: 00318  CodePage: 0
```

Figure 8-11
Resources hierarchy for CLOCK.EXE.

Each resource directory entry is a structure of type IMAGE_RESOURCE_
DIRECTORY_ENTRY (boy, these names are getting long!). Each IMAGE_
RESOURCE_DIRECTORY_ENTRY has the following format:

DWORD   *Name*

This field contains either an integer ID or a pointer to a structure that contains
a string name. If the high bit (0x80000000) is 0, this field is interpreted as
an integer ID. If the high bit is nonzero, the lower 31 bits are an offset
(relative to the start of the resource section) to an IMAGE_RESOURCE_
DIR_STRING_U structure. This structure contains a WORD character count,
followed by a Unicode string with the resource name. Yes, even PE files
intended for non-Unicode Win32 implementations use Unicode here. To convert the Unicode string to an ANSI string, see the WideCharToMultiByte()
function.

DWORD   *OffsetToData*

This field is either an offset to another resource directory or a pointer to
information about a specific resource instance. If the high bit (0x80000000)
is set, this directory entry refers to a subdirectory. The lower 31 bits are an
offset (relative to the start of the resources) to another IMAGE_RESOURCE_
DIRECTORY. If the high bit isn't set, the lower 31 bits are an offset (relative
to the resource section) to an IMAGE_RESOURCE_DATA_ENTRY structure.
The IMAGE_RESOURCE_DATA_ENTRY structure contains the location of
the resource's raw data, its size, and its code page.

To go further into the resource formats, I'd need to discuss the format of
the individual resource types (dialogs, menus, and so on). Covering these
topics could easily fill an entire chapter; and besides, I'd like to save some
trees. If you're interested, read the RESFMT.TXT file from the Win32 SDK,
which has a detailed description of all the resource type formats. The
PEDUMP program shows the resource hierarchy, but doesn't decompose
individual resources instances.

PE File Base Relocations

When the linker creates an EXE file, it makes an assumption about where
the file will be mapped into memory and then puts the assumed addresses of
code and data items into the executable file. If the executable ends up being
loaded somewhere else in the virtual address space, the addresses the linker

plugged into the image were incorrect. The information stored in the .reloc section allows the PE loader to correct these addresses in the loaded module. If the loader *was* able to load the file at the base address assumed by the linker, the .reloc section data isn't needed, and is ignored. The entries in the .reloc section are called base relocations since their usage depends on the base address of the loaded image.

Unlike relocations in the NE file format, PE file base relocations are extremely simple. They don't refer to external DLLs or even to other sections in the module. Instead, the base relocations boil down to a list of locations in the image that need a value added to them.

Here's an example to show how base relocations work: Let's say an executable file is linked assuming a base address of 0x400000. At offset 0x2134 within the image is a pointer containing the address of a string. The string starts at physical address 0x404002, so the pointer contains the value 0x404002. You then load the file, but the loader decides that it needs to map the image starting at physical address 0x600000. The difference between the linker-assumed base load address and the actual load address is called the *delta*. In this case, the delta is 0x200000 (0x600000 – 0x400000). Since the entire image is 0x200000 bytes higher in memory, so is the string (now at address 0x604002). The pointer to the string is now incorrect. It needs to have the value of the delta (0x200000 in this case) added to it to make it correct again.

To let the Windows loader do this adjustment, the executable file contains a base relocation for the memory location where the pointer resides (at offset 0x2134 in the image). To resolve a base relocation, the loader adds the delta value to the original value at the base relocation address. In this case, the loader would add 0x200000 to the original pointer value (0x404002), and store the result (0x604002) back into the pointer's memory. Since the string really is at 0x604002, everything is once again correct. Figure 8-12 shows what this process looks like.

The formation of the base relocation data is somewhat quirky. The relocations are packaged in a series of contiguous chunks of variable length. Each chunk describes the relocations for one 4K page in the image, and starts out with an IMAGE_BASE_RELOCATION structure that looks like this:

DWORD   VirtualAddress
This field contains the starting RVA for this chunk of relocations. The offset of each relocation that follows is added to this value to form the actual RVA where the relocation needs to be applied.

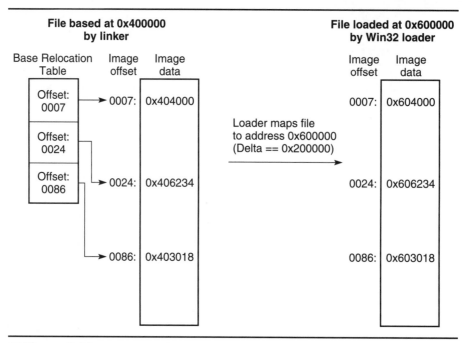

Figure 8-12
PE file base relocations.

DWORD   SizeOfBlock
The size of this structure, plus all the WORD relocations that follow. To determine the number of relocations in this block, subtract the size of an IMAGE_BASE_RELOCATION (8 bytes) from the value of this field, and then divide by 2 (the size of a WORD). For example, if this field contains 44, there are 18 relocations that immediately follow:

```
( 44 - sizeof(IMAGE_BASE_RELOCATION) ) / sizeof(WORD) = 18
```

WORD   TypeOffset
This isn't just a single WORD but rather an array of WORDs, the number of which is calculated by the formula in the previous DWORD description. The bottom 12 bits of each WORD are a relocation offset, and need to be added to the value of the Virtual Address field from this relocation block's header. The high 4 bits of each WORD are a relocation type. For PE files that run on Intel CPUs, you'll see only two types of relocations:

- 0 (IMAGE_REL_BASED_ABSOLUTE): This relocation is meaningless, and is used only as a placeholder to round the relocation information up to a DWORD multiple size.

- 3 (IMAGE_REL_BASED_HIGHLOW): Relocation means add both the high and low 16 bits of the delta to the DWORD specified by the calculated RVA.

There are other relocations defined in WINNT.H, most of which are specific to architectures other than the i386.

Figure 8-13 depicts some base relocations as shown by PEDUMP. Note that the RVA values shown in the figure have already been biased by the VirtualAddress in the IMAGE_BASE_RELOCATION field.

```
Virtual Address: 00001000  size: 0000012C
  00001032 HIGHLOW
  0000106D HIGHLOW
  000010AF HIGHLOW
  000010C5 HIGHLOW
  // Rest of chunk omitted...
Virtual Address: 00002000  size: 0000009C
  000020A6 HIGHLOW
  00002110 HIGHLOW
  00002136 HIGHLOW
  00002156 HIGHLOW
  // Rest of chunk omitted...
Virtual Address: 00003000  size: 00000114
  0000300A HIGHLOW
  0000301E HIGHLOW
  0000303B HIGHLOW
  0000306A HIGHLOW
  // Rest of relocations omitted...
```

Figure 8-13
The base relocations from an EXE file.

THE COFF SYMBOL TABLE

If you're just interested in the actual portions of the PE file used by the operating system, you can skip this section and the section that follows (The "COFF Debug Information"). You can continue reading again at the section called "Differences Between PE Files and COFF OBJ Files."

In any COFF-style OBJ file produced by a Microsoft compiler, you'll find a symbol table. Unlike CodeView information, this symbol table isn't just extra baggage that's only used if you link the executable file with debugging information. Rather, this symbol table holds the information about all public and external symbols referenced by the module. The fixup information emitted by the compiler refers to specific entries in this symbol table. The format of the COFF symbol table is surprisingly simple — in fact, it's so simple that it puts the Microsoft/Intel OMF format scheme with its LNAMEs, PUBDEFs, and EXTDEFs to shame.

If you compile without debugging information enabled, you'll get only the bare minimum number of symbols in the OBJ's symbol table. If you turn debugging information on (with /Zi), the compiler adds additional information about the beginning, length, and end of each function in the module. If you then link with either /DEBUGTYPE:COFF or /DEBUGTYPE:BOTH, the linker will output a COFF-style symbol table into the resulting EXE.

Why would you want COFF information when there's the much-more-complete CodeView information available? If you intend to use the NT system debugger (NTSD) or the NT Kernel debugger (KD), COFF is the only game in town. In addition, if your PE program crashes under Windows NT, DRWTSN32 can use this information to produce a useful symbolic postmortem dump.

For both EXE and OBJ files, you find the location and size of the COFF symbol table by looking in the IMAGE_FILE_HEADER (see "The PE Header" section that is presented earlier in this chapter if you need a refresher on this structure). The symbol table is reasonably simple in structure, and is composed of an array of IMAGE_SYMBOL structures. The number of elements in the array is given by the NumberOfSymbols field in the IMAGE_FILE_HEADER structure. Figure 8-14 shows a sampling of symbols output by the PEDUMP program.

```
Symbol Table - 433 entries  (* = auxiliary symbol)
Indx Name                   Value    Section     cAux  Type    Storage
---- --------------------   -------- ----------  ----- ------- --------
0000 .file                  0000005B sect:DEBUG aux:1 type:00 st:FILE
     * EXEDUMP.c
0002 .debug$S               0001B457 sect:7      aux:1 type:00 st:STATIC
     * Section: 0000 Len: 017C8 Relocs: 002C LineNums: 0000
0004 .data                  0000B040 sect:4      aux:1 type:00 st:STATIC
     * Section: 0000 Len: 006CA Relocs: 0020 LineNums: 0000
0006 _SzRelocTypes          0000B1E0 sect:4      aux:0 type:00 st:EXTERNAL
0007 _SzResourceTypes       0000B148 sect:4      aux:0 type:00 st:EXTERNAL
```

```
0008 _SzDebugFormats      0000B088 sect:4    aux:0 type:00 st:EXTERNAL
0009 _PCOFFDebugInfo       0000B040 sect:4    aux:0 type:00 st:EXTERNAL
000A .text                 000026A0 sect:1    aux:1 type:00 st:STATIC
     * Section: 0000  Len: 00CE0  Relocs: 00A3 LineNums: 00D0
000C _DumpDebugDirectory   000026A0 sect:1    aux:1 type:20 st:EXTERNAL
     * tag: 000E  size: 01A4  Line #'s: 00009220  next fn: 0013
000E .bf                   00000000 sect:4    aux:1 type:00 st:FUNCTION
0010 .lf                   0000001A sect:4    aux:0 type:00 st:FUNCTION
0011 .ef                   000001A4 sect:4    aux:1 type:00 st:FUNCTION
0013 _GetResourceTypeName 00002844 sect:1    aux:1 type:20 st:EXTERNAL
     * tag: 0015  size: 004A  Line #'s: 000092BC  next fn: 001A
0015 .bf                   000001A4 sect:4    aux:1 type:00 st:FUNCTION
0017 .lf                   00000006 sect:4    aux:0 type:00 st:FUNCTION
0018 .ef                   000001EE sect:4    aux:1 type:00 st:FUNCTION
// Rest of symbols omitted...
```

▌ Figure 8-14
A typical COFF symbol table.

Each IMAGE_SYMBOL structure has the following format:

```
typedef struct _IMAGE_SYMBOL {
    union {
        BYTE    ShortName[8];
        struct {
            DWORD   Short;      // If 0, use LongName.
            DWORD   Long;       // Offset into string table.
        } Name;
        PBYTE   LongName[2];
    } N;
    DWORD   Value;
    SHORT   SectionNumber;
    WORD    Type;
    BYTE    StorageClass;
    BYTE    NumberOfAuxSymbols;
} IMAGE_SYMBOL;
typedef IMAGE_SYMBOL UNALIGNED *PIMAGE_SYMBOL;
```

Let's examine each of these fields in detail:

union N   (Symbol name union)
The symbol name can be represented in two ways, depending on its length. If the symbol name has 8 characters or less, the ShortName member of the union contains the ASCIIZ symbol name. Be careful if the symbol name is exactly 8 characters long; if it is, the string isn't null terminated. If the Name.Short field is nonzero, you have to use the ShortName member of the union.

The second way to represent a symbol name occurs when the Name.Short field is 0. In this situation, the Name.Long field is a byte offset into the string table. The string table is nothing more than an array of ASCIIZ strings one after the other in memory. The table starts immediately after the symbol table in memory. To find the string table's starting address, multiply by the number of symbols by the size of an IMAGE_SYMBOL. Add that result to the beginning address of the symbol table. The length of the string table is specified in bytes via a DWORD at offset 0 in the string table.

DWORD   Value

This field contains the value associated with the symbol. For normal and data symbols (that is, functions and global variables), the Value field contains the RVA of the item that the symbol refers to. The value is interpreted differently for some other symbols. Table 8-2 provides a short list of some meanings for the Value field of special symbols.

Table 8-2

Special Symbols in COFF Symbol Tables

Symbol Name	Usage
.file	The symbol table index of the next .file symbol. You can use this index to quickly traverse the list of all files in the EXE.
.data	The starting RVA for a region of data. This region is defined by the source file given by the preceding .file symbol.
.text	The starting RVA for a region of code. This region is defined by the source file given by the preceding .file symbol.
.lf	The number of entries in the line number table for a function. The function is specified by the preceding symbol that defines the function.

SHORT   SectionNumber

The SectionNumber field contains the section number that the symbol belongs in. For example, symbols for global variables will typically have the section number of the .data section. Besides the standard sections in a PE file, three other special section values are defined:

- 0 (IMAGE_SYM_UNDEFINED): The symbol is undefined. This section number is used in OBJ files to represent symbols outside the module, for instance, external functions and external global variables.

- -1 (IMAGE_SYM_ABSOLUTE): The symbol is an absolute value and is not associated with any given section. Examples include local and register variables.
- -2 (IMAGE_SYM_DEBUG): The symbol is used only by the debugger, and isn't visible to the program. The .file symbols that give the name of a source file are examples of this symbol section.

WORD   Type

The type of the symbol. The WINNT.H file defines a fairly rich set of symbol types (int, struct, enum, and so on). (See the IMAGE_SYM_TYPE_xxx #defines for the complete list.) Unfortunately, the Microsoft tools don't seem to generate all the various symbol types. Instead, all global variables and functions are either of type NULL or of type function returning NULL.

BYTE   StorageClass

The storage class of the symbol. As with the symbol types, WINNT.H defines a rich set of storage classes (automatic, static, register, label, and so on). (See the IMAGE_SYM_CLASS_xxx #defines for a complete list.) Again, as with types, the Microsoft tools appear to generate only the bare minimum of information. All global variables and functions are of storage class external. There doesn't seem to be a way to get symbols for local variables, register variables, and so on.

BYTE   NumberOfAuxSymbols

Okay, I lied. The symbol table isn't precisely an array of IMAGE_SYMBOL structures. If a symbol has a nonzero value in its NumberOfAuxSymbols record, the symbol is followed by that same number of IMAGE_AUX_ SYMBOL structures. For example, a .file symbol is followed by as many IMAGE_AUX_SYMBOL structures as it takes to contain the entire pathname for a source file.

Luckily, the size of an IMAGE_AUX_SYMBOL is the same as an IMAGE_SYMBOL, so you can still treat the symbol table as an array of IMAGE_SYMBOLs. Remember that a symbol index should be treated as an array index, even though some of the elements may be auxiliary records. To calculate the index of the next regular symbol, you need to add in the number of auxiliary structures that the symbol uses. For example, let's say you have a symbol with index 1. If it uses 3 auxiliary symbols, the next regular symbol index will be 4.

An IMAGE_AUX_SYMBOL is a messy union of fields. To determine which union members to use, you need to know the type of the regular symbol associated with the auxiliary symbol. Although I haven't figured out which auxiliary union fields should be used in each case, I was able to figure out these two:

- Symbols of storage class IMAGE_SYM_CLASS_FILE use the File union member in the IMAGE_AUX_SYMBOL structure.

- Symbols of storage class IMAGE_SYM_CLASS_STATIC use the Section union member in the IMAGE_AUX_SYMBOL structure.

The sum total of my knowledge of how to interpret the auxiliary symbols is contained in the DumpAuxSymbols() routine in the COMMON.C source file from PEDUMP. If you figure more out on your own, feel free to add to this routine.

If you examine the information within the symbols section, you'll see that the symbols aren't ordered randomly. Instead, they're grouped by the object module (or source file, if you prefer) that they came from. The first record in the COFF symbol table is a .file record. The value of a .file record is a symbol table index to the next .file record. By following the .file record value chain, you can iterate through each of the object modules in the EXE. Immediately following each .file record are other records that are associated with the source file. For example, all the public symbols (global variables and functions) that are declared in a source file follow the .file record representing that source file. For a regular source module, the "hierarchy" of symbol records looks like this:

```
Source File record                      // Name of the source file.
    Data Section record (e.g., ".data") // Data declared in file.
        GlobalVariable1 record          // Information about variable.
        GlobalVariable2 record
        // Rest of global variable records
    Code Section record (e.g., ".text") // Code declared in file.
        Function1 record                // Information about function.
            .BF record                  // Function begin info.
            .LF record                  // Function length info.
            .EF record                  // Function end info.
        Function2 record
            .BF record
            .LF record
            .EF record
        // Rest of function records
```

THE COFF DEBUG INFORMATION

To the average PC programmer, the term *debug information* includes both symbol and line-number information. In the COFF format, the symbol and line-number records are in separate regions of the file. (In the Borland or CodeView symbol table formats, line numbers and symbol information come from the same part of the file.) I discussed the COFF symbol table portion first because it appears in both the OBJ and EXE files. Also, very early in the process of learning the PE format, you come across the PointerToSymbolTable field in the IMAGE_FILE_HEADER. For these reasons I chose to describe the symbol table as a separate entity.

The entire COFF symbol table in an EXE file is composed of three parts: a header, the line-number information, and the symbol table. They don't have to be contiguous in memory, but the Microsoft linker lays them out this way. A complete COFF symbol table looks like this:

IMAGE_COFF_SYMBOLS_HEADER structure

Line Number tables

Symbol Table (previously discussed)

The IMAGE_COFF_SYMBOLS_HEADER structure is intended to allow debuggers to get a quick fix on the important information they need to know. This structure contains pointers to the line number and symbol tables, as well as information that can be found elsewhere in the file.

To find the IMAGE_COFF_SYMBOLS_HEADER structure, look in the array of IMAGE_DEBUG_DIRECTORY structures in the .rdata section of the file. The IMAGE_DEBUG_DIRECTORY that has a Type field containing the value 1 (IMAGE_DEBUG_TYPE_COFF) contains a pointer to the COFF symbol table. To quickly recap this process: The data directory (at the end of the PE header) contains an RVA to an array of IMAGE_DEBUG_DIRECTORYs. There is one IMAGE_DEBUG_DIRECTORY for each type of debug information present in the file. If one of these IMAGE_DEBUG_DIRECTORYs refers to COFF style debug information, then it contains an RVA to a IMAGE_COFF_SYMBOLS_HEADER structure. The IMAGE_COFF_SYMBOLS_HEADER structure in turn contains pointers to the COFF symbol table and line-number information. The IMAGE_COFF_SYMBOLS_HEADER structure has the following format:

```
typedef struct _IMAGE_COFF_SYMBOLS_HEADER {
    DWORD    NumberOfSymbols;
    DWORD    LvaToFirstSymbol;
    DWORD    NumberOfLinenumbers;
    DWORD    LvaToFirstLinenumber;
    DWORD    RvaToFirstByteOfCode;
    DWORD    RvaToLastByteOfCode;
    DWORD    RvaToFirstByteOfData;
    DWORD    RvaToLastByteOfData;
} IMAGE_COFF_SYMBOLS_HEADER, *PIMAGE_COFF_SYMBOLS_HEADER;
```

Let's look at the fields of the IMAGE_COFF_SYMBOLS_HEADER in detail:

DWORD   NumberOfSymbols
The number of symbols in the COFF symbol table. This field contains the same value as the IMAGE_FILE_HEADER.NumberOfSymbols field, as discussed in "The PE Header" section earlier in this chapter.

DWORD   LvaToFirstSymbol
The byte offset to the COFF symbol table, relative to the start of this structure. Adding this value to the RVA of this IMAGE_COFF_SYMBOLS_HEADER will yield the same result as the IMAGE_FILE_HEADER.PointerToSymbolTable field.

DWORD   NumberOfLinenumbers
The number of entries in the line number table (see Figure 8-15).

DWORD   LvaToFirstLinenumber
The byte offset to the COFF line number table, relative to the start of this structure.

DWORD   RvaToFirstByteOfCode
The RVA of the first byte of executable code in the image. This field is usually the same as the RVA of the .text section. This value could also be found by scanning the executable's section table.

DWORD   RvaToLastByteOfCode
The RVA of the last byte of executable code in the image. Assuming you only have one code section (.text), this field will be equal to the section's RVA plus its raw data size. This value could also be found by scanning the section table.

```
Line Numbers
SymIndex: C (_DumpDebugDirectory)
 Addr: 016A9  Line: 0008
 Addr: 016B5  Line: 0009
 Addr: 016BF  Line: 000A
 Addr: 016C4  Line: 000E
 // Rest of line number for function omitted...
SymIndex: 13 (_GetResourceTypeName)
 Addr: 0184A  Line: 0001
 Addr: 01854  Line: 0002
 Addr: 0186F  Line: 0003
 Addr: 01874  Line: 0004
 // Rest of line number for function omitted...
SymIndex: 1A (_GetResourceNameFromId)
 Addr: 01897  Line: 0004
 Addr: 018A1  Line: 0006
 Addr: 018B6  Line: 0007
 Addr: 018BB  Line: 000A
 // Rest of line numbers omitted...
```

Figure 8-15
Typical COFF line-number information in an EXE file.

DWORD   RvaToFirstByteOfData
The RVA of the first byte of data in the image. This field is usually the same as the RVA of the .bss section.

DWORD   RvaToLastByteOfData
The RVA of the last byte of program accessible data in the image. The region encompassed by the FirstByteOfData and the LastByteOfData fields may span several sections (for instance, .bss, .rdata, and .data).

THE COFF LINE-NUMBER TABLE

The COFF line-number table pointed to by the IMAGE_COFF_SYMBOLS_ HEADER structure is very simple: It's just an array of IMAGE_LINENUM- BER structures. Each structure correlates one line of source code to its RVA in the executable image. Figure 8-15 shows a sample line-number table as shown by PEDUMP. The format of an IMAGE_LINENUMBER has two fields, a union and word.

```
union {
DWORD   SymbolTableIndex
DWORD   VirtualAddress
} Type
```

If the Linenumber field (below) is nonzero, this field should be treated as an RVA for a line of code. If the Linenumber field is 0, this field contains an index into the symbol table. The symbol record referred to by this index identifies a function. All the line-number records for that function follow this special record. From looking at the PEDUMP output, you can see that the line-number table is comprised of a symbol table index record, followed by regular line-number records, followed by another symbol table index record, and so on.

```
WORD      Linenumber
```

Contains a line number, relative to the start of the function. This field *is not* a line number in the file. To convert this field to a usable line number in the file, look up the starting line number for the associated function in the symbol table. The associated function is the function with a 0 in this field in the most recent line-number record. See the PEDUMP output in Figure 8-15 if this is unclear.

If you want to access only the line numbers for a given code section, you can look up just the relevant range of line-number entries from the section table. A section's IMAGE_SECTION_HEADER contains a file offset and a count for its line numbers within the table. COFF format OBJs also contain line-number information in the format I've just described. Since there is no IMAGE_COFF_SYMBOLS_HEADER structure in an OBJ file, you'll need to find the line-number records through the IMAGE_SECTION_HEADER structures.

DIFFERENCES BETWEEN PE FILES AND COFF OBJ FILES

At many points throughout the preceding discussion, I've noted that many structures and tables are the same in both a COFF OBJ file and the PE file that's created from it. Both COFF OBJ and PE files have an IMAGE_FILE_ HEADER at or near their beginning. This header is followed by a section table that contains information about all the sections in the file. The two formats also share the same line number and symbol table formats, although the PE file can have additional non-COFF symbol tables as well. The amount of commonality between the two formats can be seen in the PEDUMP source code. The largest file in the program is COMMON.C.

This source file contains all the routines that can be used by both the PE- and OBJ-dumping portions of the program.

This similarity between the two file formats isn't happenstance. The goal of this design is to make the linker's job as easy as possible. Theoretically, creating an EXE file from a single OBJ should be just a matter of inserting a few tables and modifying a couple of file offsets within the image. With this in mind, you can think of a COFF file as an embryonic PE file. Only a few things are missing or different, so I'll list them here.

- COFF OBJ files start immediately with an IMAGE_FILE_HEADER. There's no DOS stub preceding the header, nor is there a PE signature preceding the IMAGE_FILE_HEADER.

- OBJ files don't have the IMAGE_OPTIONAL_HEADER. In a PE file, this structure immediately follows the IMAGE_FILE_HEADER. Interestingly, some OBJs inside COFF LIB files do have an IMAGE_OPTIONAL_HEADER.

- OBJ files don't have base relocations. Instead, they have regular symbol-based fixups. I haven't gone into the format of the COFF OBJ file relocations because they're fairly obscure. If you want to dig into this particular area, the PointerToRelocations and NumberOfRelocations fields in the section table entries point to the relocations for each section. The relocations are an array of IMAGE_RELOCATION structures, which is defined in WINNT.H. The PEDUMP program can show OBJ file relocations if you enable the proper switch.

- The CodeView information in an OBJ file is stored in two sections (.debug$S and .debug$T). When the linker processes the OBJ files, it doesn't put these sections in the PE file. Instead, it collects all these sections and builds a single symbol table that's stored at the end of the file. This symbol table isn't a formal section (that is, there's no entry for it in the PE's section table).

COFF LIB Files

Once you understand COFF OBJ files, using COFF LIB files isn't much harder. COFF LIB files are essentially just a collection of COFF OBJ files, along with some initial sections that let you quickly look up the location of a desired OBJ file embedded within the library. The sparse documentation for the COFF LIB format refers to LIB files as archives, so I'll do so here to remain consistent.

All LIB files start out the same 8-byte signature. This signature is defined in WINNT.H:

```
#define IMAGE_ARCHIVE_START                    "!<arch>\n"
```

The remainder of the file is a series of variable-length records, with each record starting with an IMAGE_ARCHIVE_MEMBER_HEADER structure:

```
typedef struct _IMAGE_ARCHIVE_MEMBER_HEADER {
    BYTE     Name[16];
    BYTE     Date[12];
    BYTE     UserID[6];
    BYTE     GroupID[6];
    BYTE     Mode[8];
    BYTE     Size[10];
    BYTE     EndHeader[2];
} IMAGE_ARCHIVE_MEMBER_HEADER, *PIMAGE_ARCHIVE_MEMBER_HEADER;
```

Each IMAGE_ARCHIVE_MEMBER_HEADER corresponds to either an OBJ file within the library or to one of a small collection of special records. These special records come at the beginning of the library, and exist to let the linker quickly look up OBJ files later in the file. The raw data for the archive member immediately follows the IMAGE_ARCHIVE_MEM-BER_HEADER that starts each record. For most archive member records, the raw data is exactly the same file as an OBJ file would contain. In fact, when dumping out LIB files, the PEDUMP program calls the same OBJ dumping routines that PEDUMP would use if it were processing an OBJ file. Figure 8-16 shows the format of LIB files.

Let's look at the fields of the IMAGE_ARCHIVE_MEMBER_HEADER:

BYTE   Name[16]

The name of the archive member. If a / appears after an ASCII string (for example, FOO.OBJ/), then the string preceding the / is the member name. If the name starts with a / followed by a decimal number (for example, /104), the number is the offset of the archive member name within the Longnames member of the LIB file. In the previous example, the member name would start 104 bytes into the Longname area.

There are also special names that identify the special archive members:

```
#define IMAGE_ARCHIVE_LINKER_MEMBER        "/               "
#define IMAGE_ARCHIVE_LONGNAMES_MEMBER     "//              "
```

```
                    "!<arch>\n"

        IMAGE_ARCHIVE_MEMBER_HEADER ("/")

              First Linker Member data

        IMAGE_ARCHIVE_MEMBER_HEADER ("/")

             Second Linker Member data

        IMAGE_ARCHIVE_MEMBER_HEADER ("//")

              Longnames Member Data

    IMAGE_ARCHIVE_MEMBER_HEADER ("FOO.OBJ")

                  OBJ file data

     IMAGE_ARCHIVE_MEMBER_HEADER ("/104")

                  OBJ file data

                     ...
```

Figure 8-16
The layout of COFF format LIB files.

For OBJ files within an import library, this field is the name of the DLL containing the functions to be imported.

BYTE   Date[12]
The date/time that this member was created. This number is stored in ASCII decimal form.

BYTE   UserID[6]
ASCII decimal representation of the user ID. Appears to always be a NULL string.

BYTE   GroupID[6]
ASCII decimal representation of the group ID. Appears to always be a NULL string.

BYTE   Mode[8]
ASCII decimal representation of the file's mode. Appears to always be 0.

BYTE   Size[10]
The size of the member data to follow, represented in ASCII decimal form. The format of the data depends on what type it is (indicated in the previously described Name field).

BYTE   EndHeader[2]
The ASCII string \n.

Linker members

Every LIB file has two Linker member sections that act as a table of contents for the rest of the file. Both members have the name /, and are differentiated by the order in which they appear in the file. The first Linker member is the first archive member with the name /, while the second Linker member is the second archive member with the name /.

Both Linker members are essentially lists of the public symbols in the LIB file, along with the file offsets to the OBJ members that contains the public symbol. The two Linker members have different formats. Why two copies of the same information? The first Linker member stores its information sorted by the order in which the OBJs appear later in the LIB file. This leads to non-optimal searching. The second Linker member has its symbols sorted in alphabetical order, thereby making it much more useful to the linker. According to the Microsoft documentation, the linker ignores the first Linker member, and always uses the second Linker member.

The first Linker member has the following format:

DWORD   NumberOfSymbols
This is the number of public symbols in this library. This number is in big-endian format (reflecting COFF's heritage in machines other than the i386). The ConvertBigEndian function in PEDUMP's LIBDUMP.C file can handle switching from big-ending format to the little-endian format that the i386 uses.

DWORD   Offsets[NumberOfSymbols]
This is an array of file offsets to other archive members. The offsets are in big-endian format. Each of these members is an OBJ-type member. Each element of this array corresponds to the equivalently ordered symbol name in the list of ASCII strings that immediately follows.

BYTE   *StringTable[?]*
This is an unbroken series of C-style strings in memory.

Essentially, each element in the Offsets array corresponds to one public symbol whose name appears in the StringTable area. For example, the third element of the Offsets array is associated with the third string in the StringTable area. The PEDUMP output makes this clearer:

```
First Linker Member:
  Symbols:        00000006
  MbrOffs   Name
  --------  ----
  00000180  _DumpCAP@0
  00000180  _StartCAP@0
  00000180  _StopCAP@0
  ...
```

The format of the second Linker member is more complex because of the addition of an array necessary for fast symbol lookup. The format of the second Linker member is as follows:

DWORD   *NumberOfMembers*
This DWORD contains the number of OBJ file archive members that appear later in the file.

DWORD   *Offsets[NumberOfSymbols]*
This is an array of file offsets to other archive members. Unlike the first Linker member, these offsets are in the native format of the machine (that is, in little-endian format for i386 machines).

DWORD   *NumberOfSymbols*
This is the number of public symbols in the StringTable array (and hence, the number of public symbols in the library). This field also contains the number of elements in the Indices array that immediately follows.

WORD   *Indices[NumberOfSymbols]*
This array holds 1-based indexes into the Offsets array (described two fields up). This array runs parallel to the strings in the StringTable array.

BYTE   *StringTable[NumberOfSymbols]*
This is an unbroken series of C-style strings in memory.

To find the OBJ file that corresponds to a given symbol using the second Linker member, the linker first searches the StringTable array and calculates the relative index of the string in the array. Next, the linker uses the index to look up a WORD in the Indices array. Finally, the linker subtracts 1 from this Indices array WORD and uses the result as an index into the Offsets array. The Offsets array DWORD that's looked up is the file offset of the OBJ file that contains the public symbol. The DumpSecondLinkerMember function in PEDUMP's LIBDUMP.C shows this process in action.

The Longnames member

The data in the Longnames archive member section is simply a collection of C-style strings, one after the other. A string is placed into the Longnames section if its too big to fit into the 16 bytes reserved in the Name field of an IMAGE_ARCHIVE_MEMBER_HEADER structure. In this case, the Name field contains a /, followed by an ASCII decimal representation of the string's offset in the Longnames section.

SUMMARY

With the advent of Win32, Microsoft made a sweeping change in the OBJ and executable file formats. This change allowed Microsoft to save time by building on work previously done for other operating systems. A primary goal of these revamped file formats is to enhance portability across different platforms. The COFF OBJ format existed before Win32 was created. The PE format is an extension to the COFF format and was designed for use with Win32 platforms.

The useful part of both the OBJ and executable files begins with an IMAGE_FILE_HEADER structure. Following that structure (and possibly an additional optional structure) is a section table. The section table contains the location and attributes of all the sections in the file. A section is a collection of code or data that logically belongs together. To facilitate finding information quickly, the PE file contains a data directory that points to useful locations in the file (for example, the location of the file's export table). Besides the header(s), section tables, and raw section data, COFF OBJ files and PE files can also contain information regarding symbolic names and line numbers. This information is stored at the end of the file, after all the headers and section data.

SPELUNKING ON YOUR OWN

9

*U*nlike the rest of this book, this chapter doesn't focus on the workings or architecture of Windows 95. Instead, it describes some of the more basic elements of exploring code on your own. Consider the adage "Give someone a fish and they'll eat for a day. Teach someone to fish and they'll eat for a lifetime." The other chapters in this book give you fish. This chapter teaches you how to fish for Windows secrets on your own.

Of course, what you'll learn here can also be applied to other situations, such as to device drivers and end-user applications.

In the ideal world, you would be able to find all the operating system information you needed in the documentation, allowing you to treat the operating system components as a black box. You wouldn't need to understand the internal behaviors and data structures of such an operating system because understanding and using the documented interfaces would be sufficient to write your program, library, or device driver.

In the absence of complete documentation (ah, that perfect world is starting to crumble . . .), the operating system's source code can act as a surrogate source of information. Although you have to look at other people's code (shudder!), the answer to almost every operating system question can be found with enough digging through the operating system sources. In fact, Eric S. Raymond's *The New Hacker's Dictionary* contains an entry for UTSL, an acronym for Use the Source Luke.

In the UNIX world, access to the operating system sources is fairly common. Unfortunately for us programmers who work with Windows, source code isn't available. Granted, some actual Windows 95 code appears in the DDK. For the most part though, the majority of programming questions concern topics that neither the SDK nor the DDK provide source code for. Microsoft's documentation in these areas has improved markedly in recent years, but there are still many holes in the Windows SDK documentation that real source code would fill.

Insufficient documentation and source code unavailability aren't the only problems you can encounter when working with the operating system. Your application may need to interact with another application whose exact behavior is unknown to you. The prototypical example of this is the programmer who is forced to spend a great deal of time trying to pin down what DDE messages Microsoft Excel sends, and in what order. Another example from Windows 3.1 is the program that, when run, causes other programs to be unable to run. The problem in this case is that some program is sucking up all the memory below 1MB in the address space.

In this chapter I discuss the following methods of spelunking used by Windows programmers:

- File-dumping utilities
- API and message spy programs (such as APISPY32 from Chapter 10)
- Disassembly

In each section I describe the commonly available tools and give examples of how to use these tools to find useful information. The final section on disassembly techniques is especially detailed because disassembly is considered to be a form of "black magic" and is rarely covered in print. A lot of the art of reading assembler listings and stepping through code in a debugger is just knowing common compiler code-generation patterns. There's also a certain amount of real-world experience involved, but I'll save a full discussion of that for later.

Most of this chapter describes general spelunking concepts that beginning and intermediate programmers will find helpful. But the final section of this chapter is a collection of advanced tips and tricks for the serious spelunker. After all, I've learned a lot of lessons the hard way, and those of you who are interested might as well benefit from my hard-won knowledge.

Although Windows 95 is a Win32 operating system, vital parts of it still use 16-bit code and the 16-bit NE file format. Describing Win16 spelunking techniques is therefore a must for this chapter. Although some spelunking techniques carry over from Win16 to Win32, there are significant differences. Therefore, I'll cover tools and techniques for Win32 programs as well.

SPELUNKING OVERVIEW

The easiest and most readily available method of learning the details of a piece of code is to use file-display programs such as Borland's TDUMP, Microsoft's EXEHDR and DUMPBIN, or the PEDUMP program from Chapter 8. These programs can tell you such things as what DLLs and API functions a program uses, but won't be able to provide you with information about internal algorithms and data structures. Think of it this way: File dumping is to spelunking rather what looking out your front window is to conducting a full-scale surveillance operation on the house across the street. It's relatively easy, but you may not be able to get all the information you need.

For more sophisticated snooping into the internals of a program, you can use a spy program. Programs such as SPY from the Microsoft Windows SDK and WinSight from Borland C++ show the window messages that a program sends and receives. Recently, programs such as Nu-Mega's BoundsChecker products and Periscope's WinScope added the capability to see your program's calls to the operating system API functions. And Chapter 10 offers an extensible Win32 API spy program that you can use. With all this information and a little bit of work, you can figure out how almost any nifty piece of code is implemented. I'll give an example of spelunking with a spy program later in this chapter. Returning to our spying-on-the-house analogy, spy programs can be thought of as intercepting the mail and phone conversations going into and out of the house.

Finally, when you need to know a program or DLL's internal algorithms or data structures, you can pull out all the stops by using disassembly. Although you can do limited disassembly work with just a good debugger, you'll probably want to use a file-based disassembler such as V-Communications' Sourcer or Win2Asm from Eclectic Software. The capability to add your own comments and formatting to the listing file makes file-based disassemblers a far better choice than your favorite debugger for serious disassembly. To carry our house surveillance analogy one step further, disassembly is like breaking down the front door and rifling through the contents of the house. I'll describe disassembly tools and techniques in the "Spelunking Using Disassembly" section.

SPELUNKING WITH FILE-DUMPING TOOLS

The usual first step in spelunking a program is to dump out the file's contents. This is a quick and easy way to get a handle on what type of file you're dealing with and what the file might be used for. Table 9-1 lists the capabilities of some well-known tools that are expressly written to dissect a file's contents.

Table 9-1

Capabilities of common file-dissection tools

File type	DUMPBIN	DUMPEXE	EXEHDR	TDUMP
MZ files (DOS)		X	X	X
NE files (WIN16)		X	X	X
PE files (Win32)	X	X		X
Debug Info	X	X		X
Disassembly	X			
OBJs	X			X
Resources	X	X		X

Notes:
DUMPBIN is from Microsoft Win32 SDK and Visual C++.
DUMPEXE is from Symantec C++
EXEHDR is from Microsoft Visual C++
TDUMP is from Borland C++

If you develop with Borland C++, try out TDUMP.EXE from the BIN subdirectory. If you develop with 16-bit Microsoft C/C++, EXEHDR is probably your tool of choice. If you use Visual C++ or the Win32 SDK, the DUMPBIN program in the BIN directory works with Portable Executables (PEs) and the COFF format OBJs produced by the Microsoft 32-bit compilers. As Table 9-1 shows, no one program does everything, so it's a good idea to have at least a couple of programs on hand. The combination of TDUMP and DUMPBIN is a good one that should cover most bases.

The most useful information you get from a file-dumping program is usually the names of the DLLs and functions that a program or DLL imports. Often just knowing that a program uses a certain function is enough to get you going when you're stuck. For example, in Windows 3.0 there was no documented way to change the desktop wallpaper, yet the Control Panel application was able to change the wallpaper. The capability had to exist somewhere in Windows. By running TDUMP or EXEHDR on the Windows 3.0

control panel program, you would have seen that the program made use of the undocumented SetDeskWallPaper function. (In Windows 3.1 the documented SystemParametersInfo API took over this functionality.)

Finding the functions that a 16-bit New Executable (NE) program or DLL uses is a two-step process. The NE file doesn't contain a simple list of all functions imported from other DLLs. Therefore, the first step in this process is to find the fixup data for the executable's segments. If you use EXEHDR, you'll have to use the /VERBOSE switch to get the fixup information. This output shows the TDUMP version of a typical sequence of fixups that occurs in the Windows 3.1 CALC.EXE:

```
...
PTR     0AD9h   GDI.91
PTR     0121h   GDI.93
PTR     00EAh   USER.89
PTR     0223h   USER.90
PTR     04ADh   USER.91
PTR     1DCAh   USER.92
...
```

The important information in this output is the module name and import ordinal at the end of each line. In this case, the program is importing six functions, two from GDI and four from USER. Function names such as GDI.91 aren't particularly useful by themselves, so the second step of the process is to convert the module name (GDI) and ordinal (91) to a real function name.

When an EXE or a DLL exports functions, the function names and their associated export ordinal values are stored in the executable file, as well as in an import library. Since there's no easy way for Microsoft users to dump the contents of a 16-bit import library, I'll show you how to get the function name from the DLL directly. But back to our second step: We have to figure out what GDI.91 is. That means dumping out GDI.EXE to see what exported function 91 is. The output that follows shows a fragment of the Non-Resident Name Table section produced by running TDUMP on GDI.EXE. If you use EXEHDR, you'll find similar information in the section titled "Exports":

```
Non-Resident Name Table      offset: 0C41h
    Module Description: 'Microsoft Windows Graphics Device Interface'
    Name: GETWINDOWEXTEX              Entry:   474
    ....
    Name: GETTEXTEXTENT               Entry:    91
```

Looking at the TDUMP output for GDI.EXE, notice that the function GetTextExtent corresponds to GDI.91. Putting two and two together, it's evident that CALC.EXE calls GetTextExtent (GDI.91). The names of the other imported functions can be determined by repeating the two-step process I just described. Bear in mind that this method won't find functions that a program links to at runtime by calling GetProcAddress. In that particular case, you'll have to resort to disassembly to find these calls.

Finding the functions that a 32-bit PE file imports is much simpler. Running DUMPBIN or PEDUMP from Chapter 10 on a Win32 program shows that a PE file contains a simple list of all the functions it imports. (The list looks simple in the dump. Inside the file, the imports section is fairly complex. For a complete description of the exports section and the PE format in general, see Chapter 8.) The list of imported functions is even sorted by module. This output contains fragments of the imports section emitted by running DUMPBIN on the Windows NT 3.5 USER32.DLL:

```
ntdll.dll
Hint/Name Table: 0002F31C
TimeDateStamp:    2E67E68D
ForwarderChain:   FFFFFFFF
First thunk RVA: 0002F050
Ordn  Name
  78  NtCreateSection
 226  NtUnmapViewOfSection
 503  RtlUnwind
 901  strrchr
 890  sscanf
 ...  rest of functions omitted

KERNEL32.dll
Hint/Name Table: 0002F3CC
TimeDateStamp:    2E67E68D
ForwarderChain:   FFFFFFFF
First thunk RVA: 0002F100
Ordn  Name
 119  FindClose
 150  GetAtomNameW
 378  LocalReAlloc
 368  LoadLibraryW
 236  GetModuleFileNameW
 ...  rest of functions omitted
```

In this output, the first number on each line containing a function name is the hint ordinal. Win32 operating systems import functions by name, but the hint ordinal can speed up the process. It gives the loader a hint of where it should start its binary search for the API name in the DLL that exports the functions.

By looking at USER32.DLL's import table (in the output), we can see that it calls KERNEL32 functions such as GetAtomNameW and LocalReAlloc. It's interesting to note that when the NT USER32.DLL has a choice of calling either an ASCII or a Unicode API, it calls the Unicode version (GetAtomNameW, LoadLibraryW, and so on). This is consistent with Microsoft's claim that Windows NT uses Unicode strings internally.

This output also shows that NT's USER32.DLL uses many functions from NTDLL.DLL. NTDLL.DLL is an entire DLL of undocumented functions! Interestingly, in NT, KERNEL32.DLL relies heavily on functions in NTDLL.DLL. In contrast, NTDLL.DLL still exists in Windows 95, but KERNEL32.DLL doesn't appear to use it for anything. In fact, the Windows 95 NTDLL.DLL is the opposite of the NT version, and relies heavily on KERNEL32 functions.

Although it's useful to know what APIs an EXE or a DLL uses, the flip side is equally important. File-dumping programs can show you what APIs a DLL exports for use by other programs and DLLs. The exported functions are often a dead giveaway to the purpose and capabilities of the DLL. Sometimes a name by itself is enough information to guess what the parameters are to an undocumented function. Other times you'll need to use the disassembly techniques along with the exported API names to figure out how to call an undocumented DLL function.

The next output shows the TDUMP output of the exports from a 16-bit NE file, SPELL.DLL. This DLL comes with Microsoft Word for Windows 2.0, but its APIs aren't documented.

```
Non-Resident Name Table      offset: 02A8h
     Module Description: 'Word for Windows v. 2.0 Spell Checker DLL'
     Name: SPELLOPENUDR                Entry:     8
     Name: SPELLGETSIZEUDR             Entry:    13
     Name: SPELLADDUDR                 Entry:     9
     Name: SPELLOPTIONS                Entry:     3
     Name: SPELLDELUDR                 Entry:    11
     Name: SPELLTERMINATE              Entry:     5
     Name: SPELLADDCHANGEUDR           Entry:    10
     Name: SPELLINIT                   Entry:     2
     Name: SPELLVER                    Entry:     1
     Name: SPELLCLOSEMDR               Entry:    15
     Name: SPELLCHECK                  Entry:     4
     Name: SPELLVERIFYMDR              Entry:     6
     Name: SPELLOPENMDR                Entry:     7
     Name: SPELLCLOSEUDR               Entry:    16
     Name: SPELLCLEARUDR               Entry:    12
     Name: SPELLGETLISTUDR             Entry:    14
```

Some of the function names give obvious clues as to what the DLL does, as well as an idea of how you might call that function. For example, the SpellVer() function probably doesn't take any parameters, and probably returns a version number in the AX or DX:AX registers. It's very easy to write a small program that tests this theory. Just do a LoadLibrary on SPELL.DLL, call GetProcAddress to get the address of SpellVer(), and then call it.

News flash: Having written a small program to test this, I discovered that the function always returns 0 when called in this manner. Resorting to disassembly, I discovered that the SpellVer function actually takes three far pointers to WORDs (LPWORD) that it fills in. The lesson here: Although file-dumping is the easiest form of spelunking, it can't give you adequate information in all cases.

Returning to the other functions exported from SPELL.DLL, note that there are SpellInit(), SpellCheck(), and SpellTerminate functions — so the DLL probably expects to be initialized, called to check some text, and then shut down. What we don't know is what sort of parameters these APIs expect. Again, this is where disassembly comes into play.

If you want to see what new and exciting things changed between different versions of a product, a good way to start is to compare the exports of two corresponding DLLs. Table 9-2 shows the difference between the functions exported by KRNL386 in Windows 3.1 and Windows 95. To obtain this information, I used EXEHDR to dump the exports of the Windows 3.1 KRNL386.EXE and the Windows 95 KRNL386.EXE to separate files. Next, I sorted the list of functions in each file alphabetically. Finally, I ran a DIFF program to show the differences.

As Table 9-2 shows, some obsolete functions were deleted and a whole bunch of intriguing new functions were added. Some of the new functions are documented (for example, GetPrivateProfileStruct), but many are undocumented (for instance, Piglet_361 and GetVDMPointer32W). Noticeably missing from the table are numerous new exported KRNL386 functions that are exported by ordinal only, and that don't have names in KRNL386's resident or nonresident names tables.

In Table 9-2, notice that some function names are hidden by referring to them as, for example, K209 and K210. If we knew the names of these functions, it would sure make it easier to guess what their purpose is. As it turns out, some of the new K*xxx* functions (such as K209) are for allocating or freeing memory in a Win32 heap from a 16-bit application. A good example of code that uses the K*xxx* functions is USER.EXE, which stores the WND structures in the upper part of the USER DGROUP (above the 64K limit that plagued programmers prior to Windows 95). Chapter 5 contains more information on these functions.

Table 9-2
Windows 95 versus Windows 3.1 KRNL386 exported functions:
What's new, what's been deleted

	KRNL386 exported functions
New in Windows 95	CALLPROC32W, CREATEDIRECTORY, DELETEFILE, FINDCLOSE, FINDFIRSTFILE, FINDNEXTFILE, FREELIBRARY32W, GETCURRENTDIRECTORY, GETDISKFREESPACE, GETFILEATTRIBUTES, GETLASTERROR, GETMODULENAME, GETPRIVATEPROFILESECTION, GETPRIVATEPROFILESECTIONNAMES, GETPRIVATEPROFILESTRUCT, GETPROCADDRESS32W, GETPRODUCTNAME, GETPROFILESECTION, GETPROFILESECTIONNAMES, GETVDMPOINTER32W, GETVERSIONEX, GLOBALSMARTPAGELOCK, GLOBALSMARTPAGEUNLOCK, INVALIDATENLSCACHE, ISBADFLATREADWRITEPTR, K208, K209, K210, K211, K213, K214, K215, K228, K229, K237, LOADLIBRARYEX32W, LSTRCATN, OPENFILEEX, PIGLET_361, REGCLOSEKEY, REGCREATEKEY, REGDELETEKEY, REGDELETEVALUE, REGENUMKEY, REGENUMVALUE, REGFLUSHKEY, REGISTERSERVICEPROCESS, REGLOADKEY, REGOPENKEY, REGQUERYVALUE, REGQUERYVALUEEX, REGSAVEKEY, REGSETVALUE, REGSETVALUEEX, REGUNLOADKEY, REMOVEDIRECTORY, SETCURRENTDIRECTORY, SETFILEATTRIBUTES, SETLASTERROR, WRITEPRIVATEPROFILESECTION, WRITEPRIVATEPROFILESTRUCT, WRITEPROFILESECTION, _CALLPROCEX32W
Deleted in Windows 95	DIAGOUTPUT, DIAGQUERY, DOSIGNAL, EMSCOPY, GETFREEMEMINFO, GETTASKQUEUEDS, GETTASKQUEUEES, GETWINOLDAPHOOKS, INITTASK1, K327, K329, K403, K404, REGISTERWINOLDAPHOOK, RESERVED1, RESERVED2, RESERVED3, RESERVED4, RESERVED5, SETSIGHANDLER, SETTASKQUEUE, SETTASKSIGNALPROC, WINOLDAPCALL

On the Win32 side of things, here's a fragment of the output from running DUMPBIN on the Windows 95 version of KERNEL32.DLL:

```
1    0    AddAtomA  (00040475)
2    1    AddAtomW  (000134aa)
3    2    AddConsoleAliasA  (00014a6a)
4    3    AddConsoleAliasW  (00014ab1)
5    4    AllocConsole  (0001c4f2)
6    5    AllocLSCallback  (00029d84)
7    6    AllocMappedBuffer  (0003ea55)
8    7    AllocSLCallback  (00029db7)
9    8    BackupRead  (0001490d)
A    9    BackupSeek  (00014733)
B    A    BackupWrite  (00014928)
```

There are two important things to note in this output. First, several of the exported APIs come with two variations — for example, AddAtomA and AddAtomW. AddAtomA is the version of AddAtom that uses ASCII strings, and AddAtomW is the equivalent function that uses Unicode strings. (In Windows 95 and Win32s, most of the Unicode versions of the functions simply pop their parameters and return, since these Win32 platforms don't support Unicode.)

The second thing to note in the output is the number at the end of each line. This number is the relative virtual address (RVA) of the function in the module. This is great news! The exports section contains enough information to connect a symbolic name to a code address. As you'll see later, having symbolic names increases the ease of spelunking by several orders of magnitude.

The following output shows a small portion of the DUMPBIN display of the exported functions from the Windows NT 3.5 NTDLL.DLL.

```
ordinal hint   name
   ...
   13     12    DbgBreakPoint  (0000aa58)
   14     13    DbgPrint  (0000aa5e)
   15     14    DbgPrompt  (0000aaa2)
   ...
   24     23    LdrGetProcedureAddress  (000082ff)
   25     24    LdrInitializeThunk  (00001108)
   ...
   39     38    NtAllocateVirtualMemory  (00001198)
   3A     39    NtCancelIoFile  (000011a8)
   ...
   49     48    NtCreateMutant  (00001298)
   4A     49    NtCreateNamedPipeFile  (000012a8)
   4B     4A    NtCreatePagingFile  (000012b8)
   4C     4B    NtCreatePort  (000012c8)
   4D     4C    NtCreateProcess  (000012d8)
   4E     4D    NtCreateProfile  (000012e8)
   4F     4E    NtCreateSection  (000012f8)
   50     4F    NtCreateSemaphore  (00001308)
   ...
   A1     A0    NtQuerySystemInformation  (00001800)
   ...
   19E    19D   RtlLocalTimeToSystemTime  (00019b3c)
   19F    19E   RtlLockHeap  (00011178)
   1A0    19F   RtlLogStackBackTrace  (0001b120)
   1A1    1A0   RtlLookupElementGenericTable  (0001a104)
   1A2    1A1   RtlLookupSymbolByAddress  (0001bcdf)
   1A3    1A2   RtlLookupSymbolByName  (0001bb8b)
   ...
```

With functions like DbgPrint(), NtCreateProcess(), and NtQuerySystem-Information(), NTDLL.DLL has a lot of intriguing functionality buried in it. In Windows NT, many of these undocumented APIs uncovered with DUMPBIN do the real work of creating processes, managing memory, and so on. For numerous API functions in Windows NT, KERNEL32.DLL is nothing more than a very thin layer over the real code in NTDLL.DLL. You might be thinking, "This is nice, but I probably can't use NTDLL.DLL myself." Wrong! If you run DUMPBIN or PEDUMP on some NT programs such as WPERF.EXE, you'll see that they call undocumented NTDLL.DLL functions such as NtQuerySystemInformation.

You can often gain additional insight into the file by examining some of the text strings it contains. One of the most useful text strings is the description field. The linker puts whatever you specify on the DESCRIPTION line of the .DEF file into the executable's description field. In 16-bit NE files, the description string is the first entry in the nonresident names table. The output that follows shows some typical description strings in the files from the Windows 95 \WINDOWS directory.

```
RUMOR.EXE:     Party Line
WINBUG10.DLL:  DLL for LZ compression functions for WINBUG
DEFRAG.EXE:    Disk Defragmenter (Optimizer)
MCIOLE.DLL:    OLE handler DLL for MCI objects
SCANDSKW.EXE:  ScanDisk for Windows
CARDS.DLL:     Card Display Technology
WINPOPUP.EXE:  Microsoft Windows Message Popup Application
MORICONS.DLL:  MS-DOS Application Icons For Windows 3.1
CHARMAP.EXE:   Utility for easily selecting special characters.
PROGMAN.EXE:   Windows Program Manager 3.1
RUNDLL.EXE:    Turn a DLL into an App
WINFILE.EXE:   Windows File System 3.1
DIALER.EXE:    Microsoft Windows Telephony Dialer
```

In 32-bit PE files, the linker puts the description string somewhere in the .rdata section. Unfortunately, there doesn't appear to be any consistent pattern to its placement. If you want to see these strings, your best bet is to do a raw hex dump of the .rdata section and look for an embedded ASCII string. Also, since the Microsoft Win32 tools generally don't need a .DEF file, you'll find many files that don't have a description string.

Another interesting place to get useful strings from dumping an EXE or a DLL is the resource section. In both Win16 and Win32 programming you can specify resources by ordinal number or by name. Sometimes dialogs have interesting names or hidden controls that are outside the dialog rectangle.

Stringtable resources often contain goodies that you may ordinarily never see. For instance, in the Microsoft game TAIPEI.EXE, the program rewards you with a proverb if you win a game. If you want to see all the possible proverbs, you can either master the game, or you can cheat like I did and just dump out the string tables.

There are numerous ways to get at the resources in a file. Programs like Borland's Resource Workshop let you view and edit the resources in any file interactively. If you like doing things from the command line, Eclectic Software's disassembler (Win2Asm) comes with a utility that reads in the binary resources from an executable file. It emits a proper .RC file that you can feed back into the resource compiler if you need to.

When using file-dumping programs, the jackpot is when you encounter a file that still contains debugging information. Debugging information contains all sorts of goodies about a program. Modern compiler debug information includes the names of all your variables and functions, your source file names, the layout of your structure definitions, your class hierarchy, and many other things. In short, in the hands of those who know what they're looking for, debug information is almost as good as source code.

Borland's TDUMP dumps out both flavors of Borland debug information (16 and 32 bits), in addition to Microsoft C7 debugging information. Microsoft users can use CVDUMP to break apart CodeView information into readable text. In addition to CodeView information, Microsoft's 32-bit compiler produces another type of debugging information called COFF. (DUMPBIN.EXE and PEDUMP.EXE from Chapter 8 can break apart COFF debug information.) Finally, the DBG2MAP from Nu-Mega's SoftIce/W can create a human-readable .MAP file from both Borland and Microsoft 32-bit debug formats.

.SYM files are another form of debug information that can be useful for spelunking. Although .SYM files are relatively old and crude, they're still helpful if you happen to get hold of them. Microsoft ships .SYM files for some of the debug binaries as part of the Windows 95 SDK. Alas, there aren't good .SYM files for the system DLLs that most people would want to examine.

The first and most obvious thing that debugging information (with the exception of .SYM files) tells you is which company's linker was used to produce the executable. (You can also find that information by looking at the copyright strings that the compiler runtime libraries put into the program's data area.) More importantly, however, you can learn the names of all the executable's functions and variables. Along with the functions and variables names, the debug information also contains the address of these symbols. If you need to resort to disassembly, having symbolic names will increase the odds of success manyfold.

Beside symbolic names, the debug information might contain the types of the variables, the argument lists for the functions, and the layout of the structures and classes. In short, the debugging information contains almost everything about your program that you wouldn't want a competitor to know about. I once shocked a programmer by telling him about a GP fault in his code, and on what line it occurred. I had downloaded the program from a bulletin board and didn't have the source. The debug information alone was enough for me to pinpoint the problem and the source line number. Your competitors may not be so nice! That's why it's important for you to check that you don't ship debugging information with your product. Many companies, including Microsoft, Borland, and Delrina, have been guilty of this in the past. You can see this yourself by running TDUMP or CVDUMP on SOUNDREC.EXE from Windows 3.1.

Even if you don't leave debugging information in your EXEs and DLLs, there's still a lot that can be learned about a file by dumping its contents and analyzing the results. In the July 1993 issue of *Microsoft Systems Journal*, I presented a utility called EXESIZE that scans 16-bit NE files and looks for wasted space caused by inefficient or lazy coding practices. EXESIZE determines if the file alignment should be smaller, if inefficient real-mode code is being generated, if you've left debug information in the file, and so on. In some cases EXESIZE found files that wasted well over 100K. Over time, I found that in most cases, the files that wasted the most space were created by sloppy practices or unknowing programmers. Put another way, if an executable passed all the EXESIZE tests, it was probably created by seasoned professionals who pay attention to the details.

While I've been focusing on file dumping of EXEs and DLLs, don't overlook the wealth of information that can be found in other related files. In particular, OBJ and LIB files contain quite a bit of information about a given source module (or collection of modules). Borland's TDUMP takes apart Intel OMF OBJ files to show you public and external symbols, segment names, and so on. Symantec C++ includes the OBJ2ASM utility that symbolically disassembles the code contained in an Intel OMF OBJ file. Microsoft's DUMPBIN and my PEDUMP program both perform general-purpose COFF OBJ and LIB file dumping. DUMPBIN can even disassemble COFF OBJ/LIB files.

SPELUNKING WITH SPYING TOOLS

While file dumping can be interesting and informative, it often doesn't tell you everything you need to know about the code in question. Tools that let you spy on a program's interactions with the operating system are often much better suited to this task. The most well-known Windows spying tools are the message-spying programs: SPY from Microsoft and WINSIGHT from Borland. Message-spying programs show the messages that a window receives, and how the program responds to these messages.

Although this information can be useful, programmers often need even more information to get to the root of what they're trying to figure out. Programs such as Nu-Mega's BoundsChecker for Windows and Periscope's WinScope have raised spy tools to a new level. Besides window messages, these programs intercept API calls that a program or its DLLs make. Additionally, some spy programs monitor and log hook callbacks, TOOLHELP notifications, and other callbacks. The idea behind these programs is to put "probes" at all the well-defined places where controls enter or exit the program's code (window procedures, API calls, and so on). The information that passes across these boundaries is located in consistent places. For example, all window procedures are called with a consistent set of parameters on the stack (the HWND is at [BP+0E], the MSG number is at [BP+0C] and so on). Spy programs take advantage of this knowledge to save off, analyze, and display the information.

The best spying tools are those that don't require any modification of the code that's being spied on. These programs rely solely on the information in the executable file and the calls it makes to insert their probes. As I'll show later in this section, this allows these programs to spy on almost any EXE or DLL, even those that you can't relink or modify in some way.

Another group of spying tools requires you to relink the code you want to spy on. These tools work by fooling the linker into resolving the program's API calls to point to the tool's own code rather than to the operating system DLLs. A closely related class of tools modifies the executable file after it's been linked. The effect is still the same. The spy program redirects API calls to the tool's own code, which logs the call before passing control on to the operating system.

A variety of spying tools are available for 16-bit Windows applications. Although the primary purpose of BoundsChecker/W (BCHKW) is to find bugs, it accomplishes this by intercepting all the Windows API and certain of the C library calls that a program makes, and validating the parameters.

Since BCHKW has already done the hard work of intercepting all API function calls, it wasn't much more work to make BCHKW retain the information in a trace buffer. To give a clearer picture of the sequence of events that lead up to a bug, BCHKW also watches window and dialog messages, hook callbacks, TOOLHELP notifications, and other assorted callbacks.

If you choose to save the trace information to a disk, you can use the BCHKW's TVIEW program to get two different views of your program's actions: an expandable view and a collapsible hierarchical view. TVIEW includes a variety of event filters that do things like removing repetitive sequences of APIs and messages that you're probably not interested in. A typical sequence of this sort would be: GetMessage/TranslateMessage/DispatchMessage/Window Message/DefWindowProc.

Although BCHKW takes advantage of debugging information for its bug-finding roles, it isn't necessary for its spying capabilities. As a result, you can run BCHKW with just about any Windows program, not just your own programs during development.

Another popular spying program for 16-bit programs is Periscope's WinScope. Unlike BoundsChecker/W, which concentrates on one program at a time, WinScope is a systemwide spy tool. WinScope shows you all the API calls, hooks, and messages that occur anywhere in the system. Sometimes this is very useful; other times it leads to information overflow.

Luckily, WinScope provides a very high level of customization for what you want to spy on. You can enable or disable spying on individual APIs or on groups of APIs. You can also enable or disable spying on windows messages and hooks. Like BoundsChecker/W, WinScope can save off a copy of the memory that an API's far pointer parameters point to. This enables you to see the strings and data structures that were passed to CreateWindow, GetPrivateProfileString, and so on. WinScope can also save timing information for each event, allowing WinScope to function as a crude profiler. WinScope uses the information in an NE file to hook API calls, so you don't need to relink the code you want to spy on.

If you're willing to sacrifice usability and features in exchange for saving some money, you might consider Microsoft's API parameter profiler. Although both 16- and 32-bit versions of this spying tool appear on the Windows NT SDK, very few people know of its existence.

The Microsoft profiler is crude in its implementation and requires you to modify any EXEs or DLLs that you want to examine. The core of this spy tool is a collection of DLLs (ZERNEL.DLL, ZSER.DLL, ZERNEL32.DLL, ZSER32.DLL, and so on). Each DLL has the same base filename as an operating system DLL, but with the first letter changed to Z. These DLLs have a small stub for each API exported from the DLL they replace. For example, USER.EXE exports the function CreateWindow(). Therefore, ZSER.DLL also exports a CreateWindow() function. You connect your program or DLL to these special DLLs with the APFCNVRT program (or APF32CVT for you Win32 users). The APFCNVRT and APF32CVT programs modify your program so that it imports its functions from the parameter profiling DLLs rather than the normal operating system DLLs. When you run the modified program, all calls to the affected DLLs go through the parameter spying DLLs before they're passed to the operating system. The parameter profiler saves its collected information to a disk file for viewing. For 32-bit programs, Microsoft provides an alternative set of DLLs that do real profiling rather than API logging.

Besides the 32-bit version of Microsoft's parameter profiler, Nu-Mega's BoundsChecker32 (BCHK32) programs (for NT, Windows 95, and Win32s) also spy on API calls and window messages in Win32 programs. For the purposes of API spying, BCHK32 is similar to BoundsChecker/W. However, it has a few new features not present in its Win16 sibling. First, when an API call fails, the API usually stores an error code with SetLastError(), indicating why the call failed. BCHK32 knows when an API fails and records the error code. Second, since Win32 supports threads, BCHK32 saves the thread ID for each API call and window message. The TVIEW program uses the thread information to provide additional filtering options, such as showing only the events for a specified thread.

The final Win32 API spy program I'll mention here is my APISPY32 program from Chapter 10. Although APISPY32 isn't nearly as full-featured as BoundsChecker32, it does provide the rudimentary elements of API spying (including showing function parameters and return values). It's easily extensible to monitor any Win32 DLL that you want to spy on, and doesn't require any modification to your programs.

A key thing to consider when evaluating spying tools is which parts of the system the various tools allow you to watch. WinScope spies on calls to a dozen of the standard Windows DLLs (USER, KERNEL, GDI, and so on). More importantly, WinScope has the capability to spy on other DLLs through scripts that you write. BoundsChecker/W spies on ten standard DLLs (roughly the same set that WinScope includes by default). In contrast, the Microsoft parameter profile watches only the main three system DLLs (USER, KERNEL, and GDI). BoundsChecker32 currently spies on calls to KERNEL32, USER32, GDI32, and ADVAPI32, and on several other important DLLs.

In API spying, the information the spy tool can't show you is often the difference between figuring out what's going on and scratching your head in confusion. As a rule of thumb, the more data points (that is, API calls, window messages, hook callbacks, TOOLHELP notifications, and so on) you record, the better. For instance, the Microsoft parameter profiler is useless if you're trying to figure out how a program uses TOOLHELP to perform some action.

Enough descriptions of API spying tools! Let's solve a real-world problem so you can see these tools in action. Many times on programming forums I see questions relating to the Windows CLOCK.EXE program. The most common query is, "How do I make my program switch between having a title bar and not having a title bar, like CLOCK.EXE does?" You can find the answer by using a spy program to determine what API calls CLOCK.EXE makes when it toggles the title bar on and off. Here, I'm going to use the 32-bit CLOCK.EXE program from Windows NT. I could just as easily have used the 16-bit CLOCK.EXE. (Windows 95 doesn't include a separate CLOCK program, but you can run the NT CLOCK.EXE on Windows 95.)

For my tool, I'll use BoundsChecker32/NT, although any of the tools I've mentioned would do. If you have one of these programs, you can follow along with the steps I'll show, although it's not necessary to do so in order to understand the key points.

The first step is to run the program in question and collect the trace information. To do this, run BoundsChecker, select CLOCK.EXE from the FILE|LOAD dialog, and choose Run. After CLOCK starts up, go to CLOCK's Settings menu and select No Title. (I'm assuming that when CLOCK started there was a title bar and a menu.) Shut the Clock program down.

The next step is to examine the trace output and find the spot where the program responded to the No Title command. The following output shows a text file version of the relevant parts of the trace.

```
WNDMSG:  HWND:0049016E  MSG:WM_COMMAND(0111)  WPARAM:00000006  LPARAM:00000000
APICALL: GetWindowLong(HWND:0049016E, WINDOWLONG:GWL_STYLE)
APIRET:  GetWindowLong returns LONG:14CF0000
APICALL: SetWindowLong(HWND:0049016E, WINDOWLONG:GWL_ID, DWORD:00000000)
APIRET:  SetWindowLong returns LONG:BE00F2
APICALL: SetWindowLong(HWND:0049016E, WINDOWLONG:GWL_STYLE, DWORD:14840000)
APIRET:  SetWindowLong returns LONG:14CF0000
APICALL: SetWindowPos(HWND:0049016E, HWND:00000000, DWORD:00000000,
         DWORD:00000000, DWORD:00000000, DWORD:00000000,
         SWP_FLAGS:00000027:
         SWP_NOSIZE:SWP_NOMOVE:SWP_NOZORDER:SWP_FRAMECHANGED)
```

You may be wondering, "How am I supposed to know where to look for the information I need?" The answer is incredibly simple. Whenever you select

something from a menu, Windows delivers a WM_COMMAND message to
your program. Therefore, the first thing you need to do to find this sequence of
events is to search for the string WM_COMMAND. If you followed the steps
given above, there should be only one WM_COMMAND message in the entire
event log. However, for completeness, let's verify that the WM_COMMAND
message in the output is the correct one.

In a WM_COMMAND message, the WPARAM parameter holds the ID
of the selected menu item. In the output, WPARAM is 6. If you examine the
resources in CLOCK.EXE with Resource Workshop or some other similar
program, you'll see that the No Title menu item has an ID of 6. We're now
sure that we're looking at the right section of the event log.

After receiving the WM_COMMAND message telling CLOCK to turn
off its title bar, the first thing CLOCK does is call GetWindowLong(), passing the GWL_STYLE parameter. The next line of output shows that
GetWindowLong() returns a DWORD of 0x14CF0000. This value represents
the WS_*xxx* style bits passed to CreateWindow. You can decode these bits
yourself by looking in WINDOWS.H:

```
#define WS_VISIBLE        0x10000000L
#define WS_CLIPSIBLINGS   0x04000000L
#define WS_BORDER         0x00800000L
#define WS_DLGFRAME       0x00400000L
#define WS_SYSMENU        0x00080000L
#define WS_THICKFRAME     0x00040000L
#define WS_MINIMIZEBOX    0x00020000L
#define WS_MAXIMIZEBOX    0x00010000L
                          ===========
                          0x14CF0000
```

For now, temporarily ignore the next two lines in the output (I'll come
back to them momentarily). After CLOCK has retrieved its style bits with
GetWindowLong(), it turns around and sets a slightly different set of style
bits with the call to SetWindowLong(). In this call, the style bits are
0x14840000. It looks like CLOCK retrieves its WS_*xxx* style bits, modifies
a few of them, and sets the revised style bits back out to the window. So
what styles did CLOCK change? Comparing the original 0x14CF0000 to
the new 0x14840000, the new style DWORD is missing the following styles
from the original value:

```
#define WS_DLGFRAME       0x00400000L
#define WS_SYSMENU        0x00080000L
#define WS_MINIMIZEBOX    0x00020000L
#define WS_MAXIMIZEBOX    0x00010000L
```

This is consistent with CLOCK's behavior. When you select the No Title menu item, the system menu and the minimize and maximize buttons go away.

Now I'll return to the two lines in the output that I previously skipped. The first of these lines is a call to SetWindowLong(). This line appears to be setting the windows control ID (GWL_ID) to 0. With only that bit of information to go on, you're probably confused as to what the intent of the code is. To keep things moving, I'll let you in on the secret. All windows have an internal field that can be *either* a menu handle *or* a control ID. Top-level windows (such as CLOCK.EXE's) use this field to hold a menu handle (HMENU). Child windows (such as dialog box controls) use this field to hold their control ID. For official verification of this, refer to the hMenu field description in the documentation for CreateWindow().

Knowing this obscure factoid, we can see that CLOCK.EXE is setting its window's HMENU to 0. It probably would have been better (and clearer) for CLOCK to have used SetMenu() to change its HMENU value. However, there may have been underlying reasons why CLOCK's author(s) didn't use SetMenu(). One possible reason is that SetMenu() forces the menu area to be redrawn to reflect the change in menus.

The last line in the output is a call to SetWindowPos(). SetWindowPos() is an all-purpose routine that can move windows, change their Z-order, or cause Windows to recalculate and redraw the window. That last part (causing Windows to recalculate and redraw the window) probably has something to do with why SetMenu() wasn't used in CLOCK. Here's why: After CLOCK has twiddled the style bits and the HMENU, it needs to redraw itself using the new styles. Calling SetMenu() would cause parts of the window to be redrawn. The subsequent call to SetWindowPos() would then cause the window to be redrawn again, causing window flicker. CLOCK's implementors may have figured that it was okay to reduce flicker by directly bashing the new HMENU value into the window with SetWindowWord(). They knew that the window would be redrawn later by calling SetWindowPos().

The parameters that CLOCK passes to SetWindowPos() are interesting. The only nonzero parameters are the HWND and the SWP_*xxx* flags. The first three flags tell Windows that CLOCK doesn't want the window's size, screen position, or Z-ordering changed. The last parameter is the important one. It tells Windows that the window's frame has changed. This forces Windows to recalculate the client and nonclient areas, and to repaint the entire window. If I were to show more of the event trace, you'd see that the SetWindowPos() calls set off a flurry of messages and API calls that doesn't quiet down for several hundred lines. I highly encourage you to check this out for yourself. Also, if you want to see for yourself that the event trace mirrors reality, Microsoft supplies the source for CLOCK.EXE in the SAMPLES\DDEML\CLOCK\ directory of the Win32 SDK.

In examining CLOCK.EXE, we've seen how spying tools can show you how a visual effect (removing the title bar) is implemented. Spy tools are also useful for learning about what's going on underneath the surface, hidden from view. A favorite trick among programmers is to add some undocumented behavior or functionality to their program. For instance, the programmer might want the program to be able to write out debugging diagnostics to a file. Since this feature would only be used in rare situations, the programmer doesn't want to confuse the end user by having additional options in the user interface. Also, adding this option to the user interface requires describing it and documenting it, taking up additional precious time for a rarely used feature. The end result? Undocumented features.

One technique you can use to find these undocumented features is to look for entries in the program's .INI file that wouldn't appear there normally. In other words, the program looks for a particular .INI file entry, but never writes out a value for that entry when saving its options. To use the undocumented entry, the user of the program has to know the entry exists, and has to add the entry to the .INI file by hand. Although this discussion focuses on the .INI files, the same thing applies to the Win32 registry, which for the most part, replaces .INI files.

Finding situations such as I've just described is particularly easy with spying tools that save a copy of what an APIs pointer parameters refer to. Although I could have used BoundsChecker/W or WinScope, I've chosen to show an example of this using the Microsoft Parameter profiler. The following output shows a snippet of the event trace from running the Windows 3.1 WINMINE.EXE program.

```
01|APICALL:GetPrivateProfileInt "Minesweeper"  "Ypos"  50  "winmine.ini"
01|APIRET:GetPrivateProfileInt 105
01|APICALL:GetPrivateProfileInt "Minesweeper"  "Ypos"  50  "winmine.ini"
01|APIRET:GetPrivateProfileInt 105
01|APICALL:GetPrivateProfileInt "Minesweeper"  "Ypos"  50  "winmine.ini"
01|APIRET:GetPrivateProfileInt 105
01|APICALL:GetPrivateProfileInt "Minesweeper"  "Ypos"  50  "winmine.ini"
01|APIRET:GetPrivateProfileInt 105
01|APICALL:GetPrivateProfileInt "Minesweeper"  "Sound"  0  "winmine.ini"
01|APIRET:GetPrivateProfileInt 0
01|APICALL:GetPrivateProfileInt "Minesweeper"  "Sound"  0  "winmine.ini"
01|APIRET:GetPrivateProfileInt 0
01|APICALL:GetPrivateProfileInt "Minesweeper"  "Sound"  0  "winmine.ini"
01|APIRET:GetPrivateProfileInt 0
01|APICALL:GetPrivateProfileInt "Minesweeper"  "Sound"  0  "winmine.ini"
01|APIRET:GetPrivateProfileInt 0
```

```
01|APICALL:GetPrivateProfileInt "Minesweeper"  "Tick"  0  "winmine.ini"
01|APIRET:GetPrivateProfileInt 0
01|APICALL:GetPrivateProfileInt "Minesweeper"  "Tick"  0  "winmine.ini"
01|APIRET:GetPrivateProfileInt 0
01|APICALL:GetPrivateProfileInt "Minesweeper"  "Tick"  0  "winmine.ini"
01|APIRET:GetPrivateProfileInt 0
01|APICALL:GetPrivateProfileInt "Minesweeper"  "Tick"  0  "winmine.ini"
01|APIRET:GetPrivateProfileInt 0
01|APICALL:GetPrivateProfileInt "Minesweeper"  "Menu"  0  "winmine.ini"
01|APIRET:GetPrivateProfileInt 1
... 3 more "Menu" calls not shown...
```

The first part of each "APICALL:" line in the output is the call nesting level. In the output, all the calls are at level 01, the topmost level. This means that WINMINE didn't call the functions while in the middle of another API function. After the "APICALL:" is the name of the function, followed by its parameters. The Microsoft parameter profiler is nice enough to show actual ASCII strings rather than pointer values (for example, 0x10b7:003A). GetPrivateProfileInt takes three LPSTR parameters, so this feature is particularly helpful in this case.

In examining the fragment of WINMINE's event trace, notice that the code looks for each INI entry four times. Why it does this is a mystery to me. Trying to figure out strange sequences like this is part of the fun of spelunking.

Putting that behavior aside, look at the second parameter of each APICALL line. This parameter is the name of an entry in one of the INI's sections. The first group of APICALLs is looking for an entry called Ypos. If you look in the WINMINE.INI file, you'll see that there is in fact an entry called Ypos. However, if you continue and look for the next three entries (Sound, Tick, and Menu), you won't find them anywhere in the INI file. Looking further on in the event trace where WINMINE writes out new INI file values as part of its shutdown sequence, you won't find Sound, Tick, or Menu in there either.

What we've uncovered are three undocumented ways to affect WINMINE's behavior. I experimented with WINMINE by adding those three entries to the WINMINE.INI file myself. Although I didn't get any effect with Tick, adding the entry "Menu=1" caused WINMINE to not display a main menu. Adding an entry "Sound=3" (or a higher number) makes WINMINE play a little song when you win or lose a game.

SPELUNKING USING DISASSEMBLY

Although disassembly is complex and difficult, it's often the only way to crack open a mysterious algorithm or technique.

Disassembling a program or DLL isn't necessarily something you do only with other people's code either. When you encounter a strange bug in your code that's not immediately apparent from viewing the source, knowing how to correlate high-level language code to the compiler-generated assembler code is an incredibly valuable skill. Disassembling your own code also lets you to see whether the compiler has generated optimal code for a heavily used routine. Yet another situation in which you might disassemble your own code is when your program is mysteriously GP faulting at a customer site. If the user can give you the address where the program blows up, you can disassemble your code at that address to see what the program is doing.

Before continuing, I want to emphasize that disassembly is not for those who don't like to dive in details. If the sight of an assembler opcode strikes the remotest hint of fear in your heart, disassembly is not for you. You have to either know assembly language programming or be willing to learn it. This is not to say that you must *program* in assembly language yourself. It's perfectly fine to prefer to work in a high-level language. You just have to be willing to work at the very low level of machine opcodes and register values.

Your choice in disassemblers is sometimes constrained by the type of files you want to take apart. To do any sort of decent job, a disassembler needs to know quite a bit about the executable file format it will be working with. The simplest file disassembler isn't much more than the brains of a file-dumping program connected to a disassembly "engine" that takes raw bytes as input, and outputs assembler mnemonics. A perfect of example of this is the /DUMPBIN /DISASM option in the Visual C++ 32-bit edition linker. More advanced disassemblers can read in symbolic data that associates a symbolic name with a program address. These disassemblers can produce assembly listings that use real variable and function names rather than hexadecimal addresses.

The most well-known PC-based disassembler is probably Sourcer, from V-Communication's. By itself, Sourcer works with DOS EXE and COM files. With additional add-on components that produce script files, Sourcer also takes apart 16-bit NE files, VxDs (LE files), and Win32 PE files. Eclectic Software has the Win2Asm disassembler, which works with NE, LE, and PE files natively. RJ Swantek has the DisDoc Profesional disassembler, which works with the same types of files as Win2Asm. If you're only concerned with Win32 files and if price is a concern, it's hard to beat the DUMPBIN program that comes with Microsoft's Win32 SDK. I'll give an example using DUMPBIN shortly.

In case you're wondering what I used to do the research for this book, I have a pair of disassemblers of my own devising (one for Win16 NE files, the other for Win32 PE files and VxDs). Although they aren't multi-pass like Sourcer, they do just fine for me. The advantage of writing my own disassemblers is that I can modify them to take advantage of special tricks I've learned as well as making them read symbol information from a variety of sources. Neither one of them is currently being marketed.

If you just want to tinker with the disassembly techniques I'll describe, you might be able to get away with using the disassembler in your debugger. This is assuming that you don't use one of those battery-powered integrated development environment debuggers that doesn't have an assembly window. Some debuggers can dump the contents of their windows to a file. By dumping the contents of several disassembly windows in a row, you can get a somewhat reasonable listing. However, this is tedious and time-consuming, especially if the routine in question calls other functions elsewhere in the program. If you're at all serious about disassembly, get a real disassembler such as Sourcer, DisDoc, or Win2Asm. They're inexpensive, especially when you consider all the power they give you.

Zen and the art of disassembly

There is no single correct approach to disassembling a piece of code. What I'll describe here is what works for me. If some other methodology works for you, by all means use it! My basic approach to disassembly can be summed up as "divide and conquer." Starting with the raw output from a disassembler, I don't tackle the entire function or section in one big piece. Instead, I go through a series of steps that manipulate and break up the raw listing into small manageable pieces. I then attack the small pieces with a much greater chance of success. My ultimate goal is to work a disassembly listing into a piece of commented C code that I can refer to later.

Depending on the code you're working with, the importance and order of the following steps to break up a piece of code can vary. First, I'll describe in general terms the steps I take to disassemble a function. Afterward, I'll jump into the nitty-gritty details of identifying parameters, local variables, branch statements, function calls, and so on. Finally, I'll show a real example of how to work a raw disassembly listing into something usable. The steps you need to take to disassemble a function are discussed in the following sections.

Step 1: Disassemble the file

Run the executable through your disassembler to get a listing file. If your disassembler takes additional symbolic input (for instance from .SYM files or debug information), give it to the disassembler now.

If you're interested in one particular function, you might find it helpful to delete other code in the listing that comes before or after that function. This makes the file more manageable in your editor. For instance, some disassembly listings I've made started out as 3MB files. This caused my editor to take a long time to load and save the file. Cutting out the uninteresting code really speeds up this process.

Step 2: Label known entities

Go through the function and label all the known entities with more descriptive names. By known entities, I mean arguments to the function, local variables, and global variables. The idea of this phase is to do all the easy work first. When doing a jigsaw puzzle, most people do the easy parts such as the borders and the distinctive portions first. This reduces the number of unknown pieces that you have to sort through. It also gives you a better context from which to fill in the remaining pieces. This same concept applies to disassembly.

Assuming you know the arguments and calling convention for the function, you can easily identify the stack-based arguments to the function and replace them all with meaningful names (for example, hWnd). (I'll discuss identifying stack-based arguments later on.)

Unless there's debugging information in the executable, determining names for the local variables will be more difficult than labeling the parameters. Don't worry if you can't figure out every single name at this point. If a local variable jumps out at you though, by all means replace it with a meaningful symbolic name.

If you have symbolic information for global variables, the disassembler may have already replaced the global variable addresses with the symbolic name. However, if it didn't, you should do it by hand now.

Step 3: Break up instruction sequences

Disassembly listings often contain long sequences of instructions with no intervening blank lines. I find it helpful to insert blank lines between instruction sequences that logically belong together. This sounds vague, but it's not hard in practice. An example of such a sequence is the function's prologue code. Another sequence of instructions that logically belong together is the code that pushes parameters onto the stack and calls another function. A third logical instruction sequence is where the code performs some calculation and stores the result to a variable. A helpful (but not ironclad) guideline is to try to create sequences of instructions that form one statement in the program's source code. Put a blank line between each group of instructions to break up the listing visually.

Later on in the disassembly process you may need to decode branch statements. In high-level languages, these are statements such as if, while, do, switch, and so on. I've found that putting a blank line after each conditional or unconditional jump instruction makes it much easier to understand the listing. If your disassembler doesn't do this for your automatically, do it yourself. I used to do this quickly with an editor macro that searches for instructions that start with the letter *J* and then inserts a blank line following that instruction. Lately, I've modified my disassembler to automatically do this for me (yet another reason why I prefer to write my own disassembler).

Step 4: Add in string literals

If the function looks like it uses any string literal values, add comments that contain the string. Put the comments near the function calls that use the string. Later on, this will help reduce several lines of assembler code down to one C statement.

Step 5: Condense instructions into single C statements

Condense function calls and interrupts into single statements. At this point the function should be broken up into numerous little pieces. Find the instruction sequences that include calls to other functions for which you know the name and parameters. Study what's being pushed on the stack and try to construct what the arguments to the function should look like.

Step 6: Identify branch statements

Identify and convert conditional branch statements into the high-level language equivalent. If you see a TEST or a CMP instruction immediately followed by a conditional jump instruction (such as JE), you're probably looking at an if statement in a high-level language. The location where the J*xx* instruction jumps to is usually the end of a compound statement. In C, a compound statement is everything between matching {}'s. In Pascal, a compound statement is everything inside a BEGIN/END combination.

If you see a long series of test and conditional jumps, you're probably looking at a C switch statement or a Pascal case statement. Figuring out the conditional branching code is a tricky task. Multiple tests in a high-level language if statement can really make it challenging to figure out what the generated assembler code is doing. A C statement like:

```
if ( (GetModuleHandle("MYDLL.DLL") != 0)
      && ( (hWnd != GetDesktopWindow()) || ( styleFlags & WS_POPUP)) )
```

generates a rat's nest of conditional jumps, temporary results stored in registers, and so on. If nothing else, you'll end up with a newfound respect for compiler writers. It's not uncommon to stare at the same 20 or so instructions for an hour and still not have the faintest clue of what the code's intent is. That's why I recommend spelunking only as a last resort.

Step 7: Repeat as necessary

Repeat the preceding steps as necessary. This might sound trite, but it's not intended to be; this is an iterative process. You make a pass through the code, doing as much as you can with the information you currently have. You then step back, look at how the picture has changed, and make another pass. By figuring out one piece of the puzzle, a dozen more may fall into place quickly. In some ways, spelunking is like playing "Connect the Dots." The more dots you have, and the more you connect, the clearer the rest of the picture becomes.

Recognizing common code sequences and conventions

Having discussed in broad strokes how you might go about disassembling a function, I'll now examine some common code sequences and code-generation conventions. This will help you to mentally translate raw assembler code into its high-level language equivalent.

Identifying functions and procedures

The first thing to do when looking at the raw output from a disassembler is to figure out where a function (or procedure for you Pascal types) starts and ends. The easiest way to find the start of a function is to look for some sort of standard prologue code generated by a compiler. For 16-bit code, the standard prologue code is some variation of this process:

- Save original BP register on stack
- Assign stack pointer to BP register
- Decrement the stack pointer to make room for local variables
- Save the calling function's register variables on the stack

Expressed in assembly language, the same information looks like this:

```
PUSH   BP       ;; Save caller's BP frame.
MOV    BP,SP    ;; Set up new BP frame.
SUB    SP,XX    ;; XX is the number of bytes need for local variables.
PUSH   SI       ;; DI and SI are commonly used as register variables.
PUSH   DI
```

or, when 80286 or better code-generation is enabled:

```
ENTER  XX,0     ;; XX is the number of bytes needed for locals
PUSH   SI       ;; DI and SI are commonly used as register variables
PUSH   DI
```

These stack frames are what compilers generate for code that should run only in 16-bit protected mode. Back in the bad old days of real mode, Windows itself would often need to walk the stack of a program when moving segments around in memory. Since it can be quite tricky to walk a program stack that contains a mix of near and far calls, the compilers helped out via the odd BP stack frames. When odd BP-frame code generation is enabled, all far functions increment the BP register before pushing it on the stack (near functions leave BP alone). After restoring the original BP in a far function's epilogue, the code decrements the BP register. When walking the stack frames, if Windows saw an odd value for a saved BP, it knew that the function was a far function. The standard stack frame for an odd BP-style far function looks like this:

```
INC    BP       ;; Indicate a far frame.
PUSH   BP       ;; Save caller's BP frame.
MOV    BP,SP    ;; Set up new BP frame.
SUB    SP,XX    ;; XX is the number of bytes need for local variables.
PUSH   SI       ;; DI and SI are commonly used as register variables.
PUSH   DI
```

Moving now to 32-bit programs, the standard prologue code looks like this:

```
PUSH    EBP         ;; Save caller's EBP frame.
MOV     EBP, ESP    ;; Set up new EBP frame.
SUB     ESP, XX     ;; Make space for local variables on stack.
PUSH    ESI         ;; ESI, EDI, and EBX are commonly used as
PUSH    EDI         ;; register variables.
PUSH    EBX
```

or:

```
ENTER   XX,0    ;; XX is the number of bytes needed for locals.
PUSH    ESI
PUSH    EDI
PUSH    EBX
```

The previous sequences are the full-blown prologues. In real-world code, parts or all of the prologue may be missing or different:

- If the function's code doesn't alter a register-variable register (for example, ESI, EDI, and EBX), it won't bother to save it in the prologue code. Also, in 32-bit code, EBX is sometimes used as a register variable, while in 16-bit code it usually isn't.

- In 16-bit code, if the function doesn't take any parameters or use any local variables, the compiler may omit the PUSH BP / MOV BP,SP sequence.

- In 32-bit code, even if the function takes parameters and uses local variables, the compiler may still not set up an EBP frame. The 32-bit addressing modes of the 386 and better CPUs allow the compiler to address parameters and locals with the ESP register, for instance:

```
MOV EAX,[ESP+1C].
```

Recognizing the function epilogue is a little trickier. If the compiler's optimizer is turned on, there may be multiple places within the function where it does a RET or RETF to the caller. Assuming the function has a single epilogue at the end of the function, the full-blown, 16-bit epilogue will look something like this:

```
POP     DI  ;; Restore caller's register variables
POP     SI
LEAVE       ;; or ADD SP,XX / POP BP
RETF        ;; far return. Near return is a RET.
```

For 32-bit code, the epilogue will look like this:

```
POP     EBX ;; Restore caller's register variables.
POP     EDI
POP     ESI
LEAVE
RET         ;; A 32-bit near return.
```

When determining where one routine starts and another ends, remember that right after the end of one routine, you're likely to find the start of another. If you see something that looks like it's epilogue code, verify it by looking for something that looks like prologue code for another function after it. If you don't see this, either the compiler has optimized away the prologue code for the next function, or the current function has multiple points of exit.

Function return values

When functions return a value, they return the result in a register or in a combination of registers. To determine if a routine's return value is being used, examine the register usage in the code that calls the routine. If you see code that calls a routine and then uses the return value register(s) without explicitly setting them, you know the code uses the function's return value. For example, if you see code that calls a function and them uses the AX afterward without setting its value, you know that the called function returns its value in the AX register.

In 32-bit code, the convention is that functions return their values in EAX. 16-bit code uses AX for returning 16-bit values, and the DX:AX combination for returning 32-bit values. If the code is written in assembly language, however, all bets are off because assembly-language programmers can return values however they want. One common assembler convention is that if the routine only needs to return a success or failure code, the routine sets or clears the carry flag (CF) as appropriate. You can ferret out these routines by looking for JC and JNC instructions immediately after CALL instructions.

Identifying parameters

If you know the parameters for the function you're taking apart, labeling them in the assembler code is particularly easy. With one exception (which I'll cover later in this section), compilers always pass arguments to a function or procedure on the stack. By adding up the sizes of each parameter that's passed, you can quickly locate where each parameter resides on the stack. Before I show an example of this, however, I first need to do a quick review of compiler calling conventions used in Windows and Win32.

In 16-bit Windows code, most exported functions use the Pascal calling convention. In the Pascal calling convention, the calling code pushes parameters onto the stack from the leftmost parameter to the rightmost parameter. As an example, the 16-bit code generated for a call to "foo(0x10, 0x20, 0x30)" would look something like this:

```
PUSH 0010h
PUSH 0020h
PUSH 0030h
CALL FAR PTR FOO
```

Besides specifying that parameters are passed from right to left, the Pascal calling convention also dictates that the called function must remove the arguments from the stack before returning. In the example I just cited, the foo function needs to pop 6 bytes off the stack before it returns. It will probably do this with a RETF 6 instruction.

The immediate opposite of the Pascal calling convention is the C calling convention. The standard C/C++ runtime library functions use the C calling convention. In the C calling convention, the parameters are passed from the rightmost to the leftmost. (The primary advantage of passing arguments from right to left is to support functions such as printf that take a variable number of arguments.) The code that calls a C-style function is responsible for removing the parameters from the stack after the call returns. A call to "foo(0x10, 0x20, 0x30)" using the C calling convention would look like this:

```
PUSH 0030h       ;; Parameters pushed right to left.
PUSH 0020h
PUSH 0010h
CALL FAR PTR FOO
ADD  SP,06h      ;; Remove parameters from the stack.
```

You shouldn't expect to always see an "ADD (E)SP,XX" after a C-style call. If the compiler pushes only one or two parameters, it sometimes POPs them into an unneeded register to remove them from the stack. The Borland C++ compiler is known for this particular code-generation sequence.

For Win32, Microsoft has adopted the stdcall calling convention for almost all functions exported by the operating system DLLs. The stdcall convention is a hybrid of the C and Pascal conventions. The caller pushes the parameters from right to left, as in the C style. The callee function cleans the parameters off the stack like the Pascal style does. Incidentally, when you use a stdcall declared function with Microsoft's C++, the compiler internally adds on an "@*xx*" to the end of the function name. The *xx* is a string representing the number of bytes that the function expects as parameters, for instance, _GetWindowLong@8 or _PeekMessage@20.

After you've figured out the calling convention of the function you're examining, you can determine where the parameters are on the stack. Knowing the offset of the parameter relative to the stack frame, you can look for the instructions that reference that memory location and then replace the assembly language address with a symbolic name. Having symbolic names around when staring at a disassembly listing is extremely helpful when figuring out what the code's intent is.

After a function has executed its prologue code, the stack frame looks like the one shown here:

Parameters
return address   (placed here by the CALL instruction)
previous (E)BP   (pushed by the prologue code)

As you can see, the (E)BP register points to where the previous (E)BP value is saved. Within the function, all the parameters can now be accessed as positive displacements from BP or EBP. This is an important point worth restating: Instructions that access memory using addresses such as [BP+*xx*] or [EBP+*xx*] are probably using the routine's parameters.

For a far 16-bit function like the APIs exported by 16-bit Windows, the actual stack frame looks like this:

Parameters   (starting at BP+06)
return CS   (at BP+04)
return IP   (at BP+02)
Previous BP   (at BP+00)

Assuming WORD-sized parameters and the Pascal calling convention, the last parameter to the function will be at [BP+06], the second-to-last parameter at [BP+08], and so on. If there are any DWORD parameters, the calculations need to be adjusted accordingly. Also, if the function was a near function, the locations given would again need adjustment because there's only a return IP on the stack, and no return CS.

Let's look at a real-world example now to get a better feel for what I've just described. A window procedure for a 16-bit program has the following declaration:

```
LRESULT WINAPI WndProc(HWND hWnd, UINT msg, WPARAM wParam, LPARAM lParam);
```

Inside the WndProc code, the stack frame looks like this:

```
hWnd          WORD PTR  [BP+0E]   ;; Parameters pushed left to right.
msg           WORD PTR  [BP+0C]
wParam        WORD PTR  [BP+0A]
lParam        DWORD PTR [BP+06]
return CS     WORD PTR  [BP+04]
return IP     WORD PTR  [BP+02]
previous BP   WORD PTR  [BP+00]
```

Armed with this knowledge, you can use your editor's search and replace feature to find all the references to [BP+0E] and replace them with the much more meaningful [hWnd]. Likewise, you can replace [BP+0C] with [msg], and so forth.

Now let's look at the 32-bit equivalent to the above window procedure. In Win32, all parameters are 32 bits. The return address is a 32-bit near pointer, and the code uses EBP rather than BP. And don't forget that the window procedure uses the stdcall convention, making the parameters appear in the reverse order from the equivalent 16-bit code. The stack frame for a 32-bit window procedure therefore looks like this:

```
lParam        DWORD PTR [EBP+14]   ;; Parameters pushed right to left.
wParam        DWORD PTR [EBP+10]
msg           DWORD PTR [EBP+0C]
hWnd          DWORD PTR [EBP+08]
return EIP    DWORD PTR [EBP+04]
previous EBP  DWORD PTR [EBP+00]
```

Now that I've described the normal stack frame for a 32-bit function, I'll spring some bad news on you. 32-bit compilers have the option of not generating standard EBP frames. They do this to save time and space by not including the code to set up and take down the stack frame.

The problem is that the generated code doesn't address parameters and local variables with an offset from EBP anymore. Instead, the code may address the parameters with an offset from ESP (for example, [ESP+14]). If this thought alarms you, it should! The value of ESP changes throughout the function as it pushes parameters in preparation for calling other routines. Thus, an [lParam] that's at [ESP+14] early on in the function could later be found at [ESP+18] if the code pushes a DWORD onto the stack. If the code pushes a second DWORD, [lParam] will now be at [ESP+1C]. This makes it nearly impossible to search and replace memory references like MOV EAX,[ESP+14] with references like MOV EAX,[lParam]. Because of this, you'll need to mentally track the relative location of ESP throughout the function, giving symbolic names to parameters on an instruction by instruction basis. Yuck! Your only real hope is that the compiler has copied a parameter into a register and used the register's copy of the value wherever it was needed.

If you're taking apart a function that you don't know the parameters for, there are still some small things you can do to make this process easier on yourself. For instance, you'll most definitely want to figure out how many bytes of parameters the function is passed. To do this, look at the exit epilogue of the function. Does it pop stuff off the stack with something like RETF 8? If so, you know how many bytes of parameters the function takes (in this case, 8). If the function's exit code doesn't remove anything from the stack, find a place in the code where there's a call to the function. Is the next instruction after the CALL instruction something like ADD ESP,12? If so, then the function takes 12 bytes of parameters.

Beyond knowing how many bytes of parameters a function takes, you can often glean more information by studying the code that pushes parameters on the stack in preparation for calling the function. For instance, let's say you saw the following disassembly listing fragment from a Win32 program:

```
CALL    GetFocus
PUSH    EAX
CALL    GetCurrentThread
PUSH    EAX
CALL    DoSomething
```

From this code fragment, you can determine that the DoSomething function takes two parameters, an HWND and a thread HANDLE. How did I figure that out? Both GetFocus() and GetCurrentThread() are Win32 APIs that return a value in EAX. After calling GetFocus(), EAX holds an

HWND value. After calling GetCurrentThread(), EAX holds a thread HANDLE. By logical deduction, the DoSomething() function expects an HWND and a HANDLE as parameters.

Although parameters are usually passed on the stack, it's also possible to pass parameters in registers. This calling convention is usually called the *fastcall* convention because passing parameters in registers can be faster than passing them on the stack. For instance, many KRNL386 internal heap management routines pass parameters around in registers to speed things up. The compiler or assembly language programmer decides whether register parameters will be used on a function by function basis. The Microsoft compilers preface function names that use the fastcall style with an "@" (asterisk) character. Function "Foo" in your source code shows up as "@Foo" in the MAP file or debug information if the compiler used the fast-call convention. Fastcall style functions aren't limited to register parameters only. The compiler can pass some parameters and registers and others on the stack.

Finally, if the code you're examining uses interrupts, get out your interrupt list documentation and look up which parameters go in which registers. (You do have Ralf Brown's Interrupt List, right?) Add a comment to the INT instruction that describes what the instruction does. For instance,

```
MOV AX,0500
LES DI,[myBuffer]
INT 31
```

would become something like:

```
MOV AX,0500
LES DI,[myBuffer]    ; DPMI function 0500h - Get Free Memory Information
INT 31               ; ES:DI -> structure to fill with information
```

Identifying local variables

Like function parameters, a routine's local variables are also usually found on the stack. The key difference in distinguishing between a parameter and a local variable is that the code references local variables with a *negative* offset from the stack frame. For example, in 16-bit code, [BP-04], or in 32-bit code, [EBP-04].

Unlike parameters, there's no semi-mechanical method for determining the types, uses, and locations of local variables. Instead, you have to examine how the function's code uses a particular memory location. Sometimes it's fairly easy to determine a local variable's meaning. For example, look at the following Win32 code snippet:

```
PUSH DWORD PTR [EBP+08]
CALL GetParent
MOV  [EBP-0C],EAX
```

The GetParent() function is a Win32 API that takes an HWND parameter and returns that window's parent HWND in EAX. Since the code snippet copies EAX into [EBP-0C], it's obvious that [EBP-0C] is an HWND. Additionally, you can make a wild guess that this variable is probably called something like "hWndParent" in the original source code. Once you've gotten that far, it's time to use your editor's search and replace feature to change all occurrences of [EBP-0C] to [hWndParent]. Look at your disassembly listing after you do this. Odds are, it's starting to become clearer.

Some of you may be saying, "That's nice Matt, but not every local variable is going to be such easy picking." True, but there's more than one way to attack problems like this. Sometimes it's easier to identify locals from their use as parameters to other functions. This Win32 assembly fragment shows such an example:

```
LEA  EAX,[EBP-30]      ; Get address of EBP-30h into EAX.
PUSH EAX               ; Push it as an LPRECT.
PUSH [EBP+08]          ; Push an HWND (a parameter).
CALL GetWindowRect     ; Call into USER32 to get the RECT coordinates.
```

Looking up GetWindowRect() in the SDK documentation, we know that it takes an HWND and a pointer to a RECT structure to be filled in. Since GetWindowRect is a stdcall function, the RECT pointer should be pushed first, followed by the HWND. In the listing, we see that for the LPRECT parameter, the code pushes an address 30h bytes below the EBP value. Therefore, there must be a local variable of type RECT at [EBP-30]. This is a bonanza of information! Since WINDEF.H contains the format of a RECT structure (4 DWORDS), we can figure out where all the RECT's fields are on the stack:

```
RECT.left   = [EBP-30]
RECT.top    = [EBP-2C]
RECT.right  = [EBP-28]
RECT.bottom = [EBP-24]
```

Again, use this opportunity to search and replace those [EBP-*xx*]'s with more meaningful symbolic names.

Compilers can copy local variables (and parameters) into registers temporarily. The code uses the register wherever it needs the variable's value. This saves both code space and clock cycles. When working with a disassembly listing, you need to be on the lookout for places where the code begins using a register variable. Wherever you see this register used afterward, substitute the variable name you've figured out. Be aware, however, that the compiler (or assembler programmer) may use the same register for different variables at different places within the function.

In 16-bit programs, the SI and DI variables are most commonly used as register variables. Since these registers are only 16 bits long, they usually aren't used for pointers because most pointers in 16-bit Windows code are 32-bit far pointers. Instead, SI and DI are typically used for 16-bit values such as HWNDs and DCs. In Win32 programs, the ESI, EDI, and EBX registers are the most common register variables. In Win32, pointers are 32-bit near pointers, so it's common to see these registers used as pointers in addition to other types of variables. None of these guidelines are hard and fast, however. Use your own intuition and judgment when dealing with register variables.

Identifying global variables

Determining that a program is using a global variable is particularly easy. Almost any memory reference that uses a hardcoded address is a global variable. Put another way, global variables don't require the assistance of registers like EBP to address them. In 32-bit code, a global variable reference would look something like this:

```
MOV EAX,[00464398]
```

If you're lucky and have symbol information, the disassembler may already have replaced the "[00464398]" with the name used in the program's source. If it hasn't, you should find all the instructions that use that memory location and replace the address with the symbolic name. If you don't have symbolic information, try to figure out what the variable is used for and make up your own name.

In 16-bit code, identifying global variables is much the same as in 32-bit code, albeit with 16- rather than 32-bit addresses. If the code you're working with has multiple data segments, however, you'll need to be extra careful.

The problem is that the same offset can be in use in several data segments. When accessing global variables in a segment other than the default DGROUP, the code sets up a segment register (usually ES) to point to that segment. The code then accesses variables within the segment with hard-coded offsets — for instance, MOV AX,ES:[001C]. The lesson here is to be careful when replacing global variable addresses with symbolic names.

If you have symbolic information for an executable file, but encounter a memory location that's not in the list of global variables, you might be facing one of two likely situations. In the first situation, that memory location might be used for a static variable. If your symbol information includes only public symbols, the variable won't show up in the list. In the second situation, you might be looking at a member of a structure or an array. For instance, a 16-bit program has a global variable "MSG MyMsg;" that ends up in the program's DGROUP segment at offset 0364h. Four bytes into the MSG structure lies the wParam field. MyMsg.wParam will therefore be at offset 0368h in the data segment. Symbol information generated for this executable will include a public symbol called "MyMsg" at offset 0364h, but will contain nothing about offset 0368h.

To illustrate this process, imagine you're watching over my shoulder as I examine a disassembly listing. As I'm working along, I encounter an instruction that reads the value at offset 0368h. To my chagrin, the symbol information doesn't show any symbols at this offset.

All is not lost, though. By looking for the closest symbol occurring before address 0368h, I see there's something called "MyMsg" at offset 0364. Based on that name and a hunch, I hypothesize that the MyMsg symbol at offset 0364h is a MSG structure. I then need to test this theory. If offset 0364h really is a MSG structure, will offset 0368h be the address of one of the structure's fields? In this case, yes!

However, before I assume that I've guessed correctly, I would look for other code that backs up the theory. Does the memory location 0368h look like it's being used as a WPARAM? Does the next structure field (at offset 036Ah) look like it's being used as an LPARAM? Unfortunately, there are no hard and fast techniques that I can use here. I've got to make reasonable guesses about what's going on and test those guesses until I'm sufficiently confident in my theory.

One nice aspect of global variables is that the compiler rarely puts them into register variables. It's generally not a good idea to enregister global variables. If the only correct copy of the variable was in a register, interrupt service routines and callback functions could fail if they tried to use the memory version of the global variable.

Identifying string literals

Many API functions take strings as parameters. By matching up the ASCII strings with the functions that use them, you can often get a much better idea of what the code is doing. For instance, in a 16-bit program you might encounter the following instruction sequence:

```
PUSH DS
PUSH 0437
CALL GETMODULEHANDLE
```

or in a 32-bit program, something like this:

```
PUSH 00471784
CALL GETMODULEHANDLE
```

Turning to your trusty API documentation, which you should *always* have at your fingertips, you see that GetModuleHandle() takes one argument, a pointer to a string. Those PUSH instructions are pushing the address of a string onto the stack as the parameter to GetModuleHandle(). Therefore, at address 00471784 (or DS:0437 for you 16-bit types), there must be a null-terminated string (for example, "USER32"). If your disassembler has done a hex/ASCII dump for the data sections of the file, go to the address and retrieve the string. Back in the code that referenced the string literal, make a comment that includes the retrieved string. For instance:

```
PUSH 00471784        ;; "USER32"
CALL GETMODULEHANDLE
```

If the code you're disassembling uses a lot of string literals, you'll be amazed at how much clearer the code becomes after you do this. Filling in string literals is one of the trickier and more time-consuming aspects of disassembly.

Some executables contain string literals in the code sections themselves. Often the string occurs in memory immediately after the code that references the string. A good disassembler can pick up on this situation and switch to a hex dump mode temporarily. However, disassemblers often make mistakes. Sometimes you'll need to examine the surrounding code to look for clues that tell you where the code starts and the data ends. Often, embedded data like switch statement JMP tables creates temporary garbage in your disassembly listing. By looking at the surrounding code, you can frequently gain clues as to what's really code and what's embedded data in a code area. You can then feed this information back into the disassembler and make a second listing that correctly differentiates the code from the data. Nobody said this stuff was easy!

Identifying if statements

The simplest type of conditional execution code to figure out is a simple if statement:

```
if ( some test ) {
    do some sequence of code
}
```

Before discussing variations of this statement, I want to show what it looks like in assembly language. Viewed from the disassembly listing level, there are three major types of tests that you encounter:

- Equality tests: if (a == b), if (a != b), and so on . . .
- Boolean TRUE/FALSE tests: if (a), if (!a), and so on . . .
- Bitfield tests: if (a & 0x0040), and so on . . .

Although compilers generate different code sequences for each type of test, the goal in each case is to set or clear the CPU's Zero Flag (ZF). After setting or clearing the Zero flag, the code uses the JZ (Jump if Zero) or JNZ (Jump if Not Zero) conditional branch instruction to either execute or skip over the next section of code. In the spirit of keeping assembly language confusing, the JZ instruction mnemonic can also be expressed as JE (Jump if Equal) and JNZ can also be written as JNE (Jump if Not Equal).

The basic algorithm of the "test, then conditionally jump" model is as follows: If the test expression resolves to a FALSE result, the CPU takes the conditional jump, and the following code inside the {}'s or BEGIN/END block doesn't get executed. If the expression evaluates to TRUE, the conditional jump isn't taken, and control falls into the code inside the {} block.

Warning: What I've just described here is the simple version of what occurs. In the real world, the generated code might be more complex. For example, in 16-bit code there might be a JZ or JNZ instruction that's only job is to jump over a regular JMP statement. This would happen if the code inside the "if" block was longer than 127 bytes, the limit of a conditional jump instruction in 16-bit code. The basic premise of what I've just described still applies, though.

For equality tests, compilers uses the CMP instruction. This snippet of output produced with "DUMPBIN /DISASM" shows an example:

```
0000101E:  cmp  dword ptr [ebp-04],04
00001022:  jne  0000102E
00001028:  inc  byte ptr [ebp-04]
0000102B:  inc  byte ptr [ebp-08]
0000102E:  ...
```

The first instruction compares the DWORD at [EBP-04] to the value 4. If they're the same, the CMP instructions sets the Zero flag; otherwise, it clears the Zero flag. The next instruction (the JNE) jumps over the code that follows, but only if the Zero flag was clear. Therefore, the two INC instructions execute only if the Zero flag was set. The Zero flag could be set only if [EBP-04] was equal to 4. Expressed in C code, the above snippet could look something like this:

```
if ( SomeVariable1 == 4 )
{
    SomeVariable1++;    // INC [EBP-04]
    SomeVariable2++;    // INC [EBP-08]
}
```

When the expression in the if statement is only concerned with whether the expression is TRUE or FALSE, the compiler has a choice of code-generation options. In some cases, the generated code can look like the if statement code described earlier. For example, the expression "if (MyVariable)" could also be written as "if (MyVariable != 0)". The other situation to consider is when the expression's value is in a register. When this occurs, the compiler can use a smaller instruction to determine if the value is TRUE (nonzero) or FALSE (zero). The shorter instruction is an "OR register,register" instruction, like this:

```
0000102E:  call  00001000
00001033:  or    eax,eax
00001035:  je    0000103E
0000103B:  inc   byte ptr [ebp-04]
0000103E:  ...
```

In this code, the first instruction calls a function that returns its value in EAX. Rather than using three bytes with a "CMP EAX,0", the compiler uses an OR instruction. The OR instruction does a logical OR on all the bits in EAX. The Zero flag is set only if none of these bit are set (and hence, EAX == 0).

The third instruction sequence you'll see in conjunction with if statements occurs when individual bits are involved. Many WORDs and DWORDs in Windows programming are composed of a set of 1-bit flags, such as the WS_*xxx* style bits that you pass to CreateWindow() in a DWORD. Code that needs to see if a bit is set uses the languages bitwise AND operator (in C, the "&" operator). Consider the following C fragment:

```
DWORD winFlags = GetWinFlags();
if ( winFlags & WF_CPU386 )
    is386 = TRUE;
```

The assembler code generated for the if statement looks like this:

```
0000102E:  test  byte ptr [ebp-08],04    ;; WF_CPU386 == 0004h
00001032:  je    0000103F
00001038:  mov   dword ptr [ebp-0C],00000001
0000103F:  sub   eax,eax
```

The first instruction uses the CPU's TEST instruction to see if the bit representing the value 4 is set. The TEST instruction performs a logical AND of the corresponding bits in the two operands, but doesn't overwrite either of the operands. Instead, TEST sets the Zero flag if the result doesn't have any bits set. If any bits were set, TEST clears the Zero flag. If the bit representing the value 4 was set in [EBP-08], the Zero flag should be clear. As a result, the JE instruction won't jump and the DWORD at [EBP-0C] will be incremented.

If you look carefully at the TEST instruction in the previous snippet, you'll notice something strange. In the C code, "winFlags" is a DWORD, yet the generated assembler code looks only at the bottommost BYTE. The compiler is optimizing, and using the smallest instruction possible. The unoptimized version of the instruction that TEST'ed the entire DWORD would use three more bytes, and would be:

```
TEST DWORD PTR [EBP-08],00000004
```

I mention this not because of the optimization, but because you need to be on your toes when looking at TEST instructions. The address and bitmask being TEST'ed may not be what you expect. For example, in the previous example, let's change the test to look for WF_80x87, which has a value of 00000400h. The TEST instruction should therefore change to "test [ebp-08],00000400h", right? Wrong! The actual instruction the compiler generates is: "test [ebp-07],04". The code is looking one byte higher in memory than the start of the winFlags DWORD (at EBP-08). To compensate, the compiler shifts the bit flags to be tested to the right by 8 bits. Sneaky! If the bits to be tested are even further into the variable, the compiler bumps up the address and shifts the testing bits accordingly.

Now that we've seen the three basic ways that simple if statements can be encoded, let's move on to bigger things. Only slightly more complicated than an if statement is an if-else statement. Consider the following elaboration of a previous example:

```
if ( i == 4 )
{
    i++;
    j++;
}
else
    j--;
```

The compiler generates the following code:

```
0000101E:  cmp  dword ptr [ebp-04],04
00001022:  jne  00001033
00001028:  inc  byte ptr [ebp-04]
0000102B:  inc  byte ptr [ebp-08]
0000102E:  jmp  00001036
00001033:  dec  byte ptr [ebp-08]
00001036:  ...
```

The first two instructions look identical to the code for a plain if statement. The JMP instruction a bit farther down is the key. After executing the code for when the expression is true, the JMP instruction skips over the code generated for the "else" clause. The target address of the JMP instruction is a huge clue as to where the "else" clause's code ends.

Here are the two main things to look for when you're trying to identify an if-else statement: Does the initial JE/JNE instruction jump to an instruction that's immediately after a JMP instruction? Does the JMP instruction transfer to a higher address (that is, does it go forward in memory rather than backward)?

Another more complicated form of the if statement is the expression with multiple conditions. For example:

```
if ( (i == 4) && (j == 2) && (k == 6) )
{
    i++;
    j++;
}
```

The compiler generates the following code:

```
0000101E:  cmp   dword ptr [ebp-08],04
00001022:  jne   00001042 ;; Jump past code inside {}'s.
00001028:  cmp   dword ptr [ebp-0C],02
0000102C:  jne   00001042 ;; Jump past code inside {}'s.
00001032:  cmp   dword ptr [ebp-04],06
00001036:  jne   00001042 ;; Jump past code inside {}'s.
0000103C:  inc   byte ptr [ebp-08]
0000103F:  inc   byte ptr [ebp-0C]
00001042:  ...
```

The code here is straightforward, with three tests in succession. If any of them fails, the code skips any remaining tests and the code inside the {}'s. If you see a series of test and branch combinations that all jump to a common spot, you're probably dealing with an if statement with multiple conditions that each must be true.

The code generated for the OR case — in which there are multiple tests, any one of which can be true — is similar to the code generated for the AND case. You'll see a series of consecutive test and branches. All tests except the last one jump to the code inside the {}'s if they resolve to TRUE. If a test fails, the code simply falls through to the next test. If the last test resolves to TRUE, it falls into the code inside the {}'s. If the last test fails, it jumps around the {} code.

This section has just covered the basics; for instance, I didn't discuss "for" loops or "while" loops. You're certain to encounter things that are more complicated. However, almost everything you'll encounter can be broken down into combinations and variations of the code sequences I've described here.

Identifying switch statements

Until the advent of class libraries like MFC and OWL, most Windows programs had a large switch statement very near the beginning of their window procedures. The switch statement directs the various window messages to their appropriate handler code. If you need to see a program's window procedure to discover what it does with a particular message, you'll need to know how to crack a switch statement. Luckily, that's not hard to do.

The general process for cracking a switch statement is this: For each conditional jump, go to where the target code is. Immediately above the code, put a big bold comment that labels which case that code handles. This is especially helpful for decoding the switch statements that so often occur in window procedures. For each message that the code checks for, put the corresponding WM_*xxx* message name above the section of code that handles it. For example:

```
; CASE WM_NCHITTEST
00413254:   XOR      EAX,EAX
00413256:   JMP      00413454

; CASE WM_GETTEXTLENGTH
0041325B:   MOV      EAX,[cbTextBuffer]
00413260:   JMP      00413454
```

Recognizing a switch statement is incredibly easy, although there are three common variations in how they're encoded. The easiest switch statement to decode is what I call the "idiot encoding." It's very easy to follow but wastes a lot of space in the process. The assembler code will look something like this:

```
MOV EAX,[EBP+0C]
CMP EAX,00000045
JE  someAddress
CMP EAX,00000169
JE  someAddress2
CMP EAX,00000265
JE  someAddress3
```

The first instruction loads the switch statement's argument into a register. In this example, the register is EAX, but it could just as easily be some other register, such as EDI. 16-bit code seems to always use AX, though.

After loading a register with the test value, the code enters a series of CMP/JE combinations. For each "case" clause within the switch statement, there's a corresponding CMP/JE combination. As a result, it's easy to find the handler code for a given switch input value. If a program uses a switch statement to dispatch messages inside a window proc, just look up the WM_*xxx* values for the windows messages of interest. It's then a simple matter to look for the CMP instruction that tests for that value. The JE instruction that follows has the address of the code that handles that message.

If you want to take apart the entire routine to see how it handles every message, it's helpful to find the handler code for each message and label it prominently with the message name.

The second variation of switch statements is closely related to the one I've just described. The difference is that the testing instructions use fewer bytes and require you to keep track of intermediate values. Consider the following code sequence:

```
MOV EAX,[EBP+0C]
SUB EAX,2
JE  someAddress
DEC EAX
JE  someAddress2
DEC EAX
JE  someAddress3
SUB EAX,5
JE  someAddress4
```

At first glance, this code is confusing. It doesn't compare any values like the first switch statement variation does. The only real action is that EAX's value keeps dropping. To make sense of the code, you need to know that the DEC and SUB instructions set the Zero flag if the result of their operation is 0. Each SUB or DEC instruction eats away at the input value. If the value ever drops to exactly 0, its time is up and a JE instruction dispatches it to the appropriate handler. Lower initial values will be taken out early on, while higher input values are dispatched later on.

To see which value is being tested at a given JE instruction, you need to sum up all the values that have been previously subtracted. When taking apart a switch statement of this type, I find it helpful to label each JE instruction with the current running total. Here's how I would annotate the above sequence:

```
MOV EAX,[EBP+0C]    ; Load EAX with the switch() argument.
SUB EAX,2
JE  someAddress     ; 2 (Jumps only if EAX was initially 2.)
DEC EAX
JE  someAddress2    ; 3 (Jumps only if EAX was initially 3.)
DEC EAX
JE  someAddress3    ; 4 (Jumps only if EAX was initially 4.)
SUB EAX,5
JE  someAddress4    ; 9 (Jumps only if EAX was initially 9.)
```

The third type of switch statement encoding you'll encounter is called a *jump table*. If a series of input values are sufficiently close together, the compiler may decide to build an array of addresses. Each array entry corresponds to one case value. The advantage of jump tables is that they're fast. The code doesn't need to include a test for every possible case value. The following C code shows a switch statement that the compiler could use a jump table for:

```
switch ( i )
{
    case 0x0:   i = 2; break;
    case 0x1:   j = 2; break;
    case 0x2:   k = 3; break;
    // Cases 3 through 8 not shown.
    case 0x9:   j = j + k + i; break;
}
```

The meat of the code that the compiler generates comes down to this:

```
00001008:   mov  eax,dword ptr [ebp-0C]
0000100B:   cmp  eax,09
0000100E:   ja   00001068
00001010:   jmp  dword ptr [eax*4+0040108F]
```

The first instruction loads the switch statement's input value into EAX. The next two instructions determine if the input value is within the range of listed case values. If not, the JA instruction jumps to the code after the switch statement. The final instruction uses EAX as an index into the handler address array, and jumps to that location.

In the previous code, the compiler put the handler address array into the data area of the executable. However, don't be surprised if the array comes immediately after the JMP instruction. This is especially prevalent in 16-bit programs. It's easy to tell when this occurs because the JMP instruction uses a CS override as part of the memory address. If the handler address array follows the JMP statement, you may see garbage instructions for awhile. This is because the disassembler doesn't know that those bytes are really data rather than code. A good disassembler will either recognize these situations or, at the minimum, let you tell it which areas of code are really data.

A disassembly example

Now that I've covered the basics of disassemblers, let's look at a real-world example to show how these concepts can be applied. For this example, I'm going to use the routine in the Windows NT CLOCK.EXE that switches the program between having a titlebar and not having a titlebar. I chose this function for two reasons. First, since I've already examined this routine from the perspective of spy programs, we can do a bit of sanity checking by comparing the results of the two methods. And second, the source for CLOCK comes with the samples that Microsoft ships for Win32 programming. With this, you'll be able to judge how accurate the disassembly process was.

For this example, I'll use the output from my own disassembler. I could just as easily have used Microsoft's own DUMPBIN program. However, my disassembler automates some of the things that you'd have to do by hand with the DUMPBIN program, in particular, matching up the call to an API function with its symbolic name. Here's the initial output from the disassembler for the routine in question:

```
12F3B00:    PUSH    ESI
12F3B01:    PUSH    EDI
12F3B02:    MOV     ESI,DWORD PTR [ESP+0C]
12F3B06:    PUSH    F0
12F3B08:    PUSH    ESI
12F3B09:    CALL    GetWindowLongA
12F3B0E:    MOV     EDI,EAX
12F3B10:    CMP     DWORD PTR [012F612C],00
12F3B17:    JE      012F3B30
12F3B19:    AND     EDI,FFB4FFFF
12F3B1F:    PUSH    00
12F3B21:    PUSH    F4
12F3B23:    PUSH    ESI
12F3B24:    CALL    SetWindowLongA
12F3B29:    MOV     [012F6000],EAX
12F3B2E:    JMP     012F3B44
12F3B30:    OR      EDI,00CF0000
12F3B36:    MOV     EAX,[012F6000]
12F3B3B:    PUSH    EAX
12F3B3C:    PUSH    F4
12F3B3E:    PUSH    ESI
12F3B3F:    CALL    SetWindowLongA
12F3B44:    PUSH    EDI
12F3B45:    PUSH    F0
12F3B47:    PUSH    ESI
12F3B48:    CALL    SetWindowLongA
```

```
12F3B4D:    PUSH    27
12F3B4F:    PUSH    00
12F3B51:    PUSH    00
12F3B53:    PUSH    00
12F3B55:    PUSH    00
12F3B57:    PUSH    00
12F3B59:    PUSH    ESI
12F3B5A:    CALL    SetWindowPos
12F3B5F:    PUSH    05
12F3B61:    PUSH    ESI
12F3B62:    CALL    ShowWindow
12F3B67:    POP     EDI
12F3B68:    POP     ESI
12F3B69:    RET     0004
```

The first two lines and the last three lines are readily identifiable as the prologue and epilogue. They're of no real interest except for two things: The "RET 0004" tells us that the function takes one parameter (all parameters in 32-bit code are 4 bytes). Second, the code doesn't set up an EBP stack frame, so we'll need to keep track of what's on the stack to determine where the parameters are.

As luck would have it, there's only one instruction in the entire routine that references parameters on the stack. That's the "MOV ESI,DWORD PTR [ESP+0C]" instruction right after the prologue. The instruction copies a parameter into ESI, which is then seen in several other spots throughout the function. It's likely that ESI is some kind of register variable. Hmmm . . . what possible meaning could ESI have? Scanning through the routine, we see that ESI is passed as a parameter to GetWindowLong(), SetWindowLong(), SetWindowPos(), and ShowWindow(). Might ESI be holding an HWND? It sure looks like it!

Let's take this opportunity to rewrite the previous listing to take advantage of what we've already found, break up the instructions into manageable sequences, and eliminate the prologue and epilogue code.

```
12F3B02:    MOV     hWnd(ESI),DWORD PTR [ESP+0C]

12F3B06:    PUSH    F0
12F3B08:    PUSH    hWnd(ESI)
12F3B09:    CALL    GetWindowLongA
12F3B0E:    MOV     EDI,EAX

12F3B10:    CMP     DWORD PTR [012F612C],00
12F3B17:    JE      012F3B30

12F3B19:    AND     EDI,FFB4FFFF
```

```
12F3B1F:    PUSH    00
12F3B21:    PUSH    F4
12F3B23:    PUSH    hWnd(ESI)
12F3B24:    CALL    SetWindowLongA
12F3B29:    MOV     [012F6000],EAX
12F3B2E:    JMP     012F3B44

12F3B30:    OR      EDI,00CF0000
12F3B36:    MOV     EAX,[012F6000]
12F3B3B:    PUSH    EAX
12F3B3C:    PUSH    F4
12F3B3E:    PUSH    hWnd(ESI)
12F3B3F:    CALL    SetWindowLongA

12F3B44:    PUSH    EDI
12F3B45:    PUSH    F0
12F3B47:    PUSH    hWnd(ESI)
12F3B48:    CALL    SetWindowLongA

12F3B4D:    PUSH    27
12F3B4F:    PUSH    00
12F3B51:    PUSH    00
12F3B53:    PUSH    00
12F3B55:    PUSH    00
12F3B57:    PUSH    00
12F3B59:    PUSH    hWnd(ESI)
12F3B5A:    CALL    SetWindowPos

12F3B5F:    PUSH    05
12F3B61:    PUSH    hWnd(ESI)
12F3B62:    CALL    ShowWindow
```

At this point, several function calls — in particular, GetWindowLong(), the first SetWindowLong(), SetWindowPos(), and ShowWindow() — are screaming to be turned into their C equivalents. Each parameter to these routines is either the hWnd we discovered or a numeric value that we can look up in WINDOWS.H. Let's rewrite the routine yet again to condense some of these instruction sequences into a single C statement:

```
12F3B02:    MOV     hWnd(ESI),DWORD PTR [ESP+0C]

GetWindowLong( hWnd, GWL_STYLE );   // GWL_STYLE == -16 == 0F0h
12F3B0E:    MOV     EDI,EAX

12F3B10:    CMP     DWORD PTR [012F612C],00
12F3B17:    JE      012F3B30
```

```
12F3B19:    AND     EDI,FFB4FFFF

SetWindowLong( hWnd, GWL_ID, 0 );   // GWL_ID == -12 == 0F4h
12F3B29:    MOV     [012F6000],EAX

12F3B2E:    JMP     012F3B44

12F3B30:    OR      EDI,00CF0000
12F3B36:    MOV     EAX,[012F6000]
12F3B3B:    PUSH    EAX
12F3B3C:    PUSH    F4
12F3B3E:    PUSH    hWnd(ESI)
12F3B3F:    CALL    SetWindowLongA

12F3B44:    PUSH    EDI
12F3B45:    PUSH    F0
12F3B47:    PUSH    hWnd(ESI)
12F3B48:    CALL    SetWindowLongA

SetWindowPos( hWnd,0,0,0,0,    // 0x27 == the flags on the next line
              SWP_NOSIZE | SWP_NOMOVE | SWP_NOZORDER | SWP_FRAMECHANGED);

ShowWindow( hWnd, SW_SHOW );
```

While we were able to rewrite some of the function calls in their C equivalent, we didn't know enough about the parameters to the last two SetWindowLong()'s to condense them. In one case we need to know what EDI contains, while in the other we need to know what the global variable at address [012F6000] is.

Wait a minute! We've already seen that the GetWindowLong() retrieved the window's style value and copied it into EDI. EDI could be another register variable for holding the window's style bits. As for the global variable [012F6000], notice that the code saves the return value from the SetWindowLong(GWL_ID) into it. Earlier, I described how the window ID field (GWL_ID) is used to store the HMENU for top-level windows. Combined with the fact that SetWindowLong() returns the previous value of the field, you can guess that [012F6000] is a global variable containing a menu handle (HMENU).

Let's rewrite the routine once again to take advantage of these two new discoveries (the window style variable in EDI and the HMENU global variable):

```
winStyle = GetWindowLong( hWnd, GWL_STYLE );

12F3B10:     CMP      DWORD PTR [012F612C],00
12F3B17:     JE       012F3B30

winStyle &= ~(WS_DLGFRAME | WS_SYSMENU | WS_MINIMIZEBOX | WS_MAXIMIZEBOX);

HMenu = SetWindowLong( hWnd, GWL_ID, 0 );

12F3B2E:     JMP      012F3B44

12F3B30:
winStyle |= (WS_BORDER | WS_DLGFRAME | WS_SYSMENU |
             WS_THICKFRAME|WS_MINIMIZEBOX|WS_MAXIMIZEBOX);
SetWindowLong( hWnd, GWL_ID, HMenu );

12F3B44:
SetWindowLong(hWnd, GWL_STYLE, winStyle);

SetWindowPos( hWnd,0,0,0,0,0,
              SWP_NOSIZE | SWP_NOMOVE | SWP_NOZORDER | SWP_FRAMECHANGED);

ShowWindow( hWnd, SW_SHOW );
```

At this point, all we're left with is the conditional branch statement at address 012F3B10. The CMP instruction compares the global variable at address [012F612C] to 0. The destination of the conditional jump is immediately preceded by a JMP instruction. This looks like the classic if-else statement that I described earlier. The global variable at [012F612C] looks like it's some sort of boolean. Let's give it a name (for example, "MyBool"), stick in some {}'s and indentation, and see if the code starts to make sense:

```
winStyle = GetWindowLong( hWnd, GWL_STYLE );

if ( MyBool != 0 )
{
    // Turn off the style bits need for the titlebar, boxes, and menu.
    winStyle &= ~(WS_DLGFRAME | WS_SYSMENU | WS_MINIMIZEBOX | WS_MAXIMIZEBOX);
    // Set the window's HMENU field to 0.
    HMenu = SetWindowLong( hWnd, GWL_ID, 0 );
}
else
{
    // Turn on the style bits needed for a titlebar, boxes, and menu.
    winStyle |= (WS_BORDER | WS_DLGFRAME | WS_SYSMENU |
                 WS_THICKFRAME|WS_MINIMIZEBOX|WS_MAXIMIZEBOX);
```

```
        // Set the window's HMENU field back to whatever it was before.
        SetWindowLong( hWnd, GWL_ID, HMenu );
    }

    // Blast the style bits into the window.
    SetWindowLong(hWnd, GWL_STYLE, winStyle);

    // Force Windows to recalculate and repaint what the window should look like.
    SetWindowPos( hWnd,0,0,0,0,0,
                SWP_NOSIZE | SWP_NOMOVE | SWP_NOZORDER | SWP_FRAMECHANGED);

    ShowWindow( hWnd, SW_SHOW );
```

Amazing! We've taken some raw assembler code and worked it back into readable C code. If you compare this code to what we obtained from spying tools, you'll see that they're entirely consistent. However, the disassembly listing contains more information than you could have obtained via spy tools. For instance, the spy tools didn't give any indication that there were two global variables involved (the HMenu and the boolean).

To some of you, the series of steps from raw assembler code to C code may have gone a little fast. It's true that not every disassembly attempt goes this smoothly or this quickly. However, I hope that I've shown how disassembling a function is an iterative process. As you hypothesize and find things out about the code, you feed that information back into the listing in the hope that it'll shake something else loose.

As a final note on disassembly, don't hesitate to load the code in question into a debugger and step through it yourself. Seeing the code execute with real live values can often break a mental block about the code's purpose. Many times I've been unable to figure out what a function returns. By stepping through the code in a debugger and seeing actual return values, I've often been able to deduce a pattern in the returned values. For example, a routine may always return a global memory handle. The point is, every scrap of information can help. You'd be surprised how the tiniest thing can help you break a piece of code wide open.

ADVANCED HACKING TIPS

Before finishing this chapter, I thought it would be useful to throw in some general-purpose tips that don't fall into the general topics I've already described.

Using SoftIce/Windows

If you're at all serious about exploring, SoftIce/Windows is a must. Before I go any further, I'm obligated to point out that I work for Nu-Mega, the company that makes SoftIce/Windows. The only tool that can even remotely compare to SoftIce/W is Microsoft's WDEB386 system-level debugger, which doesn't have nearly as many commands to dump data structures or use symbolic debug information.

SoftIce/W gets its capabilities because it's a system-level debugger. Unlike application-level debuggers like Turbo Debugger, CodeView, or the debuggers built into your compilers IDE, SoftIce/W doesn't rely on Windows for anything. It operates between Windows and the hardware itself. Because of this, SoftIce/W can step through any code in the system, including ring 0 VxDs and real mode DOS code. This makes it very useful for studying code like the Windows scheduler and the routines for switching memory contexts. Don't even think about trying something like that with a regular debugger. They just won't work.

In fairness to Microsoft, WDEB386 has similar capabilities in this particular area. One pitfall of Windows 95 is that you can't step through the ring 3 system DLLs (like KERNEl32.DLL) with an application debugger. The problem is that Windows 95 shares this code with all processes, so placing INT 3's in this code would almost always crash the system. Since SoftIce/W operates underneath the system, it doesn't have these restrictions, and can easily step through any system code.

Unlike regular debuggers, you don't load SoftIce/W from within Windows. Nor do you have to explicitly debug a program to use it. Instead, SoftIce/W loads underneath Windows and is always present. Unless you press its hotkey to bring up its user interface, SoftIce/W silently sits underneath the rest of Windows. For this reason, you can load SoftIce/W every time you load Windows. When you need it, just pop it up. Otherwise, you can ignore its presence. Rather than a program, it's much more like a super version of Windows that you can stop and poke around in at will. Sort of like the ultimate Windows TSR.

Unlike WDEB386, SoftIce/W contains numerous commands to dump out data structures and lists at all levels of the system. At the lowest level, it can dump out the CPU's page tables and selectors in the global and local descriptor tables. Moving up a level, it can display important VxD-related items such as the list of VxDs, the device descriptor block for a VxD, and the context tables used to maintain per-process address spaces. In fact, SoftIce/W can even switch address contexts to any arbitrary memory context, allowing you to see all the memory of any process in the system. Up yet another level, SoftIce/W can list out all the processes, threads, modules, and Win16 tasks, along with detailed information about each item. This is invaluable when your code is using a system-supplied handle and you need to know what the handle refers to. At the highest level, SoftIce/W can display detailed information on windows and window classes. The point of all this isn't to praise SoftIce/W. Rather, it's to give you a feeling for how much system information is at your fingertips.

A couple of SoftIce/W features are particularly useful and simply must be mentioned here. When stepping through 16-bit code, you'll often be working with handles that look like they could be global heap handles. Simply give that handle to the SoftIce/W HEAP command, and you can instantly verify whether or not it's a valid global heap handle. If it is a valid heap handle, SoftIce/W will tell you what the handle's purpose is (Who owns it? Is it code, data or a resource? If it's code, which segment in the NE file does it correspond to?).

In either 16- or 32-bit code, the SoftIce/W U and D commands come in very handy. Given a code address, you can feed it to the U command and quickly disassemble at that address. Likewise, the D command lets you view anything in memory in a variety of formats. Unlike application debuggers or other programs, these commands aren't restricted to where they can disassemble or view memory.

Another thing SoftIce/W has over other debuggers is that it can load the exported function information from 16- and 32-bit EXE/DLL files, and use this as a pseudo symbol table. Thus, wherever you're stopped in Windows, SoftIce/W can tell you what EXE/DLL/VxD you're in, and often can pinpoint the exact routine. It even uses this information in its disassembler so that instead of seeing something like:

```
CALL  BFFB0149
```

You'll instead see:

```
CALL  GetModuleHandleA
```

Another nifty SoftIce/W command (added for Win32s and Windows 95 support) is the MAP32 command. With MAP32, you can easily determine where all the sections of an EXE and its DLLs (including system DLLs) reside in memory. Yet another handy feature of SoftIce/W is the STACK command. Wherever you're stopped in the system, you can almost always get a call stack that shows how you got there. Also, at any given time, if you need to know what the current task or thread is, try the TASK and THREAD commands. These commands quickly let you know what process and thread you're executing in.

Using hardware breakpoints

If you need to step through code when a certain condition is true, you can often use the CPU's hardware breakpoints to quickly get to that point in the code. For example, a coworker of mine wanted to know when a certain rarely used thread was activated. By using the SoftIce/W THREAD command, we were able to find out the thread ID of the thread we were interested in. We set a breakpoint on the code that executes after the thread switch, but that approach turned out to be hopeless because the system is constantly switching threads. The breakpoint was constantly going off, but the current thread was never the thread we were interested in.

To get around this problem, we found the DWORD in memory where the system keeps the current thread ID (hint: unassemble at the GetCurrentThreadId function). We then set a conditional hardware breakpoint on the DWORD holding the thread ID. The condition was that the breakpoint would trigger only when the thread ID we were interested in was written to the thread ID DWORD. Problem solved. The system ran normally until we undertook the action that made the thread in question wake up.

Another example: One of my programs was using SetThreadContext to change the EIP of another program. SetThreadContext was reporting success, yet the other process was always bombing. To see what was happening, I set a hardware breakpoint on the DWORD in the thread context structure where the new EIP value should have been written to. Upon running the program, I found that SetThreadContext was indeed copying the EIP value to the right location. Unfortunately, the breakpoint went off again a bit later, and I could see that KERNEL32.DLL was overwriting my EIP value with a garbage value. Without using hardware breakpoints, I'd probably still be wondering if my code was doing something wrong or if there was a bug in Windows 95.

The VxD . (dot) commands

Users of WDEB386 and SoftIce/W have quite a bit of system information available to them through the "." (dot) commands. The dot commands (so called because they all start with a ".") are implemented in various VxDs. To use them, break into your system-level debugger and, at the prompt, enter the command name (which always starts with a "."). Some of them are available all the time, while others are available only in the debug version. Some commands to try include:

..?	.vtd
.m?	.dosmgr
.vmm	.vmpoll
.vxdldr	.vtdapi
.vpicd	

The VAR2MAP utility

In Windows 95, the Win32 system DLLs such as USER32, KERNEL32, and so on are "based." That is, they always load at the same linear address every time you start Windows 95. You can take advantage of this fact to add your hard-won knowledge about where functions and variables are located to WDEB386 or SoftIce/W. Doing this lets you use these symbols when stepping through system code. How's this? Take a look at the code for the GetSystemDefaultLangID function in KERNEL32.DLL:

```
GetSystemDefaultLangID proc
BFFB69FD:      MOV      AX,[BFFD44D0]
BFFB6A03:      RET
```

It's pretty obvious that the address BFFD44D0h holds a global variable called SystemDefaultLangID (or something to that effect). And since KERNEL32.DLL has a unique base address in the linear address space, the SystemDefaultLangID variable will always be at address BFFD44D0h. Wouldn't it be great if you could tell your system debugger this fact and have it automatically replace the address "BFFD44D0h" with "SystemDefaultLangID" in its disassembly? I thought so, too, so I wrote the VAR2MAP program.

To use VAR2MAP, you create a file that contains a list of 32-bit addresses and their associated names (you have to come up with the names). The file can contain both variable names and function names. The only restriction is that all the names and addresses must be in the same EXE or DLL. VAR2MAP takes the file you create as input and emits a .MAP file. What good is a .MAP file? Well, you can run the .MAP file through a program like Microsoft's MAP-SYM or Nu-Mega's MSYM. Either of these programs will create a .SYM file from the supplied .MAP file. Both WDEB386 and SoftIce/W know how to load .SYM files for use with symbolic disassembly. I used VAR2MAP throughout the writing of this book to give meaningful symbolic names to functions in KERNEL32.DLL and other system modules.

A typical input file to VAR2MAP is shown in the following code snippet. The first line of the file must contain the path to the EXE or DLL that will contain these addresses. Why is this necessary? If you look at a .MAP file, you'll see that all the addresses for public symbols are given in logical addresses, that is, ObjectNumber:Offset (for example, 0004:00013484). VAR2MAP needs the EXE or DLL file to figure out where each of the code and data sections will be mapped to in memory. This allows VAR2MAP to translate the linear address that you give it into a logical address like 0004:00013484.

```
FILE = C:\WINDOWS\SYSTEM\KERNEL32.DLL
lGetProcAddress = BFF81DC1
lGlobalHandle = BFF76E78
lLocalReAlloc = BFF833C8
lLocalSize = BFF890CB
ppCurrentThread = BFFCB3D4
ppCurrentProcess = BFFCB3D8
ppCurrentTDBX = BFFCB3DC
pWin16Mutex = BFFD34D0
pK16SysVar = BFFD33A4
pKrn32Mutex = BFFCB3FC
```

The rest of the lines should be of the form:

```
SymbolName = AddressInHex
```

After creating the input file, run VAR2MAP and pass it the name of the input file on the command line (for example, VAR2MAP KERNEL32.VAR). The output .MAP file will be placed in the same directory as the file whose name is on the "FILE =" line of the input file. This makes sense, because the .SYM file you create must be in the same directory as the EXE or DLL it corresponds to. Otherwise, the debugger won't know to load the .SYM file. See your debugger documentation for information on loading .SYM files.

Identifying VxD services

For this type of exploration, it's helpful to know how calls to VxD services are made and implemented. A *VXD service* is a function that's exported from a VxD for use by other VxDs. A VxD doesn't directly call services in other VxDs (at least not when it's first loaded). Instead, you invoke a VxD service from another VxD with an INT 20h. A quick look at the VxDCall macro in the DDK's VMM.INC shows this in action. The INT 20h is handled by the VMM, which in turn changes the INT 20h instruction into a call to the address of the actual VxD service code.

How does the INT 20h handler know which VxD service you're invoking? Immediately following the INT 20h is a DWORD that specifies the service to be invoked. The high WORD of this DWORD is the device ID of the VxD containing the service to be invoked. The low WORD contains the service number in the VxD's service table. A value of 0 in the low WORD means the first service in that particular VxD, a value of 1 means the second service, and so on.

The device ID in the high WORD is either one of the standard VxD IDs defined in VMM.INC, or one of your company's VxD IDs (which are assigned by Microsoft). The first 16 VxD device IDs are listed here:

VMM_DEVICE_ID	1h	REBOOT_DEVICE_ID	9h
DEBUG_DEVICE_ID	2h	VDD_DEVICE_ID	0Ah
VPICD_DEVICE_ID	3h	VSD_DEVICE_ID	0Bh
VDMAD_DEVICE_ID	4h	VMD_DEVICE_ID	0Ch
VTD_DEVICE_ID	5h	VKD_DEVICE_ID	0Dh
V86MMGR_DEVICE_ID	6h	VCD_DEVICE_ID	0Eh
PAGESWAP_DEVICE_ID	7h	VPD_DEVICE_ID	0Fh
PARITY_DEVICE_ID	8h	BLOCKDEV_DEVICE_ID	10h

If you're working with one of the standard VxDs, you can usually find a list of the VxDs services by looking at the .H or .INC file for that VxD in the DDK. The Begin_Service_Table macro indicates the start of the services list. Each service provided in that VxD has its own line that starts with <VxD Name>_Service (for example, VPICD_Service). The first service listed in the table will have a low WORD of 0 in the INT 20h DWORD, the next service will have a value of 1, and so forth. Armed with this knowledge, you can easily figure out the DWORD that must follow an INT 20h in order to invoke a given function. For example, knowing that the VMM VxD has a device ID of 1 (which will go in the high WORD), you can easily calculate the DWORDs for each of VMM's services, as shown here:

Begin_Service_Table VMM, VMM	00010000h
VMM_Service Get_VMM_Version	00010001h
VMM_Service Get_Cur_VM_Handle	00010002h
VMM_Service Test_Cur_VM_Handle	00010003h
VMM_Service Get_Sys_VM_Handle	00010004h
VMM_Service Test_Sys_VM_Handle	00010005h

Debuggers or disassemblers that give the actual names of the services that will be invoked via an INT 20h simply keep a big table that matches up DWORD values to function names. Earlier, I mentioned that the INT 20h handler patches the INT 20h instruction and its following DWORD into a CALL instruction. That isn't strictly true. If the service number in the low WORD has its high bit set, the INT 20h will instead be patched to a JMP instruction. For example, using the VMM services shown in the preceding list, an INT 20h followed by a DWORD of 00018001 would become a JMP to the Get_Cur_VM_handle function, rather than a CALL. To generate a JMP to a VxD service, you'd use the VxDJmp macro in VMM.INC, rather than the normal VxDCall macro.

Identifying Win32 VxD services

One of the nifty new features in Windows 95 is the addition of Win32 VxD services. The Win32 services are sort of like VxD services, except that they can be called by ring 3 application code. To invoke a Win32 service, a program calls the VxDCall0 function exported by KERNEL32.DLL.

One of the parameters to the VxDCall0 function is a DWORD that's similar in nature to the VxD service ID I described in the previous section. The high WORD of the DWORD is the device ID (just like a regular INT 20h DWORD would have). The low WORD is the Win32 service number. This WORD corresponds to the relative order of the Win32 services within the Win32 service table. 0 is the first service, 1 the second service, and so on.

Let's look at an example to make this clearer. This short snippet of code is from GetThreadContext in KERNEL32.DLL:

```
BFFABD8D:    PUSH    EAX
BFFABD8E:    PUSH    DWORD PTR [EBX+5C]
BFFABD91:    PUSH    002A0014
BFFABD96:    CALL    VxDCall0
```

The first two PUSH instructions are parameters for the Win32 service. The final PUSH of 002A0014 informs the VxDCall0 function that it should invoke the 0x15th Win32 service in device 2Ah. What's device 2Ah? Nothing more than VWIN32, the source of much of KERNEL32's functionality.

Identifying parameter validation and Ixxx functions

In Windows 3.1, Microsoft introduced parameter-validated functions. These are API functions that check the validity of the parameters you pass to it. If your parameters aren't up to standard (if you have an invalid pointer, for instance), the functions simply return to you without doing anything. In the debug version, the function may also emit a warning diagnostic to the debug terminal.

The complete code for a function with parameter validation typically exists in two separate places. The code that validates the parameters is always found at the beginning of the function. Assuming all the validity test are passed, the code then JMPs to the real code. In Windows 3.1, the real code for a function had its own name — an *I*, followed by the function name. For example, there's an exported WinExec function that checks its parameters and then JMPs to an internal IWinExec function. In this book, I've followed the same convention for Win32 code.

A commented listing of theWindows 95 32-bit WinExec function follows. The code sets up a structured exception handling (SEH) frame and then verifies that all characters in the string pointed to by the lpszCmdLine parameter can be accessed. If the validation fails, a page fault occurs, and the SEH frame causes the function to return through another code path not shown here. If the validation succeeds, the code removes the SEH frame and then JMPs to the IWinExec code.

```
WinExec proc
BFFB2569:    PUSH    EDI                    ; Preserve EDI.

BFFB256A:    PUSH    22                     ; Set up a structured exception
BFFB256C:    SUB     EDX,EDX                ; handler frame in case the
BFFB256E:    PUSH    BFFB1172               ; following validations cause a
BFFB2573:    PUSH    DWORD PTR FS:[EDX]     ; fault.
```

```
BFFB2576:    MOV      DWORD PTR FS:[EDX],ESP

BFFB2579:    MOV      EDI,DWORD PTR [ESP+14]    ; Validate the lpszCmdLine
BFFB257D:    SUB      EAX,EAX                   ; parameter by touching every
BFFB257F:    LEA      ECX,[EAX-01]              ; character in the string. A
BFFB2582:    REPNE    SCASB                     ; page fault will trigger the
                                                ; exception handler above.

BFFB2584:    POP      DWORD PTR FS:[EDX]        ; If we got here, everything was
BFFB2587:    ADD      ESP,08                    ; OK. Remove the SEH frame.

BFFB258A:    POP      EDI                       ; Restore EDI.

BFFB258B:    JMP      IWinExec                  ; JMP to the real WinExec code.
```

A key point here is identifying the *I* version of the function. When you see code that looks similar to what I've shown here and that ends with a JMP elsewhere, it's probably a function with parameter validation. The destination of the JMP instruction is most likely the address of the *I* version of the code. You can use this knowledge to build up the addresses of additional symbols. For example, in "The VAR2MAP utility" section, I showed four functions that fall into this category:

> IGetProcAddress = BFF81DC1
>
> IGlobalHandle = BFF76E78
>
> ILocalReAlloc = BFF833C8
>
> ILocalSize = BFF890CB

If you add these internal names to your debugger, stepping through the system code can be much easier. It appears that the parameter validation stubs are lumped together in one location, while the real code for the functions is spread throughout the module. Adding in additional symbols for internal functions gives you a fighting chance of figuring out where you are in a given system module. It also greatly enhances the usability of stack traces.

Using the debug version

Beyond just finding bugs in your code, the debug version of Windows makes it much easier to figure out what Windows is doing. The various debug versions of system DLLs that come in the SDK are littered with helpful diagnostic trace messages. These strings often contain the name of the function that they're being emitted from as part of the message. Likewise, there are many messages that print out or otherwise comment on the value of system variables. You can usually go back a few instructions in the code to find the variable that they're referring to. For example, consider this code:

```
BFFC788A:   PUSH    DWORD PTR [ESI+18]
BFFC788D:   PUSH    BFFDBF9C ;;    Default Heap: %8x\n
BFFC7892:   CALL    BFFC6092
```

Here, ESI is pointing to the Win32 process database structure. The second instruction is passing a pointer to a printf-style format string. From this information, it's fairly easy to figure out that you'll find the process's heap handle at offset 18h.

Another way the debug version of Windows is helpful is in all of the sanity checking and assert-like code. The debug DLLs are always checking the parameters to their functions and the state of system variables. You can use all this sanity-checking code to confirm or disprove your guesses about what a certain piece of code is doing or working with.

Pentium-optimized code

One of Microsoft's claims about Windows 95 is that it is optimized for the Pentium. I'm here to tell you that this claim certainly appears to be true. The main optimization that compilers do specific to the Pentium CPU is to reorganize the instruction sequences to let the Pentium's two execution units execute together without stalling. Consider this code snippet from KERNEL32.DLL:

```
1) PUSH    EBP
2) MOV     EBP,ESP
3) SUB     ESP,04
4) CMP     DWORD PTR [EBP+0C],0FFFFF98
5) PUSH    EBX
6) PUSH    ESI
7) PUSH    EDI
8) JBE     BFF741AB
```

Instructions 1,2,3,5,6, and 7 together make up the prologue that sets up the function's stack frame and preserve the register variable registers. Instructions 4 and 8 together make up the standard instructions for an if statement. Were Pentium optimizations not enabled, the code would make much more sense. The JBE instruction would occur immediately after the CMP instruction, rather than four instructions later.

Why am I bringing this up? When stepping through Pentium-optimized code (such as the Windows 95 system DLLs), the instruction sequences may not immediately make sense. You have to be aware of this and look for instruction sequences that are doing two different things. I try to keep these sequences straight by rearranging the instructions into two groups. In most cases, the two groups correspond to two different C source code statements. After rearranging the instructions, I focus first on one group, then on the other.

SUMMARY

In this chapter, I've shown several different methods of exploration.. On the low end, the methods center around simplistic file-dumping programs. In the middle are spying tools that are extremely useful if you're interested in the interactions between a program and the operating system. At the high end, you and your disassembler can go head to head with an optimizing compiler to crack open practically every aspect of a program. Disassembly is messy, imprecise, and frustrating work. On the other hand, it can be an extremely valuable asset that few programmers take the time to learn.

If you're not already using the tools and techniques I've described, I hope this discussion has taken away enough of their mystique so that you're willing to try them if you need to do so. Although some of the things these tools do seem like magic, they're really not. If you have a firm grounding in hardware and operating system basics, these tools and techniques can be viewed as just another part of your toolbox, rather than as something reserved for programming wizards.

WRITING A WIN32 API SPY

*A*s programmers, we often see another programmer's code and wonder, "How does it do that?" In these situations, programming tools that let you peer under the hood of a running application are invaluable in tracking down what some program or DLL is doing. For live analysis of a running program, nothing beats an API spy program (a *spy*).

API spying tools show you which Windows functions are called by a program and its DLLs. In addition to showing the names of the API functions in the order in which they're called, API spy programs also record the parameter values to the API functions, as well as the return value for the function. More advanced API spy programs may even record additional pertinent information such as window messages, hook callbacks, and other program events. With all this information on tap, it's usually easy to figure out what a given section of code is doing. Chapter 10 discusses the more popular API spy programs, and has an example showing how to use the output from an API spy. In this chapter, I'm going to construct a simple but powerful Win32 API spying tool that's easily extensible.

The technique I'll be using to intercept API function calls for the API spy program can also be easily adapted for use in your own Win32 programs. For example, let's say you wanted to replace the Win32 lstrcpy function with your own routine.

Doing this is only a function call away with the code I'll be presenting. If you're just interested in getting the code to intercept API function calls, skip ahead to the last section in this chapter ("Intercepting Functions in Your Own Programs"). However, if you're interested in Win32 system-level programming and learning how this technique works, read on.

Why bother writing a simple API spy program when more powerful ones, such as BoundsChecker32, are available commercially? By writing you own API spy for Win32 programs, you can gain a thorough understanding of the Win32 operating system philosophy, and develop an in-depth knowledge about the important differences between the three Win32 implementations (Windows NT, Windows 95, and Win32s).

On the surface, the subject of this chapter appears to be "How to build an API spy program." However, my real goal is to present a set of real-world Win32 programming problems, and show how they can be solved. In the process, you should see many facets of the Win32 architecture. As you'll soon realize, writing an API spy for Win32 programs forces you to come into contact with such issues as address spaces, multithreading, dynamic linking, debugging mechanisms, process management, and thread control. In short, the program I'll be building will give you a good tour of many core Win32 concepts.

Before jumping into details about the program, I need to list the API spy program specifications:

1. For a given Win32 process, the program should log the function calls it makes to a given list of DLLs.

2. The set of DLLs to be monitored should be extendible by the user via a configuration file.

3. If the parameters to a function are known, they can be specified in the configuration file, and their values will be logged along with the function name.

4. The spy program must log the return values of functions.

5. The spy program should be able to run on Windows NT, Windows 95, and Win32s.

6. No modification to the program's source code or executable file should be required.

7. Log output should go to a disk file, rather than being shown live.

When this program is completed (at the end of the chapter), it will be able to do several things: it will let you pick another program to spy on, it will run that program, and it will produce an ASCII text file with the logged information. After the chosen program terminates, you can view the text file with an editor or viewer of your choice.

An important limitation of this spy program — and one that needs to be pointed out very clearly — is that this program is a per-process API spy. Unlike programs such as the Win16 WinScope spy program, my Win32 API spy doesn't watch calls made by all processes in the system. Rather, it watches only the calls made by a single process. In a system with separate address space for each process, writing a global API spy is a significant undertaking and beyond the scope of this chapter. (How's that for truth in advertising?)

INTERCEPTING THE FUNCTIONS

The basic idea behind any sort of spy program is that the spy program inserts itself into the flow of control of the program being spied on. The spy program gets control before the intended target of the call is reached, and does whatever logging it needs to before transferring control to the original intended target of the call. The first problem we're faced with is how to let our spy program gain control somewhere between the "spyee's" call to a DLL function, and the execution of the function in the DLL.

One approach to this problem that's been used in the past is to make your own DLL that exports functions with the same names as the functions you want to intercept. For example, if you wanted to intercept calls to the GetProcAddress function in KERNEL32.DLL, you'd make your own DLL with an exported GetProcAddress function. By putting this DLL's import library first in the list of import libraries, the linker will fix up calls to GetProcAddress to point to your interception DLL, rather than to KERNEL32.DLL. The interception DLL logs the information about the call before jumping to the real function (for example, GetProcAddress in KERNEL32.DLL). As an alternative to creating an import library, you could just alias the imported functions in your DEF file. However, both of these approaches share the common characteristic of requiring the linker to set up the API interception at link time — something that's not an option if the program you're spying on isn't one you wrote.

This method of intercepting calls to API functions is exactly what the Microsoft API parameter profiler in the Win32 SDK does. Included with this profiler are five DLLs: ZDI32.DLL, ZDVAPI32.DLL, ZERNEL32.DLL, ZRTDLL.DLL, and ZSER32.DLL; these DLLs intercept calls to GDI32.DLL, ADVAPI32.DLL, KERNEL32.DLL, CRTDLL.DLL, and USER32.DLL, respectively. Instead of linking with these DLLs, you run a program (APF32CVT) that modifies the EXE you want to spy on. The net effect is the same as if you had linked with the import libraries. At least no source code is required to use APF32CVT.

For our purposes, there are two problems with this dummy DLL approach. First, it's not easy to extend it to accommodate new DLLs. For each new API function you want to intercept, you need to modify the interception DLL and rebuild it. You also have to relink or modify the EXE to be spied on. The second, and bigger, problem is that this approach requires changing the program to be spied on, which is a direct violation of one of our design specifications.

Another approach to intercepting calls to API functions is to somehow modify the target of the call. By changing the initial portion of the function being called, a program can enable itself to get control before the body of the function is executed. There are two methods of modifying a function's prologue code to transfer control elsewhere. The first and most obvious method is to place a breakpoint instruction (opcode 0xCC) at the first byte in the function's code. When the function is called, an interrupt handler installed by the spy program gets control and does its logging. The spy program then restores the original byte of the function before making the CPU execute exactly one instruction (via the trap flag single-step mechanism). In its single-step exception handler, the API spy program then reinserts the breakpoint opcode so that subsequent calls to the function will be caught.

Although some Win16 spy programs use breakpoints to intercept calls to DLL functions, trying to do something similar under Win32 would be more difficult. For starters, under Win32, one process can't see another process's exceptions unless it's acting as a debugger to that process. Next, forcing every call to an API function to go through the Win32 structured exception-handling code could seriously impair performance. Also, the separate address spaces of processes under Win32 would force the spy program to use ReadProcessMemory to see the target applications's function parameters. This is far clunkier than being able to read the memory directly.

The second method of modifying a function's prologue code to transfer control to the spying code is to insert a JMP or CALL instruction at the start of the function. One problem with this approach is that in 32-bit code, a JMP or a CALL instruction will take at least 5 bytes. If the DLL has functions less than 5 bytes apart (yes, this has happened!), patching in a JMP or CALL becomes impractical because the function that comes later in the code will start in the middle of a JMP or CALL instruction. Unlike breakpoints that can be handled by another process, patching in JMPs and CALLs requires your code to be running in the process context of the program being spied on. To run in any arbitrary process requires that your code be in a DLL. However, as you'll see later, running your spy code in the context of the process being spied on isn't such a bad idea. Still, patching JMPs or CALLs into the process being spied on is a real nuisance, especially with the need to constantly switch between the original code and your JMP/CALL instructions.

Having looked at and discarded two obvious approaches to interception (linking to a custom DLL and patching the API function's code), let's look at a third approach that's not so obvious. Nothing in the rule book says that the target code in the API function has to be patched. It's equally valid to modify the call to the API function. If the spy program can somehow find the CALLs to the API functions, it can modify the CALL to point to the spy program's logging code. As in a previously discussed method, the spy program's logging code will need to execute in the process context of the program being spied on. The "Injecting a DLL into Another Process" section will show how it's possible to "inject" a DLL into the address space of a process. Here, we're concentrating on the interception part of the problem.

You might be thinking to yourself, "A program might have hundreds or even thousands of calls to API functions in just the system DLLs alone. How on earth can I hope to find all those CALL instructions?" Never fear, the manner in which Win32 EXEs and DLLs dynamically link to each other makes this almost incredibly easy: All calls to a given API function end up traveling through the same spot in the executable file. By patching that one location to point at the spy's logging code, you intercept all calls made by the EXE to that function.

To see how this works, let's look at the actual code generated for three separate calls to the GetVersion() API function in KERNEL32.DLL. Let's start with the following small C program:

```c
int main()
{
    GetVersion();
    GetVersion();
    GetVersion();
}
```

From this program, the compiler generates the following assembler code:

```
410052: CALL     0042003C
410057: CALL     0042003C
41005C: CALL     0042003C
...
42003C: JMP      DWORD PTR [00440064]
```

The important thing to notice here is that CALL instructions don't call directly to the GetVersion() code in KERNEL32.DLL. Instead, each call transfers control to a JMP statement elsewhere in the EXE's code. That JMP instruction dereferences a DWORD in memory and jumps to that location. In the above example, the DWORD is at address 00440064. What's the address stored in this DWORD? As you might suspect, it's the address of GetVersion() in KERNEL32.DLL. All calls to API functions end up going through a JMP DWORD PTR [XXXXXXXX] thunk. For each function that an executable imports, there's a corresponding JMP DWORD PTR [XXXXXXXX]. Who generates these JMP thunks? In Microsoft compilers, the JMP thunks are code in the import libraries for the DLLs being linked to. In Borland C++, the linker (TLINK) generates the JMP thunks.

The questions that naturally arise from this JMP thunk mechanism are "Where is the DWORD with the function's address found?" and "Who's responsible for initializing it?" The DWORD containing the imported function's address is found in what is known as the *import address table* (or IAT, for short). The IAT typically resides in the .idata (import data) section of each executable. For each DLL that an executable links to, there's an associated array of DWORDs containing addresses of functions in the imported DLL. When the Win32 loader brings an executable into memory, it fills in the array of DWORD with the proper addresses, as shown in Figure 10-1. In the executable file prior to loading, each DWORD contains an offset to an ASCIIZ string that names the desired function (for example GetVersion). When the loader brings the executable into memory, it overwrites the array of names offsets with the actual addresses of the functions.

Having seen how an executable imports functions from other DLLs, it's easy to understand how a spy program can intercept and log those functions with a minimum of fuss and overhead. The spy program merely needs to find the array of function addresses in the executable's imports section and overwrite those addresses with the addresses of its own logging routines. No actual code patching is required, so there's no need to constantly switch between the original code and the code as modified by the spy program. The executable ends up calling the API spy's code directly, so the only overhead is that of the logging functions. After the spy code has logged the function's data, it JMPs to the original intended target of the JMP DWORD PTR [XXXXXXXX] thunk. Simple, no?

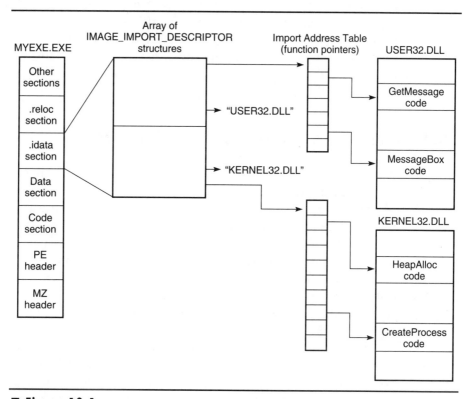

Figure 10-1
The .idata section of the executable usually holds the DWORD containing the imported function's address, although the imports table can be located elsewhere.

Even if spying isn't your goal, you can use this trick of modifying the addresses in the imports section to selectively intercept APIs. For example, you might want to replace a function in a DLL with your own custom-written code. It's easy to implement a function that takes a DLL name and function name and returns a pointer to the DWORD in the imported data section that holds the functions's address. Your code would then overwrite the DWORD with the address of your own custom function. If you want to chain on to the original address, simply save off the original DWORD value before overwriting it.

In the spy program I'll be building in this chapter, I've chosen to inter-cept calls to API functions in the manner just described. In making this deci-sion, I've committed myself to running the spy's logging code in the process context of the application being spied on. Since the design goals for the API spy program don't allow relinking or modification of the target application, I need to somehow force the logging code into the target program's address space. It also means that the majority of the API spy program's code must reside in a DLL.

INJECTING A **DLL** INTO **ANOTHER PROCESS**

Now that we know how we'll intercept calls to API functions, the next hurdle is to force the spying code into the target application's address space. In 16-bit Windows, this wouldn't be an issue since all programs share a common address space. In Win32, however, each process has its own address space, and its own set of loaded DLLs. Just because one process is using a DLL doesn't mean that another process can use it. Each process that wants to use a DLL needs to load the DLL for its own use, either by implicitly linking to it, or by calling LoadLibrary(). Since the programs we'll want to spy on have no knowl-edge of our API spy DLL, we'll need to resort to dirty tricks to force the DLL into their address space.

There are at least three ways to inject a DLL into the context of an arbitrary process. Jeffrey Richter's May 1994 *Microsoft Systems Journal* article describes each approach in quite a bit of detail. Here, I'll give a brief overview of the two methods that we won't take advantage of, and then spend more time on the DLL injection method that the API spy program will actually use. The final method that Richter chooses for a general-purpose implementation is similar (but not identical) to the method I'll use for our spy program. The key difference is that Richter's method uses the CreateRemoteThread function, which isn't available in Win32s or Windows 95. My version of injecting the DLL is portable to all three platforms.

The first and best known way to force a DLL into another process's address space is to install a windows hook using SetWindowsHookEx(). If you specify an hThread for a different process, or if you request a systemwide hook, the operating system automatically loads the DLL containing the hook procedure into the address spaces of all processes affected by the hook. Installing a windows hook to force our API spy DLL to load is ineffective for two reasons. The first reason is that you have to have an existing process to install the hook for. By the time this occurs, the target process has undoubtedly called API functions. The spy program would miss all the API function calls made by the target process up to that point. The second reason is that the hook DLL won't actually be loaded in the target process until that process takes some action that causes the hook callback to be invoked. Trying to use hooks to force a DLL to load in another process context just doesn't offer enough precision with regard to when the DLL loads.

A second way to force a DLL into the address space of a process falls into the barely documented category. It seems there's an obscure registry key value buried deep down in the registry hierarchy:

```
HKEY_LOCAL_MACHINE\Software\Microsoft\Windows NT\CurrentVersion\Windows\APPINIT_DLLS
```

By adding your DLL's name to this key, the operating system automatically loads the DLL into the address space of each process as the process starts up. There are several reasons why this method isn't suitable for a spy program. The primary reason is that this change to the registry won't have an effect until the next time the system is booted. To spy on a program, you'd have to reboot the system first. Not feasible! Another downside to this approach is that the spy DLL will need to determine on a case by case basis if it wants to spy on the process it was just loaded for. For applications you don't want to spy on, the API spy DLL should return 0 in its DllMain() procedure in response to the DLL_PROCESS_ATTACH notification. Returning 0 from DllMain tells the operating system that this DLL shouldn't be loaded for this process. Yet another problem is that the operating system will try to load the DLL in every process, even in those hidden processes that you don't interact with (like MPREXE.EXE). This slows down the entire system.

The third way to inject a DLL into another process is the brute-force approach; this is the approach I'll use in the API spy program. In an ideal world, we would somehow convey to the target process that it should call LoadLibrary to load our spy DLL, and that it should call LoadLibrary immediately upon starting up. While we can't do this directly, there's no reason why we can't trick the process into loading the DLL for us.

Let's look at an analogy to get a better feel for what I'm proposing. Suppose you wanted access to a vault that's locked via a voice-recognition lock. Only one person has the proper voice pattern to unlock the door, and you're not that person. The person with the proper voice won't willingly unlock the door for you. However, you could hypnotize the person, and while they're in the trance, tell them to speak the words to unlock the door. Before bringing them out of the hypnotic state, you tell them to forget everything that just happened.

So, how does this apply to loading a DLL? If we can freeze (or hypnotize, if you prefer) the target process, we can modify the process's memory and registers so that it looks like the process is calling LoadLibrary of its own volition. After setting up the registers and memory properly, we unfreeze the program and let it execute. The end result is that the target process calls LoadLibrary, and the operating system obliges by loading the API spying DLL into the target process's address space. After the LoadLibrary call returns, we freeze the target process again, restore the memory and registers to their original values, and let the process resume as if nothing happened.

As you might imagine, the code to fake the target process into calling LoadLibrary is complex. It'll be modifying the code of the target process, so the first step is to calculate which code page it will modify and save that page away for later restoration. The injection code also needs to modify registers in the target process, so it should save away a copy of all the original register values. Luckily, Win32 provides the GetThreadContext function, which retrieves all the register values for a given thread into a C structure.

Next, my code creates a code snippet to call LoadLibrary from within the context of the target process. Included in this code snippet is an ASCII string with the name of the spy DLL (APISPY32.DLL). Immediately after the call to LoadLibrary in the code snippet is a breakpoint instruction that allows the loader program to gain control immediately after the LoadLibrary executes. Once the code snippet is created, I write it out to the first page of the target process with the WriteProcessMemory function. Immediately after, I'll change the EIP register in the target process so that execution will resume at the beginning of my code snippet.

After setting up the memory and registers just so, the API spy program lets the target process execute. If all goes according to plan, the process successfully executes the LoadLibrary code and returns to the breakpoint I set. When it hits the breakpoint, the target process is temporarily frozen again. The spy program takes this opportunity to restore the original code page it saved away, and to restore the original register values (again, using SetThreadContext()). With everything back to the way it was originally (except for the addition of our API spy DLL to the process's address space), the breakpoint handler lets the target process resume execution. I'll come back to this method of forcing another process to load a DLL in more detail when I show the code for the program in "The APISPY32 Code" section.

USING THE DEBUG API TO CONTROL THE TARGET PROCESS

When loading a DLL in another process's context, it's essential to have precise control over the child process's execution. The Win32 debug API provides all the essential information we'll need. In particular, we need to know exactly when the target process is about to execute the first instruction so that we can inject the spy's DLL. We'll also need the debug API to know when the target process terminates. In addition, when we're performing surgery in the target process's address space, we need to be sure that the process isn't going to take off and start executing while we're in the middle of it. Using the debugging API takes care of this problem. Whenever the debugged process reports something to the debugger, all threads in the debuggee are suspended until the debugger tells the operating system to let the debuggee resume execution.

If we were writing a spy program for 16-bit Windows programs, the TOOLHELP NotifyRegister and InterruptRegister functions would be just the ticket. The TOOLHELP NFY_STARTTASK notification would allow us to know when the new task is about to begin execution, but before it actually executes any of the task's code. Unfortunately, the TOOLHELP model of notification callbacks assumes a single address space for all processes. The TOOLHELP notification callback model won't work under the separate address spaces of NT and Windows 95, so we'll need to use the closest equivalent, the Win32 debug API.

Using the Win32 debug API to monitor the target process's execution imposes a certain architecture on our API spy program. The API spy will consist of two components. The first component is the code that intercepts the API functions in the target process and logs them. This code must reside in a DLL since we'll be injecting it into the address space of the process to be spied on. The second component of the API spy consists of a loader program that loads the process to be spied upon. After loading the program, the spy executable enters into a debugging loop, which consists primarily of calls to WaitForDebugEvent() and ContinueDebugEvent(). As debugging events are returned by WaitForDebugEvent(), the loader program examines the events and takes whatever action is necessary. The type of events that can be returned by WaitForDebugEvent()are

```
EXCEPTION_DEBUG_EVENT
CREATE_THREAD_DEBUG_EVENT
CREATE_PROCESS_DEBUG_EVENT
```

```
EXIT_THREAD_DEBUG_EVENT
EXIT_PROCESS_DEBUG_EVENT
LOAD_DLL_DEBUG_EVENT
UNLOAD_DLL_DEBUG_EVENT
OUTPUT_DEBUG_STRING_EVENT
RIP_EVENT
```

Incidentally, if you compare the Win32 debug events to the notifications returned by a Win16 NotifyRegister callback function, you'll notice a striking similarity. Also, if you want a program that uses WaitForDebugEvent and displays all the possible information returned by it, check out the DEB sample program in the Win32 SDK.

Once our loader program has handled the debug event notification, it calls ContinueDebugEvent() to inform the operating system that it's okay for the debuggee to resume execution. By putting WaitForDebugEvent and ContineDebugEvent() in a loop, the loader can see all significant events in the life of the process being spied on.

The most important debug event for our API spy program is the EXCEPTION_DEBUG_EVENT. Immediately before a process is about to begin execution, WaitForDebugEvent() returns an EXCEPTION_DEBUG_EVENT notification, with the exception being of type STATUS_BREAKPOINT. The API spy loader program takes this as its cue to force the spy DLL into the process's address space in the manner I described earlier. When the LoadLibrary call returns to the breakpoint we inserted into the process's code area, the loader program sees another STATUS_BREAKPOINT exception. The loader program uses this to know when it should restore the original registers and memory pages that we modified earlier.

Once the loader program has executed the target process past the two breakpoint exceptions, its work is mostly done. However, the Win32 API apparently doesn't offer a way for a debugger to tell the system that it doesn't want to receive debug notifications anymore. Once you begin using the debug API on a process, that process will be suspended each time it generates a debug event. A debugger call to ContinueDebugEvent for each debug event is the only way to keep the debuggee process running. Because of this, the API spy loader program needs to spin around in a WaitForDebugEvent and ContinueDebugEvent loop until the target process terminates. Even though we only really need a couple of the debug events, we're forced to receive them all. We can ignore any debug event that we're not interested in, and call ContinueDebugEvent without any further processing. In pseudocode form, the API spy loader looks like this:

```
Load Process to be spied on
while ( TRUE )
{
    WaitForDebugEvent()

    if ( debug event is a breakpoint )
    {
        if ( first breakpoint )
            modify debuggee to make it load the spy DLL
        else if ( second breakpoint )
            restore original register and data pages of debuggee
    }
    else if ( debug event is an EXIT_PROCESS )
        break out of loop

    ContinueDebugEvent()
}
```

BUILDING STUBS TO LOG API FUNCTIONS

At this point, we've worked out the major architectural questions relating to the operating system:

- How API functions will be intercepted
- How to load the spy DLL into the target process's address space
- How to precisely control the target process's execution

There are still other issues to deal with, but they're not as directly related to operating system concerns. One such area is the code that will handle the redirected API function calls. While it would be tempting to try to make a single entry point for all the function calls we redirect to our spy DLL, that just isn't feasible. There would be no way for a single entry point in the spy DLL to know which function call it's currently logging. Instead, we'll need to create a unique block of code for each function that we intercept. The word *thunk* is commonly used to describe short pieces of code that do some processing before transferring control elsewhere. While the blocks of code I'll be creating could be called thunks, I'll use the term *stub* to avoid ambiguity between my code and Window's thunks. All the code stubs for our spy program will be similar, but will differ slightly. When each stub receives a redirected function call, it pushes information unique to that function onto the stack before calling a common routine to log the call.

If all we needed to do was to intercept a known fixed set of functions, it would be easy to create some macros and generate all the code stubs at compile time. Since our specification dictates that this API spy be extendible, building the stubs when we compile the spy program isn't an option. Instead, we'll need to dynamically create the stubs based on information in a configuration file. Luckily, under Win32 this isn't hard.

For each stub we need, we can simply allocate some memory and write the appropriate code into it. Under 16-bit Windows this would be harder, since we would need to somehow allocate memory in code segments, rather than in the data segments returned by memory allocation functions. Once we had proper code segments, we couldn't just write our stub code into the memory block because writing into code segments isn't allowed. To write to the code stubs, we'd have to use alias selectors or the TOOLHELP MemoryWrite() function. Under Win32 these issues don't come up since both the code data segments map to the identical range of addresses. We can write out our code using regular flat model data pointers and later execute through that code.

To build the stubs, the spy DLL reads an input file (APISPY32.API) that contains the following information about each function to be intercepted:

- The DLL containing the function
- The name of the function
- Optional information about the function's parameters

For each function, the spy DLL builds a stub containing code and data, and which is of the form shown in Figure 10-2. The code portion of the stub first preserves all the general-purpose 32-bit registers. This isn't strictly necessary, but good coding practice dictates that you leave things the way you found them. Next, the stub pushes three pointers on the stack in preparation for the call to the logging function. The three pointers point at the function's name, its return address and parameters on the stack, and information about the function's parameters. (I'll come back to the parameter information in a bit.) After the logging function has done its work, the stub code restores all the general-purpose registers and JMPs to the code that originally should have been called (had we not intercepted the call).

```
DWORD RealAddressOfInterceptedFunction;

pushad                          ; Preserve all registers.
lea     EAX, [ESP+32]
push    EAX                     ; Push pointer to the return addr and params.
push    [pParamInfo]            ; Push pointer to byte-encoded parameter info.
push    [pszFunctionName]       ; Push pointer to the function's name.
call    LogCall                 ; Call function that does logging.
popad                           ; Restore original registers.
jmp     [RealAddressOfInterceptedFunction]  ; Jump to the original code.

char    szFunctionName[]        ; ASCIIZ name of the function.
BYTE    paramInfo[]             ; Optional byte-encoded parameter info.
                                ; First byte is the length of the info.
```

█ Figure 10-2
For each intercepted function, the SPY DLL builds a stub containing code and data.

As you might expect, the entire collection of stubs needs to be built before we can start the redirection of API function calls. As the spy DLL builds each stub, it adds that stub's address to an array of stub pointers. Redirecting the function calls in the target program to the appropriate stub is easy. For each imported function in the target process, the spy DLL retrieves the address of the imported function. The imported function's addresses are kept in a table pointed to by the DataDirectory[IMAGE DIRECTORY ENTRY IMPORT].VirtualAddress field in the PE header. Next, the spy DLL iterates through the array of stubs it's built, searching for a stub containing the same address in the stub's first DWORD. If it finds a match, the spy DLL patches the appropriate DWORD in the target program's imports table with the address of the stub's first instruction. This process is shown in Figure 10-3.

PARAMETER INFORMATION ENCODING

A large part of the usefulness of API spy programs comes from the fact that they show the actual values of the parameters to API functions. It would be prohibitively expensive for the logging function to have a separate section of code for each function and its parameters. In addition, you'd have to add code and recompile the API spy in order to add new functions.

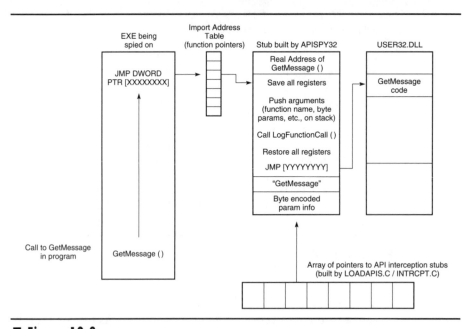

Figure 10-3
The imported function addresses are redirected through stubs built on the fly. These stubs invoke the APISPY32 code that logs the function call's name and parameters.

A better approach is to represent the function parameters in a condensed format that can be interpreted as part of logging a function call. Since there's a limited number of parameter types in Win32 programming, I decided to encode each of the basic types as a unique BYTE value. These fundamentals types include BYTEs, WORDs, DWORDs, and LPSTRs. To keep things simple, I encoded all pointers to data as an LPDATA type, with the exception of LPSTRs and LPWSTRs. If you want to make the spy program fancier, you can expand the parameter encodings to include other types, including pointers to specific data structures (for example, an LPRECT). The logging code could use this additional parameter type information to display more details about the parameters (such as what the fields in the LPRECT were). However, as I said, my goal was to keep things simple, so there are only ten unique parameter types in the supplied code.

In our API spy program, the parameter information is kept at the very end of the stub that's built for each API function. The first byte of the parameter information holds the number of parameters for that function. The BYTE codes for each parameter come immediately afterward, in the order of their appearance in the function declaration. For example, let's say that

HWND parameters are represented by the BYTE value 8, while DWORD parameters use the value 1. The parameter encoding for the GetWindow-Word(HWND,DWORD) function would be: 2,8,1 (two parameters, the first an HWND (8) and the second a DWORD (1)). A function that has no arguments is represented by a single 0 value.

Decoding the parameter information to display the parameter values is very simple. One of the values that the API function's stub passes to the logging function is a pointer to the top of the stack (the ESP register) immediately upon entry to the function. The DWORD at the top of the stack is the return address that control will return to after the API function has completed. Immediately higher in memory are the parameters that the calling function pushed on the stack. To decode the parameters, the logging function iterates through the BYTE-encoded parameter information. For each encoded parameter, the logging function retrieves a DWORD from the stack and emits a string containing the parameter type and its value (for instance: LPSTR:00410068).

After each parameter, the code increments the pointer to the stack area by 4 bytes to point at the next parameter. One nice advantage to the Win32 API is that parameters are pushed in last-to-first order, making the first parameter appear at the lowest address. If the Win32 API used the pascal calling convention (first-to-last) like the Win16 API does, decoding the parameters would be more difficult because the first parameter would appear at different locations on the stack for different APIs.

FUNCTION RETURN VALUES

At this point, we've got the mechanics of intercepting functions and logging their parameters well in hand. We could go off now and start implementing code. However, our design specification says that we need to log the value that the function returns. This makes things more difficult, and in more ways than one. While all calls to a given function end up being routed through one place (allowing us to intercept them all), the API function can return to a multitude of different places. How can we get control at that point to retrieve the value of the EAX register, which is where return values are placed?

Before we let the API function's real code execute, the only thing we know about what the function returns is the address that it will RET to. One obvious solution that springs to mind is to set a breakpoint at that address. A related method would be to stick in a JMP to our logging code. While both of these methods would work (usually), they're messy and have the same set of problems I described earlier when talking about intercepting the function call. A less obvious but cleaner solution (and one that doesn't require code modification) is to change the return address on the stack to point at the spy DLL's return value logging code. Of course, you would have to temporarily remember the original address, doing all this before you let the real API function code execute. After letting the original function code execute, the return value logging code will be entered. After logging the function's return value, the logging code copies the original return address back to the stack so that when the logging code returns, control ends up back in the target program.

Lest you think that the above method of obtaining function return values is too simple, be aware that there is a catch. In both Win16 and Win32, an API function might be in the middle of executing when it needs to call another API function. The classic example of this is DispatchMessage. DispatchMessage is the code that calls your program's window procedure. When you call Windows functions in your window procedure, you're actually calling an API function from within another API function (DispatchMessage, in this case). So what's wrong with that? In the simple method of grabbing return values that I just described, a single variable holds the original return address. If you get into a situation with nested APIs, only the most recent call's return address will be saved. The return addresses of the more deeply nested functions will be lost.

To deal with this problem of nested API functions, I've implemented a stack of return addresses. Whenever the code patches a function call's return address to point at our logging code, it adds the original return address to the top of our return address stack. When the return value logging code is ready to return to the calling program, it grabs the topmost entry off the return address stack and returns to that address. Our function return address stack is similar to the real program stack in some ways. The key difference is that the return address stack doesn't hold parameters, and only contains address for functions that are intercepted by the spy DLL.

With this situation of nested API function calls taken care of, we're ready to start coding, right? Not so fast. Programs under Windows NT and Windows 95 support multiple threads of execution. Each thread uses its own separate stack and is oblivious to what the other threads are doing. To deal with multiple threads, the API spy DLL maintains a separate return address stack for each thread that the target program starts up. Since the spy program can't know ahead of time how many threads the process to be monitored will start up, the memory for the per-thread return address stack is allocated whenever a new thread starts up. Luckily for our spy program, Win32 makes it easy to know when a thread is created. The operating system calls the entry point of all DLLs (for example, DllMain) each time it starts a new thread. As you'll see in the next section, where I present the spy program's code, the DllMain function allocates memory to hold a per-thread stack for each thread that starts.

The pointer to the per-thread return address stack is stored using the Win32 Thread Local Storage (TLS) mechanism. Thread local storage allows you to store a collection of unique DWORDs for each thread, but retrieve them in a consistent manner, no matter which thread is executing. Chapter 3 describes the implementation of thread local storage in detail. To use thread local storage, you first allocate an index value with the TlsAlloc function and store the index in a global variable. Thereafter, each thread can retrieve its thread-specific data by passing the index to TlsGetValue. To save away a per-thread value, you call TlsSetValue, passing both the TLS index allocated earlier and the value you want to save for the currently executing thread. In the case of our API spy DLL, the per-thread value we want to save is a pointer to our return address stack for that thread. The API spy DLL allocates the TLS index value when the DLL is first loaded and is processing the DLL_PROCESS_ATTACH code in DllMain.

Some of you Win32 programmers might be aware of the _ _declspec(thread) compiler directive. Using _ _declspec(thread) is a convenient way to create per-thread variables without using the TlsXXX functions. (See the description of the .tls section in Chapter 8 for more information on how _ _declspec(thread) works.) Wouldn't it be easier to make the per-thread stack a _ _declspec(thread) variable, rather than use the TlsXXX functions? Unfortunately, _ _declspec(thread) variables don't work properly in a DLL that's loaded with LoadLibrary (they work fine in implicitly loaded DLLs, though). Our API spy DLL is loaded with LoadLibrary, so _ _declspec(thread) variables are useless to us.

You might be wondering about what our spy program will do under Win32s, since Win32s doesn't support multithreading. Microsoft did the right thing and included the TLS functions in the Win32s libraries. Although the TLS data for a Win32s program is essentially just global data, the important thing is that our API spy DLL can use the TlsXXX functions without worrying about which operating system it's running on.

As you can see, grabbing the return value from API functions is quite a bit more difficult than it initially appears. Not only do we need to maintain a stack of return addresses, but we have to have such a stack for each thread in the target process. Things can't get any more complicated than that, can they? Guess again.

One of the neat features of the Win32 API is structured exception handling, which is related to exceptions in C++, but isn't quite the same thing. (For details on how structured exception handling works, see Chapter 3.) The problem with structured exception handling is that it can play havoc with our API return address stack. Let's say that you placed a try/except{} block around a call to DispatchMessage. Inside the window procedure that DispatchMessage eventually calls, your code generates an exception (a STATUS_ACCESS_VIOLATION, for instance). The except block that ends up handling the exception is the except{} block after the DispatchMessage code. The problem is that the CPU will effectively jump to the except{} block without ever returning from DispatchMessage. Since our return value logging code won't be called by the return from DispatchMessage, we don't know to remove the DispatchMessage return address off our per-thread return address stack. If this situation occurs repeatedly, the per-thread return address stack will eventually overflow.

Unlike the other problems we've encountered with return value logging, there is no elegant, clean solution to the problem caused by structured exception handling. There are messy, complex, and incomplete solutions to this problem that I've used in commercial programs (the BoundsChecker32 series), but I haven't included similar code in the API spy DLL because it complicates the code greatly. In defense of my decision to ignore structured exception handling difficulties, programs that actually bounce out of nested API functions without returning are rare. To date, I've never seen a program that has structured exception handling troubles with the logging code as presented here, with the exception of contrived test programs I've written.

One nice side effect of the return address stack is that we can use the stack pointer to figure out how deeply nested in API function calls we are. The logging code takes advantage of this to indent the function call and return lines for functions that are called inside another API function. The more deeply nested the API function, the more indented it appears in the log file. When the logging code is about to write out a function call or return value line, it checks the per-thread return address stack pointer and indents the beginning of the line accordingly. In the log file, it's easy to match up a return value with its call line by looking for the next line that starts at the same indentation level. For instance, here you can easily see the call line (at the top) that matches the return value (at the bottom):

```
DispatchMessageA(LPDATA:80B6AE68)
   LoadCursorA(HANDLE:00000000,LPSTR:00007F00)
   LoadCursorA returns: 2CE
   SetCursor()
   SetCursor returns: 2CE
DispatchMessageA returns: 0
```

THE APISPY32 CODE

Now that we've explored the theory involved in how we'll be implementing the spying code, it's time to discuss the actual code I wrote to implement the API spy program. I'll first describe the component functions of the DLL, and then show the loader program code. Don't worry, there's not a whole ton of code to go through here. I was pleasantly surprised by how little code was needed.

The name of the API spy program I've constructed is APISPY32, which is also the source file name of the spy DLL's entry point. The first important part of APISPY32.C is shown in Figure 10-4.

```
HINSTANCE HInstance;
BOOL FChicago = FALSE;
#if defined(_ _BORLANDC_ _)
#define DllMain DllEntryPoint
#endif

INT WINAPI DllMain
(
    HANDLE hInst,
    ULONG ul_reason_being_called,
    LPVOID lpReserved
)
{
    // OutputDebugString("In APISPY32.C\r\n");

    switch (ul_reason_being_called)
    {
        case DLL_PROCESS_ATTACH:
            HInstance = hInst;
            FChicago = (BOOL)((GetVersion() & 0xC0000000) == 0xC0000000);

            if ( InitializeAPISpy32() == FALSE )
                return 0;
            if ( InitThreadReturnStack() == FALSE )
                return 0;
            break;
```

```
            case DLL_THREAD_ATTACH:
                if ( InitThreadReturnStack() == FALSE )
                    return 0;
                break;

            case DLL_THREAD_DETACH:
                if ( ShutdownThreadReturnStack() == FALSE )
                    return 0;
                break;

            case DLL_PROCESS_DETACH:
                ShutDownAPISpy32();

                if ( ShutdownThreadReturnStack() == FALSE )
                    return 0;
                break;
        }

        return 1;
    }
```

▌ Figure 10-4
▌ *The first part of the DllMain functions in APISPY32.C.*

The DllMain function has a switch statement to direct the four important process/thread events to the appropriate handler. When I say "event" in the following description, I'm really talking about an invocation of DllMain with the dwReason field set to a specific value. The DLL_PROCESS_ATTACH event is our clue to intercept all the target processes calls and set up other things related to function logging.

For the initial thread in a process, the operating system doesn't call DllMain with a DLL_THREAD_ATTACH event. Instead, you need to consider DLL_PROCESS_ATTACH as also containing an implicit DLL_THREAD_ATTACH event. We'll need a per-thread return address stack for all threads in the target process, so both the DLL_PROCESS_ATTACH and DLL_THREAD_ATTACH handlers call InitThreadReturn-Stack to create the per-thread stack. The implicit assumption being made here is that both of these notifications are made in the context of newly created threads. The DLL_THREAD_DETACH event handler calls ShutdownThreadReturnStack to free the memory used by a per-thread return address stack. The last event, DLL_PROCESS_DETACH, calls ShutDownAPISpy32. Currently this function doesn't do much except close the log file so that the operating system's internal buffers will be written to the disk. We could actually go and patch back all the original addresses in the imports section of the EXE, but there's really no reason to. As with thread creation, there's no explicit DLL_THREAD_DETACH for the last thread in the process. The DLL_PROCESS_ATTACH handler therefore also calls ShutdownThreadReturnStack to get rid of the last remaining return address stack.

The remaining parts of APISPY32.C are shown in Figure 10-5. The first action of the InitializeAPISpy32 function is to invoke the LoadAPIConfig-File routine. LoadAPIConfigFile loads the .API file containing API functions and parameter information and builds the stubs with that data. (I'll discuss this function in more detail later on in the code walkthrough.)

```
BOOL InitializeAPISpy32(void)
{
    HMODULE hModExe;
    DWORD moduleBase;

    if ( LoadAPIConfigFile() == FALSE )
        return FALSE;

    if ( OpenLogFile() == FALSE )
        return FALSE;

    hModExe = GetModuleHandle(0);
    if ( !hModExe )
        return FALSE;

    if ( (GetVersion() & 0xC0000000) == 0x80000000 )    // Win32s???
        moduleBase = GetModuleBaseFromWin32sHMod(hModExe);
    else
        moduleBase = (DWORD)hModExe;

    if ( !moduleBase )
        return FALSE;

    return InterceptFunctionsInModule( (HMODULE)moduleBase );
}

BOOL ShutDownAPISpy32(void)
{
    CloseLogFile();

    return TRUE;
}
```

■ Figure 10-5
The APISPY32.C initialization and shutdown functions.

After building the API function stubs, the next step in the initialization is to open up the output file that the spy DLL writes its function call and return value information to. The final portion of the initialization is to call InterceptFunctionsInModule to redirect the target program's function calls to the stubs we built earlier. The InterceptFunctionsInModule function needs to know the base load address of the target process in memory so that it can go find the imported functions section table. In Windows NT and Windows 95 (Windows 4.0), the HMODULE of a running program is the same as its base load address. Since our DLL isn't the main EXE, its HMODULE isn't the one we need. Instead, we call GetModuleHandle(0), which under Win32 gives you the EXE's HMODULE, no matter where you call it from. Under Win32s, we need to take an extra step, since an HMODULE isn't the same as a base address. To get the base address of a Win32s module, I wrote the GetModuleBaseFromWin32sHMod function. This routine uses two undocumented Win32s functions to convert a Win32s HMODULE to a base address, and is in the W32SSUPP.C file. Shutting down the API spy is much simpler than the initialization code, and consists of a call to CloseLogFile.

The code in Figure 10-6 is responsible for reading in the APISPY32.API file. After reading in the definition for one function, it calls AddAPIFunction in INTRCPT.C to actually allocate memory for the function stub and initialize it accordingly. The APISPY32.API file is a line-oriented ASCII text file. Whitespace before lines and blank lines are tolerated, but extra characters at the end of an otherwise valid line are not. Any line that isn't recognized is ignored and processing continues with the next line.

The syntax for the API definition is extremely simple. For each function you want to intercept, add a line of the following form:

```
API:ModuleName:FunctionName
```

For instance:

```
API:USER32.dll:GetMessageA
```

Immediately after a new function definition, you can place parameter information about that function, one parameter per line. For example:

```
API:USER32.dll:GetMessageA
LPDATA
HWND
DWORD
DWORD
```

The valid parameter keywords are stored in the ParamEncodings array, and consist of the following:

```
DWORD      ; Any general-purpose 4-byte value (DWORD, UINT, int, etc.)
WORD       ; Any general-purpose 2-byte value (WORD, USHORT, short, etc.)
BYTE       ; Any general-purpose 1-byte value (BYTE, char, etc.)
LPSTR      ; Pointer to a null terminated ASCII string.
LPWSTR     ; Pointer to a null terminated Unicode (wide) string.
LPDATA     ; Pointer to any data, other than LPSTRs and LPWSTRs.
HANDLE     ; A handle value (other than HWNDs).
HWND       ; An HWND.
BOOL       ; A BOOL parameter.
LPCODE     ; Pointer to code (e.g., FARPROC, WNDPROC, etc.).
```

To allow you to use APISPY32 with a minimum of initial fuss, I've included an APISPY32.API file containing function and parameter information for KERNEL32.DLL, USER32.DLL, and GDI32.DLL, and ADVAPI32.DLL. You can add additional functions definitions to this file. A likely candidate would be COMCTL32.DLL. If you want to use APISPY32 with several different projects and DLLs, you might want to extend the LoadAPIConfigFile function to read in multiple .API files.

In the parameter types I've defined, there is some overlap. For example, an HWND could also be encoded as a HANDLE or a DWORD. My goal in defining this set of keywords was to break out the most commonly encountered types to allow some flexibility in how the parameters will be displayed in the output. By having separate LPSTR and LPDATA parameter types, we can show a snippet of the actual string when we encounter an LPSTR parameter. If we lumped LPSTR parameters in with LPDATA parameters, we wouldn't know which parameters to try to show characters from the string for. Another possibility that I haven't implemented would be to show TRUE or FALSE for BOOL parameters, rather than their numeric value. Yet another option would be to take HWND parameters and include a portion of the window title in the output. This makes it easier to connect an HWND value to a specific window when viewing the log file.

If you're ambitious, feel free to extend the parameter encodings I've defined here. Adding a new parameter type is easy. In the PARMTYPE.H file is an enumeration called PARAMTYPE. Add your new parameter type to the end of the enumeration. Then, add the name of the parameter as it should appear in the API file, and your enumeration to the end of the ParamEncodings array. Finally, in the logging code in LOG.C, add the code to print out whatever you want for your new parameter. One obvious thing to do would be to define more specific pointer types. For example, an LPMSG is a common parameter. By defining an LPMSG parameter, the logging code could dereference the LPMSG pointer to add the values of the MSG structure members to the log. Figure 10-6 shows the beginning of LOADAPIS.C, the .API file-parsing code.

```c
BOOL IsNewAPILine(PSTR pszInputLine);
BOOL ParseNewAPILine(PSTR pszInput, PSTR pszDLLName, PSTR pszAPIName);
PARAMTYPE GetParameterEncoding(PSTR pszParam);
PSTR SkipWhitespace(PSTR pszInputLine);

extern HINSTANCE HInstance;

BOOL LoadAPIConfigFile(void)
{
    FILE *pFile;
    char szInput[256];
    BYTE params[33];
    BOOL fBuilding = FALSE;
    char szAPIFunctionFile[MAX_PATH];
    PSTR p;

    // Create a string with the path to the API function file. This
    // file will be in the same directory as this DLL.
    GetModuleFileName(HInstance, szAPIFunctionFile, sizeof(szAPIFunctionFile));
    p = strrchr(szAPIFunctionFile, '\\')+1;
    strcpy(p, "APISPY32.API");

    pFile = fopen(szAPIFunctionFile, "rt");
    if ( !pFile )
        return FALSE;

    //
    // Format of a line is moduleName:APIName
    // (e.g., "KERNEL32.DLL:LoadLibraryA")
    //
    while ( fgets(szInput, sizeof(szInput), pFile) )
    {
        PSTR pszNewline, pszInput;
        char szAPIName[128], szDLLName[128];

        pszInput = SkipWhitespace(szInput);

        if ( *pszInput == '\n' )    // Go to next line if this line is blank.
            continue;
```

```
        pszNewline = strrchr(pszInput, '\n');   // Look for the newline.
        if ( pszNewline )
            *pszNewline = 0;                     // Hack off the newline.

        if ( IsNewAPILine(pszInput) )
        {
            // Dispense with the old one we've been building.
            if ( fBuilding )
                AddAPIFunction(szDLLName, szAPIName, params);

            if ( ParseNewAPILine(pszInput, szDLLName, szAPIName) )
                fBuilding = TRUE;
            else
                fBuilding = FALSE;

            params[0] = 0;  // New set of parameters.
        }
        else    // A parameter line
        {
            BYTE param = (BYTE)GetParameterEncoding(pszInput);
            if ( param != PARAM_NONE )
            {
                params[ params[0] +1 ] = param; // Add param to end of list.
                params[0]++;                    // Update the param count.
            }
            else
            {
                if ( (*pszInput != 0) && (stricmp(pszInput, "VOID") != 0) )
                {
                    char errBuff[256];
                    wsprintf(errBuff, "Unknown param %s in %s\r\n",
                            pszInput, szAPIName);
                    OutputDebugString(errBuff);
                }
            }
        }
    }

    fclose( pFile );

    return TRUE;
}


// Returns TRUE if this line is the start of an API definition. It assumes
// that any whitespace has already been skipped over.
BOOL IsNewAPILine(PSTR pszInputLine)
{
```

```
        return 0 == strnicmp(pszInputLine, "API:", 4);
}


// Break apart a function definition line into a module name and a function
// name. Returns those strings in the passed PSTR buffers.
BOOL ParseNewAPILine(PSTR pszInput, PSTR pszDLLName, PSTR pszAPIName)
{
    PSTR pszColonSeparator;

    pszDLLName[0] = pszAPIName[0] = 0;

    pszInput += 4;  // Skip over "API:"

    pszColonSeparator = strchr(pszInput, ':');
    if ( !pszColonSeparator )
        return FALSE;

    *pszColonSeparator++ = 0;   // Null terminate module name, bump up
                                // pointer to API name.

    strcpy(pszDLLName, pszInput);
    strcpy(pszAPIName, pszColonSeparator);

    return TRUE;
}



typedef struct tagPARAM_ENCODING
{
    PSTR        pszName;    // Parameter name as it appears in APISPY32.API
    PARAMTYPE   value;      // Associated PARAM_xxx enum from PARMTYPE.H
} PARAM_ENCODING, * PPARAM_ENCODING;

PARAM_ENCODING ParamEncodings[] =
{
{"DWORD", PARAM_DWORD},
{"WORD", PARAM_WORD},
{"BYTE", PARAM_BYTE},
{"LPSTR", PARAM_LPSTR},
{"LPWSTR", PARAM_LPWSTR},
{"LPDATA", PARAM_LPDATA},
{"HANDLE", PARAM_HANDLE},
{"HWND", PARAM_HWND},
{"BOOL", PARAM_BOOL},
{"LPCODE", PARAM_LPCODE},
};
```

```
// Given a line that's possibly a parameter line, returns the PARAM_xxx
// encoding for that parameter type. Lines that don't match any of the
// strings in the ParamEncodings cause the function to return PARAM_NONE.
PARAMTYPE GetParameterEncoding(PSTR pszParam)
{
    unsigned i;
    PPARAM_ENCODING pParamEncoding = ParamEncodings;

    for ( i=0; i < (sizeof(ParamEncodings)/sizeof(PARAM_ENCODING)); i++ )
    {
        if ( stricmp(pParamEncoding->pszName, pszParam) == 0 )
            return pParamEncoding->value;

        pParamEncoding++;
    }

    return PARAM_NONE;
}

// Given a pointer to an ASCIIZ string, return a pointer to the first
// non-whitespace character in the line.
PSTR SkipWhitespace(PSTR pszInputLine)
{
    while ( *pszInputLine && isspace(*pszInputLine) )
        pszInputLine++;
    return pszInputLine;
}
```

▋ Figure 10-6
The beginning of the .API file-parsing process in LOADAPIS.C.

The INTRCPT.C source module contains all the code related to intercepting functions calls from the target process. The first routine in INTR-
CPT.C is AddAPIFunction. After the LOADAPIS.C code has read in all the
information for one function, it passes the function name, the name of the
DLL that contains the function, and the byte-encoded parameter information to AddAPIFunction. AddAPIFunction's two jobs are to construct
the function interception stub and to add that stub to the list of stubs.
AddAPIFunction delegates the grunge work of constructing the stub to the
BuildAPIStub routine.

BuildAPIstub first uses the function and module name to call
GetProcAddress to retrieve the address of the specified function. Assuming
GetProcAddress succeeds, the BuildAPIStub code calculates how much
memory will be needed for the stub (the API name and the parameter

encodings are of variable length), and allocates the memory. Next BuildAPIStub fills in the fields of the stub, the initial portions of which are defined by the APIFunction structure given in INTRCPT2.H. At the end of the allocated stub memory, BuildAPIStub copies the function's name and its byte-encoded parameter information.

Besides building and maintaining the function interception stubs, the other important duty of INTRCPT.C is to rummage through the target process's memory image and redirect its JMP DWORD PTR [XXXXXXXX] calls to point at the stubs built earlier. The InterceptFunctionsInModule function doesn't need anything except the load address of the module in memory to find the imported functions table, which I described in an earlier section. The function first verifies that a valid module base address was found by looking for the DOS MZ and Win32 PE signatures in the file. Once the function knows that it has a valid base address, it uses the data directory at the end of the IMAGE_NT_HEADERS structure to get a pointer to the .idata section of the module.

To find all the functions that the EXE imports, InterceptFunctionsInModule iterates through the array of IMAGE_IMPORT_DESCRIPTOR structures at the beginning of the .idata section. The PEDUMP from Chapter 8 does something similar to this. There is one IMAGE_IMPORT_DESCRIPTOR for each DLL that the EXE implicitly links to. Each IMAGE_IMPORT_DESCRIPTOR contains a relative offset to an array of IMAGE_THUNK_DATA structures, with one IMAGE_THUNK_DATA structure for each imported function.

Using two nested loops, InterceptFunctionsInModule walks through all the functions imported by the EXE and retrieves the address of the imported function. This address is stored as part of the IMAGE_THUNK_DATA structure. For each imported function, our routine passes the imported function's address to LookupInterceptedAPI. LookupInterceptedAPI scans through the array of function stubs we built, looking for a stub that has the same address in its first DWORD. If a stub is found, InterceptFunctionsInModule overwrites the original imported function address in the IMAGE_THUNK_DATA structure with a pointer to code in the stub we just looked up (as shown in Figure 10-7). From this point on, whenever the process to be spied on calls an imported function, its JMP DWORD PTR [XXXXXXXX] thunk in the import address table will jump to our interception stub rather than to the intended API function. Only after we've logged the function call will our stub pass control along to the imported function.

```
PAPIFunction BuildAPIStub(PSTR pszModule, PSTR pszFuncName, PBYTE params);

// MakePtr is a macro that allows you to easily add to values (including
// pointers) together without dealing with C's pointer arithmetic.  It
// essentially treats the last two parameters as DWORDs. The first
// parameter is used to typecast the result to the appropriate pointer type.
#define MakePtr( cast, ptr, addValue ) (cast)( (DWORD)(ptr)+(DWORD)(addValue))

#define MAX_INTERCEPTED_APIS 2048
unsigned InterceptedAPICount = 0;
PAPIFunction InterceptedAPIArray[MAX_INTERCEPTED_APIS];

extern BOOL FChicago;
extern FILE * PLogFile;

BOOL AddAPIFunction
(
    PSTR pszModule,     // Exporting DLL name.
    PSTR pszFuncName,   // Exported function name.
    PBYTE params        // Opcode encoded parameters of exported function.
)
{
    PAPIFunction pNewFunction;

    if ( InterceptedAPICount >= MAX_INTERCEPTED_APIS )
        return FALSE;

    pNewFunction = BuildAPIStub(pszModule, pszFuncName, params);
    if ( !pNewFunction )
        return FALSE;

    InterceptedAPIArray[ InterceptedAPICount++ ] = pNewFunction;

    return TRUE;
}


PAPIFunction BuildAPIStub(PSTR pszModule, PSTR pszFuncName, PBYTE params)
{
    UINT allocSize;
    PAPIFunction pNewFunction;
    PVOID realProcAddress;
    UINT cbFuncName;
    HMODULE hModule;

    hModule = GetModuleHandle(pszModule);
    if ( !hModule )
        return 0;

    realProcAddress = GetProcAddress( hModule, pszFuncName );
    if ( !realProcAddress )
```

```
            return 0;

        cbFuncName = strlen(pszFuncName);
        allocSize = sizeof(APIFunction) + cbFuncName +1 + *params + 1;

        pNewFunction = malloc(allocSize);
        if ( !pNewFunction )
            return 0;

        pNewFunction->RealProcAddress = realProcAddress;
        pNewFunction->instr_pushad = 0x60;
        pNewFunction->instr_lea_eax_esp_plus_32 = 0x2024448D;
        pNewFunction->instr_push_eax = 0x50;
        pNewFunction->instr_push_offset_params = 0x68;
        pNewFunction->offset_params = (DWORD)(pNewFunction + 1) + cbFuncName + 1;
        pNewFunction->instr_push_offset_funcName = 0x68;
        pNewFunction->offset_funcName = (DWORD)(pNewFunction + 1);
        pNewFunction->instr_call_LogFunction = 0xE8;
        pNewFunction->offset_LogFunction
            = (DWORD)LogCall - (DWORD)&pNewFunction->instr_popad;
        pNewFunction->instr_popad = 0x61;
        pNewFunction->instr_jmp_dword_ptr_RealProcAddress = 0x25FF;
        pNewFunction->offset_dword_ptr_RealProcAddrss = (DWORD)pNewFunction;

        strcpy( (PSTR)pNewFunction->offset_funcName, pszFuncName );
        memcpy( (PVOID)pNewFunction->offset_params, params, *params+1 );

        return pNewFunction;
    }


PAPIFunction LookupInterceptedAPI( PVOID address )
{
    unsigned i;
    PVOID stubAddress;

    for ( i=0; i < InterceptedAPICount; i++ )
    {
        if ( InterceptedAPIArray[i]->RealProcAddress == address )
            return InterceptedAPIArray[i];
    }

    // If it's Windows 95, and the app is being debugged (as this app is)
    // the loader doesn't fix up the calls to point directly at the
    // DLL's entry point. Instead, the address in the .idata section
    // points to a PUSH xxxxxxxx / JMP yyyyyyyy stub. The address in
    // xxxxxxxx points to another stub: PUSH aaaaaaaa / JMP bbbbbbbb.
    // The address in aaaaaaaa is the real address of the function in the
    // DLL. This ugly code verifies we're looking at this stub setup,
    // and if so, grabs the real DLL entry point, and scans through
    // the InterceptedAPIArray list of addresses again.
```

```
        // ***WARNING*** ***WARNING*** ***WARNING*** ***WARNING***
        // This code is subject to change!
        if ( FChicago )
        {
            if ( address < (PVOID)0x80000000 )  // Only shared, system DLLs
                return 0;                        // have stubs.

            if ( IsBadReadPtr(address, 9) || (*(PBYTE)address != 0x68)
                || (*((PBYTE)address+5) != 0xE9) )
                return 0;

            stubAddress = (PVOID) *(PDWORD)((PBYTE)address+1);

            for ( i=0; i < InterceptedAPICount; i++ )
            {
                PVOID lunacy;

                if ( InterceptedAPIArray[i]->RealProcAddress == stubAddress )
                    return InterceptedAPIArray[i];

                lunacy = InterceptedAPIArray[i]->RealProcAddress;

                if ( !IsBadReadPtr(lunacy, 9) && (*(PBYTE)lunacy == 0x68)
                    && (*((PBYTE)lunacy+5) == 0xE9) )
                {
                    lunacy = (PVOID)*(PDWORD)((PBYTE)lunacy+1);
                    if ( lunacy == stubAddress )
                        return InterceptedAPIArray[i];
                }
            }
        }

        return 0;
}

BOOL InterceptFunctionsInModule(PVOID baseAddress)
{
    PIMAGE_DOS_HEADER pDOSHeader = (PIMAGE_DOS_HEADER)baseAddress;
    PIMAGE_NT_HEADERS pNTHeader;
    PIMAGE_IMPORT_DESCRIPTOR pImportDesc;

    if ( IsBadReadPtr(baseAddress, sizeof(PIMAGE_NT_HEADERS)) )
        return FALSE;

    if ( pDOSHeader->e_magic != IMAGE_DOS_SIGNATURE )
        return FALSE;

    pNTHeader = MakePtr(PIMAGE_NT_HEADERS, pDOSHeader, pDOSHeader->e_lfanew);
    if ( pNTHeader->Signature != IMAGE_NT_SIGNATURE )
        return FALSE;
```

```
        pImportDesc = MakePtr(PIMAGE_IMPORT_DESCRIPTOR, baseAddress,
                            pNTHeader->OptionalHeader.
                            DataDirectory[IMAGE_DIRECTORY_ENTRY_IMPORT].
                            VirtualAddress);

    // Bail out if the RVA of the imports section is 0 (it doesn't exist)
    if ( pImportDesc == (PIMAGE_IMPORT_DESCRIPTOR)pNTHeader )
        return FALSE;

    while ( pImportDesc->Name )
    {
        PIMAGE_THUNK_DATA pThunk;

        pThunk = MakePtr(PIMAGE_THUNK_DATA,
                        baseAddress, pImportDesc->FirstThunk);

        while ( pThunk->u1.Function )
        {
            PAPIFunction pInterceptedFunction;

            pInterceptedFunction = LookupInterceptedAPI(pThunk->u1.Function);

            if ( pInterceptedFunction )
            {
                DWORD cBytesMoved;
                DWORD src = (DWORD)&pInterceptedFunction->instr_pushad;

                // Bash the import thunk.  We have to use WriteProcessMemory,
                // since the import table may be in a code section (courtesy
                // of the NT 3.51 team!).

                WriteProcessMemory( GetCurrentProcess(),
                            &pThunk->u1.Function,
                            &src, sizeof(DWORD), &cBytesMoved );
            }

            pThunk++;
        }

        pImportDesc++;
    }

    return TRUE;
}
```

█ Figure 10-7
The beginning of stub building and function interception in INTRCPT.C.

The LOG.C file contains all code related to writing the function call and return information to the output file. The first routine, OpenLogFile, opens the output file in the directory where the program to be spied on resides. The output file has the same name as the executable file, but with a OUT extension. Calling GetModuleFileName with the HMODULE of the target program conveniently gives us the program's directory and filename, so all we have to do is replace the EXE extension with OUT. OpenLogFile doesn't take read-only media into account, so if you run the executable from a CD-ROM, the fopen call will fail and you won't get a trace file.

The LogCall routine in LOG.C is the high-level routine responsible for adding the information about a function call to the output file. LogCall is called by the intercepted function stubs, and expects a pointer to the function name, a pointer to the byte-encoded parameter information, and a pointer to the stack upon entry to the stub code. The first thing LogCall does is pass off the tedious job of decoding and formatting the function parameters to the DecodeParamsToString function.

Afterward, LogCall emits a new line to the trace file with the function name and its decoded parameters inside ()'s. If the intercepted function is nested inside another intercepted function, the line will be indented with space characters proportional to the nesting level. The final act of the LogCall code is to call InterceptFunctionReturn. This routine (in RETURN.C) patches the return address of the intercepted function to point at our return-value logging code.

The DecodeParamsToString helper function accepts a pointer to the stack upon entry to the intercepted function stub, a pointer to the byte-encoded function parameters, and a pointer to a buffer to write to. The function first bumps up the stack frame pointer by 4 bytes to get past the intercepted function's return address. Next, a for loop iterates through all the byte-encoded parameters, grabs the associated DWORD out of the stack frame, and formats the parameter accordingly. The general form of each parameter is <type>:<value>, for instance, HWND:000200AC. If the parameter is of type LPSTR, the function calls the GetLPSTR helper function to get a snippet (10 bytes maximum) of the string that the parameter points to. If a valid string is pointed to, the string is appended to the other information, separated by a : (a colon), as shown here:

```
LPSTR:80B70018:"FreeCellIc"
```

As DecodeParamsToString formats each parameter, it tacks the string on to the end of the buffer passed in to the function. If there are multiple parameters, a "," (a comma) separates them, just as it would in real C/C++ code. The goal is to make the parameter information look as realistic as possible, for example:

```
LoadAcceleratorsA(HANDLE:00001C9E,LPSTR:80B70004:"FreeMenu")
```

The flip side of logging the function's parameters is logging its return value, which is performed by the LogReturn function. LogReturn is considerably simpler than LogCall, and consists of indenting the return line appropriately for its nesting level and then printing out the function name and return value.

Some of you may have noticed the complete lack of any thread synchronization code in the LOG.C. Normally in a multithreading program that does file I/O, you need critical sections or mutexes to prevent problems if a thread gets switched away from at an inopportune time. The LOG.C doesn't need to use thread synchronization since it doesn't use any global variables that it modifies (neither the PLogFile pointer nor the TlsIndex variables will change during program execution). But what about the fprintf() calls? Won't there be problems if a thread switches in the middle of one of them? If you don't pay attention, the answer is yes. However, the APISPY32 DLL is linked using the multithreading runtime library LIBCMT.LIB for Visual C++). These multithreading libraries internally use synchronization mechanisms so that the user of the functions doesn't have to. Interestingly enough, if you look through all the code for APISPY32, you won't find any synchronization code. This is largely because global variables are written to only during the initialization phase, and never change afterward. Figure 10-8 shows LOG.C, which writes the API function names and parameters to the output file.

```
// Helper function prototypes
void MakeIndentString(PSTR buffer, UINT level);
void DecodeParamsToString(PBYTE pParams, PDWORD pFrame, PSTR pszParams);
BOOL GetLPSTR( PSTR ptr, PSTR buffer );

FILE *PLogFile = 0;
extern DWORD TlsIndex;          // Defined in RETURN.C

BOOL OpenLogFile(void)
{
    char szFilename[MAX_PATH];
    PSTR pszExtension;

    GetModuleFileName( GetModuleHandle(0), szFilename, sizeof(szFilename) );
```

```
    pszExtension = strrchr(szFilename, '.');
    if ( !pszExtension )
        return FALSE;

    strcpy(pszExtension, ".out");

    PLogFile = fopen(szFilename, "wt");

    return (BOOL)PLogFile;
}


BOOL CloseLogFile(void)
{
    if ( PLogFile )
        fclose( PLogFile );
    return TRUE;
}


void _ _stdcall LogCall(PSTR pszName, PBYTE pParams, PDWORD pFrame)
{
    char szParams[512];
    char szIndent[128];
    PPER_THREAD_DATA pStack;

    if ( !PLogFile )
        return;

    DecodeParamsToString(pParams, pFrame, szParams);

    pStack = (PPER_THREAD_DATA)TlsGetValue(TlsIndex);
    if ( !pStack )
        return;

    MakeIndentString(szIndent, pStack->FunctionStackPtr);

    fprintf(PLogFile, "%s%s(%s)\n", szIndent, pszName, szParams);
    fflush(PLogFile);

    // Patch the return address of this function so that returns to us.
    InterceptFunctionReturn(pszName, pFrame);
}

void DecodeParamsToString(PBYTE pParams, PDWORD pFrame, PSTR pszParams)
{
```

```
    unsigned i;
    unsigned paramCount;
    unsigned paramShowSize;
    PSTR pszParamName;

    pszParams[0] = 0;   // Null out string in case there's no parameters.

    paramCount = *pParams++;    // Get number of parameters and advance
                                // to first encoded param.
    pFrame++;                   // Bump past the DWORD return address.

    for ( i=0; i < paramCount; i++ )
    {
        switch ( *pParams )
        {
            case PARAM_DWORD:
                pszParamName = "DWORD"; paramShowSize = 4; break;
            case PARAM_WORD:
                pszParamName = "WORD"; paramShowSize = 2; break;
            case PARAM_BYTE:
                pszParamName = "BYTE"; paramShowSize = 1; break;
            case PARAM_LPSTR:
                pszParamName = "LPSTR"; paramShowSize = 4; break;
            case PARAM_LPWSTR:
                pszParamName = "LPWSTR"; paramShowSize = 4; break;
            case PARAM_LPDATA:
                pszParamName = "LPDATA"; paramShowSize = 4; break;
            case PARAM_HANDLE:
                pszParamName = "HANDLE"; paramShowSize = 4; break;
            case PARAM_HWND:
                pszParamName = "HWND"; paramShowSize = 4; break;
            case PARAM_BOOL:
                pszParamName = "BOOL"; paramShowSize = 4; break;
            case PARAM_LPCODE:
                pszParamName = "LPCODE"; paramShowSize = 4; break;
            default:
                pszParamName = "<unknown>"; paramShowSize = 0;
        }

        pszParams += wsprintf(pszParams, "%s:", pszParamName);

        switch ( paramShowSize )
        {
            case 4: pszParamName = "%08X"; break;
            case 2: pszParamName = "%04X"; break;
            case 1: pszParamName = "%02X"; break;
        }
```

```
            pszParams += wsprintf(pszParams, pszParamName, *pFrame) ;

            // Tack on the string literal value if it's a PARAM_LPSTR
            if ( *pParams == PARAM_LPSTR )
            {
                char buffer[30];

                if ( GetLPSTR( (PSTR)*pFrame, buffer ) )
                {
                    strcpy(pszParams, buffer);
                    pszParams += strlen(buffer);
                }
            }

            if ( (paramCount - i) != 1 )    // Tack on a comma if not last
                *pszParams++ = ',';         // parameter.

        pFrame++;   // Bump frame up to the next DWORD value
        pParams++;  // advance to next encoded parameter.
    }               // End of for() statement.
}


BOOL GetLPSTR( PSTR ptr, PSTR buffer )
{
    PSTR p = buffer;
    int i;

    *p++ = ':';     // Write out initial -> :" <-
    *p++ = '\"';

    for ( i=0; i < 10; i++ )
    {
        if ( !IsBadReadPtr( ptr, 1 ) && *ptr )
        {
            *p = *ptr++;
            if ( *p == '\r' ) { *p++ = '\\'; *p = 'r'; }
            else if ( *p == '\n' ) { *p++ = '\\'; *p = 'n'; }
            else if ( *p == '\t' ) { *p++ = '\\'; *p = 't'; }

            p++;
        }
        else
            break;
    }
```

```
        if ( i == 0 )   // Not a valid string
            return FALSE;

        *p++ = '\"';    // Valid string ptr - end quote and null
        *p++ = 0;       // terminate the string

        return TRUE;
    }


void LogReturn(PSTR pszName, DWORD returnValue, DWORD level)
{
    char szIndent[128];

    if ( !PLogFile )
        return;

    MakeIndentString(szIndent, level);
    fprintf(PLogFile, "%s%s returns: %X\n", szIndent, pszName, returnValue);
    fflush(PLogFile);
}


void MakeIndentString(PSTR buffer, UINT level)
{
    DWORD cBytes = level * 2;
    memset(buffer, ' ', cBytes);
    buffer[cBytes] = 0;
}
```

▌ Figure 10-8
▌ *LOG.C writes the API function names and parameters to this output file.*

The code in RETURN.C all relates to intercepting the return from an API function in order to get its return value. The first two functions, InitThreadReturnStack and ShutdownThreadReturnStack, are called once for each thread in the target process. InitThreadReturnStack allocates a block of memory the size of a PER_THREAD_DATA structure and initializes it (see PERTHRED.H). The PER_THREAD_DATA structure holds the two components necessary for that thread's return address stack: an array of HOOKED_FUNCTION structures and a stack pointer (see Figure 10-9).

Each time an intercepted function is called, its original return address and name pointer are written to the next available HOOKED_FUNCTION structure. Afterward, the stack pointer is incremented by 1. Implementing the stack in this way allows the stack pointer (really an index, not a pointer) to correspond to the current nesting level. The logging routines take advantage of this to indent the call and return lines as appropriate for the current function-nesting level. The pointer to the PER_THREAD_DATA structure is stored in the Thread Local Storage slot allocated for it at DLL initialization.

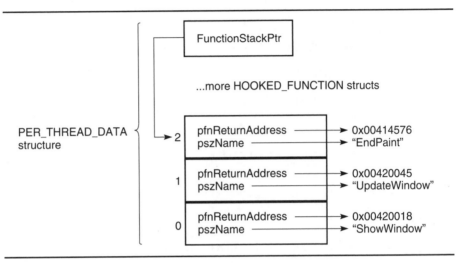

Figure 10-9
The PER_THREAD_DATA structure contains the stack pointer and the array of HOOKED_FUNCTION structures that hold that thread's return address stack.

The InterceptFunctionReturn is called by the function-call logging code, just prior to letting control jump to the originally intended API function code. The InterceptFunctionReturn first adds the intercepted function's return address and name to the return address stack. Afterward, it overwrites the return address with the address of the AsmCommonReturnPoint routine in ASMRETRN.ASM.

The final function in RETURN.C is CCommonReturnPoint, which is invoked by the assembler code in AsmCommonReturnPoint. Although I could have had the assembler code do everything, I wanted to keep as much of APISPY32 in C as possible. CCommonReturnPoint first calls LogReturn to log the intercepted function's return value. It then writes the original return value into a special space in the stack reserved for that purpose by the assembler code, and returns to the assembler code. Figure 10-10 shows RETURN.C, which handles the details of logging the function's return value.

```
void AsmCommonReturnPoint(void);

DWORD TlsIndex = 0xFFFFFFFF;

BOOL InitThreadReturnStack(void)
{
    PPER_THREAD_DATA pPerThreadData;

    static BOOL firstTime = TRUE;

    if ( firstTime )
    {
        TlsIndex = TlsAlloc();
        firstTime = FALSE;
    }

    if ( TlsIndex == 0xFFFFFFFF )
        return FALSE;

    pPerThreadData = malloc( sizeof(PER_THREAD_DATA) );
    if ( !pPerThreadData )
        return FALSE;

    pPerThreadData->FunctionStackPtr = 0;

    TlsSetValue(TlsIndex, pPerThreadData);

    return TRUE;
}

BOOL ShutdownThreadReturnStack(void)
{
    PPER_THREAD_DATA pPerThreadData;

    if ( TlsIndex == 0xFFFFFFFF )
        return FALSE;

    pPerThreadData = TlsGetValue( TlsIndex );
    if ( pPerThreadData )
        free( pPerThreadData );

    return TRUE;
}

BOOL InterceptFunctionReturn(PSTR pszName, PDWORD pFrame)
{
    PPER_THREAD_DATA pStack;
    DWORD i;

    pStack = (PPER_THREAD_DATA)TlsGetValue(TlsIndex);
    if ( !pStack )
        return FALSE;
```

```
        if ( pStack->FunctionStackPtr >= (MAX_HOOKED_FUNCTIONS-1) )
            return FALSE;

        i = pStack->FunctionStackPtr;

        pStack->FunctionStack[i].pfnReturnAddress = (PVOID)pFrame[0];
        pStack->FunctionStack[i].pszName = pszName;
        pStack->FunctionStackPtr++;

        pFrame[0] = (DWORD)AsmCommonReturnPoint;

        return TRUE;
}

// return_address <- pFrame[8]
// EAX            <- pFrame[7]
// ECX            <- pFrame[6]
// EDX            <- pFrame[5]
// EBX            <- pFrame[4]
// ESP            <- pFrame[3]
// EBP            <- pFrame[2]
// ESI            <- pFrame[1]
// EDI            <- pFrame[0]


//
// Common return point for all functions that we've intercepted.
// Called by _AsmCommonReturnPoint in ASMRETRN.ASM
// pFrame is a pointer to the stack frame set up by the PUSHAD
// (see above comment for the layout of this frame)
//
void CCommonReturnPoint( PDWORD pFrame )
{
    PPER_THREAD_DATA pStack;
    DWORD i;

    // Get the function stack for the current thread
    pStack = (PPER_THREAD_DATA)TlsGetValue(TlsIndex);
    if ( !pStack )
        return;

    i = --pStack->FunctionStackPtr;

    // Emit the information about the function return value to the logging
    // mechanism.
    LogReturn(pStack->FunctionStack[i].pszName, pFrame[7], i);

    // Patch the return address back to what it was when the function
    // was originally called.
    pFrame[8] = (DWORD)pStack->FunctionStack[i].pfnReturnAddress;
}
```

Figure 10-10
RETURN.C logs the function's return value.

When I set out to write APISPY32, I wanted to keep it entirely in C code. Unfortunately, given the stack games we played to get control when an intercepted function returns, I couldn't find a way to do it cleanly in C. Also, C routines are allowed to trash registers. I wanted the APISPY32 code to have as little effect as possible on the target process, so I chose to push and pop all the general-purpose registers around the call to the C routines. The ASMRETRN.ASM code does the bare minimum. It first subtracts 4 from the ESP register to reserve space for the original return address. The C code eventually fills in that DWORD with the correct address, so that when the assembler code returns, it will return to the correct location, and with the stack pointer exactly as it was when the routine was entered. The remainder of the code, shown in Figure 10-11, is just a PUSHAD and POPAD around a call to the CCommonReturnPoint function.

```
.386
.model flat

extrn _CCommonReturnPoint:proc

.code

public _AsmCommonReturnPoint

_AsmCommonReturnPoint proc
    SUB     ESP,4   ; Make space for return address
    PUSHAD
    MOV     EAX,ESP
    PUSH    EAX
    CALL    _CCommonReturnPoint
    ADD     ESP,4
    POPAD
    RET
_AsmCommonReturnPoint endp

END
```

▌ Figure 10-11
The assembler portion of the function return hooking code in ASMRETRN.

Win32s-Specific Code

The last remaining bit of code in APISPY32.DLL is specific to Win32s, and comes from the W32SSUPP.C file. The one function from this module, GetModuleBaseFromWin32sHMod, is shown in Figure 10-12. The function's task is to take a Win32s hModule (which isn't a base load address of a module in memory), and convert it into a base address. Browsing through the Win32s documentation, I couldn't find any clean (or even documented) way to do the conversion. However, I did know that functions like the Win32 GetProcAddress would need to do something similar. Stepping through the Win32s libraries in SoftIce/W revealed that two exported (but undocumented) functions in W32SKRNL.DLL did exactly what I needed. The first function is _ImteFromHModule@4, which takes a Win32s HMODULE and returns an internal handle known as an IMTE. (IMTEs were described in Chapter 3.) The second function I found is BaseAddrFromImte, which takes one of these IMTEs as a parameter and returns a 32-bit linear base address where the module is loaded.

Since these functions are specific to Win32s, I couldn't directly call them from the APISPY32 DLL, since the DLL wouldn't then be able to load under Windows 95 or Windows NT. Calling the functions directly would place a fixup to those functions in the DLL, and the loader wouldn't be able to find them when it brings APISPY32.DLL into memory. Therefore, I used the standard technique of using GetProcAddress to get a pointer to the two functions and then called through the pointer.

```
typedef DWORD (_ _stdcall *XPROC)(DWORD);
```

```
DWORD GetModuleBaseFromWin32sHMod(HMODULE hMod)
{
    XPROC ImteFromHModule, BaseAddrFromImte;
    HMODULE hModule;
    DWORD imte;

    hModule = GetModuleHandle("W32SKRNL.DLL");
    if( !hModule )
        return 0;

    ImteFromHModule = (XPROC)GetProcAddress(hModule, "_ImteFromHModule@4");
    if ( !ImteFromHModule )
        return 0;
```

```
        BaseAddrFromImte = (XPROC)GetProcAddress(hModule, "_BaseAddrFromImte@4");
        if ( !BaseAddrFromImte )
            return 0;

        imte = ImteFromHModule( (DWORD)hMod);
        if ( !imte )
            return 0;

        return BaseAddrFromImte(imte);
    }
```

Figure 10-12
W32SSUPP.C is the Win32s-specific code.

THE APISPYLD CODE

With the code for the API spy DLL behind us, all that remains is the program
loader. The program loader is itself a program, and uses CreateProcess to
start the process to be spied upon. Before the target process can execute any
code, the program loader injects the API spy DLL (APISPY32.DLL) into the
target process. Once injected, the program loader doesn't have much to do
except spin in a WaitForDebugEvent loop until the target process terminates.
I've named the program loader APISPYLD. Its source file is larger than the
other source files in the project, so I'll break up APISPYLD.C into several
pieces for examination.

The first portion of APISPYLD.C is the minimal user-interface code and
the code that loads the target process. The WinMain is a simple while loop
that cycles until a program has been successfully spied on or until the user
elects to quit the spy program. The while loop first invokes a dialog box to
get the program name to spy on. If the DialogBox returns nonzero, WinMain
calls LoadProcessForSpying. If the process is successfully started, WinMain
calls DebugLoop where it APISPYLD remains, pumping through all the debug
messages until the target process terminates.

The dialog box for APISPYLD is minimal, as you can see from Figure 10-13.
The single edit control is for typing in the command line (including parameters)
of the program to be spied on. For the sake of Convenience, the File. . . button brings up the GetOpenFileName common dialog box, enabling you to

click your way to the filename, rather than tediously typing in the path by hand. Clicking on Run dismisses the dialog and attempts to load the specified process for spying. Clicking on Cancel dismisses the dialog and exits the program.

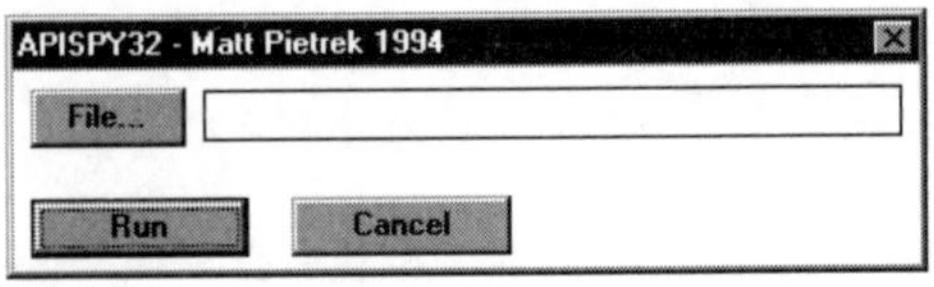

Figure 10-13
The APISPYLD dialog box lets you indicate the program to be spied on.

The dialog procedure code in APISPY32DlgProc is extremely simple, and responds to only three messages: WM_INITDIALOG, WM_COMMAND, and WM_CLOSE. The WM_INITDIALOG handler allows us the opportunity to retrieve the last command line we gave to APISPYLD, and stuff it into the edit control. The previous command line is stored in a private .INI file called APISPY32.INI.

The meat of the dialog code is for processing WM_COMMAND messages; it resides in the Handle_WM_COMMAND helper function. The only WM_COMMAND messages handled are for the three buttons. The File... button code calls the GetProgramName helper function, which is a wrapper around the Common Dialog GetOpenFileName function. If GetProgram-Name succeeds, the program name will be in the dialog's edit control. Clicking on the Run button tells APISPYLD to copy whatever is in the edit control into the SzCmdLine global variable and exit from the dialog with a code of 1. The Cancel button also exits the dialog, but tells it to return 0 so that WinMain won't try to load anything.

If the user correctly enters a proper command line and hits the Run button, the dialog box will exit and control returns to WinMain. WinMain then calls LoadProcessForSpying, passing it the contents of the SzCmdLine global variable. LoadProcessForSpying is just a shell around the Win32 CreateProcess API function. The only interesting part of this particular CreateProcess call is that the fdwCreate flags parameter specifies DEBUG_ONLY_THIS_PROCESS. This tells the operating system that our program (APISPYLD) wants to act as a debugger for the program being loaded. It also informs the operating system that we're interested only in debug events for this particular process, and not in any of the newly created process's

children. Had I specified DEBUG_PROCESS instead of DEBUG_ONLY_
THIS_PROCESS, APISPYLD would also get debug notifications for any
programs that the target process created. Figure 10-14 shows the beginning
of the APISPYLD.C user interface and process loading procedures.

```
char SzINISection[] = "Options";
char SzINICmdLineKey[] = "CommandLine";
char SzINIFile[] = "APISPY32.INI";
char SzCmdLine[MAX_PATH];

BOOL FFirstBreakpointHit = FALSE, FSecondBreakpointHit = FALSE;

PROCESS_INFORMATION ProcessInformation;
CREATE_PROCESS_DEBUG_INFO ProcessDebugInfo;

CONTEXT OriginalThreadContext, FakeLoadLibraryContext;
PVOID PInjectionPage;

#define PAGE_SIZE 4096
BYTE OriginalCodePage[PAGE_SIZE];
BYTE NewCodePage[PAGE_SIZE];

//======================== Code =========================================

//
// Function prototypes
//
BOOL  CALLBACK APISPY32DlgProc(HWND, UINT, WPARAM, LPARAM);
void  Handle_WM_COMMAND(HWND hWndDlg, WPARAM wParam, LPARAM lParam);
void  Handle_WM_INITDIALOG(HWND hWndDlg, WPARAM wParam, LPARAM lParam);
BOOL  GetProgramName(HWND hWndOwner, PSTR szFile, unsigned nFileBuffSize);
BOOL  LoadProcessForSpying(PSTR SzCmdLine);
void  DebugLoop(void);
DWORD HandleDebugEvent( DEBUG_EVENT * event );
void  HandleException(LPDEBUG_EVENT lpEvent, PDWORD continueStatus);
void  EmptyMsgQueueOfUselessMessages(void);
BOOL  InjectSpyDll(void);
BOOL  ReplaceOriginalPagesAndContext(void);
PVOID FindUsablePage(HANDLE hProcess, PVOID PProcessBase);
BOOL  GetSpyDllName(PSTR buffer, UINT cBytes);


int APIENTRY WinMain( HANDLE hInstance, HANDLE hPrevInstance,
                      LPSTR lpszCmdLine, int nCmdShow )
{
```

```
    // This dialog returns 0 if the user pressed cancel
    while ( 0 != DialogBox(hInstance, "APISPY32_LOAD_DLG", 0,
                            (DLGPROC)APISPY32DlgProc) )
    {
        if ( LoadProcessForSpying(SzCmdLine) )
        {
            DebugLoop();
            break;
        }

        MessageBox(0, "Unable to start program", 0, MB_OK);
    }

    return 0;
}

BOOL CALLBACK APISPY32DlgProc(HWND hWndDlg, UINT msg,
                                WPARAM wParam, LPARAM lParam)
{
    switch ( msg )
    {
        case WM_COMMAND:
            Handle_WM_COMMAND(hWndDlg, wParam, lParam);
            return TRUE;
        case WM_INITDIALOG:
            Handle_WM_INITDIALOG(hWndDlg, wParam, lParam);
            return TRUE;
        case WM_CLOSE:
            EndDialog(hWndDlg, 0);
            return FALSE;
    }

    return FALSE;
}

void Handle_WM_COMMAND(HWND hWndDlg, WPARAM wParam, LPARAM lParam)
{
    if ( wParam == IDC_RUN )
    {
        if ( GetWindowText( GetDlgItem(hWndDlg, IDC_CMDLINE),
                            SzCmdLine, sizeof(SzCmdLine)) )
        {
            WritePrivateProfileString(SzINISection, SzINICmdLineKey,
                                        SzCmdLine, SzINIFile);
            EndDialog(hWndDlg, 1);  // Return TRUE
        }
```

```
            else
            {
                MessageBox( hWndDlg, "No program selected", 0, MB_OK);
            }
        }
        else if ( wParam == IDC_FILE )
        {
            if ( GetProgramName(hWndDlg, SzCmdLine, sizeof(SzCmdLine)) )
                SetWindowText( GetDlgItem(hWndDlg, IDC_CMDLINE), SzCmdLine );
        }
        else if ( wParam == IDCANCEL )
        {
            EndDialog(hWndDlg, 0);
        }
    }


    void Handle_WM_INITDIALOG(HWND hWndDlg, WPARAM wParam, LPARAM lParam)
    {
        GetPrivateProfileString(SzINISection, SzINICmdLineKey, "", SzCmdLine,
                            sizeof(SzCmdLine), SzINIFile);
        SetWindowText( GetDlgItem(hWndDlg, IDC_CMDLINE), SzCmdLine );
    }


    static char szFilter1[] = "Programs (*.EXE)\0*.EXE\0";

    BOOL GetProgramName(HWND hWndOwner, PSTR szFile, unsigned nFileBuffSize)
    {
        OPENFILENAME ofn;

        szFile[0] = 0;

        memset(&ofn, 0, sizeof(OPENFILENAME));

        ofn.lStructSize = sizeof(OPENFILENAME);
        ofn.hwndOwner = hWndOwner;
        ofn.lpstrFilter = szFilter1;
        ofn.nFilterIndex = 1;
        ofn.lpstrFile= szFile;
        ofn.nMaxFile = nFileBuffSize;
        ofn.lpstrFileTitle = 0;
        ofn.nMaxFileTitle = 0;
        ofn.lpstrInitialDir = 0;
        ofn.Flags = OFN_PATHMUSTEXIST | OFN_FILEMUSTEXIST;

        return GetOpenFileName(&ofn);
    }
```

```
BOOL LoadProcessForSpying(PSTR SzCmdLine)
{
    STARTUPINFO startupInfo;

    memset(&startupInfo, 0, sizeof(startupInfo));
    startupInfo.cb = sizeof(startupInfo);

    return CreateProcess(
            0,                          // lpszImageName
            SzCmdLine,                  // lpszCommandLine
            0,                          // lpsaProcess
            0,                          // lpsaThread
            FALSE,                      // fInheritHandles
            DEBUG_ONLY_THIS_PROCESS,    // fdwCreate
            0,                          // lpvEnvironment
            0,                          // lpszCurDir
            &startupInfo,               // lpsiStartupInfo
            &ProcessInformation         // lppiProcInfo
            );
}
```

■ Figure 10-14
The beginning of the APISPYLD.C user interface and process loading functions.

The middle portion of APISPYLD.C is devoted to the debug loop: a loop that calls WaitForDebugEvent and ContinueDebugEvent until the process we're spying terminates. Each time WaitForDebugEvent returns, there's a new XXX_DEBUG_EVENT (for instance, EXCEPTION_DEBUG_EVENT or CREATE_THREAD_DEBUG_EVENT). The DebugLoop passes each debug event to the HandleDebugEvent helper function to let it do whatever processing is necessary. For the most part, the code in HandleDebugEvent ignores most of the events and passes DBG_CONTINUE to ContinueDebugEvent. However, two EXCEPTION_DEBUG_EVENTs that occur during the lifetime of the target process are of interest to our program loader. For this reason, I broke out the handling of exceptions into yet another helper function, HandleException.

The first EXCEPTION_DEBUG_EVENT that our program loader should see is the breakpoint exception, EXCEPTION_BREAKPOINT (from WINBASE.H). This breakpoint isn't in the target process's code. Rather, there's an embedded INT 3 in the operating system code that's executed right before the first instruction of the new process. Our HandleException routine explicitly looks for this first breakpoint exception; when it sees the exception, it injects the spy DLL into the address space of the child (using InjectSpyDll, described later in this section).

The second exception that HandleException looks for is the breakpoint that InjectSpyDll injects into the code so that we'll get control after APISPY32.DLL loads. When this breakpoint occurs, APISPYLD knows that the target process has finished loading APISPY32.DLL. The original memory pages and thread context modified by InjectSpyDll need to be put back the way they were when the first breakpoint went off. HandleException uses the ReplaceOriginalPagesAndContext helper function to perform this chore.

The final bit of code in this portion of APISPYLD is for Win32s only. Earlier, I said that when WaitForDebugEvent returns, a new debug event is waiting to be processed. Under Win32s this isn't necessarily true. Instead, the Win32s WaitForDebugEvent returns TRUE if there's another message waiting and FALSE if there's not. Another undocumented oddity under Win32s is that the system posts window messages with NULL window handles to the debugger's (APISPYLD's) message queue. The window messages posted to the queue have message numbers that Win32s obtained by making this call:

```
RegisterWindowMessage("W32S_Debug_Msg");
```

If you don't empty these messages out of your queue, your message queue will fill up and real window messages won't go into the queue. To handle both of these strange Win32s behaviors, our debug loop calls EmptyMsgQueueOfUselessMessages if WaitForDebugEvent returns FALSE and if the program is running under Win32s.

EmptyMsgQueueOfUselessMessages is a simple routine that calls PeekMessage(PM_REMOVE) until PeekMessage returns FALSE. Any message with a nonzero HWND is given to DispatchMessage — but to date, I haven't seen any messages with valid HWNDs come through this routine. After emptying the queue of these messages, DebugLoop again calls WaitForDebugEvent. This time WaitForDebugEvent blocks until there's really a waiting debug event. Figure 10-15 shows the beginning of the debug loop and debug event processing in APISPYLD.C.

```
void DebugLoop(void)
{
    DEBUG_EVENT event;
    DWORD continueStatus;
    BOOL fWin32s;
    BOOL fWaitResult;

    fWin32s = (GetVersion() & 0xC0000000) == 0x80000000;
```

```
    while ( 1 )
    {
        fWaitResult = WaitForDebugEvent(&event, INFINITE);

        if ( (fWaitResult == FALSE) && fWin32s )
        {
            EmptyMsgQueueOfUselessMessages();
            continue;
        }

        continueStatus = HandleDebugEvent( &event );

        if ( event.dwDebugEventCode == EXIT_PROCESS_DEBUG_EVENT )
            return;

        ContinueDebugEvent( event.dwProcessId,
                            event.dwThreadId,
                            continueStatus );
    }
}

PSTR SzDebugEventTypes[] =
{
"",
"EXCEPTION",
"CREATE_THREAD",
"CREATE_PROCESS",
"EXIT_THREAD",
"EXIT_PROCESS",
"LOAD_DLL",
"UNLOAD_DLL",
"OUTPUT_DEBUG_STRING",
"RIP",
};

DWORD HandleDebugEvent( DEBUG_EVENT * event )
{
    DWORD continueStatus = DBG_CONTINUE;
    // char buffer[1024];

    // wsprintf(buffer, "Event: %s\r\n",
    //          SzDebugEventTypes[event->dwDebugEventCode]);
    // OutputDebugString(buffer);


    if ( event->dwDebugEventCode == CREATE_PROCESS_DEBUG_EVENT )
    {
        ProcessDebugInfo = event->u.CreateProcessInfo;
    }
    else if ( event->dwDebugEventCode == EXCEPTION_DEBUG_EVENT )
    {
```

```
            HandleException(event, &continueStatus);
        }

    return continueStatus;
}

void HandleException(LPDEBUG_EVENT lpEvent, PDWORD continueStatus)
{
    // char buffer[128];
    // wsprintf(buffer, "Exception code: %X  Addr: %08X\r\n",
    //           lpEvent->u.Exception.ExceptionRecord.ExceptionCode,
    //           lpEvent->u.Exception.ExceptionRecord.ExceptionAddress);
    // OutputDebugString(buffer);


    if ( lpEvent->u.Exception.ExceptionRecord.ExceptionCode
         == EXCEPTION_BREAKPOINT )
    {
        if ( FFirstBreakpointHit == FALSE )
        {
            InjectSpyDll();
            FFirstBreakpointHit = TRUE;
        }
        else if ( FSecondBreakpointHit == FALSE )
        {
            ReplaceOriginalPagesAndContext();
            FSecondBreakpointHit = TRUE;
        }

        *continueStatus = DBG_CONTINUE;
    }
    else
    {
        *continueStatus = DBG_EXCEPTION_NOT_HANDLED;
    }
}


void EmptyMsgQueueOfUselessMessages(void)
{
    MSG msg;          // See PeekMessage loop for explanation of idiocy.

    // Win32s idiocy puts W32s_Debug_Msg message in our message queue.
    // Dispose of them! They're useless!
    while ( PeekMessage(&msg, 0, 0, 0, PM_REMOVE) )
    {
        if ( msg.hwnd )
            DispatchMessage(&msg);
    }
}
```

Figure 10-15
The beginning of the APISPYLD.C debug loop and debug event processing.

The final portion of our APISPYLD code is for injecting the APISPY32 DLL into the address space of the process to be spied on after it hits the first breakpoint. InjectSpyDll is a complicated routine that can be roughly broken up into three phases. The first phase of InjectSpyDll is for locating important addresses in the child process. Of primary interest at this stage is the address of the first writeable data page in the target process that's not in the .idata section. Also important is the address of the LoadLibrary routine in KERNEL32.DLL, the name of the DLL to load (APISPY32.DLL), and saving the original thread context of the process's initial thread.

In its second phase, InjectSpyDll copies the contents of the first writeable data page into a global variable called OriginalCodePage. (This variable is badly named, by the way. Early versions of APISPY32 used the first code page (instead of the first writeable data page) to store their injection code. I simply haven't gotten around to changing the variable's name.) It's important to note here that in order to make a copy of the page we'll be modifying, it's necessary to call ReadProcessMemory. The page we're saving a copy of is in another process, and the loader can't directly access that memory.

The third phase of InjectSpyDll sets things up so that when the target process resumes execution, it calls LoadLibrary, telling the operating system to load APISPY32.DLL. The code that will call LoadLibrary is constructed by filling in the fields of the FAKE_LOADLIBRARY_CODE structure. Each of the fields of this structure is either an assembler opcode or an operand for the preceding instruction. At the end of the structure is a copy of the spy DLL name. I put the DLL name in the structure because the DLL name needs to be visible in the context of the target process, not the APISPYLD program. After the structure is all filled in, I use WriteProcessMemory to copy the structure into the appropriate page of the target process. Afterward, the InjectSpyDll functions uses SetThreadContext to change the EIP value that the target process thread will use when it resumes execution. Specifically, the EIP register will be set to the first instruction of the code snippet as it appears in the target process's address space.

Assuming InjectSpyDll worked correctly, the target process executes the LoadLibrary code when it resumes execution. When LoadLibrary returns, the CPU will be at the breakpoint instruction after the LoadLibrary call. This causes the target process to again be frozen, and the call to WaitFor-DebugEvent in the APISPYLD process to return with an EXCEPTION_DEBUG_EVENT. When the HandleException function sees this particular exception, it knows that it's time to restore the original page we modified earlier, as well as the thread context. The code to restore the thread to its original state is in the ReplaceOriginalPagesAndContext helper function. In this routine, we use WriteProcessMemory to write the modified page back, and then do a SetThreadContext, passing the thread context we saved off before we injected the DLL. Figure 10-16 shows the InjectSpyDll section of APISPYLD.C.

```c
#pragma pack ( 1 )
typedef struct
{
    WORD    instr_SUB;
    DWORD   operand_SUB_value;
    BYTE    instr_PUSH;
    DWORD   operand_PUSH_value;
    BYTE    instr_CALL;
    DWORD   operand_CALL_offset;
    BYTE    instr_INT_3;
    char    data_DllName[1];
} FAKE_LOADLIBRARY_CODE, * PFAKE_LOADLIBRARY_CODE;

BOOL InjectSpyDll(void)
{
    BOOL retCode;
    DWORD cBytesMoved;
    char szSpyDllName[MAX_PATH];
    FARPROC pfnLoadLibrary;
    PFAKE_LOADLIBRARY_CODE pNewCode;

    // =======================================================================
    // Phase 1 - Locating addresses of important things
    // =======================================================================

    pfnLoadLibrary = GetProcAddress( GetModuleHandle("KERNEL32.DLL"),
                                     "LoadLibraryA" );
    if ( !pfnLoadLibrary )
        return FALSE;

    PInjectionPage = FindUsablePage(ProcessInformation.hProcess,
                                    ProcessDebugInfo.lpBaseOfImage);
    if ( !PInjectionPage )
        return FALSE;

    if ( !GetSpyDllName(szSpyDllName, sizeof(szSpyDllName)) )
        return FALSE;

    OriginalThreadContext.ContextFlags = CONTEXT_CONTROL;
    if ( !GetThreadContext(ProcessInformation.hThread,&OriginalThreadContext))
        return FALSE;
```

```
// =======================================================================
// Phase 2 - Saving the original code page away
// =======================================================================

// Save off the original code page
retCode = ReadProcessMemory(ProcessInformation.hProcess, PInjectionPage,
                            OriginalCodePage, sizeof(OriginalCodePage),
                            &cBytesMoved);
if ( !retCode || (cBytesMoved != sizeof(OriginalCodePage)) )
    return FALSE;


// =======================================================================
// Phase 3 - Writing new code page and changing the thread context
// =======================================================================

pNewCode = (PFAKE_LOADLIBRARY_CODE)NewCodePage;

pNewCode->instr_SUB = 0xEC81;
pNewCode->operand_SUB_value = 0x1000;

pNewCode->instr_PUSH = 0x68;
pNewCode->operand_PUSH_value = (DWORD)PInjectionPage
                        + offsetof(FAKE_LOADLIBRARY_CODE, data_DllName);

pNewCode->instr_CALL = 0xE8;
pNewCode->operand_CALL_offset =
        (DWORD)pfnLoadLibrary - (DWORD)PInjectionPage
        - offsetof(FAKE_LOADLIBRARY_CODE,instr_CALL) - 5;

pNewCode->instr_INT_3 = 0xCC;

lstrcpy(pNewCode->data_DllName, szSpyDllName); // Copy DLL name.

// Write out the new code page
retCode = WriteProcessMemory(ProcessInformation.hProcess, PInjectionPage,
                            &NewCodePage, sizeof(NewCodePage),
                            &cBytesMoved);
if ( !retCode || (cBytesMoved != sizeof(NewCodePage)) )
    return FALSE;

FakeLoadLibraryContext = OriginalThreadContext;
FakeLoadLibraryContext.Eip = (DWORD)PInjectionPage;

if ( !SetThreadContext(ProcessInformation.hThread,
                        &FakeLoadLibraryContext) )
    return FALSE;

return TRUE;
}
```

```c
BOOL ReplaceOriginalPagesAndContext(void)
{
    BOOL retCode;
    DWORD cBytesMoved;

    retCode = WriteProcessMemory(ProcessInformation.hProcess, PInjectionPage,
                            OriginalCodePage, sizeof(OriginalCodePage),
                            &cBytesMoved);
    if ( !retCode || (cBytesMoved != sizeof(OriginalCodePage)) )
        return FALSE;

    if ( !SetThreadContext(ProcessInformation.hThread,
                            &OriginalThreadContext) )
        return FALSE;

    return TRUE;
}

PVOID FindUsablePage(HANDLE hProcess, PVOID PProcessBase)
{
    DWORD peHdrOffset;
    DWORD cBytesMoved;
    IMAGE_NT_HEADERS ntHdr;
    PIMAGE_SECTION_HEADER pSection;
    unsigned i;

    // Read in the offset of the PE header within the debuggee
    if ( !ReadProcessMemory(ProcessInformation.hProcess,
                            (PBYTE)PProcessBase + 0x3C,
                            &peHdrOffset,
                            sizeof(peHdrOffset),
                            &cBytesMoved) )
        return FALSE;


    // Read in the IMAGE_NT_HEADERS.OptionalHeader.BaseOfCode field
    if ( !ReadProcessMemory(ProcessInformation.hProcess,
                            (PBYTE)PProcessBase + peHdrOffset,
                            &ntHdr, sizeof(ntHdr), &cBytesMoved) )
        return FALSE;

    pSection = (PIMAGE_SECTION_HEADER)
                ((PBYTE)PProcessBase + peHdrOffset + 4
                + sizeof(ntHdr.FileHeader)
                + ntHdr.FileHeader.SizeOfOptionalHeader);

    for ( i=0; i < ntHdr.FileHeader.NumberOfSections; i++ )
    {
```

```
        IMAGE_SECTION_HEADER section;

        if ( !ReadProcessMemory( ProcessInformation.hProcess,
                                 pSection, &section, sizeof(section),
                                 &cBytesMoved) )
            return FALSE;

        // OutputDebugString( "trying section: " );
        // OutputDebugString( section.Name );
        // OutputDebugString( "\r\n" );

        // If it's writeable, and not the .idata section, we'll go with it
        if ( (section.Characteristics & IMAGE_SCN_MEM_WRITE)
            && strncmp(section.Name, ".idata", 6) )
        {
            // OutputDebugString( "using section: " );
            // OutputDebugString( section.Name );
            // OutputDebugString( "\r\n" );

            return (PVOID) ((DWORD)PProcessBase + section.VirtualAddress);
        }

        pSection++; // Not this section. Advance to next section.
    }

    return 0;
}

BOOL GetSpyDllName(PSTR buffer, UINT cBytes)
{
    char szBuffer[MAX_PATH];
    PSTR pszFilename;

    // Get the complete path to this EXE - The spy dll should be in the
    // same directory.
    GetModuleFileName(0, szBuffer, sizeof(szBuffer));

    pszFilename = strrchr(szBuffer, '\\');
    if ( !pszFilename )
        return FALSE;

    lstrcpy(pszFilename+1, "APISPY32.DLL");
    strncpy(buffer, szBuffer, cBytes);
    return TRUE;
}
```

Figure 10-16
The APISPYLD.C DLL injection routines.

Notes on Using APISPY32

To spy on a program with APISPY32, run the APISPYLD program. In the edit control, type in a command line, or use the File... button to browse for the executable. Once the executable name is entered, click the Run button. The APISPYLD dialog will go away, and the selected program should begin running. After your target program has completed, there should be a file with a OUT extension in the same directory as the executable. Figure 10-17 shows a portion of the output from running APISPY32 on the Win32 CLOCK program.

```
KillTimer(HWND:000026F4,DWORD:00000001)
KillTimer returns: 1
SetTimer(HWND:000026F4,DWORD:00000001,DWORD:000001C2,LPDATA:00000000)
SetTimer returns: 1
CheckMenuItem(HANDLE:00001EF0,DWORD:00000008,DWORD:00000008)
CheckMenuItem returns: 0
wsprintfA(LPSTR:80E3AD68,LPSTR:80DEE190:"%s - %s")
wsprintfA returns: F
SetWindowTextA(HWND:000026F4,LPSTR:80E3AD68:"Clock - 4/")

    DefWindowProcA(HWND:000026F4,DWORD:0000000C,DWORD:00000000,DWORD:80E3AD68)
    DefWindowProcA returns: 0
SetWindowTextA returns: 1
GetSystemMenu(HWND:000026F4,BOOL:00000000)
GetSystemMenu returns: 1F68
AppendMenuA(HANDLE:00001F68,DWORD:00000800,DWORD:00000000,LPSTR:00000000)
AppendMenuA returns: 1
```

▌ Figure 10-17
CLOCK32 output from APISPY32.

Most of the time, a line in the OUT file for a function call is immediately followed by a line with the return value from the function. However, this isn't always the case. Notice (in Figure 10-17) how the DefWindowProcA function and return lines are indented. This indicates that the function was called during the execution of the surrounding function (in this case, SetWindowTextA). This particular sequence makes sense, as the second parameter to DefWindowProc (the message parameter) is shown with a value of 0xC. Looking up the number in WINUSER.H, you'll find that message 0xC (12) is WM_SETTEXT. Since the DefWindowProc was called within the call to SetWindowText, it's a safe assumption that SetWindow-Text sent a WM_SETTEXT message to the program's window procedure, and that program didn't handle the message, but simply passed it on to DefWindowProc. In this output from APISPY32, there was only one level of nesting. It's not uncommon to have nested functions that are 4 or 5 levels deep, especially during the program's shutdown sequence when the main window gets a WM_CLOSE message.

When looking at LPSTR parameters, bear in mind that the complete string may not be shown. Since garbage strings might be passed as buffers, I had no way to know ahead of time how many characters to display for each LPSTR parameter. The solution I decided on was to print out either the first 10 characters or up until the first NULL byte. Also, tabs, carriage returns and linefeeds are represented by \t, \r, and \n, respectively. If I were to have printed out the raw characters, the lines in the OUT file would be formatted improperly.

If you run APISPY32 under early versions of Win32s (versions prior to Win32s 1.2), you'll get numerous RIPs if you run the debug 16-bit USER.EXE. This is a bug in Win32s related to message translations between Win16 and Win32. In the transition from Win16 to Win32, several messages were renumbered. The Win32s thunking layer needs to convert the numbers of certain messages when a message passes between 16- and 32-bit code. To know which messages to translate, Win32s needs to know which class the window is for, so Win32s calls GetClassName in USER.EXE. The problem arises when a message with an HWND of 0 is encountered. The debugging version of GetClassName RIPs if a 0 HWND is passed to it. Where does our spy program get messages with HWNDs of 0? As I described earlier, the Win32s WaitForDebugEvent function posts RegisterWindowMessage-(W32S_Debug_Msg) messages to the debugger's message queue.

If you build the APISPY32 program using Borland C++, you won't have much luck when spying on multithreaded programs. The Borland C++ multithreading library uses per-thread data for certain functions (in APISPY32, the function of interest is fprintf). In the Borland runtime library, the code doesn't pay attention to the DLL_THREAD_ATTACH notifications. Instead, the runtime library relies on the program's call to the _beginthread function to know when to allocate its per-thread data. Unfortunately, this method breaks down when a thread is created in a different module than yours. In the case of our spy program, the Borland runtime library code in APISPY32.DLL won't see _beginthread calls made in the EXE being spied on. Borland has acknowledged this as a bug, but it still hasn't managed to fix this problem as of BC++ 4.5.

INTERCEPTING FUNCTIONS IN YOUR OWN PROGRAMS

At the beginning of the chapter, I promised you a method by which you could use the APISPY32 function interception technique in your own code. The code to do this is in HOOKAPI.C, which is shown in Figure 10-18. The HookImportedFunction in HOOKAPI.C allows you to intercept all the calls that one module makes to a given function in another module. For example, if you use a DLL called FOO.DLL, you could intercept all of FOO.DLL's calls to the MessageBeep routine (even if you don't have source for FOO.DLL). If you also wanted to intercept MessageBeep calls made by BAR.DLL and BAZ.DLL, you'd also need to call the HookImportedFunction routine once for each of those DLLs.

Another important point to remember is that this interception technique only intercepts imported functions within your own process. It can't intercept API function calls made by other processes. In other words, you can only intercept calls that your EXE and its DLLs make. You couldn't use it to do something like intercepting all calls that WINFILE makes to OpenFile. Your interception code won't be mapped into the address space of the WINFILE process.

The first parameter to HookImportedFunction is the module handle of the EXE or DLL that you want to intercept calls from (in the above example, FOO.DLL). The second parameter is the module name of the module that contains the function you want to intercept. The third parameter to Hook-ImportedFunction is the name of the function you want to intercept. The final parameter is the address of the function that you want called. Hook-ImportedFunction returns the original address of the function you just intercepted. You can use this address to chain on to the original code if necessary. Using the above example, the call to HookImportedFunction looks like this:

```
pfnOriginalProc = HookImportedFunction( GetModuleHandle("BAR.DLL"),
                                        "USER32.DLL",
                                        "MessageBeep",
                                        MyMessageBeepHandler );
```

```
// Macro for adding pointers/DWORDs together without C arithmetic interfering.
#define MakePtr( cast, ptr, addValue ) (cast)( (DWORD)(ptr)+(DWORD)(addValue))

DWORD GetModuleBaseFromWin32sHMod(HMODULE hMod); // Prototype (defined below)
```

```
PROC WINAPI HookImportedFunction(
        HMODULE hFromModule,        // Module to intercept calls from.
        PSTR    pszFunctionModule,  // Module to intercept calls to.
        PSTR    pszFunctionName,    // Function to intercept calls to.
        PROC    pfnNewProc          // New function (replaces old function).
        )
{
    PROC pfnOriginalProc;
    PIMAGE_DOS_HEADER pDosHeader;
    PIMAGE_NT_HEADERS pNTHeader;
    PIMAGE_IMPORT_DESCRIPTOR pImportDesc;
    PIMAGE_THUNK_DATA pThunk;

    if ( IsBadCodePtr(pfnNewProc) ) // Verify that a valid pfn was passed.
        return 0;

    // First, verify the module and function names passed to use are valid.
    pfnOriginalProc = GetProcAddress( GetModuleHandle(pszFunctionModule),
                                      pszFunctionName );
    if ( !pfnOriginalProc )
        return 0;

    if ( (GetVersion() & 0xC0000000) == 0x80000000 )
        pDosHeader =                                        // Win32s
            (PIMAGE_DOS_HEADER)GetModuleBaseFromWin32sHMod(hFromModule);
    else
        pDosHeader = (PIMAGE_DOS_HEADER)hFromModule;        // other

    // Tests to make sure we're looking at a module image (the MZ header).
    if ( IsBadReadPtr(pDosHeader, sizeof(IMAGE_DOS_HEADER)) )
        return 0;
    if ( pDosHeader->e_magic != IMAGE_DOS_SIGNATURE )
        return 0;

    // The MZ header has a pointer to the PE header.
    pNTHeader = MakePtr(PIMAGE_NT_HEADERS, pDosHeader, pDosHeader->e_lfanew);

    // More tests to make sure we're looking at a "PE" image.
    if ( IsBadReadPtr(pNTHeader, sizeof(IMAGE_NT_HEADERS)) )
        return 0;
    if ( pNTHeader->Signature != IMAGE_NT_SIGNATURE )
        return 0;

    // We know have a valid pointer to the module's PE header. Now go
    // get a pointer to its imports section.
    pImportDesc = MakePtr(PIMAGE_IMPORT_DESCRIPTOR, pDosHeader,
                          pNTHeader->OptionalHeader.
```

```
                              DataDirectory[IMAGE_DIRECTORY_ENTRY_IMPORT].
                              VirtualAddress);

    // Bail out if the RVA of the imports section is 0 (it doesn't exist).
    if ( pImportDesc == (PIMAGE_IMPORT_DESCRIPTOR)pNTHeader )
        return 0;

    // Iterate through the array of imported module descriptors, looking
    // for the module whose name matches the pszFunctionModule parameter.
    while ( pImportDesc->Name )
    {
        PSTR pszModName = MakePtr(PSTR, pDosHeader, pImportDesc->Name);

        if ( stricmp(pszModName, pszFunctionModule) == 0 )
            break;

        pImportDesc++;  // Advance to next imported module descriptor.
    }

    // Bail out if we didn't find the import module descriptor for the
    // specified module. pImportDesc->Name will be nonzero if we found it.
    if ( pImportDesc->Name == 0 )
        return 0;

    // Get a pointer to the found module's import address table (IAT).
    pThunk = MakePtr(PIMAGE_THUNK_DATA, pDosHeader, pImportDesc->FirstThunk);

    // Blast through the table of import addresses, looking for the one
    // that matches the address we got back from GetProcAddress above.
    while ( pThunk->u1.Function )
    {
        if ( pThunk->u1.Function == (PDWORD)pfnOriginalProc )
        {
            // We found it! Overwrite the original address with the
            // address of the interception function. Return the original
            // address to the caller so that they can chain on to it.
            pThunk->u1.Function = (PDWORD)pfnNewProc;
            return pfnOriginalProc;
        }

        pThunk++;   // Advance to next imported function address.
    }

    return 0;   // Function not found.
}
```

```
typedef DWORD (_ _stdcall *XPROC)(DWORD);

// Converts an HMODULE under Win32s to a base address in memory.
DWORD GetModuleBaseFromWin32sHMod(HMODULE hMod)
{
    XPROC ImteFromHModule, BaseAddrFromImte;
    HMODULE hModule;
    DWORD imte;

    hModule = GetModuleHandle("W32SKRNL.DLL");
    if( !hModule )
        return 0;

    ImteFromHModule = (XPROC)GetProcAddress(hModule, "_ImteFromHModule@4");
    if ( !ImteFromHModule )
        return 0;

    BaseAddrFromImte = (XPROC)GetProcAddress(hModule, "_BaseAddrFromImte@4");
    if ( !BaseAddrFromImte )
        return 0;

    imte = ImteFromHModule( (DWORD)hMod);
    if ( !imte )
        return 0;

    return BaseAddrFromImte(imte);
}
```

Figure 10-18

HOOKAPI.C lets you intercept function calls from your own programs.

Your function that's called instead of the original API function should be prototyped exactly the same as the function you're intercepting. This allows you to access all the function's parameters, and causes the compiler to pop the correct number of bytes off the stack when the function returns. If you want to pass control to the original API function as part of your handling, call through the function pointer returned by HookImportedFunction. Typically, you'll do this as the last thing in your handler function, and you'll return whatever value the original API function returns to your code.

To demonstrate the use of HookImportedFunction, I've written the SimonSez program. The program is extremely simple, and consists of intercepting SimonSez's calls to MessageBox and prepending the string "Simon Sez:" on to the message to be displayed. Since SimonSez has previously intercepted the MessageBox function, the installed handler function

(MyMessageBox) will be called, rather than the MessageBox in USER32.DLL.
Afterward MyMessageBox calls the original MessageBox function in
USER32.DLL. The SIMONSEZ.C program is shown in Figure 10-19.

```c
//==================================
// SIMONSEZ - Matt Pietrek 1995
// FILE: HOOKAPI.C
//==================================
#include <windows.h>
#include <malloc.h>
#include "hookapi.h"

// Make a typedef for the WINAPI function we're going to intercept
typedef int (_ _stdcall *MESSAGEBOXPROC)(HWND, LPCSTR, LPCSTR, UINT);

MESSAGEBOXPROC PfnOriginalMessageBox;    // For storing original. address

//
// A special version of MessageBox that always prepends "Simon Sez: "
// to the text that will be displayed.
//
int WINAPI MyMessageBox( HWND hWnd, LPCSTR lpText,
                         LPCSTR lpCaption, UINT uType )
{
    int retValue;              // Real MessageBox return value.
    PSTR lpszRevisedString;    // Pointer to our modified string.

    // Allocate space for our revised string - add 40 bytes for new stuff.
    lpszRevisedString = malloc( lstrlen(lpText) + 40 );

    // Now modify the original string to first say "Simon Sez: ".
    if ( lpszRevisedString )
    {
        lstrcpy(lpszRevisedString, "Simon Sez: ");
        lstrcat(lpszRevisedString, lpText);
    }
    else                                // If malloc() failed, just
        lpszRevisedString = (PSTR)lpText;   // use the original string.

    // Chain on to the original function in USER32.DLL.
    retValue = PfnOriginalMessageBox(hWnd,lpszRevisedString,lpCaption,uType);

    if ( lpszRevisedString != lpText )  // If we successfully allocated string
        free( lpszRevisedString );       // memory, then free it.
```

```
        return retValue;    // Return whatever the real MessageBox returned.
}

int APIENTRY WinMain( HANDLE hInstance, HANDLE hPrevInstance,
                      LPSTR lpszCmdLine, int nCmdShow )
{
    MessageBox(0, "MessageBox Isn't Intercepted Yet", "Test", MB_OK);

    // Intercept the calls that this module (TESTHOOK) makes to
    // MessageBox() in USER32.DLL. The function that intercepts the
    // calls will be MyMessageBox(), above.

    PfnOriginalMessageBox = (MESSAGEBOXPROC) HookImportedFunction(
                GetModuleHandle(0),     // Hook our own module
                "USER32.DLL",           // MessageBox is in. USE32.DLL
                "MessageBoxA",          // Function to intercept.
                (PROC)MyMessageBox);    // Interception function.

    if ( !PfnOriginalMessageBox )   // Make sure the interception worked.
    {
        MessageBox(0, "Couldn't hook function", 0, MB_OK);
        return 0;
    }

    // !!!!!!!!!!!!!!!!!!!!!!!!  WARNING  !!!!!!!!!!!!!!!!!!!!!!!!!!!!!!!!!!!!
    // When built with optimizations, the VC++ compiler loads a
    // register with the address of MessageBoxA, and then makes all
    // subsequent calls through it. This can cause the MessageBox call
    // below to not go through the Import Address table that we just patched.
    // For this reason, the .MAK file for this program does not use the
    // /O2 or /O1 switches. This usually won't be a problem, but it
    // was in this particularly simple program.  ACCKK!!!!

    // Call MessageBox again. However, since we've now intercepted
    // MessageBox, control should first go to our own function
    // (MyMessageBox), rather than the MessageBox() code in USER32.DLL.

    MessageBox(0, "MessageBox Is Now Intercepted", "Test", MB_OK);

    return 0;
}
```

Figure 10-19

This simple SIMONSEZ.C program demonstrates the use of HookImportedFunction.

How does HookImportedFunction work? As I described earlier, when a Win32 program calls a function imported from another module, the call actually transfers control to a JMP DWORD PTR [XXXXXXXX] thunk. The DWORD at memory location XXXXXXXX contains the address of the imported function (for example, the address of MessageBox in USER32.DLL).

All the HookImportedFunction code does is search through the import address table to find the particular DWORD with the address of the function you want to intercept. Once it finds that location, HookImportedFunction overwrites the address of the imported function with the address of your handler function.

The first parameter to HookImportedFuction is an HMODULE identifying the EXE or DLL that you want to intercept calls from. In Windows NT and Windows 95, an HMODULE is nothing more than the linear address where the module begins in memory. This address is known as the module's base address. Since Win32 uses memory mapped files, the memory at the module's base address is a DOS MZ header (refer to the IMAGE_DOS_HEADER in WINNT.H). Using the value in the e_lfanew field, HookImported-Function locates the address of the PE header (the IMAGE_NT_HEADERS structure in WINNT.H). At the end of the IMAGE_NT_HEADERS structure is an array of structures that contain addresses for important areas in the module. Of particular interest to our HookImportedFunction routine is the start of the import address table. This table (which typically resides in the .idata section of the module) contains information about the functions imported by this module. Somewhere in the import address table is the DWORD that HookImportedFunction needs to overwrite with the address of your handler function.

At the beginning of the import address table is an array of IMAGE_IMPORT_DESCRIPTOR structures (again, see WINNT.H). There is one of these structures for each DLL that this module imports functions from. The end of the IMAGE_IMPORT_DESCRIPTOR array is indicated by an IMAGE_IMPORT_DESCRIPTOR whose fields are all 0s. Each IMAGE_IMPORT_DESCRIPTOR has a pointer to the name of the associated DLL, as well as a pointer to the import address table (the array of function addresses mentioned earlier). HookImportedFunction walks through the IMAGE_IMPORT_DESCRIPTORs until it finds the one whose name matches the pszFunction-Module parameter passed to HookImportedFunction. The routine uses the information in the IMAGE_IMPORT_DESCRIPTOR to create a pointer to the import address table.

Near the beginning of HookImportedFunction, the code called GetProc-Address to get the address of the function we want to intercept calls to. That address should be among the addresses in the import address table we just located. The HookImportedFunction code walks through the array of addresses until it finds the slot with an address identical to what GetProc-Address returned. All that remains is to copy the new function's address (the pfnNewProc parameter) into that slot and return the original function's address.

SUMMARY

Win32 programming provides a whole new set of challenges for programmers from the Win16 environment. In general, Win32 system programming is more restrictive and complicated because of issues such as separate addresses and multiple threads of execution. In this chapter, we've met these issues head-on in building an API spy program and in creating a general-purpose mechanism for intercepting API function calls. We've also seen that, despite Microsoft's claim that "There's just one Win32 API," there are occasional differences when you get down to the details. However, by understanding these issues, you can write industrial-strength programs that work across all the Win32 platforms.

The Undocumented KERNEL32.DLL Import Library

*T*he first 100 entries in the Windows 95 KERNEL32.DLL exports table are exported by ordinal only. In contrast, all normal Win32 API functions that Microsoft provides are exported both by name and by ordinal. Exporting a function by name is what allows you to pass a function name to GetProcAddress and get back the address where the function can be called.

Clearly, since Microsoft didn't export these first 100 functions by name, it didn't intend for you to call or use them. Put another way, these are "undocumented" functions. As we all know, undocumented functions can be extremely useful. In fact, sometimes the only way you can accomplish a particular goal is to use an undocumented function. However, since these functions aren't exported by name, you can't just call GetProcAddress and use them as you might expect.

Normally in a situation like this, determined hackers wouldn't be deterred because they know that GetProcAddress can be passed a function's export ordinal rather than its name. Alas, as you saw in Chapter 3, Microsoft's KERNEL32 coders also blocked off this backdoor approach. The GetProcAddress function intentionally fails any calls that attempt to look up addresses in KERNEL32.DLL by their ordinal value. Interestingly, it's only KERNEL32.DLL that GetProcAddress doesn't allow ordinal lookups on, so it's apparent that Microsoft is trying to prevent people from using these 100 functions in KERNEL32.DLL.

Never fear. As you've seen elsewhere in this book, these artificial restrictions on calling undocumented KERNEL32.DLL functions can be overcome. One approach is to write your own GetProcAddress function. It's really not hard to do, since the format of a loaded PE module in memory is well documented. Chapter 3 even gives the pseudocode for GetProcAddress if you want to see how Windows implements it.

The problem with the "roll-your-own" GetProcAddress approach is that it's a pain to have to call GetProcAddress and then save away its return value in a function pointer. A much simpler way to use these undocumented functions is to use an import library that includes these functions. We all know that Microsoft isn't going to willingly hand over such an import library. Thus, this appendix provides you with the tools to create your own import library for use with Visual C++ or other Microsoft compilers/linkers. Figure A-1 shows K32LIB.DEF, which contains most of the 100 or so exported, undocumented KERNEL32.DLL functions.

```
LIBRARY KERNEL32
EXPORTS
    VxDCall0@0                        @1
    VxDCall1@8                        @2
    VxDCall2@12                       @3
    VxDCall3@16                       @4
    VxDCall4@20                       @5
    VxDCall5@24                       @6
    VxDCall6@28                       @7
    VxDCall7@32                       @8

    CharToOemA@8                      @10 ; USER32's version calls straight here.
    CharToOemBuffA@12                 @11 ; USER32's version calls straight here.
    OemToCharA@8                      @12 ; USER32's version calls straight here.
    OemToCharBuffA@12                 @13 ; USER32's version calls straight here.
    LoadStringA@16                    @14 ; USER32's version calls straight here.
    wsprintfA@8                       @15 ; USER32's version calls straight here.
    wvsprintfA@4                      @16 ; USER32's version calls straight here.
    CommonUnimpStub@0                 @17 ; Non-implemented APIs call here.
    GetProcessDWORD@8                 @18

    DosFileHandleToWin32Handle@4      @20
    Win32HandleToDosFileHandle@4      @21
    DisposeLZ32Handle@4               @22
    GDIReallyCares@4                  @23
    GlobalAlloc16@8                   @24
    GlobalLock16@4                    @25
```

```
GlobalUnlock16@4                      @26
GlobalFix16@4                         @27
GlobalUnfix16@4                       @28
GlobalWire16@4                        @29
GlobalUnWire16@4                      @30
GlobalFree16@4                        @31
GlobalSize16@4                        @32
HouseCleanLogicallyDeadHandles@0      @33
GetWin16DOSEnv                        @34
LoadLibrary16@4                       @35
FreeLibrary16@4                       @36
GetProcAddress16@8                    @37
AllocMappedBuffer                     @38
FreeMappedBuffer                      @39
OT_32ThkLSF                           @40
ThunkInitLSF@20                       @41
LogApiThkLSF@4                        @42
ThunkInitLS@20                        @43
LogApiThkSL@4                         @44
Common32ThkLS                         @45
ThunkInitSL@20                        @46
LogCBThkSL@4                          @47
ReleaseThunkLock@4                    @48
RestoreThunkLock@4                    @49

W32S_BackTo32                         @51
GetThunkBuff@0                        @52
GetThunkStuff@8                       @53
K32WOWCallback16@8                    @54
K32WOWCallback16Ex@20                 @55
K32WOWGetVDMPointer@12                @56

WOWGlobalAlloc16@8                         @59
WOWGlobalLock16@4                          @60
WOWGlobalUnlock16@4                        @61
WOWGlobalFree16@4                          @62
WOWGlobalAllocLock16@12                    @63
WOWGlobalUnlockFree16@4                    @64
WOWGlobalLockSize16@8                      @65
WOWYield16@0                               @66
WOWDirectedYield16@4                       @67
K32WOWGetVDMPointerFix@12                  @68
K32WOWGetVDMPointerUnfix@4                 @69
K32WOWGetDescriptor@8                      @70
IsThreadId@4                               @71
K32RtlLargeIntegerAdd@16                   @72
K32RtlEnlargedIntegerMultiply@8            @73
K32RtlEnlargedUnsignedMultiply@8           @74
```

```
K32RtlEnlargedUnsignedDivide@16          @75
K32RtlExtendedLargeIntegerDivide@16      @76
K32RtlExtendedMagicDivide@20             @77
K32RtlExtendedIntegerMultiply@12         @78
K32RtlLargeIntegerShiftLeft@12           @79
K32RtlLargeIntegerShiftRight@12          @80
K32RtlLargeIntegerArithmeticShift@12     @81
K32RtlLargeIntegerNegate@8               @82
K32RtlLargeIntegerSubtract@16            @83
K32RtlConvertLongToLargeInteger@4        @84
K32RtlConvertUlongToLargeInteger@4       @85

FT_PrologPrime          @89
QT_ThunkPrime           @90
PK16FNF@0               @91
GetPK16SysVar@0         @92
GetpWin16Lock@4         @93 : Returns a pointer to the Win16Mutex.
_CheckNotSysLevel@4     @94
ConfirmSysLevel@4       @95
_ConfirmWin16Lock@0     @96
EnterSysLevel@4         @97 : Acquire a mutex (e.g., Win16Mutex).
LeaveSysLevel@4         @98 : Release a mutex (e.g., Win16Mutex).
```

▌Figure A-1
You can use these undocumented KERNEL32.DLL functions to create your own import library to use with Visual C++ or other compilers and linkers.

You've probably noticed that I haven't included prototypes for all the undocumented functions listed in Figure A-1. Although it would be possible to write an entire *Undocumented Windows*-like chapter that prototypes and documents these functions, that task isn't the purpose of this book. No doubt these functions will be documented and described in the future in some other text. Note that certain of the functions, such as VxDCall0@0, are referenced and used elsewhere in this book, and that you can easily figure out the parameters and actions of some of the other functions.

K32LIB.DEF and K32LIB.LIB (for Microsoft VC++) are included on the disk that accompanies this book; you'll find them in the APPENDIX directory in the source tree for the files. Normally, the Microsoft linker creates an import library for a DLL when it links the DLL. However, the Microsoft LIB.EXE program can create an import library from a .DEF file. To rebuild the import library from K32LIB.DEF, you can use the MAKE.BAT in the same directory as K32LIB.DEF. MAKE.BAT is nothing more than the following:

```
lib /MACHINE:IX86 /DEF:K32LIB.DEF
```

To use K32LIB.LIB in your project, you should place it immediately after KERNEL32.LIB in the list of import libraries. This forces the Microsoft linker to place the code and data from K32LIB.LIB contiguous with the code and data brought in from KERNEL32.LIB. You'll see two references to KERNEL32.DLL in the resulting executable. Don't be too concerned, though. You're getting two IMAGE_IMPORT_DESCRIPTOR headers for KERNEL32.DLL, but not two copies of all the data that describes each imported function. (To explain what the Microsoft linker is doing at this level would be a long story, so don't ask. . .)

Borland C++ users can take K32LIB.DEF and run it through IMPORT.LIB to create an import library in the proper format for TLINK. The command line in this case is:

```
IMPLIB K32LIB.LIB K32LIB.DEF
```

You can place K32LIB.LIB anywhere in the import library list; TLINK doesn't care about the order in which it appears.

As you've seen in many of the other programs throughout this book, K32LIB.LIB is invaluable for calling Windows 95 functions that Microsoft doesn't want you to use. Of course, you should avoid using undocumented functions if that's at all possible. One very good reason for this is that if you do use undocumented functions, your programs won't run under Windows NT and may break in future versions of Windows. The programs in this book are tied to Windows 95 and are explicitly designed to show what's really happening in Windows 95. There was no way for me to avoid using these functions in this book's programs.

If you absolutely must use these functions in your code, put version tests and other sanity checks in your code so that your program fails gracefully. To do this (while avoiding loadtime failures), you'll have to use GetProcAddress rather than calling the functions directly. Such are the risks of working on the fringe of the documented operating system APIs.

INDEX

{} (braces), 663
: (colon), 199
$ (dollar sign), 585–586
+ (plus sign), 181, 237, 467, 547

A

About dialog box, 202–203
AddAPIFunction, 713
AddAtomA, 630
AddAtomW, 630
addresses. *See also* address spaces
    calculating, 292–294
    converting, 303–305
    linear, 276, 278
    physical, 276, 300
    RVAs (Relative Virtual Addresses), 86,
        295, 560–561, 563, 573, 585, 587,
        591, 595, 603, 608, 630
AddressOfEntryPoint, 566
AddressOfFunctions, 594, 595, 596
AddressOf_i, 289
AddressOfNameOrdinals, 595–596
AddressOfNames, 594, 595, 596
address space(s), 3–4, 11. *See also*
        addresses
    basic description of, 50–52, 276
    design flaws and, 63
    layout, 275
    protected subsystems and, 7–8
    of a Windows 95 Win32 process,
        279–286
ADVAPI32.DLL, 38, 59, 438–439,
    440, 709

Alpha, 3
alternatePID, 231
Animate control type, 59
ANSI characters, 92
anti–hacking code, 64–65
APF32CVT, 688
APFCNVRT, 636
APISPY32, 170, 705–728, 744–745
APISPY32.API, 698
APISPY32.DLL, 170, 720–724
APISPYLD.C, 730–743
APISuspendCount, 134
ASCII format, 18, 221, 480, 535, 551
    PE files and, 563, 588, 597,
        617–619, 620
    spelunking and, 627, 630, 631, 641, 658
    spy programs and, 687, 694, 708
ASCIIZ strings, 607–608, 690
audio-system analogy, 5–6
AUTOEXEC.BAT, 18, 21
AX register, 229, 428, 537, 540, 649

B

BAR.DLL, 746
base_GDI_FSR_percentage, 204
BaseOfCode, 566
BaseOfData, 566
BasePriority, 112
base relocations, 581–582
base_USER_FSR_percentage, 204
Begin_Service_Table, 678
_beginthread method, 745
Beziers, 33, 263

BLOCKDEV, 39
BlockedOnID, 456
BlockHandle, 455
_BlockOnID, 439–440
BlockState, 455
BM_GETSTATE, 29
BN_CLICKED, 228
bootup sequence, 17–23
BoundsChecker (BCKHW), 623, 634, 635, 640,
    686, 703
BP register, 647, 651
braces ({}), 663
branch statements, 645–646
BreakEvent, 119
BreakHandlers, 119
breakpoints, 675, 688
BreakSem, 119
BreakThreadID, 119
BreakType, 119
BSEXCPT.H, 159
.bss section, 580
BuildAPIStub, 713
BUILDFSR.BAT, 209
Bunny_351, 447
Button class, 233

C

Cairo, 14, 556
CALC.EXE, 75, 77, 469–471, 521, 532, 625–626
CalculateNewPriority, 141–142, 143
CB_SETEDITSEL, 30
cbClsExtra, 226
cbFileName, 75
cbFileName2, 77
cbModName, 76
cbModName2, 77
cbWndExtra, 226
cClsWnds, 225
CCommonReturnPoint, 725, 728
CDPSCSI, 39
cHandles, 132
ChangeBits, 220
CheckSum, 339, 567
ChecksumHeapBlock, 335, 351–352
classAtom, 231
ClassFirst, 27, 234
classNameAtom, 225
ClassNext, 27, 234
CL.EXE, 13
Client_Reg_Struc, 430

CLOCK32, 744
CLOCK.EXE, 601, 637–640, 667–672
cMsgs, 219
cNotTermThreads, 109
CodeView, 574, 584–585, 606, 615, 632, 673
COFF (common object file format), 3, 49, 555–620
    debug information, 611–613
    .LIB files, basic description of, 615–620
    line-number tables, 613–614
    .OBJ files, PE files and, difference between,
        614–616
    section flags, 575–576
    spelunking and, 633
    symbol tables, 605–610
colon (:), 199
ComboBox class, 233
ComboLBox class, 233
COMCTL32.DLL, 60, 234
COMDLG32.DLL, 38
COMMAND.COM, 21–22
COMMCTRL.DLL, 60
COMMON.C, 610, 614–615
Common Thunk, 190–191
CommonUnimpStub, 329, 377, 378
compatibility, backward, 38, 54, 187
CONFIGMG, 39
CONFIG.SYS, 18, 21
ContinueDebugEvent(), 695–696, 735
CONTEXT_CONTROL, 150
_ContextCreate, 310–311, 439–440
CONTEXT_DEBUG_REGISTERS, 150
_ContextDestroy, 310–311, 439–440
CONTEXT_FLOATING_POINT, 150
ContextHandle, 454
CONTEXT_INTEGER, 150
CONTEXT_SEGMENTS, 150
_ContextSwitch, 306, 310–311, 439–440
ContinueDebugEvent, 62
"copy on write" mechanism, 290–291, 298–299
_CopyPageTable, 308
CopyTaskInformation, 545, 546–547
CR 3 register, 303, 304
CR command, 305
crashes
    exception handling and, 56–57
    modules and, 78
    Win32s and, 9
    in Windows NT, vs. Windows 95, 13–14
CreateDirectory, 67
CreateEvent, 46
CreateFileMapping, 51
CreateProcess, 42, 731
CREATE_PROCESS_DEBUG_EVENT, 61

CreateRemoteThread, 692
CreateSemaphores, 47
CreateThread, 44
CREATE_THREAD_DEBUG_EVENT, 61
CreateToolhelp32Snapshot, 62–63
CreateWindow, 526, 635, 636, 661
CreateWindowEx, 234
CreateWindowExA, 597
CreateWindowExW, 597
cReference, 106, 128
cRing0Threads, 109
CRITICAL_SECTION, 46, 48, 110, 337, 369, 388, 464
criticalSection, 337, 388
crst, 110
CRTDLL.DLL, 688
.CRT section, 580
cSections, 76
CS register, 188, 278
cThreads, 109
CTRDLL.DLL, 331, 420
ctrlID, 230
CurrentSS, 133
CurTDB, 217, 459, 524
cUsage, 77
CVDUMP, 632, 633

D

.data section, 579–580
Date[12], 618
DBG2MAP, 632
DbgPrint(), 631
DBWIN, 61
DDE (Dynamic Data Exchange), 622
.debug$S section, 585
.debug$T section, 585
DebugContext, 130
DEBUG_EVENT, 60–63
DebuggerThread, 133
debugging. *See also* disassembly; spelunking;
    spy programs
    the "copy on write" mechanism and, 290–291
    the debug version of Windows and, 681–682
    exception handling and, 56–57
    heap functions and, 335
    memory management and, 290–291, 314, 327, 329, 335, 411–414
    overview of, 60–63
    PE/COFF formats and, 583–585, 611–613
    virtual functions and, 314, 327, 329
DebugLoop, 730

DEBUG_ONLY_THIS_PROCESS, 731–732
DEBUGSYS.INC, 453
DEC (Digital Equipment Corporation), 3
DecodeParamsToString, 719–720
DefaultHeap, 107
.DEF files, 78, 288, 502–503, 631, 687
DefWindowProc, 245, 246
DefWindowProcA, 744
delete function, 330
DeleteObject, 263
delta, definition of, 603
DeltaPriority, 134, 139
DemandInfoStruc, 442
Desktop class, 233
DesktopWndProc, 244–247
development considerations, overview of, 13–14
DeviceIoControl, 40, 431
DGROUP, 26–27, 34–35, 50, 67
    memory management and, 280, 294–295, 298
    USER/GDI subsystems and, 188, 196–200, 204, 211–212, 225, 231–232, 239, 258–260, 264
DialogBox, 503–505
Dialog class, 233
.directive section, 585
dir/AH, 17–18, 20
disassembly, 622, 642–672
DisDoc, 642–643
DispatcherContext, 161
DispatchMessage, 702, 703, 736
DisplatchRITInput, 216
DLLENTRYPOINT, 491
DllMain(), 693, 703, 706
dollar sign ($), 585–586
DoSomething(), 653, 654
DosPDBSeg, 456
DragListBoxes, 59
Dr. Watson, 158
DS register, 52, 188, 193, 278, 504–505, 540
DTA (Disk Transfer Area), 534
DumpAuxSymbols(), 610
DUMPBIN, 558, 623–624, 626, 629–633, 643, 667
DumpExportsSection, 598
DumpSecondLinkerMember, 620
dwExStyleFlags, 230
dwFlags, 230
dwMemCommitted, 207
dwSize, 336, 388
dwStyleFlags, 230
dwTotalFree, 207
DX register, 537
DYNAPAGE, 39

E

EAX register, 188, 430, 434, 438, 701
.edata section, 581, 598
Edit class, 233
EH_EXIT_UNWIND, 162
EH_UNWINDING, 161
EIP register, 126, 302, 434
EM_SETRECT, 30
EMF (Enhanced Metafile) support, 263, 270
EmulatorData, 133
EmulatorSelector, 132
EnterCriticalSection, 48, 337
EnterSysLevel, 139, 238
EntProcAddress, 517, 519–521
entry tables, 480–481, 499–501
EnumChildWindows, 237
EnumTaskWindows, 522
EnumWindows, 237
ENVIRONMENT_DATABASE, 117–122
EnvironSelector, 113
ERROR_INVALID_PARAMETER, 120
ErrorMode, 113
EstablishFrame, 161
events, as synchronization objects, 46–47
Excel, 622
Except16List, 133
EXCEPTION_BREAKPOINT, 735
ExceptionCount, 456
EXCEPTION_DEBUG_EVENT, 61, 696,
    735, 739
EXCEPTION_DISPOSITION, 160–161
exception handling, structured. *See* SEH
    (structured exception handling)
EXCEPTION_RECORD, 161
EXCPT.H, 160
Exec_PM_Int, 424, 450
EXEHDR, 503, 623, 624, 625, 628
EXESIZE, 633
EXEUTIL, 270
EXIT_PROCESS_DEBUG_EVENT, 61, 62
EXIT_THREAD_DEBUG_EVENT, 61
.EXP files, 581
Explorer, 21, 67, 204, 245, 472
    About dialog box, 202–203
    TDB and, 530
    WNDPROC and, 213
EXPLORER.EXE, 530, 593
exporting functions
    definition of, 480
    export address tables and, 86
    PE files and, 593–598
expWinVer, 220
extraInfo, 220, 223

F

FARPROC, 540
fastcall convention, 654
fFileApisAreOem, 117
File... button, 730, 731
FileAlignment, 566
file-dumping tools, 622, 624–633
Filter... button, 467
FindClose, 450–451
FindExeFile, 506
FindExeInfo, 506, 509–510
flat memory model, 278–279
.FLT files, 467
FOO.DLL, 78, 289, 746
ForwarderChain, 587
FREE_LIST_HEADER_DEBUG, 388
FREE_LIST_HEADER_RETAIL, 336
FREECALL, 307
freelistArray[4], 336, 388
FreeRing0Callgate, 302
FSR (free system resources), 35, 67, 202–217,
    244–245, 331
FS register, 136–137, 191
FSR32, 209–211
FSR32.C, 210–211
function(s)
    GDI, available for Win16 applications,
        270–271
    heap, 329–411
    identifying, 646–649
    importing/exporting, 86, 480, 586–598
    intercepting, in your programs, 746–753
    module-related, 505–521
    return values, 649, 701–705
    task-related, 536

G

GDI, 7–10, 12, 15, 67. *See also* GDI.EXE;
    GDI32.DLL
    32-bit heaps and, 196, 200, 201
    basic description of, 33–34
    free system resources and, 202–217
    functions, available for Win16 applications,
        270–271
    modules, 260–271
    objects, 263–269
    subsystems, 185–272
    Win16Mutex and, 31–33
    Windows 95 design flaws and, 64

GDI.EXE, 10–11, 33–34, 36, 195–196, 204, 260, 264–266, 270, 488, 625–626
GDI32.DLL, 7, 10, 33–34, 38, 260, 262, 590
    GetObjectType and, 266–269
    memory management and, 284, 297
    spy programs and, 709
GDIReallyCares, 182, 183
GetActiveWindow, 241–242, 250–252
GetATaskSomehow, 539
GetAtomNameW, 627
GetCapture, 241–242, 250–252
GetClassName, 745
GetCommandLineA, 119–120
_GetCurrentContext, 310–311, 439–440
GetCurrentDirectoryA, 163–166
GetCurrentPDB, 522, 533
GetCurrentProcess, 103–104
GetCurrentProcessID, 40, 65, 103, 104, 127, 182
GetCurrentPSP, 522
GetCurrentTask, 522, 537
GetCurrentThread, 127, 653–654
GetCurrentThreadID, 65, 105, 127, 182, 183, 334
Get_Cur_VM, 678
Get_Cur_VM_Handle, 426
_GetDemandPageInfo, 415, 439–440, 442–444
GetDlgCtrlID, 256–257
GetDlgItem, 255–256
GetEnvironemnt Strings, 120
GetExePtr, 504, 506, 510–514
GetExePtrHelper, 511, 513–514
GetExitCodeProcess, 114–115
GetExitCodeThread, 131, 177–178
GetFileInformationByHandle(), 101
GetFocus, 241–242, 250–252, 653
GetFreeSystemResources, 67, 202–217, 245
GetHeapSpaces, 207
GetLastActivePopup, 231
GetLastError, 176
GetLastErrorCode, 133, 176
GetMessage, 9, 11, 28, 32, 45, 214–215, 218, 221, 223, 523, 577–578
GetMessageExtraInfo, 220, 251–252
GetMessagePos, 220, 251–252
GetMessageTime, 220, 223, 251–252
GetModuleBaseFromWin32sHMod, 729–730
GetModuleFileName, 75, 92–95, 117, 529, 549, 719
GetModuleHandle, 75–76, 78, 80, 95–97, 117, 479, 504–510, 561, 658
GetModuleUsage, 77
GetObjectType, 266–269

GetOpenFileName dialog box, 730–731
GetParent, 228, 655
GetPercentFree16BitHeap, 207–208
GetPercentFree32BitHeap, 207–208
GetPhysicalAddressFromLinear, 300
GetPriorityClass, 145–146
GetPrivateProfileSection, 67, 461
GetPrivateProfileString, 635
GetProcAddress, 64–65, 80, 89, 164, 473, 475, 628, 687, 713–714, 729, 753
    basic description of, 515–521
    Win16 modules/tasks and, 501–502, 515–521, 523
GetProcessAddress, 80–85
GetProcessHeap, 54, 195, 335, 342, 377–378
GetQueueStatus, 29, 220, 221
GetRing0Callgate, 301–302
GetStdHandle, 121
GetSystemDefaultLangID, 676
GetSystemMenu, 231
GetSystemTime, 427
GetTaskQueue(), 538–539
GetTextExtent, 625–626
GetThreadContext, 45, 62, 146–149, 694, 679–680
GetThreadHandle, 126
GetThreadPriority, 139–140
GetThreadSelectorEntry, 417–419
GetVersion(), 689, 690
Get_VMM_Version, 426
GetWindow, 228
GetWindowLong, 213, 214, 638, 668–670
GetWindowRect, 655
GetWindowThreadProcessId, 229, 243–244
GetWndPtr32, 248–250, 256
GFSR_SYSTEMRESOURCES, 205
GlobalAlloc, 53–54, 76, 278, 287, 309, 329, 331, 379, 408, 479, 510–511, 541
GlobalCompact, 411
GlobalFix, 410
GlobalFlags, 410
GlobalFree, 380, 409
GlobalHandle, 409
GlobalLock, 53, 408, 478
GlobalMemoryStatus, 414–417, 442
GlobalNotify, 531
GlobalNukeGroup, 392
GlobalPageLock(), 35–36
GlobalReAlloc, 409
GlobalSize, 409
GlobalUnfix, 411
GlobalUnlock, 409

GlobalUnWire, 410
GlobalWire, 410
GMEM_FIXED, 281
GMEM_SHARE, 51, 286–289, 511
GP faults, 52, 56, 529, 537–538, 539, 633, 642
_GPFIX, 586
GroupID[6], 618
guard pages, 44–45
GW_HWNDNEXT, 228
GWL_WNDPROC, 213, 214
GW_OWNER, 228

H

HANDLE, 41–42, 45, 49, 47
HandleDebugEvent, 735
HandleException, 735–736
HandlerFunction(), 160
hBrBackground, 226
HBRUSH, 263
hcNext, 225
hCriticalSection, 337, 388
HCursor, 226
Header control type, 59
headMsg, 219
headPDB, 524
HeadTDB, 524
heap(s)
    arenas, 332–342
    functions, overview of, 329–411
    global heap functions, 379–380, 408–411
    headers, 332–342
    local heap functions, 379–407
    typical Win32, diagram of, 333
"Heap 32" command, 198
Heap32First, 62
Heap32ListFirst, 62
Heap32ListNext, 62
Heap32Next, 62
HeapAlloc(), 54, 73, 195, 330–331, 337,
        343–344, 374, 379, 420, 422, 598
_HeapAllocate, 309–311, 439–440
HEAP.C, 421–422
HeapCompact, 377
HeapCreate, 309, 335, 337, 366–368
HeapDestroy, 55, 373–376
HeapFree, 55, 195, 330, 354–356, 420
_HeapFree, 309, 310–311, 331, 439–440
HEAP_FREE_CHECKING_ENABLED, 366
HEAP_GENERATE_EXCEPTIONS, 343, 360
HeapHandle, 109

HeapHandleBlockList, 112
HeapLock, 66, 378
HEAP_NO_SERIALIZE, 360, 369, 373, 383
HeapOwnList, 112
HeapReAlloc, 55, 73, 330, 360–361
_HeapReAllocate, 310–311, 439–440
HEAP_REALLOC_IN_PLACE_ONLY, 360
HeapSetFlags, 330, 344
HeapSize, 55, 352–353
HeapUnlock, 378
HeapValidate, 377
HEAPW32.H, 339
HeapWalk, 66, 262, 307, 379
HEAP_ZERO_MEMORY, 343, 349, 360
"Hello World" programs, 184
Help|About, 67, 203
HGDIOBJ, 263, 264, 266
HGLOBAL, 408
hGlobalHeap, 524
HIBYTE, 491–492
HIcon, 226
hIconSm, 226
HIGH_PRIORITY_CLASS, 139
hInstance, 229
HINSTANCE, 50, 76, 496, 503–505, 510–511,
        515–516, 529, 540, 561
HIWORD, 64
HKEY_CLASSES_ROOT, 57
HKEY_CURRENT_CONFIG, 57
HKEY_CURRENT_USER, 57
HKEY_DYN_DATA, 57–58
HKEY_LOCAL_MACHINE, 57
HKEY_USERS, 57
hMenu, 230
hMenuSystem, 231
HMODULE, 49, 50, 65, 70–71, 76
    spy programs and, 708, 719
    Win16 modules/tasks and, 479, 487–489, 492,
        496, 503–505, 510–511, 515–516, 522,
        535–536, 547–548
HMODULE.H, 482, 496
HOOKAPI.C, 746–753
HOOKED_FUNCTION, 724–725
HookImportedFunction, 746–753
HotKey, 60
HouseCleanLogicallyDeadHandles, 383
HPAlloc, 344–351, 380, 383, 400, 408
hpCarve, 344–345, 348–351, 357
hpCommit, 369
hpFreeSub, 357–360, 369
HPInit, 345, 366, 369–373
HPReAlloc, 362–365
hProcess, 40, 42, 114, 145, 322

hQueue, 222, 229
hQueueSend, 221
HRGN, 200
hrgnUpdate, 229
hStdErr, 118
hStdIn, 118
hStdOut, 118
hTask, 219
HTASK, 40, 512, 522, 533, 534, 538–539
hThread, 45, 692
hWnd, 213, 244, 644, 669
HWND, 25, 27–29, 69, 700
    changes to, in Windows 95, 226–233
    spelunking and, 644, 655, 656, 668–669
    USER/GDI subsystems and, 199–200,
        211–212, 223–233, 239–241, 249, 255,
        258, 262
hWnd16, 231
HWND32.H, 228
hWndActive, 226
hWndCapture, 226
hWndChild, 228
hWndNext, 228
hWndOwner, 228
hWndParent, 228

I

IATs (import address tables), 690
IBM (International Business Machines), 12
.icon section, 579
.idata section, 581, 586–593
IDLE_PRIORITY_CLASS, 139
IDTs (Interrupt Descriptor Tables), 429
IFSMGR, 39
if statements, 659–663
IGetCurrentDirectory, 165
IGetExitCodeProcess, 114–115
IGetExitCodeThread, 177–178
IGetFreeSystemResources, 204–207
IGetModuleFileName, 92–95
IGetModuleHandle, 95–97, 505–510
IGetProcAddress, 80–85, 515–521, 681
IGetThreadContext, 146–149
IGetThreadSelectorEntry, 417–419
IGetWindowThreadProcessId, 243–244
IGlobalFlags, 410
IGlobalHandle, 681
IGlobalMemoryStatus, 414–417
IHeapAlloc, 343–344
IHeapDestroy, 373–376

IHeapFree, 354–356, 374
IHeapReAlloc, 360–361
IHeapSize, 352–353
ILocalAlloc, 383–387
ILocalFree, 392–396
ILocalHandle, 400–404
ILocalLock, 387–390
ILocalReAlloc, 396–400, 681
ILocalSize, 402–404, 681
IMAGE_ARCHIVE_MEMBER_HEADER,
    616–617, 620
ImageBase, 566
IMAGE_BASE_RELOCATION, 603–604, 605
IMAGE_DEBUG_DIRECTORY, 583–585, 611
IMAGE_FILE_HEADER, 606, 611, 614–615
IMAGEHLP.DLL, 567
IMAGE_IMPORT_DESCRIPTOR, 587–588,
    591–592, 714, 752
ImageList, 60
IMAGE_NT_HEADERS, 72, 75, 76, 559, 563
IMAGE_OPTIONAL_HEADER, 615
IMAGE_RELOCATION, 615
IMAGE_RESOURCE_DATA_ENTRY, 497, 600
IMAGE_RESOURCE_DIRECTORY_ENTRY,
    599–602
IMAGE_SCN_MEM_SHARED, 288–289
IMAGE_SECTION_HEADER, 570–573, 576, 614
IMAGE_SYMBOL, 606–610
IMAGE_THUNK_DATA, 588–593, 714
IMakeProcInstance, 540–544
importing/exporting, 86, 480, 586–593
IMTEs (Internal Module Table Entries), 73–80,
    108, 179
    spy programs and, 729
    structure of, 74–78
    Win32Wlk and, 181–183
InheritConsole, 119
.INI files, 57–58, 640, 641
InitApp, 539
InitializeCriticalSection, 48, 337
InitialRing0ID, 110
InitThreadReturnStack, 724
InjectSpyDll, 735–736, 739, 740
instance handles, use of the term, 561
INT 2Fh functions, 300, 428, 429
INT 3 functions, 56, 290, 735
INT 20h functions, 426–427, 678–679
INT 21h functions, 23, 113, 165, 424,
    450–453, 531
INT 30h, 429–430, 434–435
INT 31h functions, 450, 453
INT 41h functions, 450, 453–454

Intel processors, 3, 14, 274, 277, 429, 603–604
  80386 class, 4, 16
  Pentium-optimized code and, 682–683
InterceptFunctionReturn, 725
InterceptFunctionsInModule, 714
InterruptRegister, 540, 695
INTRCPT.C, 708, 713–718
INTRCPT2.H, 714
IO.SYS, 20
ISetThreadContext, 151–164
IsGDIObject, 264–266
IsTask(), 537–538, 545
IsWindow, 239–241, 248–249
IsWindow16, 239–241
IVirtualProtect, 327–328
IVirtualQuery, 323–324
IWinExec, 680

J

JP Software, 21
jump tables, 666

K

K16PDB, 456
K16TDB, 456
K209 function, 380
K211 function, 380
K32LIB.LIB, 443
K32OBJ_CHANGE, 101
K32OBJ_CONSOLE, 101
K32OBJ_CRITICAL_SECTION, 101, 135
K32OBJ_DEVICE_IOCTL, 101
K32OBJ_EVENT, 101, 106
K32OBJ_FILE, 101
K32OBJ_MAILSHOT, 101
K32OBJ_MEM_MAPPED_FILE, 101
K32OBJ_MUTEX, 101
K32OBJ_PIP, 101
K32OBJ_PROCESS, 101, 106
K32OBJ_SCREEN_BUFFER, 101
K32OBJ_SEMAPHORE, 101
K32OBJ_SERIAL, 101
K32OBJ_SOCKET, 101
K32OBJ_THREAD, 101, 125, 128
K32OBJ_TOOLHELP_SNAPSHOT, 101
KERNEL32, 10, 42, 52, 59, 66

memory management and, 286, 291, 295,
    312, 332–333, 336, 342, 345, 366, 380,
    383, 387, 392, 396
  objects, 100–102, 123
  modules and, 73–76
  processes and, 106
  threads and, 70, 127–128, 170
  Windows 95 design flaws and, 64
KERNEL32.DLL, 10–11, 37–40, 63–66, 73,
    176–178, 216, 423–424, 433–441, 447,
    450–453, 457–466, 468, 471–481
  anti–hacking code and, 64–65
  export section, 597, 598
  memory management and, 280, 284, 297–298,
    309, 311, 343, 380
  processes and, 102–103
  SEH and, 163
  spelunking and, 627, 631, 679–680, 682
  spy programs and, 687–690, 709, 739
  threads and, 125, 139
  Win16 modules/tasks and, 477–481
KRNL386, 37, 52–53, 63–64, 182, 286,
    294–295, 298, 392, 418, 428–430
KRNL386.EXE, 10–11, 37, 40, 423–424,
    457–466
  spelunking and, 628–630
  USER/GDI subsystems and, 201, 213, 217
  Win16 modules/tasks and, 477, 480, 489

L

lastActive, 231
lastMsg, 219
lastMsg2, 220
LastTlsSetValueEIP, 136
LB_INSERTSTRING, 30
LDTAlias, 418
LDTPtr, 418
LDTs (local descriptor tables), 50–51, 52, 198,
    300, 417–418
LeaveMustComplete, 412
LeaveSysLevel, 139, 238
LIBDUMP.C, 620
LIB.EXE, 589
.LIB files, basic description of, 615–620
LibMain, 534
Linker members, 618–619
LINK.EXE, 13
ListBox class, 233
ListView, 60

LMEM_FIXED, 27, 54, 380–383, 387–388, 390, 392, 396, 400, 402–403, 405
LMEM_INVALID_HANDLE, 405
LMEM_MOVEABLE, 264, 380–383, 387, 390, 392–393, 396, 400, 402–403, 405
LOAD_DLL_DEBUG_EVENT, 61
LOADAPIS.C, 710
LoadLibrary, 72, 78, 461, 482, 569, 692–694, 703, 739
LoadModule, 42, 479, 480–481
LoadProc, 496
LoadProcessForSpying, 730
LoadTDB, 524
Local32Alloc, 201
Local32Free, 201
Local32FreeQuickly, 201
Local32Info, 207
Local32ReAlloc, 201
Local32Translate, 201
LocalAlloc, 54, 55, 195, 309, 331, 379–387, 408
LocalCompact, 408
LocalFlags, 405–407
LocalFree, 55, 382, 392–396
LocalHandle, 400–404
LocalHeap, 330
LocalHeapFreeHead, 110
LocalInit, 55
LocalLock, 53, 387–390
LocalReAlloc, 55, 396–400, 627
LocalShrink, 407
LocalSize, 55, 402–404
LocalUnlock, 390–392
LOG.C, 709–710, 719, 720
LogCall, 719, 720
logo, Microsoft, 4–5, 18
LogReturn, 720
Longnames archive member section, 620
LOWORD, 64
lp16SwitchRec, 135
lParam, 223
LPARAM, 30, 657
lpfnWndProc, 229, 236
lpIntWndClass, 235
lpMem, 354
LPRECT, 700
lpszCmdLine, 680
lpszCurDir, 164
lpszMenuName, 226
lpszPath, 92
LSTMGR.C, 102
lstrcpy, 685
LT_USER_CLASS, 234
LT_USER_PROCESS, 221

LT_USER_QMSG, 222
LT_USER_SUBSYSTEM, 222
LT_USER_VWININFO, 225
LvaToFirstLinenumber, 612
LvaToFirstSymbol, 612
LZA32.DLL, 38

M

main(), 163
MajorImageVersion, 567
MajorOperatingSystemVersion, 567
MajorVersion, 594, 599
MakeProcInstance, 535–536, 540–544
malloc, 53, 312, 330–331, 420–422
MAP32, 674
.MAP files, 494, 632, 677
MAPI (Mail API), 15
MapViewOfFile, 51
MDIClient class, 233
MEM_COMMIT, 53, 314
MEM_DECOMMIT, 319
MemMapFiles, 109
memory. *See also* addresses; address spaces; FSR (free system resources); heaps; memory management; RAM (random-access memory)
    areas of, examining, with MEM/DEBUG, 18–20
    consumption below 1MB, 35–36
    corruption, 9
    "insufficient memory" messages, 35–36
    mapped files, basic description of, 51–52, 55–56
    requirements, for Windows 95 vs. Windows NT, 4, 7, 16
    sharing, 286–289, 298, 473–475
    VxDs and, 425–426, 473–475
    windowing systems and, 25, 26
MemoryContext, 107
memory management, 52–55, 273–422
    "copy on write" mechanism and, 290–291, 298–299
    heap functions and, 329–379
    memory contexts and, 281, 303–308
    page-based, 274–289
    selectors and, 277–278
    Win32 virtual functions and, 312–379
MEMORYSTATUS, 414–417
MemoryWrite(), 698
MEM_RELEASE, 319

MEM_RESERVED, 314
MEM_TOP_DOWN, 314
MessageBox, 749–750
MessageBoxW, 257
messagePos, 223
message queue(s), 218–226
    format, 218–222
    per-queue system windows and, 224–226
    QUEUEMSG structure and, 222–224
MessageQueue, 130, 137
messageTime, 220, 223
messaging system(s). *See also* message queues
    changes, in the USER subsystem, 214–217
    overview of, 27–29
Meyer, Brian, 157
MinorImageVersion, 567
MinorOperatingSystemVersion, 567
MinorVersion, 594, 599
MMTASK, 307
MOD, 22, 196–197, 284
MODFLAGS_APPTYPE, 484
MODFLAGS_AUTODATA 485
MODFLAGS_CALL_WEP, 484
MODFLAGS_DLL, 484, 485
MODFLAGS_IMPLICIT_LOAD, 485
MODFLAGS_SELF_LOADING, 484
MODFLAGS_SINGLEDATA 485
MODFLAGS_WIN32 485
MODREF, 73, 78–80, 100, 181
MODREFlist, 110
module(s)
    basic description of, 49–50, 69–73
    database fields, new, 492
    -related functions, 505–521
    Win16, overview of, 477–554
MODULE32.H, 74–79
ModuleFirst, 481
ModuleNext, 481
MPREXE.EXE, 693
MRFromHLib, 93
MSDOS.SYS, 17–18
MSGQUEUE.H, 218, 221, 223, 225
MSGSRV32, 217
MSGSRV32.EXE, 530
MsgWaitForMultipleObjects, 47
mteIndex, 80, 108
multitasking, 11, 458
    cooperative, 523
    snapshots and, 63
    synchronization and, 45
multithreading, 9, 44
MustCompleteCount, 455
mutexes, 46, 48
MyDialog, 600

N

NE (New Executable) format, 34, 49, 479,
        491–503, 525
    basic description of, 479–480
    GDI.EXE and, 262
    PE/COFF formats and, 570, 576, 581, 584,
        599, 603
    spelunking and, 625, 635
NegStackBase, 133
new (function), 53, 312, 330–331, 420–422
nextBlock, 336, 388
nextHeap, 337, 388
nextQueue, 218
nextQueueMsg, 223
NFY_STARTTASK, 695
NORMAL_PRIORITY_CLASS, 138–139
NotifyRegister, 61, 540, 695, 696
npNext, 222, 225
npPerQueue, 219
npProcess, 219
npQMsg, 225
NtCreateProcess(), 631
NTDLL.DLL, 40, 627, 630–631
NtQuerySystemInformation(), 631
NTSD (NT system debugger), 606
NumberOfAuxSymbols, 609
NumberOfFunctions, 594
NumberOfIdEntries, 599
NumberOfLinenumbers, 574, 612
NumberOfMembers, 619
NumberOfNamedEntries, 599
NumberOfNames, 594, 596
NumberOfRelocations, 574
NumberOfRvaAndSizes, 569
NumberOfSymbols, 612, 618–619
nWndFocus, 226

O

OBJ2ASM, 633
object, use of the term, 561
OBJ_METAFILE, 266
Obsfucator values, 65, 105, 127
OEM characters, 92, 95
OFSTRUCT, 483
OFSTRUCTEX, 483–484
OpenEvent, 46
OpenFile, 746
OpenLogFile, 719
OpenProcess, 42, 115–117

OriginalCodePage, 739
OS/2, 4, 7, 12, 23, 490, 547
   LX format, 576
   SEH and, 157, 158, 159
OutputDebugString, 61
OUTPUT_DEBUG_STRING_EVENT, 61

P

_PageAttach, 308, 310–311, 439–440
_PageChangePager, 439–440
_PageCommit, 310–311, 314, 349, 439–440
_PageDecommit, 310–311, 319, 357, 439–440
page directories, 303–306
PAGEFILE, 39
_PageFlush, 310–311, 439–440
_PageFree, 310–311, 319, 374, 439–440
_PageModify, 306
_PageModifyPermissions, 306, 310–311, 315,
   439–440
_PageQuery, 439–440
_PageRegister, 310–311
_PageReserve, 310–311, 312, 314, 332, 366,
   439–440
_PagerQuery, 310–311, 439–440
_PagerRegister, 439–440
page tables, 302–305, 308
parameter(s), 650–654
   information coding, 699–701
   validation, 163–164, 680–681
Parameter profiler (Microsoft), 640
ParentPDB, 110
PARMTYPE.H, 709
Pascal, 489, 645–646, 650–652
pConsole, 111
pConsoleProvider, 113
pCreateData16, 134
pCurrentPriority, 130, 137
PDB (Process Database), 102–103, 585
   basic description of, 106–114
   Win16 modules/tasks and, 533, 534
PDBToPID, 103, 127
PE (Portable Executable) format, 3, 34, 50, 55
   COFF .OBJ file format and, difference
      between, 614–616
   concepts, basic, 559–562
   .data section, 579–580
   file exports, 593–598

file imports, 586–593
header, 562–569
.icon section, 579
modules and, 71, 72, 479, 497–498
overall layout of, diagram of, 562
overview of, 555–620
section tables and, 570–586
spelunking and, 624, 631
.text section, 577–579
PEDUMP, 12, 257, 295, 558–559, 570, 581, 584,
   586, 591, 597–598, 601–602, 605–606,
   610, 613–614, 620, 626, 631, 633
PeekMessage, 9, 11, 28, 45, 214–215, 218, 221,
   223, 523, 736
Pentium-optimized code, 682–683
PERQUEUEDATA, 225, 241, 250
pExeMODREF, 111
pfdwOldProtect, 327
pGlobalHeap, 524
PGTPTR (Page Table Pointer) values, 308
PHANDLE_TABLE, 110
pHandleTable, 110, 181
PHYS, 287–288, 291–302, 308
PHYS (command), 305
PHYS.EXE, 292–299
PID, 182, 183
PidToPDB, 104–105
Plug and Play, 15
plus sign (+), 181, 237, 467, 547
pModuleTableArray, 73–74, 80, 93, 182
pNextModRef, 79
pNTHdr, 75
PointerToLinenumbers, 574
PointerToRawData, 574
PointerToRelocations, 574
PopupMenu class, 233
portability, 3–4, 7–8, 16
POSIX, 7
PostAppMessage, 522
PostMessage, 537
ppCurrentProcess, 103
ppdb, 80, 454
pPMPSPSelector, 456
pProcess, 128
pProcess2, 130
PPROCESS_DATABASE, 110–111, 114, 116,
   128, 130, 143, 145
"Press any key..." prompt, 295
prev_structure, 159
printf(), 12, 573

PROCDB.H, 117
procedures, identifying, 646–649
process(es), 69–71. *See also* PDB (Process Database)
   16-bit representations of, reasons for, 478
   basic description of, 102–103
   handles, 103–106, 122–123
   IDs, 40, 42, 45, 103–106, 116–117
   injecting DLLs into, 692–694
   list, in Win32Wlk, 179–181, 182
   management, overview of, 40–43
   synchronization, 45–49
Process32First, 62, 106
Process32Next, 62, 106
PROCESS_DATABASE, 80, 117, 122–123, 460
ProcessDWORD, 111
PROCESSENTRY32, 106
ProcessGroup, 111
Property Sheets control type, 60
protected mode, 427–430, 446–453
pSomeCritSect1, 135
pSomeCritSect2, 135
pSomeEvent, 106, 128
pSomeHeapPtr, 112
PSP (Program Segment Prefix), 43, 69, 106, 108,
   460, 511, 522
PSPSelector, 108
pStartupInfo, 118
pszCmdLine, 118
pszCurrDirectory, 118
pszEnvironment, 118
pszFileName, 75
pszFileName2, 77
pszModName, 75, 76
pszModName2, 77
ptdb, 454
pTDBX, 132
pTIB, 129, 137
pTLSArray, 130, 137
PulseEvent, 46
pvExcept, 128, 137
PVIEW, 66
pvTLSArray, 137
PWALK, 321–322
pWin16Mutex, 135
pWin32Mutex, 135

Q

QEMMFIX, 39
QS_ALLINPUT, 221
QT_Thunk, 191–195, 208–210

QueuedSyncFuncs, 456
QUEUEMSG, 220, 222–224
QUEUEPROCESSDATA, 219, 221–222, 243

R

RAM (random-access memory), 44, 52, 56
   memory management and, 53, 274–278, 280,
      282–283, 290, 292, 295, 299–300, 303,
      313, 329, 414, 416
   VxDs and, 443
   Win16 modules and, 494, 498
Raymond, Eric S., 621
.RC files, 632
.rdata section, 583–585
ReadProcessMemory, 62, 116, 411–414, 688
realloc, 330
REALTIME_PRIORITY_CLASS, 139
REBASE.EXE, 284
RECT, 655
rectClient, 229
rectWindow, 228
_RegCloseKey, 439–440
_RegCreateKey, 439–440
_RegDeleteKey, 439–440
_RegDeleteValue, 439–440
REGEDIT, 57
_RegEnumKey, 439–440
_RegFlushKey, 439–440
RegisterClass, 234
registry, basic description of, 57–58
_RegLoadKey, 439–440
_RegOpenKey, 439–440
_RegQueryMultipleValues, 439–440
_RegQueryValueEx, 439–440
_RegRemapPreDefKey, 439–440
_RegReplaceKey, 439–440
_RegSaveKey, 439–440
_RegSetValue, 439–440
_RegSetValueEx, 439–440
_RegUnLoadKey, 439–440
ReleaseSemaphore, 47
.reloc section, 581–582
Reschedule function, 536
RESFMT.TXT, 602
resident/nonresident names tables, 501–503
resource tables, 480–481, 495–499
ResumeThread, 156–157
RETURN.C, 719, 724, 725–727
ReturnFailureCode, 166
RichEdit, 60

Richter, Jeffrey, 124, 157, 692
RING0.EXE, 300
RIP_EVENT, 61
ripString, 136
RITs (Raw Input Threads), 28, 215–216
robustness, 3, 7–8, 13–14, 25
.rsrc section, 580–581
RSW (readable, writeable, shared), 474
RtlHeapFree, 598
RtlUnwind, 159, 166
RVAs (Relative Virtual Addresses), 86, 295,
        560–561, 563, 573, 585, 587, 591, 595,
        603, 608, 630
RvaToFirstByteOfCode, 612, 613
RvaToLastByteOfCode, 612, 613

S

Scheduler (Windows), 536
Schmidt, Alex, 300
Schulman, Andrew, 10–11, 207, 216–217
SC_TASKLIST, 245
section(s)
    .bss section, 580
    .CRT section, 580
    .data section, 579–580
    .debug$S section, 585
    .debug$T section, 585
    .directive section, 585
    .edata section, 581, 598
    .icon section, 579
    .idata section, 581, 586–593
    .rdata section, 583–585
    .reloc section, 581–582
    .rsrc section, 580–581
    tables, 570–586
    .text section, 577–579
    .tls section, 582–583
    use of the term, 561
SectionAlignment, 566
SectionNumber, 608
security, 3, 16, 64
segment tables, 480–481, 492–495
SEH (structured exception handling), 44–45, 53,
        56–57, 680
    overview of, 157–168
    parameter validation and, 163–164
    TIB and, 69
SelectObject, 263
SelmanList, 129, 137
SelTableLen, 524

SelTableStart, 525
semaphores, 46, 47–48
SEM_FAILCRITICALERRORS, 113
SEM_NOALIGNMENTFAULTEXCEPT, 113
SEM_NOGPFAULTERRORBOX, 113
SEM_NOOPENFILEERRORBOX, 113
SendMessage, 213–214, 252–254, 523
SetActiveWindow, 224
SetDeskWallPaper, 625
SetErrorMode, 528–529
SetEvent, 46, 47
SetFileApisToANSI, 92
SetFileApisToOEM, 92, 117
SetFocus, 28, 189–191, 208, 224
SetLastError, 176, 177, 412, 636
SetMenu(), 639
SetMessageQueue, 222–223
SetPixel, 488, 502
SetPriorityClass, 42, 138, 143–145
SetResourceHandler, 496
SetSigHandler, 530
SetStdHandle, 121
SetTaskSignalProc, 530
SetThreadContext, 62, 151–164, 675, 694,
        739, 740
SetThreadPriority, 140
SetUnhandledExceptionFilter, 115
SetWindowLong, 233, 638–639, 668–670
SetWindowPos(), 639, 668–669
SetWindowsHookEx(), 692
SetWindowText, 745
SetWindowWord(), 639
SHELL, 39
SHELL32.DLL, 38, 204, 208, 472
ShortName, 607
SHOW16, 478, 481–482, 496, 507, 525–526,
        532, 547–554
SHOW16.EXE, 50, 70
ShowPhysicalPages, 292–294
ShowScrollBar, 69
SHOWSEH.C, 162–163
ShowWindow(), 668–669
SHOWWND, 196, 218, 221, 223, 225, 228, 234,
        237–239
SHOWWND.C, 226, 238
ShutDownAPISpy32, 706
ShutdownThreadReturnStack, 707, 724
sig2, 221
sig[3], 219
_SignalID, 439–440
SignalProc, 530
SimonSez, 749–752

SizeOfBlock, 603
SizeOfCode, 565
SizeOfHeaders, 567
SizeOfHeapCommit, 569
SizeOfHeapReserve, 569
SizeOfImage, 567
SizeOfIntializedData, 565
SizeOfRawData, 573
SizeOfStackCommit, 568
SizeOfStackReserve, 568
SizeOfUninitializedData, 585
snapshots, 63
SoftIce/W, 14, 125, 729
    32-bit heaps and, 196–199
    Addr command, 306–307, 308
    CR command, 305
    "Heap 32" command, 198
    LDT command, 198
    memory management and, 284–286, 291,
      305–308, 334
    MOD command, 196–197, 284
    QT_Thunk and, 191
    spelunking and, 632, 673–675
    THREAD command, 334
    USER/GDI subsystems and, 191, 196–199
    VxDs and, 284–286, 429, 432–433, 438–440,
      445, 453, 459
some32BitHandle, 230
somehQueue1, 225
somehQueue2, 225
SOUNDREC.EXE, 633
Sourcer, 623, 642
SpellCheck(), 628
SPELL.DLL, 627–628
SpellInit(), 628
SpellTerminate(), 628
SpellVer(), 628
spelunking, 621–683
    advanced tips for, 672–683
    using disassembly, 622, 642–672
    with file-dumping tools, 622, 624–633
    overview of, 623–624
    with spying tools, 622, 634–641
spy programs, 466–475, 685–753
    building stubs and, 697–699
    controlling target processes and, 695–697
    function return values and, 701–705
    injecting DLLs into other processes and,
      692–694
    intercepting functions and, 687–692
    parameter information coding and, 699–701
    spelunking with, 622, 634–641

SS register, 52, 188, 193, 504–505
SSTable, 134
StackBase, 132
StackLow, 129
StackSelector16, 129, 137
Start button, 467
Static class, 233
STATUS_BREAKPOINT, 696
StatusWindow, 60
STILL_ACTIVE, 177
StorageClass, 609
string literals
    adding in, 645
    identifying, 658–659
StringTable, 619–620
stubs
    building, 697–699, 713–718
    definition of, 697
SuspendCount, 455
SuspendHandle, 455
SuspendThread, 154–155, 156
switch statements, 663–666
.SYM files, 632, 644, 677
symbol(s)
    : (colon), 199
    {} (braces), 663
    $ (dollar sign), 585–586
    + (plus sign), 181, 237, 467, 547
SymbolTableIndex, 614
synchronization, 45–49, 70, 124, 440
SyncWaitCount, 456
SystemDefaultLangID, 676
SYSTEM.INI, 22
SystemParametersInfo, 625
system resource cleanup, 34–35
system resources, free. *See* FSR
    (free system resources)
SzCmdLine, 731

T

TabControl, 60
tailMsg, 219
TAIPEI.EXE, 632
TAPI (Telephony API), 15
task(s). *See also* TDB (Task Database)
    16-bit, basic description of, 521–525
    common misconceptions about, 525–526
    definition of, 40, 521
    -related functions, 536

TASKENTRY, 545
TaskFindHandle(), 544–547
TaskFirst, 523, 525
TaskNext, 523, 525
TDB (Task Database), 40, 43, 125, 468,
    510–511, 522–523
  basic description of, 526–554
  SHOW16 and, 548–549
TDB.H, 526
TDBX, 454–457, 459–460
TDUMP, 503, 558, 623, 625–626, 632
TDUMP.EXE, 624
TerminateProcess, 42
TerminationStack, 132
TerminationStatus, 107, 131, 177
Test_Cur_VM_Handle, 426–427
TEST instruction, 661
TextOut, 7
.text section, 577–579
THCBs (Thread Control Blocks), 125, 132, 454
THHOOK, 523
Thielen, Dave, 425
thread(s), 9, 11–12, 69–71. *See also* TIB
    (Thread Information Block)
  basic description of, 3–4, 43, 124–126
  contexts, 146–149
  databases, 128–136
  execution control, 146–157
  functions, miscellaneous, 176–178
  handles, 126–128
  heap functions and, 334
  IDs, 45, 126–128, 169
  list, in Win32Wlk, 179–181, 182
  management, overview of, 43–45
  per-thread message queues and, 218–226
  priorities, 138–146
  processes and, relationship of, 102
  register sets, 45
  RITs (Raw Input Threads), 28, 215–216
  synchronization and, 45–49, 70
  TLS (thread local storage) and, 169–176, 454,
    582–585
Thread32First, 62
THREADB.H, 128
ThreadContext, 133
THREAD_DATABASE, 183, 457, 460, 533
threadId, 220
ThreadList, 110
THREAD_PRIORITY_LEVEL, 138
ThreadSwitchCallback, 458–460
thunk(s), 9–10, 36
  definition of, 9, 697
  USER32 and, 189–195

ThunkConnect, 133
THUNK.EXE, 191, 208, 491
ThunkToUser16_One_Param, 190
TIB (Thread Information Block), 69, 128–130,
    179, 181–183, 533
  basic description of, 136–138
  USER and, 191
TIBFlags, 130, 137
TIB.H, 137
TIBSelector, 131
TimeDateStamp, 587, 594, 599
TimeOutHandle, 454
TIMER.DRV, 507
timeslicing, 43–44
TLHELP32.H, 62, 66, 71
TLINK32, 586, 593
TLS (thread local storage), 169–176, 454,
    582–585
.tls section, 582–583
TlsAlloc, 169, 170–172, 174, 582–583, 703
TLSArray, 134
TlsFree, 169, 174–176
TlsGetValue, 169, 170, 173–174, 583
tlsInUseBits1, 111
tlsInUseBits2, 111
TlsSetValue, 169, 170, 172–174, 583, 703
ToolBar control type, 60
TOOLHELP, 27, 43, 50, 56, 60, 158
  16-bit tasks and, 523
  spelunking and, 634, 635, 637
  spy programs and, 695, 698
  USER/GDI subsystems and, 207, 234
  Win16 modules/tasks and, 478, 481, 523, 540,
    544–545, 547
TOOLHELP32, 62–63, 66, 70–72, 106,
    181–182, 339–340, 377, 379
Toolhelp32ReadProcessMemory, 62
TOOLHELP.DLL, 27, 56, 62–63, 70, 525, 531
TOOLHELP.H, 222, 225, 263
TopOfStack, 129, 137
topPDB, 524
TraceCallBack, 456
TraceEventHandle, 456
TraceOutLastCS, 456
TraceRefData, 456
TrackBar, 60
TreeView, 60
Turbo Debugger, 291, 673
TVIEW, 635
TypeOffset, 603

U

Unicode, 6, 16, 257–260
UNIX, 16, 23, 280, 290, 622. *See also* COFF
      (common object file format)
unknown1[2], 337
unknown1[14], 339
unknown2, 338, 339
unknown3, 339
UNLOAD_DLL_DEBUG_EVENT, 61
UpdateModuleList, 549
UpDown, 60
USER, 7, 10, 12, 15, 27–30, 34–38, 67
      additions to, 59–60, 195–201
      changes to HWNDs and, 226–233
      free system resources and, 202–217
      messaging system changes in, 214–217
      subsystems, overview of, 185–272
      Win16Mutex and, 31–33
      windowing systems and, 25, 226–236
      Windows 95 design flaws and, 64
USER32, 10, 36, 189–195, 248–256
USER32.DLL, 38, 186–190, 208, 243, 248, 297
      GetDlgCtrlID in, 256
      SendMessage in, 252–254
      spelunking and, 626–627
      spy programs and, 688, 709, 750
userAPCList, 456
USER.EXE, 10–11, 25–38, 76, 186–190, 195,
      204, 208, 212–218, 233, 262
      16-bit functions in, 239–247, 250–252
      free system resources and, 204
      new controls and, 60
      resource tables and, 495–496
      spelunking and, 628, 636
      spy programs and, 745
      threads and, 137
      UserSeeUserDo in, 258–260
      Win16 modules, 480, 516
UserID[6], 618
UserPointer, 129, 137
UserSeeUserDo, 201, 258–260
UTSL (Use The Source Luke), 621
UTState, 113

V

V86 mode, 23, 113, 428, 430, 431, 435, 444
ValidateCodePtr, 540, 542
ValidateHInstance, 540, 541–542

VAR2MAP, 676–677, 681
variables
      identifying global, 656–657
      identifying local, 654–656
VCACHE, 39
VCDFSD, 39
VCOMM, 39
VCOND, 39
VDD, 39
VDDVGA, 39
VDEF, 39
VERSION.DLL, 38
VFAT, 39
VFBACKUP, 39
VFD, 39
VFLATD, 39
VirtualAddress, 573, 603, 614
VirtualAlloc, 53, 56, 277, 309, 312–318, 319,
      325, 421
VirtualCommit, 421
VirtualFree, 277, 309, 319–321
VirtualLock, 328, 378
VirtualProtect, 309, 312, 318, 327–328
VirtualProtectEx, 318, 325–332
VirtualQuery, 297, 323–324
VirtualQueryEx, 116, 321–323
VirtualSize, 573
VirtualUnlock, 328
Visual C++, 13, 65, 163, 642
      memory management and, 291, 331
      PE/COFF formats and, 556–557, 559,
        578, 585
VKD (Virtual Keyboard Device), 425
VMM (Virtual Machine Manager), 10, 38–40,
      275, 306, 309–379, 412
      heap functions and, 331–332
      registry functions and, 57–59
      threads and, 125, 138–139, 143, 145
VMM32, 21, 31
VMM32.VXD, 23, 37–40, 52, 275
VMM_AllocateThreadDataSlot, 454
VMM.H, 58, 426
VMM.HLP, 440
VMM.INC, 318, 678–679
VMM_PageAttach, 472
VMM.VXD, 40, 58, 125, 415, 424–426, 430,
      432, 435–440, 458
VMOUSE, 39
VNETBIOS, 39
VPD, 39
VSHARE, 39
VTDAPI, 39

VWIN_CreateThread, 454
VWIN32, 39–40, 48, 52, 412, 417, 322,
    477–478
VWIN32_EXIT_TIME, 447
VWIN32.H, 424, 445
VWIN32.INC, 445, 446–453
VWIN32_Int21Dispatch, 450–451, 468
VWIN32_MAKE_IDLE_SYS, 447
VWIN32_SetEvent, 468
VWIN32_sleep, 432
VWIN32_SuspendThread, 154–155
VWIN32.VXD, 40, 101, 140, 154–156, 286,
    423–425, 428–430, 433, 444–466
VxDCall, 432–438, 440, 443–444, 472–473,
    475–476, 679
VXDLDR, 39
VxDs (Virtual Device Drivers), 3–4, 8, 10, 38–40
    calling, from other VxDs, 426–427
    calling, from Win32 code, 427–438
    crash course in, 425–430
    debugging and, 673–675
    DOS functions and, 23
    .dot commands, 676
    heap functions and, 331–332
    how the Windows 95 kernels communicate
        and, 457–466
    memory management and, 300, 306,
        309–312, 331–332, 415
    new, in VMM32.VXD, 39
    overview of, 423–476
    registry code and, 57–59
    removed from VMM32.VXD, 39
    services, basic description of, 426–427
    services, calling, on your own, 441–444
    services, finding, 438–440
    services, identifying, 678–680
    service spy (W32SVSPY), 424, 466–475
    from Windows 3.1, which are found in
        Windows 95, 22

W

W16LOCK, 217, 238–239
W16TDB, 109, 129, 137
W32SPDLL.DLL, 473–475
W32SRVDB.C, 467
W32SSUPP.C, 708, 729–730
W32SVSPY, 424, 466–475
    placing, into shared memory, 473–475
    sample session, 469–472
    writing, technical challenges in, 472–475

WaitExFlags, 455
WaitForDebugEvent, 48–49, 60–62, 695–696,
    735, 736
WaitForMultipleObjects, 47–49
WaitForSingleObject, 42, 46–49
WaitMessage, 523
WaitNodeList, 132
WakeBits, 221
WakeMask, 221
WakeParam, 455
WALKHEAP, 339–342, 369, 394
WALKHEAP.C, 339
WALKHP2.EXE, 339
WDCTRL, 39
WDEB386, 125, 291, 429, 673, 676
WideCharToMultiByte(), 602
Win16Mutex, 11–12, 64, 250, 412, 461, 464
    basic description of, 31–33
    messaging systems and, 27–28, 215, 216–217
    QT_Thunk and, 192
    USER/GDI subsystems and, 192, 215–217,
        251–255
Win16MutexCount, 130, 137
Win2Asm, 623, 632, 642
Win32s
    basic description of, 3–4, 8–12
    memory management and, 273
    PE/COFF formats and, 590–591
    problems with, 3–4, 11
    spy programs and, 686, 703, 729–730
    USER and, 187
    Win32c subset and, 4
Win32SDK, 262
WIN32WLK, 70–71, 74–75, 79, 137
    basic description of, 178–184
    processes, 105–106, 123
    threads and, 128
WIN386, 53, 39
WIN386.EXE, 23, 38
WIN95MEM, 441–444
WIN95UNI.C, 257–260
WINBASE.H, 139, 145, 424, 735
WINBUG, 67
WIN.COM, 20–21
WINCON.H, 424
WINDEF.H, 655
window classes, changes to, 233–236
windowing systems, 32, 37–38, 211–213
    changes to, 226–233
    overview of, 24–29
    threads and, 137
    Z-order and, 226–227, 639–640

WINDOWS.H, 67, 230, 232, 423, 483–484, 597, 638, 669
WINERROR.H, 176
WinExec, 42, 680
WINGDI.H, 267
WINHELP, 73
WINICE, 22
WIN.INI, 464, 532
WinMain, 40, 730, 731
WINMINE, 307
WINMINE.EXE, 640–641
WINMINE.INI, 640
WINNT.H, 72, 123, 146, 150, 161, 558, 605, 609, 615–616, 752
WinScope, 623, 634, 635, 640, 687
WINSERV.DLL, 7
WinSight, 623, 634
WinSpector, 158
WinSwitch class, 233
WINUSER.H, 220, 230, 232–233, 744
WM_CANCELMODE, 245
WM_CLOSE, 731, 745
WM_COMMAND, 638, 731
WM_ERASEBKGND, 245
WM_INITDIALOG, 731
WM_LBUTTONDBLCLK, 245
WMM.INC, 306
WM_PALETTECHANGED, 246
WM_QUEUENEWPALETTE, 246
WM_SETTEXT, 745
WM_SYSCOMMAND, 245
WM_USER, 29, 30, 204–205, 245
WND, 26, 196–197, 212, 226–236, 243, 245, 258
WNDCLASS, 198, 229
WNDCLASS.H, 234
WNDPROC, 29, 204, 212–214, 229, 253
WOW (Windows on Windows), 8, 37, 36, 50
WOWChain, 135
wParam, 213
WPARAM, 30–31, 223, 244, 638, 657
wParamHigh, 223
wParamLow, 223
WPERF.EXE, 631
WritePrivateProfileSection32A, 461
WriteProcessMemory, 62, 291, 292, 298–299, 411–414, 694, 740
WS_CHILD, 226, 228, 230
WS_EX_CLIENTEDGE, 59
WS_EX_LEFTSCROLLBAR, 59
WS_EX_MDICHILD, 59
WS_EX_RIGHT, 59

WS_EX_TOOLWINDOW, 59
WS_EX_XXX, 59, 233
WS_OVERLAPPED, 226, 227, 228
WS_POPUP, 226, 227
WSHELL, 39
wStackBottom, 545
wStackMinimum, 545
wStackTop, 545

X

x_ConvertHandleToK32Object, 114, 121
x_FindAddressFromExportName, 89–92
x_FindAddressFromExportOrdinal, 86–89
x_GetHModuleFromMODREF, 96, 99–100
x_GetMODREFFromFilename, 96, 98–100
x_HeapFree, 354
x_invalid_param_2_params, 164
x_invalid_param_handler, 166–168
XOR, 65, 105, 136, 182–183, 351
x_ThreadContext_CopyRegs, 147, 150–152
xxx_Priority_CLASS, 145

Z

Zen, 643–646
ZF (Zero Flag), 659–661, 665
Z-order, 226–227, 639
ZSER.DLL, 635–636

IDG BOOKS WORLDWIDE LICENSE AGREEMENT

Important — read carefully before opening the software packet. This is a legal agreement between you (either an individual or an entity) and IDG Books Worldwide, Inc. (IDG). By opening the accompanying sealed packet containing the software disc, you acknowledge that you have read and accept the following IDG License Agreement. If you do not agree and do not want to be bound by the terms of this Agreement, promptly return the book and the unopened software packet(s) to the place you obtained them for a full refund.

1. <u>License.</u> This License Agreement (Agreement) permits you to use one copy of the enclosed Software program(s) on a single computer. The Software is in "use" on a computer when it is loaded into temporary memory (i.e., RAM) or installed into permanent memory (e.g., hard disk, CD-ROM, or other storage).

2. <u>Copyright.</u> The entire contents of this disc and the compilation of the Software are copyrighted and protected by both United States copyright laws and international treaty provisions. You may only (a) make one copy of the Software for backup or archival purposes, or (b) transfer the Software to a single hard disk, provided that you keep the original for backup or archival purposes. The individual programs on the disc are copyrighted by the authors of each program respectively. Each program has its own use permissions and limitations. To use each program, you must follow the individual requirements and restrictions detailed in this book. Do not use a program if you do not want to follow its Licensing Agreement. None of the material on this disc or listed in this Book may ever be distributed, in original or modified form, for commercial purposes.

3. <u>Other Restrictions.</u> You may not rent or lease the Software. You may transfer the Software and user documentation on a permanent basis provided you retain no copies and the recipient agrees to the terms of this Agreement. You may not reverse engineer, decompile, or disassemble the Software except to the extent that the foregoing restriction is expressly prohibited by applicable law. If the Software is an update or has been updated, any transfer must include the most recent update and all prior versions. Each shareware program has its own use permissions and limitations. These limitations are contained in the individual license agreements that are on the software discs. The restrictions include a requirement that after using the program for a period of time specified in its text, the user must pay a registration fee or discontinue use. By opening the package which contains the software disc, you will be agreeing to abide by the licenses and restrictions for these programs. Do not open the software package unless you agree to be bound by the license agreements.

4. <u>Limited Warranty.</u> IDG Warrants that the Software and disc are free from defects in materials and workmanship for a period of sixty (60) days from the date of purchase of this Book. If IDG receives notification within the warranty period of defects in material or workmanship, IDG will replace the defective disc. IDG's entire liability and your exclusive remedy shall be limited to replacement of the Software, which is returned to IDG with a copy of your receipt. This Limited Warranty is void if failure of the Software has resulted from accident, abuse, or misapplication. Any replacement Software will be warranted for the remainder of the original warranty period or thirty (30) days, whichever is longer.

5. <u>No Other Warranties.</u> To the maximum extent permitted by applicable law, IDG and the author disclaim all other warranties, express or implied, including but not limited to implied warranties of merchantability and fitness for a particular purpose, with respect to the Software, the programs, the source code contained therein and/or the techniques described in this Book. This limited warranty gives you specific legal rights. You may have others which vary from state/jurisdiction to state/jurisdiction.

6. <u>No Liability For Consequential Damages.</u> To the extent permitted by applicable law, in no event shall IDG or the author be liable for any damages whatsoever (including without limitation, damages for loss of business profits, business interruption, loss of business information, or any other pecuniary loss) arising out of the use of or inability to use the Book or the Software, even if IDG has been advised of the possibility of such damages. Because some states/jurisdictions do not allow the exclusion or limitation of liability for consequential or incidental damages, the above limitation may not apply to you.

7. <u>U.S.Government Restricted Rights.</u> Use, duplication, or disclosure of the Software by the U.S. Government is subject to restrictions stated in paragraph (c) (1) (ii) of the Rights in Technical Data and Computer Software clause of DFARS 252.227-7013, and in subparagraphs (a) through (d) of the Commercial Computer—Restricted Rights clause at FAR 52.227-19, and in similar clauses in the NASA FAR supplement, when applicable.

Foundations™ of Visual C++ Programming for Windows® 95
by Paul Yao & Joseph Yao

ISBN: 1-56884-321-6
$39.99 USA/$54.99 Canada

Software included.

About Face: The Essentials of User Interface Design
by Alan Cooper

ISBN: 1-56884-322-4
$29.99 USA/$39.99 Canada

C++ Programmer's Guide to the Standard Template Library
by Mark Nelson

ISBN: 1-56884-314-3
$49.99 USA/$69.99 Canada

Software included.

PowerPC™ Programming for Intel Programmers
by Kip McClanahan

ISBN: 1-56884-306-2
$49.99 USA/$69.99 Canada

Software included.

IDG BOOKS

Order Center: **(800) 762-2974** *(8 a.m.–6 p.m., EST, weekdays)*

5/8/95

Quantity	ISBN	Title	Price	Total

Shipping & Handling Charges

	Description	First book	Each additional book	Total
Domestic	Normal	$4.50	$1.50	$
	Two Day Air	$8.50	$2.50	$
	Overnight	$18.00	$3.00	$
International	Surface	$8.00	$8.00	$
	Airmail	$16.00	$16.00	$
	DHL Air	$17.00	$17.00	$

*For large quantities call for shipping & handling charges.
**Prices are subject to change without notice.

Ship to:

Name _____

Company _____

Address _____

City/State/Zip _____

Daytime Phone _____

Payment: ☐ Check to IDG Books (US Funds Only)

☐ VISA   ☐ MasterCard   ☐ American Express

Card # _____ Expires _____

Signature _____

Subtotal _____

CA residents add
applicable sales tax _____

IN, MA, and MD
residents add
5% sales tax _____

IL residents add
6.25% sales tax _____

RI residents add
7% sales tax _____

TX residents add
8.25% sales tax _____

Shipping _____

Total _____

Please send this order form to:

**IDG Books Worldwide
7260 Shadeland Station, Suite 100
Indianapolis, IN 46256**

*Allow up to 3 weeks for delivery.
Thank you!*

IDG BOOKS WORLDWIDE REGISTRATION CARD

RETURN THIS REGISTRATION CARD FOR FREE CATALOG

Title of this book: Windows 95 System Programming SECRETS

My overall rating of this book: ❑ Very good [1] ❑ Good [2] ❑ Satisfactory [3] ❑ Fair [4] ❑ Poor [5]

How I first heard about this book:

❑ Found in bookstore; name: [6] ❑ Book review: [7]

❑ Advertisement: [8] ❑ Catalog: [9]

❑ Word of mouth; heard about book from friend, co-worker, etc.: [10] ❑ Other: [11]

What I liked most about this book:

What I would change, add, delete, etc., in future editions of this book:

Other comments:

Number of computer books I purchase in a year: ❑ 1 [12] ❑ 2-5 [13] ❑ 6-10 [14] ❑ More than 10 [15]

I would characterize my computer skills as: ❑ Beginner [16] ❑ Intermediate [17] ❑ Advanced [18] ❑ Professional [19]

I use ❑ DOS [20] ❑ Windows [21] ❑ OS/2 [22] ❑ Unix [23] ❑ Macintosh [24] ❑ Other: [25]_____
(please specify)

I would be interested in new books on the following subjects:
(please check all that apply, and use the spaces provided to identify specific software)

❑ Word processing: [26] ❑ Spreadsheets: [27]

❑ Data bases: [28] ❑ Desktop publishing: [29]

❑ File Utilities: [30] ❑ Money management: [31]

❑ Networking: [32] ❑ Programming languages: [33]

❑ Other: [34]

I use a PC at (please check all that apply): ❑ home [35] ❑ work [36] ❑ school [37] ❑ other: [38] _____

The disks I prefer to use are ❑ 5.25 [39] ❑ 3.5 [40] ❑ other: [41]_____

I have a CD ROM: ❑ yes [42] ❑ no [43]

I plan to buy or upgrade computer hardware this year: ❑ yes [44] ❑ no [45]

I plan to buy or upgrade computer software this year: ❑ yes [46] ❑ no [47]

Name: _____ Business title: [48] _____ Type of Business: [49] _____

Address (❑ home [50] ❑ work [51] /Company name: _____)

Street/Suite# _____

City [52] /State [53] /Zipcode [54]: _____ Country [55] _____

❑ **I liked this book!** You may quote me by name in future
IDG Books Worldwide promotional materials.

My daytime phone number is _____

IDG BOOKS

THE WORLD OF COMPUTER KNOWLEDGE